FLORIDA'S

B.E.S.T. Standards for **MATH**

Algebra 1

with CalcChat® and CalcView®

Volume 1

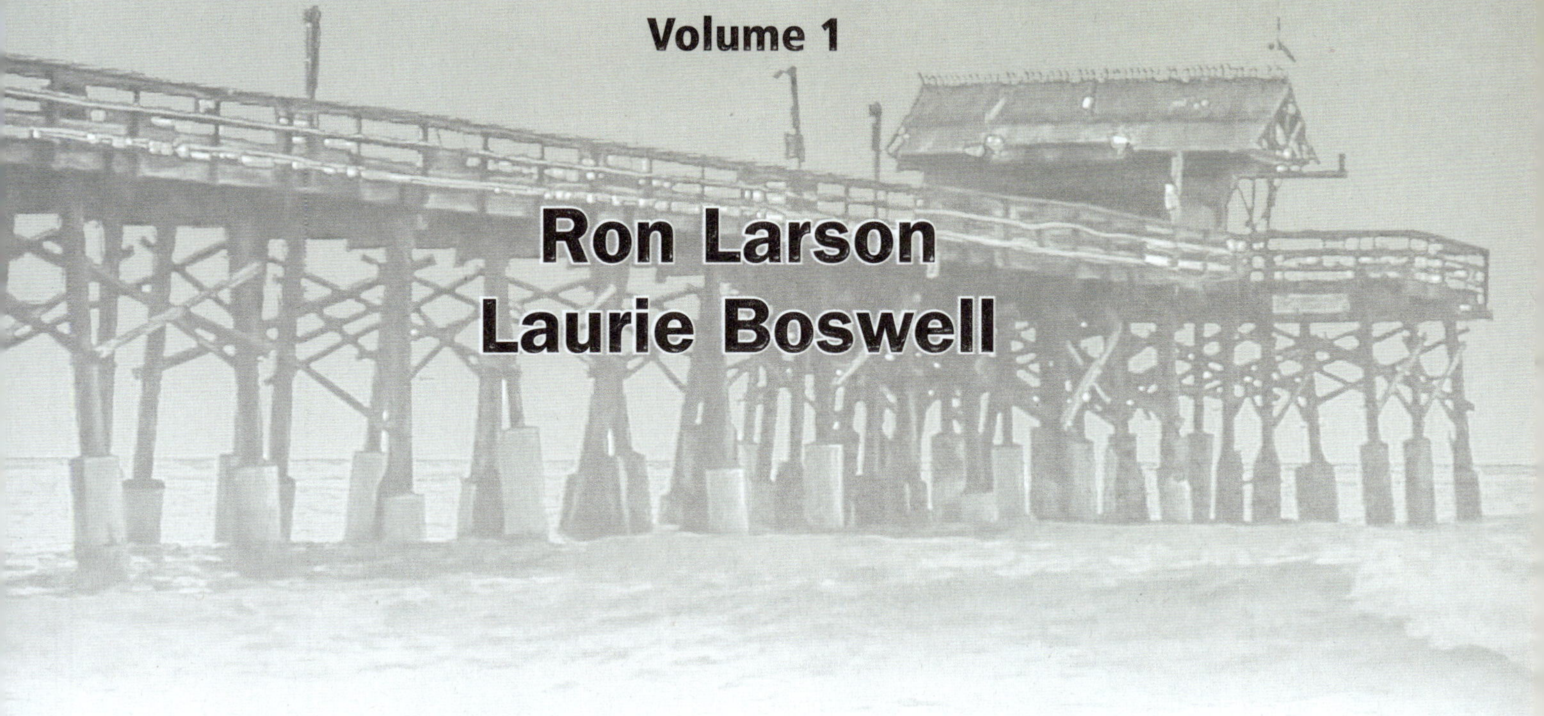

Ron Larson
Laurie Boswell

Big Ideas Learning™
Erie, Pennsylvania
BigIdeasLearning.com

Big Ideas Learning, LLC
1762 Norcross Road
Erie, PA 16510-3838
USA

For product information and customer support, contact Big Ideas Learning at **1-877-552-7766** or visit us at ***BigIdeasLearning.com***.

Cover:
Jason Sponseller/Shutterstock.com

Front Matter:
bgblue/DigitalVision Vectors/Getty Images

Printed in the United States

ISBN 13: 978-1-63896-318-9

8 9—25

A Single Authorship Team

Written by renowned authors, Dr. Ron Larson and Dr. Laurie Boswell, *Florida's B.E.S.T. Standards for MATH* offers a seamless math pedagogy from Kindergarten through Algebra 2. Together, Ron and Laurie provide a consistent voice that encourages students to make connections through cohesive progressions and clear instruction. Since 1992, Ron and Laurie have authored over 50 mathematics programs.

"Each time Laurie and I start working on a new program, we spend time putting ourselves in the position of the reader. How old is the reader? What is the reader's experience with mathematics? The answers to these questions become our writing guides. Our goal is to make the learning targets understandable and to develop these targets in a clear path that leads to student success."

Ron Larson

Ron Larson, Ph.D., is well known as lead author of a comprehensive and widely used mathematics program that ranges from elementary school through college. He holds the distinction of Professor Emeritus from Penn State Erie, The Behrend College, where he taught for nearly 40 years. He received his Ph.D. in mathematics from the University of Colorado. Dr. Larson engages in the latest research and advancements in mathematics education and consistently incorporates key pedagogical elements to ensure focus, coherence, rigor, and student self-reflection.

"My passion and goal in writing is to provide an essential resource for exploring and making sense of mathematics. Our program is guided by research around the learning and teaching of mathematics in the hopes of improving the achievement of all students. May this be a successful year for you!"

Laurie Boswell

Laurie Boswell, Ed.D., is the former Head of School at Riverside School in Lyndonville, Vermont. In addition to authoring textbooks, she provides mathematics consulting and embedded coaching sessions. Dr. Boswell received her Ed.D. from the University of Vermont in 2010. She is a recipient of the Presidential Award for Excellence in Mathematics Teaching and later served as president of CPAM. Laurie has taught math to students at all levels, elementary through college. In addition, Laurie has served on the NCTM Board of Directors and as a Regional Director for NCSM. Along with Ron, Laurie has co-authored numerous math programs and has become a popular national speaker.

1 Solving Linear Equations

2 Solving Linear Inequalities

H means the entire section is honors.

H means that the section contains honors content.

Graphing Linear Functions

3

Writing Linear Functions

4

H means the entire section is honors.

H means that the section contains honors content.

5 Solving Systems of Linear Equations

6 Exponential Functions

Polynomial Equations and Factoring

7

Graphing Quadratic Functions

8

H means the entire section is honors.

H means that the section contains honors content.

9

Solving Quadratic Equations

10

Data Analysis and Displays

Algebra 1 Course Project 944

Additional Resources

H means the entire section is honors.

H means that the section contains honors content.

Credits

Chapter 1

0 *top* ©Randall Scott/National Geographic Image Collection; *bottom* Nikolay 007/Shutterstock.com; **2** jurisam/iStock/Getty Images Plus; **6** GlobalP/iStock/Getty Images Plus; **10** Petr Toman/Shutterstock.com; **11** Harper 3D/Shutterstock.com; **12** lunamarina/Shutterstock.com; **13** 4FR/E+/Getty Images; **15** cowardlion/Shutterstock.com; **17** Willard/iStock/Getty Images Plus; **19** *right* MPFphotography/Shutterstock.com; *left* agrobacteriStock/Getty Images Plus; **24** Tom Saga/Shutterstock.com; **25** mexanichp/Shutterstock.com; **26** Dora Zett/Shutterstock.com; **27** ggyykk/iStock/Getty Images Plus; **33** Ljupco/iStock/Getty Images Plus; **38** mrdoomits/iStock/Getty Images Plus; **40** Vdovychenko Yurii/iStock/Getty Images Plus; **44** CiydemImages/iStock/Getty Images Plus; **47** Pgiam/E+/Getty Images; **51** *left* Nerthuz/iStock/Getty Images Plus; *right* stephane106/iStock/Getty Images Plus; **57** Cimmerian/iStock/Getty Images Plus; **61** *bottom* guardiano007/Shutterstock.com; *top* Nerthuz/Istock/Getty Images Plus; **63** OSTILL/iStock/Getty Images Plus; **65** *left* heinteh/iStock/Getty Images Plus; *right* Obradovic/iStock/Getty Images Plus; **67** kurtlichtenstein/iStock/Getty Images Plus; **68** kontur-vid/iStock/Getty Images Plus; **76** *top* zoooma/iStock/Getty Images Plus; *bottom* sdecoret/Shutterstock.com; **77–78** *background* pinkomelet/iStock/Getty Images Plus, **77** *top* AlessandroMassimiliano/iStock/Getty Images Plus; **79** My Life Graphic/Shutterstock.com

Chapter 2

82 *top* ©Jimmy Chin/National Geographic Image Collection; *bottom* Roberto Caucino/Shutterstock.com; **84** gutiiev/iStock/Getty Images Plus; **93** VIAVAL TOURS/Shutterstock.com; **95** saiko3p/iStock Editorial/Getty Images Plus; **96** Bet_Noire/iStock/Getty Images Plus; **97** Morozov67/iStock/Getty Images Plus; **101** Photodisc/Photodisc/Getty Images; **105** Roman Voloshyn/Shutterstock.com; **111** aldomurillo/iStock/Getty Images Plus; **116** Courtesy Peter Hutchinson Designs Ltd.; *bottom* amanalang/iStock/Getty Images Plus; **119** Picsfive/iStock/Getty Images Plus; **121** Dean Drobot/iStock/Getty Images Plus; **131** pkline/E+/Getty Images; **137** Symonenko Viktoriia/Shutterstock.com; **139** benedek/E+/Getty Images; **141** andegro4ka/iStock/Getty Images Plus; **142** mordalez/iStock/Getty Images Plus; **145** PORTRAIT IMAGES ASIA BY NONWARIT/Shutterstock.com; **150** Oleksiy Mark/Shutterstock.com; **152** GlobalP/iStock/Getty Images Plus; **156** nidwlw/iStock/Getty Images Plus; **158** *left* Dean Mitchell/E+/Getty Images; *right* skynesher/E+/Getty images; **159** thedafkish/iStock/Getty Images Plus; **162** Paolo Bona/Shutterstock.com; **163–164** *background* hadynyah/E+/Getty Images; **164** *top* Historic Images/Alamy; **167** *left* TPopova/iStock/Getty Images Plus; *right* Piotr Polaczyk/iStock/Getty Images Plus

Chapter 3

168 *top* ©Marco Grob/National Geographic Image Collection; *bottom* David Kirkland/Media Bakery; **170** cosmin4000/iStock/Getty Images Plus, Valentyna Chukhlyebova/Shutterstock.com; **173** ©iStockphoto.com/sorbetto; **179** Konstantin G/Shutterstock.com; **180** Npeter/Shutterstock.com; **182** Nerthuz/iStock/Getty Images Plus; **187** xua/iStock/Getty Images Plus; **191** Safar Aslanov/Shutterstock.com, max dallocco/Shutterstock.com; **197** domin_domin/iStock/Getty Images Plus; **203** Andyworks/iStock/Getty Images Plus; **208** OSTILL/iStock/Getty Images Plus; **213** track5/E+/Getty Images; **215** Africa Studio/Shutterstock.com; **220** Nerthuz/iStock/Getty Images Plus; **223** hatman12/iStock/Getty Images Plus; **234** michaeljung/iStock/Getty Images Plus; **241** Andrey Suslov/Shutterstock.com; **251** Tomwang112/iStock/Getty Images Plus; **259** Africa Studio/Shutterstock.com; **261** 5 second Studio/Shutterstock.com; **274** Berenika_L/E+/Getty Images; **284** scanrail/iStock/Getty Images Plus; **285** OSTILL/iStock/Getty Images Plus; **290** White Space Ukraine/Shutterstock.com; **291–292** *background* Global_Pics/E+/Getty Images; **292** *top* Pixelfeger/Shutterstock.com

Chapter 4

296 *top* ©Rebecca Hale/ National Geographic Image Collection; *bottom* ic36006/Shutterstock.com; **298** vencavolrab/iStock/Getty Images Plus; **301** PeopleImages/iStock/Getty Images Plus; **304** Image Source/DigitalVision/Getty Images; **306** pedrosala/Shutterstock.com; **309** Roman Voloshyn/Shutterstock.com; **310** Richinpit/E+/Getty Images; **318** Thomas Trompeter/Shutterstock.com; **321** Archiwiz/iStock/Getty Images Plus, LongQuattro/iStock/Getty Images Plus; **322** petesaloutos/iStock/Getty Images Plus; **325** ayprilrain/iStock/Getty Images Plus; **329** LightFieldStudios/iStock/Getty Images Plus; **335** Galina Zhigalova/iStock/Getty Images Plus; **352** Slavun/Shutterstock.com; **361** Lakeview_Images/iStock/Getty Images Plus; **365** Ljupco/iStock/Getty Images Plus; **368** Melissa Schalke/Shutterstock.com; **373** emarto/iStock/Getty Images Plus; **383–384** Mkstudi/Shutterstock.com

Chapter 5

388 *top* ©Mark Thiessen/National Geographic Creative; *bottom* George W. Bailey/Shutterstock.com; **397** Christina Richards/Shutterstock.com; **400** *Exercise 23 left to right* neamov/iStock/Getty Images Plus; tiler84/iStock/Getty Images Plus; **401** pilipphoto/iStock/Getty Images Plus; **403** aldomurillo/iStock/Getty Images Plus; **410** Odua Images/Shutterstock.com; **413** Foodio/Shutterstock.com; **417** Nerthuz/iStock/Getty Images Plus; **419** MileA/iStock /Getty Images Plus; **423** HomePixel/iStock/Getty Images Plus; **427** damedeeso/iStock/Getty Images Plus; **430** final09/iStock/Getty Images Plus, venimo/iStock/Getty Images Plus, Yeko Photo Studio/Shutterstock.com; **433** Iakov Filimonov/Shutterstock.com; **437** goinyk/iStock/Getty Images Plus; **440** Africa Studio/Shutterstock.com; **442** *left* nata_zhekova/iStock/Getty Images Plus; *right* iko636/iStock/Getty Images Plus; **443** *left* photka/iStock/Getty Images Plus; *right* Arthito/iStock/Getty Images Plus; **447** *top left* harneshkp/iStock/Getty Images Plus; *left* PixaHub/Shutterstock.com; **453** londoneye/E+/Getty Images; **459** Supertrooper/Shutterstock.com; **463** eye-blink/Shutterstock.com; **468** *left* Irina Rogova/Shutterstock.com, *right* Kostyantyn Ivanyshen/Shutterstock.com; **474** *left* choness/iStock/Getty Images Plus; *right* Vonkara1/iStock/Getty Images Plus; **475–476** *background* divedog/Shutterstock.com, Global_Pics/iStock/Getty Images Plus; **475** *in order from top to bottom* Harvepino/Shutterstock.com, Steve Nicklas/NOS, ©Mark Thiessan/National Geographic, katykin/iStock/Getty Images Plus, best works/Shutterstock.com

1 Solving Linear Equations

WATCH

NATIONAL GEOGRAPHIC EXPLORER

Dalal Hanna

Ecologist Dalal Hanna specializes in how to sustain Earth's environment. She focuses on different ways rivers contribute to human well-being, and has published research on mercury contamination in African freshwater fish. Hanna has also developed the podcast "Science Faction" which explores discoveries in all fields of science.

- What are ways that you can conserve water?
- How much water is used to take a 5-minute shower? a 10-minute shower? a 15-minute shower?
- How much water is conserved if 10,000 people each use 10 fewer gallons of water every month?

STEM

Water conservation is critical for human health and development. In the Performance Task, you will make a plan to conserve water in your own daily life.

GO DIGITAL

Water Conservation

Preparing for Chapter 1

Chapter Learning Target: Understand solving linear equations.

Chapter Success Criteria:

- ◆ I can solve simple and multi-step equations.
- ◆ I can describe how to solve equations.
- ■ I can recognize when an equation has zero, one, or infinitely many solutions.
- ■ I can apply equation-solving techniques to solve real-life problems.

◆ Surface
■ Deep

Az VOCAB

Chapter Vocabulary

Work with a partner. Discuss each of the vocabulary terms.

equation

equivalent equations

formula

solution

extraneous solution

GO DIGITAL

Mathematical Thinking and Reasoning

4 MTR **ENGAGE IN DISCUSSIONS THAT REFLECT ON THE MATHEMATICAL THINKING OF SELF AND OTHERS**

Mathematicians who engage in discussions that reflect on the mathematical thinking of self and others develop a deeper understanding of mathematical concepts.

Work with a partner. The chart shows the population and the average amount of fresh water used daily in the United States from 1960 to 2015.

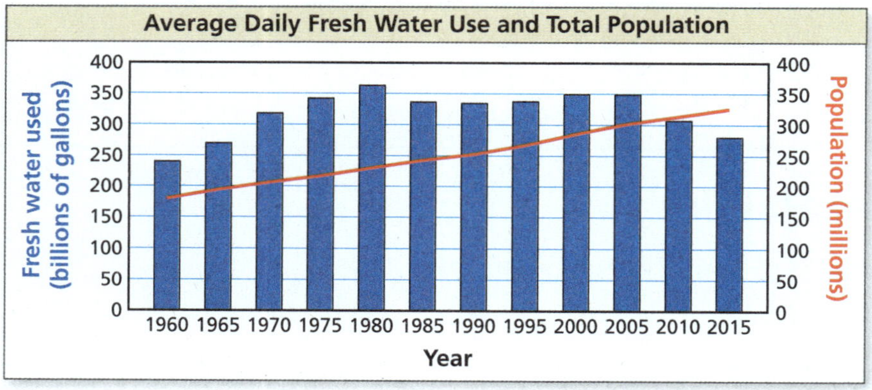

1. Make several observations about the data in the chart.

2. What conclusions can you make about water conservation efforts in the United States? Explain your reasoning to another pair.

1 Prepare WITH CalcChat®

Adding and Subtracting Rational Numbers

WATCH

Example 1 **Evaluate 4.5 + (−12.5).**

$$4.5 + (-12.5) = -8$$

$|-12.5| > |4.5|$. So, subtract $|4.5|$ from $|-12.5|$.

Use the sign of −12.5.

WATCH

Example 2 **Evaluate $-7 - \left(-\frac{5}{2}\right)$.**

$$-7 - \left(-\frac{5}{2}\right) = -7 + \frac{5}{2}$$ Add the opposite of $-\frac{5}{2}$.

$$= -\frac{9}{2}$$ Add.

Add or subtract.

1. $-5 + (-2)$

2. $0 + (-13)$

3. $-6 + 14$

4. $1.9 - (-3)$

5. $-\frac{1}{2} - \frac{3}{2}$

6. $-5.6 - (-7.2)$

7. $\frac{4}{5} + \frac{3}{10}$

8. $\frac{8}{3} + \left(-\frac{1}{3}\right)$

9. $11.5 - 5\frac{1}{2}$

GO DIGITAL

Multiplying and Dividing Rational Numbers

WATCH

Example 3 **Evaluate $-3.5 \cdot (-5)$.**

The numbers have the same sign.

$$-3.5 \cdot (-5) = 17.5$$

The product is positive.

WATCH

Example 4 **Evaluate $\frac{1}{5} \div (-3)$.**

The numbers have different signs.

$$\frac{1}{5} \div (-3) = -\frac{1}{15}$$

The quotient is negative.

Multiply or divide.

10. $-3(8)$

11. $-7 \cdot (-9)$

12. $4 \cdot (-7)$

13. $-\frac{1}{4} \div (-6)$

14. $-1.6 \div 2$

15. $1.2 \div (-3)$

16. $\frac{3}{4} \cdot \frac{1}{2}$

17. $\frac{4}{3} \div \frac{4}{9}$

18. $-3.5(-4.25)$

5 MTR **19.** **STRUCTURE** Describe the signs of two rational numbers when (a) their sum is positive, (b) their product is positive, and (c) their quotient is positive. Give examples to support your answers.

1.1 Solving Simple Equations

Learning Target: Write and solve one-step linear equations.

Success Criteria:
- I can apply properties of equality to produce equivalent equations.
- I can solve linear equations using addition, subtraction, multiplication, or division.
- I can write linear equations that model real-life situations.

Algebraic Reasoning
preparing for MA.912.AR.2.1 Given a real-world context, write and solve one-variable multi-step linear equations.

EXPLORE IT! Modeling a Real-Life Problem

Work with a partner. The Okavango Delta is the largest freshwater wetland in southern Africa and is the main source of water for one million people.

1 MTR

ANALYZE A PROBLEM
How can you use the graph to determine the quantities involved and the relationship between the quantities?

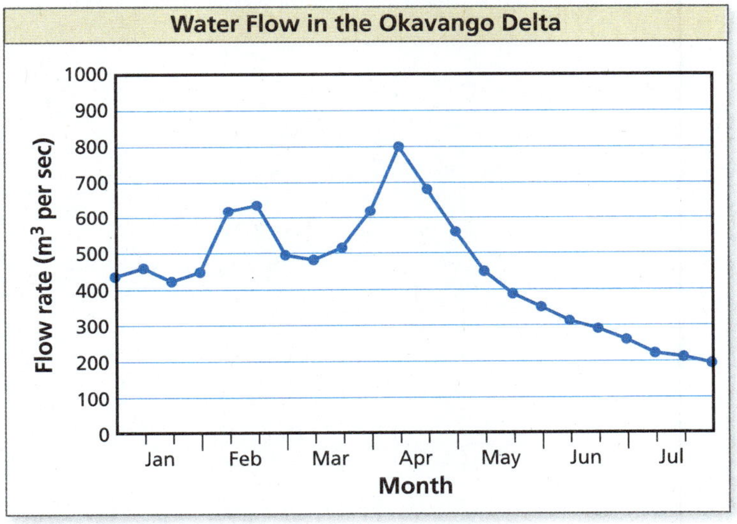

a. What does the graph show? Make several observations from the graph.

GO DIGITAL

b. When the water flow was at its peak, about how long did it take 100,000 cubic meters of water to flow past a point in the Okavango Delta? Explain your reasoning.

c. Your friend uses an equation to answer part (b) as shown. Is your friend's reasoning valid? Explain.

$$f = 800t$$

$$100{,}000 = 800t$$

$$\frac{100{,}000}{800} = t$$

$$\frac{1000}{8} = t$$

$$125 \text{ sec} = t \qquad \text{m}^3 \div \frac{\text{m}^3}{\text{sec}} = \text{m}^3 \times \frac{\text{sec}}{\text{m}^3} = \text{sec}$$

Vocabulary AZ VOCAB

equation, *p. 7*
linear equation in one variable, *p. 7*
solution, *p. 7*
equivalent equations, *p. 7*

Solving Equations Using Addition or Subtraction

An **equation** is a statement that two expressions are equal. A **linear equation in one variable** is an equation that can be written in the form $ax + b = 0$, where a and b are constants and $a \neq 0$. When you *solve an equation*, you use properties of real numbers to find a **solution**, which is a value that makes the equation true.

Equivalent equations are equations that have the same solution(s). When you perform the same operation on each side of an equation, you produce an equivalent equation.

KEY IDEAS

Addition, Subtraction, and Substitution Properties of Equality

Adding or subtracting the same number on each side of an equation produces an equivalent equation.

Addition Property of Equality If $a = b$, then $a + c = b + c$.

Subtraction Property of Equality If $a = b$, then $a - c = b - c$.

Substitution Property of Equality If $a = b$, then a can be substituted for b (or b for a) in any equation or expression.

REMEMBER

Two operations that undo each other, such as addition and subtraction, are *inverse operations*. Use inverse operations to isolate the variable.

EXAMPLE 1 Solving Equations Using Addition or Subtraction

WATCH

Solve each equation. Justify each step. Check your solution.

a. $x - 3 = -5$ **b.** $0.9 = y + 2.8$

SOLUTION

a. $x - 3 = -5$ — Write the equation.

Undo the subtraction. $\underline{+3}\quad\underline{+3}$ — Addition Property of Equality

$x = -2$ — Simplify.

▶ The solution is $x = -2$.

Check

$x - 3 = -5$

$-2 - 3 \stackrel{?}{=} -5$

$-5 = -5$ ✓

b. $0.9 = y + 2.8$ — Write the equation.

Undo the addition. $\underline{-2.8}\quad\underline{-2.8}$ — Subtraction Property of Equality

$-1.9 = y$ — Simplify.

▶ The solution is $y = -1.9$.

Check

$0.9 = y + 2.8$

$0.9 \stackrel{?}{=} -1.9 + 2.8$

$0.9 = 0.9$ ✓

GO DIGITAL

SELF-ASSESSMENT

1 I don't understand yet. 2 I can do it with help. 3 I can do it on my own. 4 I can teach someone else.

Solve the equation. Justify each step. Check your solution.

1. $n + 3 = -7$

2. $g - \frac{1}{3} = -\frac{2}{3}$

3. $-6.5 = p + 3.9$

4. VOCABULARY Are the equations $6x = -5$ and $-1 = 6x + 4$ equivalent? Explain your reasoning.

Solving Equations Using Multiplication or Division

KEY IDEAS

Multiplication and Division Properties of Equality

Multiplying or dividing each side of an equation by the same nonzero number produces an equivalent equation.

Multiplication Property of Equality If $a = b$, then $a \cdot c = b \cdot c, c \neq 0$.

Division Property of Equality If $a = b$, then $\frac{a}{c} = \frac{b}{c}, c \neq 0$.

REMEMBER

Multiplication and division are inverse operations.

EXAMPLE 2 Solving Equations Using Multiplication or Division

Solve each equation. Justify each step. Check your solution.

a. $-\frac{n}{5} = -3$ **b.** $\pi x = -2\pi$ **c.** $1.3z = 5.2$

SOLUTION

a. $-\frac{n}{5} = -3$ Write the equation.

Undo the division. → $-5 \cdot \left(-\frac{n}{5}\right) = -5 \cdot (-3)$ Multiplication Property of Equality

$n = 15$ Simplify.

▶ The solution is $n = 15$.

Check

$-\frac{n}{5} = -3$

$-\frac{15}{3} \stackrel{?}{=} -3$

$-3 = -3$ ✓

b. $\pi x = -2\pi$ Write the equation.

Undo the multiplication. → $\frac{\pi x}{\pi} = \frac{-2\pi}{\pi}$ Division Property of Equality

$x = -2$ Simplify.

▶ The solution is $x = -2$.

Check

$\pi x = -2\pi$

$\pi(-2) \stackrel{?}{=} -2\pi$

$-2\pi = -2\pi$ ✓

c. $1.3z = 5.2$ Write the equation.

Undo the multiplication. → $\frac{1.3z}{1.3} = \frac{5.2}{1.3}$ Division Property of Equality

$z = 4$ Simplify.

▶ The solution is $z = 4$.

Check

$1.3z = 5.2$

$1.3(4) \stackrel{?}{=} 5.2$

$5.2 = 5.2$ ✓

GO DIGITAL

SELF-ASSESSMENT

1 I don't understand yet. 2 I can do it with help. 3 I can do it on my own. 4 I can teach someone else.

Solve the equation. Justify each step. Check your solution.

5. $\frac{y}{3} = -6$

6. $z \div 25 = -4.5$

7. $9\pi = \pi x$

8. $0.05w = 1.4$

4 MTR **9. WHICH ONE DOESN'T BELONG?** Which equation does not belong with the other three? Explain your reasoning.

$8 = \frac{x}{2}$ $\quad$ $3 = x \div 4$ $\quad$ $x - 6 = 5$ $\quad$ $\frac{x}{3} = 9$

Solving Real-Life Problems

KEY IDEA

Problem-Solving Plan

1. **Understand the Problem** What is the unknown? What information is given? What is being asked?
2. **Make a Plan** Decide how you will solve the problem. Your plan might involve one or more of the problem-solving strategies shown on the next page.
3. **Solve and Check** Carry out your plan. Examine your solution. Then check that your solution makes sense in the original statement of the problem.

7 MTR **EXAMPLE 3** **Modeling Real Life** WATCH

In the 2016 Olympics, Usain Bolt won the 200-meter dash with a time of 19.78 seconds. Find his average speed to the nearest hundredth of a meter per second.

SOLUTION

1. **Understand the Problem** You know the winning time and the distance of the race. You are asked to find his average speed.
2. **Make a Plan** Use the Distance Formula to write an equation that represents the problem. Then solve the equation.
3. **Solve and Check**

STUDY TIP

The formula that relates distance d, rate or speed r, and time t is

$$d = rt.$$

$d = r \cdot t$	Write the Distance Formula.
$200 = r \cdot 19.78$	Substitute 200 for d and 19.78 for t.
$\frac{200}{19.78} = \frac{19.78r}{19.78}$	Division Property of Equality
$10.11 \approx r$	Simplify.

REMEMBER

The symbol $\approx$ means "approximately equal to."

▶ Bolt's average speed was about 10.11 meters per second.

Check Reasonableness Round Bolt's average speed to 10 meters per second. At this speed, it would take

$$200 \text{ m} \div \frac{10 \text{ m}}{1 \text{ sec}} = 200 \text{ m} \times \frac{1 \text{ sec}}{10 \text{ m}} = 20 \text{ sec}$$

to run 200 meters. Because 20 is close to 19.78, your solution is reasonable.

SELF-ASSESSMENT

1 I don't understand yet. 2 I can do it with help. 3 I can do it on my own. 4 I can teach someone else.

10. In 2015, an autonomous vehicle drove from the Golden Gate Bridge to New York City at an average speed of 15.7 miles per hour. The journey took 9 days. About how far did the vehicle travel?

11. In the 2012 Olympics, Usain Bolt ran the 200-meter dash at an average speed of about 10.35 meters per second. Was he faster in 2012 or in 2016? By how many seconds?

GO DIGITAL

KEY IDEA

Common Problem-Solving Strategies

Use a verbal model.	Guess, check, and revise.
Draw a diagram.	Sketch a graph or number line.
Write an equation.	Make a table.
Look for a pattern.	Make a list.
Work backward.	Break the problem into parts.

7 MTR **EXAMPLE 4** **Modeling Real Life** WATCH

On January 22, 1943, the temperature in Spearfish, South Dakota, fell from 54°F at 9:00 A.M. to −4°F at 9:27 A.M. How many degrees did the temperature fall?

SOLUTION

1. **Understand the Problem** You know the temperature before and after the temperature fell. You are asked to find how many degrees the temperature fell.
2. **Make a Plan** Use a verbal model to write an equation that represents the problem. Then solve the equation.
3. **Solve and Check**

Verbal Model Temperature at 9:27 A.M. = Temperature at 9:00 A.M. − Number of degrees the temperature fell

Variable Let T be the number of degrees Fahrenheit the temperature fell.

Equation $-4 \quad = \quad 54 \quad - \quad T$

$-4 = 54 - T$ Write the equation.

$-4 - 54 = 54 - 54 - T$ Subtraction Property of Equality

$-58 = -T$ Simplify.

$58 = T$ Divide each side by −1.

▶ The temperature fell 58°F.

Check The temperature fell from 54 degrees *above* 0 to 4 degrees *below* 0. You can use a number line to check your solution.

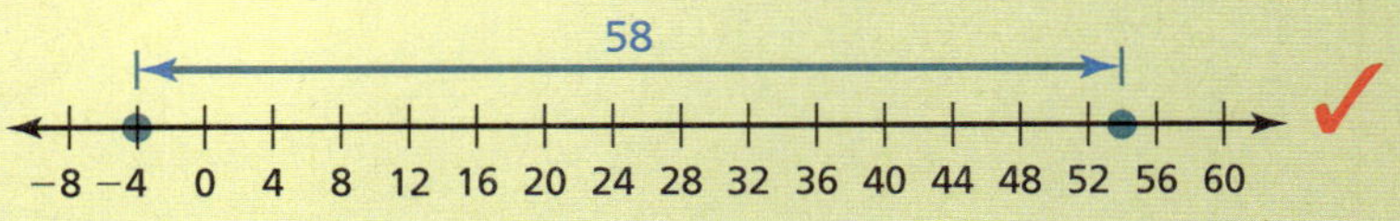

GO DIGITAL

2 MTR USE ANOTHER METHOD

How can you solve $-58 = -T$ without multiplying or dividing each side by -1?

SELF-ASSESSMENT

1 I don't understand yet. 2 I can do it with help. 3 I can do it on my own. 4 I can teach someone else.

12. You thought the balance in your savings account was \$68.33, but you forgot to record a withdrawal. Your statement lists your balance as \$26.33. How much was the withdrawal that you forgot to record?

13. In one year, a bluefin tuna releases 300% more eggs than an Atlantic sturgeon. The bluefin tuna releases about 10,000,000 eggs. About how many eggs does the Atlantic sturgeon release?

1.1 Practice WITH CalcChat® AND CalcView®

In Exercises 1–10, solve the equation. Justify each step. Check your solution. *(See Example 1.)*

1. $x + 5 = 8$

2. $m + 9 = 2$

3. $y - 4 = 3$

4. $s - 2 = 1$

5. $w + 3 = -4$

6. $n - 6 = -7$

▶ 7. $5.2 = a - 0.4$

8. $1.7 = 3.1 + c$

9. $\frac{3}{2} + t = \frac{1}{2}$

10. $z - \frac{3}{4} = -\frac{1}{3}$

7 MTR **11. MODELING REAL LIFE** An amusement park offers a ticket for \$12.95 off the original price p. Write and solve an equation to find the original price.

7 MTR **12. MODELING REAL LIFE** You and a friend are playing a board game. Your final score x is 12 points less than your friend's final score. Write and solve an equation to find your final score.

	ROUND 9	ROUND 10	FINAL SCORE
Your Friend	22	12	195
You	9	25	?

In Exercises 13–22, solve the equation. Justify each step. Check your solution. *(See Example 2.)*

13. $5g = 20$

14. $4q = 52$

15. $p \div 5 = 3$

16. $y \div 7 = 1$

17. $-54 = 9s$

18. $\frac{w}{-3} = 6$

▶ 19. $-\frac{x}{6} = 1.4$

20. $-7.8 = -2.6t$

21. $-108\pi = 9\pi r$

22. $5 = \frac{h}{4\pi}$

GO DIGITAL

In Exercises 23–32, solve the equation. Check your solution.

23. $-14 = p - 11$

24. $0 = 4 + q$

25. $-8r = 64$

26. $x \div (-2) = 8$

27. $\frac{3}{7}m = 6$

28. $-\frac{2}{5}y = 4$

29. $-3.8 = d \div 1.5$

30. $2a = \frac{1}{5}$

31. $f + 3\pi = 7\pi$

32. $-3\frac{1}{6} = k - \frac{2}{3}$

4 MTR **ERROR ANALYSIS** In Exercises 33 and 34, describe and correct the error in solving the equation.

33. ✗

$$-0.8 + r = 12.6$$
$$r = 12.6 + (-0.8)$$
$$r = 11.8$$

34. ✗

$$-\frac{m}{3} = -4$$
$$3 \cdot \left(-\frac{m}{3}\right) = 3 \cdot (-4)$$
$$m = -12$$

USING TOOLS The sum of the angle measures of a quadrilateral is 360°. In Exercises 35 and 36, write and solve an equation to find the value of x. Use a protractor to check the reasonableness of your answer.

35.

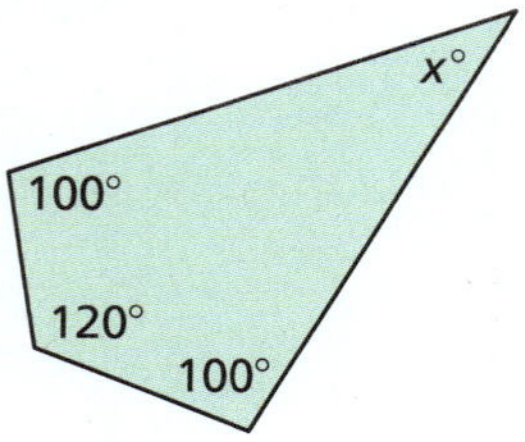

36.

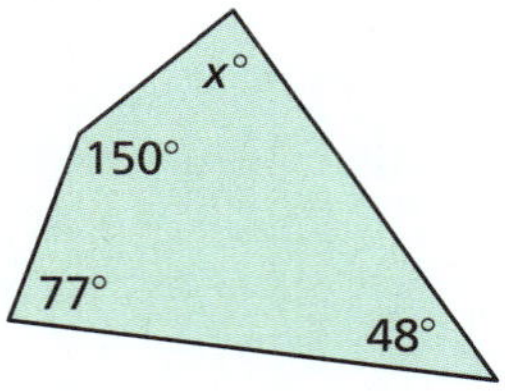

37. **B.E.S.T. TEST PREP** A baker orders 162 eggs. Each carton contains 18 eggs. Which equation can you use to find the number x of cartons? Explain your reasoning and solve the equation.

Ⓐ $162x = 18$

Ⓑ $\frac{x}{18} = 162$

Ⓒ $18x = 162$

Ⓓ $x + 18 = 162$

38. **REASONING** Are the equations equivalent? Explain.

Equation 1	$x - \frac{1}{2} = \frac{x}{4} + 3$
Equation 2	$4x - 2 = x + 12$

7 MTR MODELING REAL LIFE In Exercises 39–42, write and solve an equation to answer the question. *(See Examples 3 and 4.)*

39. A swimmer wins the 50-yard freestyle with a time of 24.76 seconds. Find the swimmer's average speed to the nearest hundredth of a yard per second.

40. The length of an American flag is 1.9 times its width. What is the width of the flag?

9.5 ft

41. The temperature at 5 P.M. is 20°F. The temperature at 10 P.M. is −5°F. How many degrees did the temperature fall?

42. The balance of an investment account is \$308.32 greater than the balance 4 years ago. The current balance is \$4708.57. What was the balance 4 years ago?

43. PROBLEM SOLVING You spend \$8.64 on 12 cans of cat food. Each can costs the same amount and is on sale for 80% of the original price. The following week, the cans are no longer on sale. You have \$10. Can you buy 12 more cans? Explain your reasoning.

44. DIG DEEPER Tatami mats are used as a floor covering in Japan. One possible layout uses four identical rectangular mats and one square mat, as shown. The area of the square mat is half the area of one of the rectangular mats. The length of a rectangular mat is twice the width. Find the dimensions of one rectangular mat. Justify your answer.

Total area = 81 ft^2

CONNECTING CONCEPTS In Exercises 45–48, find the missing dimension of the figure.

45.

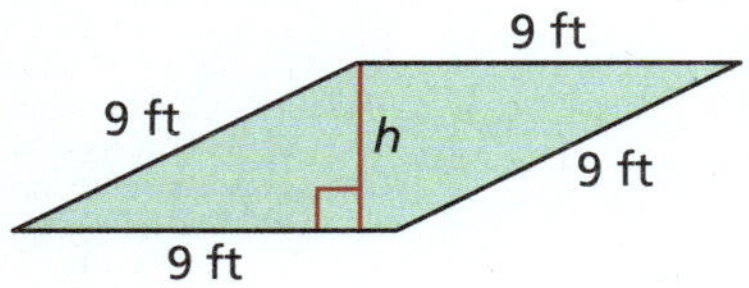

Area = 36 ft^2

46.

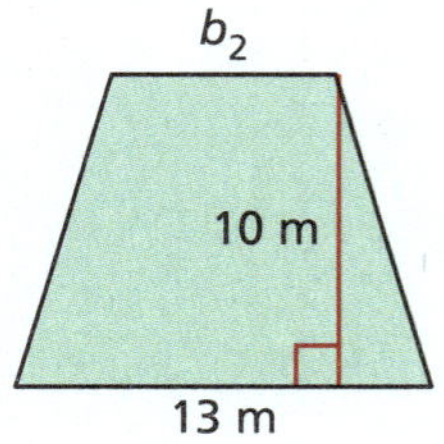

Area = 100 m^2

47.

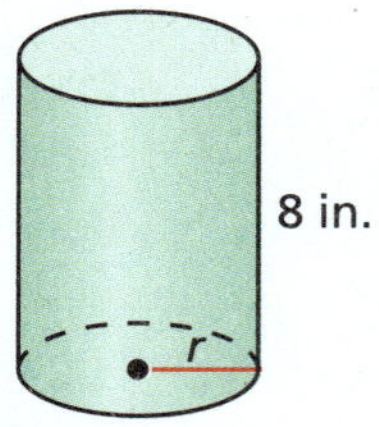

Volume = 72π in.^{3}

48.

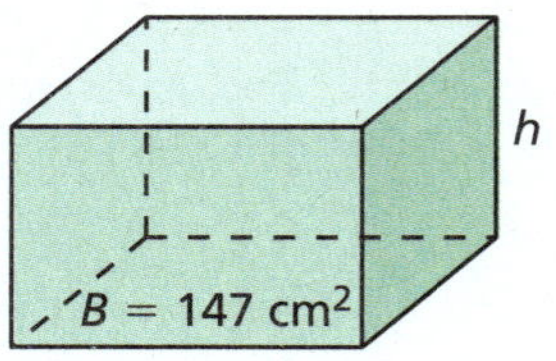

Volume = 1323 cm^3

49. STRUCTURE Use the values −2, 5, 9, and 10 to complete each statement about the equation $ax = b - 5$.

a. When a = ___ and b = ___, x is a positive integer.

b. When a = ___ and b = ___, x is a negative integer.

50. HOW DO YOU SEE IT?
The circle graph shows the adoptions from a local animal shelter in 1 year. How does the equation $7 + 9 + 5 + 48 + x = 100$ relate to the circle graph? How can you use this equation to find the percent of adoptions that were cats?

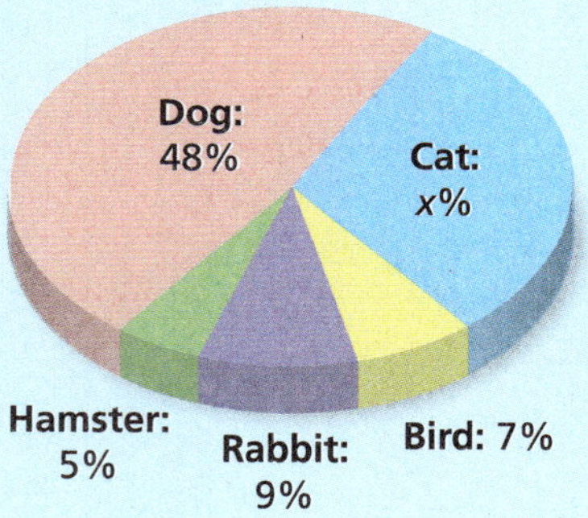

51. REASONING One-sixth of the girls and two-sevenths of the boys in a school marching band are in the percussion section. The percussion section has 6 girls and 10 boys. How many students are in the marching band? Explain.

4 MTR **52. DISCUSS MATHEMATICAL THINKING** As c increases, does the value of x *increase, decrease,* or *stay the same* for each equation? Assume c is positive.

Equation	Value of x
$x - c = 0$	
$cx = 1$	
$cx = c$	
$\frac{x}{c} = 1$	

REASONING In Exercises 53–56, the letters a, b, and c represent nonzero constants. Solve the equation for x. Then find values of a, b, and c for which the solution is positive.

53. $bx = -7$

54. $x + a = \frac{3}{4}$

55. $-\frac{x}{c} = 6.5$

56. $\frac{c}{a}x = -b$

4 MTR **57. MAKING AN ARGUMENT** In baseball, you calculate a player's batting average by dividing the number of hits by the number of at bats.

a. How many hits does Player A have?

b. Player B has 33 fewer hits than Player A but has a greater batting average. Your friend concludes that Player B has more at bats than Player A. Is your friend correct? Explain.

58. THOUGHT PROVOKING

Find the value of N such that $x - N = \frac{57}{10}$ and $\frac{x}{N} = -2.8$ are equivalent equations.

REVIEW & REFRESH

WATCH

In Exercises 59–62, multiply or divide.

59. $\frac{3}{5} \cdot \frac{4}{9}$

60. $2\frac{1}{8} \cdot \frac{2}{3}$

61. $\frac{3}{4} \div \frac{9}{10}$

62. $4\frac{1}{3} \div 1\frac{2}{5}$

63. Evaluate $15 - 6(7 + 5) \div 3^2$.

64. Find the missing values in the ratio table. Then write the equivalent ratios.

Calories	50		200	25
Servings	$\frac{1}{2}$	$\frac{3}{2}$		

In Exercises 65–67, simplify the expression.

65. $-5.9x - 4 + 2.3x - 6$

66. $4(-6m + 7)$

67. $-\frac{1}{3}(9y - 12) + 5y$

7 MTR **68.** **MODELING REAL LIFE** You have 63 red roses and 45 white roses to make floral arrangements. Each arrangement must be identical. What is the greatest number of arrangements you can make using every flower?

69. Write $\frac{7}{9}$ as a decimal and a percent.

7 MTR **70.** **MODELING REAL LIFE** A pizza shop charges \$10.99 for a large cheese pizza and \$1.50 for each topping. Write an expression that represents the cost (in dollars) of a large pizza with n toppings. How much does a large three-topping pizza cost?

71. The expression $14x + 3$ represents the perimeter of the triangle. What is the length of the third side?

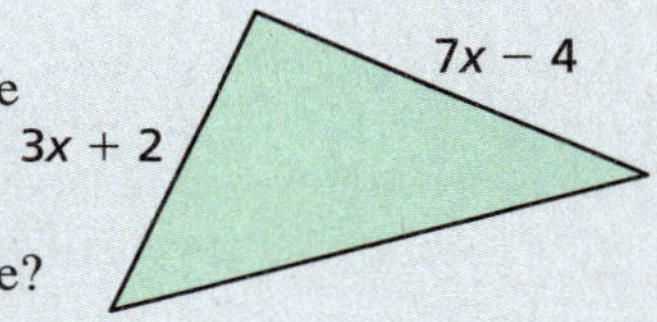

In Exercises 72–75, solve the equation. Justify each step. Check your solution.

72. $7 + x = -5$

73. $-\frac{b}{9} = 3$

74. $-1.8t = -4.5$

75. $w - \frac{1}{4} = -\frac{5}{6}$

76. Find the mean of the data.

Data usage (gigabytes)			
2.5	1.7	3.6	5.4
3.2	1.5	1.8	2.8
4.8	3.5	3.1	4.5

1.2 Solving Multi-Step Equations

Learning Target: Write and solve multi-step linear equations.

Success Criteria:

- I can apply more than one property of equality to produce equivalent equations.
- I can solve multi-step linear equations using inverse operations.
- I can write multi-step linear equations that model real-life situations.

Algebraic Reasoning
MA.912.AR.2.1 Given a real-world context, write and solve one-variable multi-step linear equations.

EXPLORE IT! Solving a Real-Life Problem

Work with a partner. You earn \$9.75 per hour at your part-time job. Your paycheck for last week is shown.

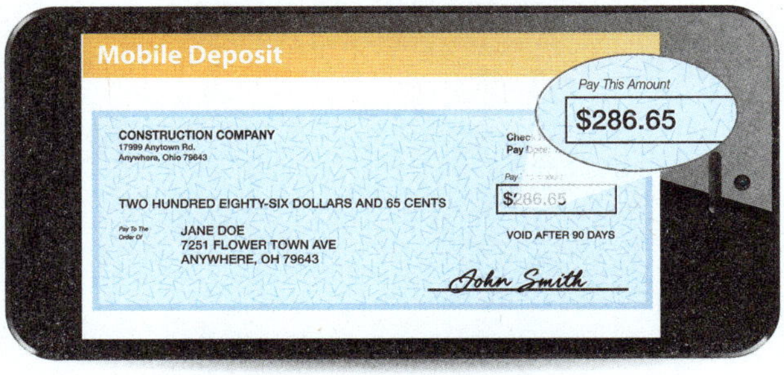

a. How many hours did you work last week? Explain how you found your answer.

b. This week you earn the same amount as last week, but that amount includes \$39 that you earn babysitting. Without solving, determine whether you work more hours at your part-time job this week than last week. Explain your reasoning.

c. Find the number of hours you work this week at your part-time job. Show two different ways to solve.

GO DIGITAL

d. The equation below represents the amount of money you will earn next week. Let h represent the number of hours you work this week.

$$9.75(h + 6) + 39 = 345.15$$

Explain what each part of the equation represents.

i. $h + 6$ **ii.** $9.75(h + 6)$ **iii.** 39

e. Solve the equation in part (d) three different ways using each of the following as the first step.

i. Subtract 39 from each side.

ii. Subtract 345.15 from each side.

iii. Divide each side by 9.75.

Compare the solution methods. Is one solution method more efficient than the other solution methods? Explain your reasoning.

4 MTR **COMMUNICATE CLEARLY**

Does it matter which step you perform first when solving? Explain your reasoning to a classmate.

Solving Multi-Step Linear Equations

KEY IDEA

Solving Multi-Step Equations

To solve a multi-step equation, simplify each side of the equation, if necessary. Then use inverse operations to isolate the variable.

EXAMPLE 1 Solving a Two-Step Equation

WATCH

Solve $2.5x - 13 = 2$. Check your solution.

SOLUTION

	$2.5x - 13 = 2$	Write the equation.
Undo the subtraction. →	$+13 \quad\quad +13$	Addition Property of Equality
	$2.5x = 15$	Simplify.
Undo the multiplication. →	$\dfrac{2.5x}{2.5} = \dfrac{15}{2.5}$	Division Property of Equality
	$x = 6$	Simplify.

▶ The solution is $x = 6$.

Check

$2.5x - 13 = 2$

$2.5(6) - 13 \stackrel{?}{=} 2$

$2 = 2$ ✓

EXAMPLE 2 Combining Like Terms to Solve an Equation

WATCH

Solve $-12 = 9x - 6x + 15$. Check your solution.

SOLUTION

	$-12 = 9x - 6x + 15$	Write the equation.
	$-12 = 3x + 15$	Combine like terms.
Undo the addition. →	$-15 \quad\quad -15$	Subtraction Property of Equality
	$-27 = 3x$	Simplify.
Undo the multiplication. →	$\dfrac{-27}{3} = \dfrac{3x}{3}$	Division Property of Equality
	$-9 = x$	Simplify.

▶ The solution is $x = -9$.

Check

$-12 = 9x - 6x + 15$

$-12 \stackrel{?}{=} 9(-9) - 6(-9) + 15$

$-12 = -12$ ✓

GO DIGITAL

SELF-ASSESSMENT

1 I don't understand yet. 2 I can do it with help. 3 I can do it on my own. 4 I can teach someone else.

Solve the equation. Check your solution.

1. $-2n + 3 = 9$

2. $-21.5 = \frac{1}{2}c - 11$

3. $-2x - 10x + 12 = 18$

4. COMPLETE THE SENTENCE To solve the equation $2x + 3x + 5 = 20$, your friend first combines $2x$ and $3x$ because they are ______________________________.

5. REASONING In Example 2, explain how you know that $-12 = 9x - 6x + 15$ and $-27 = 3x$ have the same solution.

EXAMPLE 3 Using Structure to Solve a Multi-Step Equation

WATCH

Solve $2(1 - x) + 3 = -8$. Check your solution.

SOLUTION

Method 1 One way to solve the equation is by using the Distributive Property.

$2(1 - x) + 3 = -8$	Write the equation.
$2(1) - 2(x) + 3 = -8$	Distributive Property
$2 - 2x + 3 = -8$	Multiply.
$-2x + 5 = -8$	Combine like terms.
$\underline{-5} \quad \underline{-5}$	Subtraction Property of Equality
$-2x = -13$	Simplify.
$\dfrac{-2x}{-2} = \dfrac{-13}{-2}$	Division Property of Equality
$x = 6.5$	Simplify.

▶ The solution is $x = 6.5$.

Check

$2(1 - x) + 3 = -8$

$2(1 - 6.5) + 3 \stackrel{?}{=} -8$

$-8 = -8$ ✓

REMEMBER

The Distributive Property states the following for real numbers a, b, and c.

Sum

$a(b + c) = ab + ac$

Difference

$a(b - c) = ab - ac$

GO DIGITAL

REFLECT ON YOUR METHOD 3 MTR

Explain why it is convenient to first solve for the expression $1 - x$, and then solve for x. How else could you solve the equation?

Method 2 Another way to solve the equation is by interpreting the expression $1 - x$ as a single quantity.

$2(1 - x) + 3 = -8$	Write the equation.
$\underline{-3} \quad \underline{-3}$	Subtraction Property of Equality
$2(1 - x) = -11$	Simplify.
$\frac{2(1 - x)}{2} = \frac{-11}{2}$	Division Property of Equality
$1 - x = -5.5$	Simplify.
$\underline{-1} \quad \underline{-1}$	Subtraction Property of Equality
$-x = -6.5$	Simplify.
$\frac{-x}{-1} = \frac{-6.5}{-1}$	Division Property of Equality
$x = 6.5$	Simplify.

▶ The solution is $x = 6.5$.

SELF-ASSESSMENT

1 I don't understand yet. 2 I can do it with help. 3 I can do it on my own. 4 I can teach someone else.

Solve the equation. Check your solution.

6. $3(x + 1) + 6 = -9$

7. $17 = 7 + 4(2.2d - 8.5)$

8. $13 = -2(y - 4) + 3y$

9. $2x(5 - 3) - 3x = 5$

10. $-4(2m + 5) - \frac{3}{4}m = 22$

11. $5(3 - x) + 2(3 - x) = 14$

4 MTR **12. MAKING AN ARGUMENT** Solve $2(4x - 11) = 10$ in as many ways as you can. Construct a viable argument to justify each of your solution methods.

Solving Real-Life Problems

7 MTR **EXAMPLE 4** **B.E.S.T. Test Prep: Modeling Real Life** WATCH

How many miles do you need to bike on Friday so that the mean number of miles biked per day is 5?

Day	Miles
Monday	3.5
Tuesday	5.5
Wednesday	0
Thursday	5

Ⓐ 3.5 Ⓑ 6 Ⓒ 11 Ⓓ 25

SOLUTION

1. **Understand the Problem** You know how many miles you biked Monday through Thursday. You are asked to find the distance you need to bike on Friday so that the mean number of miles biked per day is 5.
2. **Make a Plan** Use the definition of *mean* to write an equation that represents the problem. Then solve the equation.
3. **Solve and Check** The mean of a data set is the sum of the data divided by the number of data values. Let x be the number of miles you need to bike on Friday.

$$\frac{3.5 + 5.5 + 0 + 5 + x}{5} = 5$$ Write the equation.

$$\frac{14 + x}{5} = 5$$ Combine like terms.

$$5 \cdot \frac{14 + x}{5} = 5 \cdot 5$$ Multiplication Property of Equality

$$14 + x = 25$$ Simplify.

$$-14 \qquad -14$$ Subtraction Property of Equality

$$x = 11$$ Simplify.

▶ You need to bike 11 miles on Friday. So, the correct answer is Ⓒ.

Check Reasonableness Notice that on the days you did bike, the values are close to the mean. Because you did not bike on Wednesday, you need to bike about twice the mean on Friday. Eleven miles is about twice the mean. So, your solution is reasonable.

SELF-ASSESSMENT

1 I don't understand yet. 2 I can do it with help. 3 I can do it on my own. 4 I can teach someone else.

13. The formula $d = \frac{1}{2}n + 26$ relates the nozzle pressure n (in pounds per square inch) of a fire hose and the maximum horizontal distance d (in feet) the water reaches. How much pressure is needed to reach a fire 20 yards away?

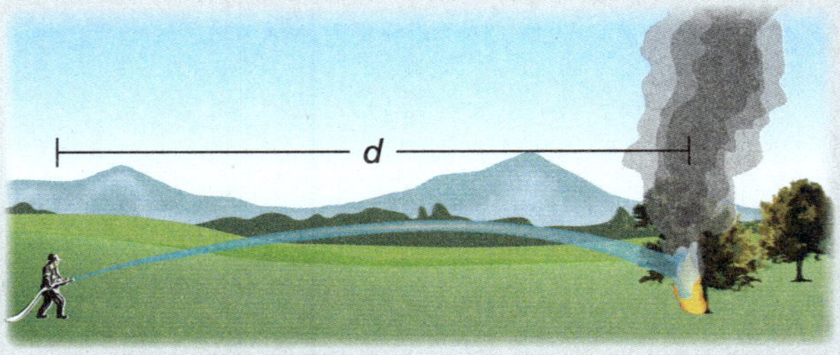

GO DIGITAL

7 MTR

EXAMPLE 5 Modeling Real Life

WATCH

One person buys a used car in Indiana and pays \$10,195, including 7% sales tax and \$425 in additional fees. Another person buys a used car in Florida and pays \$9995, including 6% sales tax and \$420 in additional fees. Compare the list prices of the used cars. (The list price is the price of the car before sales tax and fees.)

SOLUTION

1. **Understand the Problem** You know how much each person pays for a car. You also know the sales tax and additional fees in each state. You are asked to compare the list prices of the cars.
2. **Make a Plan** Use a verbal model to write equations that represent the total amount each person pays. Then solve the equations to find each list price.
3. **Solve and Check**

Verbal Model List price + Sales tax rate (written as a decimal) • List price + Other fees = Total amount paid

Variable Let p be the list price (in dollars) of the used car.

Equations

Indiana:		Florida:
$p + 0.07p + 425 = 10{,}195$	Write the equation.	$p + 0.06p + 420 = 9995$
$1.07p + 425 = 10{,}195$	Combine like terms.	$1.06p + 420 = 9995$
$-425 \quad -425$	Subtraction Property of Equality	$-420 \quad -420$
$1.07p = 9770$	Simplify.	$1.06p = 9575$
$\dfrac{1.07p}{1.07} = \dfrac{9770}{1.07}$	Division Property of Equality	$\dfrac{1.06p}{1.06} = \dfrac{9575}{1.06}$
$p \approx 9130.84$	Simplify.	$p \approx 9033.02$

REMEMBER

To write a percent as a decimal, remove the percent symbol and divide by 100.

▶ So, the list price of the car in Indiana is about \$9130.84 − \$9033.02 = \$97.82 more than the list price of the car in Florida.

Check

$$p + 0.07p + 425 = 10{,}195 \qquad p + 0.06p + 420 = 9995$$

$$9130 + 0.07(9130) + 425 \overset{?}{\approx} 10{,}195 \qquad 9030 + 0.06(9030) + 420 \overset{?}{\approx} 9995$$

$$10{,}194.10 \approx 10{,}195 \ \checkmark \qquad 9991.80 \approx 9995 \ \checkmark$$

GO DIGITAL

SELF-ASSESSMENT

1 I don't understand yet. 2 I can do it with help. 3 I can do it on my own. 4 I can teach someone else.

14. You have 96 feet of fencing to enclose a rectangular pen for your dog. To provide sufficient running space for your dog to exercise, the pen should be three times as long as it is wide. Find the dimensions of the pen.

15. You are paid 1.2 times your normal hourly rate for each hour you work over 40 hours in a week. You work 46 hours this week and earn \$462.56. What is your normal hourly rate?

1.2 Practice WITH CalcChat® AND CalcView®

In Exercises 1–12, solve the equation. Check your solution. *(See Examples 1 and 2.)*

1. $3w + 7 = 19$

2. $2g - 13 = 3$

3. $11 = 12 - q$

4. $10 = 7 - m$

5. $5 = \frac{z}{-4} - 3$

6. $\frac{a}{3} + 4 = 6$

7. $\frac{h + 6}{5} = 2$

8. $\frac{d - 8}{-2} = 12$

9. $12v + 10v + 14 = 80$

10. $24 = 13n - 4n + 9$

11. $3.8y + 5.6y - 2 = 2.7$

12. $\frac{7}{10}c - 8 - \frac{1}{2}c = -16$

7 MTR **13. MODELING REAL LIFE** The altitude a (in feet) of a plane t minutes after takeoff is given by $a = 3400t + 600$. How many minutes after takeoff is the plane at an altitude of 21,000 feet?

7 MTR **14. MODELING REAL LIFE** You are trying to use less water on laundry this month than you used on laundry last month. The amount of water w (in gallons) you save after x loads of laundry is given by $w(x) = 160 - 20x$. How many loads of laundry did you do this month if you saved 40 gallons of water?

GO DIGITAL

In Exercises 15–22, solve the equation. Check your solution. *(See Example 3.)*

15. $4(z + 5) = 32$

16. $-2(4g - 3) = 30$

17. $6 + 5(m + 1) = 26$

18. $5h + 2(11 - h) = -5$

19. $-15 = -6(3 + x) + 4(x - 6)$

20. $1 = 5(r + 9) - 2(1 - r)$

21. $83.8 = 8.6c - 7.3(6 - 2c)$

22. $3y - 2\frac{3}{4}\left(\frac{1}{2}y - 4\right) = -2$

NUMBER SENSE In Exercises 23–28, write and solve an equation to find the number.

23. The sum of twice a number and 13 is 75.

24. The difference of three times a number and 4 is -19.

25. Eight plus the quotient of a number and 3 is -2.

26. The sum of twice a number and half the number is 10.

27. Six times the sum of a number and 15 is -42.

28. Four times the difference of a number and 7 is 12.

USING TOOLS In Exercises 29 and 30, find the value of the variable. Then find the angle measures of the polygon. Use a protractor to check the reasonableness of your answer.

29.

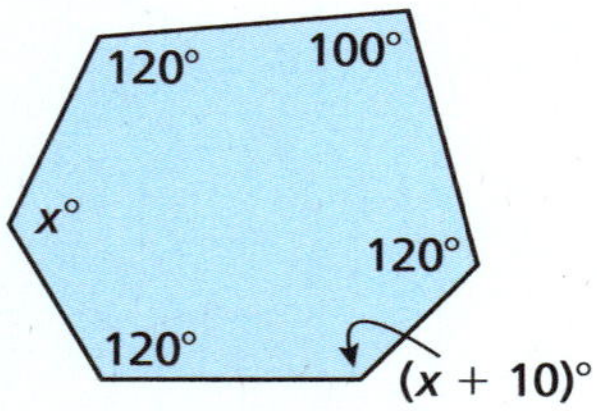

Sum of angle measures: 720°

30.

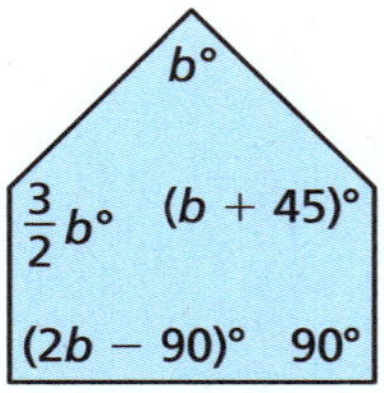

Sum of angle measures: 540°

4 MTR ERROR ANALYSIS **In Exercises 31 and 32, describe and correct the error in solving the equation.**

31. ✗

$$-2(7 - y) + 4 = -4$$
$$-14 - 2y + 4 = -4$$
$$-10 - 2y = -4$$
$$-2y = 6$$
$$y = -3$$

32. ✗

$$\tfrac{1}{4}(x - 2) + 4 = 12$$
$$\tfrac{1}{4}(x - 2) = 8$$
$$x - 2 = 2$$
$$x = 4$$

7 MTR MODELING REAL LIFE **In Exercises 33–36, write and solve an equation to answer the question.** *(See Examples 4 and 5.)*

33. During the summer, you work 30 hours per week at a gas station and earn \$8.75 per hour. You also work as a landscaper for \$11 per hour and can work as many hours as you want. You want to earn a total of \$400 per week. How many hours must you work as a landscaper?

34. The area of the surface of the swimming pool is 210 square feet. What is the length of the deep end?

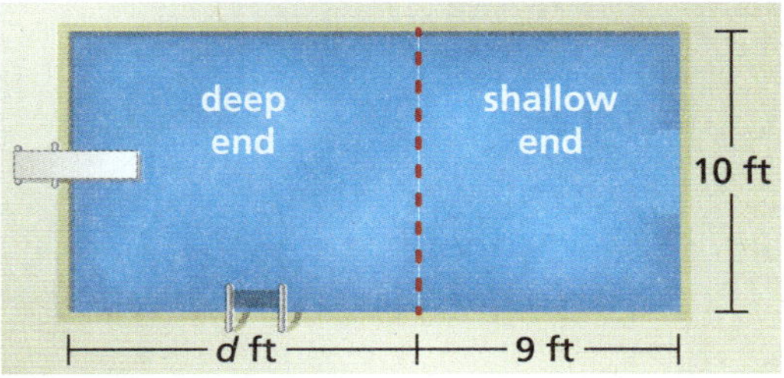

35. Your cell phone has 983.5 MB of free space. You save a 1.4-MB picture and download two songs that are the same size. Your cell phone now has 974.9 MB of free space. What is the size of each song?

36. You order two tacos and a salad. The salad costs \$2.50. You pay 6% sales tax and leave a \$3 tip. You pay a total of \$13.60. How much does one taco cost?

5 MTR CONNECTING CONCEPTS **In Exercises 37 and 38, write and solve an equation to answer the question.**

37. The perimeter of the Puerto Rican flag is 150 inches. What are the dimensions of the flag?

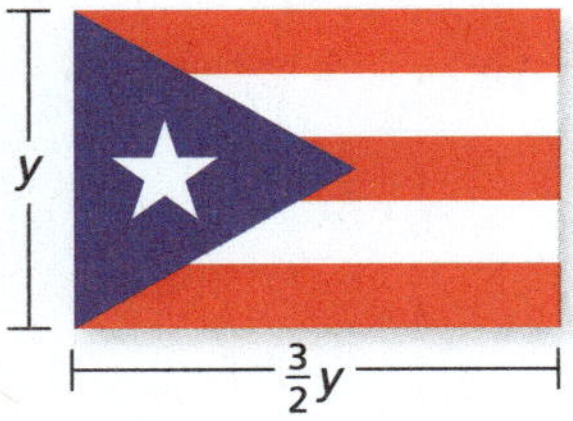

38. The perimeter of the school crossing sign is 102 inches. What is the length of each side?

JUSTIFYING STEPS **In Exercises 39 and 40, justify each step of the solution.**

39. $-\frac{1}{2}(5x - 8) - 1 = 6$ Write the equation.

$-\frac{1}{2}(5x - 8) = 7$

$5x - 8 = -14$

$5x = -6$

$x = -\frac{6}{5}$

40. $2(x + 3) + x = -9$ Write the equation.

$2(x) + 2(3) + x = -9$

$2x + 6 + x = -9$

$3x + 6 = -9$

$3x = -15$

$x = -5$

41. **CHOOSE A METHOD** Solve the equation $2(4 - 8x) + 6 = -1$ using two different methods. Which method do you prefer? Explain.

42. **HOW DO YOU SEE IT?**
The scatter plot shows the attendance for each meeting of a gaming club.

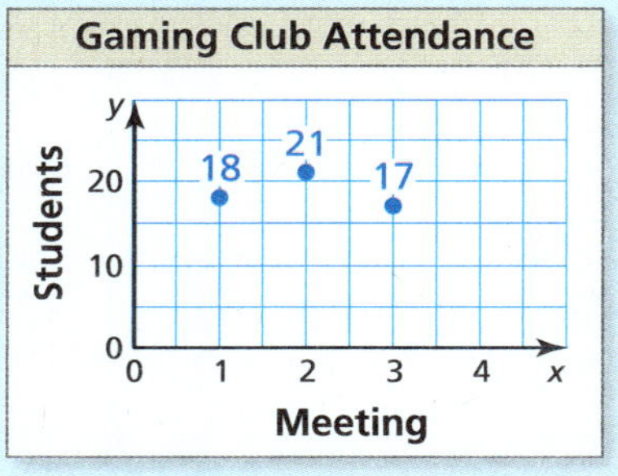

a. The mean attendance for the first four meetings is 20. Is the number of students who attended the fourth meeting greater than or less than 20? Explain.

b. Estimate the number of students who attended the fourth meeting. Describe a way you can check your estimate.

43. PROBLEM SOLVING A group of people are ordering admission tickets for Discovery Cove. The total cost for the order is \$485.04. How many people are in the group?

Charge	Amount
Admission price	\$144.00 per person
Taxes	6.5% of admission total
Resort fee (no tax)	\$4.99 per person
Service fee (no tax)	\$9.99 per order

4 MTR **44. MAKING AN ARGUMENT** You have quarters and dimes that total \$2.80. Your friend says it is possible that the number of quarters is 8 more than the number of dimes. Is your friend correct? Explain.

REASONING In Exercises 45–48, the letters *a*, *b*, and *c* represent nonzero constants. Solve the equation for *x*. Then find values of *a*, *b*, and *c* for which the solution is negative.

45. $ax - b = 12.5$

46. $ax + b = c$

47. $2bx - bx = -8$

48. $cx - 4b = 5b$

49. DIG DEEPER Find three consecutive even integers that have a sum of 54. Explain your reasoning.

50. THOUGHT PROVOKING
Your math teacher assigns a weight to each component of the class. The weight of the final exam is half your grade, and the weights of the remaining components are equal. What is the least possible score you can receive on the final exam to earn an A (90%) in the class? Explain your reasoning.

Component	Your score	Weight	Score × Weight
Class participation	92%		
Homework	96%		
Quizzes	88%		
Midterm exam	76%		
Final exam			
Total		1	

REVIEW & REFRESH

WATCH

In Exercises 51–54, find the sum or difference.

51. $-3.37 + 4.135$ **52.** $1\frac{3}{8} - \frac{7}{8}$ **53.** $18.36 - (-9.04)$ **54.** $-\frac{5}{12} + \left(-\frac{7}{3}\right)$

7 MTR **55.** **MODELING REAL LIFE** About how many times farther from the Sun is Neptune than Mercury?

Planet	Average distance from the Sun (miles)
Mercury	36,000,000
Neptune	2.795×10^9

56. Order the numbers $\frac{11}{20}$, 49%, and 0.5 from least to greatest.

57. Find the perimeter and the area of the figure.

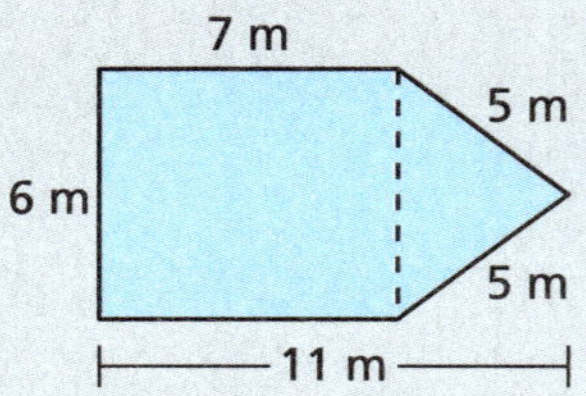

58. **NUMBER SENSE** The sum of two-thirds a number and eighteen is twenty-three. What is the number?

In Exercises 59–62, solve the equation. Check your solution.

59. $x + 9 = 7$ **60.** $8.6 = z - 3.8$ **61.** $3r + 7 = 11$ **62.** $26 = 9p - 6 - p$

63. Translate the triangle 1 unit right and 3 units up. What are the coordinates of the image?

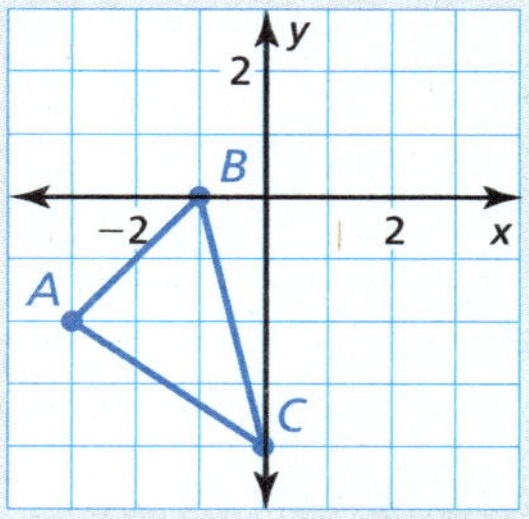

7 MTR **64.** **MODELING REAL LIFE** Your friend borrows \$7500 to buy an all-terrain vehicle (ATV). The simple annual interest rate is 6%. She pays off the loan after 5 years of equal monthly payments. How much is each payment?

65. Factor $24x + 32$ using the greatest common factor.

1.3 Solving Equations with Variables on Both Sides

Learning Target: Write and solve equations with variables on both sides.

Success Criteria:
- I can apply properties of equality using variable terms.
- I can solve equations with variables on both sides.
- I can recognize when an equation has zero, one, or infinitely many solutions.

Algebraic Reasoning
MA.912.AR.2.1 Given a real-world context, write and solve one-variable multi-step linear equations.

EXPLORE IT! Solving a Real-Life Problem

Work with a partner. You earn \$9.75 per hour at a part-time job. Your friend earns \$9.35 per hour at a part-time job. The only other income you and your friend earn is a weekly allowance.

a. Determine whether it is possible for you and your friend to work the same number of hours and earn the same total amount in a given week for the following situations. Explain your reasoning.

i. Your allowance is \$20 per week, and your friend's allowance is \$10 per week.

ii. Your allowance is \$10 per week, and your friend's allowance is \$20 per week.

iii. Your allowance is \$10 per week, your friend's allowance is \$20 per week, and your friend receives a \$0.40 raise.

iv. Your allowance is \$20 per week, your friend's allowance is \$20 per week, and your friend receives a \$0.40 raise.

GO DIGITAL

b. The following equation represents one of the situations in part (a).

$$9.75p + 10 = 9.35p + 20$$

Interpret each term and each side of the equation. Which situation does it represent?

c. Solve the equation in part (b). Explain how you solved the equation and what the solution represents. Can you start with a different first step?

d. Write and solve an equation for each of the other three situations in part (a). Compare your solutions to your answers in part (a). What do you notice?

5 MTR **USE STRUCTURE**

What do you notice about the coefficients of the variable terms in each equation? What do they tell you about the number of solutions an equation may have?

Solving Equations with Variables on Both Sides

Vocabulary

identity, *p. 36*

KEY IDEA

Solving Equations with Variables on Both Sides

To solve an equation with variables on both sides, use inverse operations to collect the variable terms on one side and the constant terms on the other side. Then isolate the variable.

EXAMPLE 1 Solving an Equation with Variables on Both Sides

Solve $10 - 4x = -9x$. Check your solution.

SOLUTION

$10 - 4x = -9x$	Write the equation.
$\underline{+\,4x} \quad \underline{+\,4x}$	Addition Property of Equality
$10 = -5x$	Simplify.
$\dfrac{10}{-5} = \dfrac{-5x}{-5}$	Division Property of Equality
$-2 = x$	Simplify.

The solution is $x = -2$.

Check

$10 - 4x = -9x$

$10 - 4(-2) \stackrel{?}{=} -9(-2)$

$18 = 18$ ✓

EXAMPLE 2 Solving an Equation with Grouping Symbols

Solve $3(3x - 4) = \frac{1}{4}(32x + 24)$.

SOLUTION

$3(3x - 4) = \frac{1}{4}(32x + 24)$	Write the equation.
$9x - 12 = 8x + 6$	Distributive Property
$\underline{+\,12} \quad \underline{+\,12}$	Addition Property of Equality
$9x = 8x + 18$	Simplify.
$\underline{-\,8x} \quad \underline{-\,8x}$	Subtraction Property of Equality
$x = 18$	Simplify.

The solution is $x = 18$.

GO DIGITAL

SELF-ASSESSMENT 1 I don't understand yet. 2 I can do it with help. 3 I can do it on my own. 4 I can teach someone else.

Solve the equation. Check your solution.

1. $-2x = 3x + 10$ **2.** $0.5(6h - 4) = -5h + 1$ **3.** $-\frac{3}{4}(8n + 12) = 3(n - 3)$

4. WRITING Describe the steps in solving the linear equation $3(3x - 8) = 4x + 6$. Explain why the steps produce a valid solution.

5. REASONING Your friend first multiplies each side of $\frac{1}{2}(x + 9) = \frac{3}{4}(5x + 1)$ by 4 when solving the equation. Why might your friend do this?

Identifying the Number of Solutions

Equations do not always have one solution. An equation that is true for all values of the variable is an **identity** and has *infinitely many solutions*. All real numbers are solutions of any identity. An equation that is not true for any value of the variable has *no solution*.

WORDS AND MATH

Think about the meaning of *identity* in everyday life. Your identity is who you are. It can be the name, distinguishing characteristics, or personality that identifies you. Your identity is the same no matter what changes in your day.

EXAMPLE 3 **Solving Equations with Variables on Both Sides** WATCH

Solve each equation.

a. $3(5x + 2) = 15x$ **b.** $\frac{n}{6} = -\frac{n}{6} + \frac{1}{2}$ **c.** $-2(4y + 1) = -8y - 2$

SOLUTION

a.

$3(5x + 2) = 15x$		Write the equation.
$15x + 6 = 15x$		Distributive Property
$-15x \quad\quad -15x$		Subtraction Property of Equality
$6 = 0$	✗	Simplify.

▶ The statement $6 = 0$ is never true. So, the equation has no solution.

GO DIGITAL

USE STRUCTURE 5 MTR

Why is it helpful to multiply each side by 6? How else could you begin to solve this equation?

b. $\frac{n}{6} = -\frac{n}{6} + \frac{1}{2}$ Write the equation.

$6 \cdot \frac{n}{6} = 6 \cdot \left(-\frac{n}{6} + \frac{1}{2}\right)$ Multiplication Property of Equality

$n = -n + 3$ Simplify.

$\underline{+n} \quad \underline{+n}$ Addition Property of Equality

$2n = 3$ Simplify.

$\frac{2n}{2} = \frac{3}{2}$ Division Property of Equality

$n = \frac{3}{2}$ Simplify.

▶ The only solution is $n = \frac{3}{2}$.

c. $-2(4y + 1) = -8y - 2$ Write the equation.

$-8y - 2 = -8y - 2$ Distributive Property

$\underline{+8y} \qquad \underline{+8y}$ Addition Property of Equality

$-2 = -2$ Simplify.

▶ Because the statement $-2 = -2$ is always true, the original equation is an identity and has infinitely many solutions. So, the solution is all real numbers.

SELF-ASSESSMENT

1 I don't understand yet. 2 I can do it with help. 3 I can do it on my own. 4 I can teach someone else.

Solve the equation.

6. $6m - m = \frac{5}{6}(-6m - 30)$

7. $10k + 7 = -3 + 10k$

8. $3(2a - 2) = 2(3a - 3)$

9. VOCABULARY Is the equation $-2(4 - x) = 2x + 8$ an identity? Explain your reasoning.

10. WRITING In Example 3, your friend says that there is enough information to determine the numbers of solutions of the equations in parts (a) and (c) once you obtain $15x + 6 = 15x$ and $-8y - 2 = -8y - 2$. Is your friend correct? Explain.

Solving Real-Life Problems

7 MTR **EXAMPLE 4** **Modeling Real Life** WATCH STEM

A boat leaves New Orleans and travels upstream on the Mississippi River for 4 hours. The return trip takes only 2.8 hours because the boat travels 3 miles per hour faster downstream due to the current. How far does the boat travel upstream?

SOLUTION

1. **Understand the Problem** You are given the amounts of time the boat travels and the difference in speeds for each direction. You are asked to find the distance the boat travels upstream.
2. **Make a Plan** Use the Distance Formula to write expressions that represent the problem. Because the distance the boat travels in both directions is the same, you can use expressions for the distance to write an equation.
3. **Solve and Check** The distance is equal to the product of speed and time.

Verbal Model Distance upstream = Distance downstream

Variable Let x be the speed (in miles per hour) of the boat traveling upstream.

Equation

$x \cdot 4 = (x + 3) \cdot 2.8$ Write the equation.

$4x = 2.8x + 8.4$ Distributive Property

$-2.8x \quad -2.8x$ Subtraction Property of Equality

$1.2x = 8.4$ Simplify.

$\frac{1.2x}{1.2} = \frac{8.4}{1.2}$ Division Property of Equality

$x = 7$ Simplify.

▶ So, the boat travels 7 miles per hour upstream. To determine how far the boat travels upstream, multiply 7 miles per hour by 4 hours to obtain 28 miles.

Check Because the speed upstream is 7 miles per hour, the speed downstream is 7 + 3 = 10 miles per hour. When you substitute each speed and time into the Distance Formula, you get the same distance upstream and downstream.

Upstream

$\text{Distance} = \frac{7 \text{ mi}}{1 \text{ h}} \cdot 4 \text{ h} = 28 \text{ mi}$

Downstream

$\text{Distance} = \frac{10 \text{ mi}}{1 \text{ h}} \cdot 2.8 \text{ h} = 28 \text{ mi}$ ✓

SELF-ASSESSMENT

1 I don't understand yet. 2 I can do it with help. 3 I can do it on my own. 4 I can teach someone else.

11. A boat travels upstream on the Missouri River for 3.5 hours. The return trip takes only 2.5 hours because the boat travels 2 miles per hour faster downstream due to the current. How far does the boat travel downstream?

12. You ask a deli clerk for x pounds of ham and x pounds of cheese. You end up getting 4 extra ounces of ham and 3 fewer ounces of cheese. The ham costs \$6.24 per pound, and the cheese costs \$4.80 per pound. You spend twice as much on ham as you do on cheese. How much do you spend in total?

GO DIGITAL

1.3 Practice WITH CalcChat® AND CalcView®

In Exercises 1–14, solve the equation. Check your solution. *(See Examples 1 and 2.)*

1. $15 - 2x = 3x$

2. $26 - 4s = 9s$

▶3. $5p - 9 = 2p + 12$

4. $8g + 10 = 35 + 3g$

5. $5t + 16 = 6 - 5t$

6. $-3r + 10 = 15r - 8$

7. $7 + 3x - 12x = 3x + 1$

8. $w - 2 + 2w = 6 + 5w$

9. $10(g + 5) = 2(g + 9)$

10. $-9(t - 2) = 4(t - 15)$

▶11. $\frac{2}{3}(3x + 9) = -2(2x + 6)$

12. $2(2t + 4) = \frac{3}{4}(24 - 8t)$

13. $1.5(3y + 2) - y = 2(8y - 6)$

14. $\frac{1}{2}(4x + 5) = 9x - 12(x - 1)$

In Exercises 15–22, solve the equation. *(See Example 3.)*

▶15. $3t + 4 = 12 + 3t$

16. $6d + 8 = 14 + 3d$

17. $2(h + 1) = 5h - 7$

18. $12y + 6 = 6(2y + 1)$

19. $-\frac{w}{5} = \frac{w}{5} - \frac{1}{10}$

20. $\frac{x}{12} + 1 = \frac{x}{3} - \frac{x}{4}$

▶21. $3(4g + 6) = 2(6g + 9)$

22. $5(1 + 2m) = \frac{1}{2}(8 + 20m)$

GO DIGITAL

23. MODELING REAL LIFE You and your friend drive toward each other. The equation $50h = 190 - 45h$ represents the number h of hours until you and your friend meet. After how many hours will you meet?

24. ERROR ANALYSIS Describe and correct the error in solving the equation.

✗

$$6(2y + 6) = 4(9 + 3y)$$
$$12y + 36 = 36 + 12y$$
$$12y = 12y$$
$$0 = 0$$

The equation has no solution.

25. MODELING REAL LIFE A cheetah that is running 90 feet per second is 120 feet behind an antelope that is running 60 feet per second. How long will it take the cheetah to catch up to the antelope? *(See Example 4.)*

26. MAKING AN ARGUMENT A cheetah can run at top speed for only about 20 seconds. If an antelope is too far away for a cheetah to catch it in 20 seconds, the antelope is probably safe. Your friend claims the antelope in Exercise 25 will not be safe if the cheetah starts running 650 feet behind it. Is your friend correct? Explain.

27. MODELING REAL LIFE You want to create a piece of pottery at an art studio. The total cost is the cost of the piece plus an hourly studio fee. The costs at two studios are shown.

a. After how many hours are the total costs the same at both studios? Justify your answer.

b. Studio B increases its hourly studio fee by $1.50. How does this affect your answer in part (a)? Explain.

28. PROBLEM SOLVING Taking a shower accounts for about 20% of your daily water usage. You use 60 gallons of water daily for other purposes. How many gallons of water do you use daily while taking a shower?

REASONING **In Exercises 29 and 30, find the value of *a* for which the equation is an identity. Explain your reasoning.**

29. $a(2x + 3) = 9x + 15 + x$

30. $8x - 8 + 3ax = 5ax - 2a$

31. **DIG DEEPER** Two times the greater of two consecutive integers is 9 less than three times the lesser integer. What are the integers?

32. **HOW DO YOU SEE IT?** The table and the graph show information about students at a high school.

	Students enrolled this year	Average rate of change
Spanish	355	9 fewer students each year
French	229	12 more students each year

a. Use the graph to determine after how many years there will be equal enrollment in both classes.

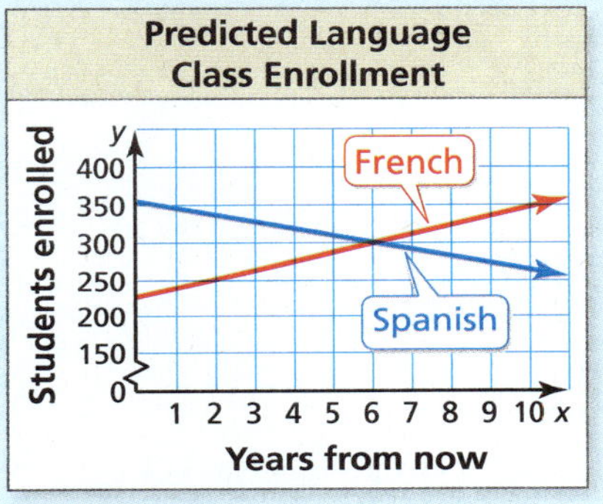

b. How does the equation $355 - 9x = 229 + 12x$ relate to the table and the graph? How can you use this equation to determine whether your answer in part (a) is reasonable?

33. **REASONING** Without solving, determine whether the equation $3n + 5 = 3n - 5$ has *one solution*, *no solution*, or *infinitely many solutions*. Explain your reasoning.

5 MTR **34.** **CONNECTING CONCEPTS** Cylinder A has a radius of 6 feet and a height that is 5.5 feet less than Cylinder B. The cylinders have the same surface area. Find the height of each cylinder.

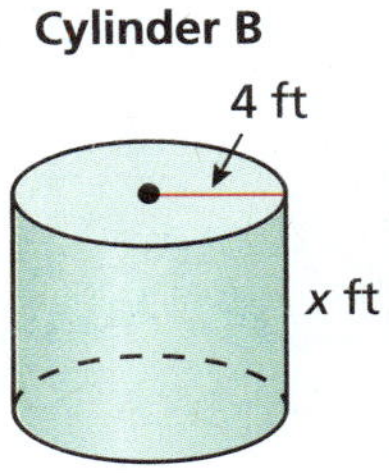

35. **B.E.S.T. TEST PREP** For which of the following values of c and d does the equation $cx - 2 = 7x + d$ have no solution? Select all that apply.

Ⓐ $c = -7, d = -2$

Ⓑ $c = 7, d = -2$

Ⓒ $c = 7, d = 0$

Ⓓ $c = 7, d = 2$

36. **THOUGHT PROVOKING** Draw a different figure that has the same perimeter as the triangle shown. Explain why your figure has the same perimeter.

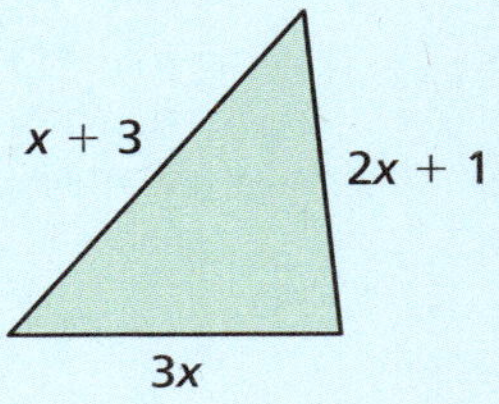

REVIEW & REFRESH

WATCH

37. The diameter of a circular watch face is 3 centimeters. Find the area of the watch face.

In Exercises 38–43, solve the equation. Check your solution.

38. $5 = 10 - v$

39. $2k - 3(2k - 3) = 45$

40. $x - \frac{1}{5} = -\frac{4}{5}$

41. $\frac{n}{7} = 4.5$

42. $7t - 20 = -50 - 8t$

43. $\frac{1}{2}(6c + 2) = -3(c - 1)$

44. Find the area of the trapezoid.

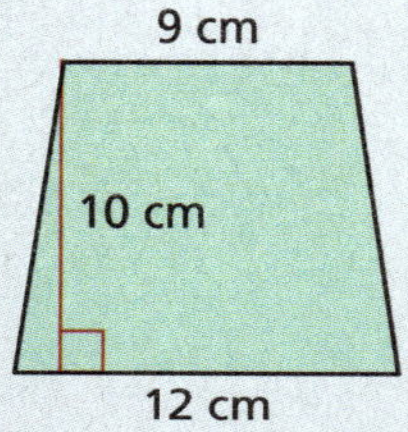

45. You type 168 words in $3\frac{1}{2}$ minutes. How many words do you type per minute?

46. Order the values from least to greatest.

$|-32|, 22, -16, -|21|, |-10|$

47. You want to find the height of a drop tower at an amusement park. You take the measurements shown in the diagram. The right triangles created by each object and its shadow are similar. How tall is the drop tower?

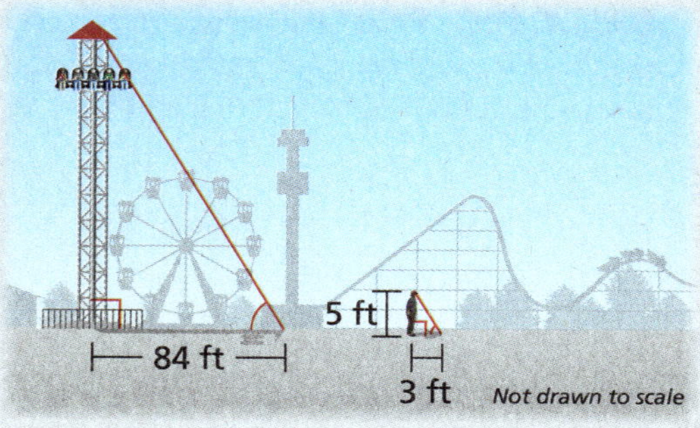

1.4 Solving Absolute Value Equations

Learning Target: Write and solve equations involving absolute value.

Success Criteria:
- I can write the two linear equations related to a given absolute value equation.
- I can solve equations involving one or two absolute values.
- I can identify special solutions of absolute value equations.

Algebraic Reasoning
MA.912.AR.4.1 Given a mathematical or real-world context, write and solve one-variable absolute value equations.

EXPLORE IT! Solving an Absolute Value Equation

Work with a partner. Consider the absolute value equation

$$|x + 2| = 3.$$

a. Explain what you think this equation means.

b. Can you find a number that makes the equation true? If so, what is the number?

c. Do you think there is another number that makes the equation true? If so, find that number. Compare your answer with your classmates'.

d. On the real number line below, locate the point for which the expression $|x + 2|$ is equal to 0.

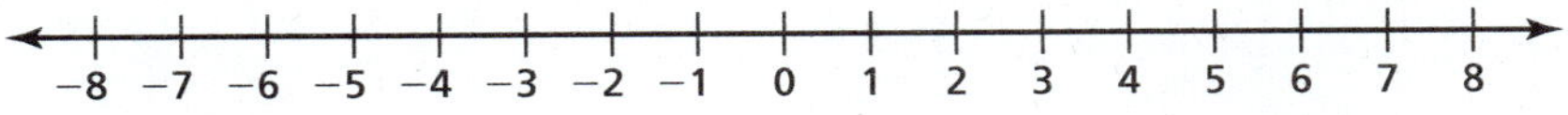

Then locate the numbers you found in parts (b) and (c) on the real number line. What do you notice?

GO DIGITAL

CONSTRUCT AN ARGUMENT 4 MTR

Construct a viable argument as to why you think there is or is not more than one solution to the absolute value equation.

e. Complete the two linear equations below so that the solutions are the values you found in parts (b) and (c).

$x + 2 =$ _____ $\qquad x + 2 =$ _____

f. Describe how to find the solutions of the absolute value equations algebraically. Then find the solutions.

i. $|x + 2| = 5$ **ii.** $|x - 3| = 1$

g. Use a spreadsheet to solve the absolute value equations in part (f). Explain your method.

	A	B
1	x	$\lvert x + 2\rvert$
2	−8	6
3	−7	
4	−6	
5	−5	
6	−4	
7	−3	
8	−2	
9	−1	
10	0	
11		

=abs(A2 + 2)

Solving Absolute Value Equations

An **absolute value equation** is an equation that contains an absolute value expression. You can solve these types of equations by solving two related linear equations.

Vocabulary

absolute value equation, *p. 45*
extraneous solution, *p. 49*

KEY IDEAS

Properties of Absolute Value

Let a and b be real numbers. Then the following properties are true.

1. $|a| \geq 0$

2. $|-a| = |a|$

3. $|ab| = |a||b|$

4. $\left|\dfrac{a}{b}\right| = \dfrac{|a|}{|b|},\ b \neq 0$

Solving Absolute Value Equations

To solve $|ax + b| = c$ when $c \geq 0$, solve the related linear equations

$$ax + b = c \quad or \quad ax + b = -c.$$

When $c < 0$, the absolute value equation $|ax + b| = c$ has no solution because absolute value represents a distance and cannot be negative.

EXAMPLE 1 Solving Absolute Value Equations

WATCH

Solve each equation. Graph the solutions, if possible.

a. $|x - 4| = 6$

b. $|3x + 1| = -5$

SOLUTION

a. Write the two related linear equations for $|x - 4| = 6$. Then solve.

$x - 4 = 6$	*or*	$x - 4 = -6$	Write related linear equations.
$x = 10$		$x = -2$	Add 4 to each side.

▶ The solutions are $x = 10$ and $x = -2$.

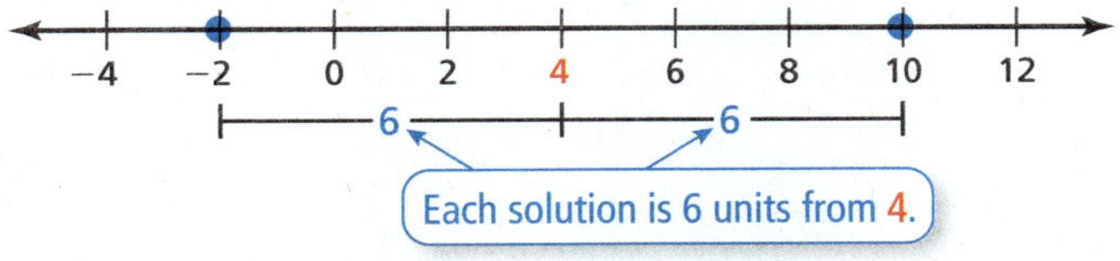

b. The absolute value of an expression must be greater than or equal to 0. The expression $|3x + 1|$ cannot equal -5.

▶ So, the equation has no solution.

GO DIGITAL

SELF-ASSESSMENT

1 I don't understand yet. **2** I can do it with help. **3** I can do it on my own. **4** I can teach someone else.

Solve the equation. Graph the solutions, if possible.

1. $|x| = 10$

2. $|x - 1| = 4$

3. $|3 + x| = -\frac{1}{2}$

4. REASONING How do you know that the equation $|4x - 7| = -1$ has no solution?

EXAMPLE 2 Solving a Multi-Step Absolute Value Equation

WATCH

Solve $|3x + 9| - 10 = -4$.

SOLUTION

First isolate the absolute value expression on one side of the equation.

$|3x + 9| - 10 = -4$ Write the equation.

$|3x + 9| = 6$ Add 10 to each side.

Now write the two related linear equations for $|3x + 9| = 6$. Then solve.

$3x + 9 = 6$ *or* $3x + 9 = -6$ Write related linear equations.

$3x = -3$ $3x = -15$ Subtract 9 from each side.

$x = -1$ $x = -5$ Divide each side by 3.

▶ The solutions are $x = -1$ and $x = -5$.

2 MTR **USE ANOTHER METHOD**

Is it valid to rewrite the equation as $3|x + 3| - 10 = -4$ and then solve? Justify your answer.

GO DIGITAL

7 MTR **EXAMPLE 3** **Modeling Real Life** WATCH

You are driving on a highway and are about 250 miles from the Florida-Georgia border. You set your cruise control at 60 miles per hour and plan to turn it off within 30 miles of the border on either side. Find the minimum and maximum numbers of hours you will have cruise control on.

SOLUTION

One way to solve is to write an absolute value equation that models the number x of hours you will have cruise control on. You know that the distance you travel will be within 30 miles of 250 miles.

distance you travel → $60x$; 30 miles from the state border → 30

$$|60x - 250| = 30$$

$|60x - 250|$: distance from state border

Write the two related linear equations for $|60x - 250| = 30$. Then solve.

$60x - 250 = 30$	*or*	$60x - 250 = -30$	Write related linear equations.
$60x = 280$		$60x = 220$	Add 250 to each side.
$x = 4\frac{2}{3}$		$x = 3\frac{2}{3}$	Divide each side by 60.

The solutions are $x = 3\frac{2}{3}$ and $x = 4\frac{2}{3}$.

▶ So, you will travel at least $3\frac{2}{3}$ hours and at most $4\frac{2}{3}$ hours with cruise control on.

Check

Minimum

$60\left(3\frac{2}{3}\right) - 250 \stackrel{?}{=} -30$

$-30 = -30$ ✓

Maximum

$60\left(4\frac{2}{3}\right) - 250 \stackrel{?}{=} 30$

$30 = 30$ ✓

SELF-ASSESSMENT

1 I don't understand yet. 2 I can do it with help. 3 I can do it on my own. 4 I can teach someone else.

Solve the equation. Check your solution.

5. $|x - 2| + 5 = 9$

6. $4|2x + 7| = 16$

7. $-2|5x - 1| - 3 = -11$

8. A plane is flying at a speed of 150 miles per hour. The pilot plans to fly at this speed for the next 160 miles, plus or minus 25 miles. Write an absolute value equation to find the minimum and maximum number of hours the plane will travel at that speed.

Solving Equations with Two Absolute Values

If the absolute values of two algebraic expressions are equal, then they must either be equal to each other or be opposites of each other.

KEY IDEA

Solving Equations with Two Absolute Values

To solve $|ax + b| = |cx + d|$, solve the related linear equations

$$ax + b = cx + d \quad \text{or} \quad ax + b = -(cx + d).$$

EXAMPLE 4 **Solving Equations with Two Absolute Values** WATCH

Solve (a) $|3x - 4| = |x|$ and (b) $|4x - 10| = 2|3x + 1|$.

SOLUTION

a. Write the two related linear equations for $|3x - 4| = |x|$. Then solve.

$$\begin{array}{rcl} 3x - 4 &=& x \\ -x && -x \\ 2x - 4 &=& 0 \\ +4 && +4 \\ 2x &=& 4 \\ \frac{2x}{2} &=& \frac{4}{2} \\ x &=& 2 \end{array} \qquad or \qquad \begin{array}{rcl} 3x - 4 &=& -x \\ +x && +x \\ 4x - 4 &=& 0 \\ +4 && +4 \\ 4x &=& 4 \\ \frac{4x}{4} &=& \frac{4}{4} \\ x &=& 1 \end{array}$$

▶ The solutions are $x = 2$ and $x = 1$.

Check

$$|3x - 4| = |x|$$
$$|3(2) - 4| \stackrel{?}{=} |2|$$
$$|2| \stackrel{?}{=} |2|$$
$$2 = 2 \checkmark$$

$$|3x - 4| = |x|$$
$$|3(1) - 4| \stackrel{?}{=} |1|$$
$$|-1| \stackrel{?}{=} |1|$$
$$1 = 1 \checkmark$$

b. Write the two related linear equations for $|4x - 10| = 2|3x + 1|$. Then solve.

$$\begin{array}{rcl} 4x - 10 &=& 2(3x + 1) \\ 4x - 10 &=& 6x + 2 \\ -6x && -6x \\ -2x - 10 &=& 2 \\ +10 && +10 \\ -2x &=& 12 \\ \frac{-2x}{-2} &=& \frac{12}{-2} \\ x &=& -6 \end{array} \qquad or \qquad \begin{array}{rcl} 4x - 10 &=& 2[-(3x + 1)] \\ 4x - 10 &=& 2(-3x - 1) \\ 4x - 10 &=& -6x - 2 \\ +6x && +6x \\ 10x - 10 &=& -2 \\ +10 && +10 \\ 10x &=& 8 \\ \frac{10x}{10} &=& \frac{8}{10} \\ x &=& 0.8 \end{array}$$

▶ The solutions are $x = -6$ and $x = 0.8$.

GO DIGITAL

Identifying Special Solutions

When you solve an absolute value equation, it is possible for a solution to be *extraneous*. An **extraneous solution** is an apparent solution that must be rejected because it does not satisfy the original equation.

WORDS AND MATH

The word *extraneous* contains the prefix *extra-*, which means "more than is necessary." Extraneous information is information that is not relevant or essential.

EXAMPLE 5 Identifying Extraneous Solutions

WATCH

Solve $|2x + 12| = 4x$. Check your solutions.

SOLUTION

Write the two related linear equations for $|2x + 12| = 4x$. Then solve.

$2x + 12 = 4x$	*or*	$2x + 12 = -4x$	Write related linear equations.
$12 = 2x$		$12 = -6x$	Subtract $2x$ from each side.
$6 = x$		$-2 = x$	Solve for x.

Check the apparent solutions to see if either is extraneous.

▶ The solution is $x = 6$. Reject $x = -2$ because it is extraneous.

Check

$|2x + 12| = 4x$

$|2(6) + 12| \stackrel{?}{=} 4(6)$

$|24| \stackrel{?}{=} 24$

$24 = 24$ ✓

$|2x + 12| = 4x$

$|2(-2) + 12| \stackrel{?}{=} 4(-2)$

$|8| \stackrel{?}{=} -8$

$8 \neq -8$ ✗

When solving equations of the form $|ax + b| = |cx + d|$, it is possible that one of the related linear equations will not have a solution.

EXAMPLE 6 Solving an Equation with Two Absolute Values

WATCH

Solve $|x + 5| = |x + 11|$.

SOLUTION

By equating the expression $x + 5$ and the opposite of $x + 11$, you obtain

$x + 5 = -(x + 11)$	Write related linear equation.
$x + 5 = -x - 11$	Distributive Property
$2x + 5 = -11$	Add x to each side.
$2x = -16$	Subtract 5 from each side.
$x = -8.$	Divide each side by 2.

However, by equating the expressions $x + 5$ and $x + 11$, you obtain

$x + 5 = x + 11$	Write related linear equation.
$x = x + 6$	Subtract 5 from each side.
$0 = 6$ ✗	Subtract x from each side.

which is a false statement. So, the original equation has only one solution.

▶ The solution is $x = -8$.

REMEMBER

Always check your solutions in the original equation to make sure they are not extraneous.

GO DIGITAL

SELF-ASSESSMENT

1 I don't understand yet. 2 I can do it with help. 3 I can do it on my own. 4 I can teach someone else.

Solve the equation. Check your solutions.

9. $|x + 8| = |2x + 1|$

10. $3|x - 4| = |2x + 5|$

11. $\frac{1}{2}|x + 8| = |4x - 1|$

Solve the equation. Check your solutions.

12. $|x + 6| = 2x$

13. $|3x - 2| = x$

14. $|2 + x| = |x - 8|$

15. $|5x - 2| = |5x + 4|$

16. WRITING How is solving an absolute value equation similar to solving an equation without an absolute value? How is it different?

1.4 Practice WITH CalcChat® AND CalcView®

In Exercises 1–8, simplify the expression.

1. $|-9|$

2. $-|15|$

3. $|14| - |-14|$

4. $|-3| + |3|$

5. $-|-5 \cdot (-7)|$

6. $|-0.8 \cdot 10|$

7. $\left|\frac{27}{-3}\right|$

8. $\left|-\frac{-12}{4}\right|$

In Exercises 9–22, solve the equation. Graph the solution(s), if possible. *(See Examples 1 and 2.)*

9. $|r| = -2$

10. $|x| = 13.4$

▶11. $|m + 3| = 7$

12. $|q - 8| = 14$

13. $\left|\frac{t}{2}\right| = 6$

14. $|-3.5d| = 15.4$

15. $|4b - 5| = 19$

16. $|x - 1| + 5 = 2$

▶17. $2|-8w + 6| = 76$

18. $\left|\frac{1}{3}y - 2\right| - 7 = 3$

19. $-4|8 - 5n| = 13$

20. $-3\left|1 - \frac{2}{3}v\right| = -9$

21. $3 = -2\left|\frac{1}{4}s - 5\right| + 3$

22. $9|4p + 2| + 8 = 35$

GO DIGITAL

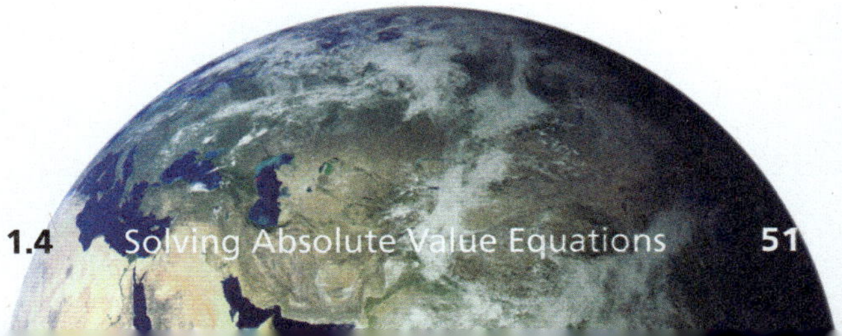

23. **MODELING REAL LIFE** The average distance from Earth to the Sun is 92.95 million miles. The actual distance varies from the average by up to 1.55 million miles. Write and solve an absolute value equation to find the minimum and maximum distance from Earth to the Sun. *(See Example 3.)*

24. **MODELING REAL LIFE** The recommended mass of a soccer ball is 0.43 kilogram. The actual mass is allowed to vary by up to 20 grams.

   a. Write and solve an absolute value equation to find the minimum and maximum acceptable soccer ball masses.

   b. A soccer ball has a mass of 423 grams. The soccer ball loses 0.016 kilogram of mass over time. Is the mass now acceptable? Explain.

STRUCTURE **In Exercises 25–28, match the absolute value equation with its graph without solving the equation.**

25. $|x + 2| = 4$

26. $|x - 4| = 2$

27. $|x - 2| = 4$

28. $|x + 4| = 2$

A.
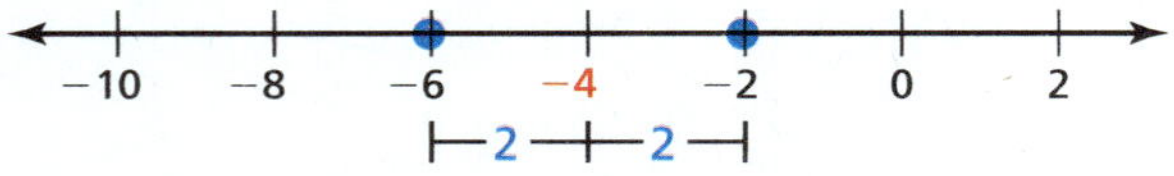

B.
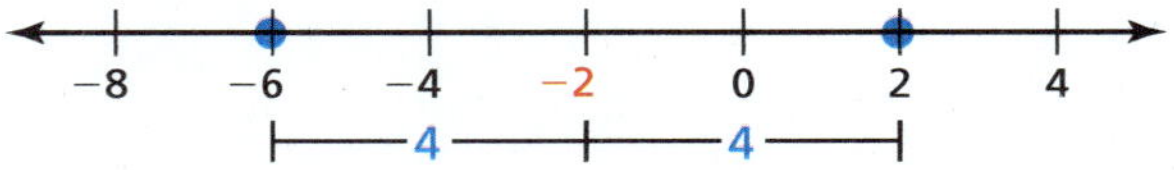

C.
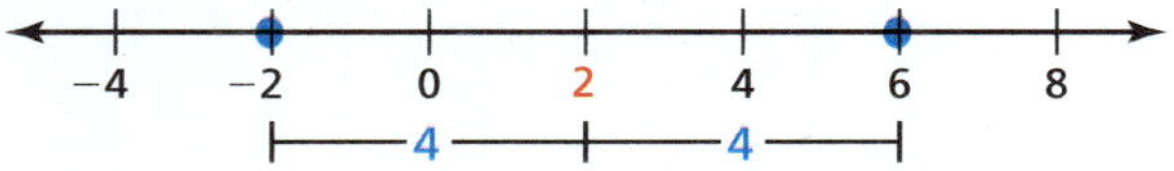

D.

In Exercises 29–38, solve the equation. Check your solutions. *(See Examples 4, 5, and 6.)*

▶29. $|4n - 15| = |n|$

30. $|2c + 8| = |10c|$

31. $|3k - 2| = 2|k + 2|$

32. $\left|\frac{1}{2}b - 8\right| = \left|\frac{1}{4}b - 1\right|$

33. $4|p - 3| = |2p + 8|$

34. $2|4w - 1| = 3|4w + 2|$

▶35. $|3h + 1| = 7h$

36. $|6a - 5| = 4a$

▶37. $\left|f - \frac{4}{3}\right| = \left|f + \frac{1}{6}\right|$

38. $|3x - 4| = |3x - 5|$

REASONING **In Exercises 39–42, write an absolute value equation that has the given solutions.**

39. $x = 8$ and $x = 18$

40. $x = -6$ and $x = 10$

41. $x = 1.5$ and $x = 8.5$

42. $x = -10$ and $x = -5$

4 MTR **ERROR ANALYSIS** **In Exercises 43 and 44, describe and correct the error in solving the equation.**

43.

✗

$$|2x - 1| = -9$$

$$2x - 1 = -9 \quad \text{or} \quad 2x - 1 = -(-9)$$

$$2x = -8 \qquad\qquad 2x = 10$$

$$x = -4 \qquad\qquad x = 5$$

The solutions are $x = -4$ and $x = 5$.

44.

✗

$$|5x + 8| = x$$

$$5x + 8 = x \quad \text{or} \quad 5x + 8 = -x$$

$$4x + 8 = 0 \qquad\qquad 6x + 8 = 0$$

$$4x = -8 \qquad\qquad 6x = -8$$

$$x = -2 \qquad\qquad x = -\frac{4}{3}$$

The solutions are $x = -2$ and $x = -\frac{4}{3}$.

7 MTR **45.** **MODELING REAL LIFE** Starting from 300 feet away, a car drives toward you. It then passes by you at a constant speed of 48 feet per second. The distance d (in feet) of the car from you after t seconds is given by the equation $d = |300 - 48t|$.

a. Explain what $48t$ represents in the given equation.

b. At what times is the car 60 feet from you?

46. **REASONING** Without solving completely, place each equation into one of the three categories. Explain your reasoning.

No solution	One solution	Two solutions

$|x - 2| + 6 = 0$ $\qquad$ $|x + 3| - 1 = 0$

$|x + 8| + 2 = 7$ $\qquad$ $|x - 1| + 4 = 4$

$|x - 6| - 5 = -9$ $\qquad$ $|x + 5| - 8 = -8$

47. **MAKING AN ARGUMENT** Your friend says that the absolute value equation $|3x + 8| - 9 = -5$ has no solution because the constant on the right side of the equation is negative. Is your friend correct? Explain.

4 MTR

48. **HOW DO YOU SEE IT?** The circle graph shows the results of a survey of registered voters the day of an election.

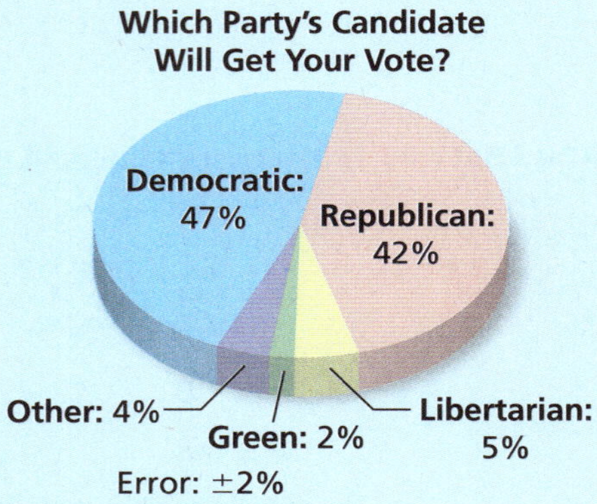

The error given in the graph means that the actual percent could be 2% more or 2% less than the percent reported by the survey.

a. What does the survey predict are the minimum and maximum percents of voters who will vote Republican? Green?

b. Write absolute value equations to represent your answers in part (a).

c. One candidate receives 44% of the vote. Which party do you think the candidate belongs to? Explain.

4 MTR **DISCUSS MATHEMATICAL THINKING** **In Exercises 49–52, complete the statement with *always*, *sometimes*, or *never*. Explain your reasoning.**

49. If $x^2 = a^2$, then $|x|$ is ________ equal to $|a|$.

50. If a and b are real numbers, then $|a - b|$ is ________ equal to $|b - a|$.

51. For any real number p, the equation $|x - 4| = p$ will ________ have two solutions.

52. For any real number p, the equation $|x - p| = 4$ will ________ have two solutions.

53. WRITING Explain why absolute value equations can have no solution, one solution, or two solutions. Give an example of each case.

5 MTR **54. STRUCTURE** Complete the equation $|x - \square| = \square$ with a, b, c, or d so that the equation is graphed correctly.

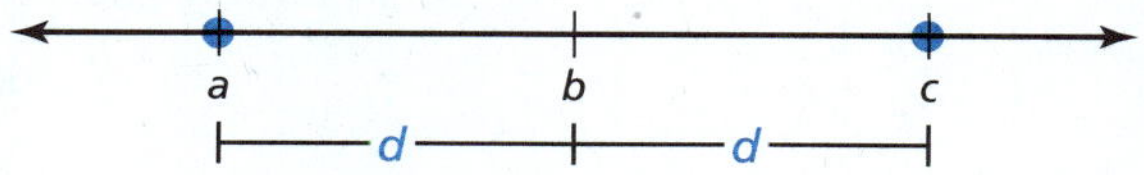

55. B.E.S.T. TEST PREP Which values are solutions of the equation $5 = -\frac{2}{3}|4x - 7| + 11$? Select all that apply.

Ⓐ $x = -\frac{1}{2}$

Ⓑ $x = \frac{1}{2}$

Ⓒ $x = \frac{3}{4}$

Ⓓ $x = \frac{11}{4}$

Ⓔ $x = 4$

Ⓕ no solution

4 MTR **56. DISCUSS MATHEMATICAL THINKING** Solve

$$8|x + 2| - 6 = 5|x + 2| + 3.$$

Explain how you found your solution(s).

57. OPEN-ENDED Describe a real-life situation that can be modeled by an absolute value equation with the solutions $x = 62$ and $x = 72$.

58. THOUGHT PROVOKING

What is the maximum number of solutions an equation of the form $\big||ax - b| + c\big| = d$ can have? Justify your reasoning with an example.

59. DIG DEEPER The minimum normal glucose level for a fasting adult is 70 mg/dL. The maximum normal level is 99 mg/dL. Write an absolute value equation that represents the minimum and maximum normal glucose levels.

60. REASONING How many solutions does the equation $a|x + b| + c = d$ have when $a > 0$ and $c = d$? when $a < 0$ and $c > d$? Explain your reasoning.

WATCH

REVIEW & REFRESH

In Exercises 61–64, solve the equation. Check your solution(s).

61. $3c + 1 = c + 1$

62. $4(6k + 9) = 8(3k - 2)$

63. $-10 - 12g = -4(3g + 2.5)$

64. $|y - 4| = |y + 10|$

65. Make a line graph of the data.

Year	1	2	3	4	5	6
Tickets sold	78	93	102	81	123	137

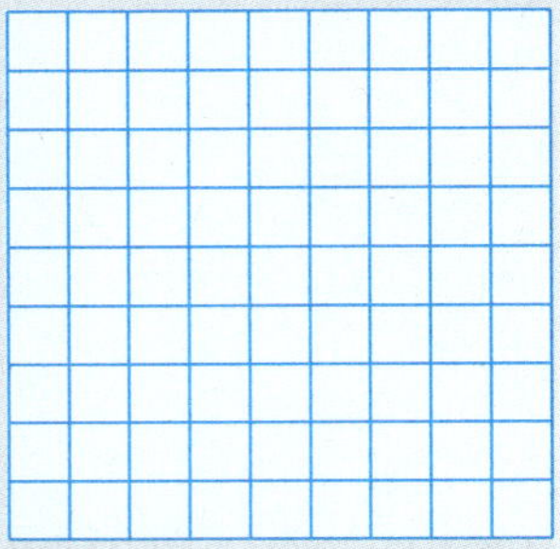

66. Simplify $12 + 5h - 3.5 + 8h$.

In Exercises 67 and 68, write the number in standard form.

67. 7×10^{-8}

68. 2.59×10^{3}

In Exercises 69 and 70, find the volume of the figure. Round your answer to the nearest tenth.

69.

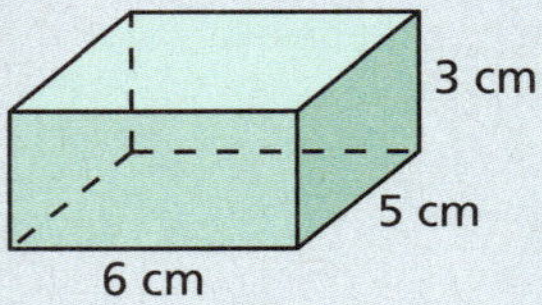

70.

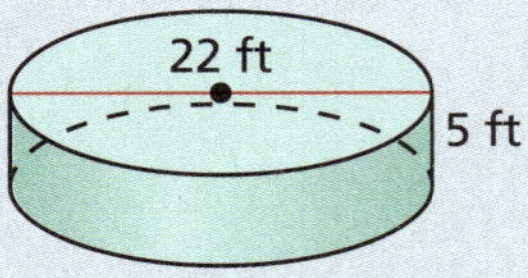

6 MTR **JUSTIFYING STEPS** **In Exercises 71 and 72, identify the property of equality that can be used to justify that Equation 1 and Equation 2 are equivalent.**

71.

Equation 1	$3x + 8 = x - 1$
Equation 2	$3x + 9 = x$

72.

Equation 1	$4y = 28$
Equation 2	$y = 7$

73. A circle has an area of 36π square inches. Find the radius.

74. A triangle has a height of 8 feet and an area of 48 square feet. Find the base.

7 MTR **75.** **MODELING REAL LIFE** You are driving your moped to school. The drive is about 12.5 miles, but the distance varies by up to 1.25 miles, depending on the route you take. You drive at a constant speed of 25 miles per hour. Find the minimum and maximum number of minutes it will take you to travel to school.

In Exercises 76–79, complete the statement. Round to the nearest hundredth, if necessary.

76. 9900 sec = ____ h

77. 0.25 T = ____ oz

78. 11.5 qt ≈ ____ mL

79. 49.6 cm ≈ ____ ft

1.5 Rewriting Equations and Formulas

Learning Target: Solve literal equations for given variables.

Success Criteria:
- I can identify a literal equation.
- I can use properties of equality to rewrite literal equations.
- I can use rewritten formulas to solve problems.

Algebraic Reasoning
MA.912.AR.1.2 Rearrange equations or formulas to isolate a quantity of interest.
Financial Literacy
MA.912.FL.1.2 Solve real-world problems involving simple, compound, and continuously compounded interest.

EXPLORE IT! Using Multiple Equations to Relate Quantities

Work with a partner. A landscaper purchases gasoline for various lawn care equipment. Consider the following quantities involved in this situation.

Number of gallons of gasoline	Price per gallon of gasoline	Total cost of gasoline

a. How are these quantities related in this situation? How can you represent this relationship?

b. Write an equation that represents the relationship among the three quantities.

Total cost of gasoline = ?

c. Write two more equations that represent the same relationship. How did you write these equations?

Price per gallon of gasoline = ?   Number of gallons of gasoline = ?

d. Why do you think it is beneficial to have solved an equation for each quantity?

e. After pumping gasoline, the landscaper sees the screen shown on the pump. Which quantity is missing? Find the missing quantity and explain how you found it.

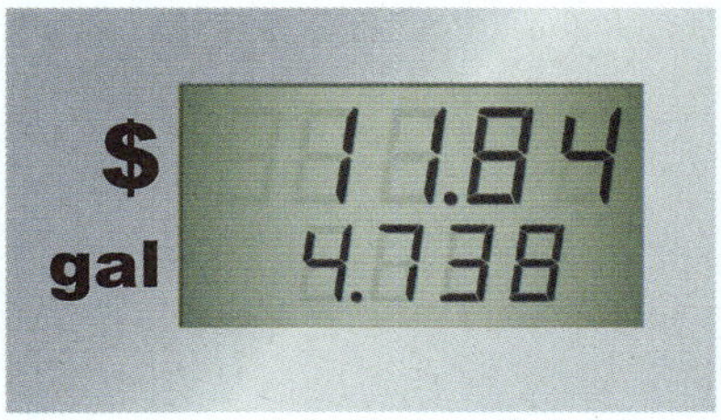

ASSESS REASONABLENESS (6 MTR)
How many decimal places did you use in your answer in part (e)? Explain your reasoning. How can you check that your answer is reasonable?

GO DIGITAL

Rewriting Literal Equations

An equation that has two or more variables is called a **literal equation**. To rewrite a literal equation, solve for one variable in terms of the other variable(s).

Vocabulary

literal equation, *p. 58*
formula, *p. 59*

EXAMPLE 1 **Rewriting a Literal Equation**

Solve the literal equation $3y + 4x = 9$ for y.

SOLUTION

$3y + 4x = 9$	Write the equation.
$3y + 4x - 4x = 9 - 4x$	Subtraction Property of Equality
$3y = 9 - 4x$	Simplify.
$\frac{3y}{3} = \frac{9 - 4x}{3}$	Division Property of Equality
$y = 3 - \frac{4}{3}x$	Simplify.

▶ The rewritten literal equation is $y = 3 - \frac{4}{3}x$.

EXAMPLE 2 **Rewriting a Literal Equation**

Solve the literal equation $y = 3x + 5xz$ for x.

SOLUTION

$y = 3x + 5xz$	Write the equation.
$y = x(3 + 5z)$	Distributive Property
$\frac{y}{3 + 5z} = \frac{x(3 + 5z)}{3 + 5z}$	Division Property of Equality
$\frac{y}{3 + 5z} = x$	Simplify.

▶ The rewritten literal equation is $x = \frac{y}{3 + 5z}$.

REMEMBER
Division by 0 is undefined.

In Example 2, you must assume that $z \neq -\frac{3}{5}$ in order to divide by $3 + 5z$. In general, when dividing by a variable or variable expression to rewrite a literal equation, assume that the variable or variable expression does not equal 0.

SELF-ASSESSMENT

1 I don't understand yet. 2 I can do it with help. 3 I can do it on my own. 4 I can teach someone else.

Solve the literal equation for *y*.

1. $3y - x = 9$

2. $2x - 2y = 5$

3. $20 = 8x + 4y$

Solve the literal equation for *x*.

4. $y = 5x - 4x$

5. $2x + kx = m$

6. $3 + 5x - kx = y$

GO DIGITAL

SELF-ASSESSMENT

1 I don't understand yet. 2 I can do it with help. 3 I can do it on my own. 4 I can teach someone else.

4 MTR **7. DIFFERENT WORDS, SAME QUESTION** Which is different? Find "both" answers.

Solve $3x + 6y = 24$ for x.	Solve $24 - 3x = 6y$ for x.	Solve $6y = 24 - 3x$ for y in terms of x.	Solve $24 - 6y = 3x$ for x in terms of y.

Rewriting and Using Formulas for Area

A **formula** shows how one variable is related to one or more other variables. A formula is a type of literal equation.

EXAMPLE 3 Rewriting a Formula for Surface Area

WATCH

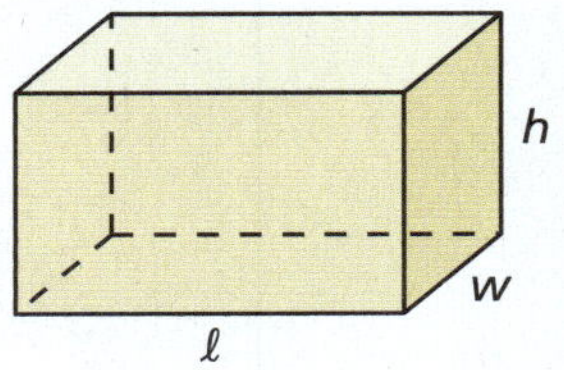

The formula for the surface area S of a rectangular prism is $S = 2\ell w + 2\ell h + 2wh$. Solve the formula for the length ℓ.

SOLUTION

$$S = 2\ell w + 2\ell h + 2wh$$ Write the equation.

$$S - 2wh = 2\ell w + 2\ell h + 2wh - 2wh$$ Subtraction Property of Equality

$$S - 2wh = 2\ell w + 2\ell h$$ Simplify.

$$S - 2wh = \ell(2w + 2h)$$ Distributive Property

$$\frac{S - 2wh}{2w + 2h} = \frac{\ell(2w + 2h)}{2w + 2h}$$ Division Property of Equality

$$\frac{S - 2wh}{2w + 2h} = \ell$$ Simplify.

▶ When you solve the formula for ℓ, you obtain $\ell = \dfrac{S - 2wh}{2w + 2h}$.

7 MTR

EXAMPLE 4 Modeling Real Life

WATCH

You own a rectangular lot that is 500 feet deep. It has an area of 100,000 square feet. To pay for a new water system, you are assessed \$5.50 per foot of lot frontage. How much are you assessed for the new water system?

SOLUTION

To find the amount assessed, first find the frontage of your lot. In the formula for the area of a rectangle, let the width w represent the lot frontage.

$$A = \ell w$$ Write the formula for area of a rectangle.

$$\frac{A}{\ell} = w$$ Divide each side by ℓ to solve for w.

$$\frac{100{,}000}{500} = w$$ Substitute 100,000 for A and 500 for ℓ.

$$200 = w$$ Simplify.

Your frontage is 200 feet. Multiply this by the cost of frontage, \$5.50 per foot.

$$\frac{\$5.50}{1\ \cancel{\text{ft}}} \cdot 200\ \cancel{\text{ft}} = \$1100$$

▶ So, you are assessed \$1100 for the new water system.

GO DIGITAL

SELF-ASSESSMENT

1 I don't understand yet. 2 I can do it with help. 3 I can do it on my own. 4 I can teach someone else.

Solve the formula for the indicated variable.

8. Area of a triangle: $A = \frac{1}{2}bh$; Solve for h.

9. Surface area of a cone: $S = \pi r^2 + \pi r\ell$; Solve for ℓ.

10. You want to enclose a rectangular region with an area of 1200 square feet and a length of 40 feet, 50 feet, or 60 feet. Find the perimeter for each possible region. Explain why you might rewrite the area formula to find the solutions.

Rewriting and Using Other Common Formulas

KEY IDEA

Common Formulas

Temperature F = degrees Fahrenheit, C = degrees Celsius

$C = \frac{5}{9}(F - 32)$

Simple Interest I = interest, P = principal,

r = annual interest rate (decimal form),

t = time (years)

$I = Prt$

Distance d = distance traveled, r = rate, t = time

$d = rt$

EXAMPLE 5 Rewriting the Formula for Temperature

WATCH

Solve the temperature formula for F.

SOLUTION

$C = \frac{5}{9}(F - 32)$	Write the temperature formula.
$\frac{9}{5}C = F - 32$	Multiply each side by $\frac{9}{5}$.
$\frac{9}{5}C + 32 = F$	Add 32 to each side.

▶ The rewritten formula is $F = \frac{9}{5}C + 32$.

GO DIGITAL

7 MTR **EXAMPLE 6** **Modeling Real Life** WATCH

Which has the greater surface temperature: Mercury or Venus?

SOLUTION

Convert the Celsius temperature of Mercury to degrees Fahrenheit.

$F = \frac{9}{5}C + 32$	Write the rewritten formula from Example 5.
$= \frac{9}{5}(427) + 32$	Substitute 427 for C.
$= 768.6 + 32$	Multiply.
$= 800.6$	Add.

▶ The surface temperature of Mercury is 800.6°F. Because 864°F is greater than 800.6°F, Venus has the greater surface temperature.

SELF-ASSESSMENT

1 I don't understand yet. 2 I can do it with help. 3 I can do it on my own. 4 I can teach someone else.

11. A fever is generally considered to be a body temperature greater than 100°F. Your friend has a temperature of 37°C. Does your friend have a fever when the temperature increases by 1°F? 1°C?

7 MTR **EXAMPLE 7** **Modeling Real Life** WATCH

You deposit $5000 in an account that earns simple interest. After 6 months, the account earns $162.50 in interest. What is the annual interest rate?

SOLUTION

One way to find the annual interest rate is to solve the simple interest formula for r.

$I = Prt$	Write the simple interest formula.
$\frac{I}{Pt} = r$	Divide each side by Pt to solve for r.
$\frac{162.50}{(5000)(0.5)} = r$	Substitute 162.50 for I, 5000 for P, and 0.5 for t.
$0.065 = r$	Simplify.

▶ The annual interest rate is 0.065, or 6.5%.

COMMON ERROR

The unit of t is years. Be sure to convert months to years.

$\frac{1 \text{ yr}}{12 \text{ mo}} \cdot 6 \text{ mo} = 0.5 \text{ yr}$

GO DIGITAL

7 MTR **EXAMPLE 8** **Modeling Real Life** WATCH

A truck driver averages 60 miles per hour while delivering freight to a customer. On the return trip, the driver averages 50 miles per hour because of construction. The total driving time is 6 hours and 36 minutes. How long does each trip take?

SOLUTION

Step 1 Rewrite the Distance Formula to write expressions that represent the two trip times. Solving the formula $d = rt$ for t, you obtain $t = \frac{d}{r}$. So, $\frac{d}{60}$ represents the delivery time, and $\frac{d}{50}$ represents the return trip time.

Step 2 Use these expressions and the total driving time to write and solve an equation to find the distance one way.

$$\frac{d}{60} + \frac{d}{50} = 6.6$$ Total driving time: $6 \text{ h} + \frac{36}{60} \text{ h} = 6.6 \text{ h}$

$$\frac{11d}{300} = 6.6$$ Add the fractions using a common denominator of 300.

$$11d = 1980$$ Multiply each side by 300.

$$d = 180$$ Divide each side by 11.

The distance one way is 180 miles.

Check Check that the sum of the driving times is equal to the total driving time.

$$\begin{array}{r} 3\text{ h} \\ +\ 3\text{ h}\ \ 36\text{ min} \\ \hline 6\text{ h}\ \ 36\text{ min} \end{array}$$ ✓

Step 3 Use the expressions from Step 1 to find the two trip times.

▶ So, the delivery takes $180 \text{ mi} \div \frac{60 \text{ mi}}{1 \text{ h}} = 3$ hours, and the return trip takes $180 \text{ mi} \div \frac{50 \text{ mi}}{1 \text{ h}} = 3.6$ hours, or 3 hours and 36 minutes.

SELF-ASSESSMENT

1 I don't understand yet. 2 I can do it with help. 3 I can do it on my own. 4 I can teach someone else.

12. How much money must you deposit in a simple interest account to earn \$500 in interest in 5 years at 4% annual interest?

13. A truck driver averages 60 miles per hour while delivering freight and 45 miles per hour on the return trip. The total driving time is 7 hours. How much longer does the return trip take than the delivery?

1.5 Practice WITH CalcChat® AND CalcView®

In Exercises 1–10, solve the literal equation for y. *(See Example 1.)*

1. $y - 3x = 13$

2. $2x + y = 7$

▶3. $2y - 18x = -26$

4. $20x + 5y = 15$

5. $9x - y = 45$

6. $6x - 3y = -6$

7. $4x - 5 = 7 + 4y$

8. $16x + 9 = 9y - 2x$

9. $2 + \frac{1}{6}y = 3x + 4$

10. $11 - \frac{1}{2}y = 3 + 6x$

In Exercises 11–20, solve the literal equation for x. *(See Example 2.)*

11. $y = 4x + 8x$

12. $m = 10x - x$

13. $a = 2x + 6xz$

14. $y = 3bx - 7x$

▶15. $y = 4x + rx + 6$

16. $z = 8 + 6x - px$

17. $sx + tx = r$

18. $a = bx + cx + d$

19. $12 - 5x - 4kx = y$

20. $x - 9 + 2wx = y$

7 MTR 21. **MODELING REAL LIFE** The total cost C (in dollars) to participate in a ski club is given by $C = 85x + 60$, where x is the number of ski trips you take.

a. Solve the equation for x.

b. How many ski trips did you take if you spent a total of \$315? \$485?

GO DIGITAL

22. **MODELING REAL LIFE** The penny size of a nail indicates the length of the nail. The penny size d of a nail that is 1 to 3 inches long is given by $d = 4n - 2$, where n is the length (in inches) of the nail.

7 MTR

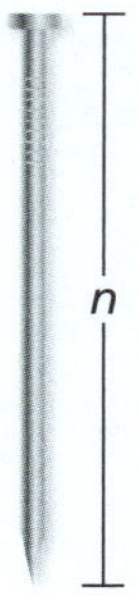

a. Solve the equation for n.

b. Find the lengths of nails with the following penny sizes: 3, 6, and 10.

4 MTR **ERROR ANALYSIS** **In Exercises 23 and 24, describe and correct the error in solving the equation for x.**

23.

$$12 - 2x = -2(y - x)$$
$$-2x = -2(y - x) - 12$$
$$x = (y - x) + 6$$

24.

$$10 = ax - 3b$$
$$10 = x(a - 3b)$$
$$\frac{10}{a - 3b} = x$$

In Exercises 25–28, solve the formula for the indicated variable. *(See Examples 3 and 5.)*

25. Profit: $P = R - C$;
Solve for C.

26. Surface area of a cylinder: $S = 2\pi r^2 + 2\pi rh$;
Solve for h.

▶ **27.** Area of a trapezoid: $A = \frac{1}{2}h(b_1 + b_2)$;
Solve for b_2.

28. Average acceleration of an object: $a = \frac{v_1 - v_0}{t}$;
Solve for v_1.

29. **STRUCTURE** A common statistic used in professional football is the quarterback rating. This rating is made up of four major factors. One factor is the completion rating given by the formula

5 MTR

$$R = 5\left(\frac{C}{A} - 0.3\right)$$

where C is the number of completed passes and A is the number of attempted passes. Solve the formula for C.

5 MTR **30.** **STRUCTURE** Newton's law of gravitation is given by the formula

$$F = G\left(\frac{m_1 m_2}{d^2}\right)$$

where F is the force between two objects of masses m_1 and m_2, G is the gravitational constant, and d is the distance between the two objects. Solve the formula for m_1.

31. **MODELING REAL LIFE** The sale price S (in dollars) of an item is given by the formula $S = L - rL$, where L is the list price (in dollars) and r is the percent of discount (in decimal form). *(See Examples 4 and 6.)*

a. Solve the formula for r.

b. The list price of the shirt is \$21.50. What is the percent of discount?

32. **MODELING REAL LIFE** The density d of a substance is given by the formula $d = \frac{m}{V}$, where m is its mass and V is its volume.

a. Solve the formula for each of the other two variables.

b. Find the mass of the pyrite sample. Explain how you found the mass.

33. **MODELING REAL LIFE** You deposit \$2000 in an account that earns simple interest at an annual rate of 4%. How long must you leave the money in the account to earn \$500 in interest? *(See Example 7.)*

34. **MODELING REAL LIFE** You deposit money into an account that earns simple interest at an annual rate of 8%. After 5 years, the account earns \$1200 in interest. How much money did you deposit into the account?

35. **MODELING REAL LIFE** You deposit \$6000 into an account that earns simple interest at an annual rate of 5%. How much interest does the account earn after 3 months?

36. **MODELING REAL LIFE** A flight averages 460 miles per hour. The return flight averages 500 miles per hour because of a tailwind. The total flying time is 4 hours and 48 minutes. How long is each flight? Explain. *(See Example 8.)*

37. **MODELING REAL LIFE** A vehicle travels 55 miles per hour and 20 miles per gallon.

7 MTR

a. Write an equation that represents the distance d (in miles) that the vehicle travels in t hours. Then write an equation that represents the distance d (in miles) that the vehicle travels using g gallons of gasoline.

b. Write an equation that relates g and t. Then solve the equation for g.

c. The vehicle travels for 6 hours. How many gallons of gasoline does the vehicle use? How far does it travel? Explain.

38. **HOW DO YOU SEE IT?**
The rectangular prism shown has square bases.

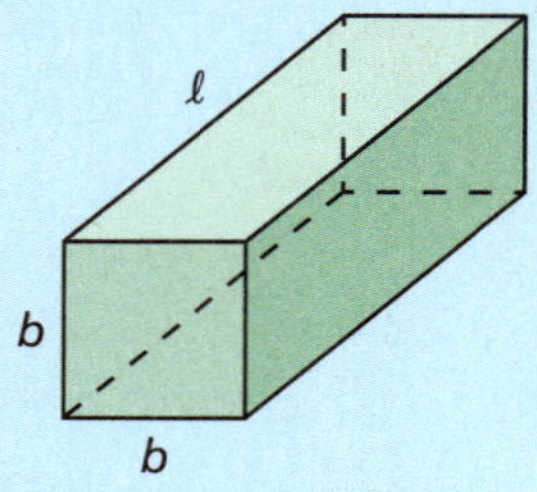

a. Use the figure to write a formula for the surface area S of the prism.

b. Your teacher asks you to solve the formula for either b or ℓ. Which would you choose? Explain.

DIG DEEPER **In Exercises 39 and 40, solve the literal equation for *a*.**

39. $x = \dfrac{a + b + c}{ab}$

40. $y = x\left(\dfrac{ab}{a - b}\right)$

41. **INVESTIGATE** The ideal gas law is given by the formula $PV = nRT$.

7 MTR

a. Research what each variable in the ideal gas law represents.

b. A container has 7.8 moles of a gas at a pressure of 0.09 standard atmosphere at a temperature of 300 Kelvin. Find the volume of the container.

7 MTR

42. **PERFORMANCE TASK** You have $2000 to deposit into a bank account that earns simple interest. Use interest rates at local banks to find how much interest different accounts earn after four years. Compare the different accounts and decide which account you should use. Consider other fees associated with each account when making your decision.

7 MTR **43. MODELING REAL LIFE** One type of stone formation found in Carlsbad Caverns in New Mexico is called a column. This stone formation connects to the ceiling and the floor of a cave.

a. What is the radius (to the nearest tenth of a foot) of a cylindrical column that has a circumference of 7 feet? 8 feet? 9 feet?

b. Explain why you might rewrite the circumference formula to find the solutions in part (a).

44. THOUGHT PROVOKING Give a possible value for h. Justify your answer. Draw and label the figure using your chosen value of h.

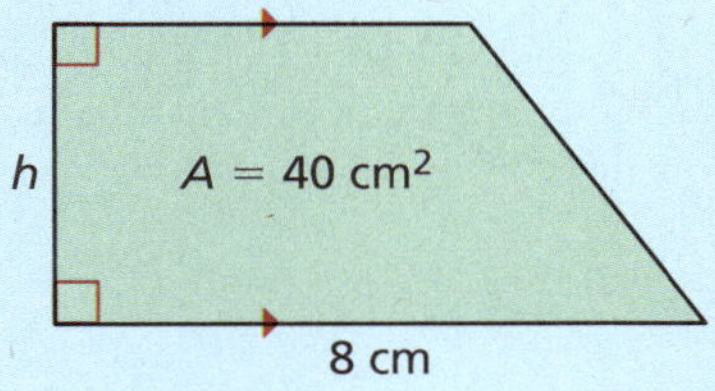

5 MTR **CONNECTING CONCEPTS** **In Exercises 45 and 46, write a formula for the area of the regular polygon. Solve the formula for the height *h*.**

45.

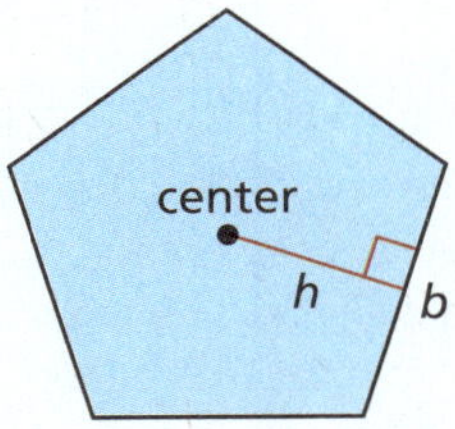

46.

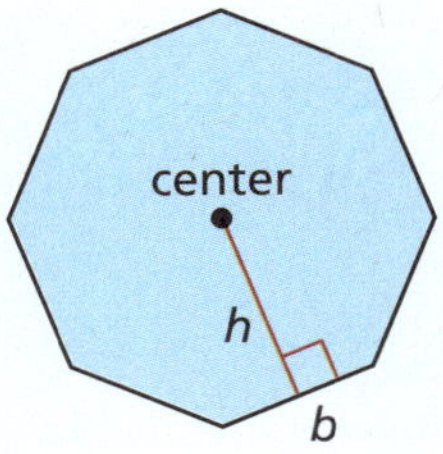

REVIEW & REFRESH

WATCH

In Exercises 47–50, evaluate the expression when $a = 5$ and $b = 2$.

47. $a^2 + 12$

48. $9b - 4$

49. $\frac{a}{b} - \frac{3}{4}$

50. $3b\left(16 - \frac{1}{10}a\right)$

51. Solve the literal equation $6x - y = 12$ for y.

52. Find the surface area of the cylinder.

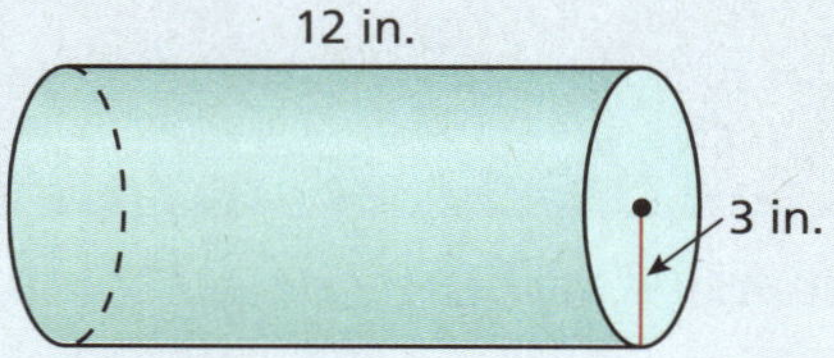

53. Tell whether the ratios 6 : 8 and 4 : 6 form a proportion.

7 MTR **54.** **MODELING REAL LIFE** The volume G of an aquarium (in gallons) is given by the formula $G = \frac{\ell wh}{231}$, where ℓ is the length of the aquarium (in inches), w is the width (in inches), and h is the height (in inches).

a. Solve the formula for h.

b. Find the height of a 20-gallon aquarium with a length of 24 inches and a width of 12 inches.

In Exercises 55–58, solve the equation. Graph the solutions, if possible.

55. $|x - 3| = 5$

56. $|3y - 12| - 7 = 2$

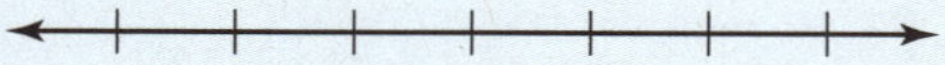

57. $2|2r + 4| = -16$

58. $-4|s + 9| = -24$

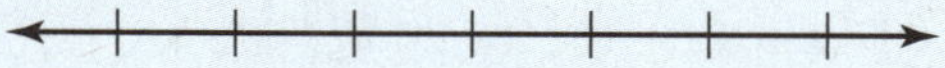

59. Tell whether the points $(-2, 3)$, $(2, 1)$, and $(3, 3)$ form a right triangle.

7 MTR **60.** **MODELING REAL LIFE** You want to rent a kayak from one of the two rental companies shown. After how many hours is the total rental cost the same at each company?

In Exercises 61–63, solve the equation. Check your solution.

61. $\frac{z}{-5} + 2 = -4$

62. $1.9t = -5.7$

63. $27 = -3(8y - 7) + 20y$

1 Chapter Review WITH CalcChat®

Chapter Learning Target: Understand solving linear equations.

Chapter Success Criteria:
- ◆ I can solve simple and multi-step equations.
- ◆ I can describe how to solve equations.
- ■ I can recognize when an equation has zero, one, or infinitely many solutions.
- ■ I can apply equation-solving techniques to solve real-life problems.

◆ Surface
■ Deep

SELF-ASSESSMENT 1 I don't understand yet. 2 I can do it with help. 3 I can do it on my own. 4 I can teach someone else.

1.1 Solving Simple Equations (pp. 5–18) WATCH

Learning Target: Write and solve one-step linear equations.

Vocabulary AZ VOCAB
equation
linear equation in one variable
solution
equivalent equations

Solve the equation. Justify each step. Check your solution.

1. $z + 3 = -6$

2. $2.6 = -0.2t$

3. $-\frac{n}{5} = -2$

4. $5.9 = y - 2.7$

5. $\pi b = -\frac{1}{9}$

6. $3\frac{3}{10} = w + 1\frac{4}{5}$

7. Which property of equality should you use to solve the equation $\frac{a}{b} + x = c$, where a and b are negative numbers? Explain your reasoning.

8. You have \$175.29 in a savings account. You deposit an additional \$48.75. How much more do you need to save to buy the cell phone?

GO DIGITAL

1.2 Solving Multi-Step Equations (pp. 19–32) WATCH

Learning Target: Write and solve multi-step linear equations.

Solve the equation. Check your solution.

9. $3y + 11 = -16$

10. $6 = 1 - b$

11. $n + 5n + 7 = 43$

12. $-4(2z + 6) - 12 = 4$

13. $\frac{3}{2}(x - 2) - 5 = 19$

14. $6 = \frac{1}{5}w + \frac{7}{5}w - 4$

15. What happens to the value of x in the equation $\frac{x}{b} + 8 = 15$ as the value of b decreases? Explain your reasoning.

16. Find three consecutive odd integers that have a sum of 75.

1.3 Solving Equations with Variables on Both Sides (pp. 33–42)

WATCH

Learning Target: Write and solve equations with variables on both sides.

Vocabulary
identity

Solve the equation. Check your solution.

17. $3n - 3 = 4n + 1$

18. $-18 + \frac{1}{2}m = m - 6$

19. $2y - 16 = \frac{1}{3}(y - 3)$

20. $5(1 + x) = 5x + 5$

21. $\frac{1}{6}(3z + 2) = -\frac{3}{4}z$

22. $3(n + 4) = \frac{1}{2}(6n + 4)$

23. Solve $7(2 + 3x) = 77x$ using two different methods. Justify each of your solution methods.

24. An airplane leaves Los Angeles and travels 5 hours to New York City. The return trip travels along the same route and takes 6 hours and 15 minutes because the plane travels 99 miles per hour slower due to a headwind. Find the distance that the plane flies between the two cities.

25. How can you modify the equation $6(3 + 4d) = 24d$ so that it has at least one solution? Write and solve your modified equation to check your answer.

26. Determine whether the equation $mx + 4 = \frac{1}{2}nx + 8$ *always*, *sometimes*, or *never* has a solution when (a) $m < n$, (b) $m = n$, and (c) $m > n$.

1.4 Solving Absolute Value Equations (pp. 43–56) WATCH

Learning Target: Write and solve equations involving absolute value.

Vocabulary
absolute value equation
extraneous solution

Solve the equation. Check your solutions.

27. $|y + 3| = 17$

28. $2|k - 3| = 18$

29. $|16g - 40| = -4|4g - 10|$

30. $-|b + 6| = |3b - 2|$

31. $-2|5w - 7| + 9 = -7$

32. $|x - 2| = |4 + x|$

Write an absolute value equation that has the given solutions.

33. $x = 7$ and $x = -7$

34. $x = 4$ and $x = -10$

35. $x = 3.4$ and $x = 9.4$

36. no solution

37. The minimum sustained wind speed of a Category 1 hurricane is 74 miles per hour. The maximum sustained wind speed is 95 miles per hour. Write an absolute value equation that represents the minimum and maximum speeds.

38. A cargo truck is traveling 70 miles per hour and plans to travel 840 miles, plus or minus 105 miles, depending on fuel levels. Find the minimum and maximum number of hours the truck will travel at that speed.

1.5 Rewriting Equations and Formulas (pp. 57–68) WATCH

Learning Target: Solve literal equations for given variables.

Vocabulary
literal equation
formula

Solve the literal equation for y.

39. $2x - 4y = 20$

40. $8x - 3 = 5 + 4y$

41. $3(2x - y) = -4x - y$

42. $a = 9y + 3yx$

Solve the literal equation for x.

43. $6y + 18x = -14$

44. $9 + 4y = -5x + 7y$

45. $y = -2bx + 7y$

46. $3(x + 2by) = 15by$

47. You deposit money in an account that earns simple interest at an annual rate of 6%. After 8 years, the account earns \$360 in interest. How much money did you deposit in the account?

48. High divers use the height of the diving platform to calculate the speed at which they enter the water. The formula $5s - 3h = 12$ models the diver's speed s (in miles per hour) and the height h (in feet) of the platform.

a. Solve the formula for s and for h.

b. At what speed does a diver enter the water when the platform is 82 feet tall?

c. A diver enters the water at 48 miles per hour. How tall is the platform?

49. The formula $F = \frac{9}{5}(K - 273.15) + 32$ converts a temperature from kelvin K to degrees Fahrenheit F.

a. Solve the formula for K.

b. Convert 180°F to kelvin. Round your answer to the nearest hundredth.

Mathematical Thinking and Reasoning

4 MTR **ENGAGE IN DISCUSSIONS THAT REFLECT ON THE MATHEMATICAL THINKING OF SELF AND OTHERS**

Mathematicians who engage in discussions that reflect on the mathematical thinking of self and others develop a deeper understanding of mathematical concepts.

1. In Exercise 37 on page 66, explain why you are able to write an equation that relates the number of gallons g of gasoline and the time t.

2. Your friend says that Equation 1 and Equation 2 are equivalent. Is your friend correct? If so, explain why the equations are equivalent. If not, correct your friend's reasoning.

Equation 1: $8x + 18 = 4x - 32$

Equation 2: $2x + 18 = x - 32$

1 Practice Test WITH CalcChat®

Solve the equation.

1. $x - 7 = 15$

2. $\frac{2}{3}x + 5 = 3$

3. $2|x - 3| - 5 = 7$

4. $|2x - 19| = 4x + 1$

5. $-2 + 5x - 7 = 3x - 9 + 2x$

6. $\frac{1}{3}(6x + 12) - 2(x - 7) = 19$

Describe the values of *c* for which the equation has no solution. Explain your reasoning.

7. $3x - 5 = 3x - c$

8. $|x - 7| = c$

Solve the literal equation for *y*.

9. $x - 3y = 18x$

10. $7(3y - x) = -21$

11. $8xy = 2(2x + y)$

12. $9(x + y) = 3ay$

13. A safety regulation says that the minimum height of a handrail is 30 inches. The maximum height is 38 inches. Write an absolute value equation that represents the minimum and maximum heights.

GO DIGITAL

14. The perimeter P (in yards) of a soccer field is represented by the formula $P = 2\ell + 2w$, where ℓ is the length (in yards) and w is the width (in yards).

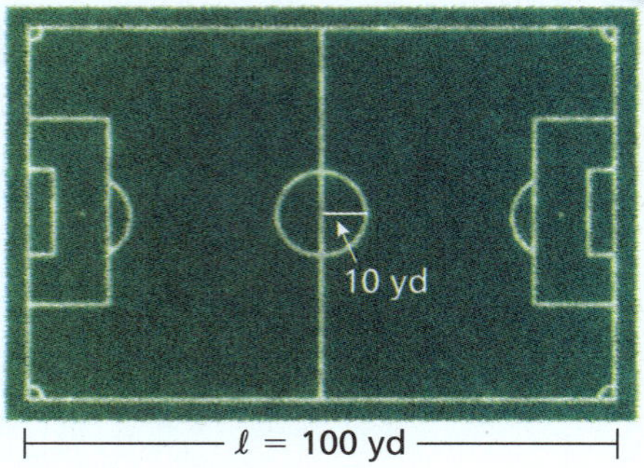

a. Solve the formula for w.

b. The perimeter of the soccer field is 330 yards. Find the width of the field.

c. About what percent of the field is inside the circle?

15. Consider the equation $|4x + 20| = 6x$. Without solving, how do you know that $x = -2$ is an extraneous solution?

16. You use the equation $\frac{M}{5} - 26 = 2\ell - \frac{1}{2}g$ to calculate the amount of money M in your account at the end of the month, where ℓ is the number of lawns mowed and g is the number of gallons of gas used.

a. Solve the equation for M.

b. What does 130 represent in your equation from part (a)?

c. How much money is in your acount at the end of the month when you mow 7 lawns and use $11\frac{1}{2}$ gallons of gas?

17. The speed of light is 11,176,920 miles per minute, and the distance from Earth to the Sun at a specific time is 92,955,807 miles. About how long does it take for sunlight to reach Earth?

1 Performance Task
Every Drop Counts

The average American family uses more than 300 gallons of water per day!

GO DIGITAL

About **60%** of an adult's body is water.

WATER LOG

Record your water activities and water consumption for one week. Then make a plan to reduce the amount of water you use each week. Determine the number of gallons you want to use for each activity, and solve equations to show how you will achieve your goal.

1 B.E.S.T. Test Prep WITH CalcChat®
Cumulative Practice

WATCH Tutorial videos are available for each exercise.

1. Which equation is equivalent to the formula for the area A of a trapezoid, $A = \frac{1}{2}h(b_1 + b_2)$?

Ⓐ $h = \dfrac{A}{2(b_1 + b_2)}$

Ⓑ $h = 2A - (b_1 + b_2)$

Ⓒ $h = \dfrac{2A - b_2}{b_1}$

Ⓓ $h = \dfrac{2A}{b_1 + b_2}$

2. Which equation is *not* equivalent to $cx - a = b$?

Ⓐ $cx - a + b = 2b$

Ⓑ $cx - a + b = 0$

Ⓒ $2cx - 2a = 2b$

Ⓓ $b + a = cx$

GRIDDED RESPONSE

3. A mountain biking park has 48 trails, 37.5% of which are beginner trails. The rest are divided evenly between intermediate and expert trails. How many expert trails are in the park?

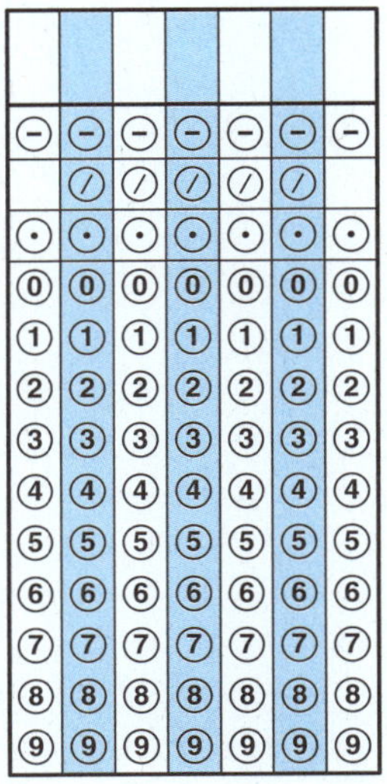

GO DIGITAL

4. Let N represent the number of solutions of the equation $3(x - a) = 3x - 6$. Which statements are correct?

Ⓐ When $a = 3$, $N < 1$.

Ⓑ When $a = -3$, $N > 1$.

Ⓒ When $a = 2$, $N > 1$.

Ⓓ When $a = -2$, $N > 1$.

Ⓔ When $a = x$, $N = 1$.

Ⓕ When $a = -x$, $N = 1$.

5. Which equation is equivalent to $5x + 3 = -7$?

Ⓐ $3x + 10 = 2x$

Ⓑ $-12 + 7x = 2x - 2$

Ⓒ $x - 1 = 4x + 11$

Ⓓ $8x + 6 = -2x - 14$

GRIDDED RESPONSE

6. You are painting your dining room white and your living room blue. You spend \$132 on 5 cans of paint. The white paint costs \$24 per can, and the blue paint costs \$28 per can. How many dollars would you save by switching the colors of the dining room and living room?

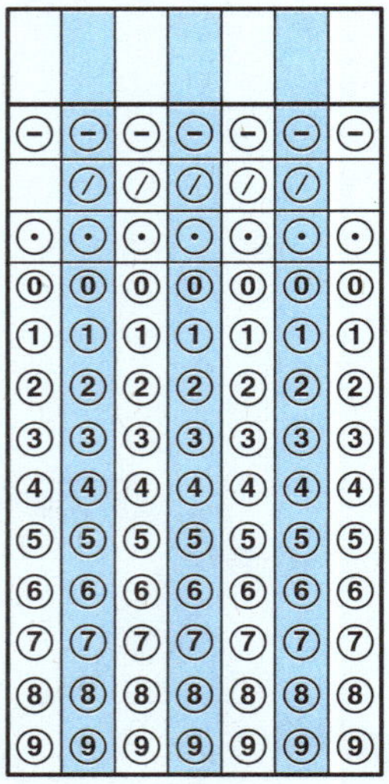

7. The perimeter of the triangle is 13 inches. What is the length of the shortest side?

Ⓐ 3 in.

Ⓑ 4 in.

Ⓒ 6 in.

Ⓓ 8 in.

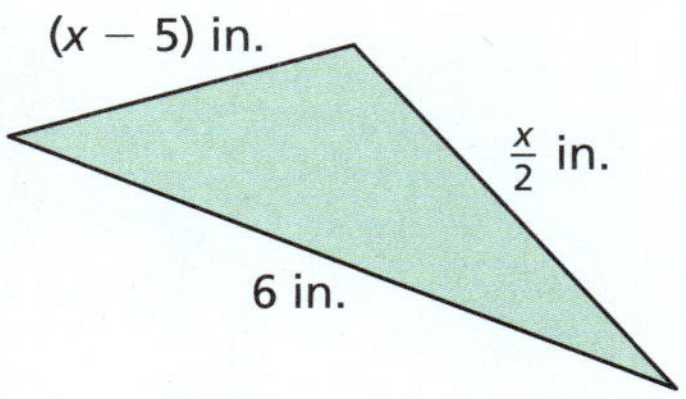

8. A line passes through the points $(-2, -3)$ and $(3, 7)$.

The slope of the line is [Ⓐ $\frac{1}{2}$ Ⓑ 1 Ⓒ 2 Ⓓ 4] and the y-intercept is [Ⓐ -2 Ⓑ 1 Ⓒ 5 Ⓓ 13].

9. Which table represents a proportional relationship?

Ⓐ

x	1	2	3	4
y	18	15	12	9

Ⓑ

x	2	4	5	8
y	7	14	17.5	28

Ⓒ

x	1	2	3	4
y	5	5	5	5

Ⓓ

x	40	20	10	5
y	1	2	4	8

10. Which equations have no solution? Select all that apply.

Ⓐ $-9 = -3|2x - 11|$

Ⓑ $-2x + 4 = 2x + 4$

Ⓒ $12x - 2x = 10x - 8$

Ⓓ $0 = |x + 13| + 2$

Ⓔ $7 - 2x = 3 - 2(x - 2)$

Ⓕ $3x - 12 = 3(x - 4) + 1$

11. The distance between Earth and Mars is approximately 4.35×10^7 miles. What is this distance in standard form?

Ⓐ 435,000 miles

Ⓑ 4,350,000 miles

Ⓒ 43,500,000 miles

Ⓓ 435,000,000 miles

2 Solving Linear Inequalities

WATCH

NATIONAL GEOGRAPHIC EXPLORER

Jimmy Kuo Wei Chin

Jimmy Chin is a photographer and mountain sports athlete known for his ability to capture extraordinary imagery while climbing and skiing in high-risk environments. In 2002, he was the cinematographer for a National Geographic trek across Tibet's Chang Tang Plateau. In 2006, he was part of the first American team to ski off the summit of Mount Everest.

- As elevation increases, the *effective oxygen level* decreases. What is the meaning of *effective oxygen level*?
- What is the effective oxygen level (in percent) at an elevation of 0 feet? 4000 feet? 8000 feet? 12,000 feet?
- What is the atmospheric pressure (in atmospheres) at an elevation of 0 feet? 4000 feet? 8000 feet? Do atmospheric pressure and elevation have a linear relationship?

STEM

Mountain climbing is one of the most dangerous sports in the world. In the Performance Task, you will assume the role of an expedition leader and use inequalities to track the progress of climbers on Mount Everest.

GO DIGITAL

Mountaineering

Preparing for Chapter 2

Chapter Learning Target: Understand solving linear inequalities.

Chapter Success Criteria:
- ◆ I can solve simple and multi-step inequalities.
- ◆ I can describe how to solve inequalities.
- ■ I can compare and contrast solving inequalities with solving equations.
- ■ I can apply techniques for solving inequalities to solve real-life problems.

◆ Surface
■ Deep

Chapter Vocabulary

AZ VOCAB

Work with a partner. Discuss each of the vocabulary terms.

inequality

compound inequality

solution of an inequality

absolute value inequality

equivalent inequalities

GO DIGITAL

Mathematical Thinking and Reasoning

1 MTR

ACTIVELY PARTICIPATE IN EFFORTFUL LEARNING BOTH INDIVIDUALLY AND COLLECTIVELY

Mathematicians who participate in effortful learning both individually and with others analyze a problem in a way that makes sense given the task.

Work with a partner. For every increase in elevation of 1000 feet, the temperature decreases about 3.5°F. A climber on K2 records a temperature of 1°F at an elevation of 17,700 feet.

The summit of K2 is the second-highest point on Earth, with an elevation of 28,251 feet.

1. Which inequality represents the elevations h (in feet) for which the temperature is less than -20°F?

$1 - 3.5h \leq -20$

$1 - 3.5\left(\frac{h - 17{,}700}{1000}\right) < -20$

$1 - 3.5h < -20$

$1 - 3.5\left(\frac{h - 17{,}700}{1000}\right) \leq -20$

2. What conclusions can you make about the values of h that make the inequality true?

3. Your friend says that the solution of the inequality is $h < 23{,}700$. Is your friend correct? Explain your reasoning.

2 Prepare WITH CalcChat®

Graphing Numbers on a Number Line

WATCH

Example 1 **Graph each number.**

a. 3

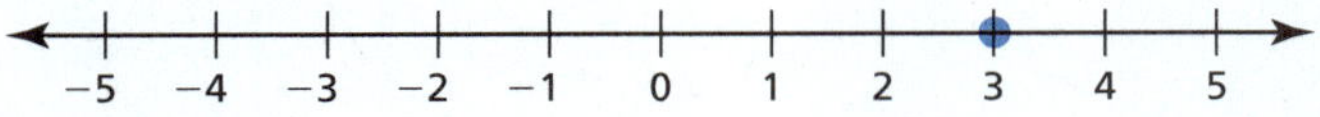

b. −0.2

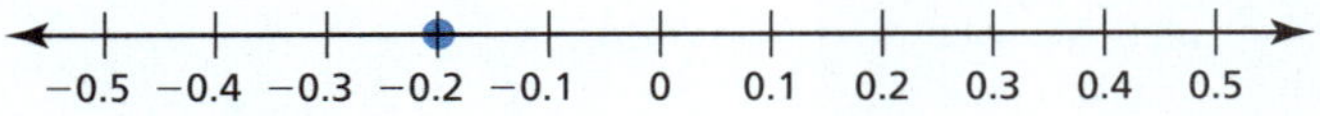

WATCH

Example 2 **Graph each number.**

a. $|4|$

The absolute value of a positive number is positive.

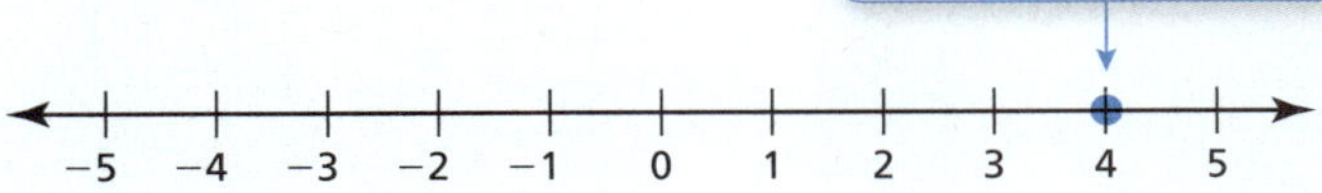

b. $\left|-1\frac{1}{3}\right|$

The absolute value of a negative number is positive.

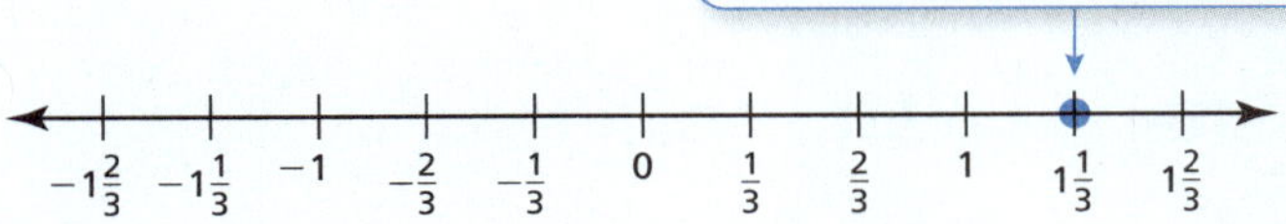

Graph the number.

1. 6

2. −5

3. $-\frac{1}{4}$

4. $|2|$

5. $|-1|$

6. $-|-2.2|$

GO DIGITAL

Comparing Real Numbers

Example 3 **Complete the statement -1 ____ -5 with <, >, or =.**

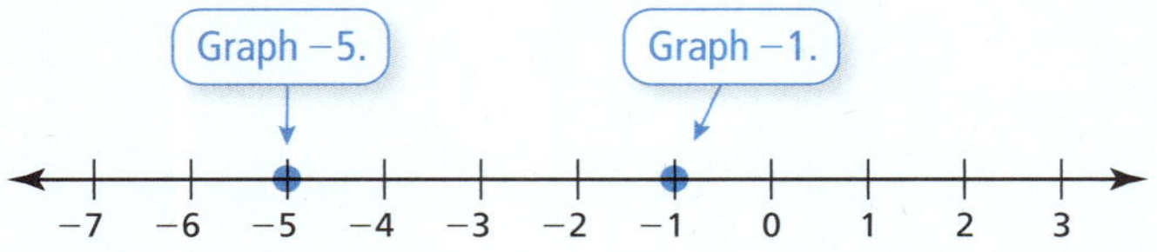

▶ -1 is to the right of -5. So, $-1 > -5$.

Complete the statement with <, >, or =.

7. 2 ____ 9

8. -6 ____ 5

9. $-\frac{1}{2}$ ____ -4

10. -7 ____ -7.5

11. $|-8|$ ____ $|8|$

12. $-1\frac{2}{5}$ ____ $\left|-3\frac{5}{8}\right|$

13. ANALYZE A PROBLEM A number a is to the left of a number b on a number line. How do the numbers $-a$ and $-b$ compare?

2.1 Writing and Graphing Inequalities

Learning Target: Write inequalities and represent solutions of inequalities on number lines.

Success Criteria:
- I can write word sentences as inequalities.
- I can determine whether a value is a solution of an inequality.
- I can graph and interpret inequalities.

Algebraic Reasoning
MA.912.AR.2.6 Given a mathematical or real-world context, write and solve one-variable linear inequalities, including compound inequalities. Represent solutions algebraically or graphically.

EXPLORE IT! Interpreting a Diagram

Work with a partner. Use the diagram shown.

Geography of Life Expectancy in the Bottom Income Quartile

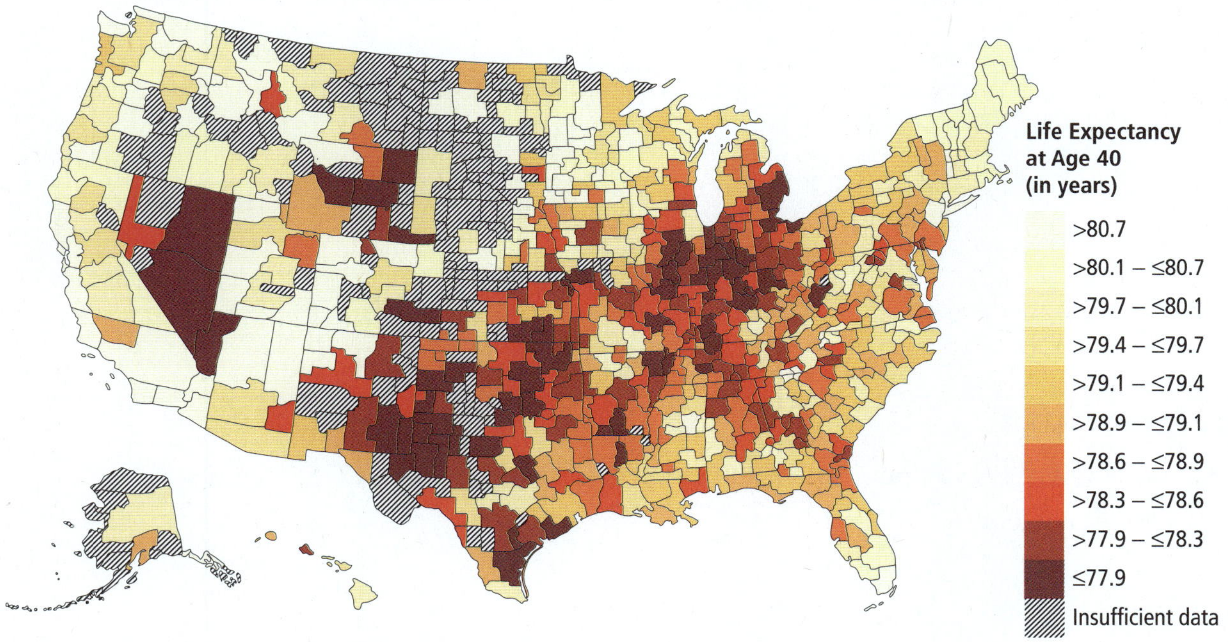

a. Explain what the diagram represents in your own words.

b. Which state do you think has the highest life expectancy for lower-income people at age 40? Which state do you think has the lowest? Explain your reasoning.

GO DIGITAL

c. Which city do you think has a higher life expectancy for lower-income people at age 40, Detroit or Miami? Explain your reasoning.

d. Write several other observations you can make from the diagram.

e. Explain how you can represent one piece of information from the diagram graphically.

7 MTR **f.** **INVESTIGATE** Use the Internet or some other reference to find a real-life data set represented by a data display that uses inequalities.

7 MTR APPLY MATHEMATICS

Why is it important to be able to interpret real-life data sets that are represented by maps, diagrams, and other data displays?

Writing Linear Inequalities

Vocabulary

inequality, *p. 89*
solution of an inequality, *p. 90*
solution set, *p. 90*
graph of an inequality, *p. 92*

An **inequality** is a mathematical sentence that compares expressions. An inequality contains the symbol $<$, $>$, $\leq$, or $\geq$. To write an inequality, look for the following phrases to determine which inequality symbol to use.

Inequality Symbols				
Symbol	$<$	$>$	$\leq$	$\geq$
Key phrases	• is less than • is fewer than	• is greater than • is more than	• is less than or equal to • is at most • is no more than	• is greater than or equal to • is at least • is no less than

EXAMPLE 1 Writing Inequalities

WATCH

Write each sentence as an inequality.

a. A number w minus 3.5 is less than or equal to -2.

b. Three is less than a number n plus 5.

c. Zero is greater than or equal to twice a number x plus 1.

SOLUTION

a. A number w minus 3.5 is less than or equal to -2.

$w - 3.5 \quad \leq \quad -2$

▶ An inequality is $w - 3.5 \leq -2$.

REMEMBER

The inequality $3 < n + 5$ is the same as $n + 5 > 3$.

b. Three is less than a number n plus 5.

$3 \quad < \quad n + 5$

▶ An inequality is $3 < n + 5$.

c. Zero is greater than or equal to twice a number x plus 1.

$0 \quad \geq \quad 2x + 1$

▶ An inequality is $0 \geq 2x + 1$.

SELF-ASSESSMENT

1 I don't understand yet. 2 I can do it with help. 3 I can do it on my own. 4 I can teach someone else.

Write the sentence as an inequality.

1. A number b is fewer than 30.4.

2. Eleven is more than a number y divided by 4.

3. $-\frac{7}{10}$ is at least twice a number k minus 4.

4. The sum of a number z and 16.2 is at most 30.

GO DIGITAL

SELF-ASSESSMENT
1 I don't understand yet. 2 I can do it with help. 3 I can do it on my own. 4 I can teach someone else.

5. **COMPLETE THE SENTENCE** A mathematical sentence using the symbols <, >, ≤, or ≥ is called a(n)____________________________.

4 MTR 6. **DIFFERENT WORDS, SAME QUESTION** Which is different? Write "both" inequalities.

w is greater than or equal to -7.	w is no less than -7.	w is no more than -7.	w is at least -7.

Sketching Graphs of Linear Inequalities

A **solution of an inequality** is a value that makes the inequality true. An inequality can have more than one solution. The set of all solutions of an inequality is called the **solution set**.

WORDS AND MATH

The word *set* can mean a collection of similar things that belong together, such as a train set, a set of dishes, or a set of cards.

Value of x	$x + 5 \geq -2$	Is the inequality true?
-6	$-6 + 5 \overset{?}{\geq} -2$ $-1 \geq -2$ ✓	yes
-7	$-7 + 5 \overset{?}{\geq} -2$ $-2 \geq -2$ ✓	yes
-8	$-8 + 5 \overset{?}{\geq} -2$ $-3 \ngeq -2$ ✗	no

REMEMBER

Recall that a diagonal line through an inequality symbol means the inequality is not true. For instance, the symbol $\ngeq$ means "is not greater than or equal to."

EXAMPLE 2 Checking Solutions of Inequalities

WATCH

Tell whether -4 is a solution of each inequality.

a. $x + 8 < -3$

b. $-4.5x > -21$

SOLUTION

a. $x + 8 < -3$ Write the inequality.

$-4 + 8 \overset{?}{<} -3$ Substitute -4 for x.

$4 \nless -3$ ✗ Simplify.

▶ So, -4 is *not* a solution of the inequality.

b. $-4.5x > -21$ Write the inequality.

$-4.5(-4) \overset{?}{>} -21$ Substitute -4 for x.

$18 > -21$ ✓ Simplify.

▶ So, -4 is a solution of the inequality.

GO DIGITAL

SELF-ASSESSMENT 1 I don't understand yet. 2 I can do it with help. 3 I can do it on my own. 4 I can teach someone else.

7. **VOCABULARY** Is 5 in the solution set of $x + 3 > 8$? Explain.

Tell whether −6 is a solution of the inequality.

8. $c + 4 < -1$

9. $10 \leq 3 - m$

10. $21 \div x \geq -3.5$

11. $4x - 25 > -2$

12. $-\frac{7}{5}d < -8$

13. $5 \leq -\frac{33}{h}$

14. **REASONING** List four solutions of the inequality in Exercise 11.

The **graph of an inequality** shows the solution set of the inequality on a number line. An open circle, ○, is used when a number is *not* a solution. A closed circle, ●, is used when a number is a solution. An arrow to the left or right shows that the graph continues in that direction.

REFLECT ON YOUR METHOD (3 MTR)

Do you always shade the number line in the direction that the inequality symbol points? Explain your reasoning.

EXAMPLE 3 Graphing Inequalities

WATCH

Graph each inequality.

a. $y \le -3$ **b.** $\frac{5}{2} < x$ **c.** $z > 0$

SOLUTION

a. Test a number to the left of -3. $y = -4$ is a solution.

Test a number to the right of -3. $y = 0$ is *not* a solution.

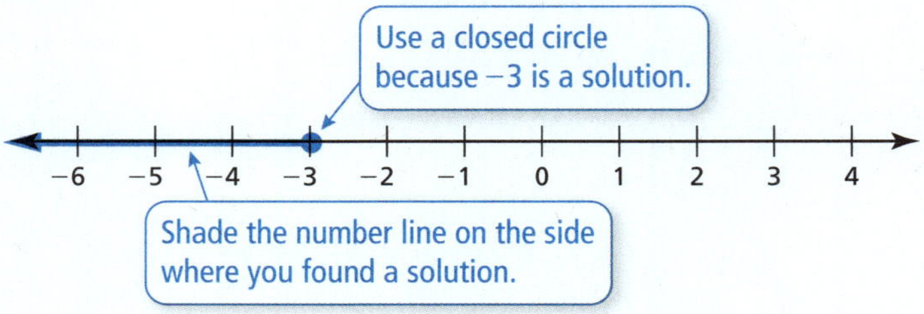

b. Test a number to the left of $\frac{5}{2}$. $x = 0$ is *not* a solution.

Test a number to the right of $\frac{5}{2}$. $x = 4$ is a solution.

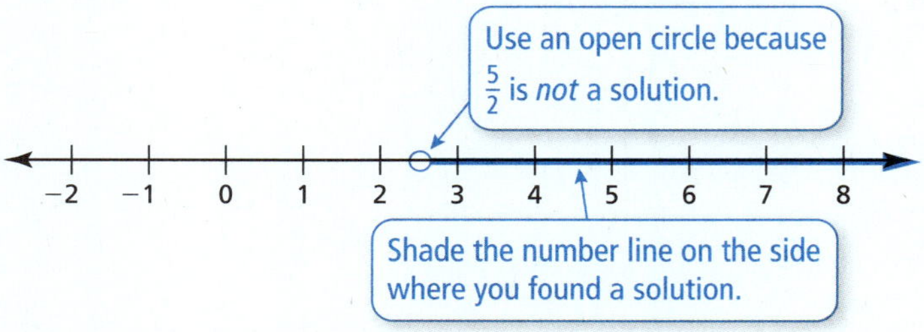

c. Just by looking at the inequality, you can see that it represents the set of all positive numbers.

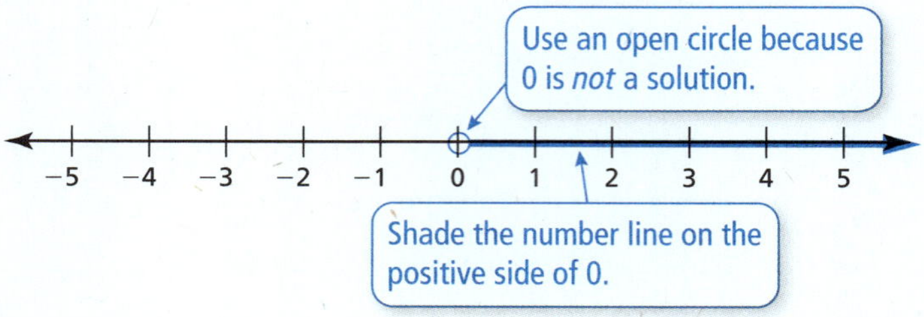

GO DIGITAL

SELF-ASSESSMENT
1 I don't understand yet. 2 I can do it with help. 3 I can do it on my own. 4 I can teach someone else.

15. WRITING Describe how to graph an inequality.

Graph the inequality.

16. $b > -8$

17. $1.4 \geq g$

18. $r < \frac{1}{2}$

19. $v \geq \sqrt{36}$

2 MTR **20. MAKE A CONNECTION** How are the graphs of $k < 0$ and $k \leq 0$ alike? How are they different?

Writing and Interpreting Inequalities

7 MTR **EXAMPLE 4** **Modeling Real Life** WATCH

The graph shows the height restriction h (in inches) for the Cheetah Hunt ride at Busch Gardens. Write and interpret an inequality that represents the height restriction.

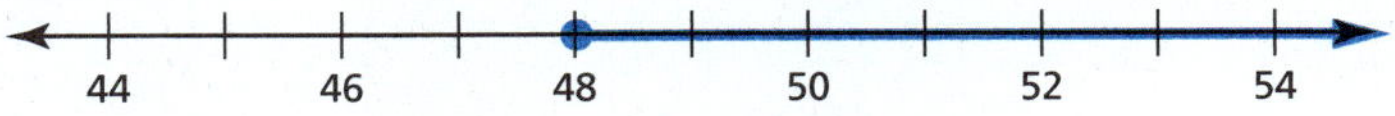

SOLUTION

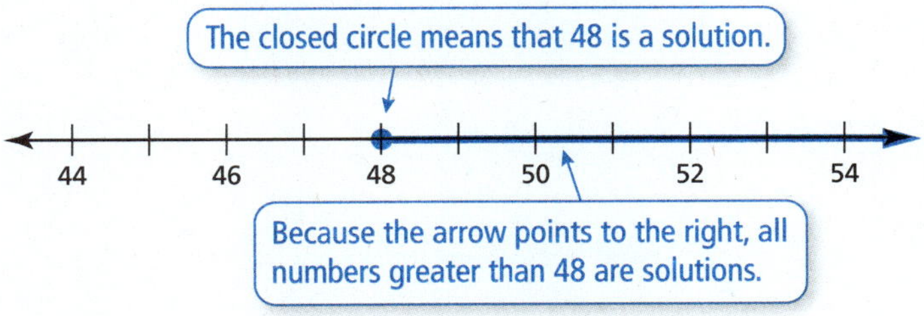

▶ So, $h \geq 48$ represents the height restriction for the ride. This means that you must be at least 48 inches tall to go on the ride.

GO DIGITAL

EXAMPLE 5 Interpreting an Inequality

WATCH

Let A represent the number of students in the school band. Let B represent the number of students in the
school choir, where B is less than A. Interpret the inequality and tell whether it is true.

$$\frac{A + B}{2} < \frac{A}{A + B}$$

SOLUTION

The sum $A + B$ represents the total number of students in the band and the choir. The mean number of students in the band and choir is $A + B$ divided by 2. So, $\frac{A + B}{2}$ is a number between B and A.

The quantity $\frac{A}{A + B}$ relates the number of band students to the number of students in both the band and the choir.

Because $A < A + B$, you can conclude that $\frac{A}{A + B}$ is less than 1.

▶ Because $\frac{A + B}{2} \not< \frac{A}{A + B}$, the inequality is not true.

SELF-ASSESSMENT

1 I don't understand yet. 2 I can do it with help. 3 I can do it on my own. 4 I can teach someone else.

21. The graph shows the height restriction h (in inches) for a ride at a water park. Write and interpret an inequality that represents the height restriction for the ride.

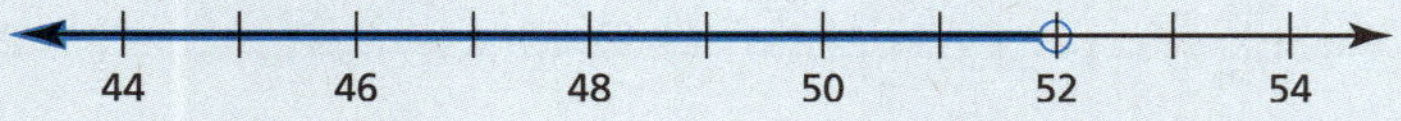

22. Use the information in Example 5 to interpret the inequality and tell whether it is true. Explain your reasoning.

a. $\frac{A}{B} < \frac{B}{A}$

b. $\frac{B}{A + B} \geq \frac{1}{2}$

2.1 Practice WITH CalcChat® AND CalcView®

In Exercises 1–8, write the sentence as an inequality. *(See Example 1.)*

1. A number x is greater than 3.

2. A number n plus 7 is less than or equal to 9.

▶3. Fifteen is no more than a number t divided by 5.

4. One-half of a number y is more than 22.

5. The sum of a number v and 6.2 is at least -4.7.

6. Four is no less than the quotient of a number x and 2.1.

7. Three times a number k minus $\frac{5}{3}$ is no more than $\frac{4}{9}$.

8. $-\frac{7}{8}$ is at most the difference of twice a number m and $\frac{5}{4}$.

In Exercises 9–18, tell whether the value is a solution of the inequality. *(See Example 2.)*

9. $r + 4 > 8;\ r = 2$

10. $5 - x < 8;\ x = -3$

▶11. $3s \leq 19;\ s = -6$

12. $17 \geq 2y;\ y = 7$

13. $-1 > -\frac{x}{2};\ x = 3$

14. $\frac{4}{z} \geq 3;\ z = 2$

15. $20 \leq \frac{10}{2z} + 20;\ z = 5$

16. $\frac{3m}{6} - 2 > 3;\ m = 8$

17. $10.4 \geq -2n + 4.6;\ n = -2.9$

18. $-5q - \frac{7}{4} + 8q < \frac{5}{8};\ q = \frac{5}{6}$

7 MTR 19. **MODELING REAL LIFE** The Xianren Bridge is in Guangxi Province, China. This arch is the world's longest natural arch, with a length of 400 feet. Write an inequality that represents the possible lengths ℓ (in *inches*) of all other natural arches.

GO DIGITAL

20. REASONING The winner of a weight-lifting competition bench-pressed 400 pounds. The other competitors all bench-pressed at least 23 pounds less.

a. Write an inequality that represents the weights that the other competitors bench-pressed.

b. Was one of the other competitors able to bench-press 379 pounds? Explain.

OPEN-ENDED In Exercises 21 and 22, describe a real-life situation that can be modeled by the inequality.

21. $12x \geq 60$

22. $23 + x \leq 31$

In Exercises 23–30, graph the inequality. *(See Example 3.)*

23. $x \geq 2$

24. $z \leq 5$

25. $-1 > t$

26. $-2 < w$

27. $v \leq -4.8$

28. $s < \frac{3}{2}$

29. $\frac{1}{4} < p$

30. $r \geq -|5|$

4 MTR **ERROR ANALYSIS In Exercises 31 and 32, describe and correct the error in graphing the inequality.**

31.

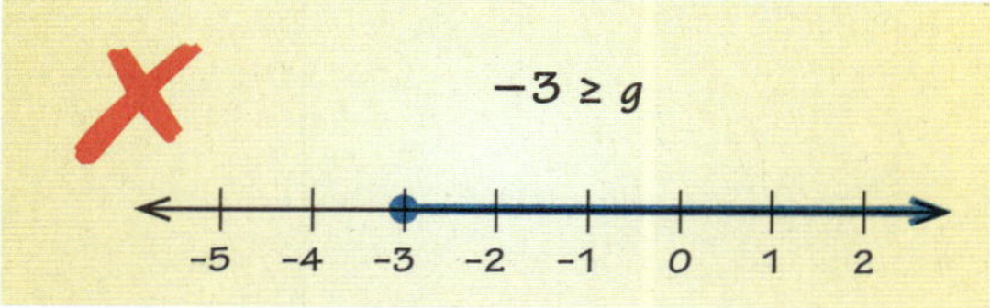

32.

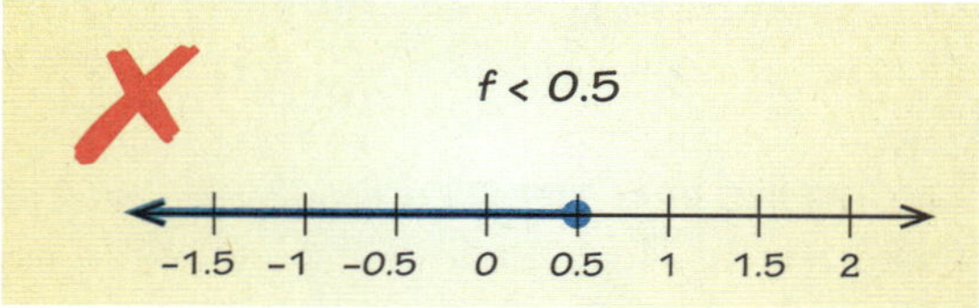

In Exercises 33 and 34, write and graph an inequality for the given scenario. Identify a solution.

33. Because of downtown Orlando's proximity to Orlando Executive Airport, the heights of the buildings are under 450 feet.

34. For safety, all dogs at a dog park who weigh more than 50 pounds must play in Area 2.

In Exercises 35 and 36, write an inequality that represents the graph.

35. 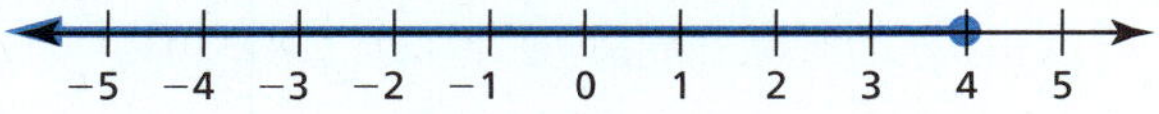

36. 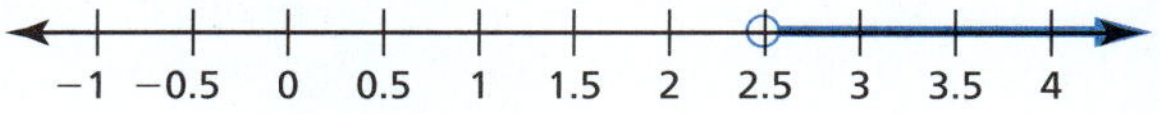

37. MODELING REAL LIFE The graph shows the hourly wage requirement m (in dollars) for employees in a state. Write and interpret an inequality that represents the state's hourly wage requirement. *(See Example 4.)*

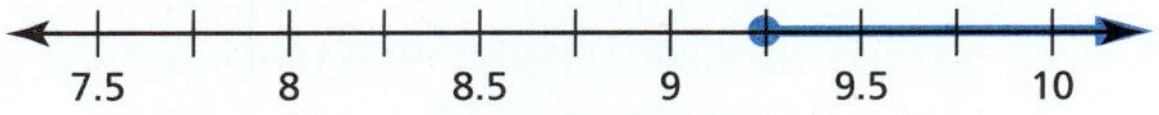

38. MODELING REAL LIFE The graphs show the weight restrictions w (in tons) for vehicles with (a) 2 axles, (b) 3 axles, and (c) 4 axles traveling on state roads. For each type of vehicle, write and interpret an inequality that represents the weight restriction (in pounds).

a. 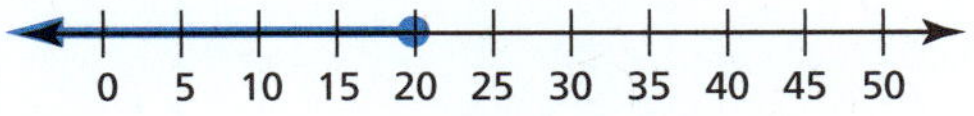

b. 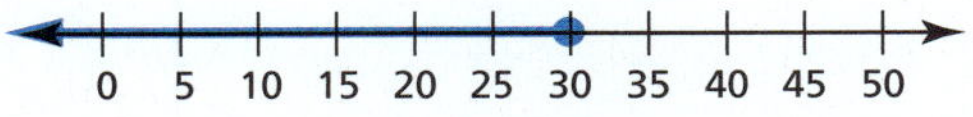

c. 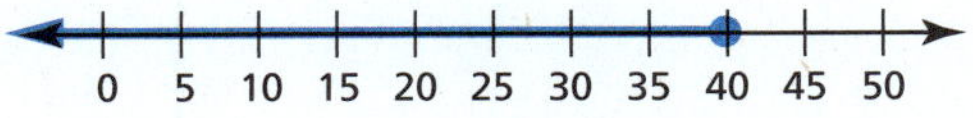

39. B.E.S.T. TEST PREP The water temperature of a swimming pool must be no less than 76°F. The temperature is currently 74°F. Which graph shows how much the temperature must increase to meet the requirement?

Ⓐ 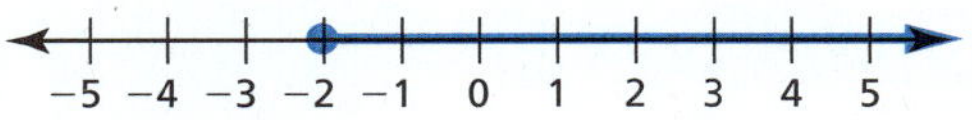

Ⓑ 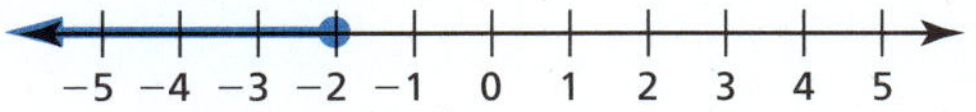

Ⓒ 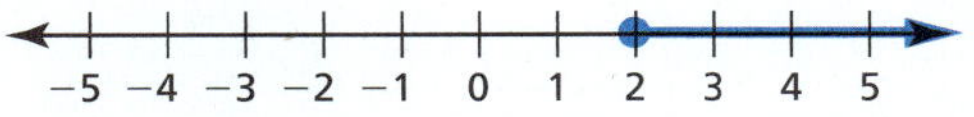

Ⓓ 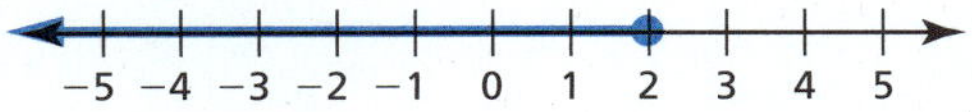

40. PROBLEM SOLVING An elevation more than 18,000 feet above sea level is considered extremely high altitude. Supplementary oxygen is recommended when climbing at extremely high altitudes. A mountaineer plans to climb a mountain with an elevation of 6282 meters. Is supplementary oxygen recommended for the climb? Explain.

In Exercises 41–44, let X and Y represent the populations of two cities, where X is greater than Y. Interpret the inequality and tell whether it is true. *(See Example 5.)*

41. $2Y > X + Y$

42. $\frac{X + Y}{X} < \frac{X + Y}{Y}$

43. $\frac{Y}{X + Y} < \frac{X}{Y}$

44. $\frac{1}{2}(X - Y) \geq X - \frac{Y}{2}$

45. REASONING Complete the inequality $2 \;\square\; |x + 5|$ with <, ≤, >, or ≥ so that $x = 3$ and $x = -3$ are both solutions of the inequality.

46. HOW DO YOU SEE IT?
The graph represents the known melting points of all metallic elements (in degrees Celsius).

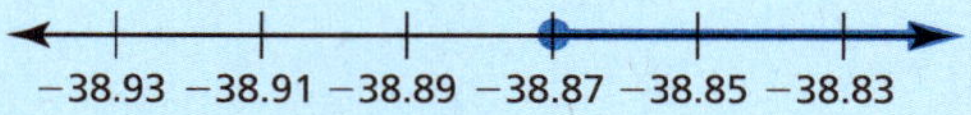

a. Write an inequality represented by the graph.

b. Write an inequality for the set of all numbers *not* represented by the graph. What does the inequality represent in this context?

5 MTR CONNECTING CONCEPTS **In Exercises 47 and 48, write an inequality that represents the missing dimension x.**

47. The area is less than 18 square centimeters.

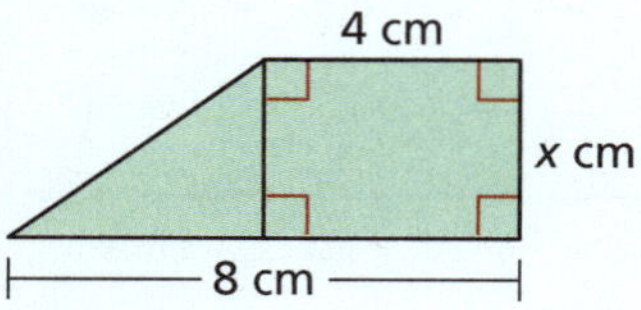

48. The area is greater than or equal to 8 square feet.

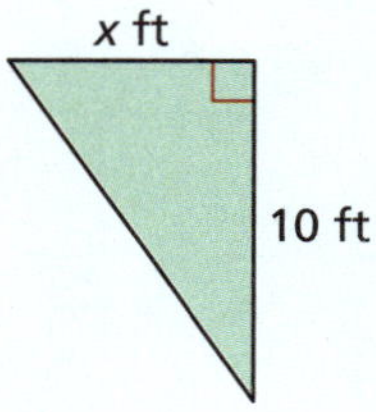

49. PROBLEM SOLVING A one-way bus ride costs \$1.65. A monthly pass costs \$52. You ride the bus twice each weekday. Should you buy the monthly pass? Explain.

50. THOUGHT PROVOKING
A company charges A dollars per unit for x units, plus an initial fee B (in dollars) for a product, where B is greater than A. Explain what $\frac{Ax + B}{x}$ represents, and write an inequality that represents its possible values.

51. DIG DEEPER A runner finishes a 200-meter dash in 35 seconds. Let r represent any speed (in meters per second) faster than the runner's speed.

a. Write an inequality that represents r. Then graph the inequality.

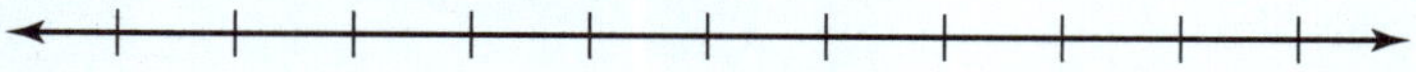

b. Every point on the graph in part (a) represents a speed faster than the runner's speed. Explain why every point may not represent the speed of a runner.

c. Show how you can use a second inequality to alter the graph in part (a) so that every point represents a possible speed of a runner.

REVIEW & REFRESH

WATCH

In Exercises 52–57, solve the equation. Check your solution.

52. $x + 2 = 3$

53. $-12 = y - 11$

54. $\frac{z}{6} = \frac{4}{3}$

55. $10 = 2.5w$

56. $3.4v - 7 + 4.6v = 17$

57. $3(5s + 2) - 9s = -42$

58. Tell whether the triangles are similar. Explain.

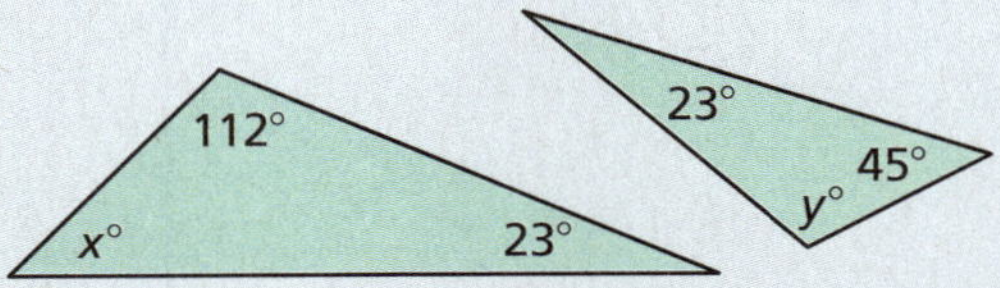

59. OPEN-ENDED Write an equation that has (a) one solution, (b) no solution, and (c) infinitely many solutions.

In Exercises 60–63, solve the equation. Check your solutions.

60. $|2a - 3| = 15$

61. $\frac{1}{4}|7 + d| - \frac{5}{2} = -5$

62. $|4g + 16| = 8g$

63. $|3h - 1| = |7 + 3h|$

7 MTR **64. MODELING REAL LIFE** A store pays $95 for a drone. What is the selling price when the markup is 25%?

In Exercises 65 and 66, complete the statement. Round to the nearest hundredth, if necessary.

65. 84 c = ☐ gal

66. 3.6 m = ☐ mm

In Exercises 67–70, solve the literal equation for x.

67. $v = x \cdot y \cdot z$

68. $s = 2r + 3x$

69. $w = 5 + 3(x - 1)$

70. $n = \dfrac{2x + 1}{2}$

71. NUMBER SENSE You use three different laser measuring devices to measure the length of a plank. The results are shown in the table. Order the measurements from least to greatest. Which measurement is closest to 12 feet?

Laser measure	1	2	3
Length (feet)	12.01	11.989	12.1

In Exercises 72 and 73, graph the inequality.

72. $q \leq -4$

73. $p > 1$

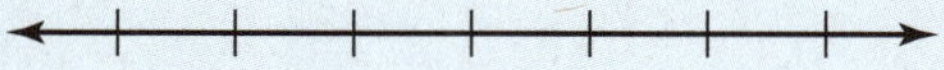

74. MODELING REAL LIFE The tallest person who ever lived was 8 feet 11.1 inches tall.

a. Write an inequality that represents the possible heights of every other person who has ever lived.

b. Is 9 feet a solution of the inequality? Explain.

75. Find the missing values in the ratio table. Then write the equivalent ratios.

Baseballs	12		72	
Gloves	3	6		9

In Exercises 76 and 77, write the sentence as an inequality.

76. Eight is less than or equal to a number z.

77. The difference of a number p and 1 is greater than 6.

2.2 Solving Inequalities Using Addition or Subtraction

Learning Target: Write and solve inequalities using addition or subtraction.

Success Criteria:
- I can apply the Addition and Subtraction Properties of Inequality to produce equivalent inequalities.
- I can solve inequalities using addition or subtraction.
- I can use inequalities to model real-life problems.

Algebraic Reasoning
MA.912.AR.2.6 Given a mathematical or real-world context, write and solve one-variable linear inequalities, including compound inequalities. Represent solutions algebraically or graphically.

EXPLORE IT! Quarterback Passing Efficiency

Work with a partner. The National Collegiate Athletic Association (NCAA) uses the following formula to rank the passing efficiencies P of quarterbacks.

$$P = \frac{8.4Y + 100C + 330T - 200N}{A}$$

Y = total length of all completed passes (in Yards)

C = Completed passes

T = passes resulting in a Touchdown

N = iNtercepted passes

A = Attempted passes

M = incoMplete passes

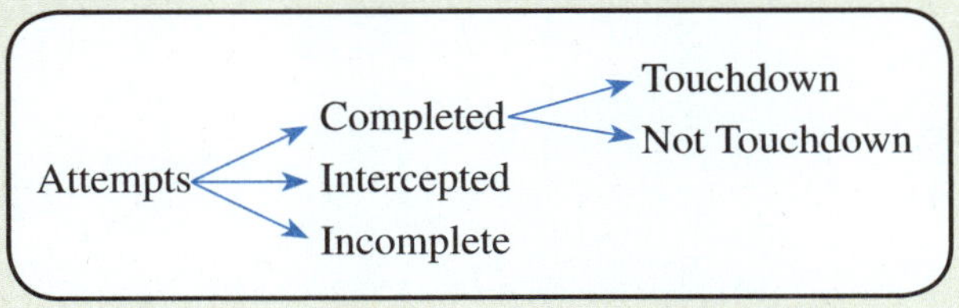

a. Determine whether each inequality must be true. Explain your reasoning.

i. $T < C$

ii. $C + N \leq A$

iii. $N < A$

iv. $A - C \geq M$

ANALYZE A PROBLEM (1 MTR)
Which has a greater effect on the value of P, a touchdown or an interception? How do you know?

GO DIGITAL

b. You have used properties of equality to solve equations involving addition or subtraction. Can you use similar properties to solve inequalities involving addition or subtraction? Explain your reasoning.

c. Use $C + N \leq A$ and $A - C \geq M$ from part (a) to support your answer in part (b).

d. For each inequality below, complete a table with passing statistics that satisfy the inequality. Then describe the values of P that make each inequality true.

i. $P < 0$

Attempts	
Completions	
Yards	
Touchdowns	
Interceptions	

ii. $P + 100 \geq 250$

Attempts	
Completions	
Yards	
Touchdowns	
Interceptions	

iii. $P - 250 > -80$

Attempts	
Completions	
Yards	
Touchdowns	
Interceptions	

Vocabulary

equivalent inequalities, p. 103

Solving Inequalities Using Addition

Just as you used the properties of equality to produce equivalent equations, you can use the properties of inequality to produce equivalent inequalities. **Equivalent inequalities** are inequalities that have the same solutions.

KEY IDEA

Addition Property of Inequality

Words Adding the same number to each side of an inequality produces an equivalent inequality.

Numbers

$$\begin{array}{rcr} -3 & < & 2 \\ \underline{+4} & & \underline{+4} \\ 1 & < & 6 \end{array} \qquad \begin{array}{rcr} -3 & \geq & -10 \\ \underline{+3} & & \underline{+3} \\ 0 & \geq & -7 \end{array}$$

Algebra If $a > b$, then $a + c > b + c$. If $a \geq b$, then $a + c \geq b + c$.

If $a < b$, then $a + c < b + c$. If $a \leq b$, then $a + c \leq b + c$.

The diagram shows one way to visualize the Addition Property of Inequality when $c > 0$.

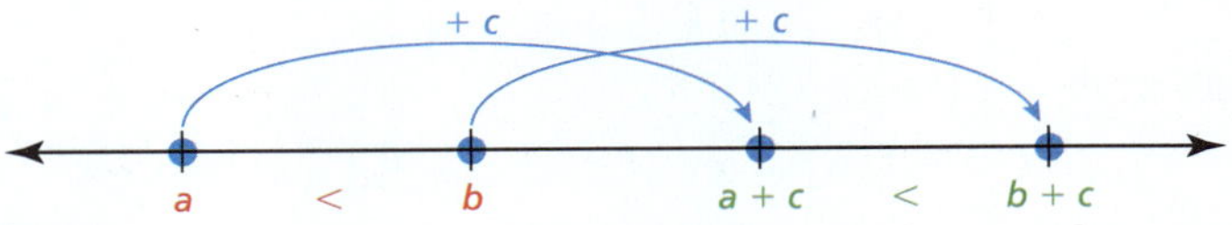

EXAMPLE 1 Solving an Inequality Using Addition

WATCH

Solve $x - 6 \geq -10$. Graph the solution.

SOLUTION

$$\begin{array}{rcrl} x - 6 & \geq & -10 & \text{Write the inequality.} \\ \underline{+6} & & \underline{+6} & \text{Addition Property of Inequality} \\ x & \geq & -4 & \text{Simplify.} \end{array}$$

Undo the subtraction.

▶ The solution is $x \geq -4$.

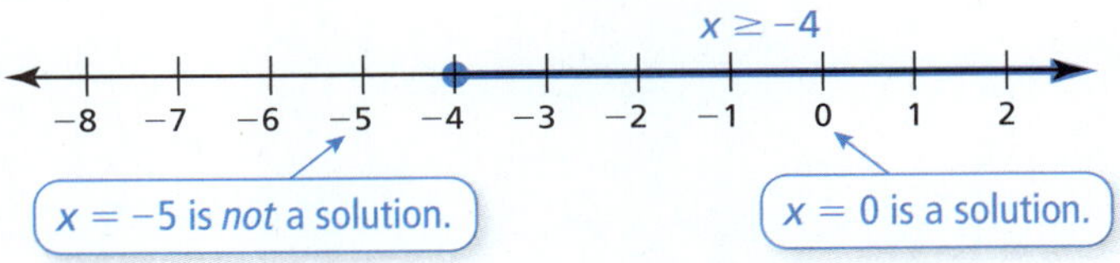

REMEMBER

To check this solution, substitute numbers to the left and right of −4 into the original inequality.

SELF-ASSESSMENT

1 I don't understand yet. 2 I can do it with help. 3 I can do it on my own. 4 I can teach someone else.

Solve the inequality. Graph the solution.

1. $b - 2 > -9$

2. $m - 3 \leq 5$

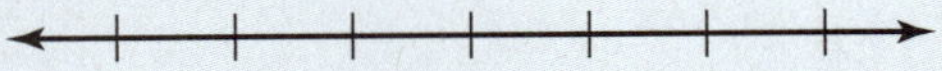

3. $\frac{1}{4} > y - \frac{1}{4}$

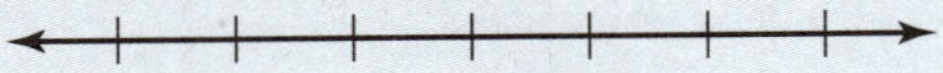

4. $0.07 \leq -4.05 + z$

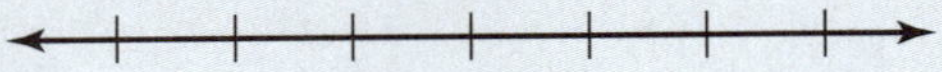

GO DIGITAL

SELF-ASSESSMENT

1 I don't understand yet. 2 I can do it with help. 3 I can do it on my own. 4 I can teach someone else.

5. VOCABULARY Is the inequality $x \le 6$ equivalent to the inequality $x - 5 \le 6 - 5$? Explain your reasoning.

6. REASONING The possible values of x are given by $x - 4 \ge -1$. What is the greatest possible value of $-5x$? Explain your reasoning.

Solving Inequalities Using Subtraction

KEY IDEA

Subtraction Property of Inequality

Words Subtracting the same number from each side of an inequality produces an equivalent inequality.

Numbers

$$\begin{array}{rcr} -3 & \le & 1 \\ \underline{-5} & & \underline{-5} \\ -8 & \le & -4 \end{array} \qquad \begin{array}{rcr} 7 & > & -20 \\ \underline{-7} & & \underline{-7} \\ 0 & > & -27 \end{array}$$

Algebra If $a > b$, then $a - c > b - c$. If $a \ge b$, then $a - c \ge b - c$.

If $a < b$, then $a - c < b - c$. If $a \le b$, then $a - c \le b - c$.

The diagram shows one way to visualize the Subtraction Property of Inequality when $c > 0$.

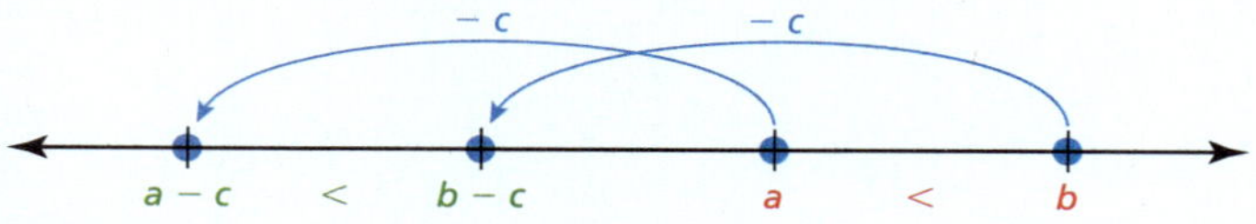

EXAMPLE 2 Solving Inequalities Using Subtraction

WATCH

Solve each inequality. Graph each solution.

a. $y + 8 \le 5$ **b.** $-8 < 1.4 + m$

SOLUTION

a.

$$\begin{array}{rcrl} y + 8 & \le & 5 & \text{Write the inequality.} \\ \underline{-8} & & \underline{-8} & \text{Subtraction Property of Inequality} \\ y & \le & -3 & \text{Simplify.} \end{array}$$

Undo the addition.

▶ The solution is $y \le -3$.

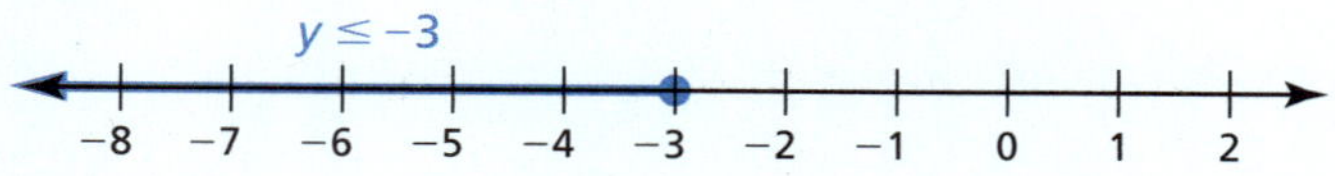

b.

$$\begin{array}{rcll} -8 & < & 1.4 + m & \text{Write the inequality.} \\ \underline{-1.4} & & \underline{-1.4} & \text{Subtraction Property of Inequality} \\ -9.4 & < & m & \text{Simplify.} \end{array}$$

▶ The solution is $m > -9.4$.

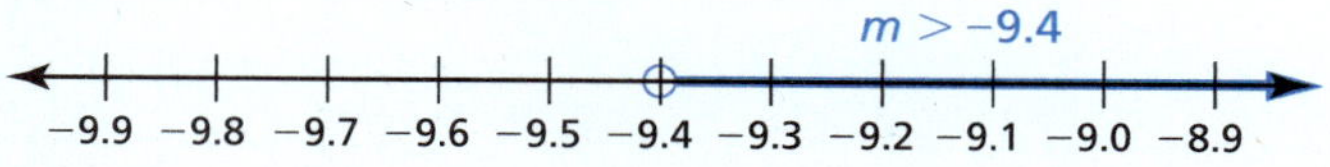

GO DIGITAL

Solving Real-Life Problems

7 MTR **EXAMPLE 3** **Modeling Real Life** WATCH STEM

A circuit overloads at 1800 watts of electricity. You plug an amplifier that uses 900 watts of electricity into the circuit. In addition to the amplifier, which of the following equipment can you plug into the circuit at the same time without overloading the circuit?

Equipment	Watts
Lighting	600
Fog machine 1	450
Fog machine 2	450
Television	200

SOLUTION

1. **Understand the Problem** You know that a circuit overloads at 1800 watts. You also know the numbers of watts used by several pieces of equipment. You are asked to determine what you can plug in without overloading the circuit.

2. **Make a Plan** Use a verbal model to write an inequality that represents the numbers of watts you can add without overloading the circuit. Then solve the inequality and identify other equipment that you can plug in without overloading the circuit.

3. **Solve and Check**

Verbal Model	Watts used by amplifier	+	Additional watts	<	Overload wattage
Variable	Let w be the additional watts you can add to the circuit.				
Inequality	900	+	w	<	1800

$$\begin{aligned} 900 + w &< 1800 && \text{Write the inequality.} \\ -900 \quad & \quad -900 && \text{Subtraction Property of Inequality} \\ w &< 900 && \text{Simplify.} \end{aligned}$$

▶ You can add up to 900 watts to the circuit. So, you can also plug in the lighting and the television, one of the fog machines and the television, or any individual piece of equipment.

Check

You can check that your answer is correct by adding the numbers of watts used by each grouping of equipment.

$900 + 600 + 200 = 1700$ $\qquad$ $900 + 450 + 200 = 1550$

The circuit will not overload because the total wattage is less than 1800 watts. ✓

GO DIGITAL

SELF-ASSESSMENT

1 I don't understand yet. 2 I can do it with help. 3 I can do it on my own. 4 I can teach someone else.

Solve the inequality. Graph the solution.

7. $k + 5 \leq -3$

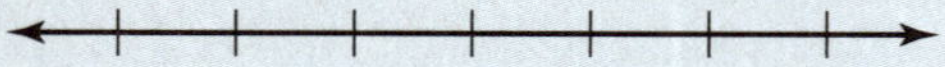

8. $75 < 58 + w$

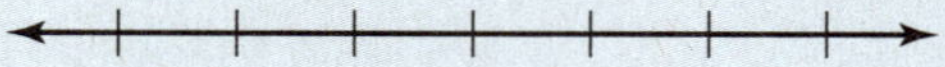

9. $\frac{5}{6} \leq z + \frac{1}{6}$

10. $p + 0.7 > -2.3$

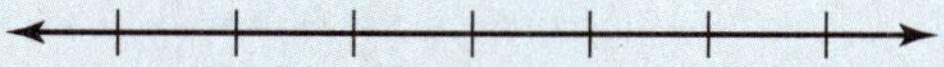

11. OPEN-ENDED Write two inequalities that have a solution of $y \geq -3$. One must require using subtraction to solve the inequality, and the other must require using addition.

12. The capacity of a flash drive is shown in the diagram. You copy two files to the flash drive, one of which is 1.92 gigabytes (GB) and the other 3.4 gigabytes. Which of the following folders can you also copy to the flash drive?

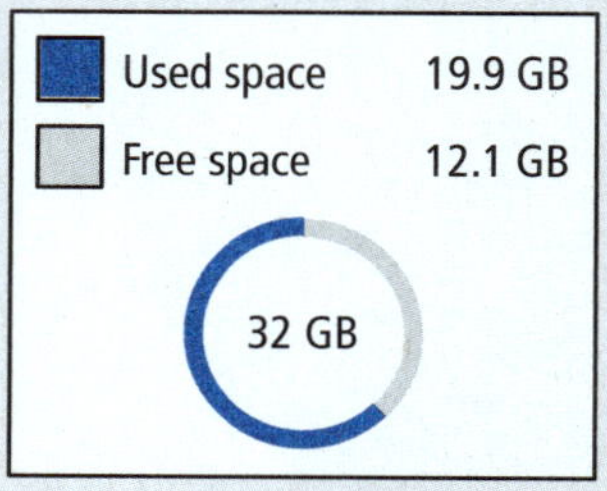

1 MTR **13. HELP A CLASSMATE** In Example 3, explain to a classmate why you cannot plug in both fog machines along with the amplifier.

2.2 Practice WITH CalcChat® AND CalcView®

In Exercises 1–14, solve the inequality. Graph the solution. *(See Examples 1 and 2.)*

1. $x - 4 < -5$

2. $1 \leq s - 8$

▶ **3.** $6 \geq m - 1$

4. $c - 12 > -4$

5. $r + 4 < 5$

6. $-8 \leq 8 + y$

▶ **7.** $9 + w > 7$

8. $15 \geq q + 3$

9. $h - (-2) \geq 10$

10. $-6 > t - (-13)$

11. $j + 1.7 < -2.1$

12. $-5.2 + y \geq -7.4$

13. $-\frac{4}{5} \geq p - \frac{2}{5}$

14. $\frac{1}{6} + z > 2\frac{2}{3}$

In Exercises 15–18, write the sentence as an inequality. Then solve the inequality.

15. A number plus 8 is greater than 11.

16. A number minus 3 is at least -5.

17. The difference of a number and 9 is fewer than 4.

18. Six is less than or equal to the sum of a number and $3\frac{1}{4}$.

GO DIGITAL

19. 7 MTR **MODELING REAL LIFE** A Tampa Bay Lightning player has 59 goals so far in a season. What are the possible numbers of additional goals the player can score to break the NHL record of 92 goals in a season?

20. 7 MTR **MODELING REAL LIFE** You want your daily sodium intake to be less than 2300 milligrams. For breakfast, you eat a cereal bar with the nutrition label shown. What are the possible amounts of sodium you can eat during the rest of the day?

4 MTR **ERROR ANALYSIS** **In Exercises 21 and 22, describe and correct the error in solving the inequality and graphing the solution.**

21.

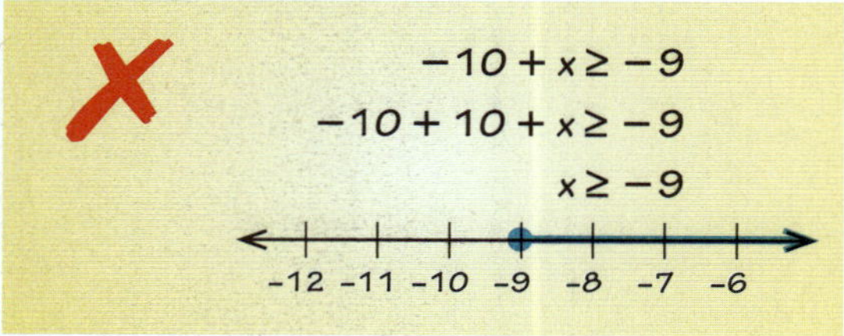

22.

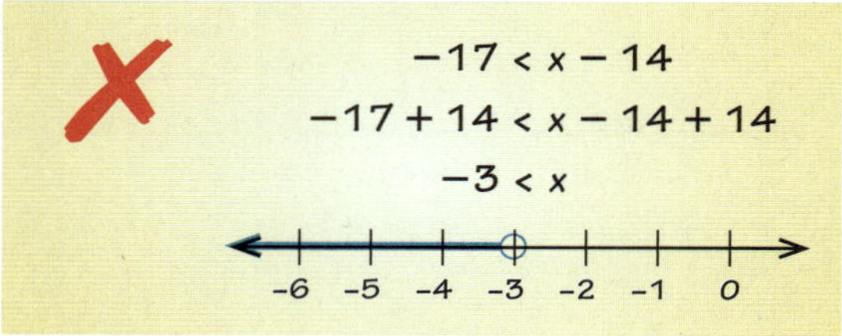

23. 7 MTR **MODELING REAL LIFE** An airline charges an extra fee for a checked bag that weighs more than 50 pounds. Your bag weighs 44.9 pounds. You have a 2.5-pound hair dryer, a 1.3-pound souvenir, and a 3.6-pound pair of boots. Which items can you add to the bag without paying the extra fee? *(See Example 3.)*

24. 7 MTR **MODELING REAL LIFE** A website offers free shipping on orders of $75 or more. You have items totaling $34.95 in your shopping cart. You want to add one sweater and one shirt to your cart. With which combination can you get free shipping and also spend the least amount of money?

Sweater	Price
A	$29.95
B	$24.50

Shirt	Price
A	$15.75
B	$12.95

5 MTR **CONNECTING CONCEPTS** **In Exercises 25 and 26, write and solve an inequality to find the possible values of x.**

25. Perimeter < 51.3 in.

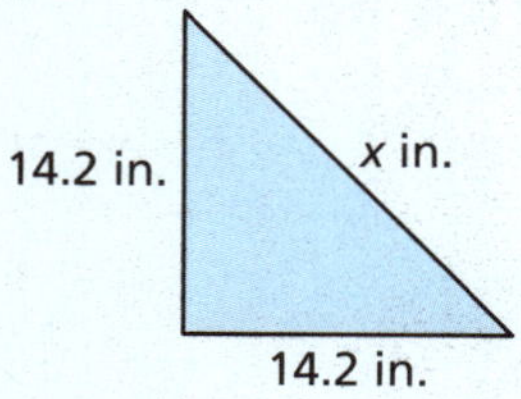

26. Perimeter ≤ 18.7 ft

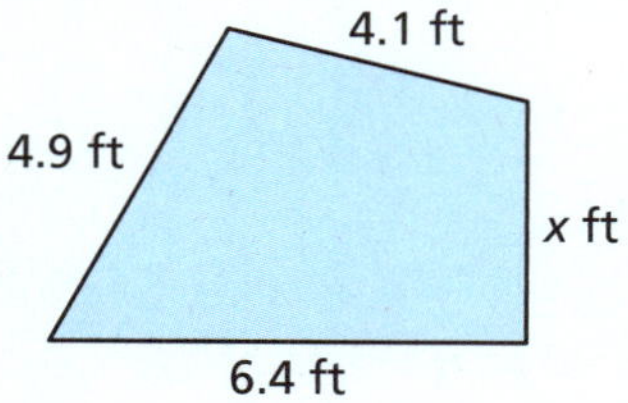

4 MTR **27. MAKING AN ARGUMENT** In an aerial ski competition, you perform two acrobatic ski jumps. The scores on the two jumps are then added together.

Ski jump	Competitor's score	Your score
1	117.1	119.5
2	119.8	

a. Describe the possible scores that you can earn on your second jump to beat your competitor.

b. Your coach says that you will beat your competitor if you score 118.4 points. A teammate says that you need only 117.5 points. Who is correct? Explain.

28. HOW DO YOU SEE IT?
The diagram represents the numbers of students in a school with brown eyes, brown hair, or both.

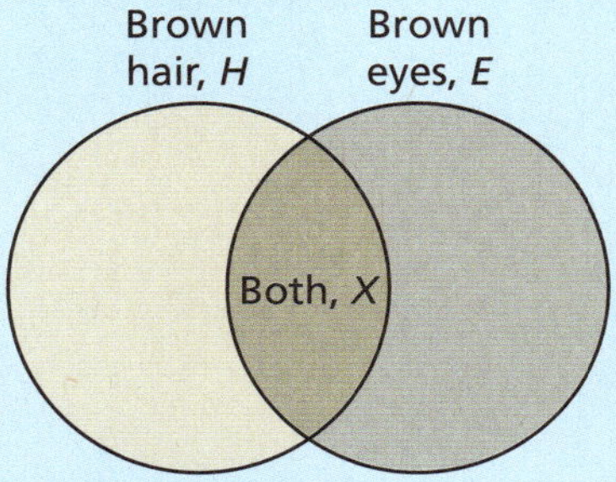

Determine whether each inequality must be true. Explain your reasoning.

a. $H \geq E$

b. $H + 10 \geq E$

c. $H \geq X$

d. $H + 10 \geq X$

e. $H > X$

f. $H + 10 > X$

29. REASONING Write and graph an inequality that represents the numbers that are *not* solutions of each inequality.

a. $x + 8 < 14$

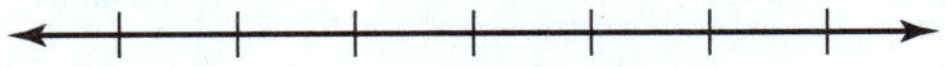

b. $x - 12 \geq 5.7$

30. REASONING What is the greatest value of $2n + 7$ when $\frac{7}{12} \geq \frac{5}{6} + n$?

31. B.E.S.T. TEST PREP Which of the following inequalities are equivalent to the inequality $x - b < 3$, where b is a constant? Select all that apply.

Ⓐ $x - b - 3 < 0$

Ⓑ $0 > b - x + 3$

Ⓒ $x < 3 - b$

Ⓓ $-3 < b - x$

32. THOUGHT PROVOKING
Use the inequalities

$$c - 3 \geq d,\ b + 4 < a + 1, \text{ and } a - 2 \leq d - 7$$

to order a, b, c, and d from least to greatest.

33. DIG DEEPER Write an inequality that requires using addition or subtraction to solve and has the solution shown in the graph. Then describe a real-life situation that can be modeled by the inequality.

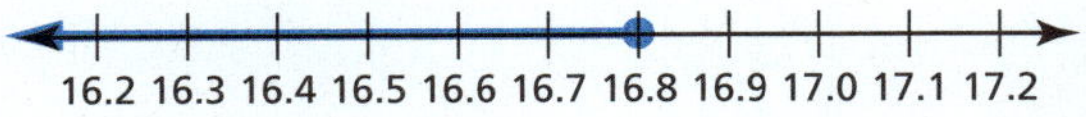

REVIEW & REFRESH

In Exercises 34–37, find the product or quotient.

34. $7 \cdot (-9)$

35. $-11 \cdot (-12)$

36. $-27 \div (-3)$

37. $20 \div (-5)$

In Exercises 38 and 39, solve the equation. Check your solution.

38. $-3y = -18$

39. $\frac{n}{4} = -7.3$

40. **MODELING REAL LIFE** The graph shows the age requirement x (in years) for obtaining a driver's license in a state. Write and interpret an inequality that represents the age requirement.

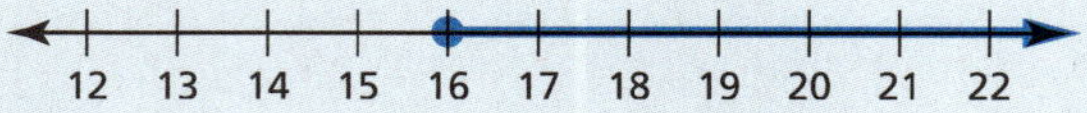

41. Solve the equation $2|x + 5| = |3x - 2|$. Check your solutions.

42. **REASONING** Describe the values of a for which the equation $|x + 12| - 10 = a$ has no solution.

43. You randomly choose one of the letters shown. What is the theoretical probability of choosing a vowel?

In Exercises 44 and 45, solve the inequality. Graph the solution.

44. $6 \geq w + 11$

45. $x - 4.5 > -1.8$

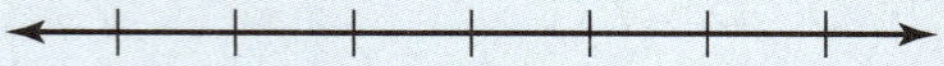

46. **MODELING REAL LIFE** You average 55 miles per hour while driving to a relative's house. On the return trip, you average 50 miles per hour because of bad weather. The total driving time is 5 hours and 15 minutes. How long does each trip take?

In Exercises 47 and 48, find the square root.

47. $\sqrt{121}$

48. $-\sqrt{\frac{4}{81}}$

2.3 Solving Inequalities Using Multiplication or Division

Learning Target: Write and solve inequalities using multiplication or division.

Success Criteria:

- I can apply the Multiplication and Division Properties of Inequality to produce equivalent inequalities.
- I can solve inequalities using multiplication or division.
- I can recognize when to reverse an inequality symbol while solving an inequality.

Algebraic Reasoning
MA.912.AR.2.6 Given a mathematical or real-world context, write and solve one-variable linear inequalities, including compound inequalities. Represent solutions algebraically or graphically.

EXPLORE IT! Solving Inequalities

Work with a partner.

a. Which graph represents the solutions of $-6 > 3x$? Does the other graph represent the solutions of $6 < -3x$? Explain your reasoning.

i.

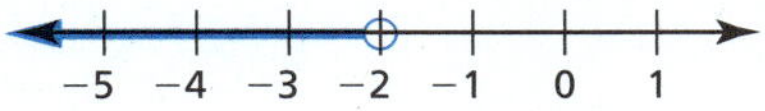

ii.

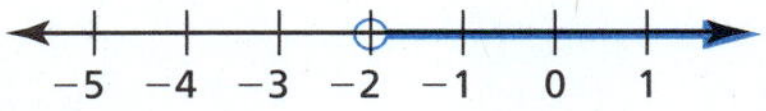

GO DIGITAL

MAKE A CONNECTION 2 MTR

How can you use a number line to convince a friend that your rules for solving $ax < b$ are valid?

b. Your friend uses properties of inequality to solve $6 < -3x$ two different ways, but gets two different answers. Is either solution correct? What did your friend do wrong?

Solution Method #1

$6 < -3x$	Write the inequality.
$-2 < x$	Divide each side by -3.

The solution is $x > -2$.

Solution Method #2

$6 < -3x$	Write the inequality.
$3x + 6 < 0$	Add $3x$ to each side.
$3x < -6$	Subtract 6 from each side.
$x < -2$	Divide each side by 3.

The solution is $x < -2$.

c. Write a rule that describes how to solve an inequality of the form $ax < b$ when a is positive and when a is negative. Explain.

Multiplying or Dividing by Positive Numbers

KEY IDEA

Multiplication and Division Properties of Inequality (*c* is positive)

Words Multiplying or dividing each side of an inequality by the same *positive* number produces an equivalent inequality.

Numbers

$-6 < 8$	$6 > -8$
$2 \cdot (-6) < 2 \cdot 8$	$\frac{6}{2} > \frac{-8}{2}$
$-12 < 16$	$3 > -4$

Algebra If $a > b$ and c is positive, then $ac > bc$. If $a > b$ and c is positive, then $\frac{a}{c} > \frac{b}{c}$.

If $a < b$ and c is positive, then $ac < bc$. If $a < b$ and c is positive, then $\frac{a}{c} < \frac{b}{c}$.

These properties are also true for ≤ and ≥.

EXAMPLE 1 Multiplying or Dividing by Positive Numbers

WATCH

Solve (a) $\frac{x}{8} > -5$ and (b) $-27 \geq 6x$. Graph each solution.

SOLUTION

a. $\frac{x}{8} > -5$ Write the inequality.

Undo the division. → $8 \cdot \frac{x}{8} > 8 \cdot (-5)$ Multiplication Property of Inequality

$x > -40$ Simplify.

▶ The solution is $x > -40$.

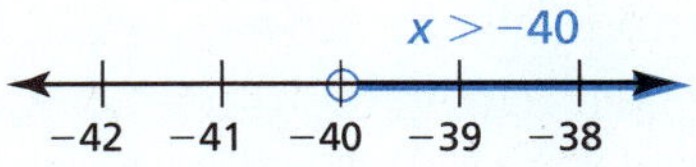

b. $-27 \geq 6x$ Write the inequality.

Undo the multiplication. → $\frac{-27}{6} \geq \frac{6x}{6}$ Division Property of Inequality

$-4\frac{1}{2} \geq x$ Simplify.

▶ The solution is $x \leq -4\frac{1}{2}$.

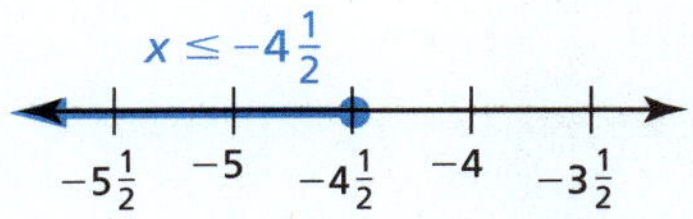

GO DIGITAL

SELF-ASSESSMENT

1 I don't understand yet. 2 I can do it with help. 3 I can do it on my own. 4 I can teach someone else.

Solve the inequality. Graph the solution.

1. $\frac{n}{7} \geq -1$

2. $-6 \geq \frac{1}{5}w$

3. $4b \geq 39$

4. $-18 > 1.5q$

5. REASONING Can you use the Multiplication Property of Inequality to solve $8m > -\frac{1}{10}$? Can you use the Division Property of Inequality to solve $-\frac{9}{2} > \frac{3}{2}n$? Explain your reasoning.

Multiplying or Dividing by Negative Numbers

KEY IDEA

Multiplication and Division Properties of Inequality (*c* is negative)

Words When multiplying or dividing each side of an inequality by the same *negative* number, the direction of the inequality symbol must be reversed to produce an equivalent inequality.

Numbers

$$-6 < 8$$
$$-2 \cdot (-6) > -2 \cdot 8$$
$$12 > -16$$

$$6 > -8$$
$$\frac{6}{-2} < \frac{-8}{-2}$$
$$-3 < 4$$

Algebra If $a > b$ and c is negative, then $ac < bc$.

If $a > b$ and c is negative, then $\frac{a}{c} < \frac{b}{c}$.

If $a < b$ and c is negative, then $ac > bc$.

If $a < b$ and c is negative, then $\frac{a}{c} > \frac{b}{c}$.

These properties are also true for $\leq$ and $\geq$.

COMMON ERROR

A negative sign in an inequality does not necessarily mean you must reverse the inequality symbol, as shown in Example 1.

Reverse the inequality symbol only when you multiply or divide each side by a negative number.

EXAMPLE 2 Multiplying or Dividing by Negative Numbers

Solve each inequality. Graph each solution.

WATCH

a. $2 < \frac{y}{-3}$ **b.** $-7y \leq -35$

SOLUTION

a. $2 < \frac{y}{-3}$ Write the inequality.

$-3 \cdot 2 > -3 \cdot \frac{y}{-3}$ Use the Multiplication Property of Inequality. Reverse the inequality symbol.

$-6 > y$ Simplify.

▶ The solution is $y < -6$.

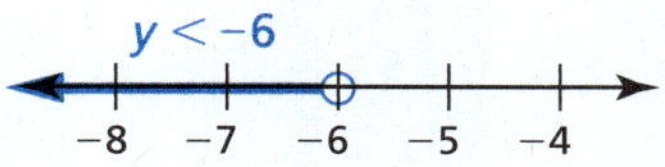

b. $-7y \leq -35$ Write the inequality.

Undo the multiplication. → $\frac{-7y}{-7} \geq \frac{-35}{-7}$ Use the Division Property of Inequality. Reverse the inequality symbol.

$y \geq 5$ Simplify.

▶ The solution is $y \geq 5$.

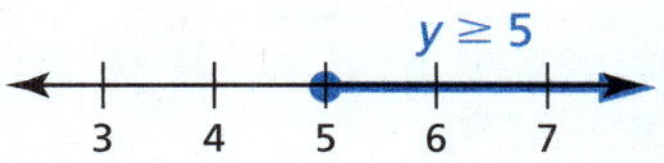

SELF-ASSESSMENT

1 I don't understand yet. 2 I can do it with help. 3 I can do it on my own. 4 I can teach someone else.

Solve the inequality. Graph the solution.

6. $\frac{x}{-5} \leq -5$

7. $1 \geq -\frac{1}{10}z$

8. $-9m > 67.5$

9. $-0.4y \geq -12$

10. WRITING Explain how solving $200x < -800$ is different from solving $-200x < 800$.

GO DIGITAL

Solving Real-Life Problems

7 MTR **EXAMPLE 3** **Modeling Real Life** WATCH

Your friend saves $150 each month to buy a down suit needed for a high-altitude mountain-climbing trip. Describe the numbers of months your friend needs to save to buy the suit.

Mountainwear Down Suit
$1249.95

SOLUTION

1. **Understand the Problem** You know how much your friend saves each month and how much the suit costs. You are asked how long your friend needs to save in order to buy the suit.
2. **Make a Plan** Use a verbal model to write an inequality. Then solve the inequality and interpret the solution.
3. **Solve and Check**

Verbal Model Monthly savings • Months ≥ Cost of suit

Variable Let m be the number of months your friend saves money.

Inequality $150 \cdot m \geq 1249.95$

$150m \geq 1249.95$ Write the inequality.

$\frac{150m}{150} \geq \frac{1249.95}{150}$ Division Property of Inequality

$m \geq 8.333$ Simplify.

▶ Your friend needs to save for more than 8 months, or at least 9 months, to buy the suit.

Check Reasonableness In 10 months, your friend would save

$\frac{\$150}{\text{mo}} \times 10 \text{ mo} = \$1500.$

Your friend would have a few hundred dollars more than the amount needed. So, your answer of 9 months or more is reasonable.

ANALYZE A PROBLEM 1 MTR
Why is the solution rounded up to 9 months in this situation?

SELF-ASSESSMENT

1 I don't understand yet. 2 I can do it with help. 3 I can do it on my own. 4 I can teach someone else.

11. You have at most $2.85 for a parking meter. Each 15-minute interval costs $0.25. Describe the amounts of time that you can park.

12. The photograph shows the speed limit for cars on a highway during the day and at night.

a. How many hours does it take a car traveling at the speed limit to travel 175 miles during the day?

b. The car in part (a) travels at or below the nighttime speed limit on the return trip. Describe how much longer the return trip could take.

GO DIGITAL

2.3 Practice WITH CalcChat® AND CalcView®

In Exercises 1–16, solve the inequality. Graph the solution. *(See Examples 1 and 2.)*

1. $3y \leq -9$

2. $-6t < 12$

3. $-15 \leq -3c$

4. $-9y > 27$

5. $-20 \leq 10n$

6. $4x < 14$

7. $29.6 < 7.4t$

8. $-\frac{5}{6} \geq -10z$

9. $\frac{x}{2} > -2$

10. $\frac{w}{-5} \leq 16$

11. $-16 \leq \frac{8}{3}t$

12. $\frac{a}{4} < 10.2$

13. $22 \geq \frac{4}{5}w$

14. $-6 > -\frac{2}{3}y$

15. $-\frac{n}{3} \geq 0.75$

16. $-7.6 < -\frac{5}{4}m$

7 MTR **17. MODELING REAL LIFE** A weather forecaster predicts that the temperature in Antarctica will decrease 8°F each hour for the next 6 hours. How many hours will it take for the temperature to drop at least 36°F? *(See Example 3.)*

7 MTR **18. MODELING REAL LIFE** You have $25 to purchase apps on your cell phone. Each app that you want costs $3.99. Describe the numbers of apps you can purchase.

GO DIGITAL

19. **ERROR ANALYSIS** Describe and correct the error in solving the inequality.

4 MTR

$$-6 > \frac{2}{3}x$$
$$\frac{3}{2} \cdot (-6) < \frac{3}{2} \cdot \frac{2}{3}x$$
$$-\frac{18}{2} < x$$
$$-9 < x$$

The solution is $x > -9$.

20. **MAKING AN ARGUMENT** Your friend says that the inequalities $x \leq \frac{4}{3}$ and $-6x \leq -8$ are equivalent. Is your friend correct? Explain.

4 MTR

USING TOOLS **In Exercises 21–24, solve the inequality. Use technology to verify your answer.**

21. $36 < 3y$

22. $17v \geq 51$

23. $4 > \frac{n}{-4}$

24. $1.1y < 4.4$

25. **MODELING REAL LIFE** The U.S. Mint pays \$0.11 to produce every \$5 bill. How many \$5 bills are produced when the U.S. Mint pays more than \$5.5 million in production costs for \$5 bills?

7 MTR

26. **HOW DO YOU SEE IT?** Let $m > 0$. Match each inequality with its graph. Explain your reasoning.

a. $\frac{x}{m} < -1$

b. $\frac{x}{m} > 1$

c. $\frac{x}{m} < 1$

d. $-\frac{x}{m} < 1$

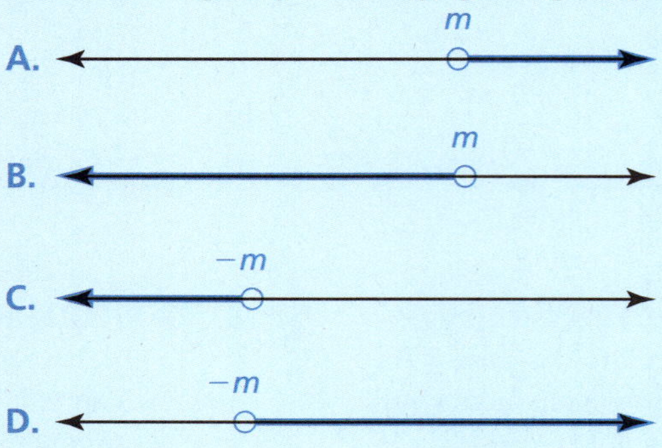

27. DIG DEEPER Your class wants to raise at least \$100 for a charity by collecting bottles. Each glass bottle earns \$0.05. Each plastic bottle earns \$0.10.

a. Describe the numbers of glass bottles your class needs to collect if no plastic bottles are collected.

b. Describe the numbers of plastic bottles your class needs to collect if no glass bottles are collected.

c. Write an inequality that represents how many of each type of bottle your class can collect to reach the goal.

28. THOUGHT PROVOKING

The inequality $\frac{x}{4} \leq 5$ has a solution of $x = p$. Write a second inequality that also has a solution of $x = p$.

29. PROBLEM SOLVING You run for 2 hours at a speed no faster than 6.3 miles per hour. You want to run a marathon, which is 26.2 miles, in less than 4 hours. If you continue to run at the same speed, will you reach your goal? Explain.

5 MTR **30. STRUCTURE** Use the number line shown to explain why the direction of the inequality symbol must be reversed when multiplying or dividing each side of an inequality by the same negative number.

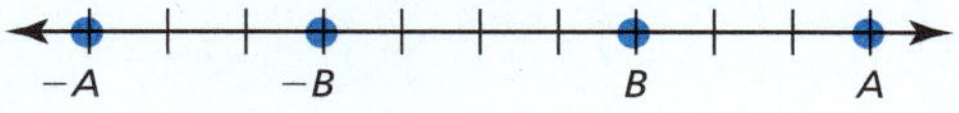

31. REASONING Explain why solving the inequality $\frac{4}{x} \geq 2$ by first multiplying each side by x might lead to an error. Assume $x \neq 0$.

5 MTR **32. CONNECTING CONCEPTS** The radius of a circle is represented by the formula $r = \frac{C}{2\pi}$. Describe the circumferences C of circles with radii greater than 5.

33. REASONING A water-skiing instructor recommends that a boat pulling a beginning skier have a speed less than 18 miles per hour. Describe the possible distances (in miles) that a beginner can travel in 45 minutes of practice time.

34. REASONING A local zoo employs 36 people to take care of the animals each day. At most, 24 of the employees work full-time. Describe the fraction of employees who work part-time.

REVIEW & REFRESH

WATCH

In Exercises 35–38, solve the equation. Check your solution.

35. $5x + 3 = 13$

36. $\frac{1}{2}y - 8 = -10$

37. $-0.4x + 2 = 3 - \frac{2}{5}x$

38. $\frac{1}{4}(6x + 8) = -5\left(2 + \frac{1}{2}x\right)$

39. The graph of a proportional relationship passes through the points (2, 56) and (x, 154). Find x.

7 MTR **40.** **MODELING REAL LIFE** You deposit \$2000 in an account that earns simple interest at an annual rate of 3.5%. How long must you leave the money in the account to earn \$175 in interest?

In Exercises 41 and 42, solve the inequality. Graph the solution.

41. $-4d < 18$

42. $7 \geq \frac{c}{3}$

43. Write the prime factorization of 72.

In Exercises 44–47, tell which number is greater.

44. 0.8, 85%

45. $\frac{7}{30}$, 25%

46. 120%, 0.12

47. 0.6%, $\frac{2}{3}$

7 MTR **48.** **MODELING REAL LIFE** You have \$15 to spend on a movie ticket, a drink, and snacks. The ticket costs \$6.99. Describe how much money you can spend on a drink and snacks.

49. The vertices of a trapezoid are $A(-4, 1)$, $B(-1, 3)$, $C(-1, -4)$, and $D(-4, -3)$. Rotate the trapezoid 90° counterclockwise about the origin. What are the coordinates of the image?

50. **NUMBER SENSE** One-fifth of the greater of two consecutive integers is 7 less than one-half of the lesser integer. What are the integers?

In Exercises 51–54, graph the inequality.

51. $y > -2$

52. $6.5 \geq k$

53. $\frac{3}{8} \leq m$

54. $p < \left|-\frac{9}{5}\right|$

55. **REASONING** An icosahedron has twenty congruent faces numbered 1 through 20. Describe the likelihood that each event will occur when you roll the icosahedron. Explain your reasoning.

a. rolling a 20

b. rolling a one-digit number

c. rolling a multiple of 4

2.4 Solving Multi-Step Inequalities

Learning Target: Write and solve multi-step inequalities.

Success Criteria:
- I can use more than one property of inequality to generate equivalent inequalities.
- I can solve multi-step inequalities using inverse operations.
- I can apply multi-step inequalities to solve real-life problems.

Algebraic Reasoning
MA.912.AR.2.6 Given a mathematical or real-world context, write and solve one-variable linear inequalities, including compound inequalities. Represent solutions algebraically or graphically.

EXPLORE IT! Solving Multi-Step Inequalities

CONSTRUCT AN ARGUMENT 4 MTR
Do you think it is possible for an inequality to have no solution? infinitely many solutions? Construct an argument that supports your answers.

Work with a partner.

- Use what you already know about solving equations and inequalities to solve each inequality. Construct a viable argument to justify each solution.
- Match each inequality with its graph.

a. $2x + 3 \leq x + 5$

b. $-2x + 3 > x + 9$

c. $27 \geq 5x + 4x$

d. $-8x + 2x - 16 < -5x + 7x$

e. $3(x - 3) - 5x > -3x - 6$

f. $-5x - 6x \leq 8 - 8x - x$

A.
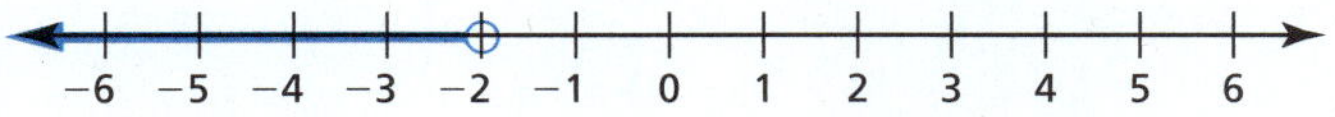

B.
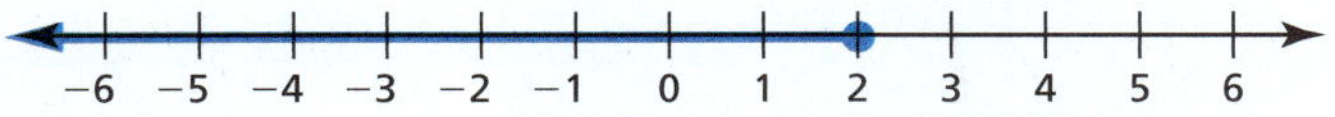

C.
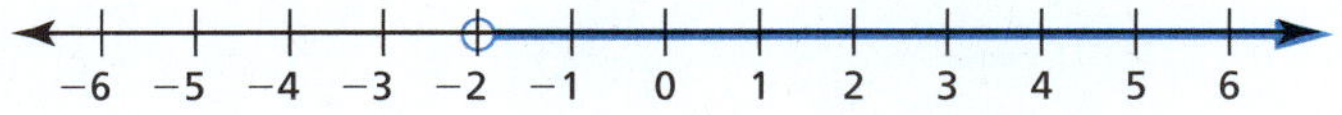

D.
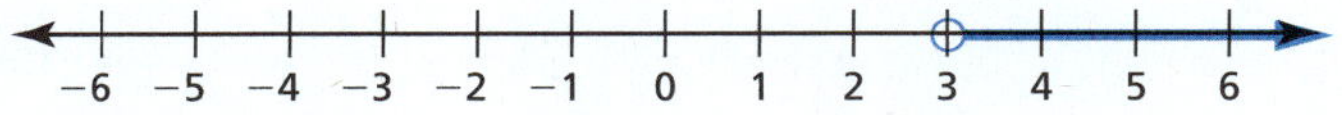

E.
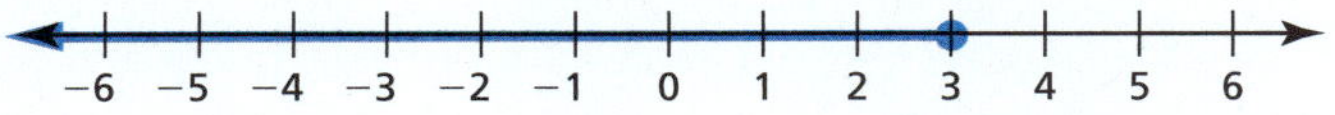

F.
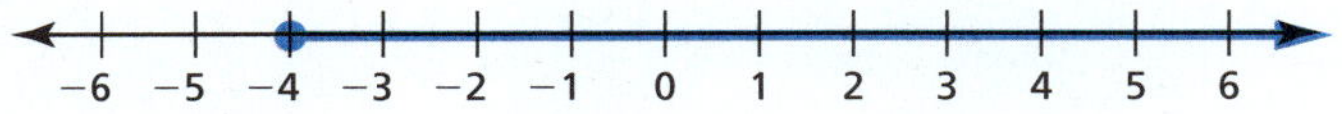

GO DIGITAL

Solving Multi-Step Inequalities

To solve multi-step inequalities, use inverse operations to isolate the variable.

EXAMPLE 1 Solving Multi-Step Inequalities

WATCH

Solve each inequality. Graph each solution.

a. $\dfrac{y}{-6} + 7 < 9$

b. $2v - 4 \geq 5$

SOLUTION

a.

$\dfrac{y}{-6} + 7 < 9$	Write the inequality.
$\quad -7 \quad -7$	Subtraction Property of Inequality
$\dfrac{y}{-6} < 2$	Simplify.
$-6 \cdot \dfrac{y}{-6} > -6 \cdot 2$	Use the Multiplication Property of Inequality. Reverse the inequality symbol.
$y > -12$	Simplify.

REMEMBER

Be sure to reverse the inequality symbol when multiplying or dividing by a negative number.

▶ The solution is $y > -12$.

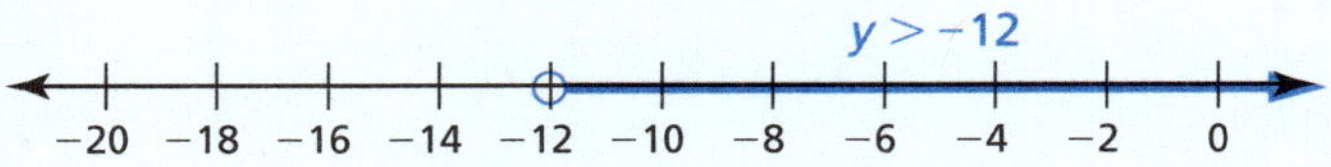

b.

$2v - 4 \geq 5$	Write the inequality.
$\quad +4 \quad +4$	Addition Property of Inequality
$2v \geq 9$	Simplify.
$\dfrac{2v}{2} \geq \dfrac{9}{2}$	Division Property of Inequality
$v \geq \dfrac{9}{2}$	Simplify.

▶ The solution is $v \geq \frac{9}{2}$.

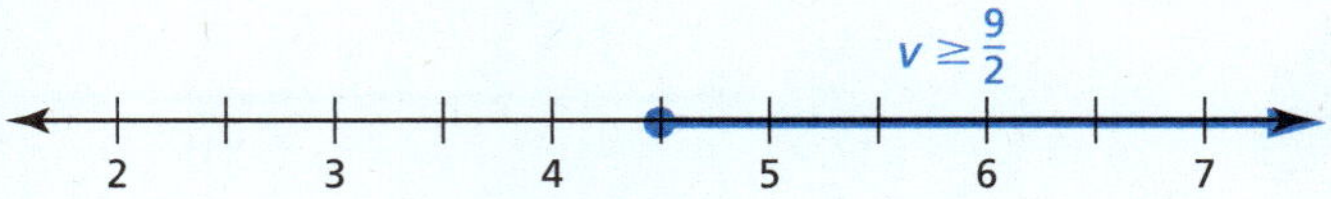

GO DIGITAL

SELF-ASSESSMENT

1 I don't understand yet. 2 I can do it with help. 3 I can do it on my own. 4 I can teach someone else.

Solve the inequality. Graph the solution.

1. $4b - 1 < 7$

2. $8 - 9c \geq -16$

3. $\frac{n}{-2} + 11 > 12$

4. $6 \geq 5 - \frac{v}{3}$

5. OPEN-ENDED Write two different multi-step inequalities whose solutions are represented by the graph.

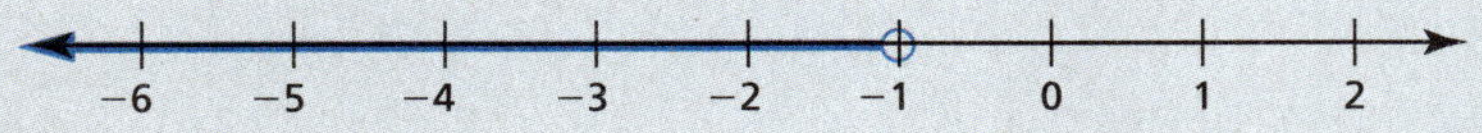

EXAMPLE 2 Solving an Inequality with Variables on Both Sides

WATCH

Solve $6x - 5 < 2x + 11$.

SOLUTION

$$
\begin{aligned}
6x - 5 &< 2x + 11 && \text{Write the inequality.} \\
\underline{+5} \quad & \quad \underline{+5} && \text{Addition Property of Inequality} \\
6x &< 2x + 16 && \text{Simplify.} \\
\underline{-2x} \quad & \quad \underline{-2x} && \text{Subtraction Property of Inequality} \\
4x &< 16 && \text{Simplify.} \\
\frac{4x}{4} &< \frac{16}{4} && \text{Division Property of Inequality} \\
x &< 4 && \text{Simplify.}
\end{aligned}
$$

▶ The solution is $x < 4$.

When solving an inequality, if you obtain an equivalent inequality that is always true, such as $-5 < 0$, the solutions of the inequality are *all real numbers*. If you obtain an equivalent inequality that is false, such as $3 \leq -2$, the inequality has *no solution*.

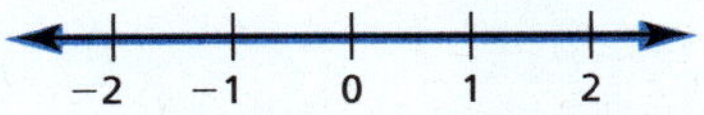

Graph of an inequality whose solutions are all real numbers

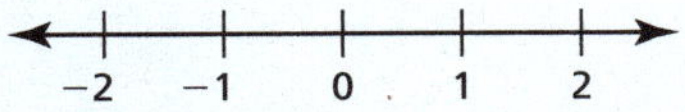

Graph of an inequality that has no solution

GO DIGITAL

ADAPT A PROCEDURE (3 MTR)

When the variable terms on each side of an inequality are the same, how can you use inspection to determine whether the inequality is true or false?

EXAMPLE 3 Inequalities with Special Solutions

WATCH

Solve (a) $8b - 3 > 4(2b + 3)$ and (b) $2(5w - 1.2) \leq 7 + 10w$.

SOLUTION

a.

$8b - 3 > 4(2b + 3)$	Write the inequality.
$8b - 3 > 8b + 12$	Distributive Property
$\underline{-8b} \quad \underline{-8b}$	Subtraction Property of Inequality
$-3 > 12$ ✗	Simplify.

▶ The inequality $-3 > 12$ is false. So, the inequality has no solution.

b.

$2(5w - 1.2) \leq 7 + 10w$	Write the inequality.
$10w - 2.4 \leq 7 + 10w$	Distributive Property
$\underline{-10w} \quad \underline{-10w}$	Subtraction Property of Inequality
$-2.4 \leq 7$	Simplify.

▶ The inequality $-2.4 \leq 7$ is always true. So, all real numbers are solutions.

SELF-ASSESSMENT

1 I don't understand yet. 2 I can do it with help. 3 I can do it on my own. 4 I can teach someone else.

Solve the inequality. Graph the solution, if possible.

6. $5x - 12 \leq 3x - 4$

7. $2(k - 5) < 2k + 5$

8. $-4(3n - 1) > -12n + 5.2$

9. $3(2a - 1) \geq \frac{3}{4}a - 17$

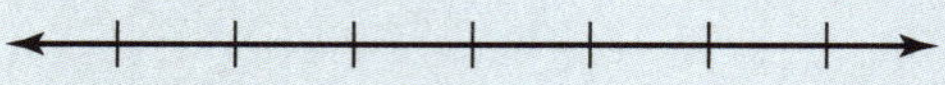

(5 MTR) **10. STRUCTURE** Without solving, how can you tell that the inequality $4x + 8 \leq 4x - 3$ has no solution?

Solving Real-Life Problems

7 MTR **EXAMPLE 4** **Modeling Real Life** WATCH

You are playing a trivia game on your cell phone. You need a mean score of at least 90 points to advance to the next round. What scores in the fifth game will allow you to advance?

SOLUTION

1. **Understand the Problem** You know the scores of your first four games. You are asked to find the scores in the fifth game that will allow you to advance.
2. **Make a Plan** Use the definition of the mean of a set of numbers to write an inequality. Then solve the inequality and answer the question.
3. **Solve and Check** Let x be your score in the fifth game.

$$\frac{95 + 91 + 77 + 89 + x}{5} \geq 90 \quad \text{Write an inequality.}$$

$$\frac{352 + x}{5} \geq 90 \quad \text{Simplify.}$$

$$5 \cdot \frac{352 + x}{5} \geq 5 \cdot 90 \quad \text{Multiplication Property of Inequality}$$

$$352 + x \geq 450 \quad \text{Simplify.}$$

$$\underline{-352} \qquad \underline{-352} \quad \text{Subtraction Property of Inequality}$$

$$x \geq 98 \quad \text{Simplify.}$$

▶ A score of at least 98 points will allow you to advance.

REMEMBER

The mean in Example 4 is equal to the sum of the game scores divided by the number of games.

Check

You can draw a diagram to check your answer. The horizontal bar graph shows the differences between the game scores and the desired mean of 90.

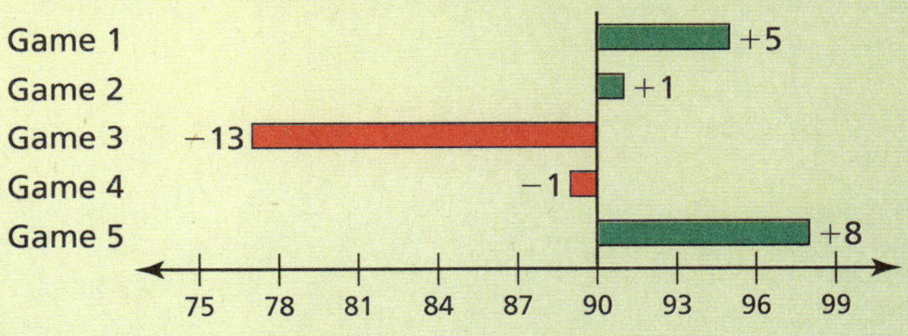

To have a mean of 90, the sum of the differences must be zero.

$$5 + 1 + (-13) + (-1) + 8 = 0 \ \checkmark$$

GO DIGITAL

SELF-ASSESSMENT

1 I don't understand yet. 2 I can do it with help. 3 I can do it on my own. 4 I can teach someone else.

11. WHAT IF? You need a mean score of at least 85 points to advance to the next round. What scores in the fifth game will allow you to advance?

12. For what amounts of sales do you earn more in the first year with Job Offer A? with Job Offer B?

Job Offer A	
Base salary	\$46,975
Commission	4.5% of sales

Job Offer B	
Base salary	\$42,550
Commission	6.5% of sales
Sign-on bonus	\$2500

2.4 Practice WITH CalcChat® AND CalcView®

In Exercises 1–10, solve the inequality. Graph the solution. *(See Example 1.)*

1. $2x - 3 > 7$

2. $5y + 9 \leq 4$

▶3. $-3 \leq 1 - 8v$

4. $-8 > -3t - 10$

5. $\frac{w}{2} + 4 > 5$

6. $1 + \frac{m}{3} \leq 6$

7. $\frac{p}{-8} - \frac{2}{5} > \frac{8}{5}$

8. $\frac{1}{2} + \frac{r}{-4} \leq \frac{5}{6}$

9. $12.6 \geq -6(a + 2)$

10. $14.7 \leq 3.5(b - 4)$

In Exercises 11–22, solve the inequality. Graph the solution, if possible. *(See Examples 2 and 3.)*

11. $4 - 2m > 7 - 3m$

12. $8n + 2 \leq 8n - 9$

▶13. $-2d - 2 < 3d + 8$

14. $8 + 10f > 14 - 2f$

15. $8g - 5g - 4 \leq -3 + 3g$

16. $3w - 5 > 2w + w - 7$

▶17. $6(\ell + 3) < 3(2\ell + 6)$

18. $2(5c - 7) \geq 10(c - 3)$

19. $4\left(\frac{1}{2}t - 2\right) > 2(t - 3)$

20. $15\left(\frac{1}{3}b + 3\right) \leq 6(b + 9)$

21. $9j - 4.5 + 6j \geq 3(5j - 1.5)$

22. $6h - 6 + 3.4h < 2(4.7h - 3)$

GO DIGITAL

4 MTR **ERROR ANALYSIS** **In Exercises 23 and 24, describe and correct the error in solving the inequality.**

23. ✗

$$\frac{x}{4} + 6 \geq 3$$
$$x + 6 \geq 12$$
$$x \geq 6$$

24. ✗

$$-2(1 - x) \leq 2x - 7$$
$$-2 + 2x \leq 2x - 7$$
$$-2 \leq -7$$

All real numbers are solutions.

25. **7 MTR** **MODELING REAL LIFE** You want an average of at least 30 active minutes each day during the week. How many active minutes do you need on Sunday to achieve your goal? Make an argument for your answer using a bar graph. *(See Example 4.)*

Day	Minutes exercising
Monday	15
Tuesday	45
Wednesday	20

Day	Minutes exercising
Thursday	0
Friday	60
Saturday	30

7 MTR **26.** **MODELING REAL LIFE** Bowling alley A charges \$3.75 to rent shoes and \$4 per game. Bowling alley B charges \$2.50 to rent shoes and \$4.50 per game.

a. For what numbers of games is the total cost, including a pair of rental shoes, less at bowling alley A? at bowling alley B?

b. Bowling alley A increases the cost per game by \$0.50. How does this affect your answer in part (a)? Explain.

27. **5 MTR** **CONNECTING CONCEPTS** The area of the rectangle is greater than 60 square feet. Find the possible values of x.

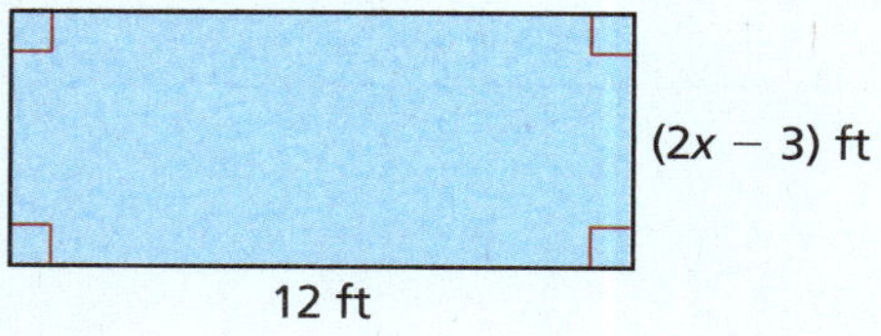

6 MTR **28.** **ASSESS REASONABLENESS** Your friend says that the inequality $5x - 2 > 5x - 4$ has no solution because the equation $5x - 2 = 5x - 4$ has no solution. Is your friend correct? Explain.

REASONING **In Exercises 29 and 30, find the value of a for which the solutions of the inequality are all real numbers.**

29. $a(x + 3) < 5x + 15 - x$

30. $3x + 8 + 2ax \geq 3ax - 4a$

5 MTR **31.** **STRUCTURE** Complete the inequality so that it has no solution.

$-3(2x + 1) <$ ____ $x +$ ____ $x +$ ____

32. **HOW DO YOU SEE IT?**

The graph shows your budget and the total cost of x gallons of gasoline and a car wash. You want to determine the possible amounts (in gallons) of gasoline you can buy within your budget.

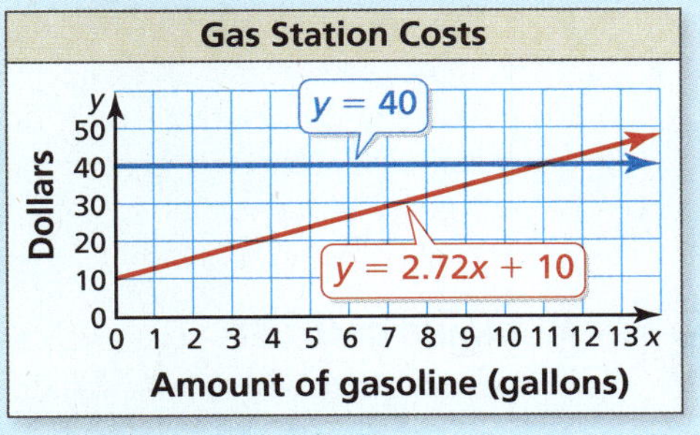

a. What is your budget?

b. How much does a gallon of gasoline cost? How much does a car wash cost?

c. Write an inequality that represents the possible amounts of gasoline you can buy.

d. Use the graph to estimate the solution of your inequality in part (c).

33. **DIG DEEPER** The height of each story of a building is about 10 feet. The bottom of the ladder on the fire truck must be at least 24 feet away from the building. How many stories can the ladder reach? Justify your answer.

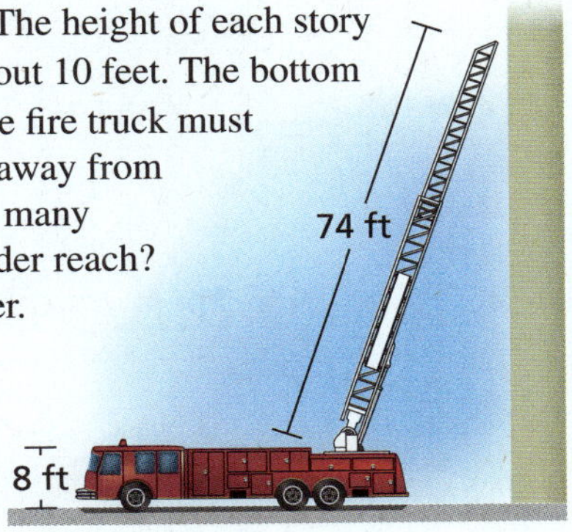

34. **THOUGHT PROVOKING**

A runner's times (in minutes) in the four races he has completed are 25.5, 24.3, 24.8, and 23.5. The runner plans to run at least two more races and wants to have an average time of less than 24 minutes. Write and solve an inequality to show how the runner can achieve his goal.

REVIEW & REFRESH

35. Solve the literal equation $6x + 5 = 3 - 2y$ for y.

36. Solve $\frac{10}{x} = \frac{25}{20}$.

In Exercises 37–40, solve the inequality. Graph the solution.

37. $n - 13 \geq -20$

38. $4 < \frac{b}{-3.8}$

39. $x + \frac{3}{7} < \frac{2}{7}$

40. $8(3g - 2) \leq 12(2g + 1)$

41. MODELING REAL LIFE You save \$20 each week to buy a smart watch that costs \$229.95.

a. Describe the numbers of months you need to save to buy the smart watch.

b. Your parents give you \$50 to help you buy the smart watch. How does this affect your answer in part (a)? Use an inequality to justify your answer.

42. Tell whether x and y are proportional.

x	3	6	9	12
y	2	4	6	8

In Exercises 43 and 44, write the sentence as an inequality.

43. Six times a number y is less than or equal to 10.

44. A number p plus 7 is greater than 24.8.

In Exercises 45 and 46, solve the equation.

45. $\frac{z}{8} + \frac{1}{4} = -\frac{z}{8}$

46. $4.9k + 6 - 1.2k = 8 + 3.7k$

47. MODELING REAL LIFE The histogram shows the numbers of hours that students in a class spent watching television last week. How many students are in the class? What percent of the students watched at least 15 hours of television?

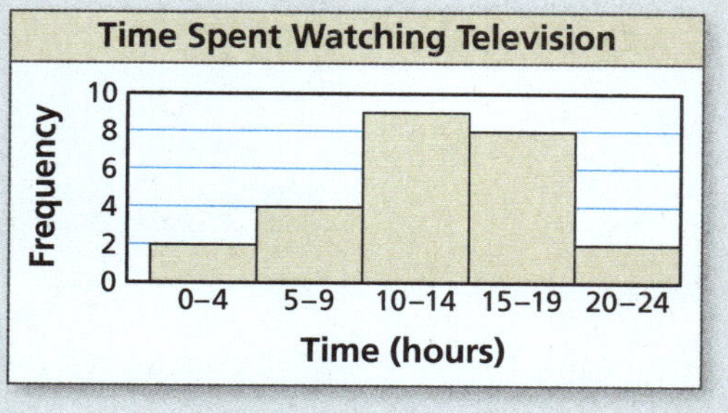

2.5 Solving Compound Inequalities

Learning Target: Write and solve compound inequalities.

Success Criteria:
- I can write word sentences as compound inequalities.
- I can solve compound inequalities.
- I can graph solutions of compound inequalities.

Algebraic Reasoning
MA.912.AR.2.6 Given a mathematical or real-world context, write and solve one-variable linear inequalities, including compound inequalities. Represent solutions algebraically or graphically.

EXPLORE IT! Describing Intervals on the Real Number Line

Work with a partner. In parts (a)–(h), use two inequalities to describe the interval. Explain your reasoning.

Half-Open Interval

a. 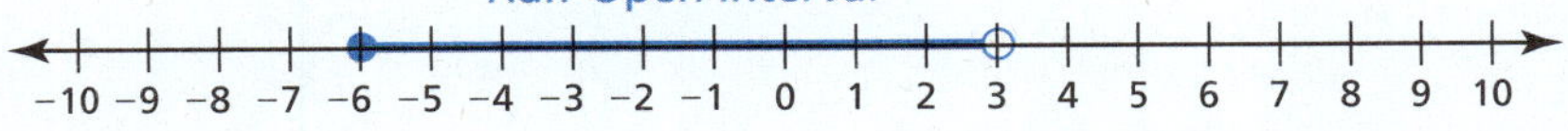

b. 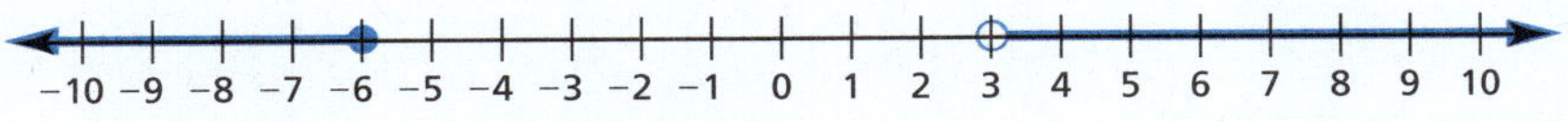

Half-Open Interval

c. 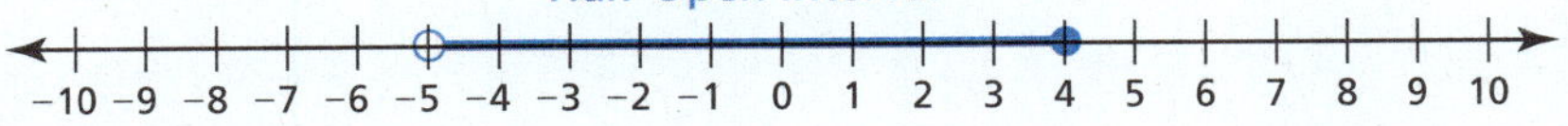

d. 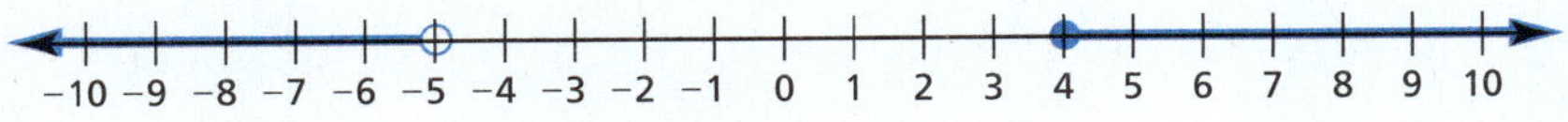

GO DIGITAL

Closed Interval

e. 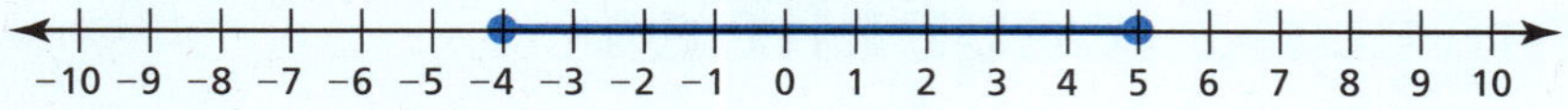

f. 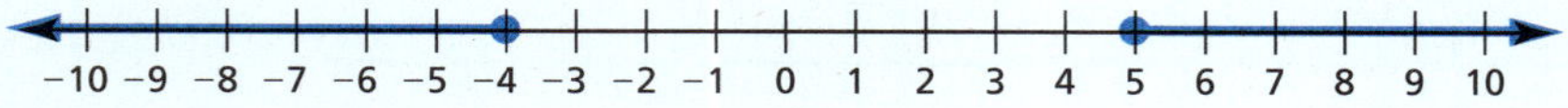

Open Interval

g. 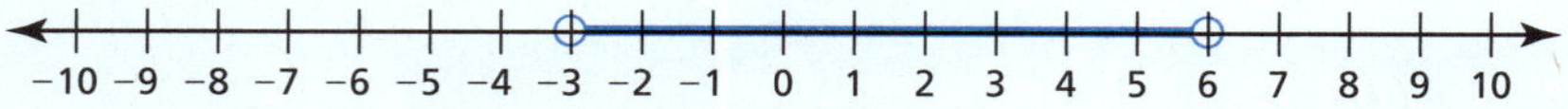

h. 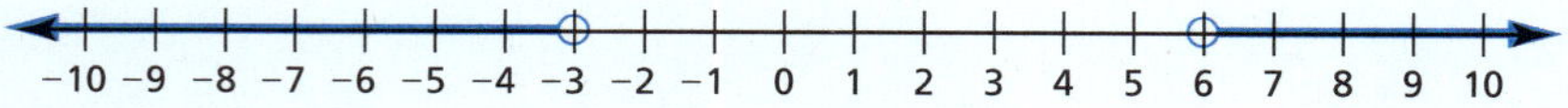

i. Do you use *and* or *or* when writing the inequalities for each graph?

4 MTR **COMMUNICATE CLEARLY**

Describe the difference between a closed interval and an open interval.

Writing and Graphing Compound Inequalities

> **WORDS AND MATH**
> The word *compound* can have many meanings, such as a chemical mixture, a group of buildings, or a word made from more than one word. All of these meanings have something in common: they represent something that is made from more than one thing.

A **compound inequality** is an inequality formed by joining two inequalities with the word *and* or the word *or*.

The graph of a compound inequality with *and* is the *intersection* of the graphs of the inequalities. The graph shows numbers that are solutions of *both* inequalities.

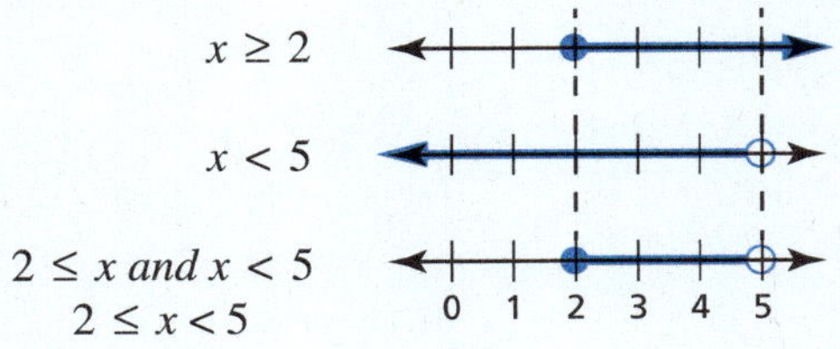

The graph of a compound inequality with *or* is the *union* of the graphs of the inequalities. The graph shows numbers that are solutions of *either* inequality.

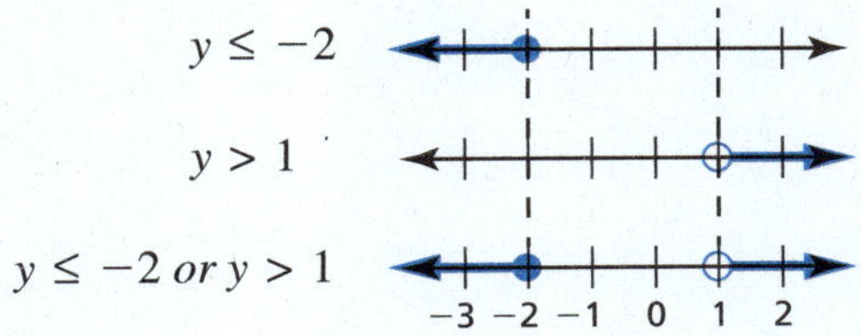

> **Vocabulary** (AZ VOCAB)
> compound inequality, *p. 133*
> set-builder notation, *p. 136*

EXAMPLE 1 **Writing and Graphing Compound Inequalities** (WATCH)

Write each sentence as an inequality. Graph each inequality.

a. A number x is greater than -8 and less than or equal to 4.

b. A number y is at most 0 or at least $\frac{3}{2}$.

SOLUTION

a. A number x is greater than -8 and less than or equal to 4.

$x > -8$ *and* $x \leq 4$

▶ An inequality is $-8 < x \leq 4$.

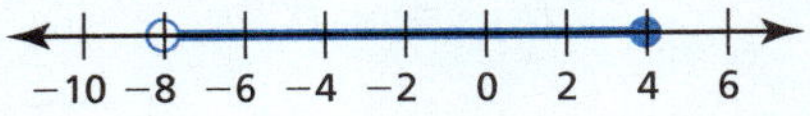

Graph the intersection of the graphs of $x > -8$ and $x \leq 4$.

b. A number y is at most 0 or at least $\frac{3}{2}$.

$y \leq 0$ *or* $y \geq \frac{3}{2}$

▶ An inequality is $y \leq 0$ *or* $y \geq \frac{3}{2}$.

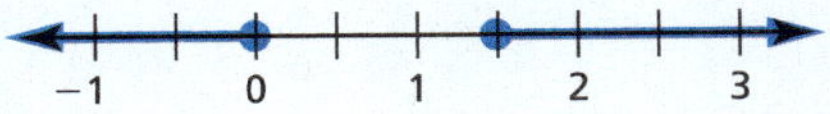

Graph the union of the graphs of $y \leq 0$ and $y \geq \frac{3}{2}$.

GO DIGITAL

SELF-ASSESSMENT

1 I don't understand yet. 2 I can do it with help. 3 I can do it on my own. 4 I can teach someone else.

Write the sentence as an inequality. Graph the inequality.

1. A number d is more than 0 and less than 10.

2. A number a is fewer than -6 or no less than -3.

3. WRITING Compare the graph of $-6 \le x \le -4$ with the graph of $x \le -6$ *or* $x \ge -4$.

4 MTR **4. WHICH ONE DOESN'T BELONG?** Which compound inequality does *not* belong with the other three? Explain your reasoning.

$a > 4$ *or* $a < -3$	$a < -2$ *or* $a > 8$	$a > 7$ *or* $a < -5$	$a < 6$ *or* $a > -9$

Solving Compound Inequalities

You can solve a compound inequality by solving two inequalities separately. When a compound inequality with *and* is written as a single inequality, you can solve the inequality by performing the same operation on each expression.

USE STRUCTURE 5 MTR

In the inequality $-4 < x - 2 < 3$, what do you know about the quantity $x - 2$? How does this help you begin to solve?

EXAMPLE 2 Solving Compound Inequalities with *And*

WATCH

Solve each inequality. Graph each solution.

a. $-4 < x - 2 < 3$ **b.** $-3 < -2x + 1 \le 9$

SOLUTION

a. Separate the compound inequality into two inequalities, then solve.

$$-4 < x - 2 \quad \text{and} \quad x - 2 < 3 \qquad \text{Write two inequalities.}$$

$$\underline{+2} \quad \underline{+2} \qquad\qquad \underline{+2} \quad \underline{+2} \qquad \text{Addition Property of Inequality}$$

$$-2 < x \quad \text{and} \quad x < 5 \qquad \text{Simplify.}$$

▶ The solution is $-2 < x < 5$.

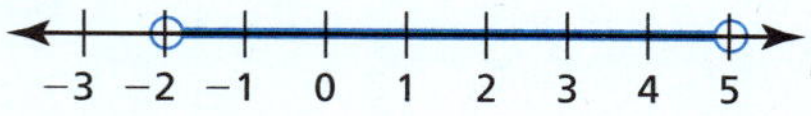

b.

$$-3 < -2x + 1 \le 9 \qquad \text{Write the inequality.}$$

$$\underline{-1} \quad \underline{-1} \quad \underline{-1} \qquad \text{Subtraction Property of Inequality}$$

$$-4 < -2x \le 8 \qquad \text{Simplify.}$$

$$\frac{-4}{-2} > \frac{-2x}{-2} \ge \frac{8}{-2} \qquad \text{Use the Division Property of Inequality. Reverse each inequality symbol.}$$

$$2 > x \ge -4 \qquad \text{Simplify.}$$

▶ The solution is $-4 \le x < 2$.

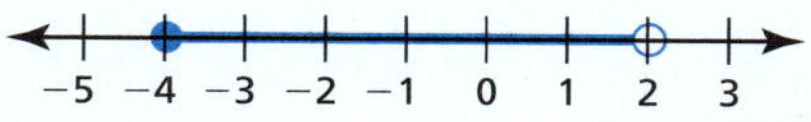

GO DIGITAL

EXAMPLE 3 Solving a Compound Inequality with *Or*

WATCH

Solve $3y - 5 < -8$ *or* $2y - 1 > 5$. Graph the solution.

SOLUTION

$3y - 5 < -8$	*or*	$2y - 1 > 5$	Write the inequality.
$+5 \quad +5$		$+1 \quad +1$	Addition Property of Inequality
$3y < -3$		$2y > 6$	Simplify.
$\frac{3y}{3} < \frac{-3}{3}$		$\frac{2y}{2} > \frac{6}{2}$	Division Property of Inequality
$y < -1$	*or*	$y > 3$	Simplify.

▶ The solution is $y < -1$ *or* $y > 3$.

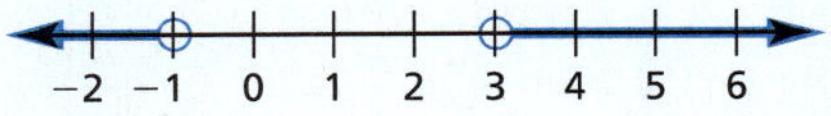

SELF-ASSESSMENT

1 I don't understand yet. 2 I can do it with help. 3 I can do it on my own. 4 I can teach someone else.

Solve the inequality. Graph the solution.

5. $5 \leq m + 4 < 10$

6. $-3 < \frac{2}{3}k - 5 < 0$

7. $4c + 3 \leq -5$ *or* $c - 8 > -1$

8. $2p + 1 < -4$ *or* $3 - 8p \leq -1$

9. OPEN-ENDED Write a compound inequality that has a solution of all real numbers.

Another way to represent solutions of inequalities is to use *set-builder notation.*

KEY IDEA

Set-Builder Notation

Set-builder notation uses symbols to define a set in terms of the properties of the members of the set.

Set-builder notation $\{x \mid x < b\}$

Words the set of all real numbers x such that x is less than b

> **READING**
> *Words* indicates how to read the set-builder notation $\{x \mid x < b\}$ aloud.

Set-Builder Notation	*Graph*
$\{x \mid x \leq a \text{ or } x > b\}$	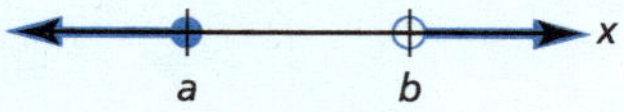
$\{x \mid x \neq a\}$	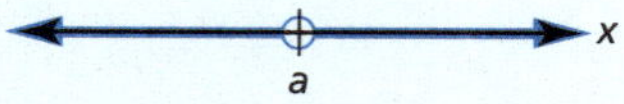

EXAMPLE 4 B.E.S.T. Test Prep: Solving a Compound Inequality

What is the solution of $-\frac{1}{2}z + 5 < 2$ *or* $3z - 4 < 14$? Select all that apply.

Ⓐ all real numbers

Ⓑ $z < 6$ *or* $z > 6$

Ⓒ $\{z \mid z < 6\}$

Ⓓ $\{z \mid z \neq 6\}$

SOLUTION

$$-\frac{1}{2}z + 5 < 2 \qquad \textit{or} \qquad 3z - 4 < 14$$

$$\underline{-5} \quad \underline{-5} \qquad\qquad \underline{+4} \quad \underline{+4}$$

$$-\frac{1}{2}z < -3 \qquad\qquad 3z < 18$$

$$-2 \cdot \left(-\frac{1}{2}z\right) > -2 \cdot (-3) \qquad\qquad \frac{3z}{3} < \frac{18}{3}$$

$$z > 6 \qquad \textit{or} \qquad z < 6$$

The solutions is $z < 6$ *or* $z > 6$. This represents all real numbers except $z = 6$.

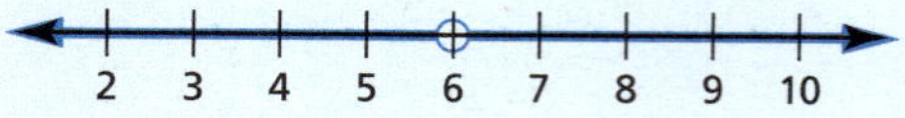

▶ So, the correct answers are Ⓑ and Ⓓ.

5 MTR USE STRUCTURE

How can you change the inequality so that Choice A is correct? so that Choice C is correct?

GO DIGITAL

SELF-ASSESSMENT

1 I don't understand yet. 2 I can do it with help. 3 I can do it on my own. 4 I can teach someone else.

Solve the inequality. Write the solution using set-builder notation.

10. $0 < 2n - 7 \leq 1$

11. $4x + 5 \leq 1$ *or* $-\frac{1}{2}x + 10 \geq 10$

12. REASONING Is it possible for a compound inequality to have no real solution? Explain your reasoning.

Operating temperature:
0°C to 35°C

Solving Real-Life Problems

7 MTR **EXAMPLE 5** **Modeling Real Life** WATCH

A smartphone may fail outside of its operating temperature range. Write an inequality that represents the possible operating temperatures (in degrees Fahrenheit) of the smartphone. Then describe a situation in which the phone may be outside of the operating range.

SOLUTION

1. **Understand the Problem** You know the operating temperature range in degrees Celsius. You are asked to represent the range in degrees Fahrenheit and to describe a situation outside of this range.

2. **Make a Plan** Write a compound inequality in degrees Celsius C. Use the formula $C = \frac{5}{9}(F - 32)$ to rewrite the inequality in degrees Fahrenheit F. Then solve the inequality and describe a situation outside of this range.

3. **Solve and Check**

$$
\begin{aligned}
0 \leq \quad C \quad &\leq 35 && \text{Write the inequality using } C.\\
0 \leq \tfrac{5}{9}(F - 32) &\leq 35 && \text{Substitute } \tfrac{5}{9}(F-32) \text{ for } C.\\
\tfrac{9}{5} \cdot 0 \leq \tfrac{9}{5} \cdot \tfrac{5}{9}(F - 32) &\leq \tfrac{9}{5} \cdot 35 && \text{Multiplication Property of Inequality}\\
0 \leq F - 32 &\leq 63 && \text{Simplify.}\\
+32 \quad\quad +32 &\quad +32 && \text{Addition Property of Inequality}\\
32 \leq F &\leq 95 && \text{Simplify.}
\end{aligned}
$$

▶ A solution is $32 \leq F \leq 95$. So, the operating temperature range of the smartphone is 32°F to 95°F. Someone might leave the phone in a car on a hot day, where temperatures can exceed 150°F.

Check
You can use the formula $C = \frac{5}{9}(F - 32)$ to check that your answer is correct. Substitute 32 and 95 for F in the formula to verify that 0°C and 35°C are the minimum and maximum operating temperatures in degrees Celsius. ✓

GO DIGITAL

SELF-ASSESSMENT 1 I don't understand yet. 2 I can do it with help. 3 I can do it on my own. 4 I can teach someone else.

13. A pair of winter boots are rated for temperatures from $-40°C$ to $15°C$. Write an inequality that represents the temperature rating (in degrees Fahrenheit) of the boots.

14. Bird-watchers record the types of birds they see or hear. The graph shows results from a location in Canada. Write an inequality that represents the range in the percents of bird-watchers who saw or heard a Black-and-white Warbler from July 1 to September 15.

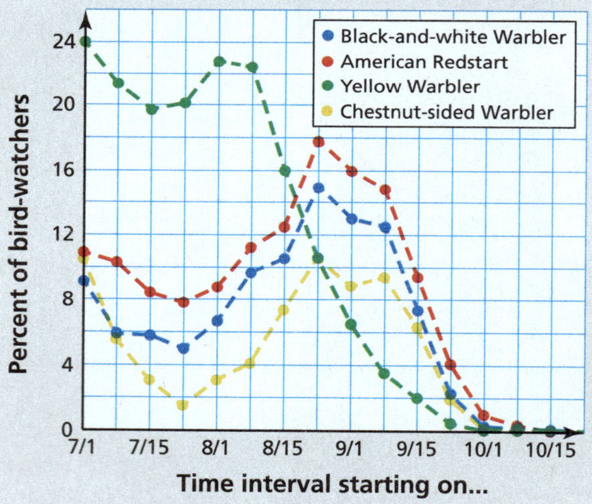

2.5 Practice WITH CalcChat® AND CalcView®

In Exercises 1–4, write the sentence as an inequality. Graph the inequality. *(See Example 1.)*

▶ **1.** A number p is less than 6 and greater than 2.

2. A number n is less than or equal to -7 or greater than 12.

3. A number m is more than $-7\frac{2}{3}$ or at most -10.

4. A number r is no less than -1.5 and fewer than 9.5.

In Exercises 5–12, solve the inequality. Graph the solution. *(See Examples 2 and 3.)*

▶ **5.** $6 < x + 5 \leq 11$

6. $24 > -3r \geq -9$

▶ **7.** $v + 8 < 3$ *or* $-8v < -40$

8. $-14 > w + 3$ *or* $3w \geq -27$

9. $\frac{1}{2}r + 3 < \frac{7}{4}$ *or* $-r + \frac{3}{4} \leq \frac{3}{8}$

10. $-6.2 < 2n + 8.6 < 21.4$

11. $-12 < \frac{1}{2}(4x + 16) < 18$

12. $35 < 7(2 - b)$ *or* $\frac{1}{3}(15b - 12) \geq 21$

7 MTR **13. MODELING REAL LIFE** The life zones on Mount Rainier, a mountain in Washington, can be approximately classified by elevation, as follows.

Write an inequality that represents the elevation range for each type of plant life.

a. trees in the low-elevation forest zone

b. flowers in the subalpine and alpine zones

Elevation of Mount Rainer: 14,410 ft

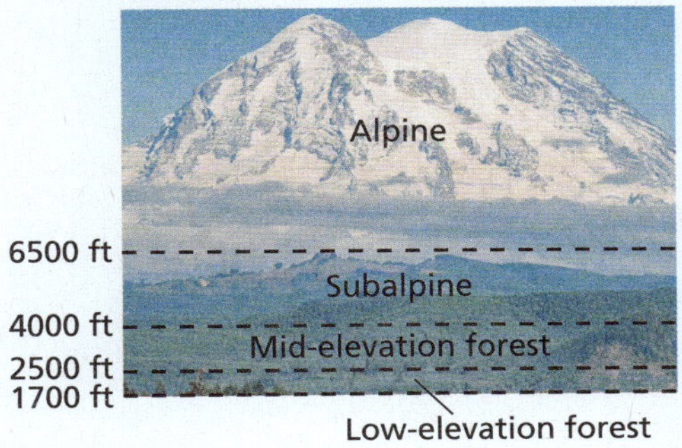

GO DIGITAL

14. ERROR ANALYSIS Describe and correct the error in solving the inequality and graphing the solution.

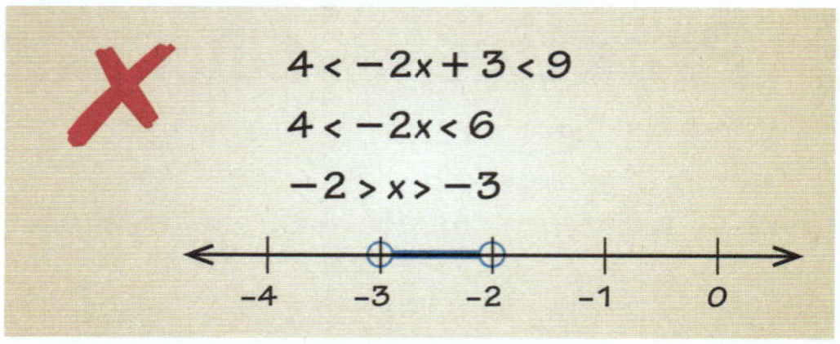

In Exercises 15–18, sketch the graph of the set of numbers.

15. $\{x \mid 3 < x < 12\}$

16. $\{x \mid -10 \leq x \leq 15\}$

17. $\{x \mid x < 5 \text{ or } x > 10\}$

18. $\{x \mid x \neq 4\}$

In Exercises 19–22, write the set of numbers in set-builder notation.

19. the set of all real numbers less than -8 or greater than or equal to -4

20. the set of all real numbers greater than 19 and less than 32

21. the set of all real numbers except 100

22. the set of all real numbers less than 50 or greater than 50

In Exercises 23–30, solve the inequality. Write the solution using set-builder notation. *(See Example 4.)*

23. $7 \leq x + 3 < 15$

24. $16 > -4v \geq -8$

25. $w + 6 \leq 2$ *or* $-6w < -48$

26. $18 \geq p + 13$ *or* $4p > -28$

27. $5 + \frac{1}{4}m > \frac{9}{2}$ *or* $7 - \frac{4}{3}m \geq \frac{1}{3}$

28. $2.3 \leq 3t + 6.2 < 8$

29. $6 \leq \frac{1}{3}(9x + 27) \leq 6$

30. $9n \geq -7.2$ *or* $1.6 \geq 2.4 + n$

7 MTR **31. MODELING REAL LIFE** Write an inequality that represents the temperatures (in degrees Fahrenheit) of the interior of the iceberg. *(See Example 5.)*

7 MTR **32. MODELING REAL LIFE** pH is measured on a scale of 0 to 14 and refers to the concentration of an acid or base in water. The recommended pH for a swimming pool is 7.2 to 7.8. Write an inequality that represents the recommended pH of the swimming pool.

In Exercises 33–38, solve the inequality. Graph the solution, if possible.

33. $22 < -3c + 4 < 14$

34. $2m - 1 \geq 5$ *or* $5m > -25$

35. $-y + 3 \leq 8$ *and* $y + 2 > 9$

36. $x - 8 \leq 4$ *or* $2x + 3 > 9$

37. $\frac{3}{2}n + 19 \leq 10 + \frac{1}{2}n$ *or* $-\frac{2}{3}n + 3 < -\frac{1}{3}n + 12$

38. $3.5x - 18 < 4.5x - 23$ *and* $9.5x - 16 < 22$

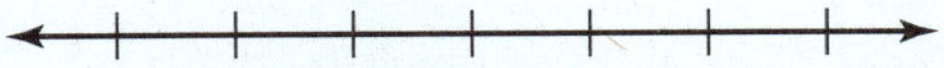

7 MTR **39. MODELING REAL LIFE** You are selling flowers to raise money for a field trip. For each flower you sell, you earn \$5 toward the trip. The total cost of the trip including the bus ride is \$75. You must sell enough flowers to cover the cost of the \$15 bus ride, and you plan to stop selling flowers if you earn enough to cover the total cost of the trip. Describe the possible numbers of flowers you sell.

7 MTR **40. MODELING REAL LIFE** A melting point is the temperature at which a solid melts to become a liquid. A boiling point is the temperature at which a liquid boils to become a gas. The table shows the melting and boiling points of several elements.

Element	Melting point (°C)	Boiling point (°C)
Gold	1064	2807
Silver	962	2212
Copper	1083	2567

a. Write an inequality that represents the temperatures (in degrees Fahrenheit) of each element as a liquid.

b. Describe a situation in which someone might need to know the melting point of one of these elements.

41. PROBLEM SOLVING A ski shop sells skis with lengths ranging from 150 centimeters to 220 centimeters. The shop says the length of the skis should be about 1.16 times a skier's height (in centimeters). Write an inequality that represents the heights of skiers (in inches) for which the shop does *not* provide skis.

42. HOW DO YOU SEE IT? The graph shows the annual profits of a company over 8 years. Write an inequality that represents the annual profits from 2013 to 2020.

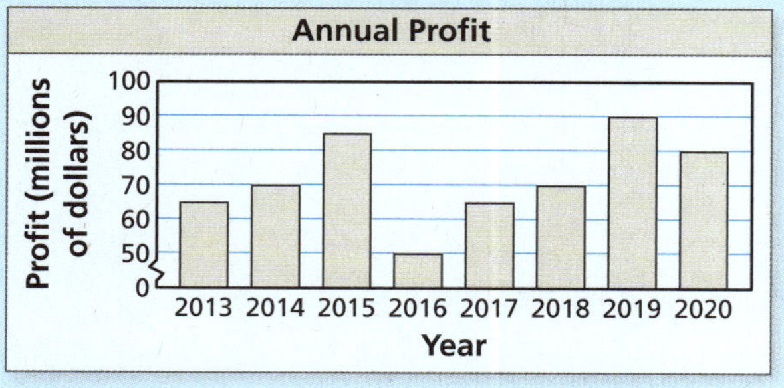

43. CONNECTING CONCEPTS You are marking a rectangular paintball zone that must be 34 meters wide and have a perimeter of at least 140 meters but not more than 260 meters. Find the possible lengths x of the rectangular paintball zone.

44. THOUGHT PROVOKING Complete the inequality

$$4(x - 6) \ \square \ 2(x - 10)$$

and

$$5(x + 2) \geq 2(x + 8)$$

with <, ≤, >, or ≥ so that the solution is only one value.

45. DIG DEEPER Determine the value of k for which the inequality $0.5 < -4x + k \leq 12 - k$ has the solution set $\{x \mid 1.25 \leq x < 2\}$.

46. PERFORMANCE TASK You and your friends want to go on a road trip. You establish a round-trip fuel budget of \$100, and plan to use a car with a fuel range of 25–34 miles per gallon. Use current gasoline prices to determine the distances you can travel. Then plan a trip to a city within the allotted distance from your location. Use inequalities to represent how much you will spend on gasoline, the maximum speeds at which you can travel, and how long the trip will take.

47. MAKING AN ARGUMENT The sum of the lengths of any two sides of a triangle is greater than the length of the third side. Write three inequalities that represent the possible values of x. Your friend claims the value of x can be 1.5. Is your friend correct? Explain.

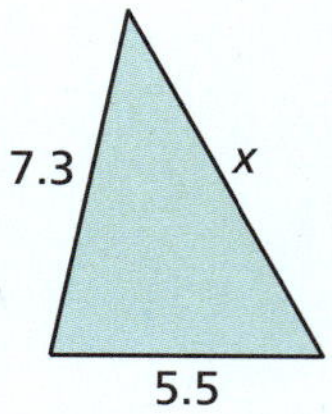

REVIEW & REFRESH

WATCH

48. The vertices of a triangle are $A(3, 3)$, $B(0, -3)$, and $C(-3, 0)$. Translate the triangle 2 units left and 1 unit up. What are the coordinates of the image?

In Exercises 49–52, solve the equation. Graph the solutions, if possible.

49. $\left|\frac{d}{9}\right| = 6$

50. $7|5p - 7| = -21$

51. $|r + 2| = 9.4$

52. $\left|\frac{1}{2}w - 6\right| = |w + 7|$

53. Describe the relationship between the data.

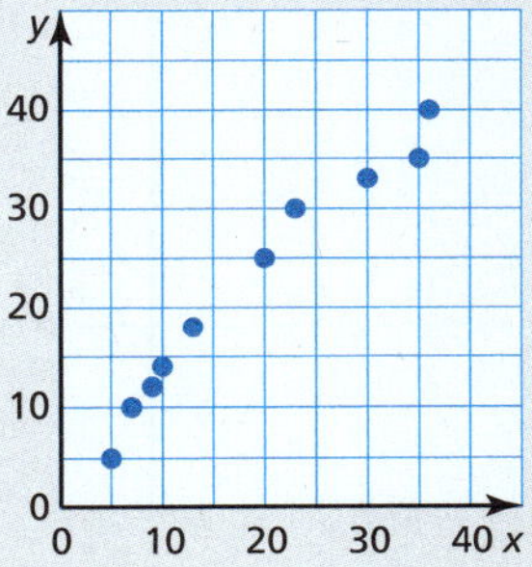

7 MTR **54.** **MODELING REAL LIFE** You have quarters, nickels, and dimes that total \$1.85. You have twice as many nickels as dimes, and 2 more quarters than dimes. How many of each coin do you have?

In Exercises 55 and 56, write an inequality that represents the graph.

55.

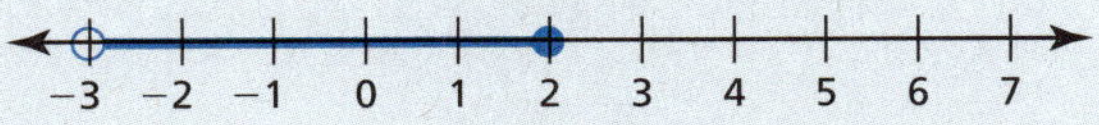

56.

57. What percent of 25 is 16?

58. REASONING Explain how you could predict the number of times you will spin a 4 in 50 spins on the spinner shown.

59. MODELING REAL LIFE You need an average exam score of at least 84% to receive a B in a class. For what scores on the fourth exam will you receive a B in the class?

Exam	Score
1	78%
2	93%
3	82%

In Exercises 60–63, solve the inequality. Graph the solution.

60. $9.4 + q \le 15.2$

61. $z - \left(-\frac{3}{5}\right) > \frac{7}{20}$

62. $2 \le -\frac{2}{9}x$

63. $2x \ge \frac{3}{4}$

64. Find the missing values in the ratio table. Then write the equivalent ratios.

Miles	$\frac{4}{3}$		4
Hours	2	4	

65. Find the area of the circle.

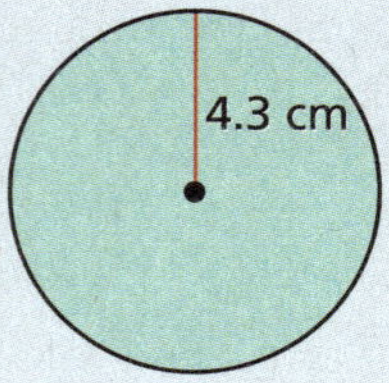

2.6 Solving Absolute Value Inequalities (H)

Learning Target: Write and solve inequalities involving absolute value.

Success Criteria:

- I can write a compound inequality related to a given absolute value inequality.
- I can solve absolute value inequalities.
- I can use absolute value inequalities to solve real-life problems.

Algebraic Reasoning

(H) **MA.912.AR.4.2** Given a mathematical or real-world context, write and solve one-variable absolute value inequalities. Represent solutions algebraically or graphically.

EXPLORE IT! Solving an Absolute Value Inequality

Work with a partner. Consider the absolute value inequality

$$|x + 2| \le 3.$$

a. Explain what you think this inequality means.

b. Can you find a number that makes the inequality true? If so, what is the number?

c. Do you think there are other numbers that make the inequality true? If so, find several of them. Compare your answers with your classmates'.

d. On the real number line below, locate the point for which the expression $|x + 2|$ is equal to 0.

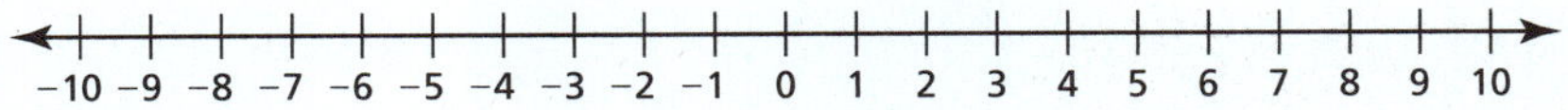

Then locate the numbers you found in parts (b) and (c) on the real number line. What do you notice?

GO DIGITAL

USE STRUCTURE 5 MTR

How can you change one of the absolute value inequalities shown so that it has no solution?

e. Can you write two linear inequalities that use the expression $x + 2$ to represent the solutions of $|x + 2| \leq 3$? Explain.

f. Repeat parts (b)–(e) for the inequality $|x + 2| \geq 3$. Compare your results with those for the inequality $|x + 2| \leq 3$.

g. Describe how to find the solutions of the absolute value inequalities algebraically. Then find the solutions.

i. $|x - 4| \leq 2$

x_1	$\lvert x_1 - 4 \rvert$
−6	10
−5	9
−4	
−3	
−2	
−1	
0	
1	
2	

ii. $|x - 4| \geq 2$

3 MTR **h. CHOOSE A METHOD** Solve the absolute value inequalities in part (g) in a different way. Explain your method.

Solving Absolute Value Inequalities

Vocabulary

absolute value inequality, *p. 147*
absolute deviation, *p. 149*

An **absolute value inequality** is an inequality that contains an absolute value expression. For example, $|x| < 2$ and $|x| > 2$ are absolute value inequalities. Recall that $|x| = 2$ means the distance between x and 0 is 2.

The inequality $|x| < 2$ means the distance between x and 0 is *less than* 2.

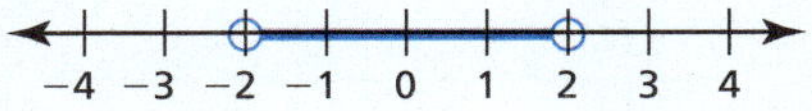

The graph of $|x| < 2$ is the graph of $x > -2$ *and* $x < 2$.

The inequality $|x| > 2$ means the distance between x and 0 is *greater than* 2.

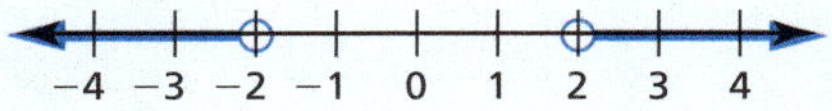

The graph of $|x| > 2$ is the graph of $x < -2$ *or* $x > 2$.

You can solve these types of inequalities by solving a compound inequality.

KEY IDEA

Solving Absolute Value Inequalities

Let c be a positive real number.

To solve $|ax + b| < c$, solve the compound inequality

$$ax + b > -c \quad \textit{and} \quad ax + b < c.$$

To solve $|ax + b| > c$, solve the compound inequality

$$ax + b < -c \quad \textit{or} \quad ax + b > c.$$

In the inequalities above, you can replace $<$ with $\leq$ and $>$ with $\geq$.

EXAMPLE 1 **Solving Absolute Value Inequalities** WATCH

Solve each inequality. Graph each solution, if possible.

a. $|x + 7| \leq 2$ **b.** $|8x - 11| < 0$

SOLUTION

a. Use $|x + 7| \leq 2$ to write a compound inequality. Then solve.

$x + 7 \geq -2$	*and*	$x + 7 \leq 2$	Write a compound inequality.
$\underline{-7} \quad \underline{-7}$		$\underline{-7} \quad \underline{-7}$	Subtraction Property of Inequality
$x \geq -9$	*and*	$x \leq -5$	Simplify.

REMEMBER

A compound inequality with *and* can be written as a single inequality.

▶ The solution is $-9 \leq x \leq -5$.

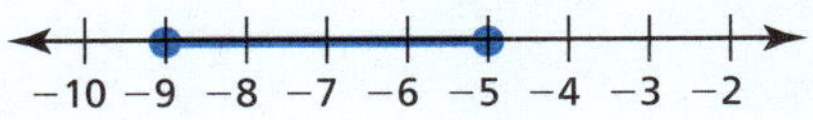

b. By definition, the absolute value of an expression must be greater than or equal to 0. The expression $|8x - 11|$ cannot be less than 0.

▶ So, the inequality has no solution.

GO DIGITAL

SELF-ASSESSMENT

1 I don't understand yet. 2 I can do it with help. 3 I can do it on my own. 4 I can teach someone else.

1. **WRITING** How do you determine whether to use a compound inequality with *and* or a compound inequality with *or* when solving an absolute value inequality?

Solve the inequality. Graph the solution, if possible.

2. $|x| \leq 3.5$

3. $|k - 3| < -1$

4. $\left|\frac{1}{2}w - 1\right| < 11$

EXAMPLE 2 Solving Absolute Value Inequalities

WATCH

Solve each inequality. Graph each solution.

a. $|c - 1| \geq 5$ **b.** $|10 - m| \geq -2$ **c.** $4|2x - 3| + 1 > 17$

SOLUTION

a. Use $|c - 1| \geq 5$ to write a compound inequality. Then solve.

$c - 1 \leq -5$ *or* $c - 1 \geq 5$ Write a compound inequality.

$\underline{+1}$ $\underline{+1}$ $\underline{+1}$ $\underline{+1}$ Addition Property of Inequality

$c \leq -4$ *or* $c \geq 6$ Simplify.

▶ The solution is $c \leq -4$ *or* $c \geq 6$.

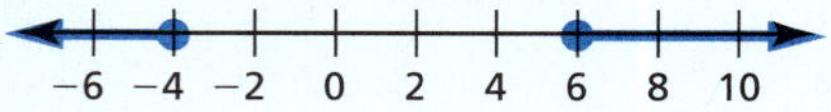

b. By definition, the absolute value of an expression must be greater than or equal to 0. The expression $|10 - m|$ will always be greater than -2.

▶ So, all real numbers are solutions.

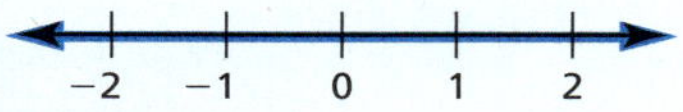

c. First isolate the absolute value expression on one side of the inequality.

$4|2x - 3| + 1 > 17$ Write the inequality.

$\underline{-1}$ $\underline{-1}$ Subtraction Property of Inequality

$4|2x - 3| > 16$ Simplify.

$\frac{4|2x - 3|}{4} > \frac{16}{4}$ Division Property of Inequality

$|2x - 3| > 4$ Simplify.

Use $|2x - 3| > 4$ to write a compound inequality. Then solve.

$2x - 3 < -4$ *or* $2x - 3 > 4$ Write a compound inequality.

$\underline{+3}$ $\underline{+3}$ $\underline{+3}$ $\underline{+3}$ Addition Property of Inequality

$2x < -1$ $2x > 7$ Simplify.

$\frac{2x}{2} < \frac{-1}{2}$ $\frac{2x}{2} > \frac{7}{2}$ Division Property of Inequality

$x < -\frac{1}{2}$ *or* $x > \frac{7}{2}$ Simplify.

▶ The solution is $x < -\frac{1}{2}$ *or* $x > \frac{7}{2}$.

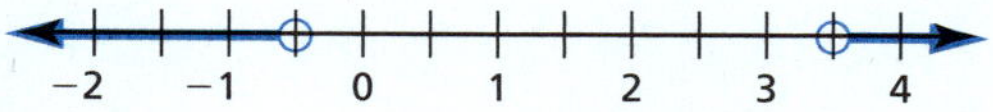

GO DIGITAL

SELF-ASSESSMENT

1 I don't understand yet. 2 I can do it with help. 3 I can do it on my own. 4 I can teach someone else.

Solve the inequality. Graph the solution.

5. $|x + 3| > 8$

6. $|n + 2| - 3.7 \geq -6$

7. $3|d + 1| - 7 \geq -2$

8. WRITING Describe how solving $|w - 9| \leq 2$ is different from solving $|w - 9| = 2$.

9. REASONING What is the solution of the inequality $|ax + b| < c$, where $c < 0$? What is the solution of the inequality $|ax + b| > c$, where $c < 0$? Explain.

Solving Real-Life Problems

WORDS AND MATH

A *deviation* is something that is different from the expected norm. In mathematics, *absolute deviation* represents how far a number deviates from a specific value.

The **absolute deviation** of a number x from a given value is the absolute value of the difference of x and the given value.

$$\text{absolute deviation} = |x - \text{given value}|$$

7 MTR **EXAMPLE 3** **Modeling Real Life** WATCH

A mountain climber wants to buy a new camera drone to help map out a safe route to a mountain's summit. The table shows the prices of several camera drones. The climber is willing to pay the mean price with an absolute deviation of at most $100. How many of the camera drone prices meet this condition?

Camera Drone Prices	
$890	$750
$650	$370
$660	$670
$450	$650
$725	$825

SOLUTION

1. **Understand the Problem** You know the prices of 10 camera drones. You are asked to find how many drones are at most $100 from the mean price.

2. **Make a Plan** Calculate the mean price by dividing the sum of the prices by the number of prices. Use the absolute deviation and the mean price to write an absolute value inequality. Then solve the inequality and use it to answer the question.

3. **Solve and Check**

The mean price is $\frac{6640}{10} = \$664$. Let x represent a price the climber is willing to pay.

$|x - 664| \leq 100$ — Write the absolute value inequality.

$-100 \leq x - 664 \leq 100$ — Write a compound inequality.

$564 \leq x \leq 764$ — Add 664 to each expression and simplify.

STUDY TIP

The absolute deviation of at most $100 from the mean, $664, is given by the inequality $|x - 664| \leq 100$.

▶ The prices the climber is willing to pay are at least $564 and at most $764. Six prices meet this condition: $750, $650, $660, $670, $650, and $725.

Check Reasonableness You can check that your answer is correct by graphing the drone prices and the mean on a number line. Any point within 100 of 664 represents a price that the climber is willing to pay.

SELF-ASSESSMENT

1 I don't understand yet. 2 I can do it with help. 3 I can do it on my own. 4 I can teach someone else.

10. **WHAT IF?** The climber is willing to pay the mean price with an absolute deviation of at most $75. Do you expect the number of prices that meet this condition to increase or decrease? Explain your reasoning. How many of the camera drone prices meet this condition?

11. A softball team is participating in a tournament where the team will spend three nights at a hotel. Each hotel offers a 50% discount for the third night. The coach wants to keep the total cost for each player at $225 with an absolute deviation of at most $25. Write and solve an absolute value inequality to find which hotels meet this condition.

Hotel	Price per night
Hotel A	$80
Hotel B	$105
Hotel C	$75
Hotel D	$90

GO DIGITAL

2.6 Practice WITH CalcChat® AND CalcView®

In Exercises 1–16, solve the inequality. Graph the solution, if possible. *(See Examples 1 and 2.)*

1. $|x| < 3$

2. $|y| \geq 4.5$

3. $|d + 9| > 3$

4. $|h - 5| \leq 10$

5. $|2s - 7| \geq -1$

6. $|4c + 5| > 7$

7. $|5p + 2| < -4$

8. $|9 - 4n| < 5$

9. $|6t - 7| - 8 \geq 3$

10. $|3j - 1| + 6 < 0$

11. $3|14 - m| > 18$

12. $-4|6b - 8| \leq 12$

13. $2|3w + 8| - 12.5 \leq -4.5$

14. $-3|2 - 4u| + 5.5 < -4.1$

15. $6\left|-\frac{1}{4}f + 3\right| + 7 > 7$

16. $\frac{2}{3}|4v + 6| - 2 \leq 10$

In Exercises 17 and 18, write the sentence as an absolute value inequality. Then solve the inequality.

17. A number is less than 6 units from 0.

18. Twice a number is no less than 10 units from -1.

19. **MODELING REAL LIFE** The rules for an essay contest require that entries have 500 words with an absolute deviation of at most 30 words. Write and solve an absolute value inequality that represents the acceptable numbers of words.

GO DIGITAL

20. **MODELING REAL LIFE** The normal body temperature of a camel is 37°C. This temperature varies by up to 3°C throughout the day. Write and solve an absolute value inequality that represents the range of normal body temperatures (in degrees Celsius) of a camel throughout the day.

ERROR ANALYSIS **In Exercises 21 and 22, describe and correct the error in solving the absolute value inequality.**

21.

✗

$$|x - 5| < 20$$
$$x - 5 < 20$$
$$x < 25$$

22.

✗

$$|x + 4| > 13$$
$$x + 4 > -13 \quad \textit{and} \quad x + 4 < 13$$
$$x > -17 \quad \textit{and} \quad x < 9$$
$$-17 < x < 9$$

23. **MODELING REAL LIFE** A manufacturer throws out gaskets with weights that have an absolute deviation of more than 0.06 pound from the mean weight of the batch. The weights (in pounds) of the gaskets in a batch are 0.58, 0.63, 0.65, 0.53, and 0.61. Which gaskets should be thrown out? Use an absolute value inequality to justify your answer. *(See Example 3.)*

24. **MODELING REAL LIFE** The table shows the total distances of four trails. You want to complete a trail in $1\frac{1}{2}$ hours with an absolute deviation of at most 15 minutes. You hike at a rate of 3 miles per hour. Which trails can you hike? Use an absolute value inequality to justify your answer.

Trail	Miles
A	$5\frac{1}{4}$
B	$4\frac{3}{4}$
C	$3\frac{1}{2}$
D	4

CONNECTING CONCEPTS **In Exercises 25 and 26, write and solve an absolute value inequality that represents the situation.**

25. The difference between the areas of the figures is less than 2.

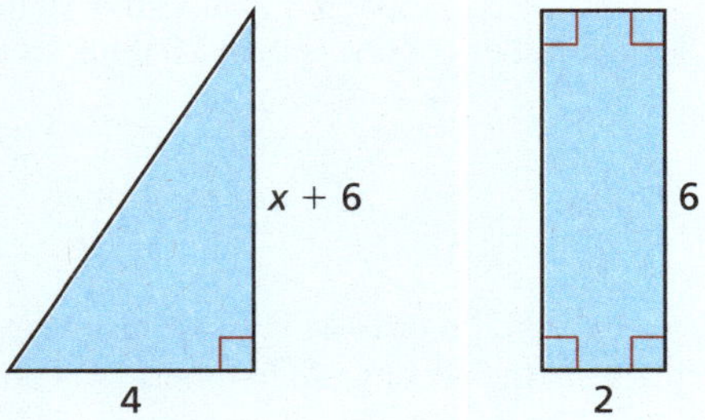

26. The difference between the perimeters of the figures is less than or equal to 3.

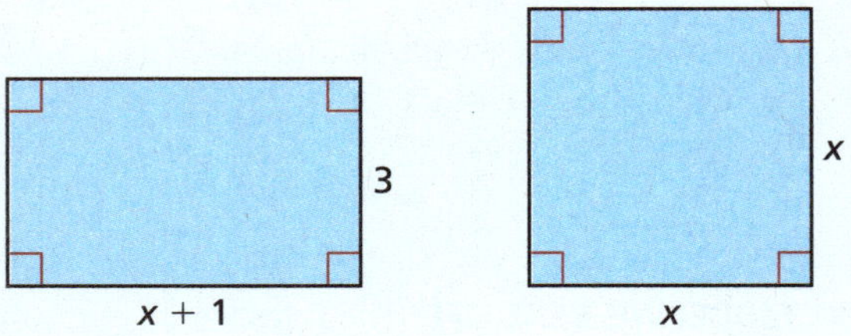

27. PROBLEM SOLVING Six students measure the acceleration (in meters per second per second) of an object in free fall. The measured values are shown. The students want to state that the absolute deviation of each measured value x from the mean is at most d. Find the value of d.

10.56, 9.52, 9.73, 9.80, 9.78, 10.91

28. HOW DO YOU SEE IT?
Write an absolute value inequality for each graph.

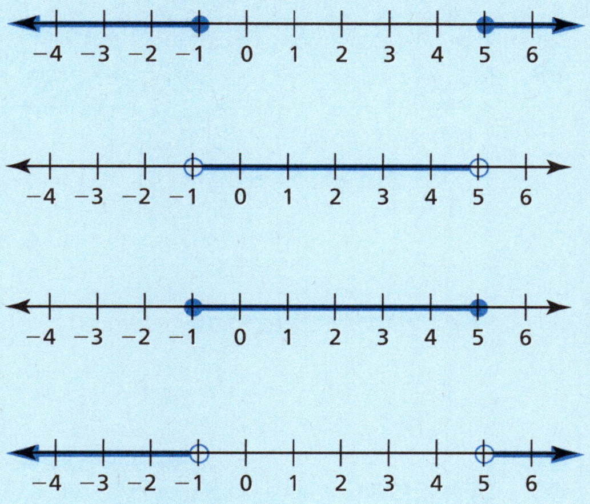

How did you decide which inequality symbol to use for each inequality?

REASONING In Exercises 29–32, tell whether the statement is *true* or *false*. If it is false, explain why.

29. If a is a solution of $|x + 3| \leq 8$, then a is also a solution of $x + 3 \geq -8$.

30. If a is a solution of $|x + 3| > 8$, then a is also a solution of $x + 3 > 8$.

31. If a is a solution of $|x + 3| \geq 8$, then a is also a solution of $x + 3 \geq -8$.

32. If a is a solution of $x + 3 \leq -8$, then a is also a solution of $|x + 3| \geq 8$.

4 MTR **33. MAKING AN ARGUMENT** One of your classmates claims that the solution of $|n| > 0$ is $\{n \mid n \neq 0\}$. Is your classmate correct? Explain your reasoning.

34. THOUGHT PROVOKING
Draw and label a geometric figure so that the perimeter P of the figure is a solution of the inequality $|P - 60| \leq 12$.

35. DIG DEEPER Solve the compound inequality $|x - 3| < 4$ *and* $|x + 2| > 8$. Describe your steps.

REVIEW & REFRESH

WATCH

In Exercises 36–39, plot the ordered pair in a coordinate plane. Describe the location of the point.

36. $A(1, 3)$

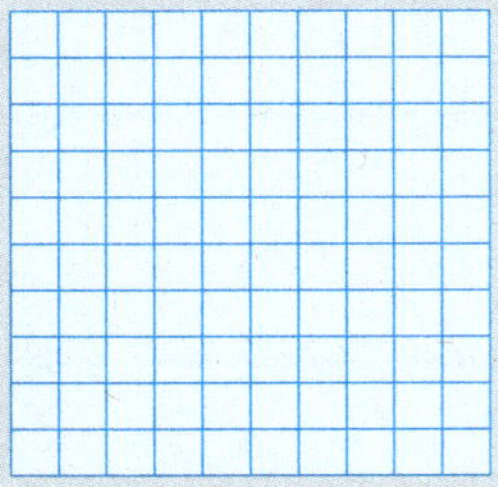

37. $B(0, -3)$

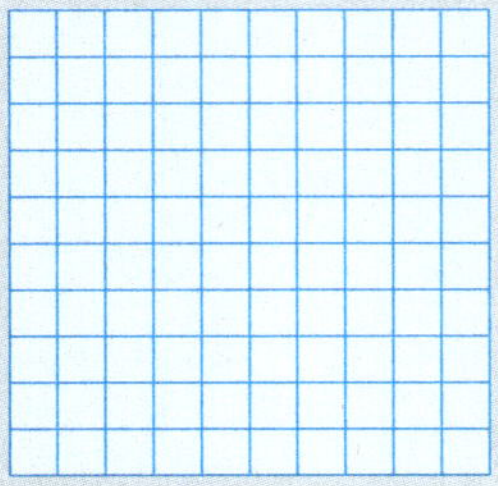

38. $C(-4, -2)$

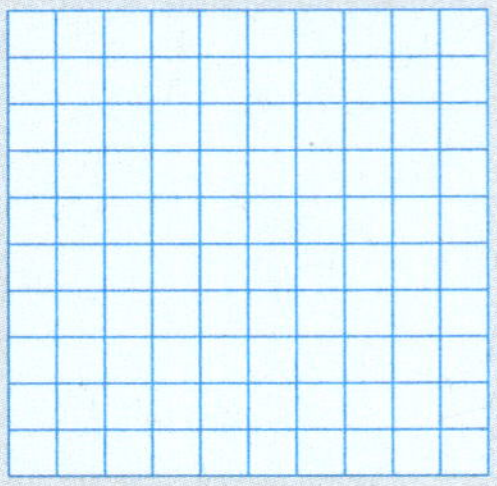

39. $D(-1, 2)$

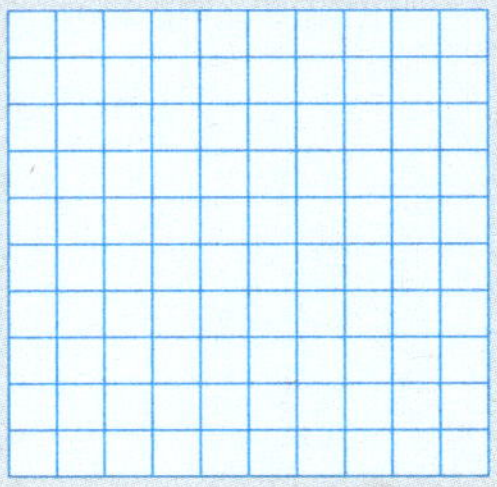

40. REASONING Can you determine the solution of $|4x - 2| \geq -6$ without solving? Explain.

41. Complete the table.

x	0	1	2	3	4
5x + 1					

In Exercises 42–44, solve the equation.

42. $3(5m - 1) - 7m = -9$

43. $|2x + 7| - 8 = -5$

44. $-\frac{1}{2}(4h - 3) = \frac{1}{4}(6 - 8h)$

45. Write an inequality that represents the graph.

REASONING In Exercises 46 and 47, let $c > 0$. Solve the inequality for x.

46. $\frac{x}{c} > -7$

47. $-cx \geq 10.5$

In Exercises 48 and 49, find the cube root.

48. $\sqrt[3]{-216}$

49. $\sqrt[3]{\frac{8}{125}}$

7 MTR **50. MODELING REAL LIFE** You bike at a speed of 12 miles per hour. Your friend bikes at a speed of 270 meters per minute. Who bikes faster?

In Exercises 51–55, solve the inequality. Graph the solution.

51. $\frac{t}{-5} - 2 \geq 1.7$

52. $15x + 3 < 6(4x + 5)$

53. $-3 < 4y + 5 \leq 9$

54. $6|3x + 2| > 60$

55. $b + \frac{1}{3} \leq \frac{5}{3}$ *or* $1 - 3b \leq -5$

In Exercises 56 and 57, evaluate the expression.

56. $(-3)^4$

57. -10^2

2 Chapter Review WITH CalcChat®

Chapter Learning Target: Understand solving linear inequalities.

Chapter Success Criteria:
- ◆ I can solve simple and multi-step inequalities.
- ◆ I can describe how to solve inequalities.
- ■ I can compare and contrast solving inequalities with solving equations.
- ■ I can apply techniques for solving inequalities to solve real-life problems.

◆ Surface
■ Deep

SELF-ASSESSMENT 1 I don't understand yet. 2 I can do it with help. 3 I can do it on my own. 4 I can teach someone else.

2.1 Writing and Graphing Inequalities *(pp. 87–100)* WATCH

Learning Target: Write inequalities and represent solutions of inequalities on number lines.

Vocabulary AZ VOCAB
- inequality
- solution of an inequality
- solution set
- graph of an inequality

Write the sentence as an inequality.

1. A number d minus 2 is less than -1.

2. Ten is at least the product of a number h and 5.

Tell whether -5 is a solution of the inequality.

3. $b + 6 > 1$

4. $\frac{3}{5}d \geq -3$

5. $w - 2.5 > -8$

Graph the inequality.

6. $x > 4$

7. $y \leq 2$

8. $-1.5 \geq z$

9. $w < \frac{2}{3}$

GO DIGITAL

Write an inequality that represents the graph.

10. 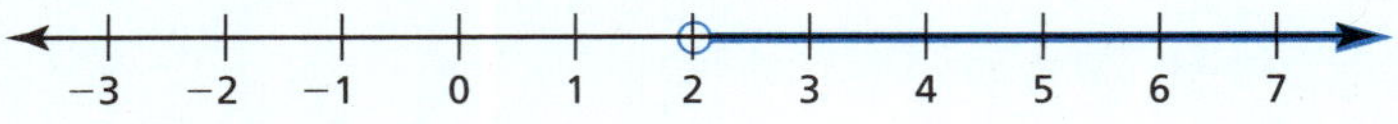

11. 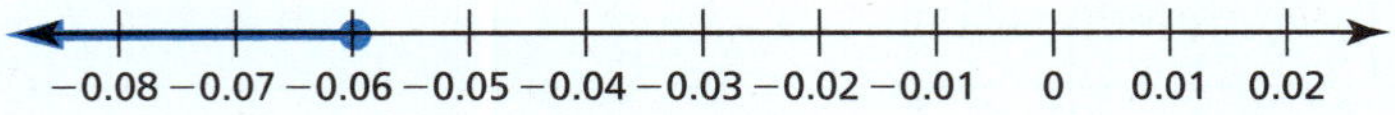

12. Three requirements for a particular lifeguard training course in Florida are shown.

a. Write and graph three inequalities that represent the requirements.

b. You can swim 915 feet, tread water for 4 minutes, and swim 18 feet underwater without taking a breath. Do you satisfy the requirements of the course? Explain.

13. Given that $M > N$, determine whether the inequality $\frac{M}{N} > \frac{N}{M}$ is *always*, *sometimes*, or *never* true. Explain your reasoning.

2.2 Solving Inequalities Using Addition or Subtraction (pp. 101–110) WATCH

Learning Target: Write and solve inequalities using addition or subtraction.

Vocabulary AZ VOCAB
equivalent inequalities

Solve the inequality. Graph the solution.

14. $p + 4 < 10$

15. $r - 4 > -6$

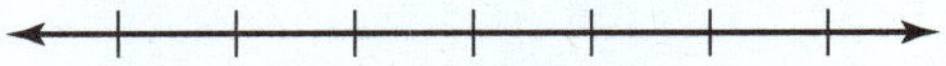

16. $2.1 \geq m - 6.7$

17. $x + 2.5 \leq -8$

18. Write an inequality that requires using addition or subtraction to solve and has a solution of $-\frac{2}{3} > b$.

19. The Douglas Sea Scale describes the roughness of a sea for navigation. Waves currently reach a height of 12.82 meters. By what amounts can the wave heights increase for the sea to be described as *phenomenal*?

Wave height (m)	2.50–4.00	4.01–6.00	6.01–9.00	9.01–14.00	> 14.00
Description	Rough	Very Rough	High	Very High	Phenomenal

2.3 Solving Inequalities Using Multiplication or Division (pp. 111–120) WATCH

Learning Target: Write and solve inequalities using multiplication or division.

Solve the inequality. Graph the solution.

20. $3x > -21$

21. $-4 \leq \frac{g}{5}$

22. $-\frac{3}{4}n \leq 3$

23. $\frac{s}{-8} \geq 11$

24. $36 < 2q$

25. $-1.2k > 6$

26. Write an inequality that requires using multiplication or division to solve and has a solution of $h \geq 3.25$.

2.4 Solving Multi-Step Inequalities (pp. 121–130) WATCH

Learning Target: Write and solve multi-step inequalities.

Solve the inequality. Graph the solution, if possible.

27. $3x - 4 > 11$

28. $-4 < \frac{b}{2} + 9$

29. $7.5 - n \leq n + 3$

30. $2(-4s + 2) \geq -5s - 10$

31. $6(2t + 9) \leq 12t - 1$

32. $2r - 8 > \frac{3}{4}(r - 6)$

33. You want to subscribe to an online streaming service for live television. For what numbers of months is the total cost of Channel Champ less than the total cost of TV Mania?

2.5 Solving Compound Inequalities (pp. 131–144)

WATCH

Learning Target: Write and solve compound inequalities.

Vocabulary

compound inequality
set-builder notation

34. A number x is more than -6 and at most 8. Write this sentence as an inequality. Graph the inequality.

Solve the inequality. Write the solution using set-builder notation. Graph the solution, if possible.

35. $19 \geq 3z + 1 \geq -5$

36. $-3p \geq -6$ *or* $4p + 1 > 13$

37. $\frac{r}{4} < -5$ *or* $-2r - 7 \leq 3$

38. $-1 \leq -2d + 7 < 10$

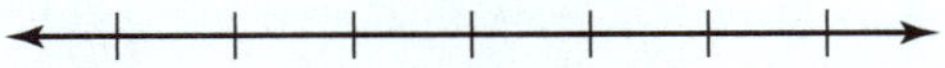

39. Mount Everest has an elevation of about 8850 meters. Any location above 8000 meters is in the *death zone*, which is the elevation at which there is not enough oxygen to sustain human life. Write an inequality that represents the possible elevations of climbers in the death zone on Mount Everest.

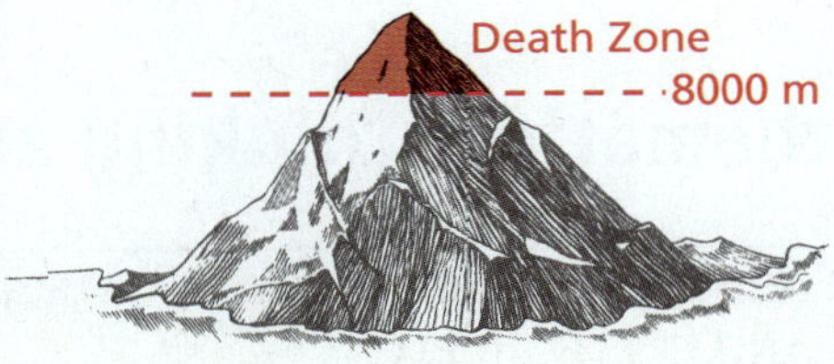

40. A highway has a minimum speed limit of 45 miles per hour and a maximum speed limit of 70 miles per hour. Write and solve an inequality that represents the legal driving speeds in kilometers per hour. Write the solution using set-builder notation.

2.6 Solving Absolute Value Inequalities (pp. 145–154)

WATCH

Learning Target: Write and solve inequalities involving absolute value.

Vocabulary

AZ VOCAB

absolute value inequality

absolute deviation

Solve the inequality. Graph the solution, if possible.

41. $|m| \geq 10$

42. $|k - 9| < -4$

43. $|-1.5g - 2| + 1 < 6$

44. $|9 - 2j| + 10 \geq 2$

45. A safety regulation says that the height of a guardrail should be 106 centimeters with an absolute deviation of no more than 7 centimeters. Write and solve an absolute value inequality that represents the acceptable heights of a guardrail.

Mathematical Thinking and Reasoning

1 MTR ACTIVELY PARTICIPATE IN EFFORTFUL LEARNING BOTH INDIVIDUALLY AND COLLECTIVELY

Mathematicians who participate in effortful learning both individually and with others analyze a problem in a way that makes sense given the task.

1. In Exercise 39 on page 97, how does reasoning about the meaning of the solution help you choose the correct graph?

2. In Exercise 31 on page 129, what assumption did you make about both sides of the inequality? How did this help you complete the inequality?

3. An inequality can be used to represent the normal weights of golden retrievers. Make a conjecture about the inequality and its graph. Explain your reasoning.

2 Practice Test WITH CalcChat®

Write the sentence as an inequality.

1. The sum of a number y and 9 is at least -1.

2. A number k is less than 3 units from 10.

Solve the inequality. Graph the solution, if possible.

3. $6m \leq -42$

4. $\frac{x}{2} - 5 \geq -9$

5. $4p + 3 \geq 2(2p + 1)$

6. $-2 \leq 4 - 3a \leq 13$

7. $-7.5 < 2 - h$ *or* $6h + 5 > 71$

8. $4|-3b + 5| - 9 < 7$

9. You start a baking business, and your goal is to earn a profit of at least \$250 in the first month. Your expenses in the first month are \$155. What are the possible revenues that you can earn to meet your goal?

10. A manufacturer of bicycle parts makes chains that have widths of 0.3 inch with an absolute deviation of at most 0.0003 inch. Write and solve an absolute value inequality that represents the possible widths.

GO DIGITAL

11. Write and graph an inequality that represents the numbers that are *not* solutions of the inequality represented by the graph. Explain your reasoning.

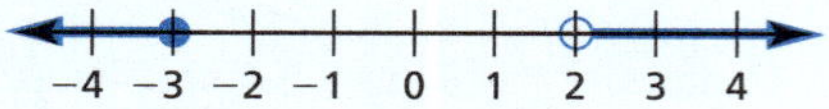

12. In a diving competition, scores range from 0 to 10. When there are three judges, the number of points awarded is calculated by multiplying the sum of the scores by the degree of difficulty. Your opponent earns 40.8 points on a dive. You perform a dive with a degree of difficulty of 2.4. Two of your scores are shown. What scores from the third judge will give you more points than your opponent?

Judge 1	Judge 2	Judge 3
$4\frac{1}{2}$	$6\frac{1}{2}$	?

13. You jog at a rate of 6 miles per hour. Your friend is 55 feet ahead of you and jogs at a rate of 6.6 feet per second. Write and solve an inequality that represents the amounts of time that your friend is ahead of you.

14. A state imposes a sales tax on items of clothing that cost more than $175. The tax applies only to the difference of the price of the item and $175.

   a. Use the receipt shown to find the tax rate.

   b. A shopper has $430 to spend on a winter coat. Find the prices p of coats that the shopper can buy. Assume that $p \geq 175$.

   c. Another state imposes a 5% sales tax on the entire price of an item of clothing. For which prices is paying the 5% tax cheaper than paying the tax described above? Justify your answer.

2 Performance Task
Summiting Everest

Most expeditions leave from the South Col around **midnight** on "summit day."

A round trip from the South Col to the summit usually takes less than **20 hours**.

Approximate Time Frames
Ascent: **9–13 hours**
Descent: **4–7 hours**

Climbers usually set an **early-afternoon** turnaround time to guard against running out of oxygen or descending in the dark.

GO DIGITAL

George Mallory was a leading member of the first British expeditions to Mount Everest in the early 1920s. In 1923, when asked why he wanted to climb the mountain, he famously responded, "Because it's there."

EXPEDITION LEADER

You are leading an expedition to the summit of Mount Everest. As the leader, you have the authority to send climbers down the mountain if they are too far behind schedule. You must set a departure time and a turnaround time, and then monitor the progress of your climbers. Use inequalities to show how you will know that the climbers are not falling behind schedule during the ascent.

2 B.E.S.T. Test Prep WITH CalcChat®
Cumulative Practice

WATCH Tutorial videos are available for each exercise.

1. The expected attendance at a school event is 65 people. The actual attendance can vary by up to 30 people. Which equation can you use to find the minimum and maximum possible attendances?

Ⓐ $|x - 65| = 30$

Ⓑ $|x + 65| = 30$

Ⓒ $|x - 30| = 65$

Ⓓ $|x + 30| = 65$

GRIDDED RESPONSE **2.** Find the maximum value of x for which the inequality $8.5x - 24.7 \leq 3x + 32.5$ is true.

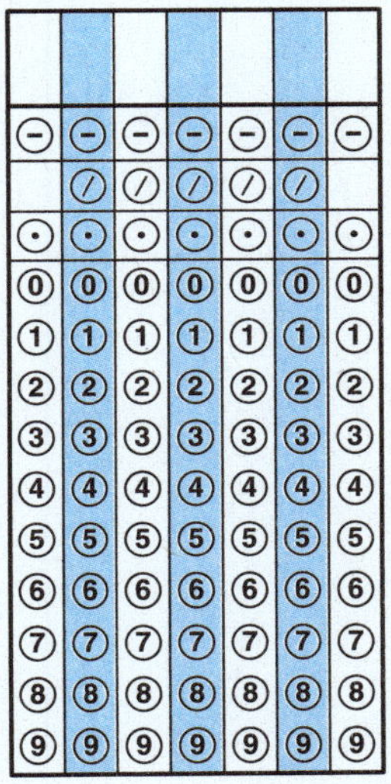

3. A round of golf costs \$45. A season pass costs \$1200. Which inequality represents the numbers x of rounds of golf you can play in order to spend less money by purchasing the season pass?

Ⓐ $45x < 1200$

Ⓑ $45x \geq 1200$

Ⓒ $1200 \geq 45x$

Ⓓ $1200 < 45x$

GO DIGITAL

4. A student solved the inequality $\frac{-x+4}{3} > \frac{x+1}{2}$ as shown. Which statements accurately describe the student's work?

$$\frac{-x+4}{3} > \frac{x+1}{2}$$

Step 1: $\frac{2}{2} \bullet \frac{-x+4}{3} > \frac{3}{3} \bullet \frac{x+1}{2}$

Step 2: $\frac{-2x+4}{6} > \frac{3x+1}{6}$

Step 3: $-2x + 4 > 3x + 1$

Step 4: $-5x > -3$

Step 5: $x > \frac{3}{5}$

Ⓐ The student made an error in Step 1.

Ⓑ The student made an error in Step 2.

Ⓒ The student made an error in Step 3.

Ⓓ The student made an error in Step 4.

Ⓔ The student made an error in Step 5.

Ⓕ The student's work is correct.

GRIDDED RESPONSE 5. Find the value of y when $7(x + y) = -8x - y$ and $x = 8$.

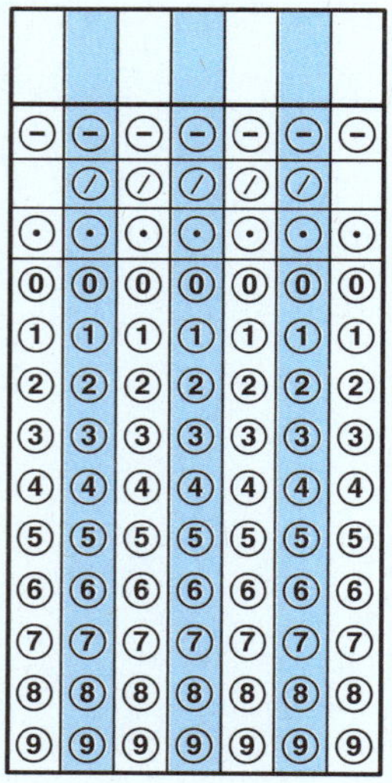

6. Which equation is *not* equivalent to $\frac{4}{3}x - \frac{1}{2} = \frac{y}{6} + 1$?

Ⓐ $4x - \frac{3}{2} = \frac{y}{2} + 3$

Ⓑ $x = \frac{y+9}{8}$

Ⓒ $x - \frac{2}{3} = \frac{2}{9}y + \frac{4}{3}$

Ⓓ $8x - 3 = y + 6$

GRIDDED RESPONSE **7.** Consider the compound inequality
$4x - 18 \leq -x - 3$ *and* $-3x - 9 \geq -3$.
Find the value that makes the statement true.

The solution of the compound inequality is $x \leq$ ____.

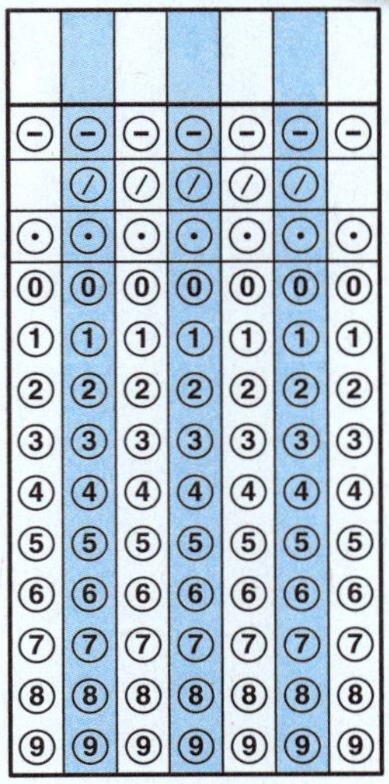

8. Which values of a make the solution of the equation $3(2x - 4) = 4(ax - 2)$ positive?

Ⓐ $a = -2$

Ⓑ $a = -1$

Ⓒ $a = 0$

Ⓓ $a = 1$

Ⓔ $a = 2$

Ⓕ $a = 3$

9. You have a \$250 gift card to use at a department store.

Which inequality represents the number of pairs of socks x you can buy when you buy 2 pairs of sneakers?

Ⓐ $160 \leq 12x - 250$ Ⓑ $12x + 160 < 250$ Ⓒ $160 \geq 250 - 12x$ Ⓓ $160 + 12x \leq 250$

10. Which statements are true regarding the equation $9a + 7 = 9x - 2$?

Ⓐ When $a = 0$, the solution of the equation is $x = 1$.

Ⓑ When $a = x$, the solution of the equation is $x = 9$.

Ⓒ When $a = x$, the equation has infinitely many solutions.

Ⓓ When $a = x$, the equation has no solution.

Ⓔ When $a = 1$, the solution of the equation is $x = 2$.

Ⓕ When $a = 1$, the equation has no solution.

3 Graphing Linear Functions

NATIONAL GEOGRAPHIC EXPLORER

WATCH

Rhian G. Waller

Dr. Rhian Waller is a professor of Marine Sciences at the University of Maine. She has led several scuba diving expeditions to some of the most remote locations in the world. Dr. Waller specializes in the ecology of cold-water organisms, with a passion for the conservation of deep-sea and polar ecosystems.

- What are some examples of deep-sea or cold-water organisms?
- What can scuba divers learn by studying some of the least accessible locations on the planet?
- How might scuba divers use mathematics when planning a diving expedition?

STEM

Divers must be sure that their scuba tank provides enough oxygen for their dive. In the Performance Task, you will plan a dive by selecting a tank size, the depth, and the amount of time you will spend underwater.

GO DIGITAL

Scuba Diving

Preparing for Chapter 3

Chapter Learning Target: Understand graphing linear functions.

Chapter Success Criteria:

- ◆ I can identify the graph of a linear function.
- ◆ I can graph linear functions written in different forms.
- ■ I can describe the characteristics of a function.
- ■ I can explain how a transformation affects the graph of a linear function.

◆ Surface
■ Deep

Chapter Vocabulary

AZ VOCAB

Work with a partner. Discuss each of the vocabulary terms.

relation

dependent variable

linear function

function

x-intercept

nonlinear function

independent variable

y-intercept

GO DIGITAL

Mathematical Thinking and Reasoning

3 MTR

COMPLETE TASKS WITH MATHEMATICAL FLUENCY

Mathematicians who complete tasks with mathematical fluency select efficient and appropriate methods for solving problems within the given context.

Work with a partner. The equation $d = 90 - 15t$ represents the depth d (in feet) of a scuba diver t minutes after beginning an ascent to the surface. How long does it take the scuba diver to reach the surface?

1. Solve the problem using each tool.

a. pencil and paper

b. online or graphing calculator

c. spreadsheet

2. Describe the advantages and disadvantages of using each tool.

3. Why is it important to know how to choose appropriate tools to solve mathematical problems?

3 Prepare WITH CalcChat®

Plotting Points

WATCH

Example 1 **Plot the point $A(-3, 4)$ in a coordinate plane. Describe the location of the point.**

Start at the origin. Move 3 units left and 4 units up. Then plot the point.
The point is in Quadrant II.

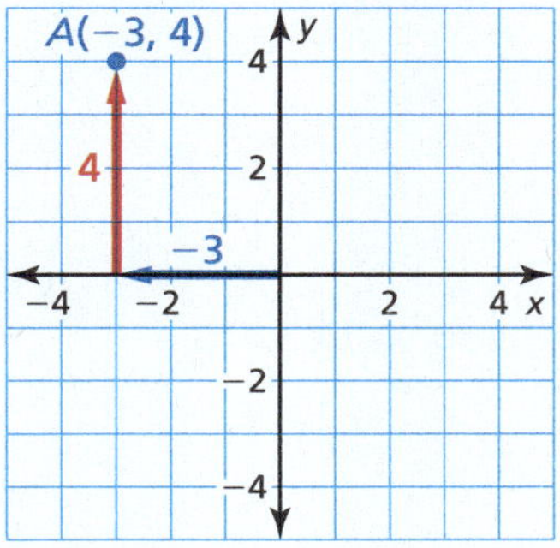

Plot the point in a coordinate plane. Describe the location of the point.

1. $A(3, 2)$

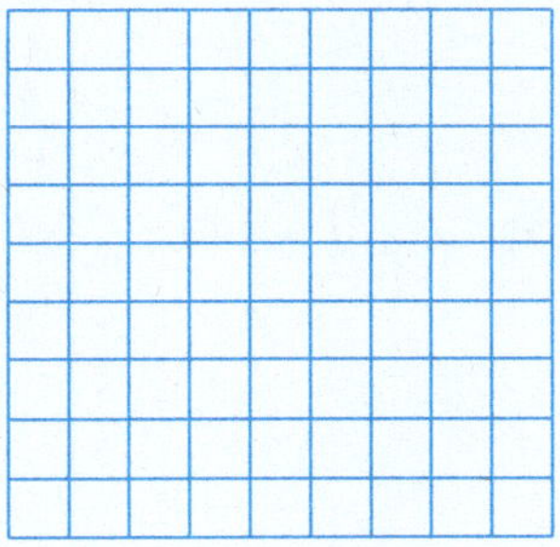

2. $B(-5, 1)$

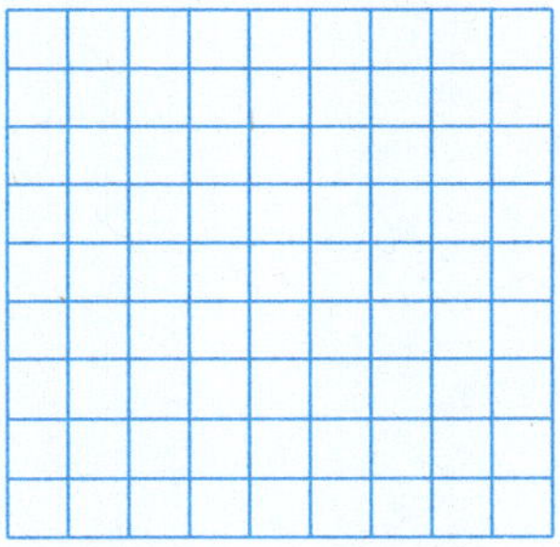

3. $C(0, 3)$

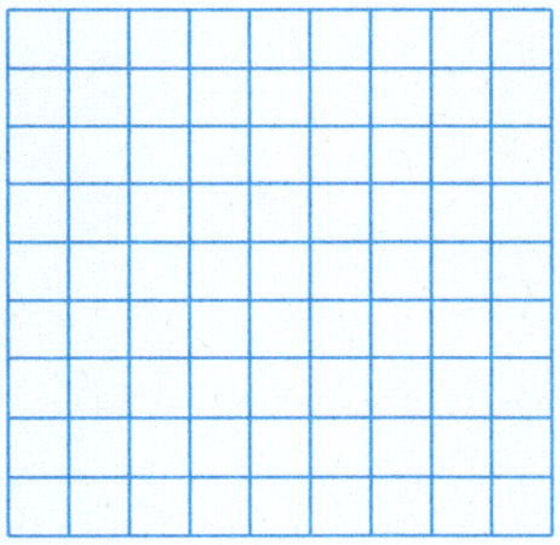

4. $D\left(-2\frac{1}{2}, -4\right)$

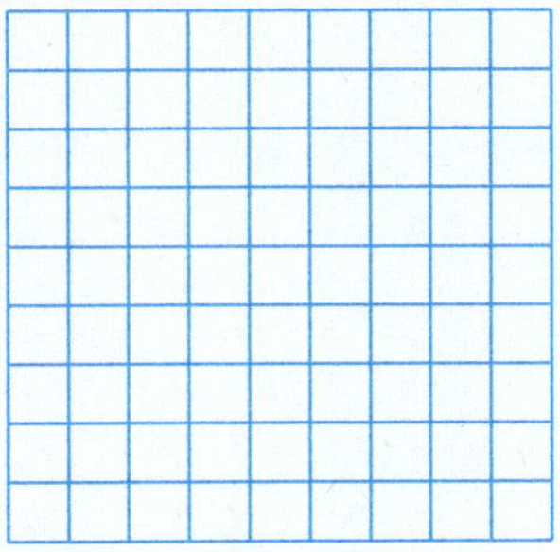

5. $E(-6.5, 0)$

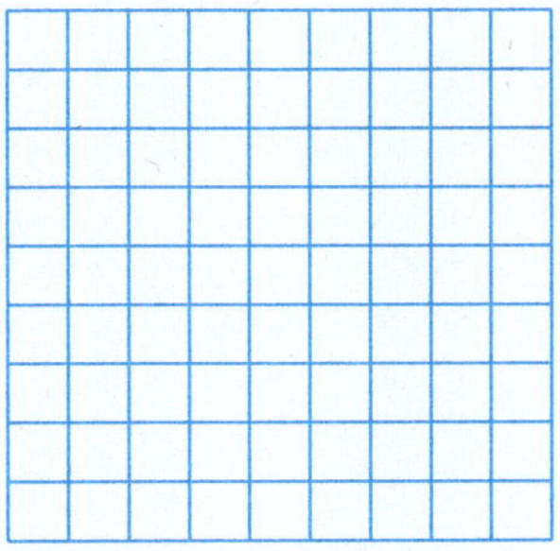

6. $F\left(\frac{5}{2}, -\frac{3}{2}\right)$

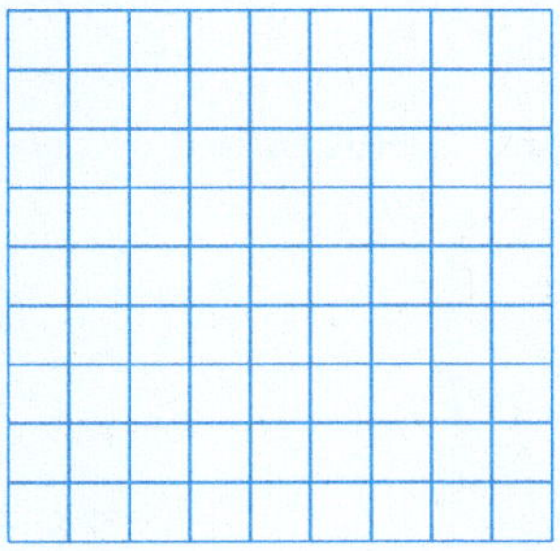

GO DIGITAL

Evaluating Expressions

WATCH

Example 2 **Evaluate $4x - 5$ when $x = 3$.**

$$4x - 5 = 4(3) - 5 \quad \text{Substitute 3 for } x.$$
$$= 12 - 5 \quad \text{Multiply.}$$
$$= 7 \quad \text{Subtract.}$$

WATCH

Example 3 **Evaluate $-2x + 9$ when $x = -8.5$.**

$$-2x + 9 = -2(-8.5) + 9 \quad \text{Substitute } -8.5 \text{ for } x.$$
$$= 17 + 9 \quad \text{Multiply.}$$
$$= 26 \quad \text{Add.}$$

Evaluate the expression for the given value of x.

7. $3x - 4; x = 7$

8. $-5x + 8; x = 3$

9. $10x + 18; x = \frac{1}{5}$

10. $-9x - 2; x = -4$

11. $24 - 8x; x = -2.25$

12. $15x + 9; x = -\frac{1}{10}$

5 MTR **13.** **STRUCTURE** Let a and b be positive real numbers. Describe how to plot (a, b), $(-a, b)$, $(a, -b)$, and $(-a, -b)$.

3.1 Functions

Learning Target: Understand the concept of a function.

Success Criteria:
- I can determine whether a relation is a function.
- I can find the domain and range of a function.
- I can distinguish between independent and dependent variables.

Algebraic Reasoning
MA.912.AR.2.5 Solve and graph mathematical and real-world problems that are modeled with linear functions. Interpret key features and determine constraints in terms of the context.

WORDS AND MATH
Think about the meanings of the compound words *input* and *output* by analyzing their prefixes and the root word *put*.

A **relation** pairs inputs with outputs. For example, the number of hours you work *and* the pay you receive form a relation. The inputs are the hours worked, and the outputs are the pay amounts. Can you think of other relations?

EXPLORE IT! Describing Relations

Work with a partner. You buy an item from the vending machine.

a. Describe two possible relations associated with the vending machine.

b. Think about each relation in part (a).
- What are the inputs?
- What are the outputs?
- Does each input pair with *exactly* one output? Explain.

GO DIGITAL

In mathematics, a **function** is a relation that pairs each input with exactly one output.

COMMUNICATE CLEARLY 4 MTR

Can you think of any mathematical relations? Are any of these relations functions?

c. How can you use a coordinate plane to represent a relation? What are the inputs? What are the outputs?

d. The graph shows a relation. Is the relation a function? Explain your reasoning.

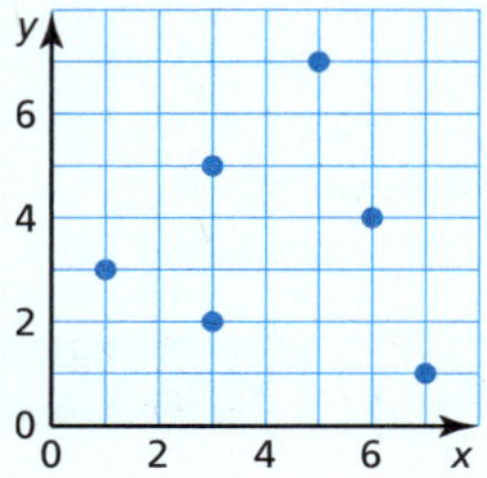

e. Draw two more graphs that represent relations, one that is a function and one that is not a function. Compare your graphs with other students in your class.

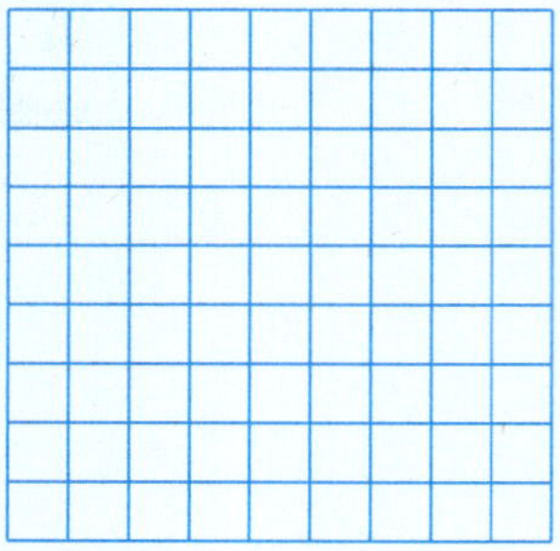

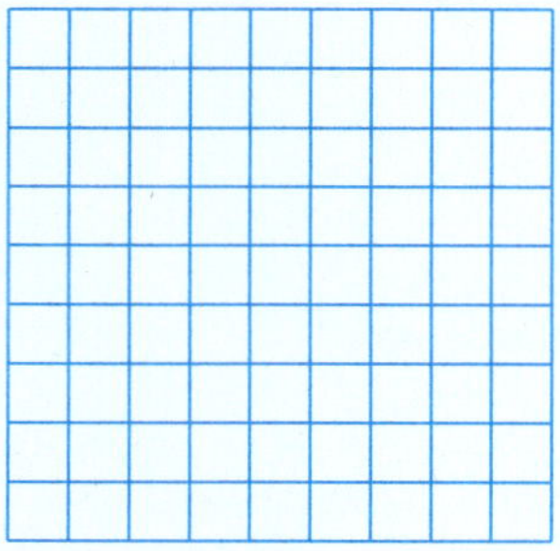

Vocabulary

AZ VOCAB

relation, *p. 175*
function, *p. 175*
domain, *p. 177*
range, *p. 177*
independent variable, *p. 179*
dependent variable, *p. 179*

Determining Whether Relations Are Functions

A **relation** pairs inputs with outputs. When a relation is given as ordered pairs, the *x*-coordinates are inputs and the *y*-coordinates are outputs. A relation that pairs each input with *exactly one* output is a **function.**

EXAMPLE 1 Determining Whether Relations Are Functions

WATCH

Determine whether each relation is a function. Explain.

a. $(-2, 2), (-1, 2), (0, 2), (1, 0), (2, 0)$

b. $(4, 0), (8, 7), (6, 4), (4, 3), (5, 2)$

c.

Input, *x*	−2	−1	0	0	1	2
Output, *y*	3	4	5	6	7	8

REMEMBER

A relation can be represented by a mapping diagram.

d. Input, *x* Output, *y*

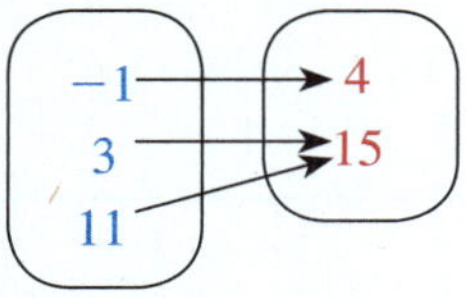

SOLUTION

a. Every input has exactly one output.

▶ So, the relation is a function.

b. The input 4 has two outputs, 0 and 3.

▶ So, the relation is *not* a function.

c. The input 0 has two outputs, 5 and 6.

▶ So, the relation is *not* a function.

d. Every input has exactly one output.

▶ So, the relation is a function.

SELF-ASSESSMENT

1 I don't understand yet. 2 I can do it with help. 3 I can do it on my own. 4 I can teach someone else.

Determine whether the relation is a function. Explain.

1. $(-5, 0), (0, 0), (5, 0), (5, 10)$

2. $(-4, 8), (-1, 2), (2, -4), (5, -10)$

3.

Input, *x*	Output, *y*
2	2.6
4	5.2
6	7.8

4. Input, *x* Output, *y*

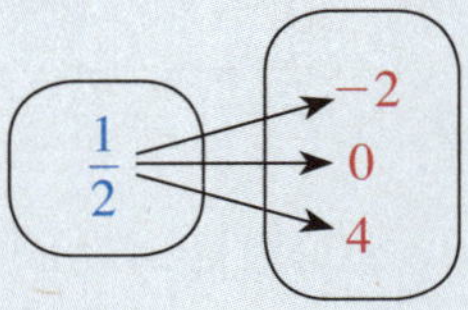

GO DIGITAL

SELF-ASSESSMENT

1 I don't understand yet. 2 I can do it with help. 3 I can do it on my own. 4 I can teach someone else.

5. **OPEN-ENDED** Write a relation that is not a function. How can you change the relation so that it is a function?

6. **REASONING** Two quantities x and y are in a proportional relationship. Do the ordered pairs (x, y) represent a function? Explain your reasoning.

KEY IDEA

Vertical Line Test

Words A graph represents a function when no vertical line passes through more than one point on the graph.

Examples Function

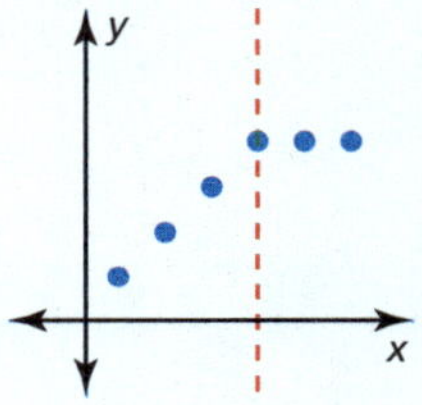

Not a function

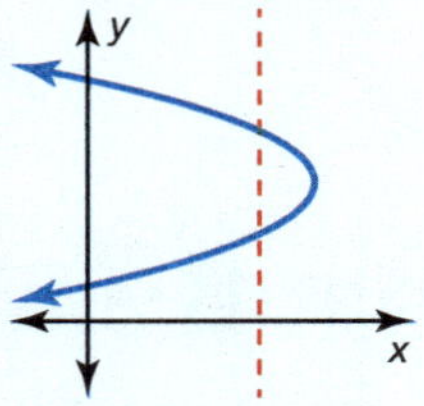

EXAMPLE 2 Using the Vertical Line Test

WATCH

Determine whether each graph represents a function. Explain.

a.

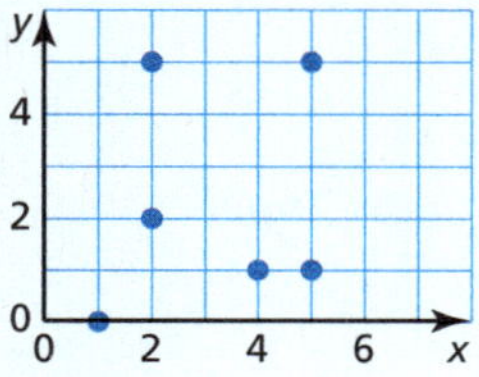

b.

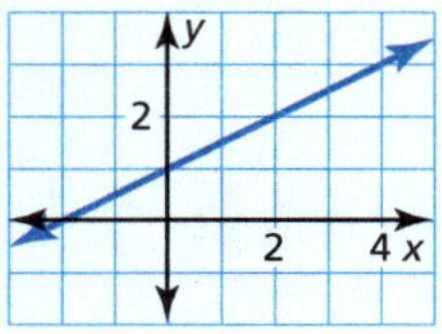

SOLUTION

a. You can draw a vertical line through (2, 2) and (2, 5).

► So, the graph does *not* represent a function.

b. No vertical line can be drawn through more than one point on the graph.

► So, the graph represents a function.

GO DIGITAL

SELF-ASSESSMENT

1 I don't understand yet. | 2 I can do it with help. | 3 I can do it on my own. | 4 I can teach someone else.

Determine whether the graph represents a function. Explain.

7.

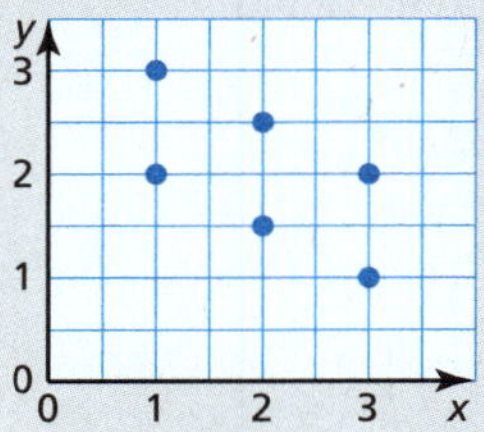

8.

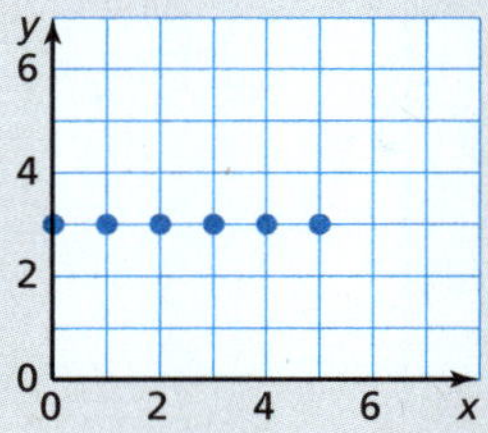

9.

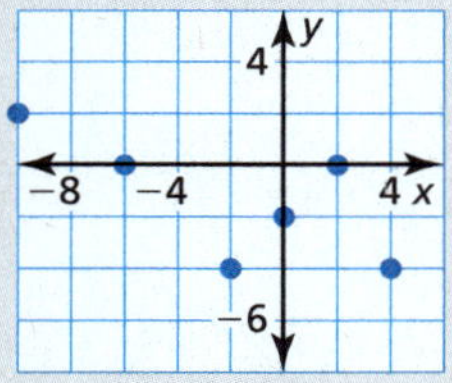

10.

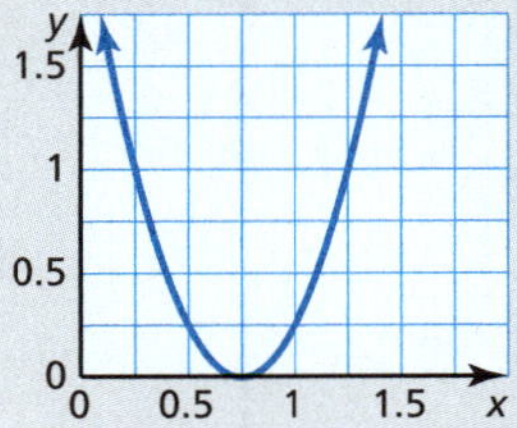

11.

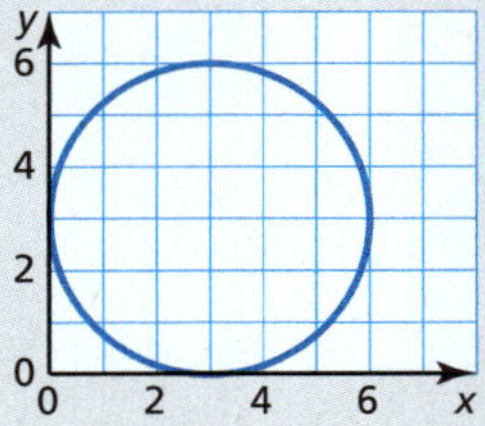

12.

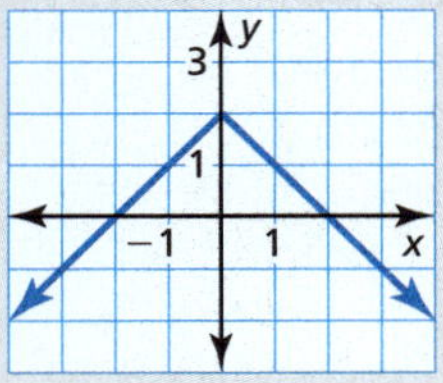

13. WRITING Explain why you can use vertical lines to determine whether a graph represents a function.

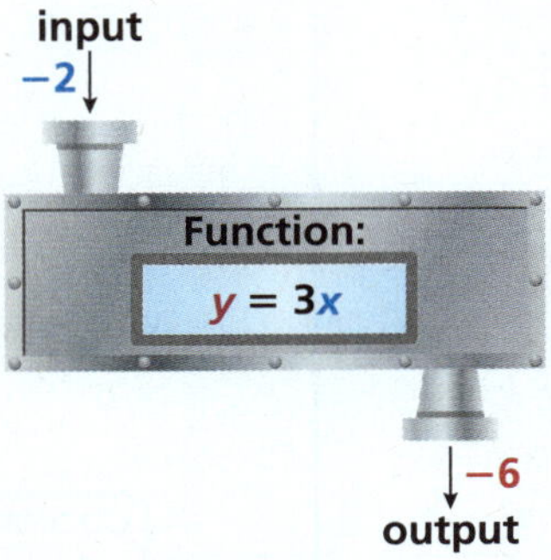

Finding the Domain and Range of a Function

KEY IDEAS

The Domain and Range of a Function

The **domain** of a function is the set of all possible input values.

The **range** of a function is the set of all possible output values.

EXAMPLE 3 Finding the Domain and Range from a Graph

Find the domain and range of the function represented by the graph.

a.

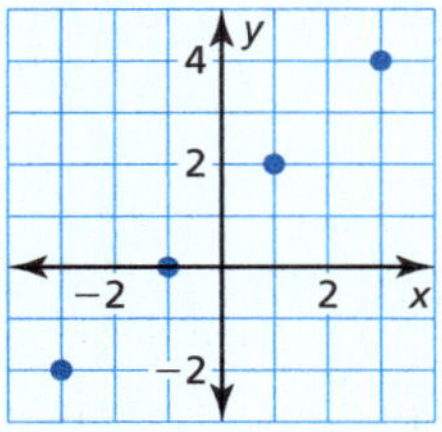

b.

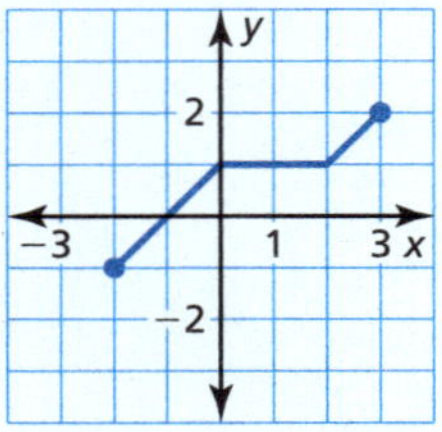

SOLUTION

a. Write the ordered pairs. Identify the inputs and outputs.

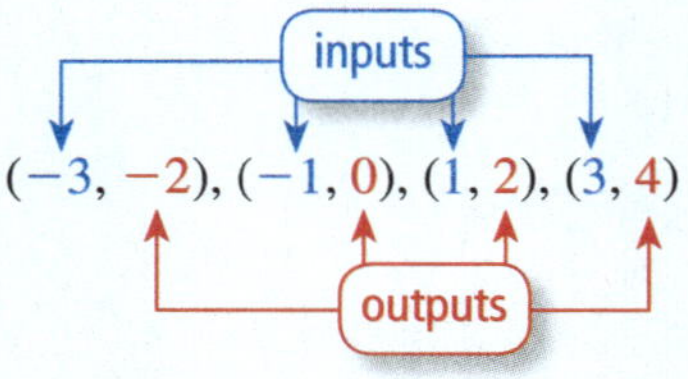

▶ The domain is −3, −1, 1, and 3.
The range is −2, 0, 2, and 4.

b. Identify the x- and y-values represented by the graph.

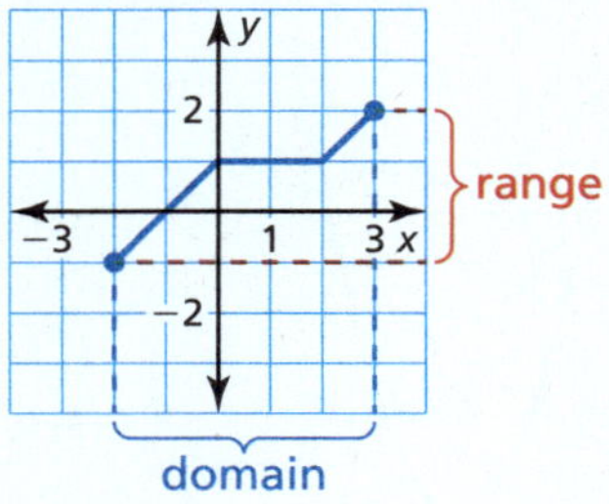

▶ The domain is $-2 \le x \le 3$.
The range is $-1 \le y \le 2$.

STUDY TIP

You can also use set-builder notation to write the domain and range of a function. In part (b), the domain is $\{x \mid -2 \le x \le 3\}$ and the range is $\{y \mid -1 \le y \le 2\}$.

SELF-ASSESSMENT

1 I don't understand yet. 2 I can do it with help. 3 I can do it on my own. 4 I can teach someone else.

Find the domain and range of the function represented by the graph.

14.

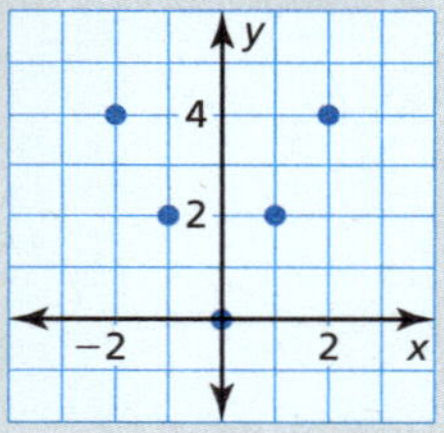

15.

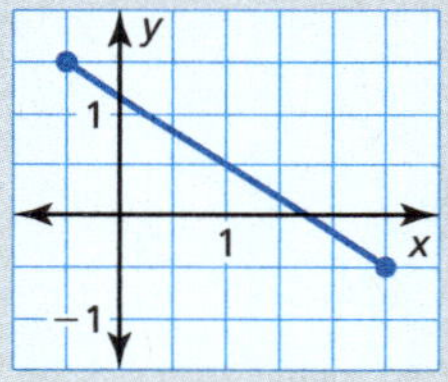

16.

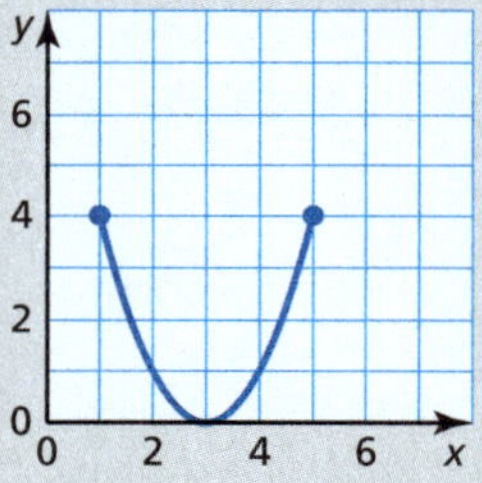

17. DIFFERENT WORDS, SAME QUESTION Which is different? Find "both" answers.

Find the range of the function represented by the table.

Find the x-values of the function represented by $(-1, 7)$, $(0, 5)$, and $(1, -1)$.

Find the inputs of the function represented by the table.

Find the domain of the function represented by $(-1, 7)$, $(0, 5)$, and $(1, -1)$.

x	y
−1	7
0	5
1	−1

GO DIGITAL

Identifying Independent and Dependent Variables

The variable that represents the input values of a function is the **independent variable** because it can be *any* value in the domain. The variable that represents the output values of a function is the **dependent variable** because it *depends* on the value of the independent variable. When an equation represents a function, the dependent variable is defined in terms of the independent variable. The statement "y is a function of x" means that y varies depending on the value of x.

A whale's rib cage safely collapses at pressures that can snap human bones.

$$y = -x + 10$$

dependent variable, y — independent variable, x

7 MTR

EXAMPLE 4 Modeling Real Life

WATCH

Water pressure is 0 psi (pounds per square inch) at sea level and increases by about 0.44 psi for every foot an object descends in water.

a. Does the situation represent a function? If so, identify the independent and dependent variables.

b. A whale dives from 1000 feet to 3500 feet. Find the domain and range.

SOLUTION

a. The water pressure depends on the depth of the water. Because the water pressure changes with any change in depth, each input has exactly one output.

▶ So, the situation represents a function in which the water pressure is the dependent variable and depth is the independent variable.

b. The whale dives from 1000 feet to 3500 feet, so the domain is any depth from 1000 feet to 3500 feet.

Because water pressure is 0 psi at sea level and increases at a constant rate, water pressure is proportional to depth. So, the water pressure y (in psi) at a depth of x feet can be represented by $y = 0.44x$. To find the range, find y when $x = 1000$ and when $x = 3500$.

REMEMBER

A proportional relationship can be represented by $y = kx$, where k is the constant of proportionality.

Input, x	$0.44x$	Output, y
1000	0.44(1000)	440
3500	0.44(3500)	1540

▶ So, the domain is $\{x \mid 1000 \le x \le 3500\}$ and the range is $\{y \mid 440 \le y \le 1540\}$.

GO DIGITAL

SELF-ASSESSMENT 1 I don't understand yet. 2 I can do it with help. 3 I can do it on my own. 4 I can teach someone else.

18. You arrange coins in stacks so that each stack has twice as many coins as the previous stack. The first stack has 2 coins.

a. Does the situation represent a function? If so, identify the independent and dependent variables.

b. You have 6 stacks of coins. Find the domain and range.

19. The total pressure exerted on an object in water is the sum of air pressure at sea level and water pressure. You are scuba diving at a depth where the total pressure is three times the air pressure at sea level. Use the information in Example 4 to find your depth. Explain how you found your answer.

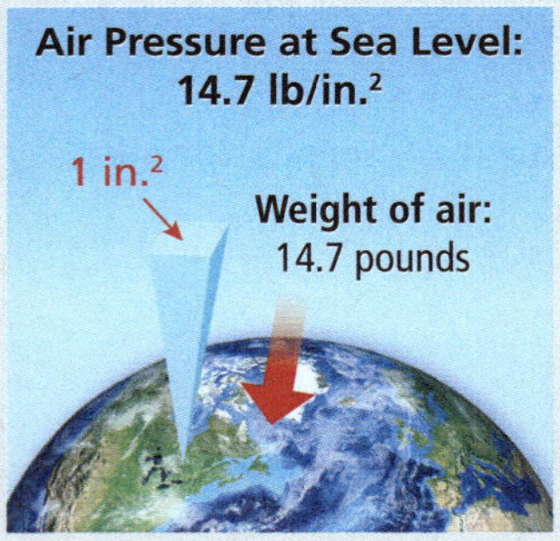

3.1 Practice WITH CalcChat® AND CalcView®

In Exercises 1–6, determine whether the relation is a function. Explain. *(See Example 1.)*

1. (1, −2), (2, 1), (3, 6), (4, 13), (5, 22)

2. (7, 4), (5, −1), (3, −8), (1, −5), (3, 6)

3.

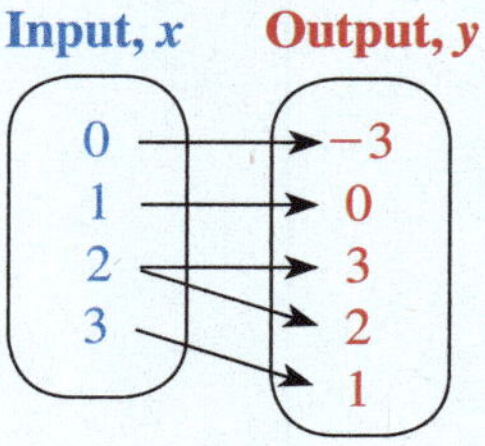

4.

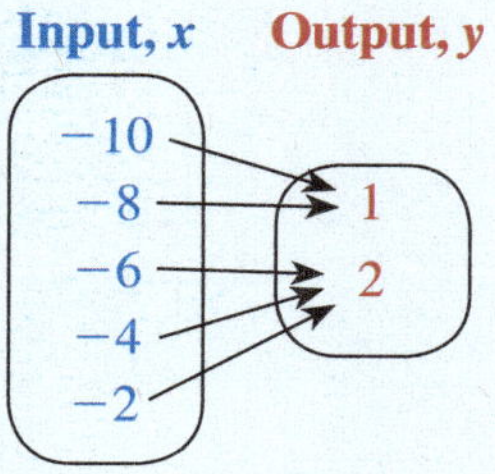

5.

Input, x	16	1	0	1	16
Output, y	−2	−1	0	1	2

6.

Input, x	−3	0	3	6	9
Output, y	$\frac{2}{3}$	$\frac{1}{3}$	0	$-\frac{1}{3}$	$-\frac{2}{3}$

In Exercises 7–10, determine whether the graph represents a function. Explain. *(See Example 2.)*

7.

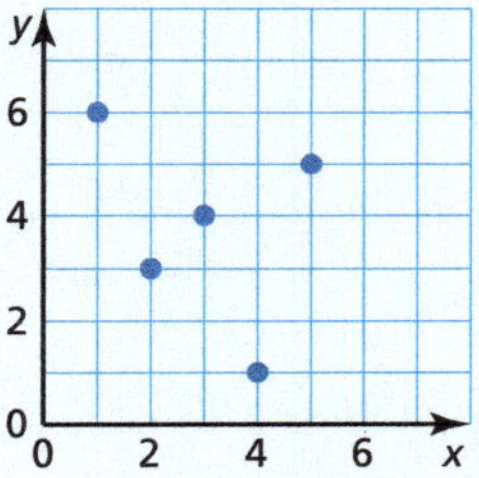

8.

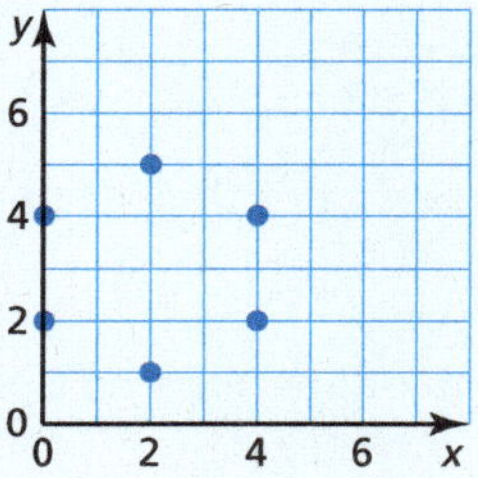

9.

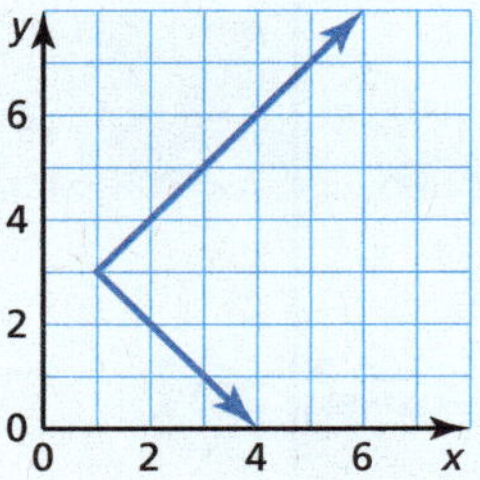

10.

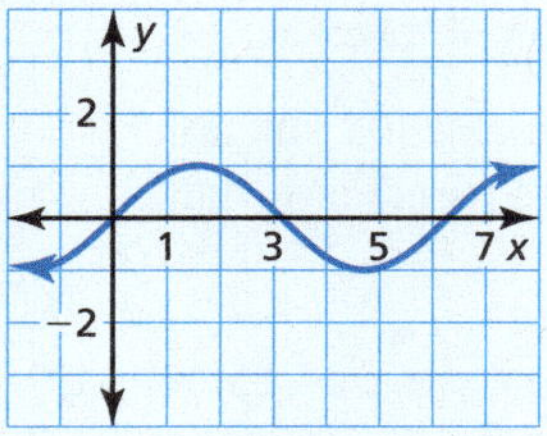

GO DIGITAL

In Exercises 11–14, find the domain and range of the function represented by the graph. *(See Example 3.)*

11.

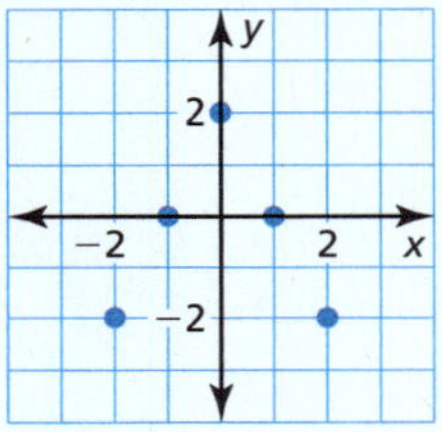

12.

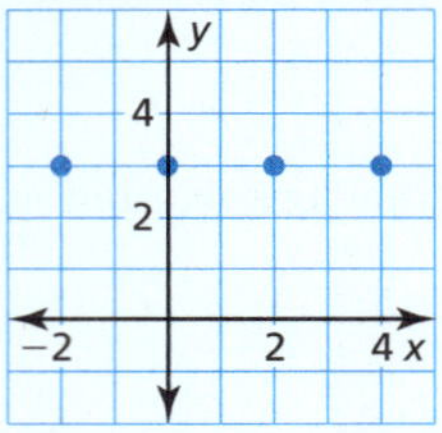

13.

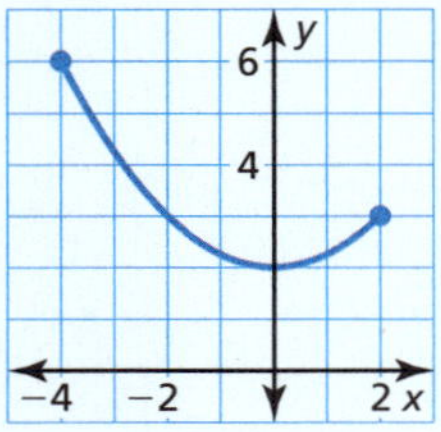

14.

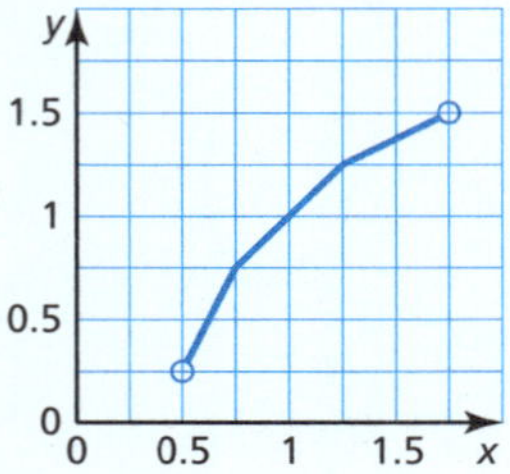

ANALYZE A PROBLEM **In Exercises 15 and 16, identify the independent and dependent variables.**

15. the number of quarters you put into a parking meter and the amount of time on the meter

16. the amount of gasoline in a car's fuel tank and the amount of time spent driving

17. **MODELING REAL LIFE** A cell phone plan costs \$30 for each line. *(See Example 4.)*

a. Does the situation represent a function? If so, identify the independent and dependent variables.

b. You can have a maximum of four lines on a plan. Find the domain and range.

18. **MODELING REAL LIFE** A taxi company charges an initial fee of \$2.80 plus \$3.50 per mile traveled.

a. Does the situation represent a function? If so, identify the independent and dependent variables.

b. You have enough money to travel at most 20 miles in the taxi. Find the domain and range.

4 MTR **ERROR ANALYSIS** **In Exercises 19 and 20, describe and correct the error in the statement about the relation shown in the table.**

Input, x	1	2	3	4	5
Output, y	$6\frac{1}{2}$	$7\frac{1}{2}$	$8\frac{1}{2}$	$6\frac{1}{2}$	$9\frac{1}{2}$

19. ✗ The relation is *not* a function. One output is paired with two inputs.

20. ✗ The relation is a function. The range is 1, 2, 3, 4, and 5.

2 MTR **21.** **MULTIPLE REPRESENTATIONS** The table shows the balance of a savings account over time. Represent the situation in words and in a coordinate plane. Does the situation represent a function? Explain.

Month, x	0	1	2	3	4
Balance (dollars), y	100	125	150	175	200

2 MTR **22.** **MULTIPLE REPRESENTATIONS** The equation $1.5x + 0.5y = 12$ represents the number x of hardcover books and the number y of softcover books you can buy at a used-book sale. Represent the situation in a table and in a coordinate plane. Does the situation represent a function? Explain.

23. **REASONING** The graph represents a function. Find the input value corresponding to an output of 2.

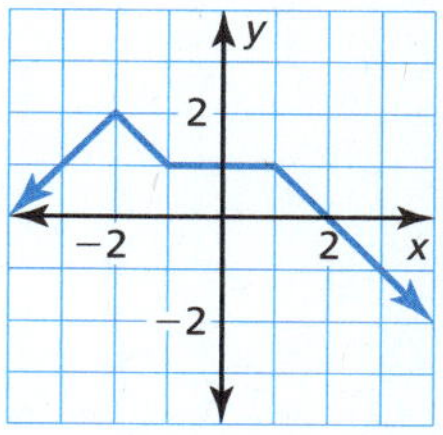

24. **OPEN-ENDED** Complete the table so that when t is the independent variable, the relation is a function, and when t is the dependent variable, the relation is not a function.

t				
v				

4 MTR **25.** **MAKING AN ARGUMENT** Your friend says that a line always represents a function. Is your friend correct? Explain.

26. **HOW DO YOU SEE IT?**
The graph represents the height h of a projectile after t seconds.

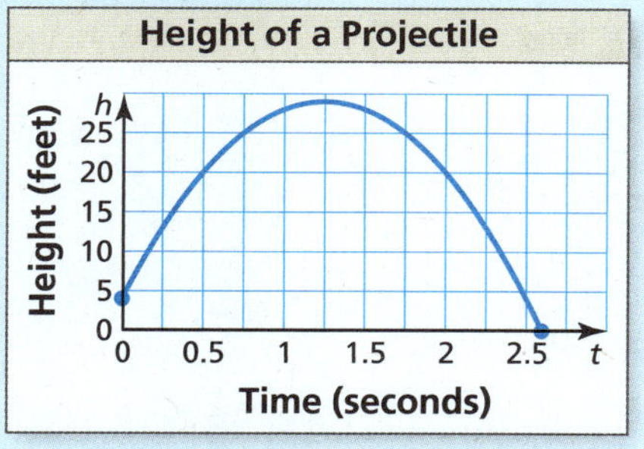

a. Is h a function of t? Explain.

b. Approximate the height of the projectile after 0.5 second and after 1.25 seconds.

c. Approximate the domain and range.

d. Is t a function of h? Explain.

3 MTR MAINTAIN ACCURACY **In Exercises 27–30, determine whether the statement uses the word *function* in a way that is mathematically correct. Explain your reasoning.**

27. The selling price of an item is a function of the cost of making the item.

28. The sales tax on a purchased item in a given state is a function of the selling price.

29. A function pairs each student in your school with a homeroom teacher.

30. A function pairs each chaperone on a school trip with 10 students.

4 MTR DISCUSS MATHEMATICAL THINKING **In Exercises 31–34, tell whether the statement is *true* or *false*. If it is false, explain why.**

31. Every function is a relation.

32. Every relation is a function.

33. When you switch the inputs and outputs of any function, the resulting relation is a function.

34. When the domain of a function has an infinite number of values, the range always has an infinite number of values.

35. B.E.S.T. TEST PREP Which of the following values of x and y make the relation a function? Select all that apply.

$$(-3, 7), (-2, 3), (0, 8), (1, -1), (x, y)$$

Ⓐ $x = -4, y = 0$

Ⓑ $x = 1, y = -2$

Ⓒ $x = 5, y = -1$

Ⓓ $x = 2, y = 8$

36. THOUGHT PROVOKING
Describe a function in which the inputs and/or the outputs are not numbers. Identify the independent and dependent variables. Then find the domain and range of the function.

DIG DEEPER **In Exercises 37–40, find the domain and range of the function.**

37. $y = |x|$

38. $y = -|x|$

39. $y = |x| - 6$

40. $y = 4 - |x|$

41. CONNECTING CONCEPTS Find the domain and range of a function that represents the perimeter of the triangle shown.
5 MTR

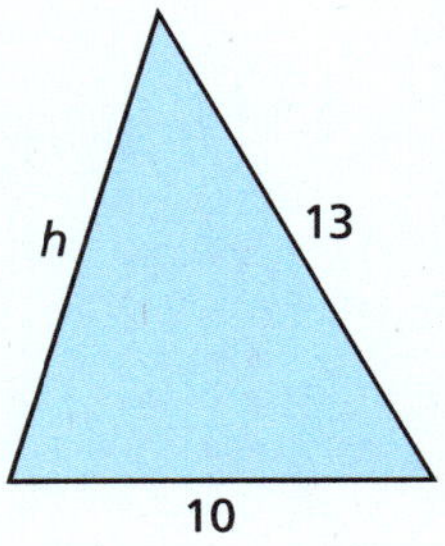

REVIEW & REFRESH

WATCH

42. Tell whether x and y are proportional.

x	4	6	12	16
y	6	8	16	20

43. What number is 60% of 35?

44. 27 is what percent of 75?

In Exercises 45–48, solve the equation.

45. $n - 5.3 = -7.4$

46. $|2x + 5| = 3x$

47. $7c + 10 - 12c = -11 - 2c$

48. $-\frac{1}{2}(3h + 8) + 2 = 13$

49. Determine whether the relation is a function. Explain.

$(0, -6), (1, -3), (3, 2), (5, 1), (2, -3)$

50. Write the sentence as an inequality.

Seven is at most the quotient of a number d and -5.

7 MTR **51.** **MODELING REAL LIFE** There is a 6% sales tax on your clothing purchase. You pay \$1.80 in tax. What is the total amount you pay?

In Exercises 52–57, solve the inequality. Graph the solution.

52. $z + 9 < 5$

53. $-5y + 9.2 \geq -18.3$

54. $\frac{x}{-7} \leq 2$

55. $7w + 6 > 3(-2 + w)$

56. $2|t - 5| + 3 \geq 9$

57. $-12 \leq 2m + 8 < 4$

58. Find the domain and range of the function represented by the graph.

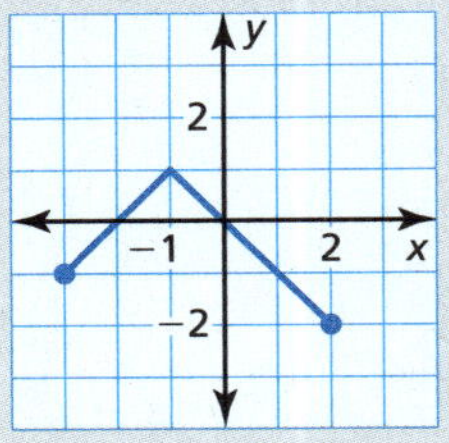

59. **REASONING** Find the value of a for which the equation

$$12x - 15 = a(5 - 4x)$$

is an identity.

60. Write an inequality that represents the graph.

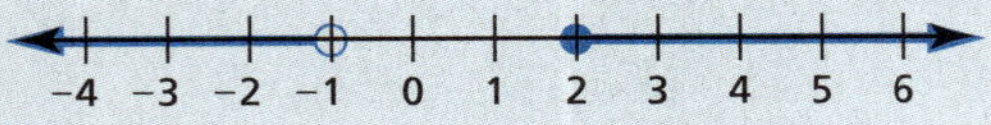

7 MTR **61.** **MODELING REAL LIFE** You want to score an average of at least 10 points per game in the last six basketball games of the season. In five of the six remaining games, you score 8, 14, 6, 12, and 8 points. How many points do you need to score in the sixth game to achieve your goal?

62. Solve the literal equation $3x - 6y = 18$ for y.

63. The volume of the rectangular prism is 105 cubic yards. What is the surface area of the prism in square feet?

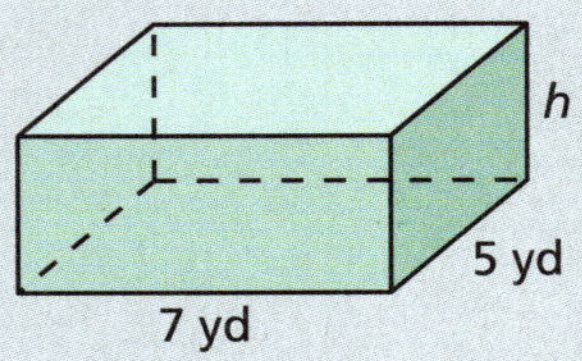

3.2 Characteristics of Functions

Learning Target: Describe characteristics of functions.

Success Criteria:
- I can estimate intercepts of a graph of a function.
- I can approximate when a function is positive, negative, increasing, or decreasing.
- I can sketch a graph of a function from a verbal description.

Algebraic Reasoning

MA.912.AR.2.5 Solve and graph mathematical and real-world problems that are modeled with linear functions. Interpret key features and determine constraints in terms of the context.

MA.912.AR.3.8 Solve and graph mathematical and real-world problems that are modeled with quadratic functions. Interpret key features and determine constraints in terms of the context.

Also MA.912.AR.2.4, MA.912.AR.3.7, MA.912.F.1.6

EXPLORE IT! Describing Characteristics of Functions

Work with a partner. Consider the function $y = x^3 - 3x$.

a. What do you think it means for a function to be *positive*? *negative*? *increasing*? *decreasing*?

b. Write a pair of numbers greater than 50 and a pair of numbers less than -50 to use as inputs for the function.

NUMBERS GREATER THAN 50	NUMBERS LESS THAN −50
First Number: ________	First Number: ________
Second Number: ______	Second Number: ______

Find the outputs for each pair of inputs. Do you think the function is increasing? decreasing? Explain your reasoning using your input-output pairs.

GO DIGITAL

c. The graph of the function is shown below. Approximate when the function is positive, negative, increasing, or decreasing over its entire domain.

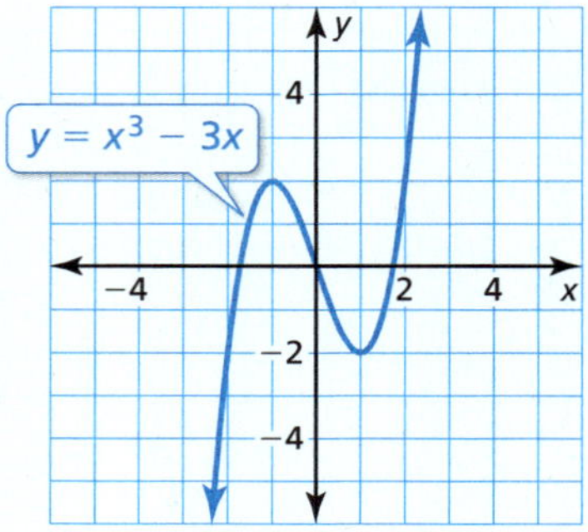

d. Explain whether it is possible for a graph to be decreasing over its entire domain but never negative. Justify your answer using a sketch.

4 MTR **COMPARE METHODS**

Compare using *input-output pairs* with using a graph when describing characteristics of a function. Which method is generally more accurate?

Intercepts of Graphs of Functions

Vocabulary

x-intercept, *p. 189*
y-intercept, *p. 189*
increasing, *p. 190*
decreasing, *p. 190*
end behavior, *p. 190*

KEY IDEA

Intercepts

An **x-intercept** of a graph is the x-coordinate of a point where the graph intersects the x-axis. It occurs when $y = 0$.

A **y-intercept** of a graph is the y-coordinate of a point where the graph intersects the y-axis. It occurs when $x = 0$.

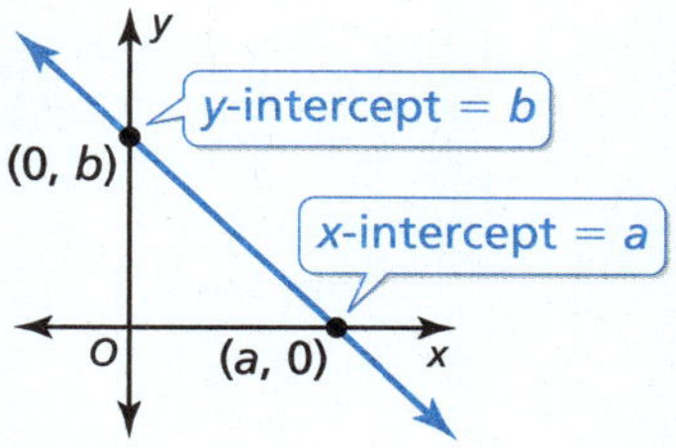

EXAMPLE 1 Estimating Intercepts

Estimate the intercepts of the graph of each function.

a.

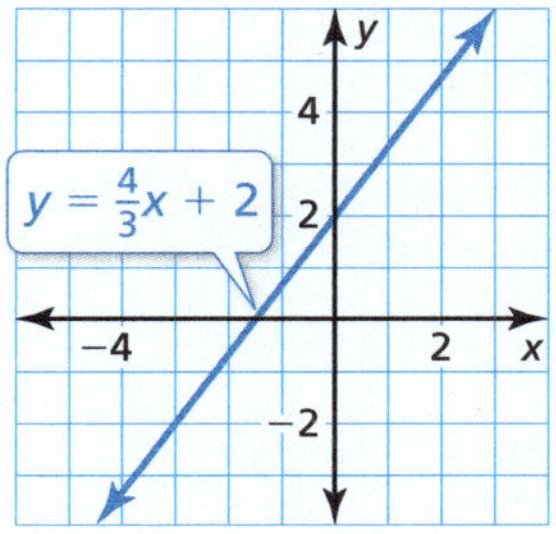

b.

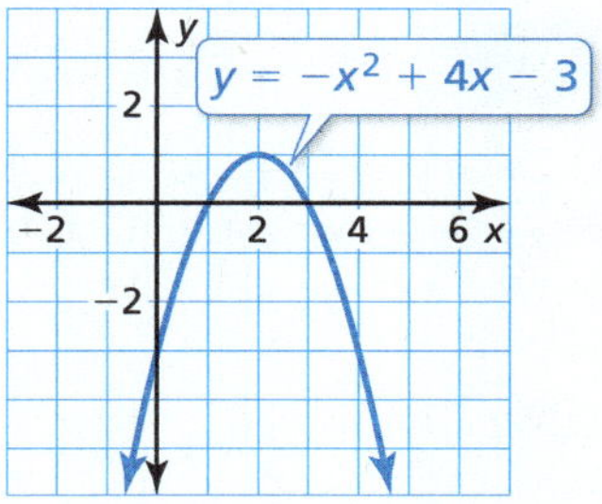

STUDY TIP

You can use a graph to estimate intercepts, but your estimates may not be exact. Substitute your estimates into the equation to check whether they are exact.

SOLUTION

a. The graph appears to intersect the x-axis at $(-1.5, 0)$. It appears to intersect the y-axis at $(0, 2)$.

► So, the x-intercept is about -1.5, and the y-intercept is about 2.

b. The graph appears to intersect the x-axis at $(1, 0)$ and $(3, 0)$. It appears to intersect the y-axis at $(0, -3)$.

► So, the x-intercepts are about 1 and 3, and the y-intercept is about -3.

SELF-ASSESSMENT 1 I don't understand yet. 2 I can do it with help. 3 I can do it on my own. 4 I can teach someone else.

Estimate the intercepts of the graph of the function.

1.

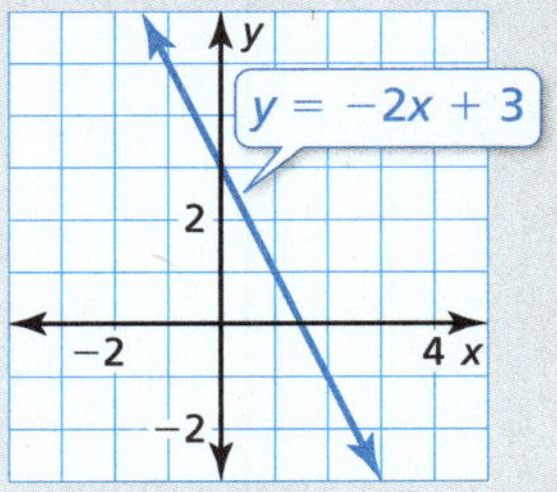

2.

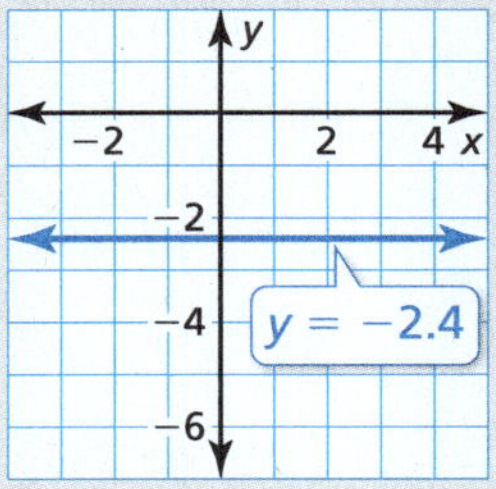

3.

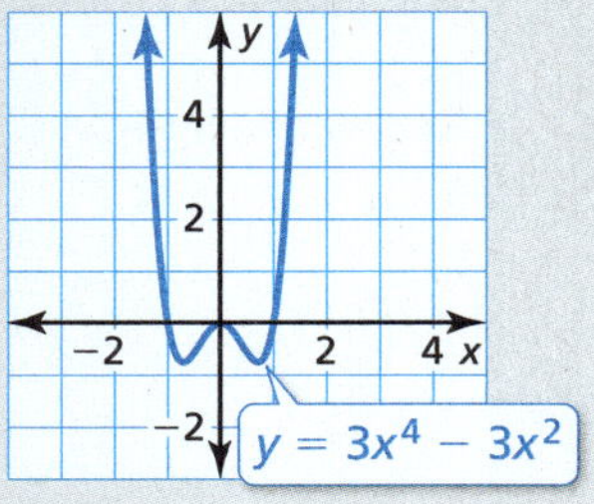

4. REASONING Can the graph of a function have more than one y-intercept? Can the graph of a function have an infinite number of x-intercepts? Explain your reasoning.

GO DIGITAL

Other Characteristics of Functions

KEY IDEAS

Positive, Negative, Increasing, Decreasing, and End Behavior

A function is *positive* when its graph lies above the x-axis. A function is *negative* when its graph lies below the x-axis.

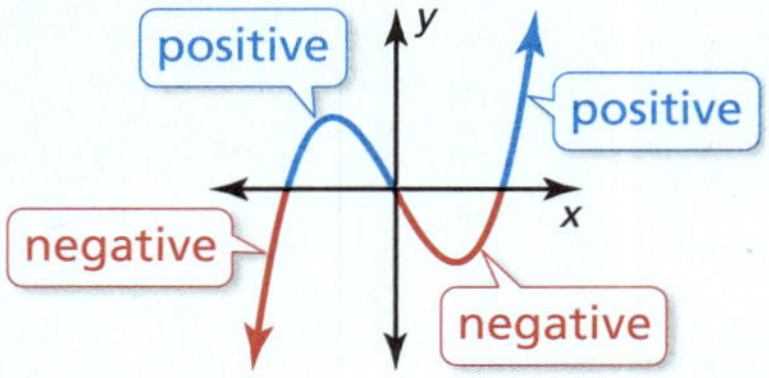

A function is **increasing** when its graph moves up as x moves to the right. A function is **decreasing** when its graph moves down as x moves to the right.

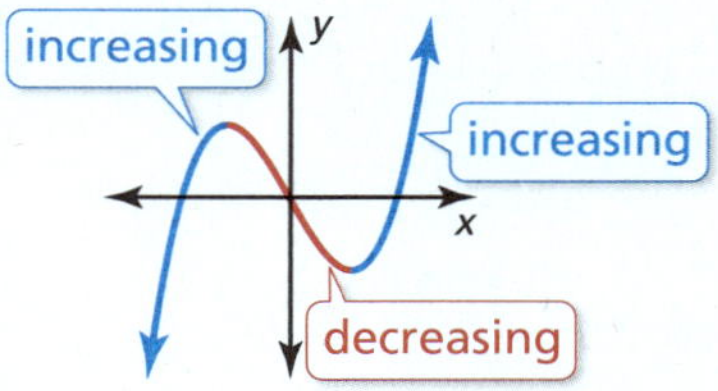

The **end behavior** of a function is the behavior of the graph as x approaches positive infinity $(+\infty)$ or negative infinity $(-\infty)$.

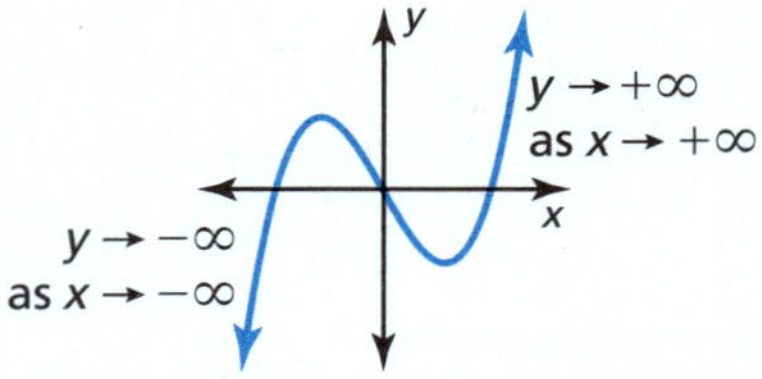

EXAMPLE 2 Describing Characteristics

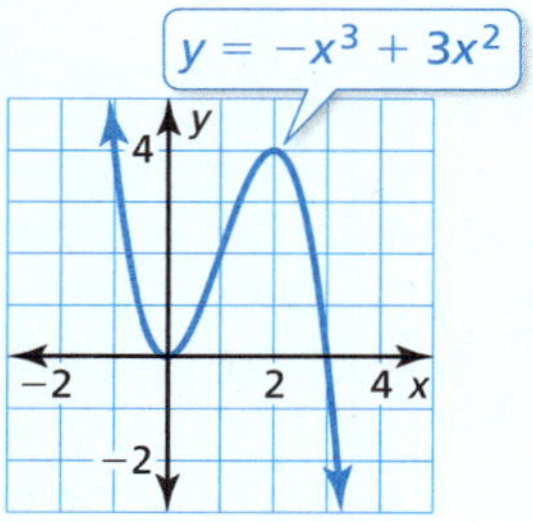

Approximate when the function $y = -x^3 + 3x^2$ is positive, negative, increasing, or decreasing. Then describe the end behavior of the function.

SOLUTION

Positive and Negative:
The function appears to be positive when $x < 0$, positive when $0 < x < 3$, and negative when $x > 3$.

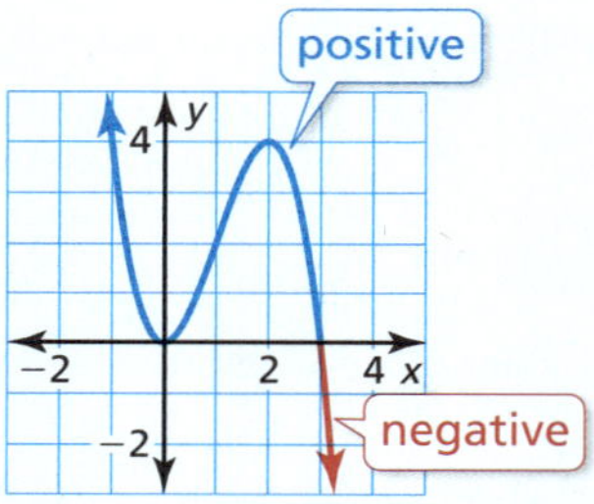

Increasing and Decreasing:
The function appears to be decreasing when $x < 0$, increasing when $0 < x < 2$, and decreasing when $x > 2$.

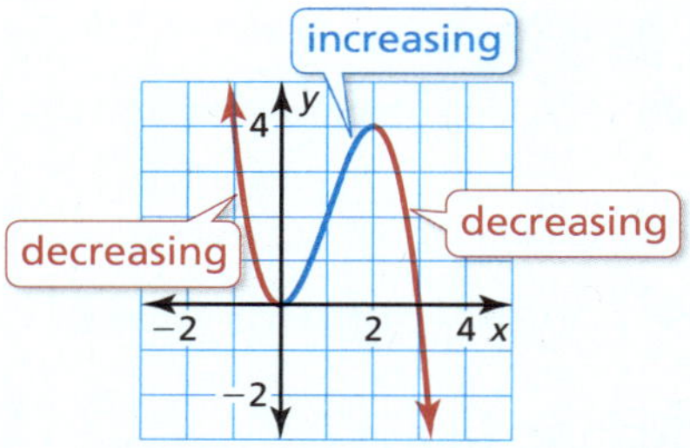

End behavior: The graph shows that the function values increase as x approaches negative infinity and the function values decrease as x approaches positive infinity. So, $y \rightarrow +\infty$ as $x \rightarrow -\infty$ and $y \rightarrow -\infty$ as $x \rightarrow +\infty$.

GO DIGITAL

SELF-ASSESSMENT

1 I don't understand yet. 2 I can do it with help. 3 I can do it on my own. 4 I can teach someone else.

Approximate when the function is positive, negative, increasing, or decreasing. Then describe the end behavior of the function.

5.

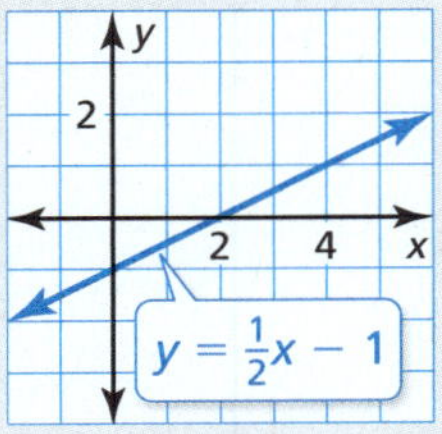

6.

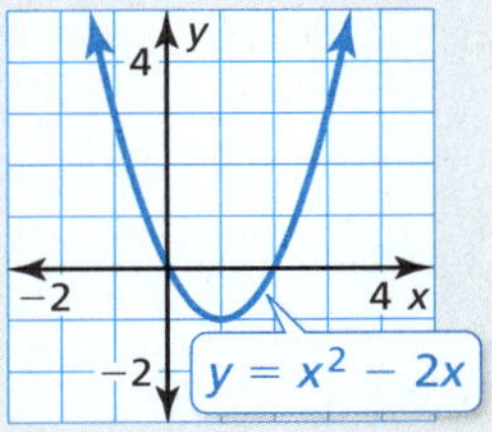

7.

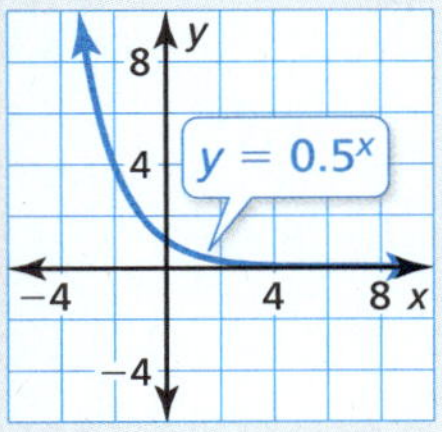

Solving Real-Life Problems

A Japanese mission used hopping robots to conduct experiments on an asteroid. Because of the asteroid's low gravity, a single hop could last 15 minutes or more.

7 MTR

EXAMPLE 3 Modeling Real Life

WATCH

Researchers send two robots to explore an asteroid. The robots move by "hopping" between locations. The graph shows the path of Robot A's first hop. Robot B lands 60 feet from where it starts its first hop, reaching a maximum height of 48 feet after traveling a horizontal distance of 30 feet. Compare the two hops.

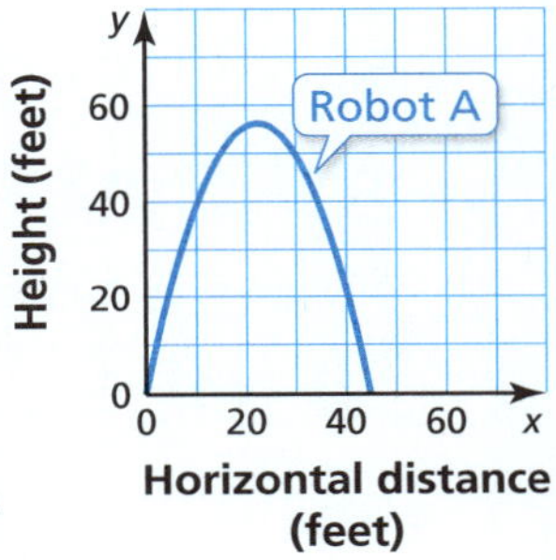

SOLUTION

Use the verbal description to sketch a graph that represents Robot B's hop. First identify several points on the graph.

- the start of the hop: (0, 0)
- the maximum height of the hop: (30, 48)
- the end of the hop: (60, 0)

So, the graph increases from (0, 0) to (30, 48) and then decreases to (60, 0). Sketch the graph using a curve similar to the graph that represents Robot A's hop.

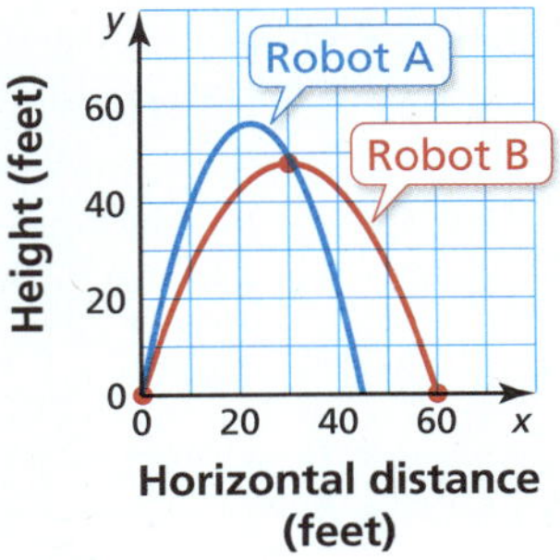

▶ **Intercepts:** Robot A's hop has x-intercepts of about 0 and 45. So, the robot lands about 45 feet from where it starts. This is about $60 - 45 = 15$ feet shorter than Robot B's hop.

Increasing and decreasing: Each hop reaches its maximum height when the height changes from increasing to decreasing. The graph shows that the maximum height of Robot A's hop is between 50 and 60, or about 55. So, Robot A's hop is about $55 - 48 = 7$ feet higher than Robot B's hop at its maximum height.

GO DIGITAL

1 MTR ANALYZE A PROBLEM

In Example 3, what are the domain and range of each function in this context? Write your answers in both inequality and set-builder notations.

SELF-ASSESSMENT

1 I don't understand yet. 2 I can do it with help. 3 I can do it on my own. 4 I can teach someone else.

8. The graph shows your distance from home while out on a walk. The next day, you jog the same route twice at a constant speed. The entire jog takes 1 hour. Compare your walk to your jog.

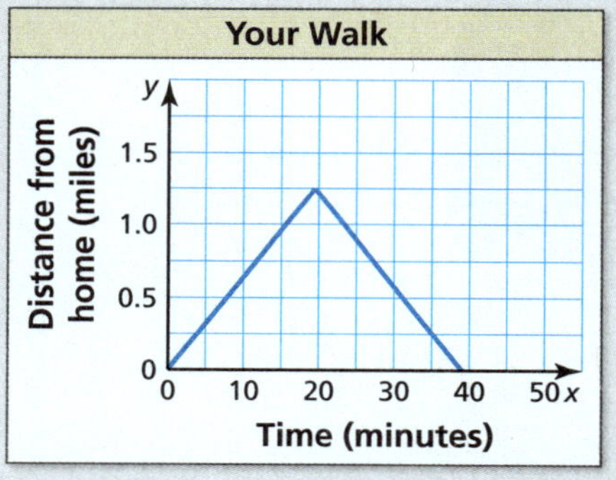

2 MTR **9. MODEL A PROBLEM** You throw a ball straight up into the air and notice that the speed of the ball decreases as it approaches its maximum height, then increases again on the way down. Sketch a graph that represents the relationship between time and height in this situation. Explain your reasoning.

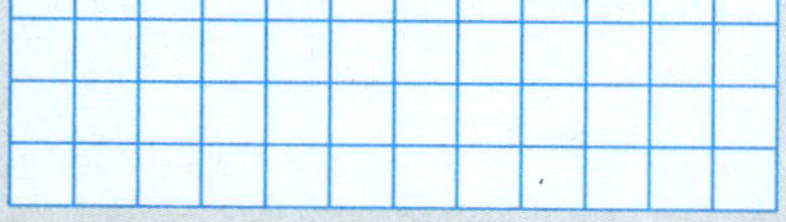

3.2 Practice WITH CalcChat® AND CalcView®

In Exercises 1–4, estimate the intercepts of the graph of the function. *(See Example 1.)*

1.
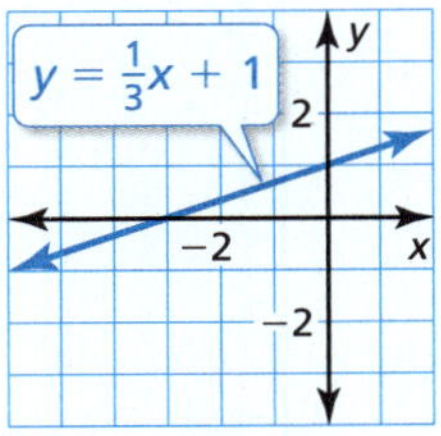

2.
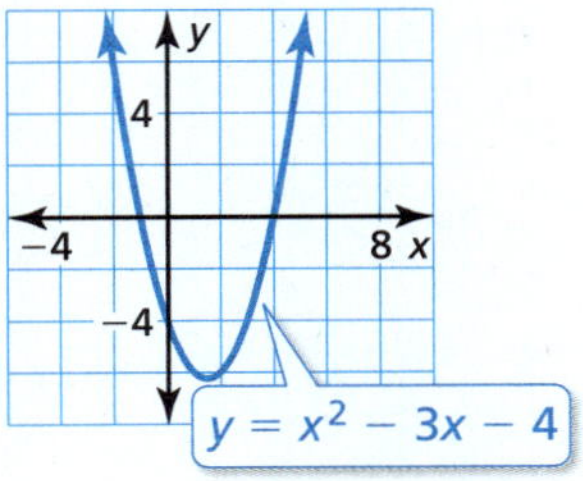

▶ 3.
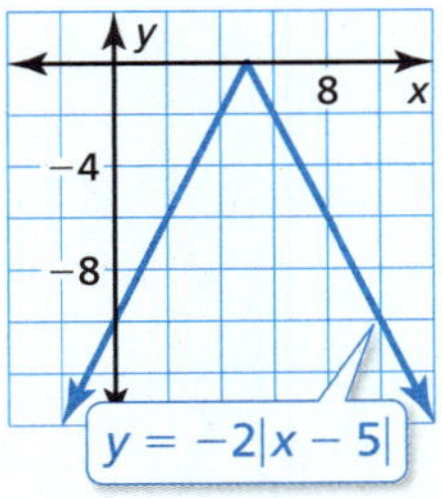

4.
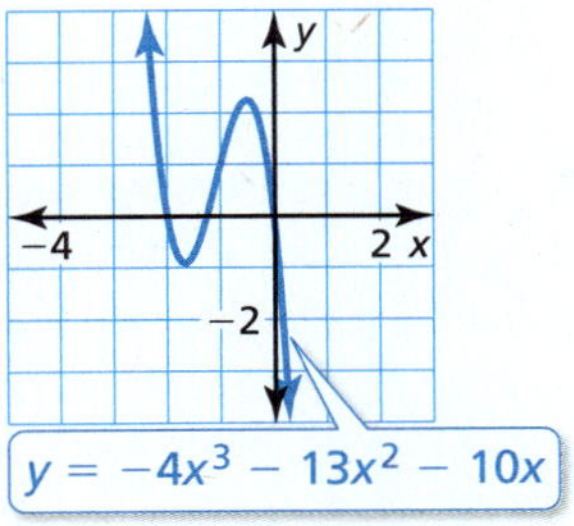

In Exercises 5–8, approximate when the function is positive, negative, increasing, or decreasing. Then describe the end behavior of the function. *(See Example 2.)*

5.
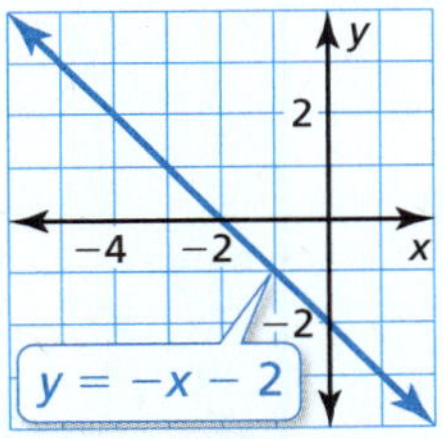

6.
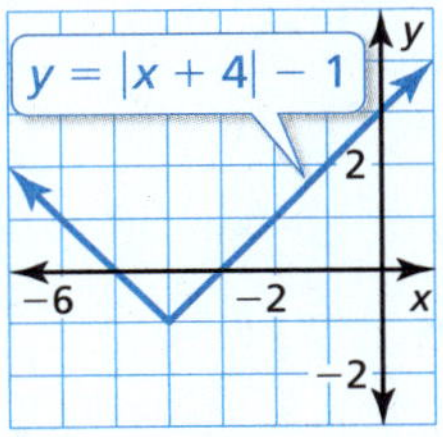

▶ 7.
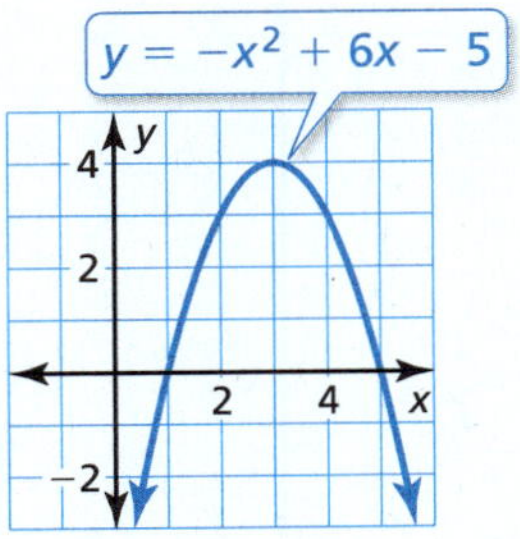

8.
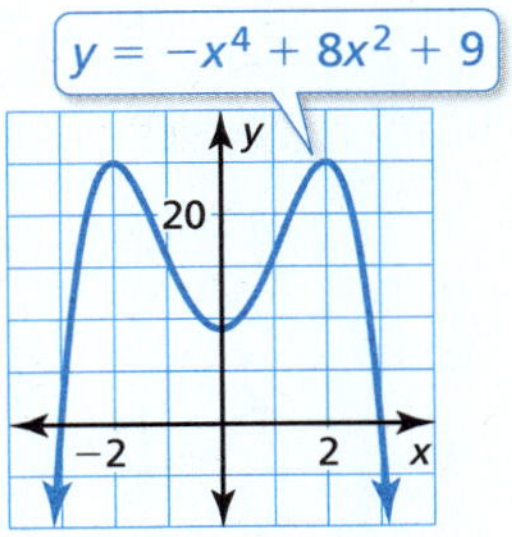

GO DIGITAL

In Exercises 9 and 10, sketch a graph of a function with the given characteristics.

9. • The function is increasing when $x < -6$ and decreasing when $x > -6$.

• The function is negative when $x < -8$, positive when $-8 < x < -4$, and negative when $x > -4$.

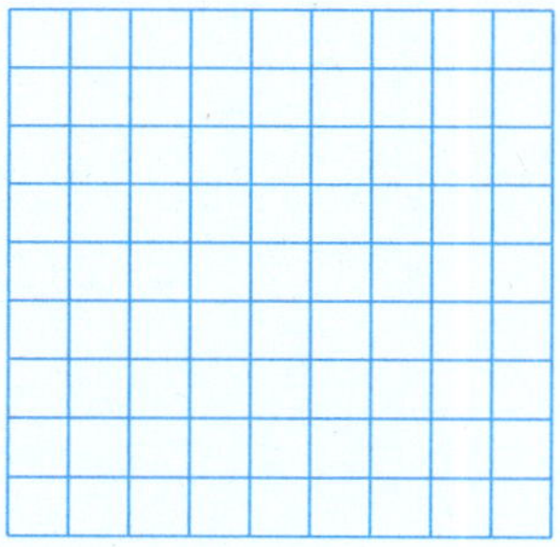

10. • The x-intercepts are -0.5, 1, and 3.25.

• $y \to +\infty$ as $x \to -\infty$ and $y \to -\infty$ as $x \to +\infty$.

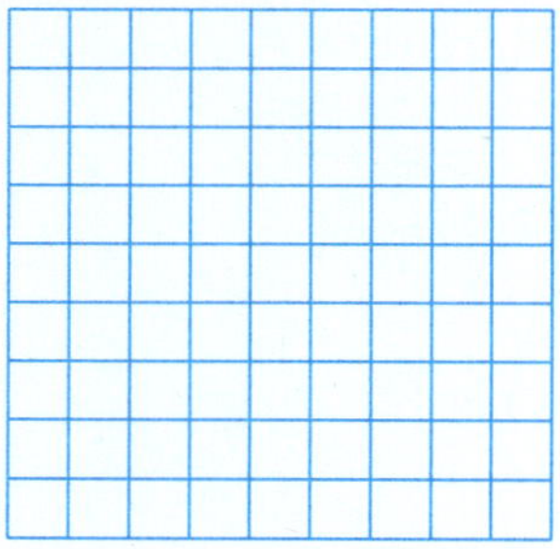

11. MODELING REAL LIFE The graph shows the speed of a blue car after the driver applies the brakes, represented by $y = -\frac{35}{3}x + 35$, where x is the time (in seconds) and y is the speed (in miles per hour). The driver of a red car applies the brakes while traveling 30 miles per hour. The speed of the red car decreases at a constant rate until the car comes to a complete stop 4 seconds later. Compare the initial speeds and stopping times. *(See Example 3.)*

7 MTR

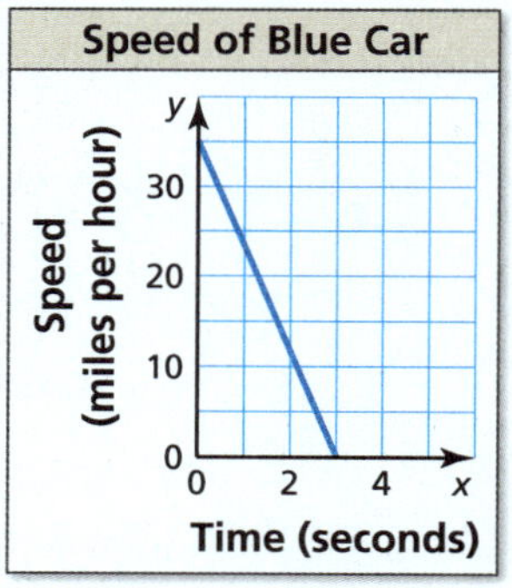

12. MODELING REAL LIFE The graphs show the path of two home runs. Compare the two home runs.

7 MTR

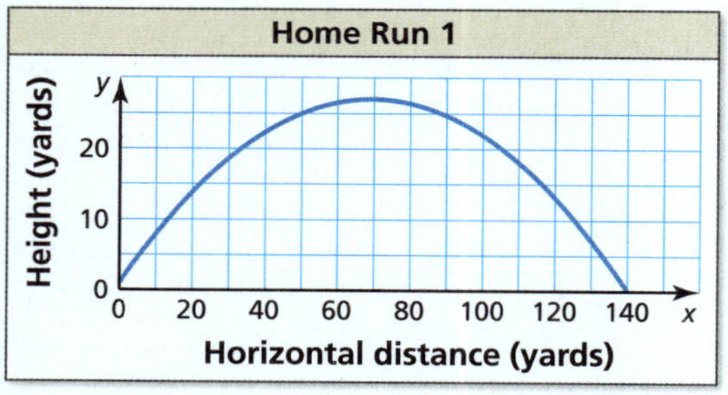

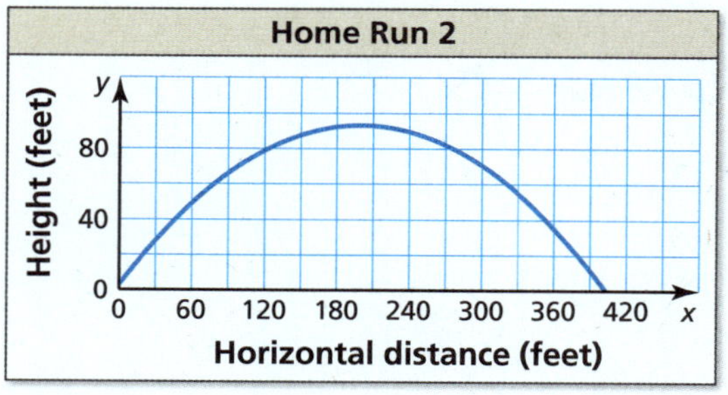

4 MTR **13. ERROR ANALYSIS** Describe and correct the error in describing characteristics of the function.

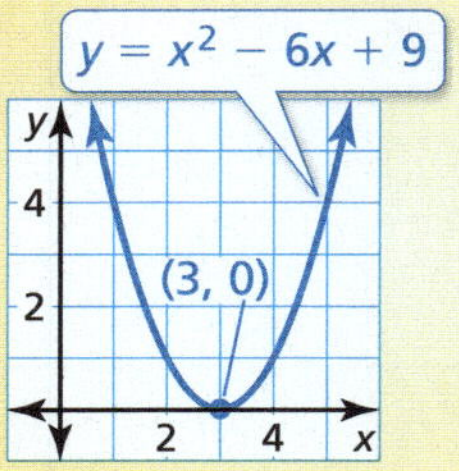

The function is positive for all values of x. The function is decreasing when $x < 3$ and increasing when $x > 3$.

14. HOW DO YOU SEE IT?
The graph of a function is shown.

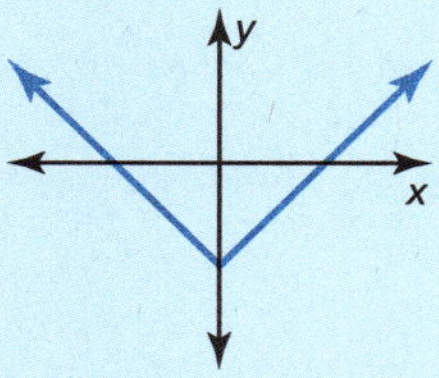

a. How many x-intercepts does the graph have? Is the y-intercept *positive* or *negative*?

b. Is the function *increasing* or *decreasing* when $x < 0$? $x > 0$?

15. B.E.S.T. TEST PREP The graph of a function is a line that is decreasing for all values of x and has an x-intercept of 4. Which of the following are true? Select all that apply.

Ⓐ The y-intercept is negative.

Ⓑ The graph has only one x-intercept.

Ⓒ The function is positive when $x < 4$ and negative when $x > 4$.

Ⓓ $y \to -\infty$ as $x \to -\infty$ and $y \to +\infty$ as $x \to +\infty$.

4 MTR **16. MAKING AN ARGUMENT** Consider the graph of a function that is negative over its entire domain. Can the graph have an x-intercept? Explain.

17. DIG DEEPER You board a car at the bottom of a Ferris wheel. The Ferris wheel then makes several complete rotations before stopping again to let you off where you boarded. Sketch a graph that represents the relationship between time and your height above the ground, and describe the relationship.

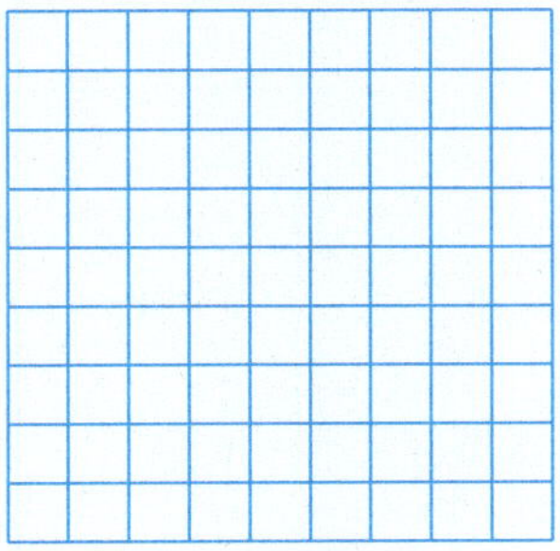

18. THOUGHT PROVOKING
Sketch a graph of a function with the given characteristics.

- The function is decreasing for $x < 0$ and increasing for $x > 0$.
- As x approaches negative infinity, the function does *not* approach positive infinity or negative infinity.
- As x approaches positive infinity, the function does *not* approach positive infinity or negative infinity.
- The graph does *not* have a y-intercept.

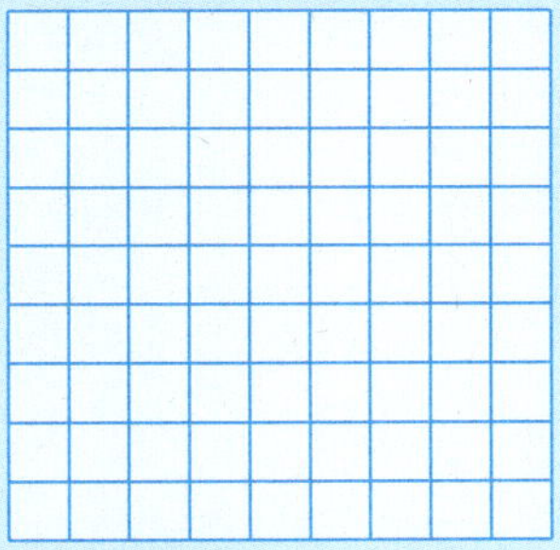

REVIEW & REFRESH

WATCH

In Exercises 19 and 20, write the sentence as an inequality. Graph the inequality.

19. A number n is greater than or equal to -5 and less than -1.

20. A number k is no more than $-\frac{1}{2}$ or at least $2\frac{1}{2}$.

In Exercises 21–24, solve the equation.

21. $7 + b = -21$

22. $-3.2x = 16$

23. $-3(t - 5) = 14$

24. $30 = 2m - 8m + 12$

7 MTR **25. MODELING REAL LIFE** You have a $25 gift card to a coffee shop. You have already used $19.85. You want to purchase one drink and one bakery item. Which pairs of items can you purchase with the amount left on the gift card?

Drink	Price
Coffee	$2.09
Cappuccino	$3.79

Bakery item	Price
Muffin	$2.59
Bagel	$1.49

26. Find the greatest common factor of 30 and 42.

27. Estimate the intercepts of the graph of the function.

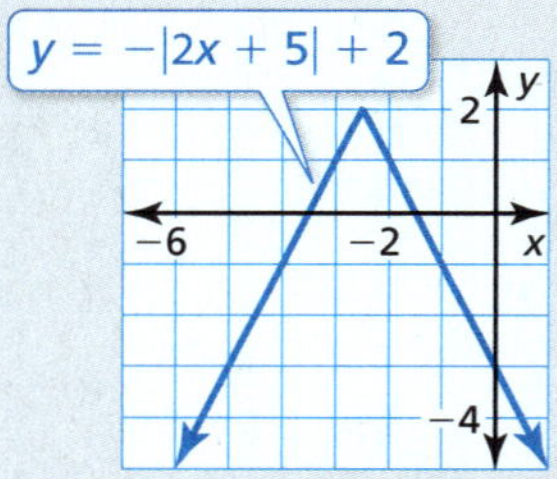

In Exercises 28–31, solve the inequality. Graph the solution.

28. $5a > 20$

29. $\frac{r}{-2} + 6 \leq 11$

30. $1.5x + 7 - 5x > 11 - 3x$

31. $\left|\frac{1}{3}x + 6\right| + 2 > 3$

32. REASONING Complete the relation so that it is (a) a function and (b) *not* a function. Explain your reasoning.

$(-6, -1), (-4, 0), (-2, 1), (2, 2),$ ______

3.3 Linear Functions

Learning Target: Identify and graph linear functions.

Success Criteria:
- I can identify linear functions using graphs, tables, and equations.
- I can determine whether a domain is discrete or continuous in a real-life situation.
- I can graph linear functions with discrete and continuous domains.

Algebraic Reasoning
MA.912.AR.2.4 Given a table, equation or written description of a linear function, graph that function, and determine and interpret its key features.
Functions
MA.912.F.1.1 Given an equation or graph that defines a function, determine the function type. Given an input-output table, determine a function type that could represent it.
Also MA.912.AR.2.5

EXPLORE IT! Finding a Pattern

Work with a partner. Use a piece of rope that is at least 100 centimeters long. Record your data in the table.

Number of knots	Length of rope
0	
1	
2	
3	
4	
5	
6	
7	
8	

a. Measure the length of the rope. Describe your measurement.

b. Make a knot in the rope, and then measure the length of the rope again. Continue to make identical knots in the rope, measuring the length of the rope after each knot is tied.

c. Write several observations about the data. What pattern(s) do you notice in the data? Explain.

d. Make a scatter plot of the data. What pattern(s) do you notice in the scatter plot? Explain.

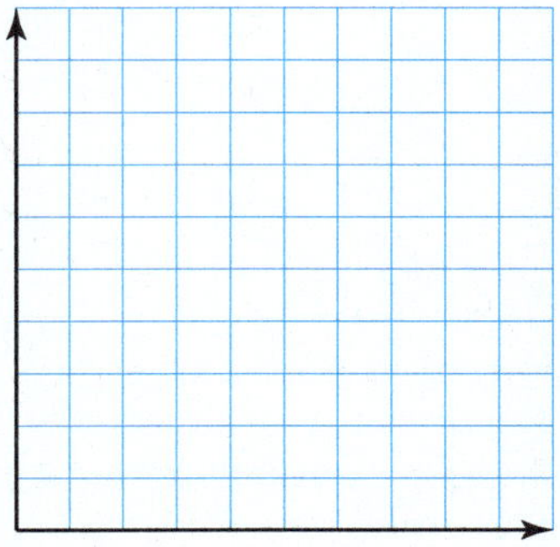

e. How can you predict the length of the rope when it has 10 knots? Explain your reasoning.

f. Does it matter where you tie the knots on the rope? Is there a maximum number of knots you can tie? Does the thickness of the rope or the type of knot you tie affect your results? Explain your reasoning.

USE ANOTHER METHOD (2 MTR)
Is there more than one way to predict the length in part (e)? Explain.

GO DIGITAL

Identifying Linear Functions

> **Vocabulary** (AZ VOCAB)
> linear equation in two variables, *p. 198*
> linear function, *p. 198*
> nonlinear function, *p. 198*
> solution of a linear equation in two variables, *p. 201*
> discrete domain, *p. 201*
> continuous domain, *p. 201*

A **linear equation in two variables**, x and y, is an equation that can be written in the form

$$y = mx + b$$

where m and b are constants. The graph of a linear equation is a line. Likewise, a **linear function** is a function whose graph is a nonvertical line. A linear function has a constant rate of change and can be represented by a linear equation in two variables. A **nonlinear function** does not have a constant rate of change. So, its graph is *not* a line.

EXAMPLE 1 Identifying Linear Functions Using Graphs

WATCH

Does the graph represent a *linear* or *nonlinear* function? Explain.

a.

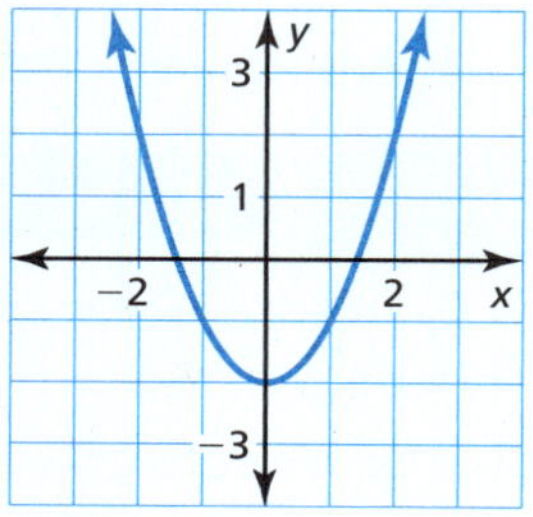

b.

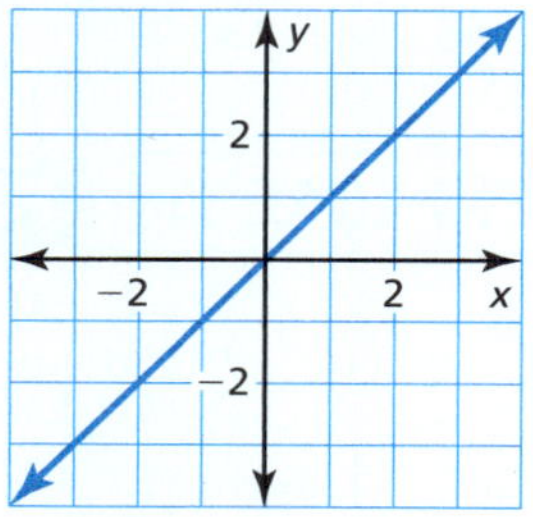

SOLUTION

a. The graph is *not* a line.

▶ So, the function is nonlinear.

b. The graph is a nonvertical line.

▶ So, the function is linear.

EXAMPLE 2 Identifying Linear Functions Using Tables

WATCH

Does the table represent a *linear* or *nonlinear* function? Explain.

a.

x	3	6	9	12
y	36	30	24	18

b.

x	1	3.5	6	8.5
y	2	9	20	35

SOLUTION

a.

	+3	+3	+3	
x	3	6	9	12
y	36	30	24	18
	−6	−6	−6	

As x increases by 3, y decreases by 6. The rate of change is constant.

▶ So, the function is linear.

b.

	+2.5	+2.5	+2.5	
x	1	3.5	6	8.5
y	2	9	20	35
	+7	+11	+15	

As x increases by 2.5, y increases by different amounts. The rate of change is *not* constant.

▶ So, the function is nonlinear.

> **STUDY TIP**
> A constant rate of change describes a quantity that changes by equal amounts over equal intervals.

GO DIGITAL

EXAMPLE 3 B.E.S.T. Test Prep: Identifying Linear Functions Using Equations

WATCH

Which of the following equations represent linear functions? Explain.

Ⓐ $0 = -x - y$ Ⓒ $y = 2^x$ Ⓔ $y = -1 + x$

Ⓑ $y = \sqrt{x}$ Ⓓ $y = |x| - 1$ Ⓕ $x^2 - y = 0$

SOLUTION

You cannot rewrite the equations $y = \sqrt{x}$, $y = 2^x$, $y = |x| - 1$, and $x^2 - y = 0$ in the form $y = mx + b$. So, they cannot represent linear functions.

You can rewrite the equation $0 = -x - y$ as $y = -x$ and the equation $y = -1 + x$ as $y = x - 1$.

▶ So, the correct answers are Ⓐ and Ⓔ.

CONCEPT SUMMARY

Representations of Functions

Words An output is 3 more than the input. **Equation** $y = x + 3$

Input-Output Table

Input, x	Output, y
−1	2
0	3
1	4
2	5

Mapping Diagram

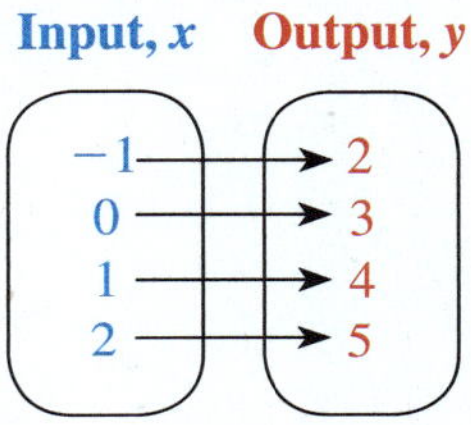

Graph

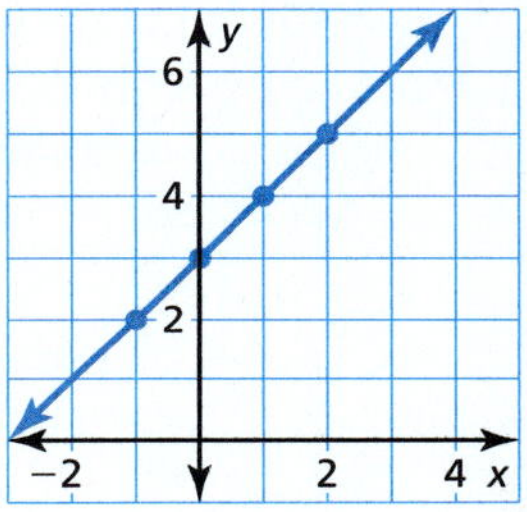

SELF-ASSESSMENT

1 I don't understand yet. 2 I can do it with help. 3 I can do it on my own. 4 I can teach someone else.

Does the graph or table represent a *linear* or *nonlinear* function? Explain.

1.

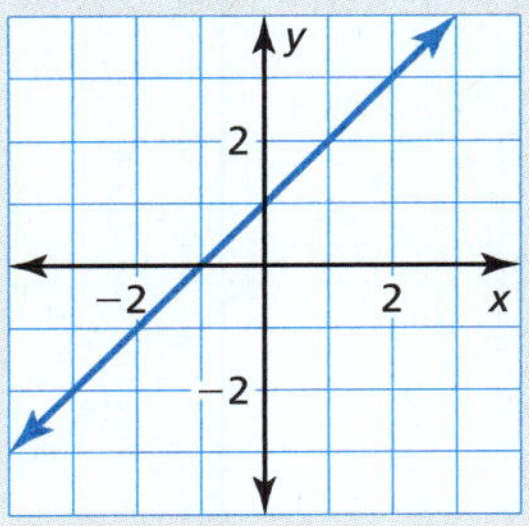

2.

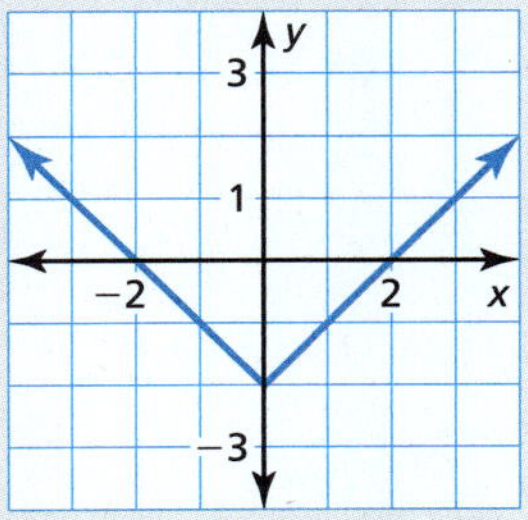

3.

x	0	1	2	3
y	3	5	7	9

4.

x	1	2	3	4
y	$\frac{1}{16}$	$\frac{1}{8}$	$\frac{1}{4}$	$\frac{1}{2}$

Does the equation represent a *linear* or *nonlinear* function? Explain.

5. $y = x + 9$ **6.** $5 = -x + y$ **7.** $y = 5 - 2x^2$

GO DIGITAL

Graphing Linear Functions

EXAMPLE 4 **Using Tables to Graph Linear Functions** WATCH

Graph the linear function represented by each table.

a.

x	y
-2	-4
0	-3
2	-2
4	-1

b.

x	y
-1	5
2	2.5
5	0
8	-2.5

SOLUTION

a. Write each ordered pair (x, y). Then plot each point in a coordinate plane and draw a line through the points.

STUDY TIP

When the domain of a linear function is not specified or cannot be obtained from a real-life context, it is understood to be all real numbers.

x	y	(x, y)
-2	-4	$(-2, -4)$
0	-3	$(0, -3)$
2	-2	$(2, -2)$
4	-1	$(4, -1)$

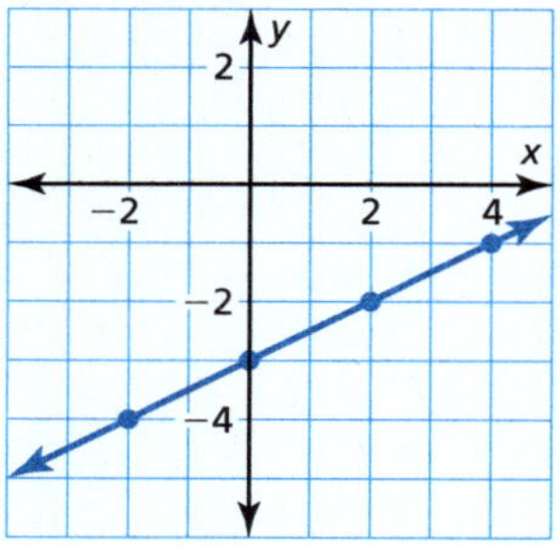

b. Write each ordered pair (x, y). Then plot each point in a coordinate plane and draw a line through the points.

x	y	(x, y)
-1	5	$(-1, 5)$
2	2.5	$(2, 2.5)$
5	0	$(5, 0)$
8	-2.5	$(8, -2.5)$

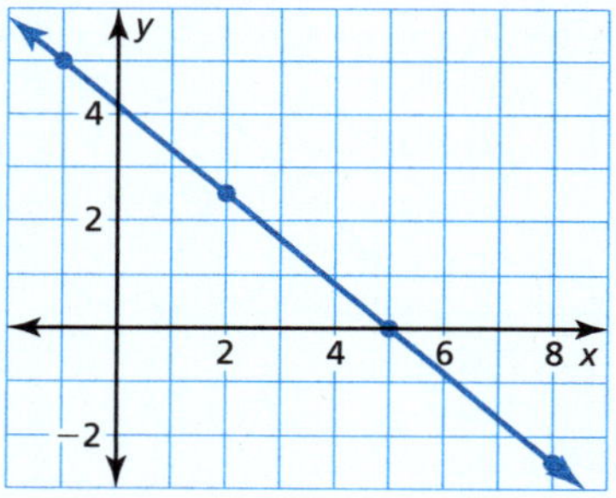

4 MTR **CONSTRUCT AN ARGUMENT**

How many points do you need in order to graph a linear function? Explain your reasoning.

GO DIGITAL

SELF-ASSESSMENT

1 I don't understand yet. 2 I can do it with help. 3 I can do it on my own. 4 I can teach someone else.

Graph the linear function represented by the table.

8.

x	0	1	2	3
y	6	4	2	0

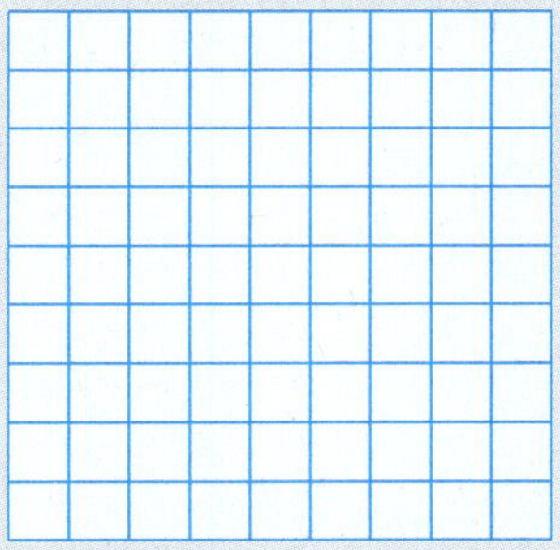

9.

x	-2	-1	0	1
y	-1	0.5	2	3.5

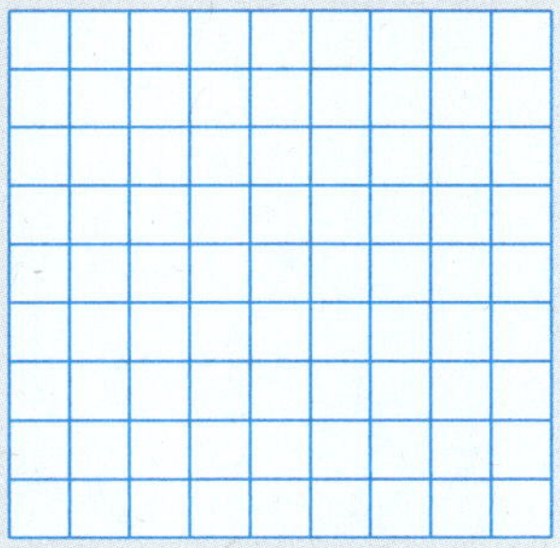

5 MTR **10. PATTERNS** The graph of a linear function passes through the point $(-3, 2.25)$. As x increases by 4, y decreases by 1.25. Graph the function.

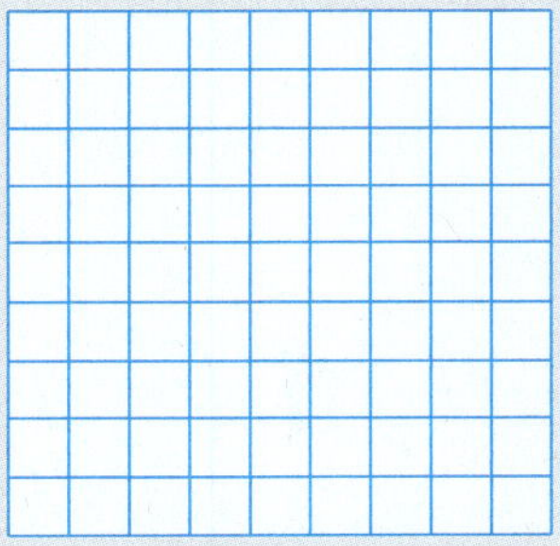

A **solution of a linear equation in two variables** is an ordered pair (x, y) that makes the equation true. The graph of a linear equation in two variables is the set of points (x, y) in a coordinate plane that represents all solutions of the equation. Sometimes the points are distinct, and other times the points are connected.

KEY IDEAS

Discrete and Continuous Domains

A **discrete domain** is a set of input values that consists of only certain numbers in an interval.

Example: Integers from 1 to 5

A **continuous domain** is a set of input values that consists of all numbers in an interval.

Example: All numbers from 1 to 5

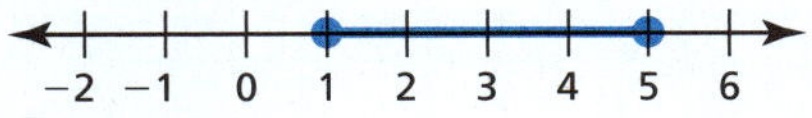

EXAMPLE 5 Graphing Discrete Data

WATCH

The linear function $y = 15.95x$ represents the cost y (in dollars) of x tickets for a museum. Each customer can buy a maximum of four tickets.

a. Find the domain of the function. Is the domain discrete or continuous? Explain.

b. Graph the function using its domain.

STUDY TIP

The domain of a function depends on the real-life context of the function, not just the equation that represents the function.

SOLUTION

a. You cannot buy part of a ticket, only a certain number of tickets. Because x represents the number of tickets, it must be a whole number. The maximum number of tickets a customer can buy is four.

▶ So, the domain is 0, 1, 2, 3, and 4, and it is discrete.

b. Step 1 Make an input-output table to find the ordered pairs.

Input, x	$15.95x$	Output, y	(x, y)
0	15.95(0)	0	(0, 0)
1	15.95(1)	15.95	(1, 15.95)
2	15.95(2)	31.9	(2, 31.9)
3	15.95(3)	47.85	(3, 47.85)
4	15.95(4)	63.8	(4, 63.8)

Step 2 Plot the ordered pairs. The domain is discrete. So, the graph consists of individual points.

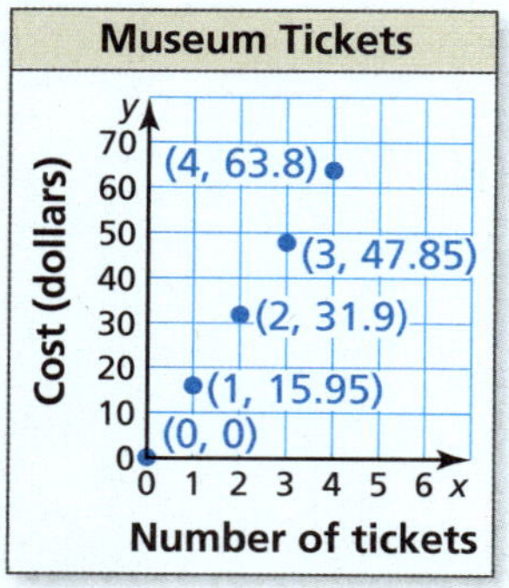

SELF-ASSESSMENT

1 I don't understand yet. 2 I can do it with help. 3 I can do it on my own. 4 I can teach someone else.

11. The linear function $m = 50 - 9d$ represents the amount m (in dollars) of money you have left after buying d DVDs.

a. Interpret the terms and coefficient in the equation.

b. Find the domain of the function. Is the domain discrete or continuous? Explain.

c. Graph the function using its domain.

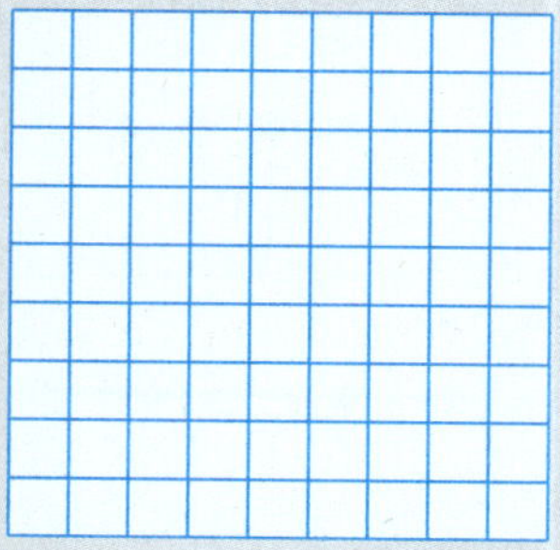

GO DIGITAL

EXAMPLE 6 Graphing Continuous Data

Each year, thousands of peregrine falcons fly over the Florida Keys as they migrate to South America. A peregrine falcon can fly 350 feet per second.

a. Explain why the distance traveled is a function of the number of seconds.

b. Find the domain of the function. Is the domain discrete or continuous? Explain.

c. Graph the function using its domain.

SOLUTION

a. As the number n of seconds increases by 1, the distance d traveled increases by 350 feet. The rate of change is constant.

▶ So, this situation represents a linear function.

b. The number n of seconds can be any value greater than or equal to 0.

▶ So, the domain is $n \geq 0$, and it is continuous.

c. Step 1 Make an input-output table to find ordered pairs.

Input, n	Output, d	(n, d)
0	0	(0, 0)
1	350	(1, 350)
2	700	(2, 700)
3	1050	(3, 1050)
4	1400	(4, 1400)

Hawk Mania is an annual bird-watching event held by the Florida Keys Audubon Society. The event teaches about the falcons, eagles, and ospreys that migrate through the Keys each fall.

Step 2 Plot the ordered pairs.

Step 3 Draw a line through the points. The line should start at (0, 0) and continue to the right. Use an arrow to indicate that the line continues without end, as shown. The domain is continuous. So, the graph is a line with a domain of $n \geq 0$.

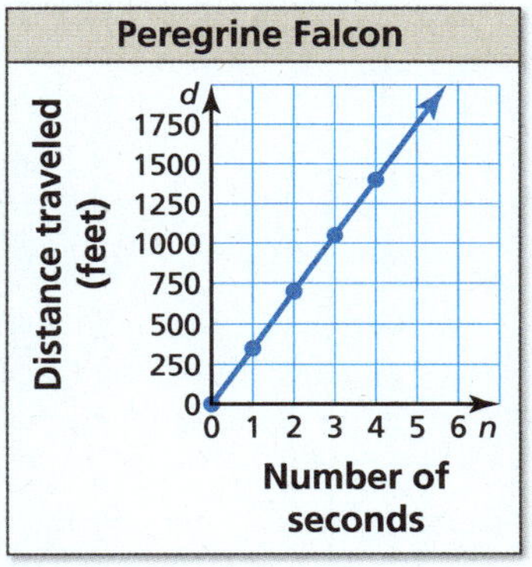

GO DIGITAL

SELF-ASSESSMENT

1 I don't understand yet. 2 I can do it with help. 3 I can do it on my own. 4 I can teach someone else.

12. A 20-gallon bathtub is draining at a rate of 2.5 gallons per minute.

a. Explain why the number of gallons remaining is a function of the number of minutes.

b. Find the domain of the function. Is the domain discrete or continuous? Explain.

c. Graph the function using its domain.

13. When feeding, a juvenile whale shark filters about 600 cubic meters of water through its mouth each hour. About 2.8 kilograms of food are filtered out from the water each hour.

a. Graph the function that represents the amount a of water filtered by the whale shark as a function of the number m of minutes.

b. The whale shark feeds for 7.5 hours each day. Graph the function that represents the amount f of food (in pounds) filtered by the whale shark as a function of the number d of days.

3.3 Practice WITH CalcChat® AND CalcView®

In Exercises 1–6, determine whether the graph represents a *linear* or *nonlinear* function. Explain. *(See Example 1.)*

1.

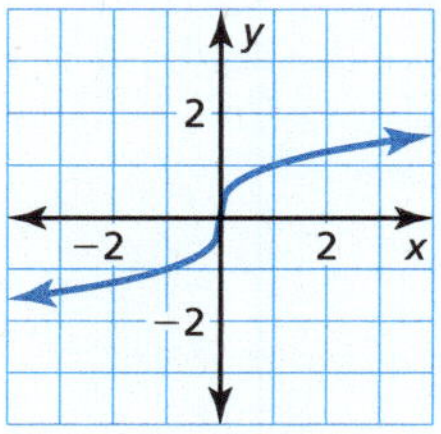

2.

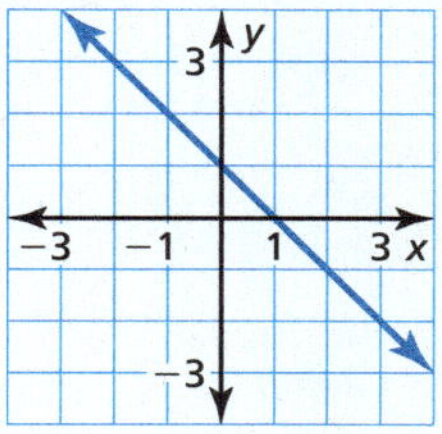

▶ 3.

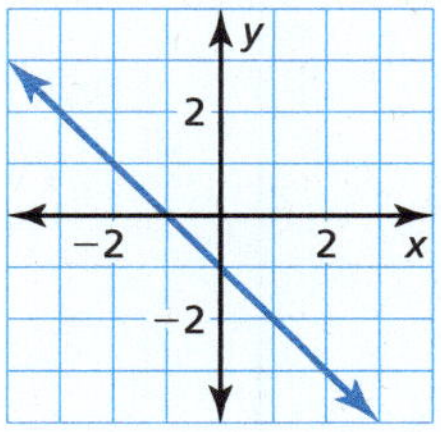

4.

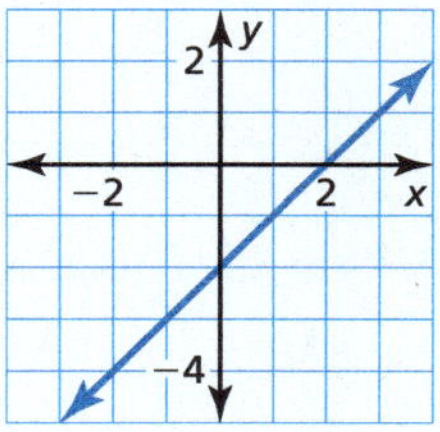

5.

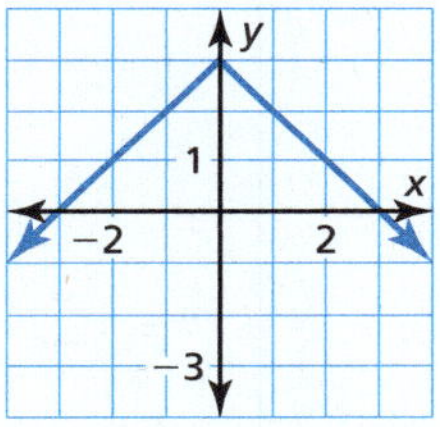

6.

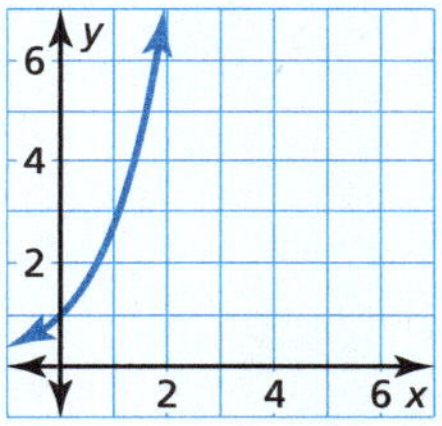

In Exercises 7–10, determine whether the table represents a *linear* or *nonlinear* function. Explain. *(See Example 2.)*

7.

x	1	2	3	4
y	5	10	15	20

8.

x	5	7	9	11
y	−9	−3	−1	3

▶ 9.

x	4	8	12	16
y	16.8	12.6	7.4	1.2

10.

x	−1	0	1	2
y	35	20	5	−10

11. REASONING Explain why a V-shaped graph does *not* represent a linear function.

12. REASONING How can you tell whether a graph shows a discrete domain or a continuous domain?

GO DIGITAL

4 MTR **ERROR ANALYSIS** **In Exercises 13 and 14, describe and correct the error in determining whether the table or graph represents a linear function.**

13. ✗

+2 +2 +2

x	2	4	6	8
y	4	16	64	256

×4 ×4 ×4

As *x* increases by 2, *y* increases by a constant factor of 4. So, the function is linear.

14. ✗

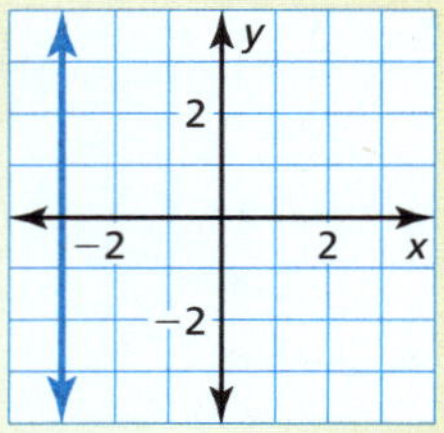

The graph is a line. So, the graph represents a linear function.

In Exercises 15–22, determine whether the equation represents a *linear* or *nonlinear* function. Explain. *(See Example 3.)*

15. $y = x^2 + 13$

16. $y = 7 - x$

▶ **17.** $y = \sqrt[3]{8} - x$

18. $y = x \cdot x \cdot x$

19. $2 + y = x + 4$

20. $7 - y = 2^x$

21. $x - y = |-54|$

22. $|x| + 12 = y$

23. **B.E.S.T. TEST PREP** Which of the following equations do *not* represent linear functions? Select all that apply.

Ⓐ $12 = -x^2 + y$

Ⓑ $y - x + 3 = 0$

Ⓒ $x = 8$

Ⓓ $-x = y$

Ⓔ $y = \left(\frac{1}{2}\right)^x + 9$

Ⓕ $y = \sqrt{x} + 3$

24. **WRITING** Compare discrete domains and continuous domains.

In Exercises 25–28, graph the linear function represented by the table. *(See Example 4.)*

25.

x	−2	−1	0	1	2
y	7	4	1	−2	−5

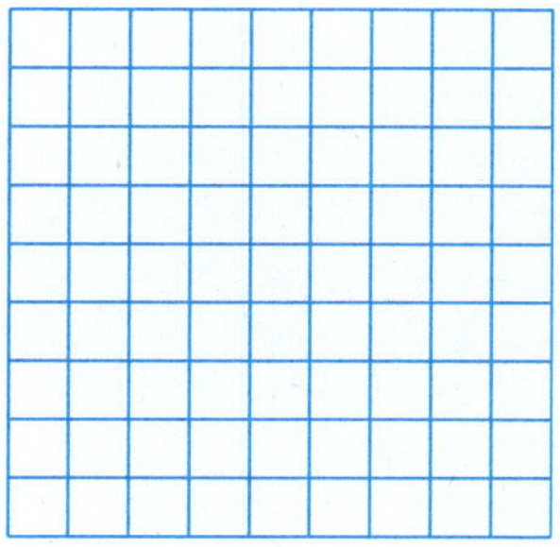

26.

x	−6	−3	0	3	6
y	−4	−3	−2	−1	0

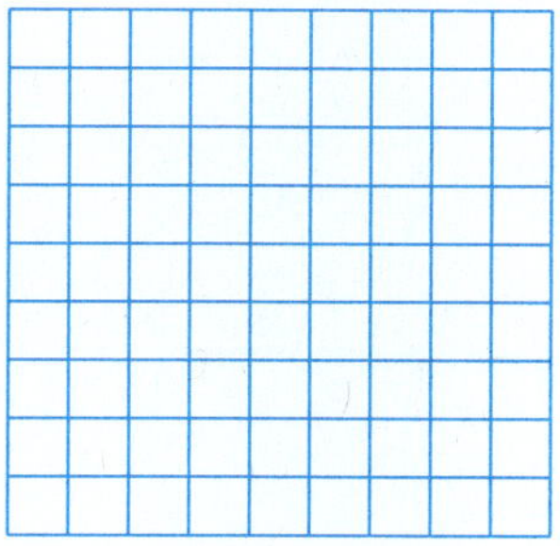

27.

x	−5	−3	3	5	8
y	−15	−11	1	5	11

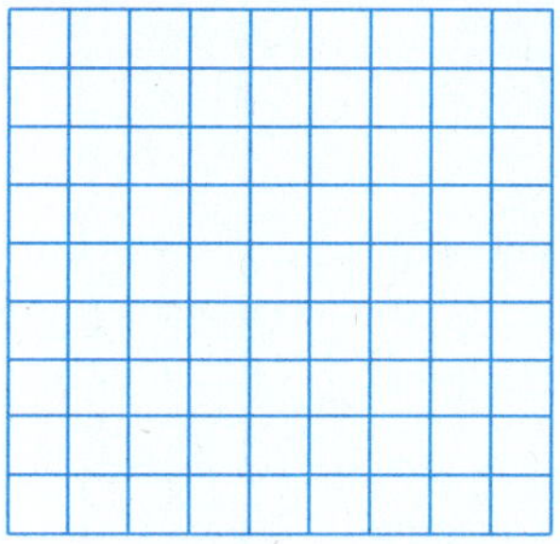

28.

x	−6.3	−3	2.1	3	7
y	9.3	6	0.9	0	−4

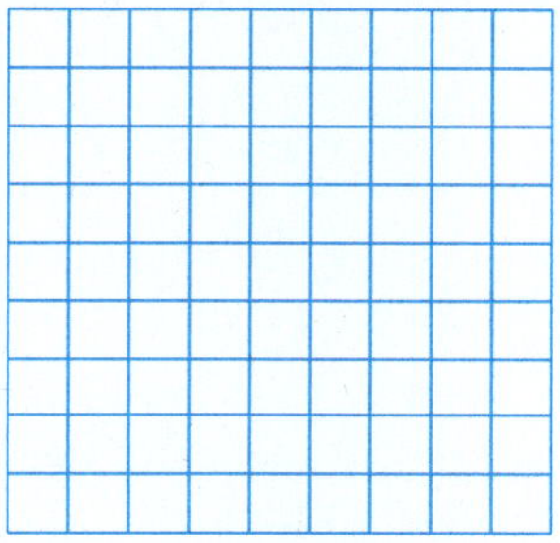

In Exercises 29 and 30, find the domain of the function represented by the graph. Determine whether the domain is *discrete* or *continuous*. Explain.

29.

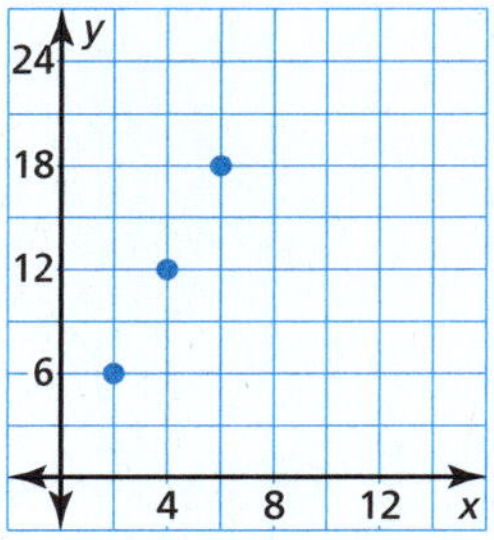

30.

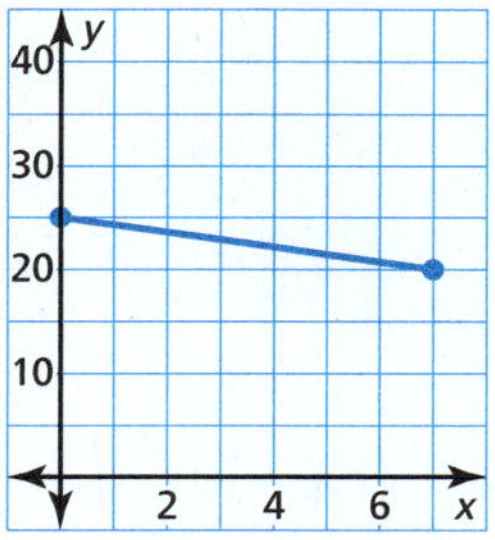

In Exercises 31 and 32, determine whether the domain is *discrete* or *continuous*. Explain.

31.

Input Time (hours), x	3	6	9
Output Distance (miles), y	150	300	450

32.

Input Relay teams, x	0	1	2
Output Athletes, y	0	4	8

33. **MODELING REAL LIFE** The linear function $m = 10 - 1.44p$ represents the amount m (in dollars) of money that you have after printing p photographs. *(See Example 5.)*

7 MTR

a. Interpret the terms and coefficient in the equation.

b. Find the domain of the function. Is the domain discrete or continuous? Explain.

c. Graph the function using its domain.

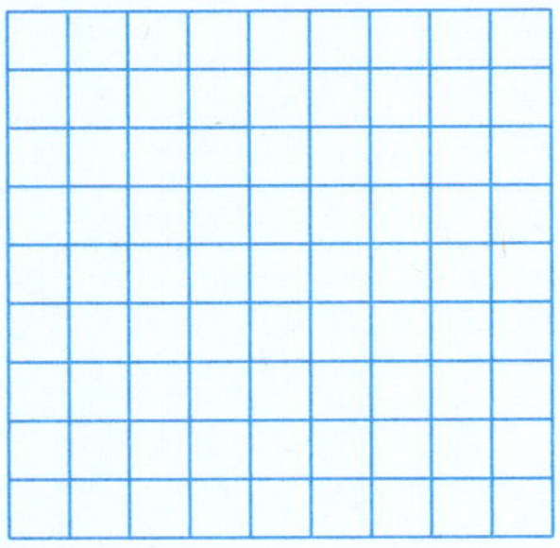

34. **MODELING REAL LIFE** The linear function $y = 145 + 30x$ represents the cost y (in dollars) of an airline ticket after adding x checked bags. At most 5 bags can be checked.

7 MTR

a. Interpret the terms and coefficient in the equation.

b. Find the domain of the function. Is the domain discrete or continuous? Explain.

c. Graph the function using its domain.

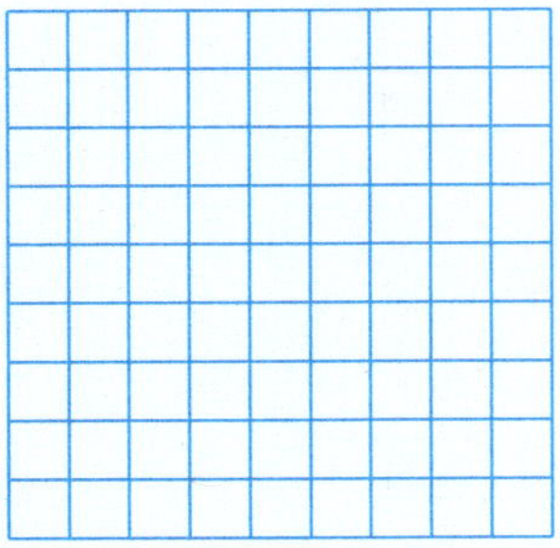

35. **MODELING REAL LIFE** You fill a swimming pool with water at a rate of 17 gallons per minute. *(See Example 6.)*

7 MTR

a. Is the amount of water in the pool a function of the number of minutes? Explain.

b. Find the domain of the function. Is the domain discrete or continuous? Explain.

c. Graph the function using its domain.

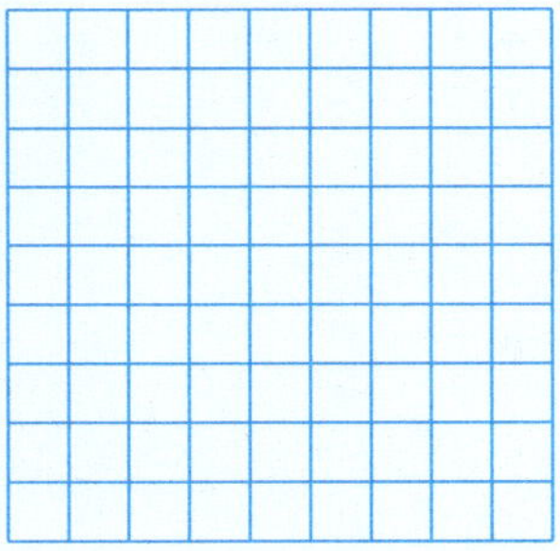

36. **MODELING REAL LIFE** The amount of air in a scuba diving tank with a capacity of 2400 liters is decreasing at a rate of 48 liters per minute.

7 MTR

a. Is the amount of air in the tank a function of the number of minutes? Explain.

b. Find the domain of the function. Is the domain discrete or continuous? Explain.

c. Graph the function using its domain.

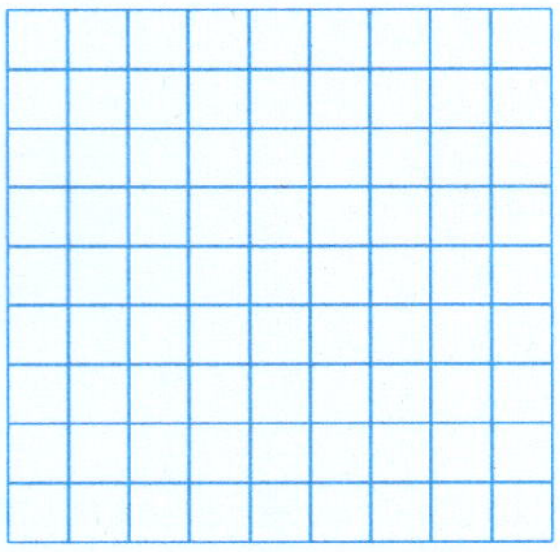

37. **STRUCTURE** Complete the table so it represents a linear function.

5 MTR

x	5	10	15	20	25
y	-1				11

38. MULTIPLE REPRESENTATIONS You are researching the speed of sound waves in dry air at 86°F. The linear function $d = 0.217t$ represents the distances d (in miles) sound waves travel in t seconds.

a. Represent the situation using a table and a graph.

b. Which of the three representations would you use to find how long it takes sound waves to travel 0.1 mile in dry air at 86°F? Explain.

39. OPEN-ENDED Identify a real-life situation where the domain is continuous. Justify your answer.

40. ASSESS REASONABLENESS You and a friend observe the Mug Race along the St. Johns River. The table shows how many sailboats you see. Graph the linear function. Your friend claims you will see 110 sailboats by hour 6. Is your friend's claim reasonable? Explain.

Time (hours), x	0	1	2	3	4
Number of boats, y	0	15	30	45	60

41. REASONING Is the function represented by the ordered pairs linear or nonlinear? Explain your reasoning.

(0, 2), (3, 14), (5, 22), (9, 38), (11, 46)

42. WRITING Describe the end behavior of an increasing linear function and a decreasing linear function.

43. STRUCTURE The table shows your earnings y (in dollars) for working x hours. You work no more than 18 hours each week.

Time (hours), x	Earnings (dollars), y
4	40.80
5	51.00
6	61.20
7	71.40

a. What is your hourly pay rate?

b. Find the domain and range of the function.

44. MAKING AN ARGUMENT The linear function $d = 50t$ represents the distance d (in miles) Car A is from a car rental store after t hours. The table shows the distances Car B is from the rental store.

Time (hours), t	Distance (miles), d
1	60
3	180
5	310
7	450
9	540

a. Does the table represent a linear or nonlinear function? Explain.

b. Which car is moving at a faster rate? Explain.

45. REASONING A water company fills two different-sized jugs. The first jug can hold x gallons of water. The second jug can hold y gallons of water. The company fills A jugs of the first size and B jugs of the second size. What does each expression represent? Does each expression represent a set of discrete or continuous values?

a. $x + y$ **b.** $A + B$ **c.** Ax **d.** $Ax + By$

46. HOW DO YOU SEE IT?
You and your friend go running. The graph shows the distances you and your friend run.

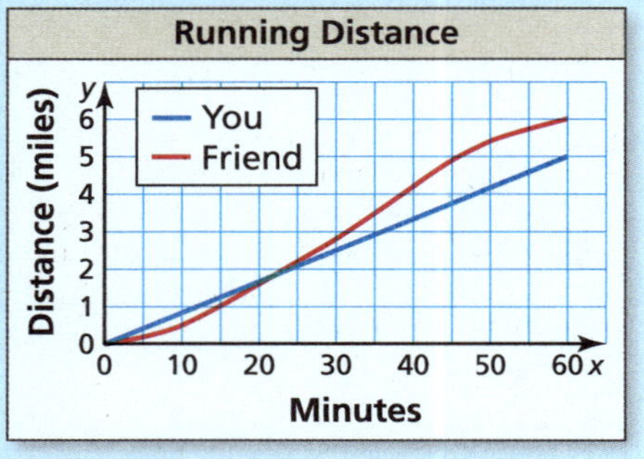

a. Describe your run and your friend's run. Who runs at a constant rate? How do you know? Why might a person not run at a constant rate?

b. Find the domain of each function. Describe the domains using the context of the problem.

7 MTR **47. PERFORMANCE TASK** You are ordering T-shirts for a school fundraiser and receive bids from three options. You are not sure exactly how many T-shirts you need, but you know it will be no more than 200 shirts. Create a proposal for the school principal. Include the number of T-shirts, which option you chose, and the cost per T-shirt.

Option 1

Charge includes an initial fee plus a cost per T-shirt. Sample pricing is shown in the table.

Number of shirts	Price (dollars)
40	200
80	340
120	480
160	620
200	760

Option 2

Cost for x T-shirts:
$c = 2x + 80$

Option 3

Cost is $5 per T-shirt.

48. THOUGHT PROVOKING
A movie complex is open from 10:00 A.M. to 2:00 A.M. daily. It contains 8 theaters, each of which has 225 seats. The number of viewers in the theaters is a function of the number of hours after 10:00 A.M. each day. Describe a reasonable domain and range of the function. Then determine whether the function must be linear. Explain.

49. REASONING Is a linear function always increasing or always decreasing? Explain.

50. DISCUSS MATHEMATICAL THINKING Explain the relationship between an equation and its graph. Why does the graph of a linear equation form a line?
4 MTR

2 MTR **51. MAKE A CONNECTION** What can you determine about the range of a linear function with a discrete domain? a continuous domain? Explain.

DIG DEEPER **In Exercises 52 and 53, describe a real-life situation for the constraints.**

52. The function has at least one negative number in the domain. The domain is continuous.

53. The function gives at least one negative number as an output. The domain is discrete.

REVIEW & REFRESH

In Exercises 54–57, solve the equation. Check your solution.

54. $h + 6 = -7$

55. $15 = 24 - 3y$

56. $9g - 12 = 6g$

57. $-18 = -2|w + 3|$

In Exercises 58–61, multiply or divide.

58. $\frac{3}{2} \cdot \frac{4}{7}$

59. $2\frac{5}{8} \cdot 3\frac{1}{3}$

60. $\frac{7}{8} \div \frac{1}{16}$

61. $\frac{8}{9} \div 4$

62. Tell whether x and y are proportional. Explain your reasoning.

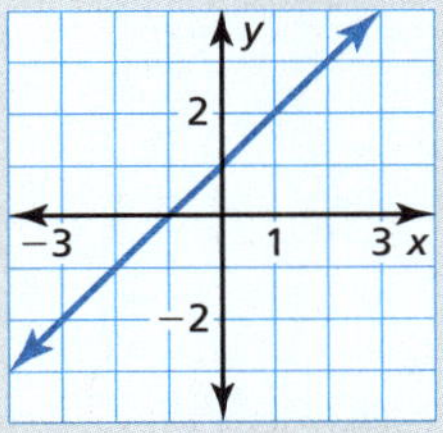

63. Write the sentence as an inequality. Then graph the inequality.

The sum of a number and 12 is at least 35.

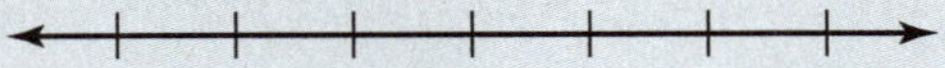

In Exercises 64 and 65, determine whether the relation is a function.

64. $(-5, 6), (0, 3), (2, 10), (4, -3), (-5, -2)$

65. $(-3, 4), (-1, -1), (1, 6), (2, 2), (4, -1)$

66. Is the domain discrete or continuous? Explain.

Input **Number of stories, *x***	1	2	3
Output **Height of building (feet), *y***	12	24	36

67. **OPEN-ENDED** Write an inequality that can be solved using the Division Property of Inequality where the inequality symbol needs to be reversed.

68. **MODELING REAL LIFE** An event center charges \$59.95 for each concert ticket.

a. Does this situation represent a function? If so, identify the independent and dependent variables.

b. There are 9350 seats in the arena. Find the domain and range. Is the domain discrete or continuous? Explain.

69. Approximate when the function is positive, negative, increasing, or decreasing. Then describe the end behavior of the function.

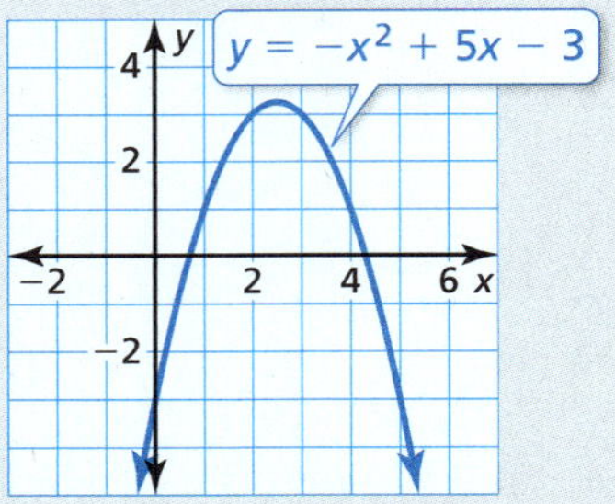

In Exercises 70–73, solve the inequality. Graph the solution.

70. $-4 < -2x + 9 \leq 32$

71. $-1 \leq q - 6$ *or* $\frac{1}{8}q < -\frac{3}{4}$

72. $|8y + 3| > -1$

73. $4|3 - 2z| - 9 \leq 3$

74. Does the graph represent a *linear* or *nonlinear* function? Explain.

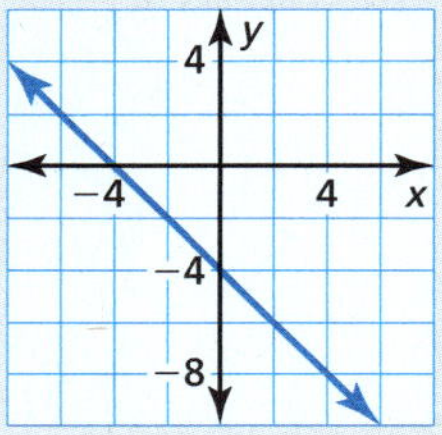

In Exercises 75 and 76, write the number in scientific notation.

75. 107,000,000

76. 0.000002

3.4 Function Notation

Learning Target: Understand and use function notation.

Success Criteria:
- I can evaluate functions using function notation.
- I can interpret statements that use function notation.
- I can graph functions represented using function notation.

Algebraic Reasoning
MA.912.AR.2.4 Given a table, equation, or written description of a linear function, graph that function, and determine and interpret its key features.
Functions
MA.912.F.1.5 Compare key features of linear functions each represented algebraically, graphically, in tables or written descriptions.
Also MA.912.AR.2.5, MA.912.F.1.2

EXPLORE IT! Using Function Notation

4 MTR COMMUNICATE CLEARLY
In part (b), for a function $y = f(x)$, explain the meaning of f, x, and $f(x)$.

Work with a partner. Consider the functions f and g represented by the graph.

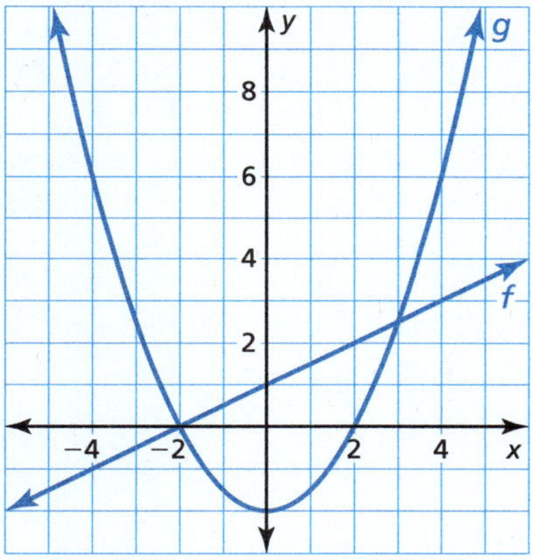

a. Find a point on g and explain how you found the point.

b. Find a point on f and explain what $f(x) = y$ means.

c. Find the points on the appropriate graph(s) at which

- $f(0) = 1$.
- $g(-2) = 0$ and $g(2) = 0$.
- $f(3) = g(3)$.
- $g(x) < f(x)$.

d. Why is it helpful to use f and g to describe the functions instead of using y?

e. Use function notation and inequalities to complete each definition.

- A function h is positive when ____________________ and negative when ____________________.
- A function h is increasing on an interval when, for any two numbers x_1 and x_2 in the interval, $x_1 < x_2$ implies ____________________.
- A function h is decreasing on an interval when, for any two numbers x_1 and x_2 in the interval, $x_1 < x_2$ implies ____________________.

GO DIGITAL

Using Function Notation to Evaluate and Interpret

Vocabulary AZ VOCAB

function notation, *p. 214*

You learned that a linear function can be written in the form $y = mx + b$. By naming a linear function f, you can also write the function using **function notation**.

$f(x) = mx + b$ Function notation

READING

The notation $f(x)$ is read as "the value of f at x" or "f of x." It does not mean "f times x."

The notation $f(x)$ is another name for y. If f is a function, and x is in its domain, then $f(x)$ represents the output of f corresponding to the input x. You can use letters other than f to name a function, such as g or h.

EXAMPLE 1 Evaluating a Function

WATCH

Evaluate $f(x) = -4x + 7$ when $x = 2$ and $x = -2$.

SOLUTION

$f(x) = -4x + 7$	Write the function.	$f(x) = -4x + 7$
$f(2) = -4(2) + 7$	Substitute for x.	$f(-2) = -4(-2) + 7$
$= -8 + 7$	Multiply.	$= 8 + 7$
$= -1$	Add.	$= 15$

▶ When $x = 2$, $f(x) = -1$, and when $x = -2$, $f(x) = 15$.

EXAMPLE 2 Interpreting Function Notation

WATCH

Let $f(t)$ be the outside temperature (in degrees Fahrenheit) t hours after 6 A.M. Explain the meaning of each statement.

a. $f(0) = 58$ **b.** $f(6) = n$ **c.** $f(3.5) < f(9)$

SOLUTION

READING

The *initial value* of f is the value of the function when $x = 0$.

a. The initial value of the function is 58. So, the temperature at 6 A.M. is 58°F.

b. The output of f when $t = 6$ is n. So, the temperature at noon (6 hours after 6 A.M.) is n°F.

c. The output of f when $t = 3.5$ is less than the output of f when $t = 9$. So, the temperature at 9:30 A.M. (3 hours and 30 minutes after 6 A.M.) is less than the temperature at 3 P.M. (9 hours after 6 A.M.).

SELF-ASSESSMENT

1 I don't understand yet. 2 I can do it with help. 3 I can do it on my own. 4 I can teach someone else.

Evaluate the function when $x = -4$, 0, and $\frac{1}{2}$.

1. $f(x) = 2x + 1$ **2.** $g(x) = -x - 1$ **3.** $n(x) = \frac{1}{2} - \frac{5}{6}x$

GO DIGITAL

SELF-ASSESSMENT 1 I don't understand yet. 2 I can do it with help. 3 I can do it on my own. 4 I can teach someone else.

4. You cook a turkey in an oven for 3 hours and 45 minutes. Let $f(t)$ be the temperature (in degrees Fahrenheit) of the turkey t hours after being placed in the oven. Explain the meaning of each statement.

a. $f(0) = 67$

b. $f(3.75) = 165$

c. $f(3) = f(4)$

d. $f(3.75) > f(4)$

Using Function Notation to Solve and Graph

EXAMPLE 3 Solving for the Independent Variable

WATCH

For $h(x) = \frac{2}{3}x - 5$, find the value of x for which $h(x) = -7$.

SOLUTION

$h(x) = \frac{2}{3}x - 5$	Write the function.
$-7 = \frac{2}{3}x - 5$	Substitute -7 for $h(x)$.
$-2 = \frac{2}{3}x$	Add 5 to each side.
$-3 = x$	Multiply each side by $\frac{3}{2}$.

▶ When $x = -3$, $h(x) = -7$.

GO DIGITAL

EXAMPLE 4 Graphing a Linear Function in Function Notation

WATCH

Graph $f(x) = 2x + 5$.

SOLUTION

Step 1 Make an input-output table to find ordered pairs.

x	-2	-1	0	1	2
$f(x)$	1	3	5	7	9

STUDY TIP

The graph of $y = f(x)$ consists of the points $(x, f(x))$.

Step 2 Plot the ordered pairs.

Step 3 Draw a line through the points.

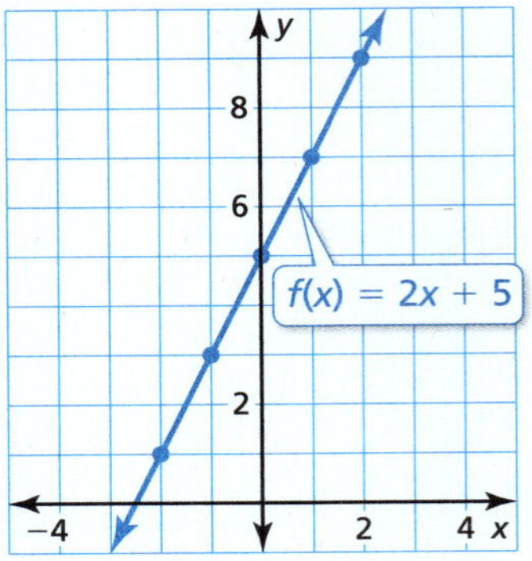

SELF-ASSESSMENT

1 I don't understand yet. 2 I can do it with help. 3 I can do it on my own. 4 I can teach someone else.

Find the value of x so that the function has the given value.

5. $f(x) = 6x + 9$; $f(x) = 21$

6. $g(x) = -\frac{1}{2}x + 3$; $g(x) = -1$

Graph the linear function.

7. $f(x) = 3x - 2$

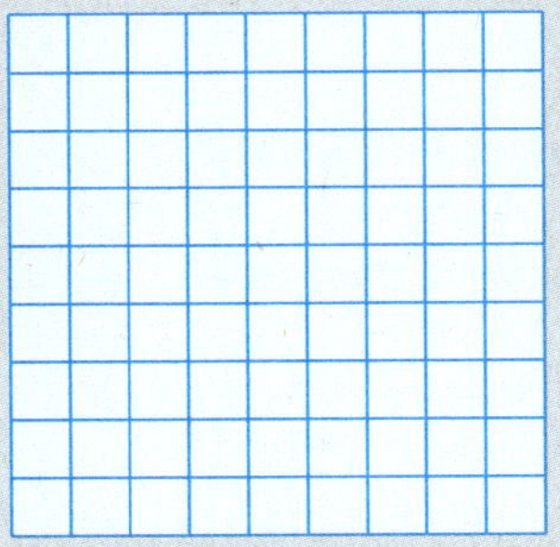

8. $g(x) = 4 - x$

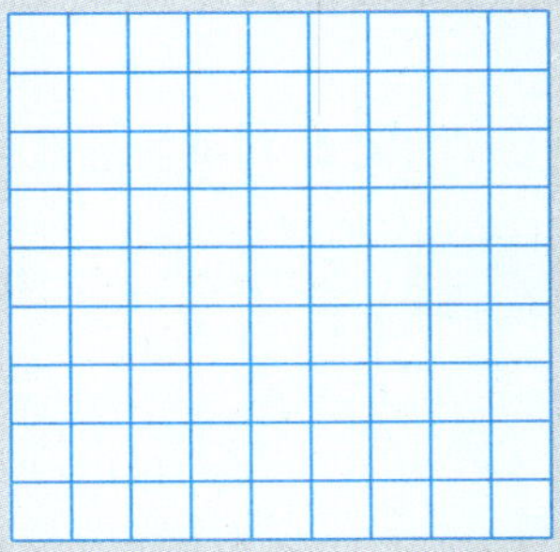

9. $h(x) = -\frac{3}{4}x - 1$

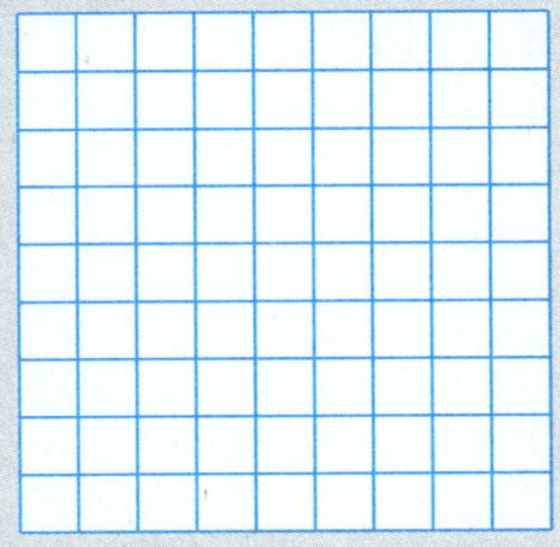

10. REASONING Let g be a function.

a. Given that $13 = g(-5)$, find a point that is on the graph of g.

b. Given that $-\frac{1}{2}$ is a solution of $g(x) = 4$, find a point that is on the graph of g.

Solving Real-Life Problems

7 MTR **EXAMPLE 5** **Modeling Real Life** WATCH

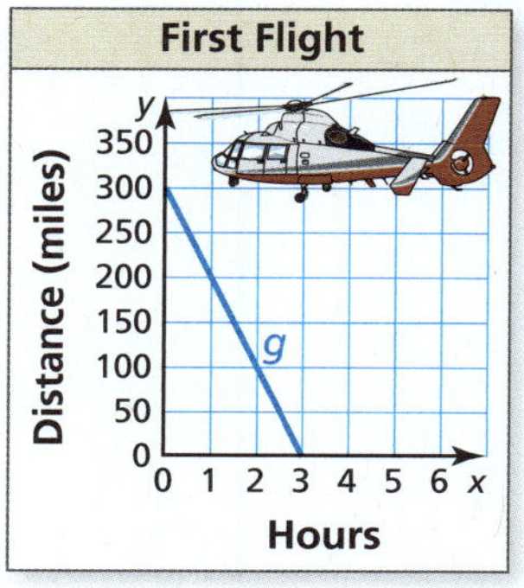

The graph of g shows how far a helicopter is from its destination after taking off. The function $f(x) = 350 - 125x$ represents a second flight, where $f(x)$ is the number of miles the helicopter is from its destination after x hours. Which flight takes less time?

SOLUTION

1. **Understand the Problem** You are given a graph of the first flight and an equation of the second flight. You are asked to determine which flight takes less time.
2. **Make a Plan** Graph the function that represents the second flight. Because both flights involve the same quantities with the same units, you can compare the graphs to determine which flight takes less time. The x-values that correspond to $f(x) = 0$ and $g(x) = 0$ represent the total flight times.
3. **Solve and Check** Graph $f(x) = 350 - 125x$.

Step 1 Make an input-output table to find the ordered pairs.

x	0	1	2	3
$f(x)$	350	225	100	-25

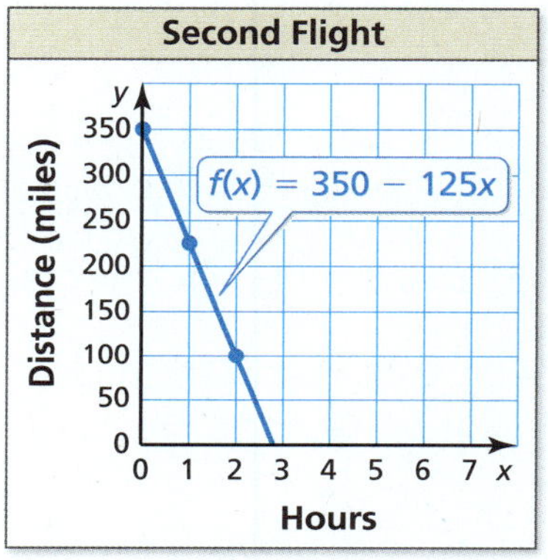

Step 2 Plot the ordered pairs. Draw a line through the points. Note that the function makes sense only when x and $f(x)$ are nonnegative. So, draw the line in the first quadrant only.

▶ From the graph of the first flight, you can see that when $g(x) = 0$, $x \approx 3$. From the graph of the second flight, you can see that when $f(x) = 0$, $x < 3$. So, the second flight takes less time.

Another Way For the second flight, use the equation to find the value of x for which $f(x) = 0$.

$f(x) = 350 - 125x$ — Write the function.

$0 = 350 - 125x$ — Substitute 0 for $f(x)$.

$-350 = -125x$ — Subtract 350 from each side.

$2.8 = x$ — Divide each side by -125.

Because $2.8 < 3$, the second flight takes less time.

2 MTR **MAKE A CONNECTION**

What happens to $f(x)$ as x increases from 2 to 3? What does this tell you about the time it takes the helicopter to reach its destination?

GO DIGITAL

SELF-ASSESSMENT 1 I don't understand yet. 2 I can do it with help. 3 I can do it on my own. 4 I can teach someone else.

11. WHAT IF? Let $f(x) = 250 - 75x$ represent the second flight in Example 5, where $f(x)$ is the number of miles the helicopter is from its destination after x hours. Which flight takes less time? Explain.

12. You stand at zero on a number line and flip a coin. When the coin is heads, you move one unit to the right. When the coin is tails, you move one unit to the left. After each flip, you record your position on the number line. Let g represent your position after the nth flip.

a. Explain why g is a function.

b. What does $g(5) = 3$ represent?

c. What is the probability that $g(3) = 0$? Explain your reasoning.

3.4 Practice WITH CalcChat® AND CalcView®

In Exercises 1–8, evaluate the function when $x = -2, 0,$ and 5. *(See Example 1.)*

1. $f(x) = x + 6$

2. $g(x) = 3x$

3. $h(x) = -2x + 9$

4. $r(x) = -x - 7$

▶5. $p(x) = -3 + \frac{1}{4}x$

6. $b(x) = 18 - 0.5x$

7. $v(x) = 12 - 2x - 5.8$

8. $n(x) = -1 - \frac{1}{3}x + 1\frac{2}{3}$

▶9. **INTERPRETING FUNCTION NOTATION** Let $c(t)$ be the number of customers in a restaurant t hours after 8 A.M. Explain the meaning of each statement. *(See Example 2.)*

a. $c(0) = 0$

b. $c(3) = c(8)$

c. $c(n) = 29$

d. $c(13.5) < c(12)$

10. **INTERPRETING FUNCTION NOTATION** Let $H(x)$ be the percent of U.S. households with Internet use x years after 1980. Explain the meaning of each statement.

a. $H(27) = 61.7$

b. $H(4) = k$

c. $H(37) > H(30)$

d. $H(17) + H(21) \approx H(29)$

In Exercises 11–16, find the value of x so that the function has the given value. *(See Example 3.)*

11. $h(x) = -7x;\ h(x) = 63$

12. $t(x) = 3x;\ t(x) = 24$

▶13. $m(x) = 4x + 15;\ m(x) = 7$

14. $k(x) = 6x - 12;\ k(x) = 15$

15. $q(x) = 0.5x - 3;\ q(x) = -4$

16. $j(x) = -\frac{4}{5}x + 7;\ j(x) = -5$

GO DIGITAL

In Exercises 17 and 18, find the value of x so that $f(x) = 7$.

17.

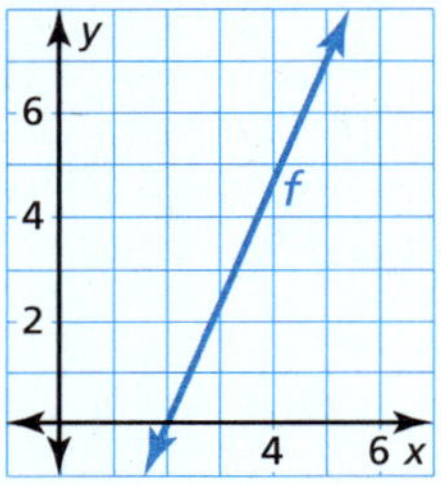

18.

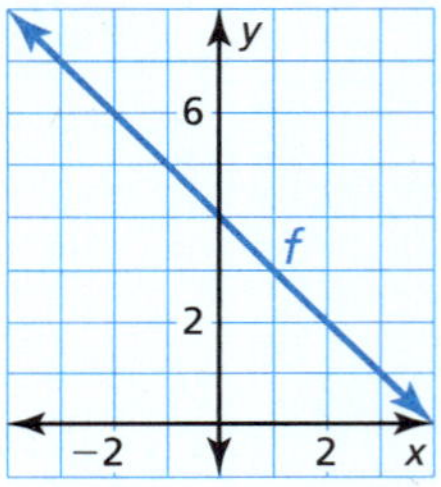

19. MODELING REAL LIFE The function $C(x) = 17.5x - 10$ represents the cost (in dollars) of buying x tickets to the orchestra with a \$10 coupon. How much does it cost to buy five tickets?

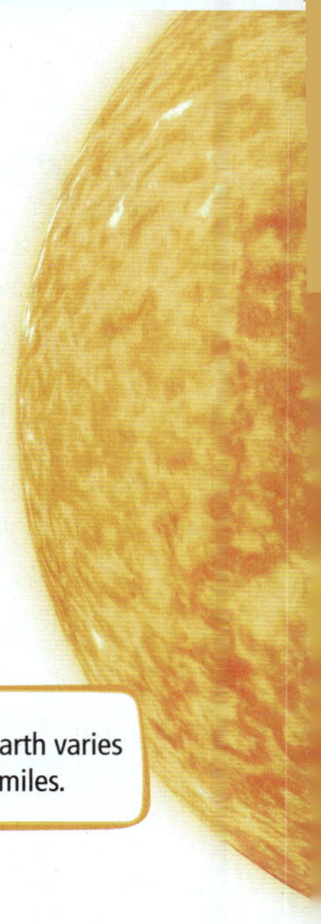

The distance from the Sun to Earth varies from 91.4 to 94.5 million miles.

20. MODELING REAL LIFE The function $d(t) = 300{,}000t$ represents the distance (in kilometers) that light travels in t seconds.

a. How far does light travel in 15 seconds?

b. How long does it take light to travel from the Sun to Earth?

In Exercises 21–28, graph the linear function. *(See Example 4.)*

21.

x	y
−2	2
0	1
2	0
4	−1

22.

x	y
−6	−1
−3	0
0	1
3	2

23. $p(x) = 4x$

24. $h(x) = -5x$

25. $d(x) = -\frac{1}{2}x - 3$

26. $w(x) = 0.6x + 2$

27. $g(x) = -4 + 7x$

28. $f(x) = 3 - 6x$

29. PROBLEM SOLVING The function $C(x) = 25x + 50$ represents the labor cost (in dollars) for Contractor A to build a deck, where x is the number of hours of labor. The table shows sample labor costs from its main competitor, Contractor B. The deck is estimated to take 8 hours of labor. Which contractor would you hire? Explain. *(See Example 5.)*

Hours	Cost
2	\$130
4	\$160
6	\$190

30. MODELING REAL LIFE The function $g(x) = 1.0 - 0.2x$ represents the percent (in decimal form) of battery power remaining on a laptop x hours after it is turned on. The function $f(x) = 0.75 - 0.125x$ represents the percent (in decimal form) of battery power remaining on a tablet x hours after it is turned on. Which device stays on longer? Explain.

31. MODELING REAL LIFE The cost of a wedding venue can be represented by the function $C(x) = 1000 + 45x$, where $C(x)$ represents the total cost of the space and x represents the number of people attending. A couple wants to spend no more than \$8900 for the venue. Graph the function in terms of the context. Then interpret the domain and range.

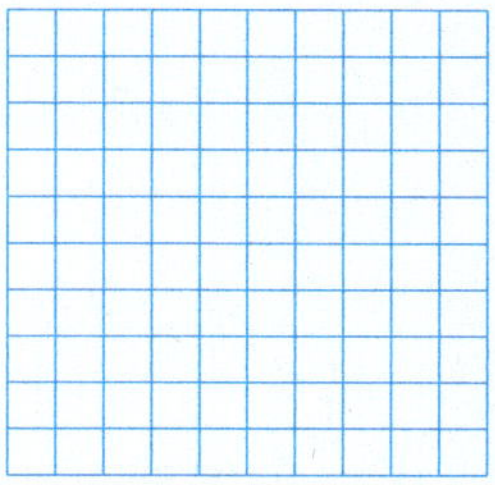

32. HOW DO YOU SEE IT? The function A represents the attendance at a high school since the beginning of a flu outbreak. The graph of the function is shown.

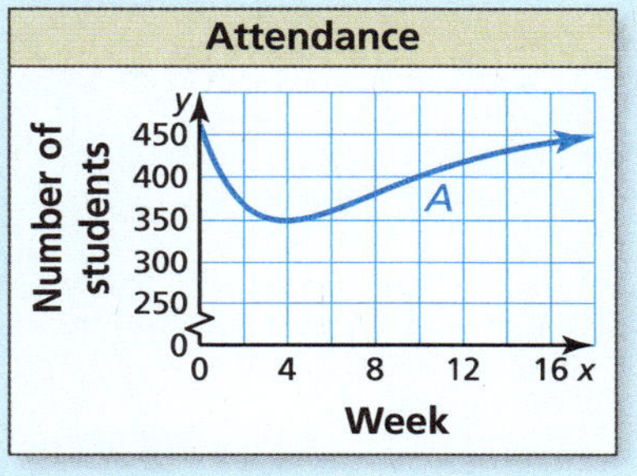

a. What happens to the school's attendance during the flu outbreak?

b. Estimate $A(13)$ and explain its meaning.

c. Use the graph to estimate the solution(s) of the equation $A(x) = 400$. Explain the meaning of the solution(s).

d. What was the least attendance? When did that occur?

e. How many students do you think are enrolled at this high school? Explain your reasoning.

33. REASONING A student's height can be represented by a function h, where the input is the student's age.

a. What does $h(14)$ represent? Can you determine the units for height? Explain.

b. What does $h(15) = 58$ represent? What can you conclude about the units for height?

34. THOUGHT PROVOKING Let $B(t)$ be your bank account balance after t days. Describe a situation in which $B(0) < B(4) < B(2)$.

35. REASONING Given a function f, tell whether the statement

$$f(a + b) = f(a) + f(b)$$

is true or false for all values of a and b. If it is false, explain why.

36. DIG DEEPER Let $f(x) = -5 - 10x$ and $g(x) = \frac{1}{5}x + 1$. Find $f(g(x))$. Simplify the expression.

REVIEW & REFRESH

37. Sketch a graph of a function with the given characteristics.

- The function is decreasing when $x < 1$ and increasing when $x > 1$.
- The function is positive when $x < -2.5$, negative when $-2.5 < x < 4.5$, and positive when $x > 4.5$.

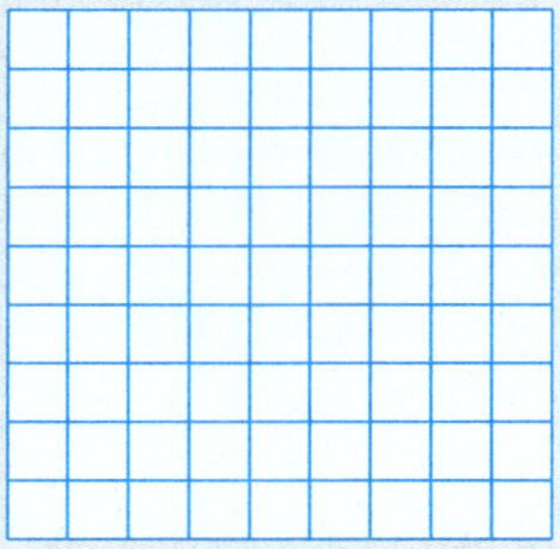

In Exercises 38 and 39, solve the inequality. Graph the solution.

38. $5a < -35$ *or* $a - 14 > 1$

39. $-16 \leq 6k + 2 < 0$

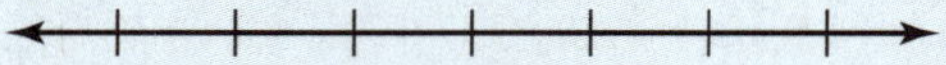

40. Determine whether the relation is a function. Explain.

Input, *x*	−1	0	1	2	3
Output, *y*	0	1	4	4	8

41. Write the sentence as an inequality.

Four times a number *n* minus 10.5 is no less than −1.5.

42. For $g(x) = 10 - 8x$, find the value of x for which $g(x) = 42$.

43. Solve the literal equation $m = 5x + 6xy$ for x.

7 MTR **44.** **MODELING REAL LIFE** You order two hamburgers and a drink. The drink costs \$1.50. You pay a total of \$5.83, including a 6% sales tax. How much does one hamburger cost?

45. Determine whether the graph represents a *linear* or *nonlinear* function. Explain.

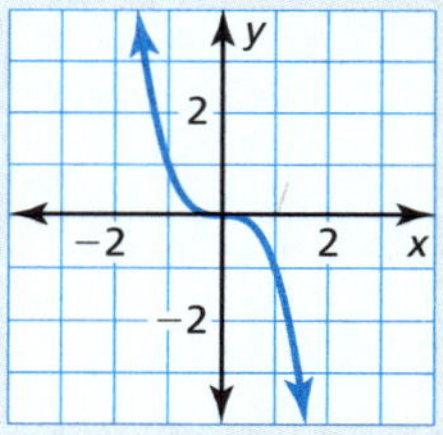

46. **NUMBER SENSE** Three times the greater of two consecutive odd integers is 15 less than two-thirds of the lesser integer. What are the integers?

47. Write $1\frac{3}{11}$ as a decimal.

48. Graph $f(x) = \frac{3}{2}x - 1$.

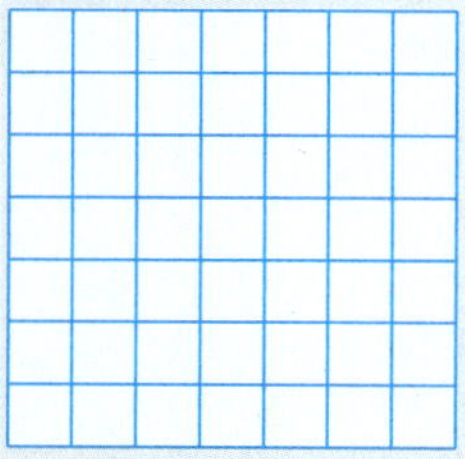

3.5 Graphing Linear Equations in Standard Form

Learning Target: Graph and interpret linear equations written in standard form.

Success Criteria:
- I can graph equations of horizontal and vertical lines.
- I can graph linear equations written in standard form using intercepts.
- I can solve real-life problems using linear equations in standard form.

Algebraic Reasoning

MA.912.AR.2.4 Given a table, equation or written description of a linear function, graph that function, and determine and interpret its key features.

MA.912.AR.2.5 Solve and graph mathematical and real-world problems that are modeled with linear functions. Interpret key features and determine constraints in terms of the context.

EXPLORE IT! Analyzing and Graphing a Linear Equation

Work with a partner. You sold a total of \$80 in tickets to a fundraiser. You lost track of how many of each type of ticket you sold. Adult tickets are \$4 each. Child tickets are \$2 each. The equation $4x + 2y = 80$ represents this situation, where x is the number of adult tickets and y is the number of child tickets.

a. If you sold a large quantity of adult tickets, does that mean you also sold a large quantity of child tickets? Explain.

b. Construct a table of values to show different combinations of tickets you might have sold. Then plot the points and describe any patterns you notice.

x					
y					

c. Graph the equation. Find the intercepts. Explain the meanings of the intercepts in the context of the problem.

GO DIGITAL

d. Use technology to check your results in parts (b) and (c). Describe the characteristics of the graph.

e. If you know how many adult tickets you sold, can you determine how many child tickets you sold? Explain your reasoning.

f. Determine whether each statement is correct. Explain your reasoning.

i. As the value of x increases, the value of $2y$ decreases.

ii. As the value of y decreases, the value of $4x$ decreases.

iii. For $x < 10$, $y > 20$.

iv. $x = 20$ makes the equation true.

2 MTR **MODEL A PROBLEM**

How many different ways did you model the problem? Describe the benefits of each representation.

Horizontal and Vertical Lines

Vocabulary (AZ VOCAB)

standard form, *p. 225*

The **standard form** of a linear equation is $Ax + By = C$, where A, B, and C are real numbers and A and B are not both zero.

Consider what happens when $A = 0$ or when $B = 0$. When $A = 0$, the equation becomes $By = C$, or $y = \frac{C}{B}$. Because $\frac{C}{B}$ is a constant, you can write $y = b$. Similarly, when $B = 0$, the equation becomes $Ax = C$, or $x = \frac{C}{A}$, and you can write $x = a$.

KEY IDEAS

Horizontal and Vertical Lines

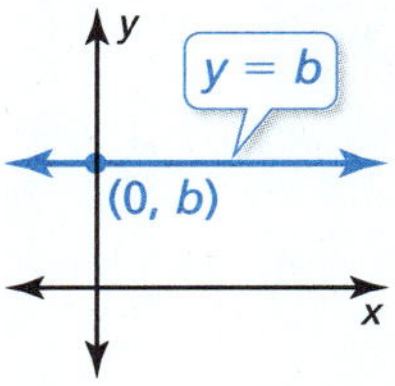

The graph of $y = b$ is a horizontal line. The line passes through the point $(0, b)$.

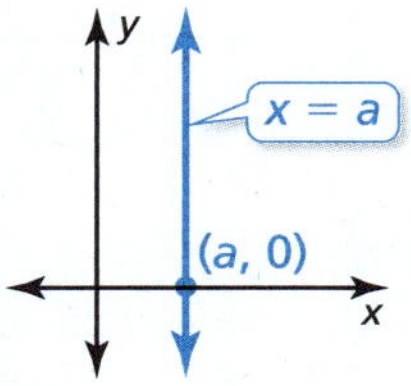

The graph of $x = a$ is a vertical line. The line passes through the point $(a, 0)$.

STUDY TIP

For a horizontal line, notice that for every value of *x*, the value of *y* is *b*.

For a vertical line, notice that for every value of *y*, the value of *x* is *a*.

EXAMPLE 1 Graphing Horizontal and Vertical Lines

WATCH

Graph each linear equation.

a. $y = 4$

b. $x = -2$

SOLUTION

a. For every value of x, the value of y is 4. The graph of the equation $y = 4$ is a horizontal line 4 units above the x-axis.

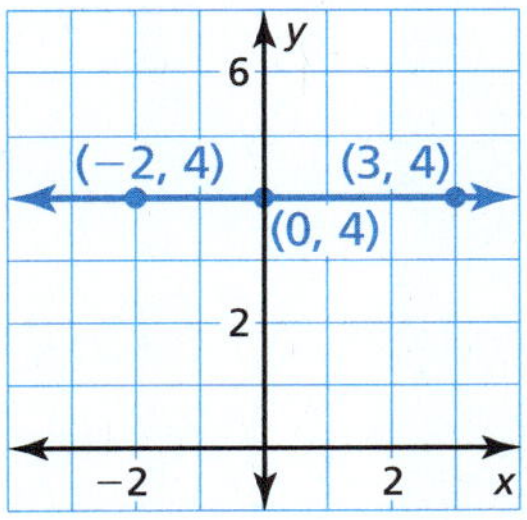

b. For every value of y, the value of x is -2. The graph of the equation $x = -2$ is a vertical line 2 units to the left of the y-axis.

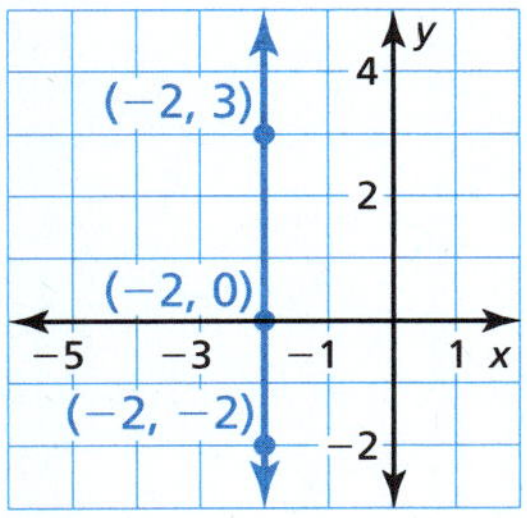

STUDY TIP

For every value of *x*, the ordered pair (*x*, 4) is a solution of *y* = 4.

GO DIGITAL

SELF-ASSESSMENT

1 I don't understand yet. 2 I can do it with help. 3 I can do it on my own. 4 I can teach someone else.

Graph the linear equation.

1. $y = -2.5$

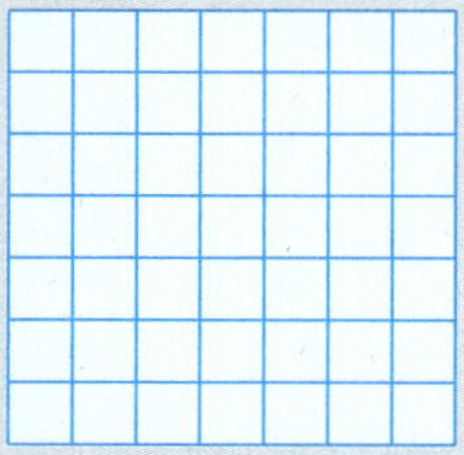

2. $x = 5$

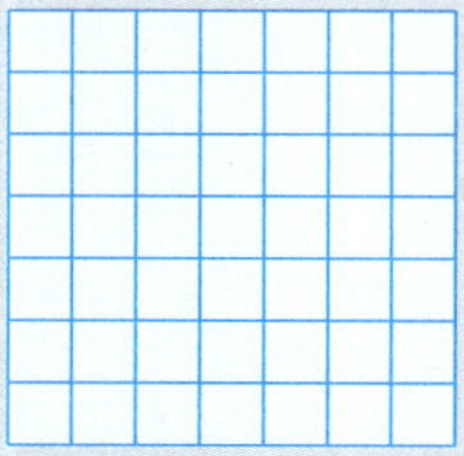

3. $x = -\frac{4}{3}$

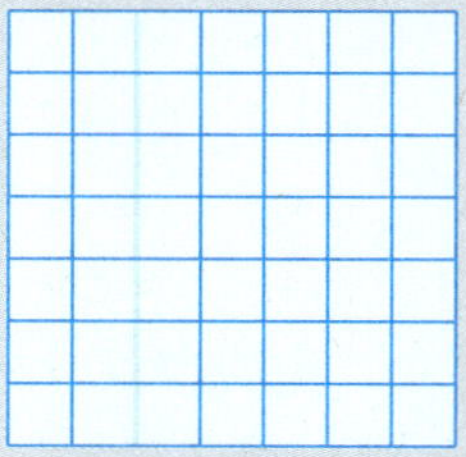

4. $y = 18$

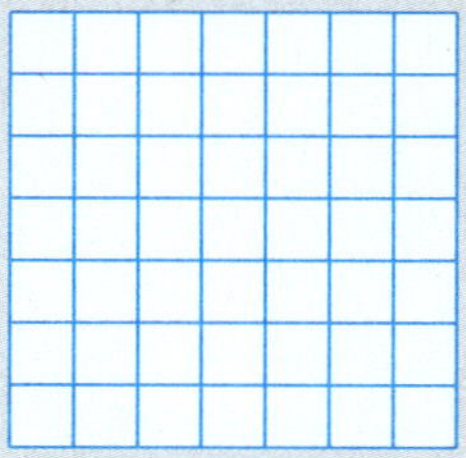

5. WRITING Describe the x- and y-intercepts of the horizontal line that passes through the origin and the vertical line that passes through the origin.

6. REASONING Graph $x = -1$ and $y = -1$. Does each graph represent a function? If so, find the domain and range.

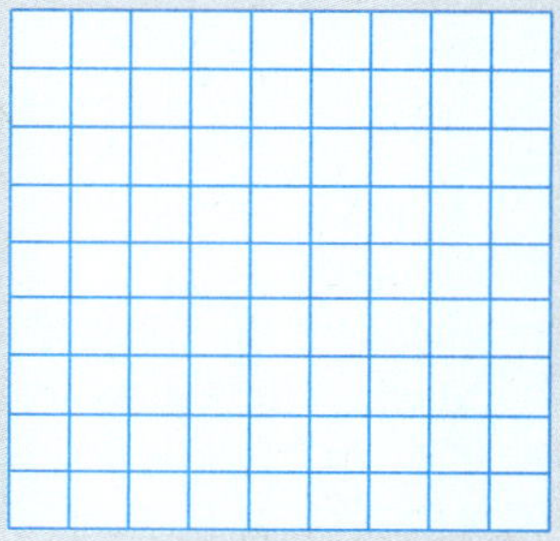

Using Intercepts to Graph Linear Equations

You can use the fact that two points determine a line to graph a linear equation. Two convenient points are the x- and y-intercepts.

KEY IDEA

Using Intercepts to Graph Equations

To graph the linear equation $Ax + By = C$ using intercepts, find the intercepts and draw the line that passes through them.

- To find the x-intercept, let $y = 0$ and solve for x.
- To find the y-intercept, let $x = 0$ and solve for y.

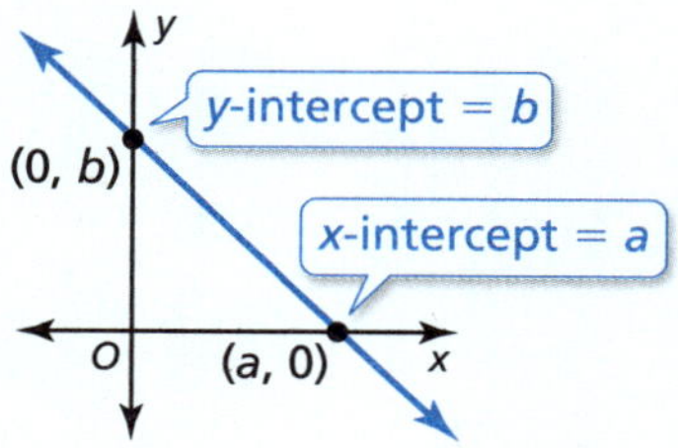

EXAMPLE 2 Using Intercepts to Graph a Linear Equation

Use intercepts to graph the equation $3x + 4y = 12$.

WATCH

SOLUTION

Step 1 Find the intercepts.

To find the x-intercept, substitute 0 for y and solve for x.

$3x + 4y = 12$ Write the original equation.

$3x + 4(0) = 12$ Substitute 0 for *y*.

$x = 4$ Solve for *x*.

To find the y-intercept, substitute 0 for x and solve for y.

$3x + 4y = 12$ Write the original equation.

$3(0) + 4y = 12$ Substitute 0 for *x*.

$y = 3$ Solve for *y*.

Step 2 Plot the points and draw the line.

The x-intercept is 4, so plot the point (4, 0).
The y-intercept is 3, so plot the point (0, 3).
Draw a line through the points.

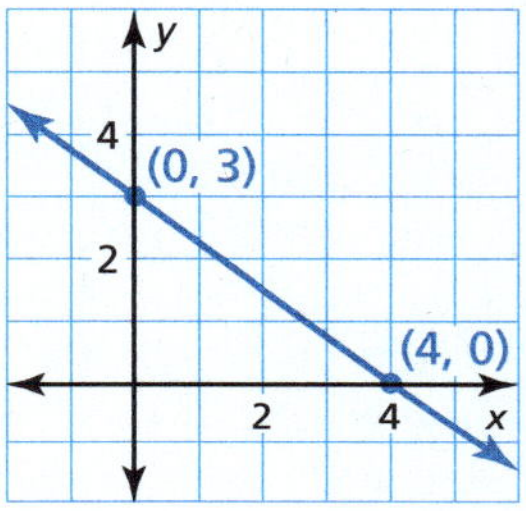

STUDY TIP

You can check your answer by finding other solutions of the equation and verifying that the corresponding points are on the graph.

SELF-ASSESSMENT

1 I don't understand yet. 2 I can do it with help. 3 I can do it on my own. 4 I can teach someone else.

4 MTR **7. DISCUSS MATHEMATICAL THINKING** What are some advantages of using the standard form of a linear equation?

Use intercepts to graph the linear equation. Label the points corresponding to the intercepts.

8. $2x - y = 4$

9. $x + 3y = -9$

10. $\frac{3}{4}x + 2y = 6$

2 MTR **11. MAKE A CONNECTION** Describe the graph of a linear equation written in the form $Ax + By = C$ when $C = 0$.

GO DIGITAL

Solving Real-Life Problems

7 MTR **EXAMPLE 3** **Modeling Real Life** WATCH

5 MTR **DECOMPOSE A PROBLEM**
What do the terms $6x$ and $10y$ represent in this situation?

You are planning an awards banquet and need to rent tables to seat 180 people. There are two table sizes available. Small tables seat 6 people, and large tables seat 10 people. The equation $6x + 10y = 180$ models this situation, where x is the number of small tables and y is the number of large tables.

a. Graph the equation. Interpret the intercepts.

b. Find three possible solutions in the context of the problem.

SOLUTION

a. Use intercepts to graph the equation. Neither x nor y can be negative, so graph the equation only in the first quadrant.

STUDY TIP
Although x and y represent discrete data, it is convenient to draw a line segment that includes points whose coordinates are not whole numbers.

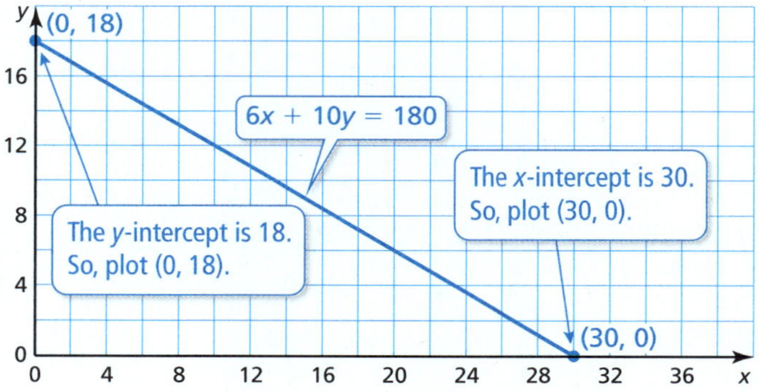

Use the graph to interpret the intercepts.

▶ The x-intercept shows that you can rent 30 small tables when you do not rent any large tables. The y-intercept shows that you can rent 18 large tables when you do not rent any small tables.

b. Only whole-number values of x and y make sense in the context of the problem. Besides the intercepts, it appears that the line passes through the point (10, 12). To verify that this point is a solution, check it in the equation.

$$6x + 10y = 180$$

$$6(10) + 10(12) \stackrel{?}{=} 180$$

$$180 = 180 \checkmark$$

▶ So, three possible combinations of tables that will seat 180 people are 0 small and 18 large, 10 small and 12 large, and 30 small and 0 large.

SELF-ASSESSMENT

1 I don't understand yet. 2 I can do it with help. 3 I can do it on my own. 4 I can teach someone else.

12. WHAT IF? You decide to rent tables from a different company. The situation can be modeled by the equation $4x + 6y = 180$, where x is the number of small tables and y is the number of large tables.

a. Interpret the terms and coefficients in the equation.

b. Graph the equation. Interpret the intercepts.

c. Find three possible solutions in the context of the problem.

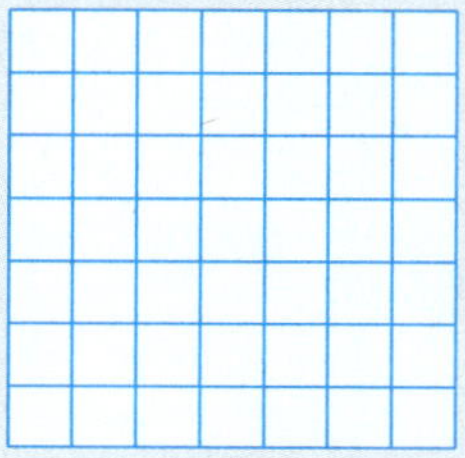

13. The number of people attending the banquet in Example 3 increases by 25%. Your friend claims that not all of the tables will be completely filled. Is your friend correct? Explain.

GO DIGITAL

3.5 Practice WITH CalcChat® AND CalcView®

In Exercises 1–4, graph the linear equation. *(See Example 1.)*

1. $x = 4$

2. $y = -3$

▶3. $y = \frac{1}{2}$

4. $x = -1.5$

In Exercises 5–8, find the x- and y-intercepts of the graph of the linear equation.

5. $2x + 3y = 12$

6. $-6x + 9y = -18$

7. $3x = 6y + 2$

8. $\frac{3}{4} + x = \frac{1}{2}y$

In Exercises 9–18, use intercepts to graph the linear equation. Label the points corresponding to the intercepts. *(See Example 2.)*

9. $5x + 3y = 30$

10. $4x + 6y = 12$

▶11. $-12x + 3y = 24$

12. $-2x + 6y = 18$

13. $-4x + 3y = -30$

14. $-2x + 7y = -21$

15. $2y - x = 7$

16. $3x + 5 = y$

17. $\frac{4}{3} + \frac{2}{3}x = \frac{1}{6}y$

18. $y = \frac{1}{4} - \frac{5}{2}x$

GO DIGITAL

2 MTR **MULTIPLE REPRESENTATIONS** **In Exercises 19–22, match the equation with its graph.**

19. $5x + 3y = 30$

20. $5x + 3y = -30$

21. $5x - 3y = 30$

22. $5x - 3y = -30$

A.

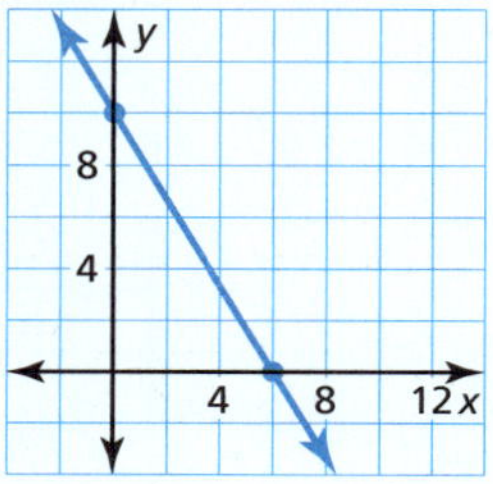

B.

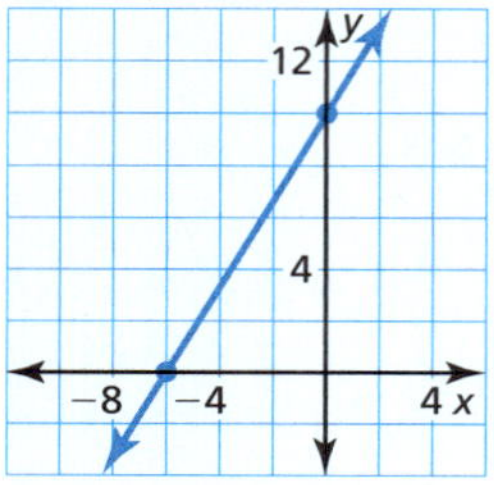

C.

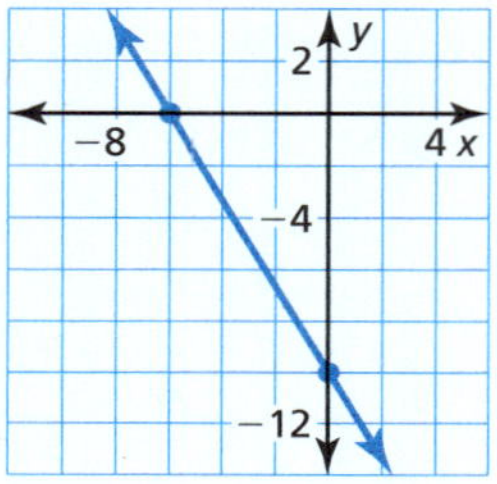

D.

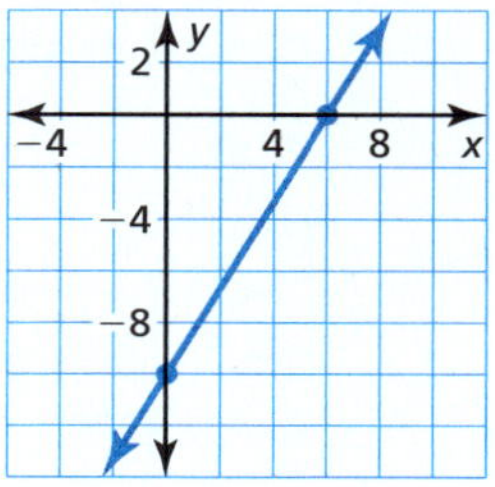

23. **MODELING REAL LIFE** You have a budget of $300 to order shirts for a math club. The equation $10x + 12y = 300$ models the total cost, where x is the number of short-sleeved shirts and y is the number of long-sleeved shirts. *(See Example 3.)* **7 MTR**

a. Interpret the terms and coefficients in the equation.

b. Graph the equation. Interpret the intercepts.

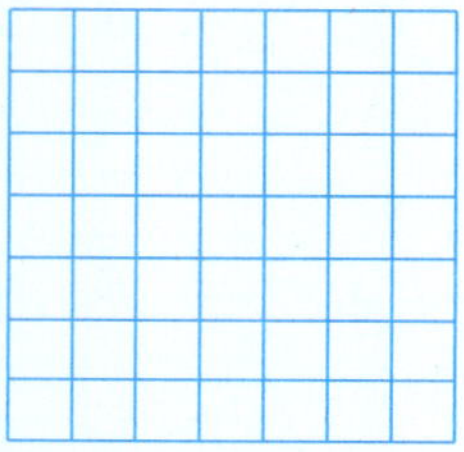

c. Find three possible solutions in the context of the problem.

7 MTR **24.** **MODELING REAL LIFE** Your goal is to bike and jog a total of 150 miles this month. You want to bike no more than 120 miles this month. The equation $12.5x + 6y = 150$ models this situation, where x is the number of hours you bike and y is the number of hours you jog.

a. Interpret the terms and coefficients in the equation.

b. Graph the equation. Interpret the intercept(s).

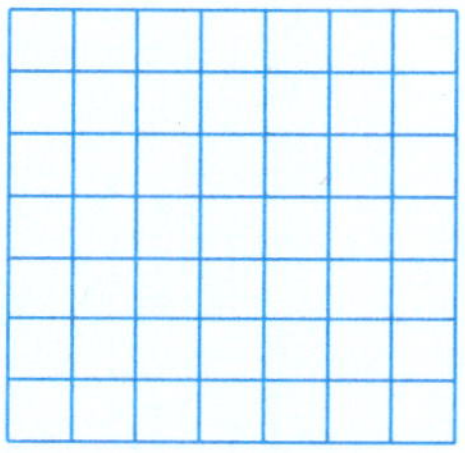

c. You bike for 9 hours this month. How many hours must you jog to reach your goal? How many miles do you bike? jog?

25. **ERROR ANALYSIS** Describe and correct the error in using intercepts to graph the linear equation $4x + 10y = 20$. **4 MTR**

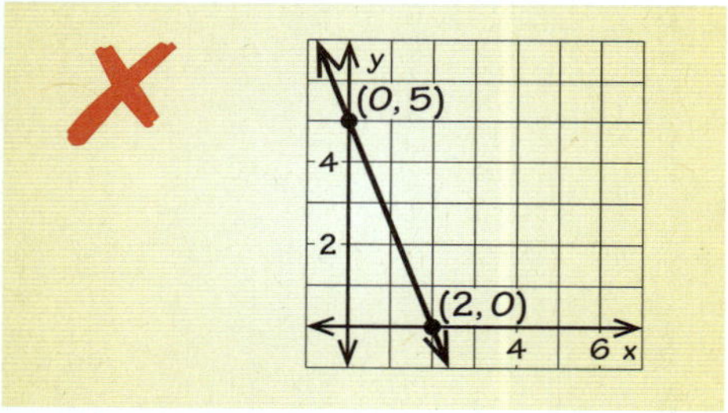

4 MTR **26.** **MAKING AN ARGUMENT** To find the x-intercept of the graph of a linear equation, can you substitute 0 for x and solve the equation? Explain.

5 MTR **CONNECTING CONCEPTS** **In Exercises 27–30, write a set of linear equations that intersect to form the enclosed shape.**

27. rectangle **28.** square **29.** right triangle **30.** trapezoid

31. REASONING Are the equations of horizontal and vertical lines written in standard form? Explain.

32. HOW DO YOU SEE IT?
An artist wants to earn a revenue of \$2700 by selling paintings for \$30 each and sculptures for \$45 each.

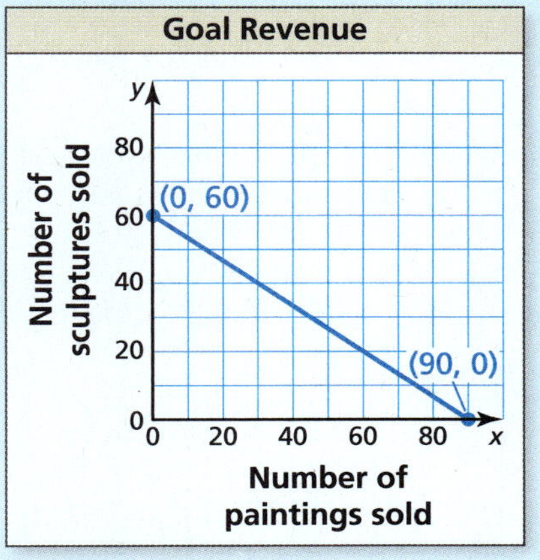

a. Interpret the intercepts of the graph.

b. Describe the domain and range in the context of the problem.

33. B.E.S.T. TEST PREP Which of the following is *not* true about the graph of $-\frac{2}{5}x + \frac{1}{10}y = -\frac{4}{5}$?

Ⓐ The x-intercept is 2 and the y-intercept is -8.

Ⓑ The function is decreasing when $x < 2$ and increasing when $x > 2$.

Ⓒ The graph passes through $(1, -4)$ and $(5, 12)$.

Ⓓ $y \rightarrow -\infty$ as $x \rightarrow -\infty$ and $y \rightarrow +\infty$ as $x \rightarrow +\infty$.

34. THOUGHT PROVOKING
The x- and y-intercepts of the graph of $ax + by = k$ are integers. Describe the possible values of k. Explain your reasoning.

35. DIG DEEPER You have \$99 to buy stamps and envelopes. A sheet of 20 stamps costs \$11. A box of 50 envelopes costs \$7.50.

a. Write an equation in standard form that models this situation. Do the intercepts of the graph make sense in this context? Explain.

b. Can you use all of the money to buy the same numbers of stamps and envelopes? Explain.

REVIEW & REFRESH

WATCH

7 MTR **36. MODELING REAL LIFE** The function $D(t) = 75 - 0.3t$ represents the number of gigabytes left after downloading a video game for t minutes.

a. How many gigabytes are left to download after 90 minutes?

b. How long will it take to download the entire video game?

37. Estimate the intercepts of the graph of the function.

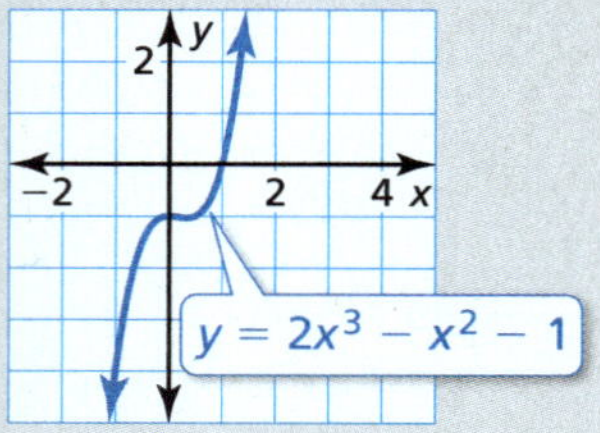

38. WRITING Explain how you can determine whether a graph represents a *linear* or a *nonlinear* function.

39. Determine whether the equation $y = x(2 - x)$ represents a *linear* or *nonlinear* function. Explain.

In Exercises 40 and 41, solve the inequality. Graph the solution.

40. $b + 5 \leq -12$

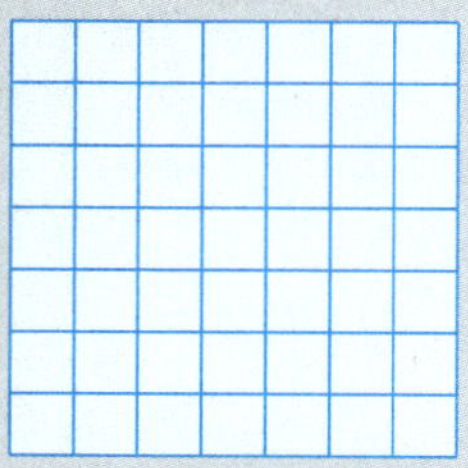

41. $-\frac{c}{3} > -15$

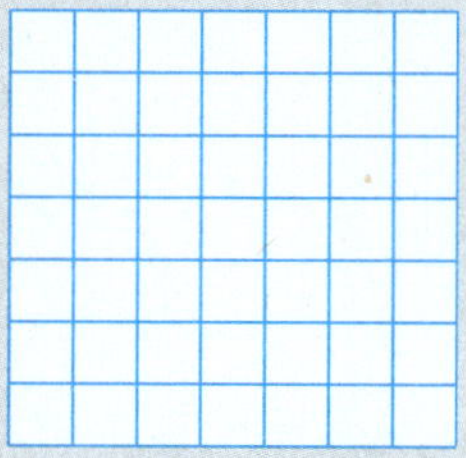

42. REASONING Complete the equation $\square x + \square y = 30$ so that the x-intercept of the graph is -10 and the y-intercept of the graph is 5.

In Exercises 43–46, solve the equation. Check your solutions.

43. $6.8 + g = 14.1$

44. $-11 = 7 - 3(h + 2)$

45. $3(4 - 8k) = -4(6k - 3)$

46. $5|6n - 9| + 4 = 29$

47. The tape diagram represents the ratio of rare cards to common cards in a collection. There are 9 rare cards. How many common cards are in the collection?

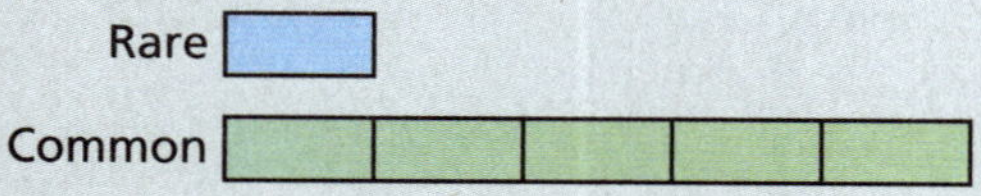

48. For $f(x) = -\frac{2}{3}x + 1$, find the value of x for which $f(x) = 9$.

49. Find the x- and y-intercepts of the graph of $-4x + 8y = -16$.

3.6 Graphing Linear Equations in Slope-Intercept Form

Learning Target: Find the slope of a line and use slope-intercept form.

Success Criteria:

- I can find the slope of a line.
- I can use the slope-intercept form of a linear equation.
- I can solve real-life problems using slopes and *y*-intercepts.

Algebraic Reasoning

MA.912.AR.2.4 Given a table, equation or written description of a linear function, graph that function, and determine and interpret its key features.

MA.912.AR.2.5 Solve and graph mathematical and real-world problems that are modeled with linear functions. Interpret key features and determine constraints in terms of the context.

Slope is the rate of change between any two points on a line. It is the measure of the *steepness* of the line.

To find the slope of a line, find the value of the ratioof the change in y (vertical change) to the change in x (horizontal change).

$$\text{slope} = \frac{\text{change in } y}{\text{change in } x}$$

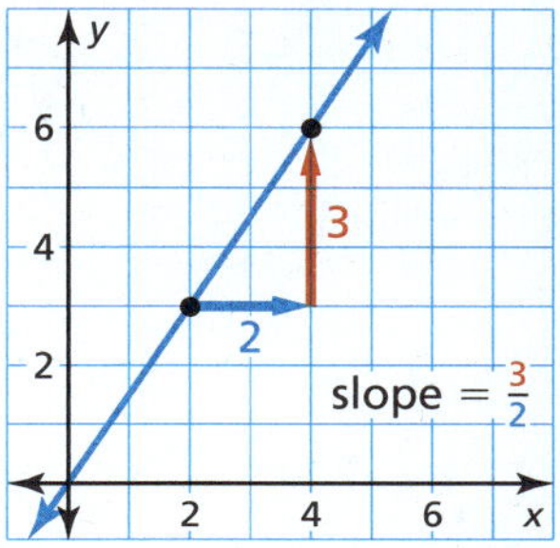

EXPLORE IT! Analyzing Linear Equations

Work with a partner.

USE STRUCTURE (5 MTR)
If you complete a similar table for a line with a negative or fractional slope or *y*-intercept, do your results change?

a. Complete the table for $y = 2x$. What do you notice about the values in Columns 2 and 4?

x	Change in x	y	Change in y
1	---	2	---
2	1	4	2
3			
4			
5			

b. Complete a similar table for each equation. Interpret your results.

i. $y = 2x + 1$

x	Change in x	y	Change in y
1	---		---
2			
3			
4			
5			

ii. $y = 4x - 3$

x	Change in x	y	Change in y
1	---		---
2			
3			
4			
5			

iii. $y = px + q$

x	Change in x	y	Change in y
1	---		---
2			
3			
4			
5			

GO DIGITAL

c. For $y = px + q$, when x increases by 1, explain why the change in y is constant and does not depend on the value of x. What does this constant represent?

d. Complete the table for each of the equations in part (a) and part (b). What do you notice?

x	Change in x	y	Change in y
1	---		---
3			
5			
7			

x	Change in x	y	Change in y
1	---		---
3			
5			
7			

x	Change in x	y	Change in y
1	---		---
3			
5			
7			

x	Change in x	y	Change in y
1	---		---
3			
5			
7			

e. For $y = px + q$, when x increases by a constant c, explain why the change in y is constant and does not depend on the valueof x. What does this constant represent?

f. What is the relationship between the graph of $y = px + q$ and the values of p and q?

The Slope of a Line

Vocabulary
- slope, *p. 235*
- rise, *p. 235*
- run, *p. 235*
- slope-intercept form, *p. 237*
- constant function, *p. 237*

READING

In the slope formula, x_1 is read as "x sub one" and y_2 is read as "y sub two." The numbers 1 and 2 in x_1 and y_2 are called *subscripts*.

KEY IDEA

Slope

The **slope** m of a nonvertical line passing through two points (x_1, y_1) and (x_2, y_2) is the value of the ratio of the **rise** (change in y) to the **run** (change in x).

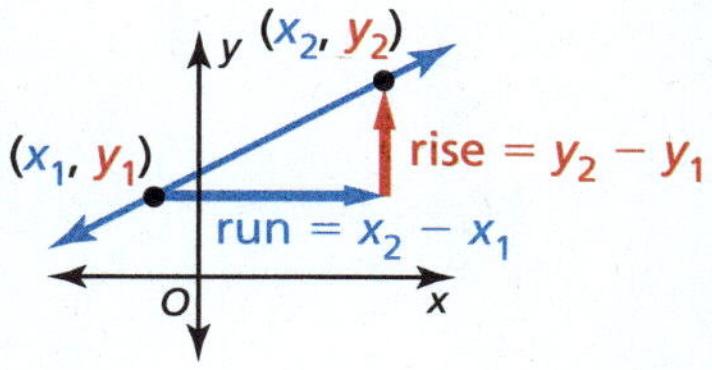

$$\text{slope} = m = \frac{\text{rise}}{\text{run}} = \frac{\text{change in } y}{\text{change in } x} = \frac{y_2 - y_1}{x_2 - x_1}$$

When the line rises from left to right, the slope is positive. When the line falls from left to right, the slope is negative.

EXAMPLE 1 Finding Slopes of Lines

Describe the slope of each line. Then find the slope.

a.

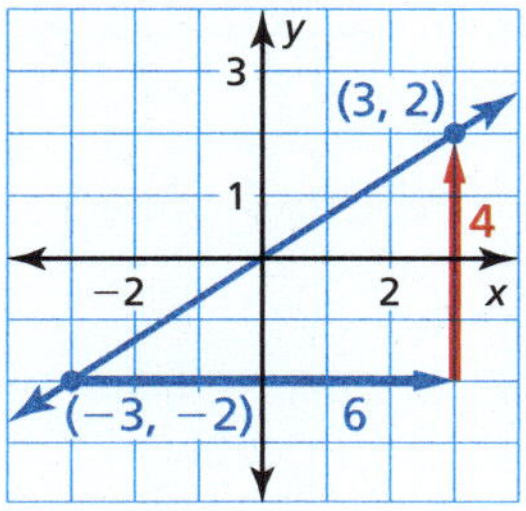

b.

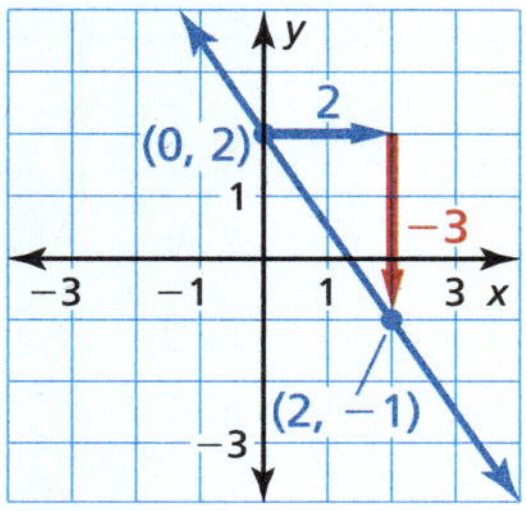

SOLUTION

a. The line rises from left to right. So, the slope is positive. Let $(x_1, y_1) = (-3, -2)$ and $(x_2, y_2) = (3, 2)$.

$$m = \frac{y_2 - y_1}{x_2 - x_1} = \frac{2 - (-2)}{3 - (-3)} = \frac{4}{6} = \frac{2}{3}$$

b. The line falls from left to right. So, the slope is negative. Let $(x_1, y_1) = (0, 2)$ and $(x_2, y_2) = (2, -1)$.

$$m = \frac{y_2 - y_1}{x_2 - x_1} = \frac{-1 - 2}{2 - 0} = \frac{-3}{2} = -\frac{3}{2}$$

SELF-ASSESSMENT

1 I don't understand yet. 2 I can do it with help. 3 I can do it on my own. 4 I can teach someone else.

Describe the slope of the line. Then find the slope.

1.

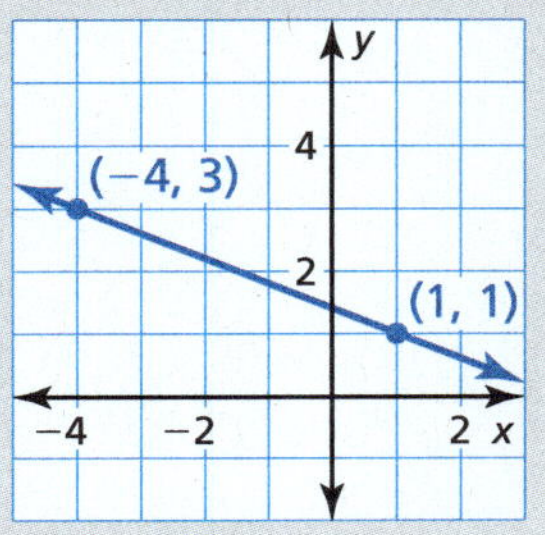

2.

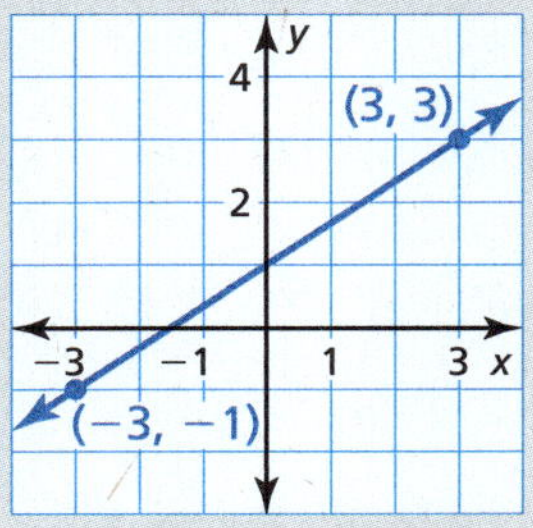

3.

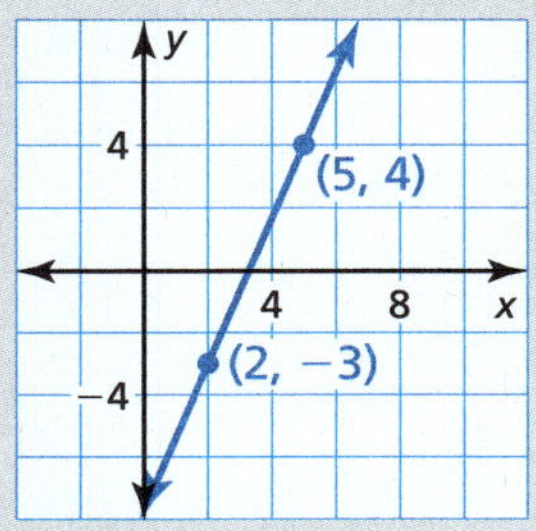

GO DIGITAL

SELF-ASSESSMENT

1 I don't understand yet. 2 I can do it with help. 3 I can do it on my own. 4 I can teach someone else.

5 MTR **4. STRUCTURE** When finding slope, can you label either point as (x_1, y_1) and (x_2, y_2)? Explain.

5. WRITING When the graph of a line is not horizontal or vertical, how can you tell whether the graph has a positive or a negative slope?

6. REASONING Line p has a slope of -4. Line q has a slope of $\frac{7}{4}$. Which line is steeper? Explain your reasoning.

EXAMPLE 2 Finding Slopes from Tables

WATCH

The points represented by each table lie on a line. How can you find the slope of each line from the table? What is the slope of each line?

a.

x	y
4	20
7	14
10	8
13	2

b.

x	y
-1	2
1	2
3	2
5	2

c.

x	y
-3	-3
-3	0
-3	6
-3	9

SOLUTION

Choose any two points from the table and use the slope formula.

a. Let $(x_1, y_1) = (4, 20)$ and $(x_2, y_2) = (7, 14)$.

$$m = \frac{y_2 - y_1}{x_2 - x_1} = \frac{14 - 20}{7 - 4} = \frac{-6}{3}, \text{ or } -2$$

▶ The slope is -2.

b. Let $(x_1, y_1) = (-1, 2)$ and $(x_2, y_2) = (5, 2)$.

$$m = \frac{y_2 - y_1}{x_2 - x_1} = \frac{2 - 2}{5 - (-1)} = \frac{0}{6}, \text{ or } 0$$

The change in y is 0.

▶ The slope is 0.

c. Let $(x_1, y_1) = (-3, 0)$ and $(x_2, y_2) = (-3, 6)$.

$$m = \frac{y_2 - y_1}{x_2 - x_1} = \frac{6 - 0}{-3 - (-3)} = \frac{6}{0} \quad ✗$$

The change in x is 0.

▶ Because division by zero is undefined, the slope of the line is undefined.

ASSESS REASONABLENESS 6 MTR

Plot the points in the table to show that your answer in part (a) is reasonable.

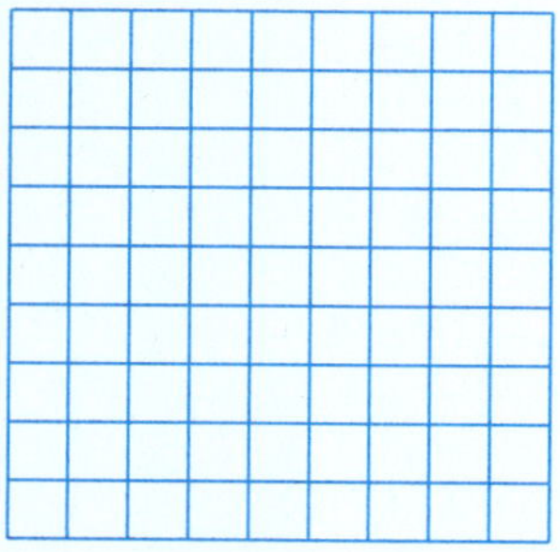

GO DIGITAL

CONCEPT SUMMARY

Slope

Positive slope

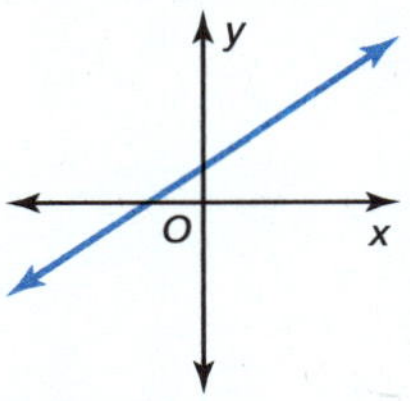

The line rises from left to right.

Negative slope

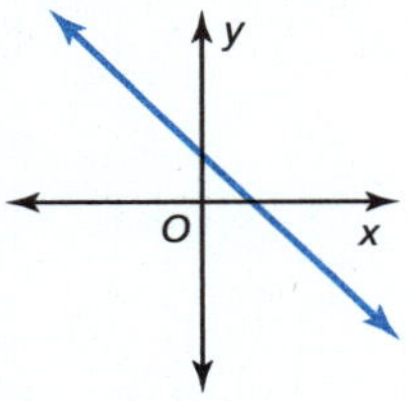

The line falls from left to right.

Slope of 0

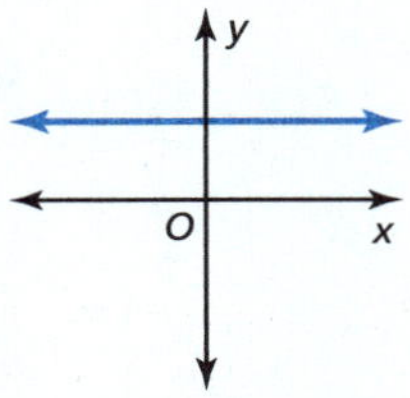

The line is horizontal.

Undefined slope

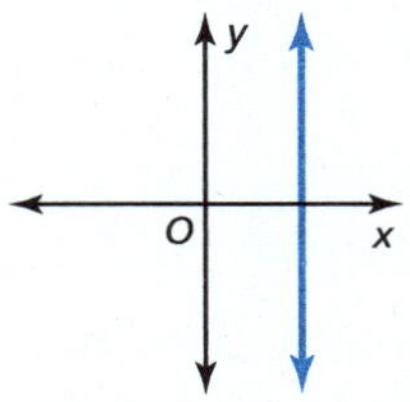

The line is vertical.

SELF-ASSESSMENT

1 I don't understand yet. 2 I can do it with help. 3 I can do it on my own. 4 I can teach someone else.

The points represented by each table lie on a line. How can you find the slope of each line from the table? What is the slope of each line?

7.

x	2	4	6	8
y	10	15	20	25

8.

x	5	5	5	5
y	-12	-9	-6	-3

Using the Slope-Intercept Form of a Linear Equation

KEY IDEA

Slope-Intercept Form

Words A linear equation written in the form $y = mx + b$ is in **slope-intercept form**. The slope of the line is m, and the y-intercept of the line is b.

Algebra $y = mx + b$

slope (m) y-intercept (b)

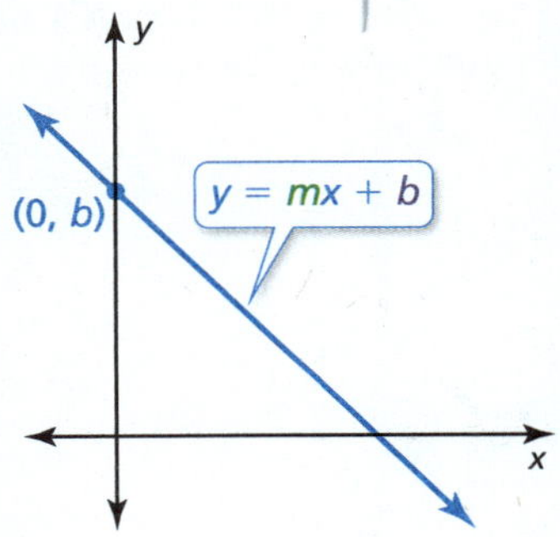

A linear equation written in the form $y = 0x + b$, or $y = b$, is a **constant function**. The graph of a constant function is a horizontal line.

EXAMPLE 3 Identifying Slopes and y-Intercepts

WATCH

Find the slope and the y-intercept of the graph of each linear equation.

a. $y = 3x - 4$ **b.** $y = 6.5$ **c.** $-5x - y = -2$

SOLUTION

a. $y = mx + b$ — Write the slope-intercept form.

slope (m) y-intercept (b)

$y = 3x + (-4)$ — Rewrite the original equation in slope-intercept form.

▶ The slope is 3, and the y-intercept is -4.

STUDY TIP

For a constant function, every input has the same output. For instance, in Example 3(b), every input has an output of 6.5.

b. The equation represents a constant function. The equation can also be written as $y = 0x + 6.5$.

▶ The slope is 0, and the y-intercept is 6.5.

STUDY TIP

When you rewrite a linear equation in slope-intercept form, you are expressing y as a function of x.

c. Rewrite the equation in slope-intercept form by solving for y.

$-5x - y = -2$ — Write the original equation.

$-y = 5x - 2$ — Add $5x$ to each side.

$y = -5x + 2$ — Divide each side by -1.

▶ The slope is -5, and the y-intercept is 2.

SELF-ASSESSMENT

1 I don't understand yet. 2 I can do it with help. 3 I can do it on my own. 4 I can teach someone else.

Find the slope and the y-intercept of the graph of the linear equation.

9. $y = -6x + 1$ **10.** $y = -\frac{1}{2}$ **11.** $x + 4y = -10$

4 MTR **12. WHICH ONE DOESN'T BELONG?** Which equation does *not* belong with the other three? Explain your reasoning.

$y = -5x - 1$ $2x - y = 8$ $y = x + 4$ $y = -3x + 13$

GO DIGITAL

EXAMPLE 4 Using Slope-Intercept Form to Graph an Equation

WATCH

STUDY TIP

You can use the slope to find points on a line in either direction. In Example 4, note that the slope can be written as $\frac{2}{-1}$. So, you can move 1 unit left and 2 units up from (0, 4) to find the point (−1, 6).

Graph $2x + y = 4$. Identify the x-intercept.

SOLUTION

Step 1 Rewrite the equation in slope-intercept form.

$$y = -2x + 4$$

Step 2 Find the slope and the y-intercept.

$$m = -2 \text{ and } b = 4$$

Step 3 The y-intercept is 4. So, plot (0, 4).

Step 4 Use the slope to find another point on the line.

$$\text{slope} = \frac{\text{rise}}{\text{run}} = \frac{-2}{1}$$

Plot the point that is 1 unit right and 2 units down from (0, 4). Draw a line through the two points.

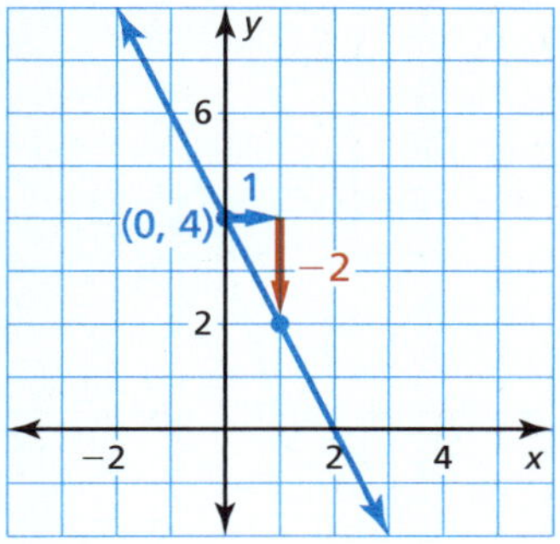

▶ The line appears to intersect the x-axis at (2, 0). So, the x-intercept is 2.

2 MTR USE ANOTHER METHOD

Show how you can find the x-intercept by substituting 0 for y in the equation.

GO DIGITAL

EXAMPLE 5 Graphing from a Verbal Description

WATCH

A linear function g models a relationship in which the dependent variable increases 3 units for every 1 unit the independent variable increases. Graph g when $g(0) = 3$. Identify the slope and the intercepts of the graph.

SOLUTION

Because the function g is linear, it has a constant rate of change. Let x represent the independent variable and y represent the dependent variable.

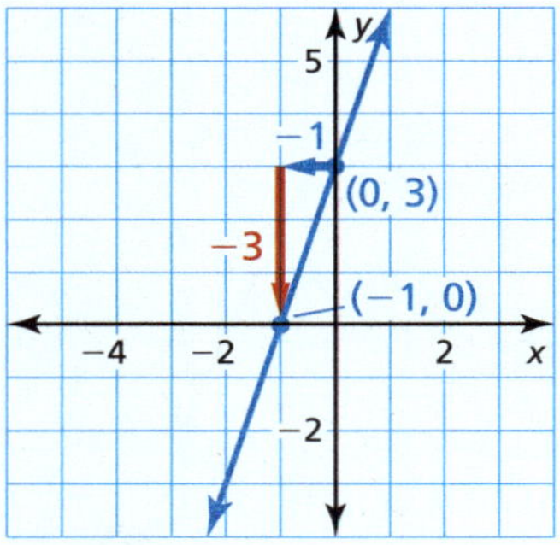

Step 1 Find the slope. When the dependent variable increases by 3, the change in y is $+3$. When the independent variable increases by 1, the change in x is $+1$. So, the slope is $\frac{3}{1}$, or 3.

Step 2 Find the y-intercept. The statement $g(0) = 3$ indicates that when $x = 0$, $y = 3$. So, the y-intercept is 3. Plot (0, 3).

Step 3 Use the slope to find another point on the line. A slope of 3 can be written as $\frac{-3}{-1}$. Plot the point that is 1 unit left and 3 units down from (0, 3). Draw a line through the two points. The line crosses the x-axis at $(-1, 0)$. So, the x-intercept is -1.

▶ The slope is 3, the y-intercept is 3, and the x-intercept is -1.

SELF-ASSESSMENT

1 I don't understand yet. 2 I can do it with help. 3 I can do it on my own. 4 I can teach someone else.

Graph the linear equation. Identify the x-intercept.

13. $y = 4x - 4$

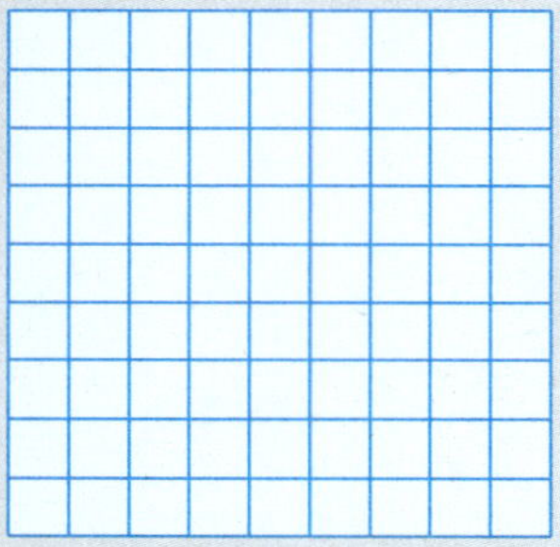

14. $3x + y = -3$

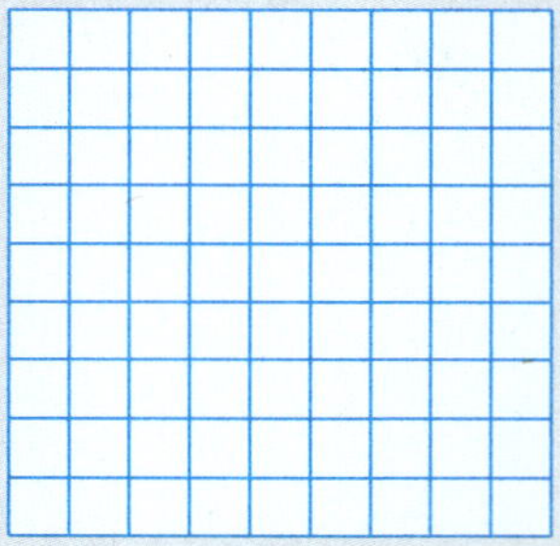

15. $x + 2y = 6$

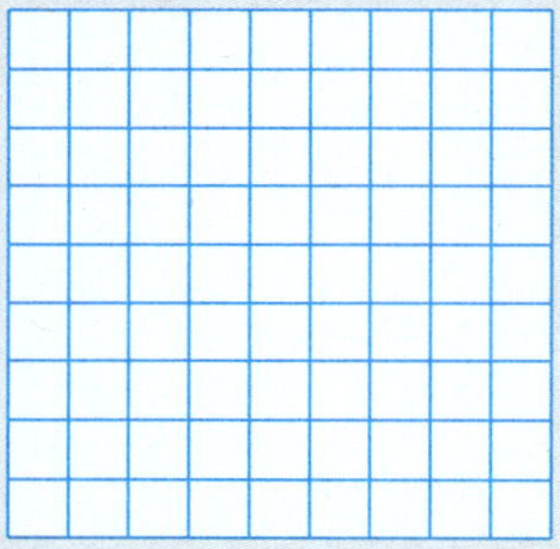

16. A linear function h models a relationship in which the dependent variable decreases 2 units for every 5 units the independent variable increases. Graph h when $h(0) = 4$. Identify the slope and the intercepts of the graph.

Solving Real-Life Problems

In most real-life problems, slope indicates a rate, such as miles per hour, dollars per hour, or people per year.

7 MTR **EXAMPLE 6** **Modeling Real Life** WATCH

The function $h(t) = -75t - 4000$ represents the elevation $h(t)$ (in feet) of a submersible t minutes after it begins to descend. The ocean floor is at a depth of 13,000 feet.

a. Find the domain and range in this context. Then graph the function.

b. Interpret the slope and the intercepts of the graph.

SOLUTION

1. **Understand the Problem** You know the function that models the elevation. You are asked to find the domain and range in this context and to graph the function. Then you are asked to interpret the slope and intercepts of the graph.

2. **Make a Plan** Use the equation to find the domain and range in this context. Then graph the function. Examine the graph to interpret the slope and the intercepts.

3. **Solve and Check**

   a. Because the ocean floor is at a depth of 13,000 feet, $h(t) \geq -13{,}000$. Find the value of t when $h(t) = -13{,}000$.

   $h(t) = -75t - 4000$ — Write the equation.

   $-13{,}000 = -75t - 4000$ — Substitute $-13{,}000$ for $h(t)$.

   $120 = t$ — Solve for t.

   The time t must be greater than or equal to 0, and the y-intercept is -4000. So, the domain is $\{t \mid 0 \leq t \leq 120\}$, and the range is $\{h(t) \mid -13{,}000 \leq h(t) \leq -4{,}000\}$. Use the slope of -75 and the y-intercept of -4000 to graph the function in this context.

Elevation of a Submersible

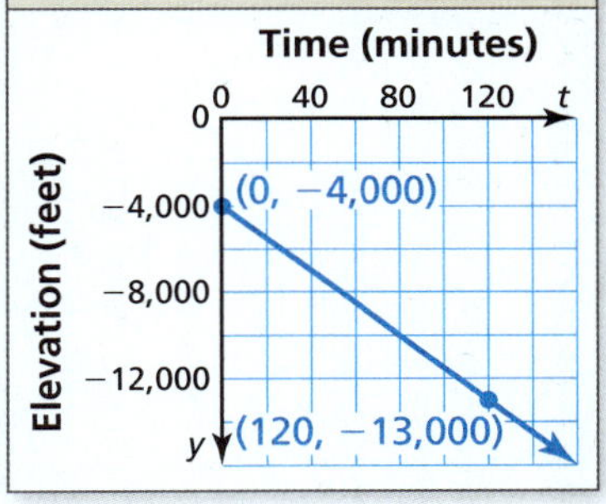

   b. The slope is -75. So, the elevation changes at a rate of -75 feet per minute. The term -4000 is the y-intercept. So, the elevation of the submersible when the descent begins is -4000 feet. There is no t-intercept in this context.

In 1975, scientists used submersibles to discover the Oculina coral reefs off Florida's east coast. The discovery led to the world's first Marine Protected Area for deepwater coral.

Look Back Show that the slope between the points $(0, -4000)$ and $(120, -13{,}000)$ is -75.

$$m = \frac{y_2 - y_1}{x_2 - x_1} = \frac{-13{,}000 - (-4000)}{120 - 0} = -75 \checkmark$$

GO DIGITAL

SELF-ASSESSMENT

1 I don't understand yet. 2 I can do it with help. 3 I can do it on my own. 4 I can teach someone else.

17. The table shows the elevation $p(t)$ (in meters) of a submersible t minutes after it begins to descend. The ocean floor is at a depth of 3810 meters.

Time (minutes), *t*	**Elevation (meters), *p*(*t*)**
0	−1800
5	−1900
10	−2000

a. Does this submersible descend faster than the submersible in Example 6? Use a graph to justify your answer.

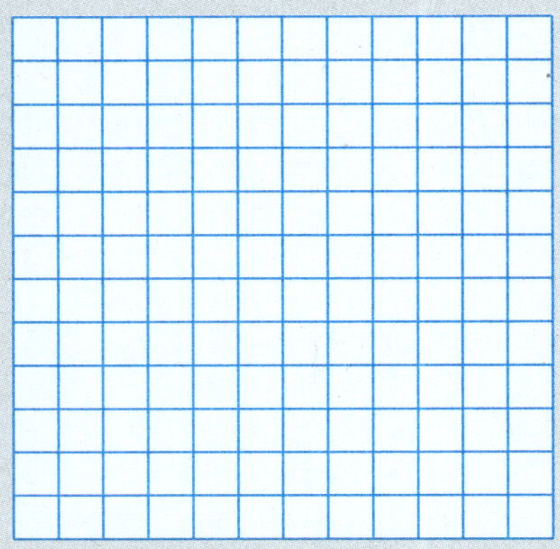

b. Both submersibles begin to descend at the same time. Which one reaches the ocean floor first? Explain.

3.6 Practice WITH CalcChat® AND CalcView®

In Exercises 1–4, describe the slope of the line. Then find the slope. *(See Example 1.)*

▶ **1.**

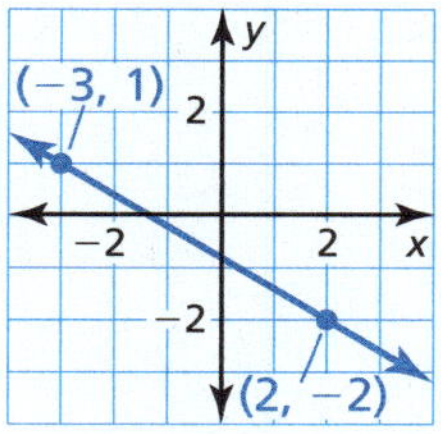

2.

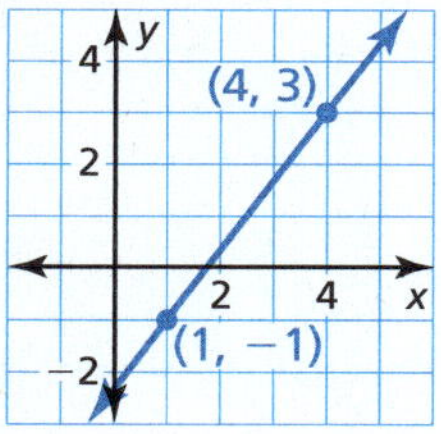

3.

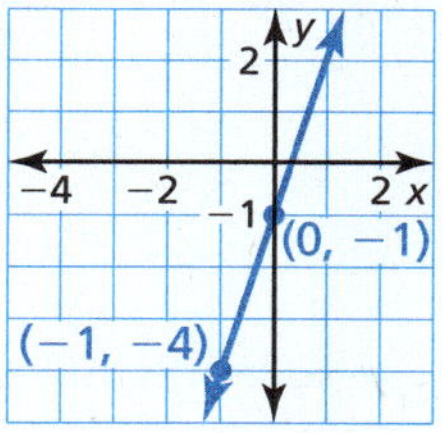

4.

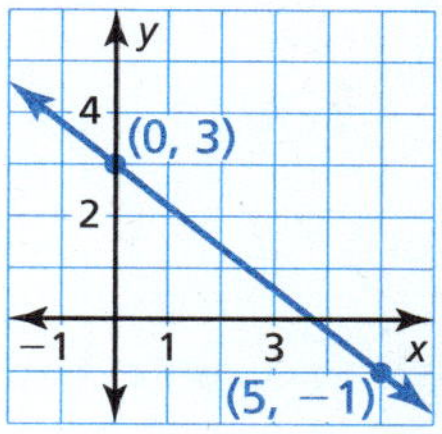

In Exercises 5 and 6, find the slope of the line that passes through the given points.

5. (1, 4), (3, −6)

6. (2, −2), (−7, −5)

In Exercises 7–10, the points represented by the table lie on a line. Find the slope of the line. *(See Example 2.)*

▶ **7.**

x	−9	−5	−1	3
y	−2	0	2	4

8.

x	−1	2	5	8
y	−6	−6	−6	−6

9.

x	0	0	0	0
y	−4	0	4	8

10.

x	−4	−3	−2	−1
y	2	−5	−12	−19

11. ANALYZING A GRAPH The graph shows the distance *y* (in miles) that a bus travels in *x* hours. Find and interpret the slope of the line.

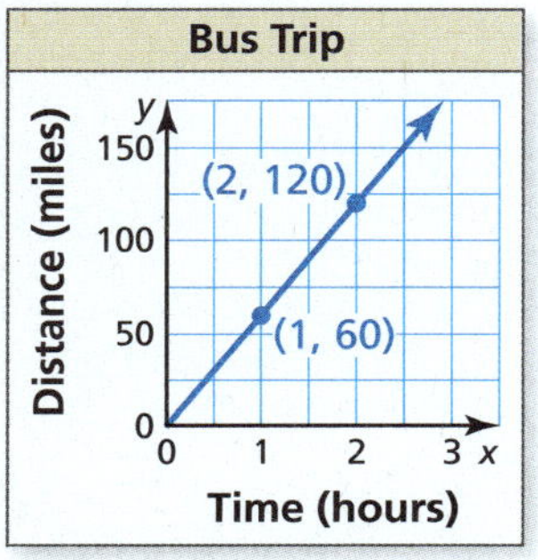

12. ANALYZING A TABLE The table shows the amount *x* (in hours) of time you spend at a theme park and the admission fee *y* (in dollars) to the park. The points represented by the table lie on a line. Find and interpret the slope of the line.

Time (hours), *x*	Admission (dollars), *y*
6	54.99
7	54.99
8	54.99

In Exercises 13–20, find the slope and the *y*-intercept of the graph of the linear equation. *(See Example 3.)*

13. $y = -3x + 2$

14. $y = 4x - 7$

15. $y = 6x$

16. $y = -1$

▶ **17.** $-0.75x + y = 4$

18. $x + y = -6\frac{1}{2}$

19. $\frac{1}{6}x = \frac{1}{3} - y$

20. $0 = 4.5 - 2y + 4.8x$

GO DIGITAL

4 MTR ERROR ANALYSIS In Exercises 21 and 22, describe and correct the error in finding the slope and the y-intercept of the graph of the equation.

21. ✗ $x = -4y$

The slope is -4, and the y-intercept is 0.

22. ✗ $y = 3x - 6$

The slope is 3, and the y-intercept is 6.

In Exercises 23–30, graph the linear equation. Identify the x-intercept. *(See Example 4.)*

23. $y = -x + 7$

24. $y = \frac{1}{2}x + 3$

25. $y = 2x$

26. $y = -x$

▶ **27.** $3x + y = -1$

28. $x + 4y = 8$

29. $-y + \frac{3}{5}x = 0$

30. $2.5x - y - 7.5 = 0$

In Exercises 31 and 32, graph the function with the given description. Identify the slope and the intercepts of the graph. *(See Example 5.)*

31. A linear function f models a relationship in which the dependent variable decreases 4 units for every 2 units the independent variable increases, and $f(0) = -2$.

32. A linear function h models a relationship in which the dependent variable increases 1 unit for every 5 units the independent variable decreases, and $h(0) = 3$.

33. **MODELING REAL LIFE** A linear function r models the growth of your right index fingernail. The length of the fingernail increases 0.7 millimeter every week. Graph r when $r(0) = 12$. Identify the slope and interpret the y-intercept of the graph.

34. **MODELING REAL LIFE** A linear function m models the amount of milk sold by a farm per month. The amount decreases 500 gallons for every \$1 increase in price. Graph m when $m(0) = 3000$. Identify the slope and interpret the intercepts of the graph.

ERROR ANALYSIS In Exercises 35 and 36, describe and correct the error in graphing the function.

35.

✗

$y + 1 = 3x$

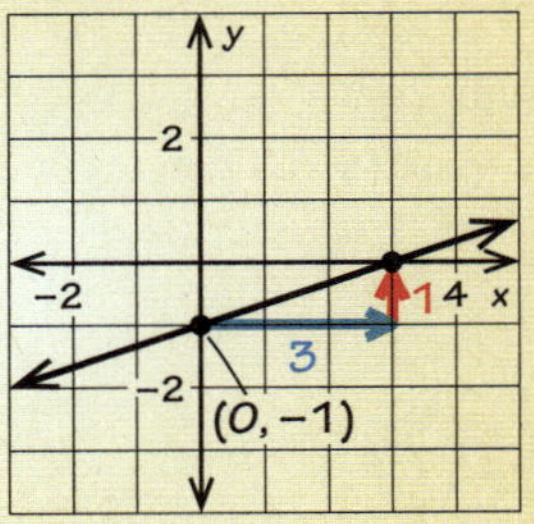

36.

✗

$-4x + y = -2$

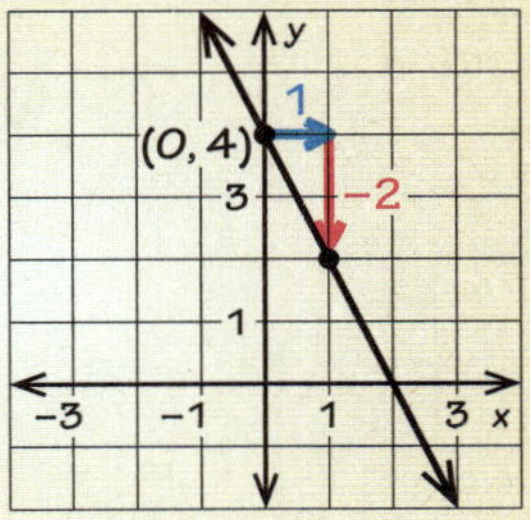

37. **MODELING REAL LIFE** The function $d(t) = \frac{1}{2}t + 2$ represents the amount (in inches) of water in a rain barrel for six rainy days, where t is the time (in days) since the rainfall began. *(See Example 6.)*

a. Find the domain and range in this context. Then graph the function.

b. Interpret the slope and intercepts of the graph.

38. MODELING REAL LIFE The function $f(x) = -200x + 1000$ represents the altitude (in feet) of a paraglider x minutes from the time the paraglider begins a descent to a landing site located 100 feet above sea level.

7 MTR

a. Find the domain and range in this context. Then graph the function.

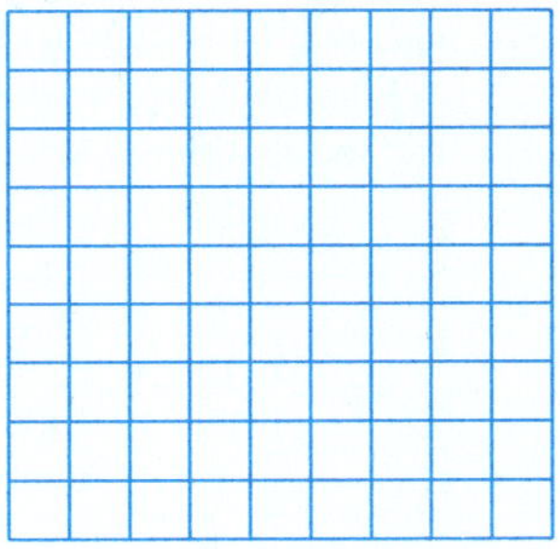

b. Interpret the slope and intercepts of the graph.

c. The function $g(x) = -150x + 900$ represents the altitude (in feet) of a second paraglider x minutes from the time the paraglider begins a descent to the same landing site. Both paragliders start their descent at the same time. Who reaches an altitude of 100 feet first? Explain.

39. CHOOSE A METHOD Describe two ways to graph the equation $4x - 6y = 18$. Which method do you prefer? Explain.

3 MTR

40. PROBLEM SOLVING A linear function represents the cost of catering an event from a Puerto Rican food truck. The table shows the cost y (in dollars) for x dishes. The function $c(x) = 9x + 600$ represents the cost (in dollars) of catering an event from a Dominican food truck, where x is the number of dishes ordered. Graph each function in terms of the context. Which truck charges a greater initial fee? Which truck can cater the greatest number of dishes for $695?

Dishes, x	Cost (dollars), y
0	500
5	550
10	600

The national dish of Puerto Rico is arroz con gandules, which features rice and pigeon peas seasoned with sofrito.

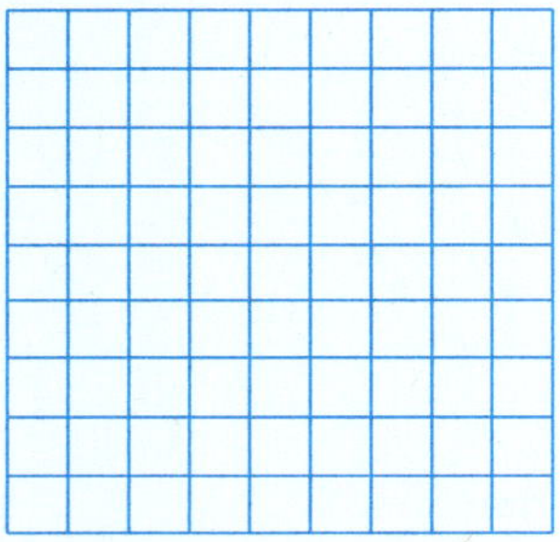

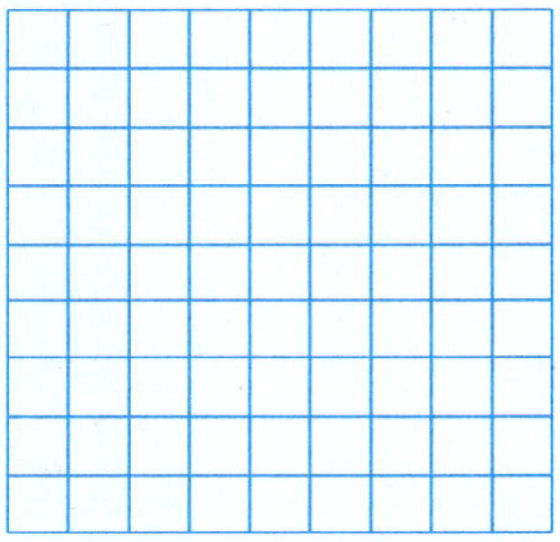

41. B.E.S.T. TEST PREP Which of the following linear functions has a slope of $-\frac{2}{3}$ and a y-intercept of 2? Select all that apply.

Ⓐ
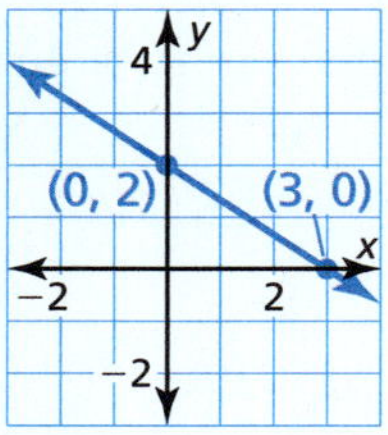

Ⓑ

x	y
−2	6
0	3
2	0
4	−3

Ⓒ $f(x)$ decreases by 3 units for every 2 units x increases, and $f(0) = 2$.

Ⓓ $-y + 2 = \frac{2}{3}x$

42. WRITING Describe the end behavior of the function $y = mx + b$ when (a) $m > 0$ and (b) $m < 0$.

5 MTR **43. CONNECTING CONCEPTS** The graph shows the relationship between the width y (in inches) and the length x (in inches) of a rectangle. The perimeter of a second rectangle is 10 inches less than the perimeter of the first rectangle.

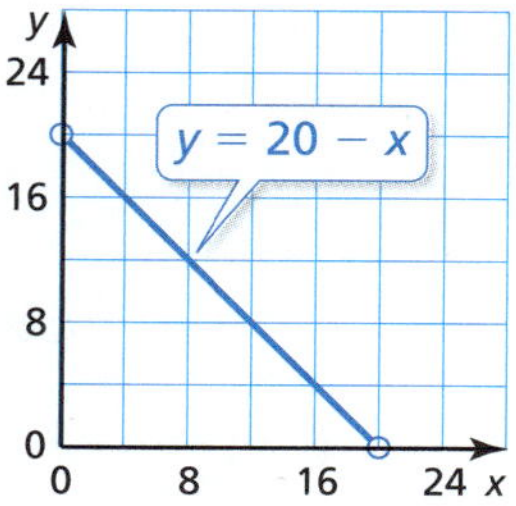

a. Graph the relationship between the width and length of the second rectangle.

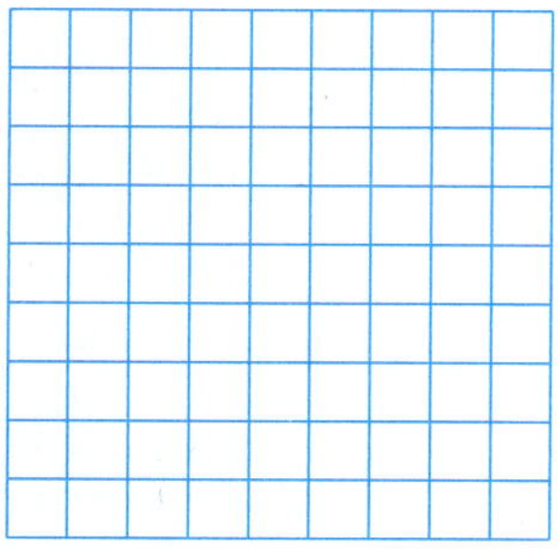

b. How does your graph in part (a) compare to the graph shown?

5 MTR **44. CONNECTING CONCEPTS** The graph shows the relationship between the base length x (in meters) and the lengths y (in meters) of the two equal sides of an isosceles triangle. The perimeter of a second isosceles triangle is 8 meters more than the perimeter of the first triangle.

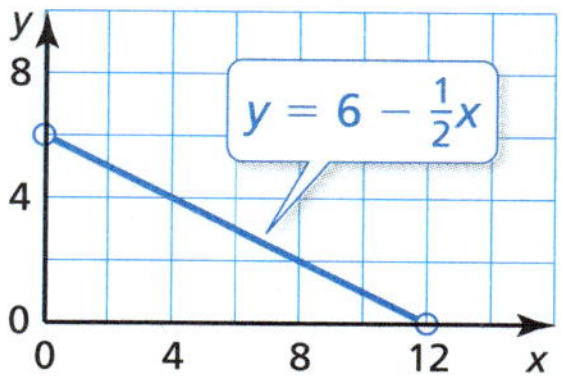

a. Graph the relationship between the base length and the side lengths of the second triangle.

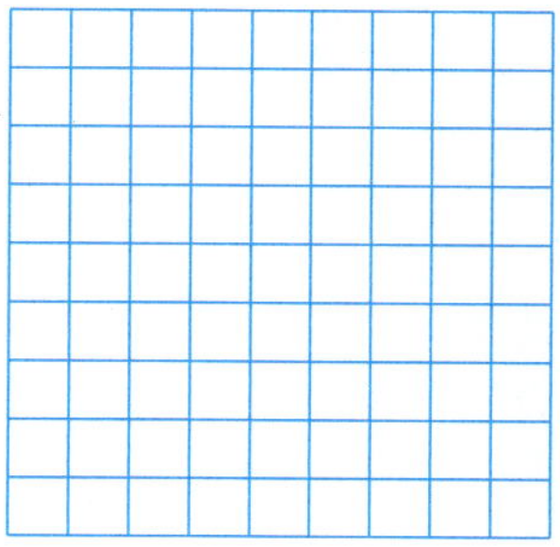

b. How does your graph in part (a) compare to the graph shown?

5 MTR **45. CONNECTING CONCEPTS** Graph the equations in the same coordinate plane. What is the area of the enclosed figure?

$3y = -9$

$2y - 14 = 4x$

$-4x + 5 - y = 0$

$y - 1 = 0$

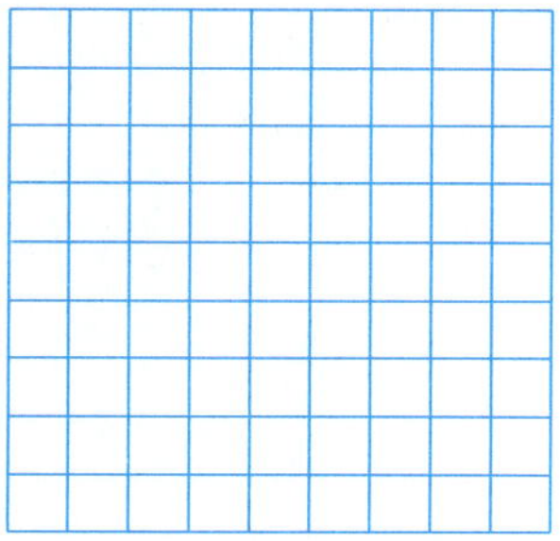

4 MTR **46. MAKING AN ARGUMENT** Your friend says that you can write the equation of any line in slope-intercept form. Is your friend correct? Explain your reasoning.

47. ANALYZING EQUATIONS Which equations could be represented by each graph? (The graphs are not drawn to scale.)

$y = -3x + 8$	$y = -x - \frac{4}{3}$
$y = -7x$	$y = 2x - 4$
$y = \frac{7}{4}x - \frac{1}{4}$	$y = \frac{1}{3}x + 5$
$y = -4x - 9$	$y = 6$

a.

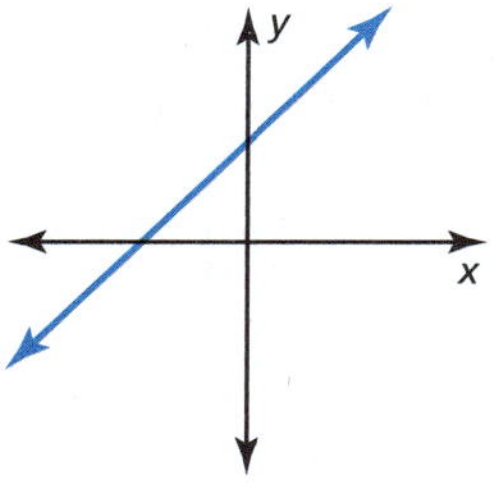

b.

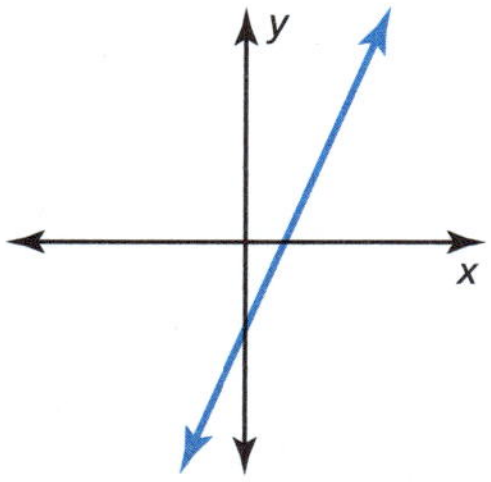

c.

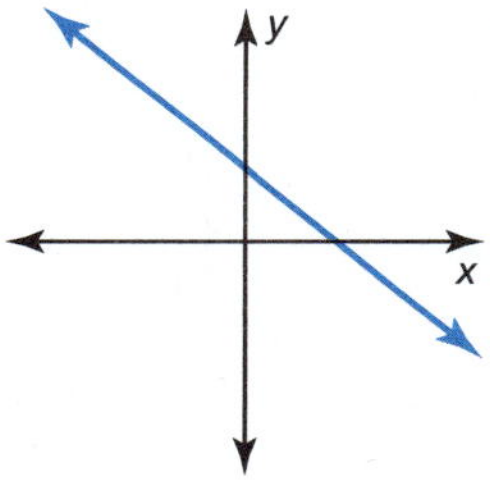

d.

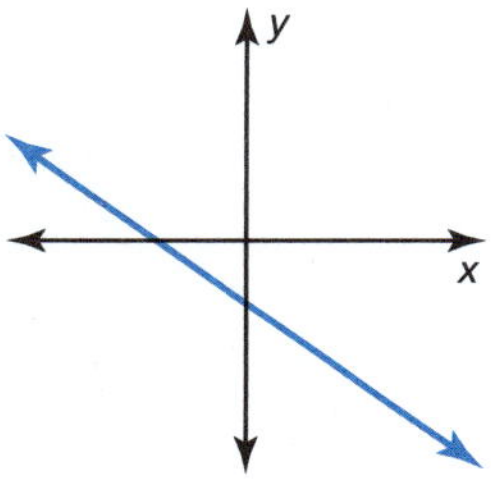

48. HOW DO YOU SEE IT? You commute to school by walking and by riding a bus. The graph represents your commute.

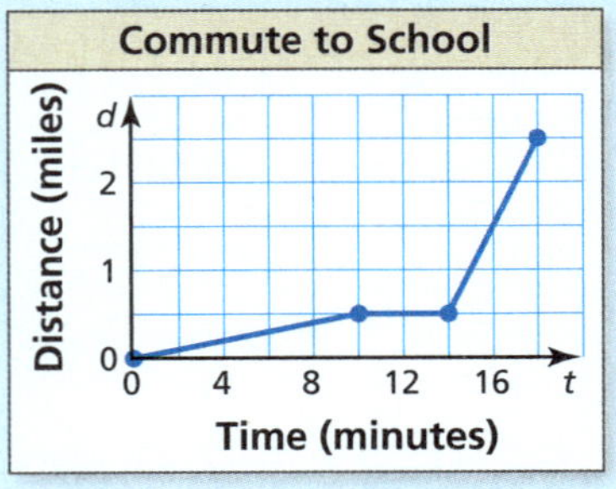

a. Describe your commute in words.

b. Calculate and interpret the slopes of the different parts of the graph.

PROBLEM SOLVING **In Exercises 49 and 50, find the value of k so that the graph of the equation has the given slope or y-intercept.**

49. $16kx - 4y = 20; m = \frac{1}{2}$

50. $\frac{2}{3}x + 2y - \frac{5}{3}k = 0; b = -10$

51. DIG DEEPER To show that the slope of a line is constant, let (x_1, y_1) and (x_2, y_2) be any two points on the line $y = mx + b$. Use the equation of the line to express y_1 in terms of x_1 and y_2 in terms of x_2. Then show that the slope between the points is m.

52. THOUGHT PROVOKING
Your family goes on vacation to a beach 300 miles from your house. You stop along the way and reach your destination 6 hours after departing. Draw a graph that describes your trip. Explain what each part of your graph represents.

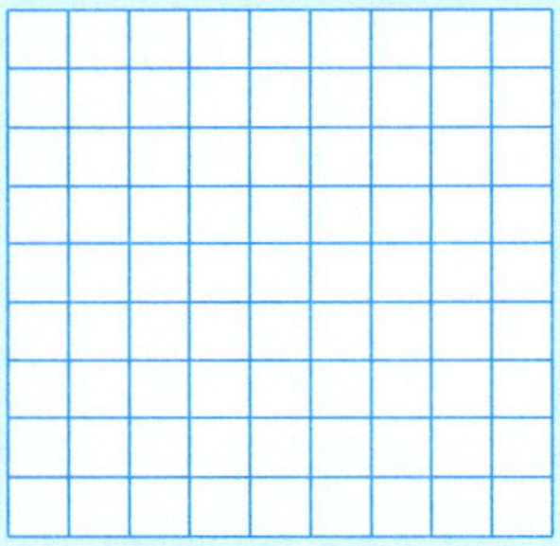

53. DIG DEEPER The graphs of the functions $g(x) = 6x + a$ and $h(x) = 2x + b$, where a and b are constants, are shown. They intersect at the point (p, q). Which is greater, $g(p + 2)$ or $h(p + 2)$? How much greater? Explain your reasoning.

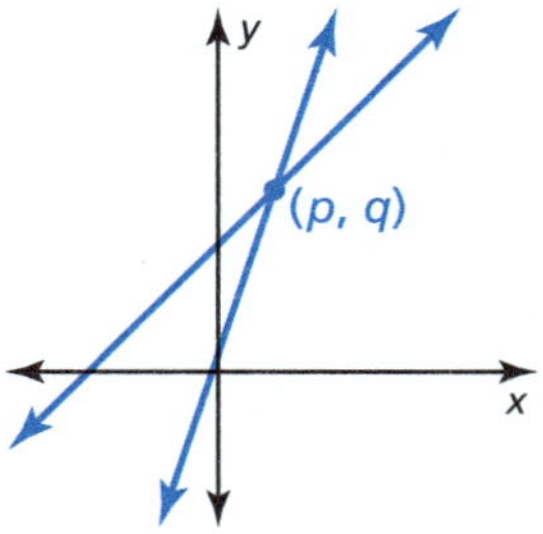

REVIEW & REFRESH

WATCH

In Exercises 54–56, find the coordinates of thefigure after the transformation.

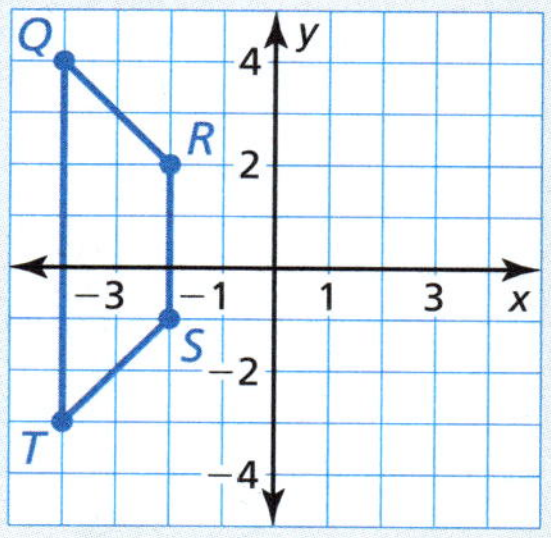

54. Translate the trapezoid 3 units right.

55. Dilate the trapezoid with respect to the origin using a scale factor of $\frac{1}{2}$.

56. Reflect the trapezoid in the y-axis.

In Exercises 57–60, solve the equation.

57. $-\frac{x}{7} = 2.5$

58. $\frac{1}{3}n - 4 = -4 + \frac{1}{3}n$

59. $-4(7 - a) + 10 = -12$

60. $5(2q - 1) = -3(q + 6)$

61. Find the slope and y-intercept of the graph of $7x - 4y = 10$.

62. The circumference of the circle is at least 14π centimeters. Find the possible values of r.

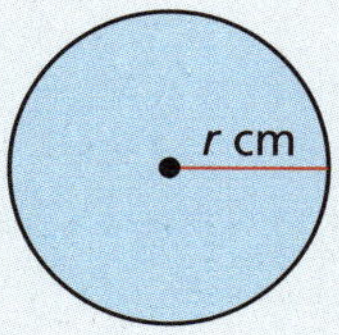

63. **MAKE A CONNECTION** Let f be a function. Use each statement to write a point on the graph of f.

a. $f(3)$ is equal to -8.

b. A solution of the equation $f(x) = \frac{3}{4}$ is -1.

64. Graph $y = -\frac{3}{2}x - 6$. Identify the x-intercept.

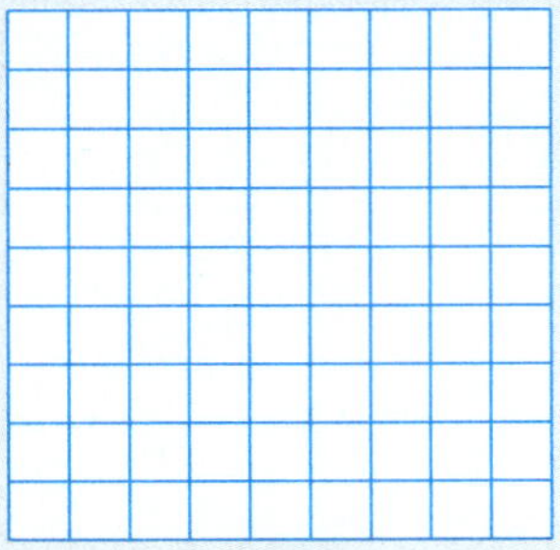

In Exercises 65 and 66, determine whether the table or equation represents a *linear* or *nonlinear* function. Explain.

65.

x	-2	-1	0	1
y	-4	-1	3	8

66. $\frac{x}{4} + \frac{y}{12} = 1$

67. **MODELING REAL LIFE** The table shows the prices of four video games. You have a coupon for 20% off one game, and you want to spend a total of \$30 with an absolute deviation of at most \$5. Which video games can you buy? Use an absolute value inequality to justify your answer.

Video game	Price
A	\$44.99
B	\$41.99
C	\$49.99
D	\$39.99

68. Use intercepts to graph the equation $-3x + 2y = 9$. Label the points corresponding to the intercepts.

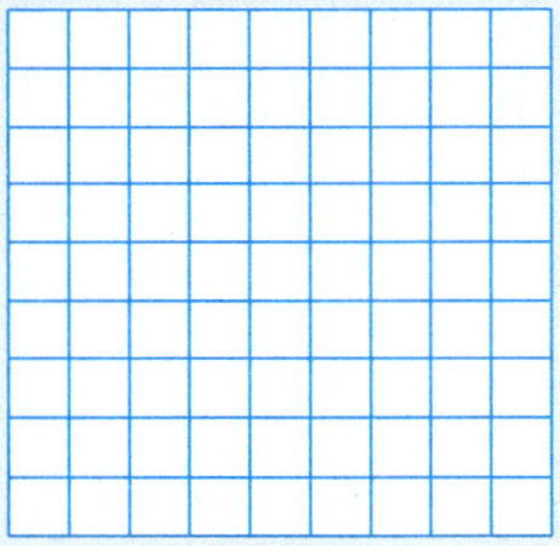

In Exercises 69 and 70, graph the inequality.

69. $h < -4$

70. $\frac{9}{2} \le t$

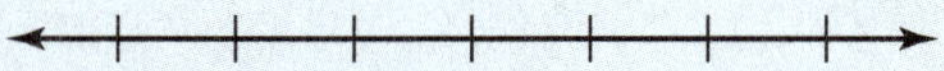

3.7 Transformations of Linear Functions

Learning Target: Graph transformations of linear functions.

Success Criteria:
- I can identify a transformation of a linear graph.
- I can graph transformations of linear functions.
- I can explain how translations, reflections, stretches, and shrinks affect graphs of functions.

Algebraic Reasoning

MA.912.F.2.1 Identify the effect on the graph or table of a given function after replacing $f(x)$ by $f(x) + k$, $kf(x)$, $f(kx)$ and $f(x + k)$ for specific values of k.

H **MA.912.F.2.3** Given the graph or table of $f(x)$ and the graph or table of $f(x) + k$, $kf(x)$, $f(kx)$ and $f(x + k)$, state the type of transformation and find the value of the real number k.

Also MA.912.AR.2.4, MA.912.AR.2.5

EXPLORE IT! Comparing Graphs of Functions

Work with a partner.

a. The graph of $f(x) = x$ is shown. Graph f and g on the same set of coordinate axes. Compare the graphs of f and g.

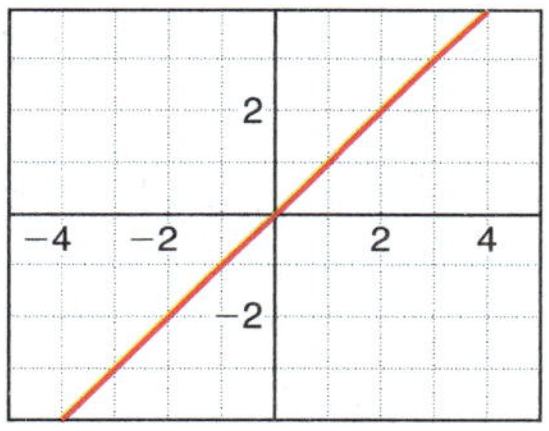

i. $g(x) = x + 4$

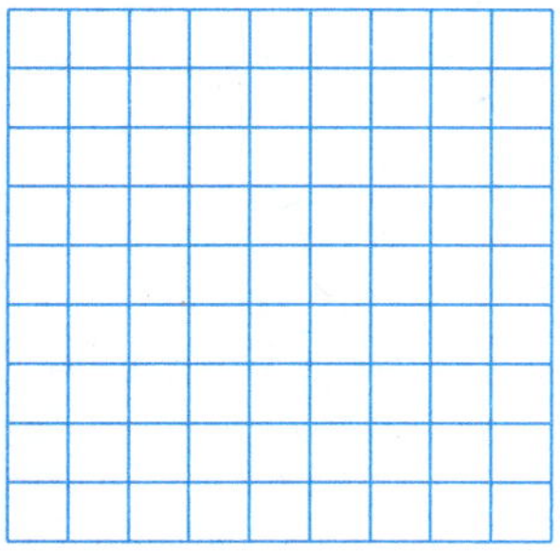

ii. $g(x) = 2x$

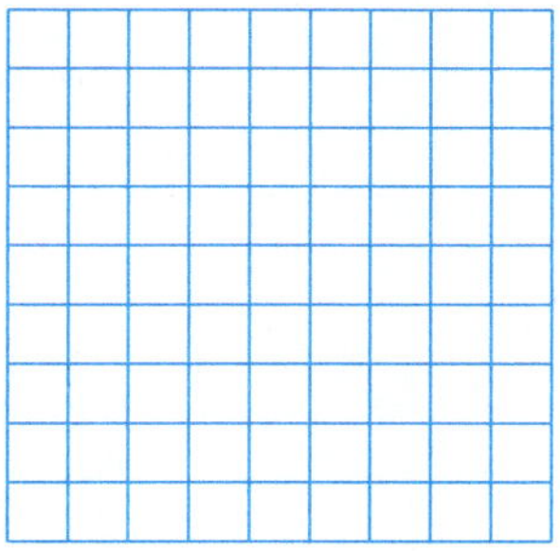

iii. $g(x) = -x$

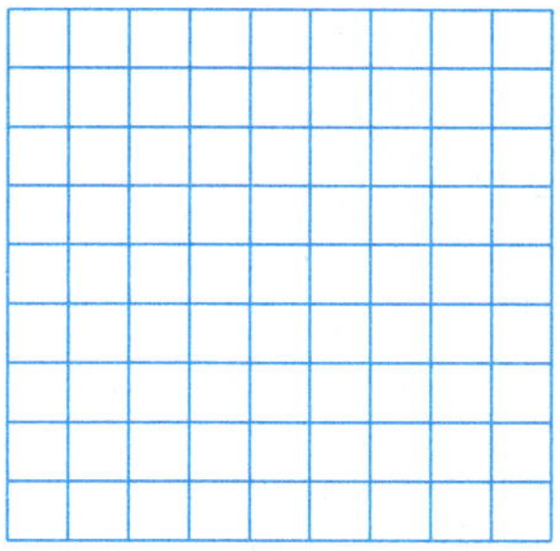

GO DIGITAL

USE STRUCTURE 5 MTR

How can you use the right side of each equation in part (b) to compare the values of $n(x)$ and $m(x)$? What does this tell you about the graph of n?

b. Write any linear function m in terms of x. Compare the graphs of m and n. Explain your reasoning.

i. $n(x) = m(x) + 3$

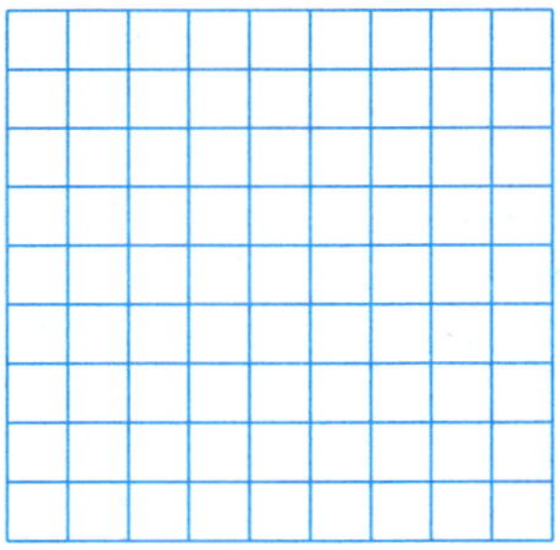

ii. $n(x) = m(x) - 3$

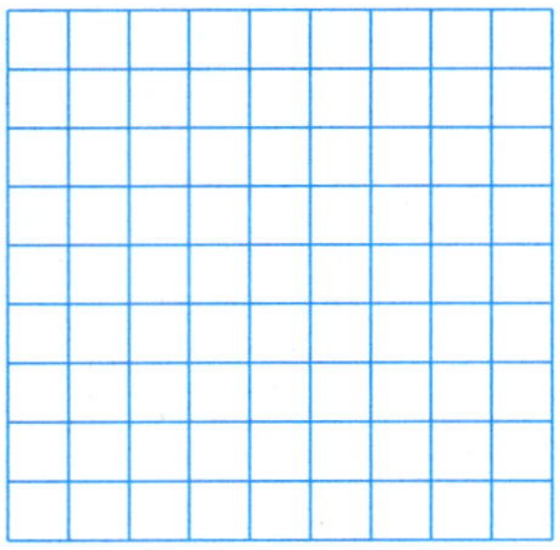

iii. $n(x) = \frac{1}{3} \cdot m(x)$

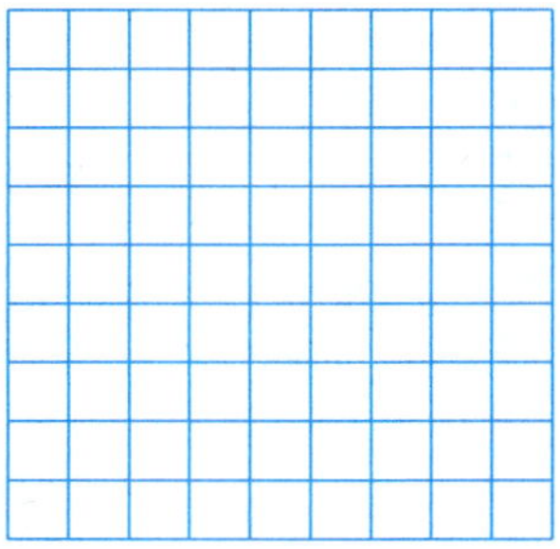

iv. $n(x) = 3 \cdot m(x)$

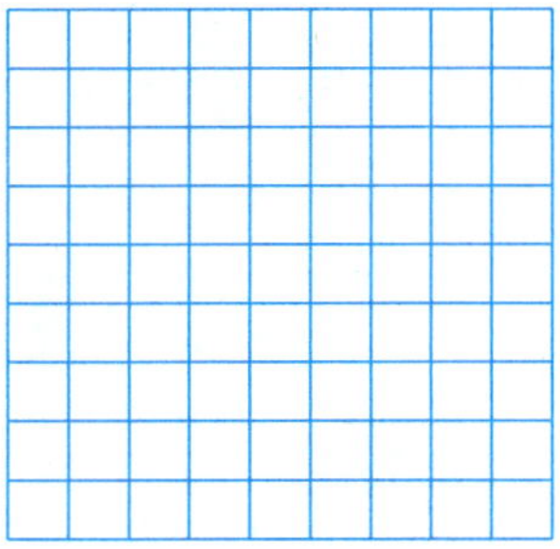

v. $n(x) = -m(x)$

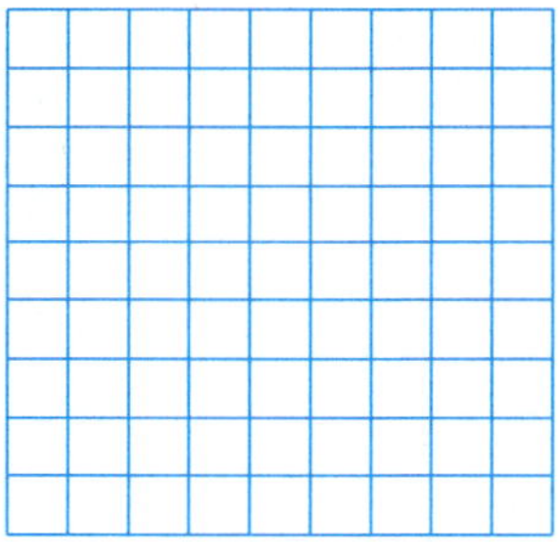

vi. $n(x) = m(-x)$

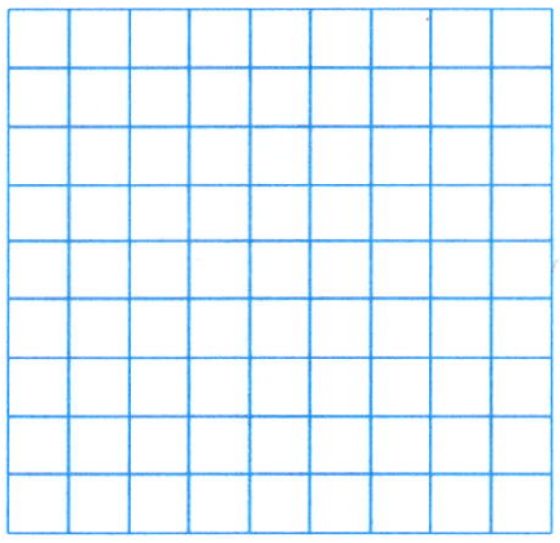

c. Discuss your results in part (b) with other students. What do you notice?

d. How does the graph of a function p compare to the graph of each of the following functions? Explain your reasoning.

i. $q(x) = p(x) + k$

ii. $q(x) = k \cdot p(x)$, where $k > 0$

iii. $q(x) = -p(x)$

iv. $q(x) = p(-x)$

Translations and Reflections

A **family of functions** is a group of functions with similar characteristics. The most basic function in a family of functions is the **parent function**. For nonconstant linear functions, the parent function is $f(x) = x$. The graphs of all other nonconstant linear functions are *transformations* of the graph of the parent function. A **transformation** changes the size, shape, position, or orientation of a graph.

WORDS AND MATH

Used as an adjective, *parent* can refer to "being the original source." A *parent function* is the original source of the family of functions.

Vocabulary (AZ VOCAB)

KEY IDEAS

A **translation** is a transformation that shifts a graph horizontally or vertically.

Horizontal Translations

The graph of $y = f(x - h)$ is a horizontal translation of the graph of $y = f(x)$, where $h \neq 0$.

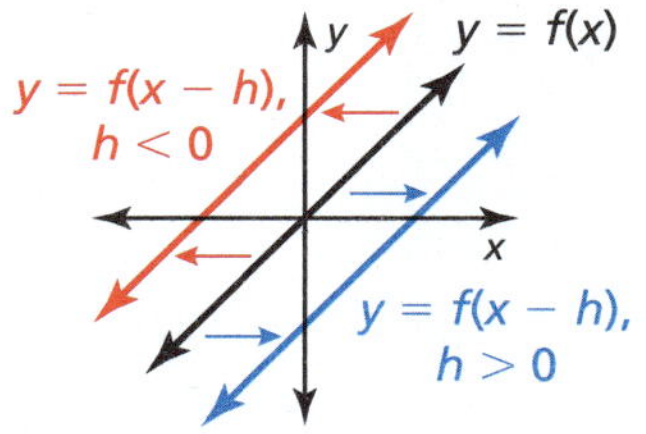

Subtracting h from the *inputs* before evaluating the function shifts the graph left when $h < 0$ and right when $h > 0$.

Vertical Translations

The graph of $y = f(x) + k$ is a vertical translation of the graph of $y = f(x)$, where $k \neq 0$.

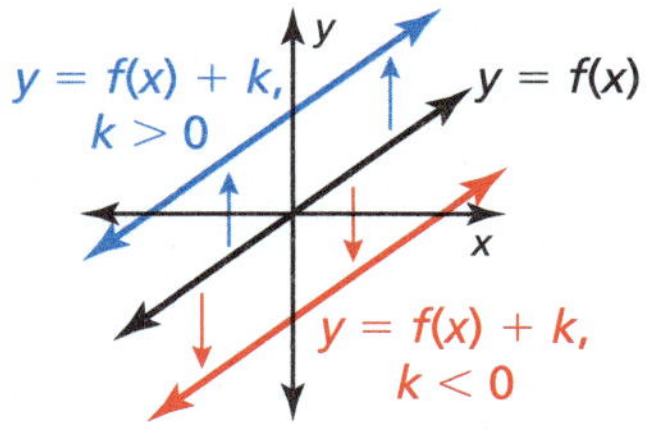

Adding k to the *outputs* shifts the graph down when $k < 0$ and up when $k > 0$.

EXAMPLE 1 **Describing Horizontal and Vertical Translations**

Let $f(x) = 2x - 1$. Graph (a) $g(x) = f(x) + 3$ and (b) $t(x) = f(x + 3)$. Describe the transformations from the graph of f to the graphs of g and t.

WATCH

SOLUTION

a. The function g is of the form $y = f(x) + k$, where $k = 3$. So, the graph of g is a vertical translation 3 units up of the graph of f.

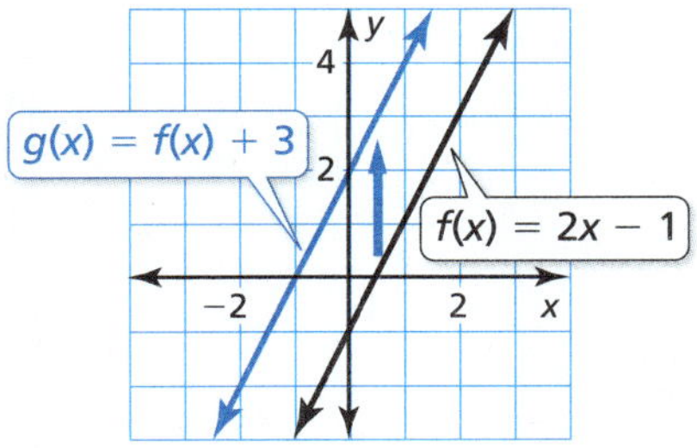

b. The function t is of the form $y = f(x - h)$, where $h = -3$. So, the graph of t is a horizontal translation 3 units left of the graph of f.

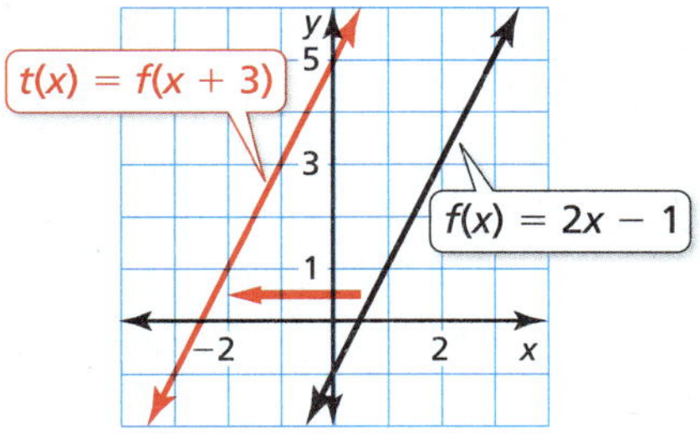

GO DIGITAL

SELF-ASSESSMENT

1 I don't understand yet. 2 I can do it with help. 3 I can do it on my own. 4 I can teach someone else.

Using *f*, graph (a) *g* and (b) *h*. Describe the transformations from the graph of *f* to the graphs of *g* and *h*.

1. $f(x) = 3x + 1$; $g(x) = f(x) - 2$; $h(x) = f(x - 2)$

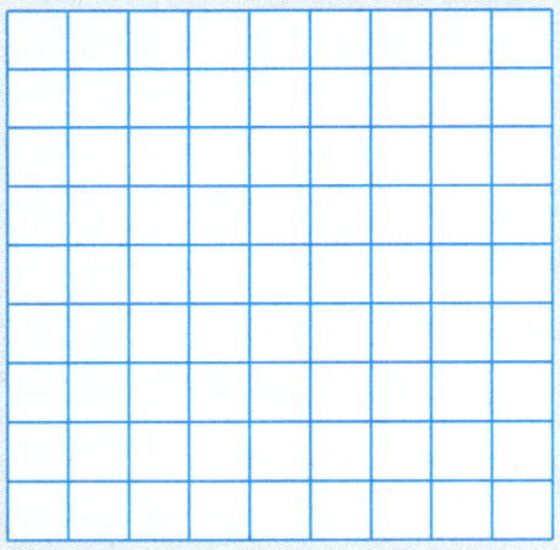

2. $f(x) = -2x$; $g(x) = f(x) + 1$; $h(x) = f(x + 1)$

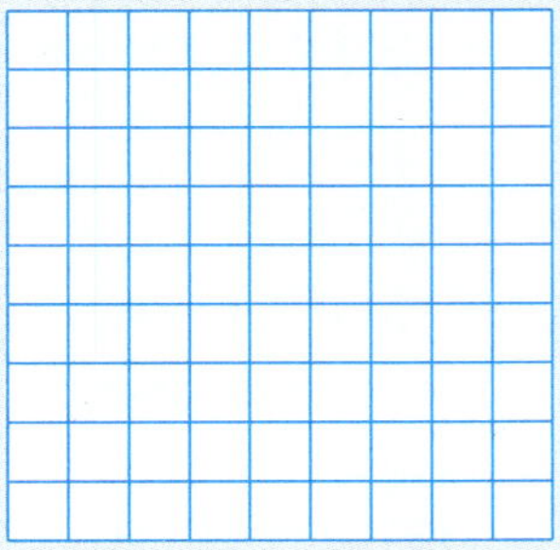

KEY IDEAS

A **reflection** is a transformation that flips a graph over a line called the *line of reflection.*

Reflections in the x-Axis

The graph of $y = -f(x)$ is a reflection in the x-axis of the graph of $y = f(x)$.

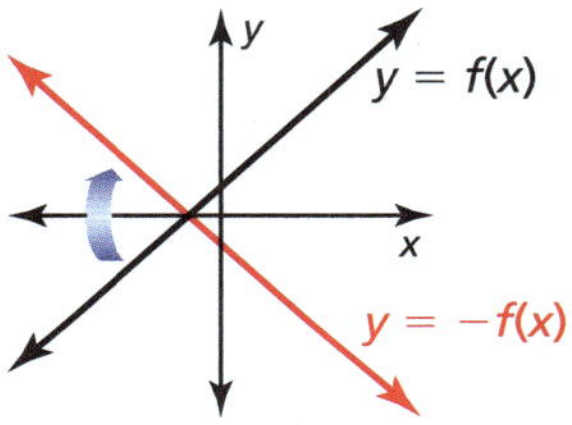

Multiplying the outputs by -1 changes their signs.

Reflections in the y-Axis

The graph of $y = f(-x)$ is a reflection in the y-axis of the graph of $y = f(x)$.

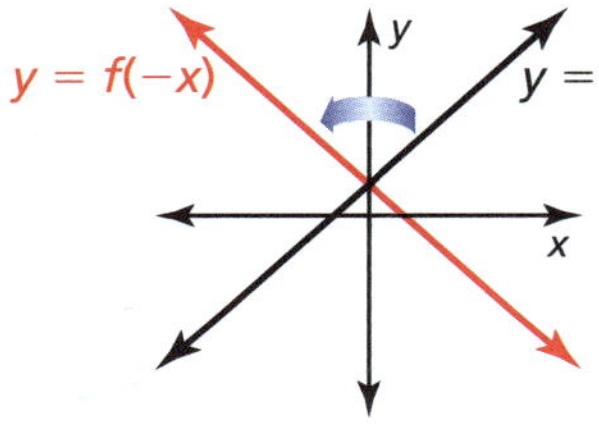

Multiplying the inputs by -1 changes their signs.

STUDY TIP

A reflected point is the same distance from the line of reflection as the original point but on the opposite side of the line.

EXAMPLE 2 Describing Reflections in the x-Axis and the y-Axis

WATCH

Let $f(x) = \frac{1}{2}x + 1$. Graph (a) $g(x) = -f(x)$ and (b) $t(x) = f(-x)$. Describe the transformations from the graph of f to the graphs of g and t.

SOLUTION

a. To find the outputs of g, multiply the outputs of f by -1. The graph of g consists of the points $(x, -f(x))$.

x	-4	-2	0
$f(x)$	-1	0	1
$-f(x)$	1	0	-1

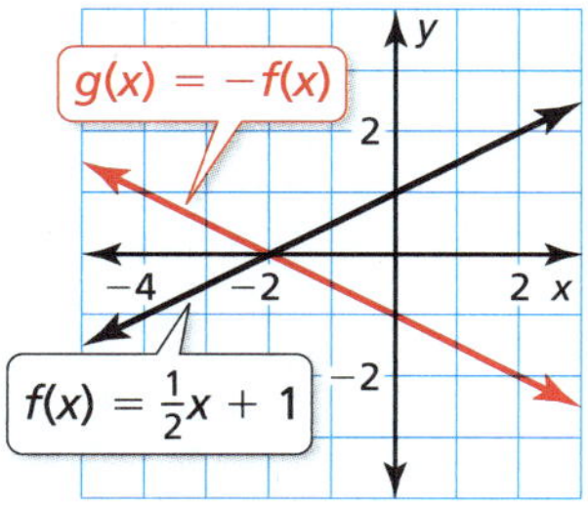

▶ The graph of g is a reflection in the x-axis of the graph of f.

b. To find the outputs of t, multiply the inputs by -1 and then evaluate f. The graph of t consists of the points $(x, f(-x))$.

x	-2	0	2
$-x$	2	0	-2
$f(-x)$	2	1	0

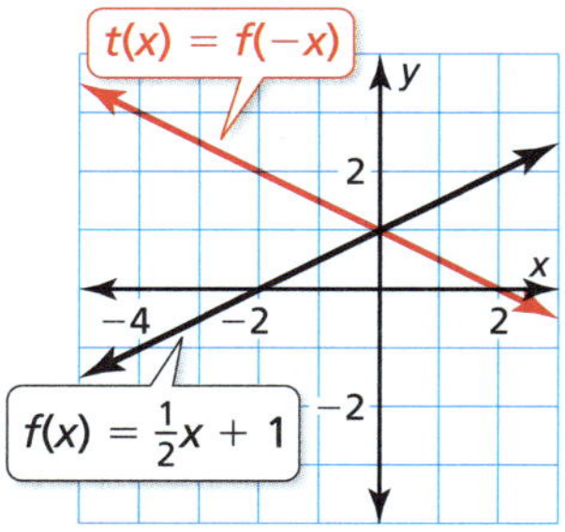

▶ The graph of t is a reflection in the y-axis of the graph of f.

GO DIGITAL

SELF-ASSESSMENT

1 I don't understand yet. **2** I can do it with help. **3** I can do it on my own. **4** I can teach someone else.

Using f, graph g. Describe the transformation from the graph of f to the graph of g.

3. $f(x) = \frac{3}{2}x + 2;\ g(x) = -f(x)$

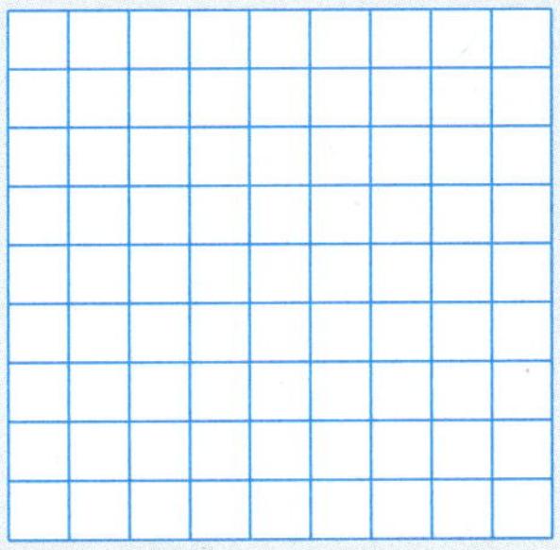

4. $f(x) = -4x - 2;\ g(x) = f(-x)$

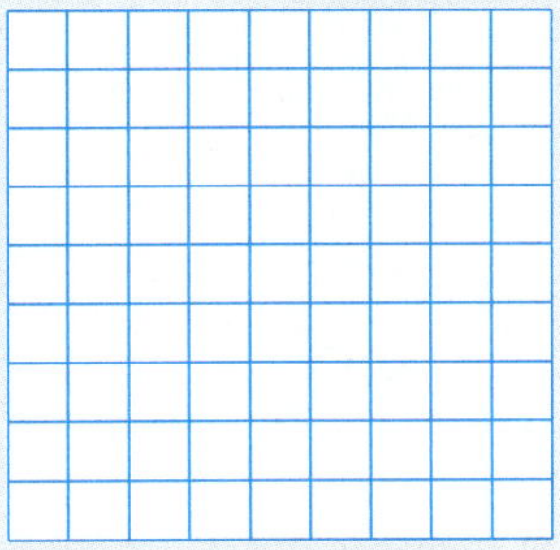

5. OPEN-ENDED Write a linear function for which a reflection in the x-axis has the same graph as a reflection in the y-axis.

Stretches and Shrinks

You can transform a function by multiplying all the inputs (x-coordinates) by the same factor a. When $a > 1$, the transformation is a **horizontal shrink** because the graph shrinks toward the y-axis. When $0 < a < 1$, the transformation is a **horizontal stretch** because the graph stretches away from the y-axis. In each case, the y-intercept stays the same.

You can also transform a function by multiplying all the outputs (y-coordinates) by the same factor a. When $a > 1$, the transformation is a **vertical stretch** because the graph stretches away from the x-axis. When $0 < a < 1$, the transformation is a **vertical shrink** because the graph shrinks toward the x-axis. In each case, the x-intercept stays the same.

KEY IDEAS

Horizontal Stretches and Shrinks

The graph of $y = f(ax)$ is a horizontal stretch or shrink by a factor of $\frac{1}{a}$ of the graph of $y = f(x)$, where $a > 0$ and $a \neq 1$.

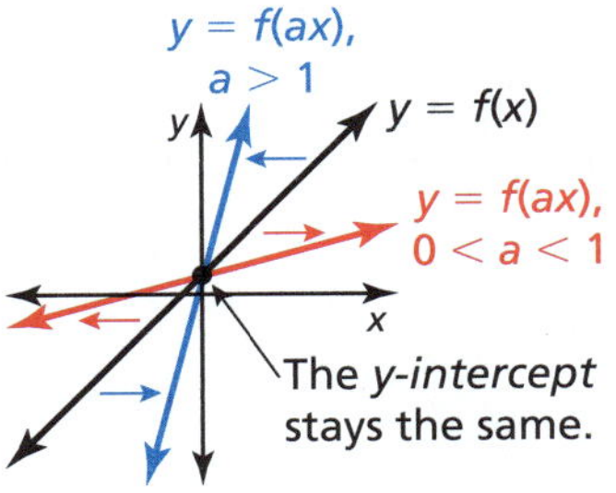

Vertical Stretches and Shrinks

The graph of $y = a \cdot f(x)$ is a vertical stretch or shrink by a factor of a of the graph of $y = f(x)$, where $a > 0$ and $a \neq 1$.

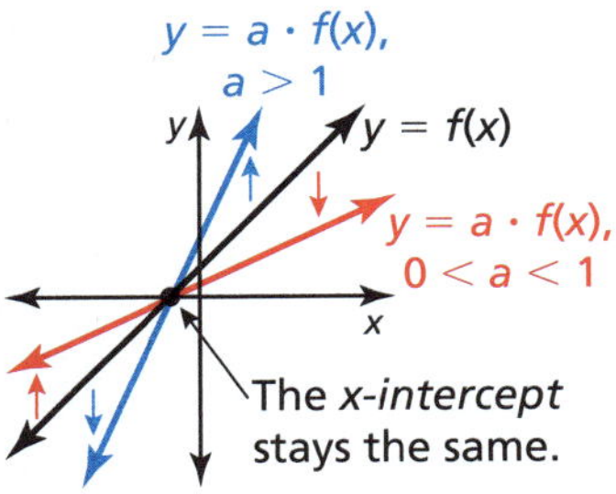

STUDY TIP

When $a < 0$ and $a \neq -1$, the graphs of $y = f(ax)$ and $y = a \cdot f(x)$ represent a stretch or shrink *and* a reflection in the x- or y-axis of the graph of $y = f(x)$.

GO DIGITAL

EXAMPLE 3 Describing Horizontal and Vertical Stretches

WATCH

Let $f(x) = x - 1$. Graph (a) $g(x) = f\left(\frac{1}{3}x\right)$ and (b) $h(x) = 3f(x)$. Describe the transformations from the graph of f to the graphs of g and h.

SOLUTION

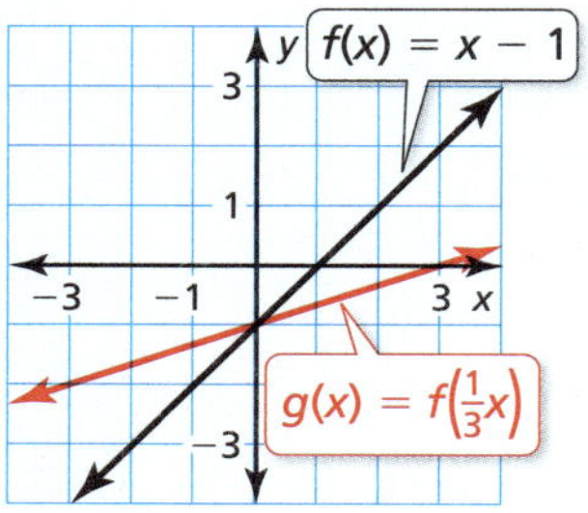

a. To find the outputs of g, multiply the inputs by $\frac{1}{3}$. Then evaluate f. The graph of g consists of the points $\left(x, f\left(\frac{1}{3}x\right)\right)$.

x	−3	0	3
$\frac{1}{3}x$	−1	0	1
$f\left(\frac{1}{3}x\right)$	−2	−1	0

▶ The graph of g is a horizontal stretch of the graph of f by a factor of $1 \div \frac{1}{3} = 3$.

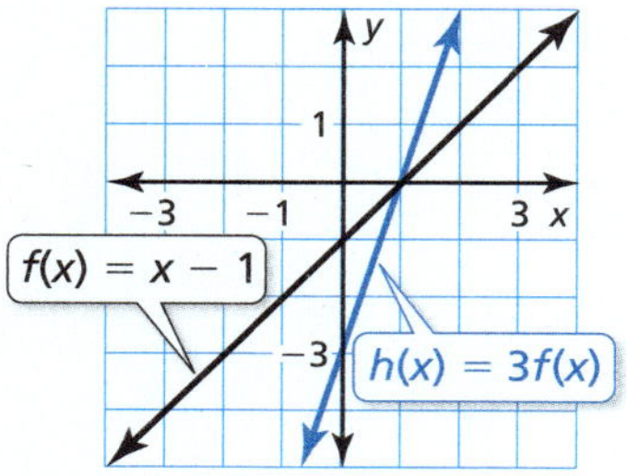

b. To find the outputs of h, multiply the outputs of f by 3. The graph of h consists of the points $(x, 3f(x))$.

x	0	1	2
$f(x)$	−1	0	1
$3f(x)$	−3	0	3

▶ The graph of h is a vertical stretch of the graph of f by a factor of 3.

EXAMPLE 4 Describing Horizontal and Vertical Shrinks

WATCH

Let $f(x) = x + 2$. Graph (a) $g(x) = f(2x)$ and (b) $h(x) = \frac{1}{4}f(x)$. Describe the transformations from the graph of f to the graphs of g and h.

SOLUTION

a. To find the outputs of g, multiply the inputs by 2. Then evaluate f. The graph of g consists of the points $(x, f(2x))$.

x	−1	0	1
$2x$	−2	0	2
$f(2x)$	0	2	4

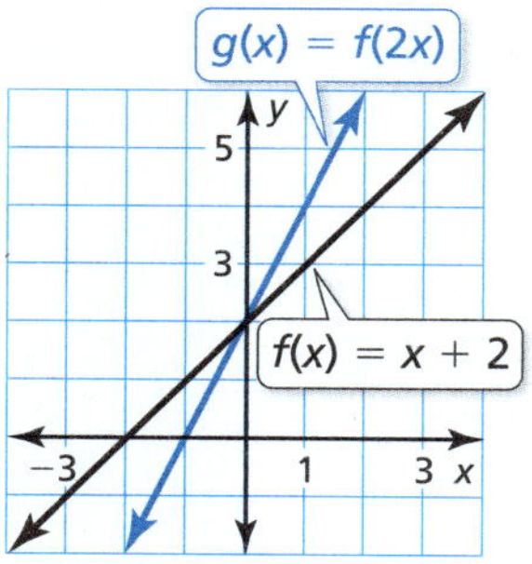

▶ The graph of g is a horizontal shrink of the graph of f by a factor of $\frac{1}{2}$.

b. To find the outputs of h, multiply the outputs of f by $\frac{1}{4}$. The graph of h consists of the points $\left(x, \frac{1}{4}f(x)\right)$.

x	−2	0	2
$f(x)$	0	2	4
$\frac{1}{4}f(x)$	0	$\frac{1}{2}$	1

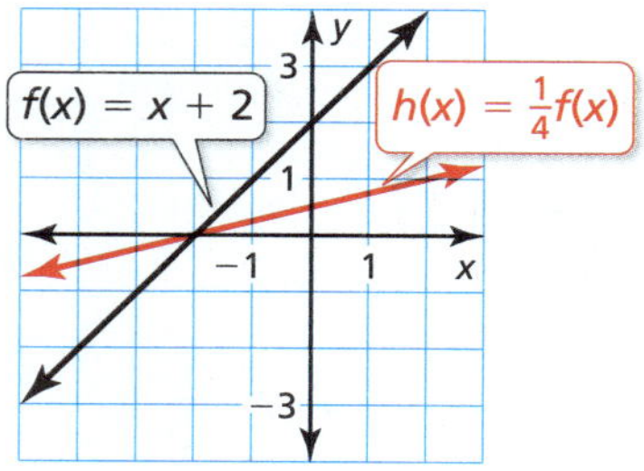

▶ The graph of h is a vertical shrink of the graph of f by a factor of $\frac{1}{4}$.

GO DIGITAL

SELF-ASSESSMENT

1 I don't understand yet. 2 I can do it with help. 3 I can do it on my own. 4 I can teach someone else.

Using f, graph (a) g and (b) h. Describe the transformations from the graph of f to the graphs of g and h.

6. $f(x) = 4x - 2$; $g(x) = f\left(\frac{1}{2}x\right)$; $h(x) = 2f(x)$

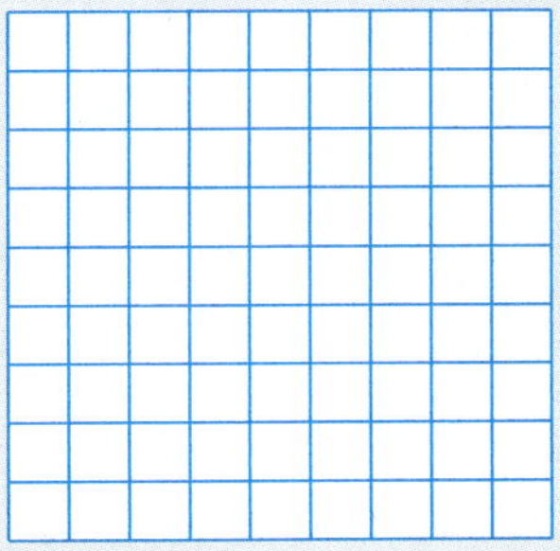

7. $f(x) = -3x + 4$; $g(x) = f(3x)$; $h(x) = \frac{1}{2}f(x)$

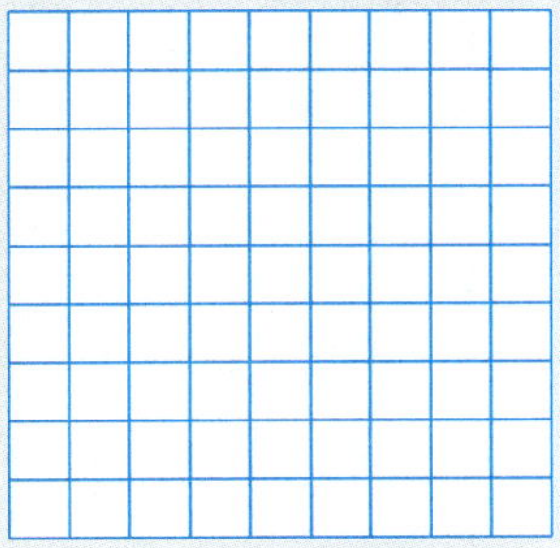

8. WRITING How does the value of a in the equation $y = h(ax)$ affect the graph of $y = h(x)$? How does the value of a in the equation $y = a \cdot h(x)$ affect the graph of $y = h(x)$?

9. REASONING The functions f and g are linear functions. The graph of g is a vertical shrink of the graph of f. What can you say about the intercepts of the graphs of f and g? Is this always true? Explain.

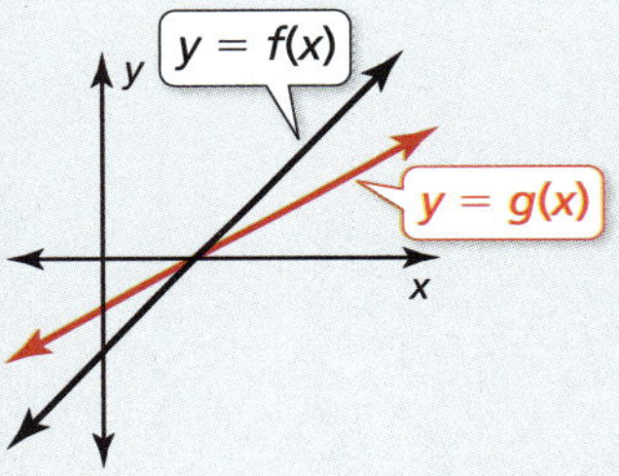

Describing Transformations

EXAMPLE 5 Describing a Transformation

WATCH H

The table represents two linear functions f and g. Describe the transformation from the graph of f to the graph of g.

x	−1	0	1	2	3
$f(x)$	−4	−1	2	5	8
$g(x)$	−2	1	4	7	10

SOLUTION

To determine the transformation, compare values of $f(x)$ and $g(x)$.

x	−1	0	1	2	3
$f(x)$	−4	−1	2	5	8
	+ 2	+ 2	+ 2	+ 2	+ 2
$g(x)$	−2	1	4	7	10

For each input, $g(x)$ is 2 more than $f(x)$. So, $g(x) = f(x) + 2$.

▶ The graph of g is a translation 2 units up of the graph of f.

GO DIGITAL

7 MTR **EXAMPLE 6** **Modeling Real Life** WATCH H

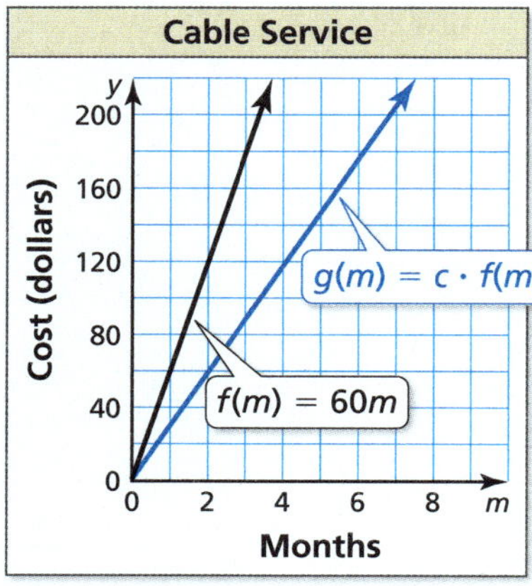

The cost (in dollars) of cable service for m months is represented by the function f. To attract new customers, the cable company multiplies the monthly fee by a factor of c. Use the graph to find and interpret the value of c.

SOLUTION

To find c, compare f and g. The function $g(m) = c \cdot f(m)$ indicates that the graph of g is a vertical stretch or shrink of the graph of f. The graphs of f and g show that for any number of months, the new cost is one-half of the original cost. For example, the cost for two months ($m = 2$) decreases from \$120 to \$60. So, $c = \frac{1}{2}$.

▶ The factor $c = \frac{1}{2}$ indicates that the monthly price is halved.

SELF-ASSESSMENT

1 I don't understand yet. 2 I can do it with help. 3 I can do it on my own. 4 I can teach someone else.

10. The table represents two linear functions f and g. Describe the transformation from the graph of f to the graph of g.

x	0	2	4	6	8
$f(x)$	−8	−4	0	4	8
$g(x)$	−2	−1	0	1	2

11. A company pays x dollars per unit for a product. The selling price is represented by the function p.

a. What does $f(x) = x$ represent in this situation? Describe a transformation of the graph of f that results in the graph of p.

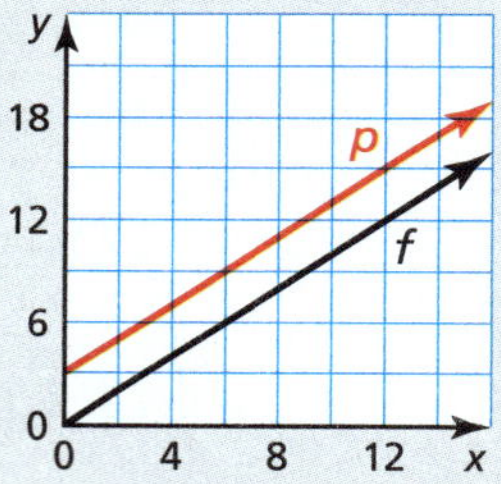

b. How does the company determine the selling price of a product?

3.7 Practice WITH CalcChat® AND CalcView®

In Exercises 1–6, use the graphs of f and g to describe the transformation from the graph of f to the graph of g. *(See Example 1.)*

1.

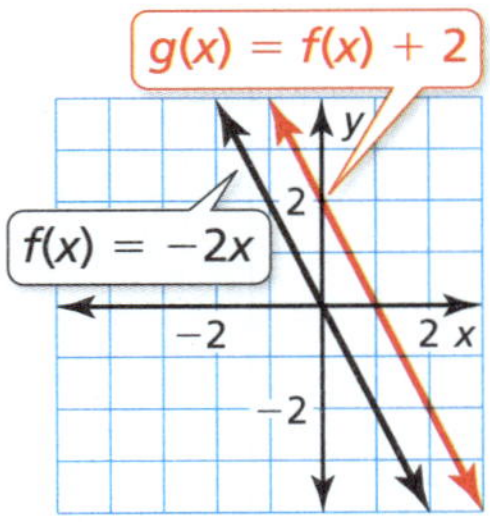

2.

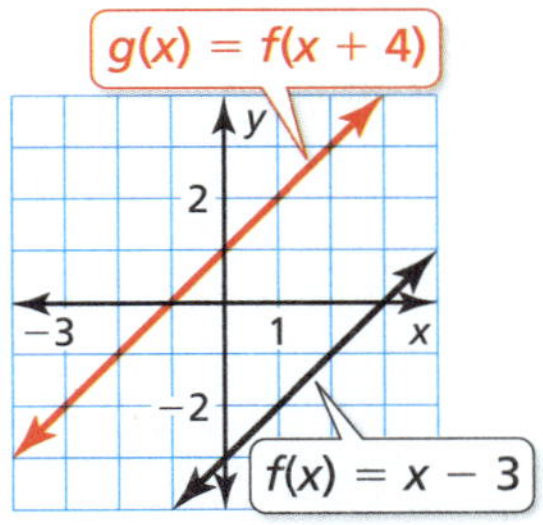

3. $f(x) = \frac{1}{3}x + 3;\ g(x) = f(x) - 3$

4. $f(x) = -3x + 4;\ g(x) = f(x) + 1$

5. $f(x) = -x - 2;\ g(x) = f(x + 5)$

6. $f(x) = \frac{1}{2}x - 5;\ g(x) = f(x - 3)$

7 MTR **7. MODELING REAL LIFE** You and your friend start biking from the same location. Your distance (in miles) after t minutes is represented by $d(t) = \frac{1}{5}t$. Your friend starts biking 5 minutes after you. Her distance is represented by $f(t) = d(t - 5)$. Describe the transformation from the graph of d to the graph of f.

7 MTR **8. MODELING REAL LIFE** The total cost (in dollars) to bowl n games is represented by $C(n) = 4.5n + 2.5$. The shoe rental price increases \$0.50. The new total cost is represented by $T(n) = C(n) + 0.5$. Describe the transformation from the graph of C to the graph of T.

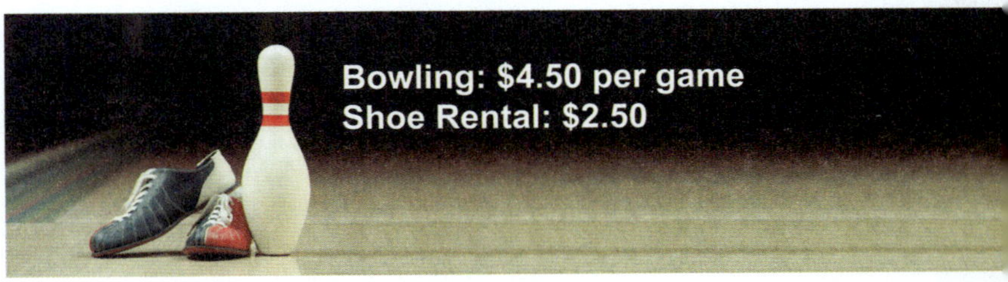

GO DIGITAL

In Exercises 9–12, use the graphs of f and h to describe the transformation from the graph of f to the graph of h. *(See Example 2.)*

9.

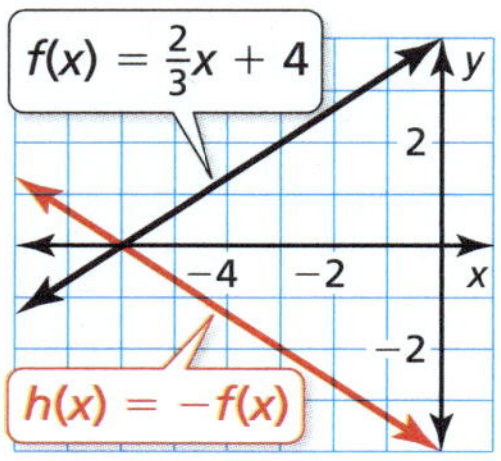

10.

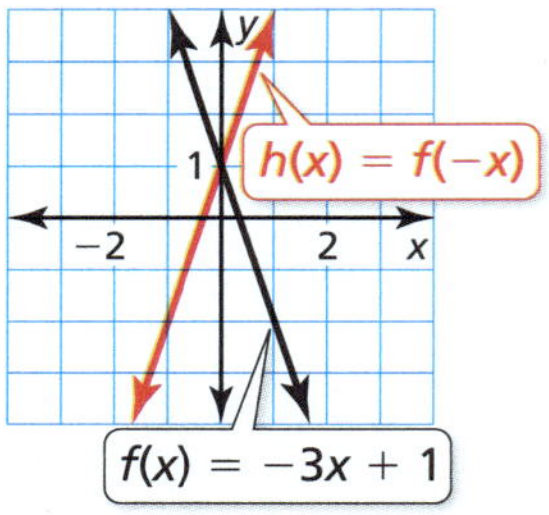

11. $f(x) = -5 - x;\ h(x) = f(-x)$

12. $f(x) = \frac{1}{4}x - 2;\ h(x) = -f(x)$

In Exercises 13–18, use the graphs of f and r to describe the transformation from the graph of f to the graph of r. *(See Example 3.)*

13.

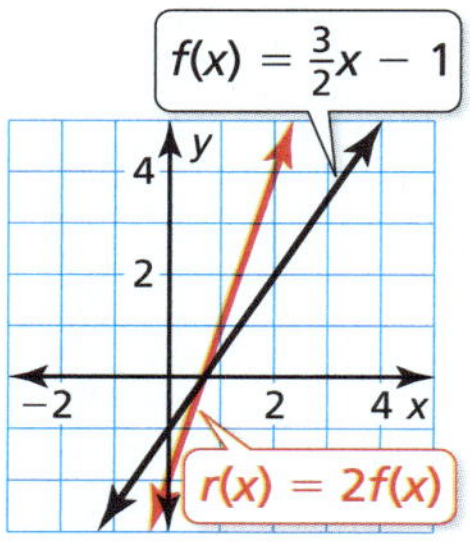

14.

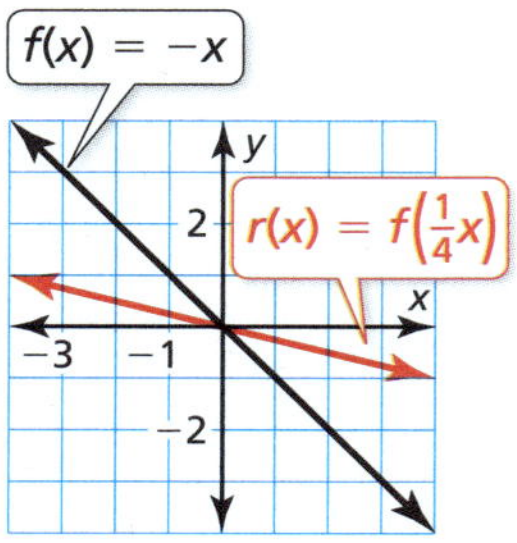

15. $f(x) = -2x - 4;\ r(x) = f\left(\frac{1}{2}x\right)$

16. $f(x) = 3x + 5;\ r(x) = f\left(\frac{1}{3}x\right)$

17. $f(x) = \frac{2}{3}x + 1;\ r(x) = 3f(x)$

18. $f(x) = -\frac{1}{4}x - 2;\ r(x) = 4f(x)$

In Exercises 19–24, use the graphs of f and h to describe the transformation from the graph of f to the graph of h. *(See Example 4.)*

19.

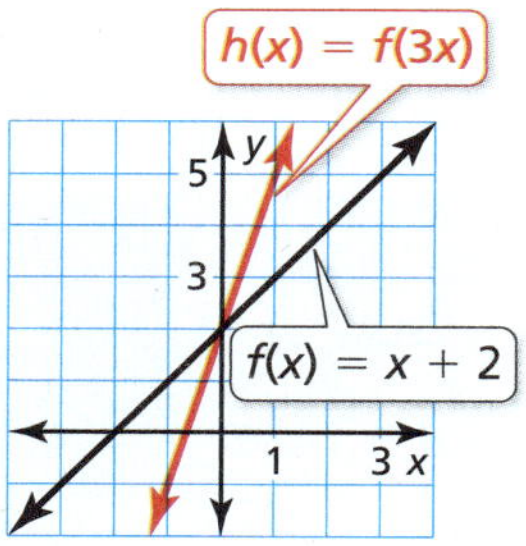

20.

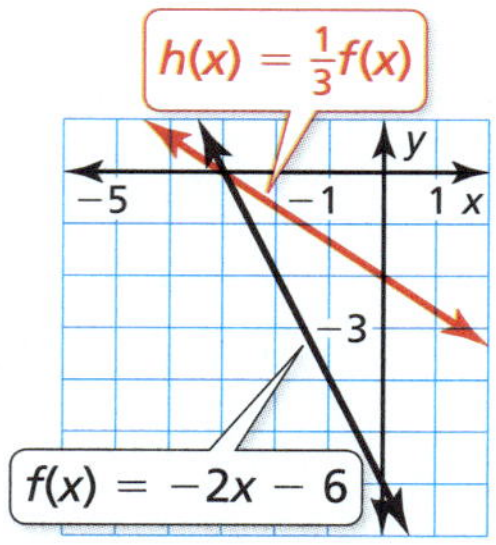

21. $f(x) = 3x - 12;\ h(x) = \frac{1}{6}f(x)$

22. $f(x) = -x + 1;\ h(x) = f(2x)$

23. $f(x) = -2x - 2;\ h(x) = f(5x)$

24. $f(x) = 4x + 8;\ h(x) = \frac{3}{4}f(x)$

25. MODELING REAL LIFE The temperature (in degrees Fahrenheit) x hours after 5 P.M. is represented by $t(x) = -4x + 72$. The temperature x hours after 10 A.M. is represented by $d(x) = 4x + 72$. Describe the transformation from the graph of t to the graph of d.

26. MODELING REAL LIFE The cost (in dollars) of a basic music streaming service for m months is represented by $B(m) = 5m$. The cost of the premium service is represented by $P(m) = 10m$. Describe the transformation from the graph of B to the graph of P.

In Exercises 27–32, use the graphs of f and g to describe the transformation from the graph of f to the graph of g.

27. $f(x) = x - 2$; $g(x) = f(x + 4)$

28. $f(x) = -4x + 8$; $g(x) = -f(x)$

29. $f(x) = -2x - 7$; $g(x) = f(x - 2)$

30. $f(x) = 3x + 8$; $g(x) = f\left(\frac{2}{3}x\right)$

31. $f(x) = x - 6$; $g(x) = 6f(x)$

32. $f(x) = -x$; $g(x) = f(x) - 3$

In Exercises 33–36, write a function g in terms of f so that the statement is true.

33. The graph of g is a horizontal translation 2 units right of the graph of f.

34. The graph of g is a reflection in the y-axis of the graph of f.

35. The graph of g is a vertical translation 4 units up of the graph of f.

36. The graph of g is a horizontal shrink by a factor of $\frac{1}{5}$ of the graph of f.

4 MTR ERROR ANALYSIS In Exercises 37 and 38, describe and correct the error in graphing *g*.

37.

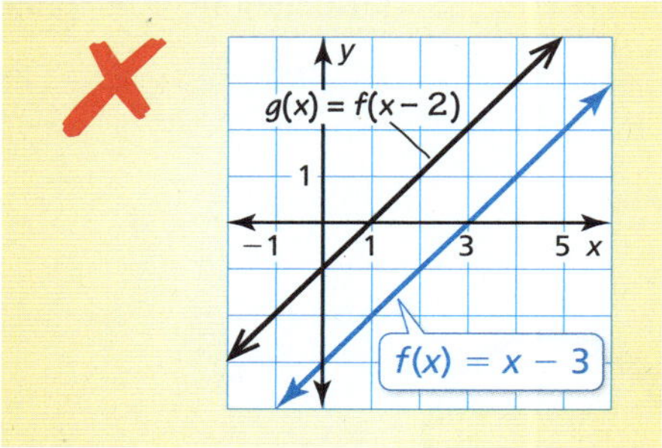

38.

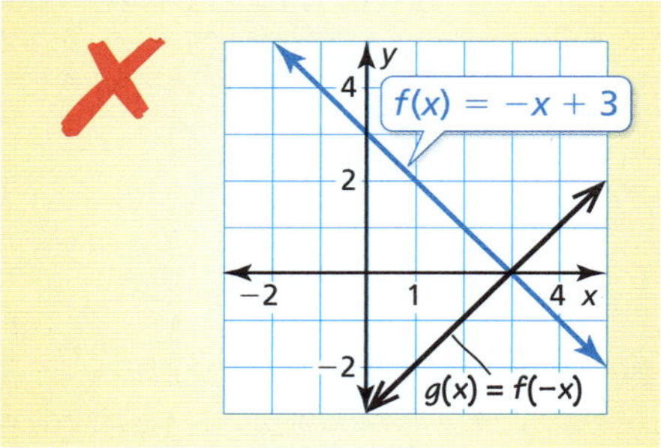

In Exercises 39–46, describe the transformation from the graph of *f* to the graph of *g*. *(See Example 5.)*

39.

x	−2	−1	0	1	2
$f(x)$	14	11	8	5	2
$g(x) = f(x + k)$	11	8	5	2	−1

40.

x	−3	−2	−1	0	1
$f(x)$	−10	−6	−2	2	6
$g(x) = f(x) + k$	−5	−1	3	7	11

41.

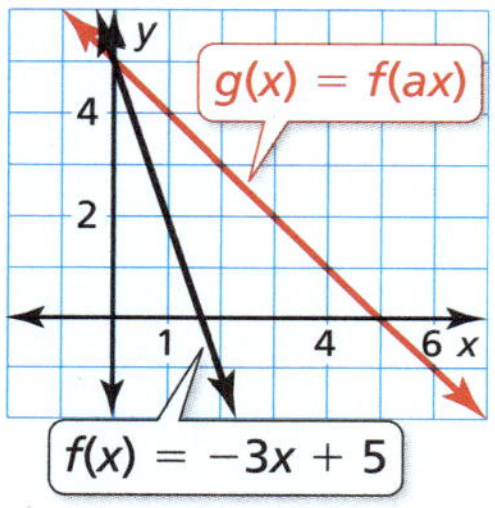

42.

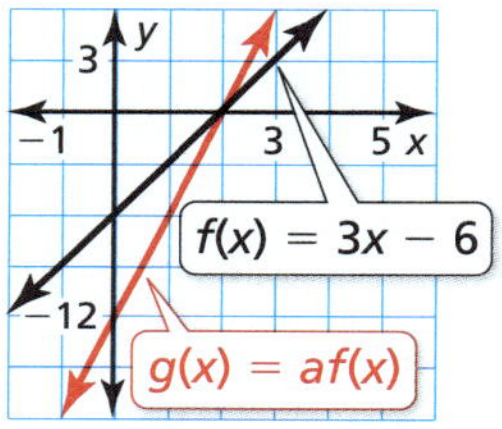

43.

x	−1	0	1	2	3
$f(x)$	6	7	8	9	10
$g(x)$	−6	−7	−8	−9	−10

44.

x	3	5	7	9	11
$f(x)$	2	0	−2	−4	−6
$g(x)$	−2	−4	−6	−8	−10

45.

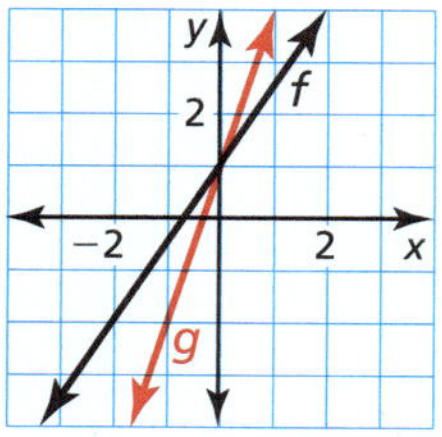

46.

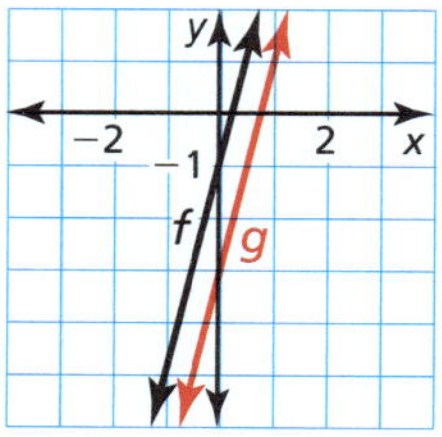

47. **MODELING REAL LIFE** The cost (in dollars) of a gym membership for m months is represented by the function g. In January, the gym multiplies the monthly fee by a factor of a. Use the graph to find and interpret the value of a. *(See Example 6.)*

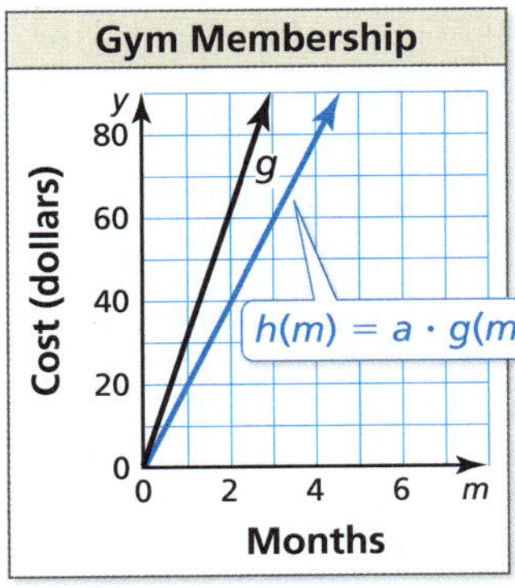

48. **MODELING REAL LIFE** The function $m(x) = 360x$ represents the amount of money (in dollars) you make at your job after x weeks. You earn a bonus of c dollars. Use the graph to find and interpret the value of c.

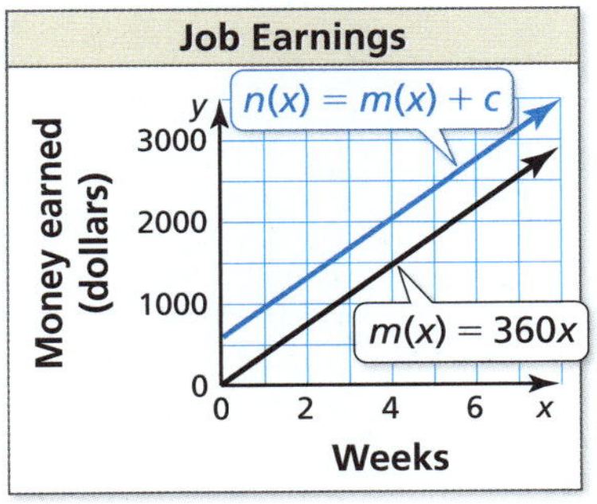

49. **B.E.S.T. TEST PREP** Which of the graphs are related by only a translation? Explain.

Ⓐ
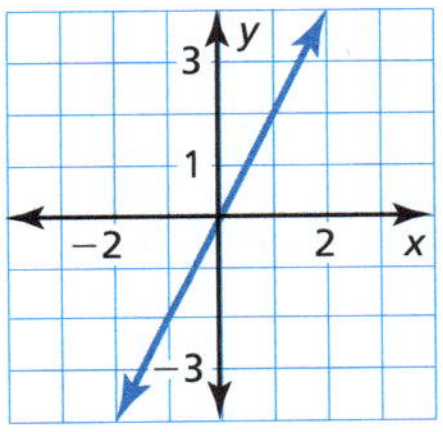

Ⓑ
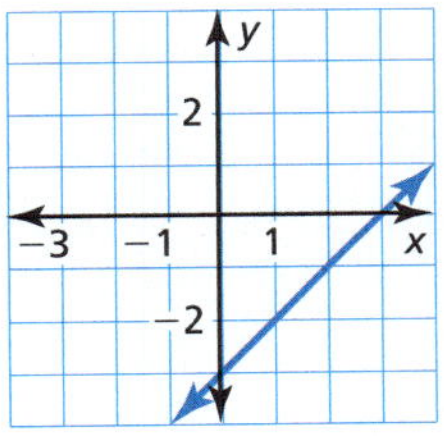

Ⓒ
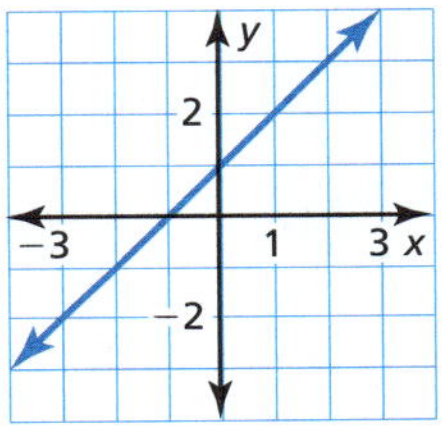

Ⓓ
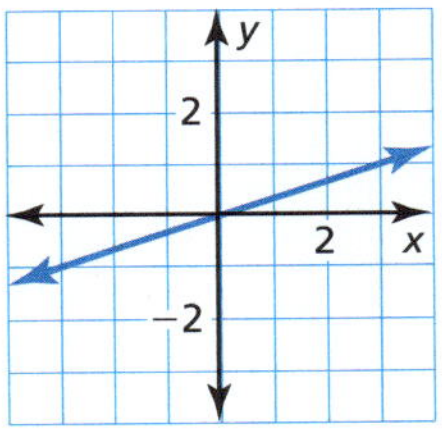

Ⓔ
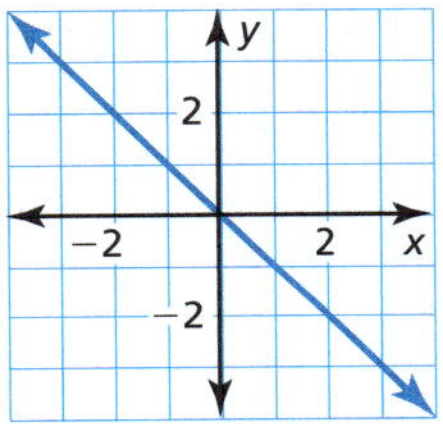

Ⓕ
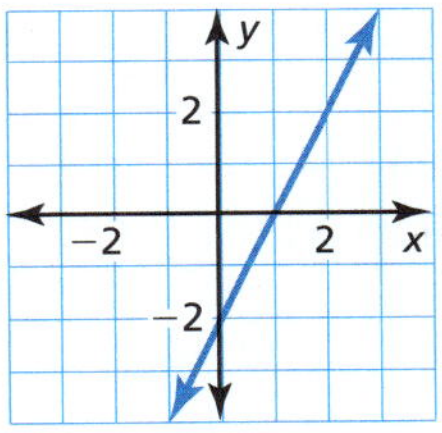

50. **WRITING** How does the value of p in the equation $y = g(x) + p$ affect the graph of $y = g(x)$? How does the value of p in the equation $y = g(x + p)$ affect the graph of $y = g(x)$?

51. **STRUCTURE** The graph of $g(x) = a \bullet f(x - b) + c$ is a transformation of the graph of the linear function f. Complete each statement.

a. The graph of g is a vertical ____________ of the graph of f when $a = 4$, $b = 0$, and $c = 0$.

b. The graph of g is a vertical translation 1 unit up of the graph of f when $a = 1$, $b = 0$, and $c =$ __________.

c. The graph of g is a reflection in the ____________ of the graph of f when $a = -1$, $b = 0$, and $c = 0$.

52. HOW DO YOU SEE IT?
Match each function with its graph. Explain.

a. $a(x) = f(-x)$

b. $g(x) = f(x) - 4$

c. $h(x) = f(x) + 2$

d. $k(x) = f(3x)$

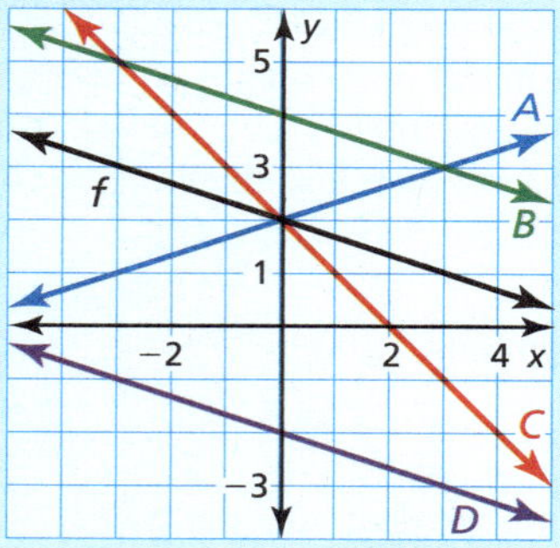

OPEN-ENDED In Exercises 53 and 54, write a function whose graph passes through the given point and is a transformation of the graph of $f(x) = x$.

53. $(4, 2)$

54. $\left(\frac{3}{2}, \frac{7}{2}\right)$

In Exercises 55–58, graph f and g. Write g in terms of f. Describe the transformation from the graph of f to the graph of g.

55. $f(x) = 2x - 5$; $g(x) = 2x - 8$

56. $f(x) = 3x + 9$; $g(x) = 3x + 15$

57. $f(x) = -x - 4$; $g(x) = x - 4$

58. $f(x) = x - 1$; $g(x) = 3x - 3$

59. REASONING The graph of $f(x) = x + 5$ is a vertical translation 5 units up of the graph of $f(x) = x$. How can you obtain the graph of $f(x) = x + 5$ from the graph of $f(x) = x$ using a horizontal translation?

60. REASONING A swimming pool is filled with water by a hose at a rate of 1020 gallons per hour. The amount (in gallons) of water in the pool after t hours is represented by the function $v(t) = 1020t$. How does the graph of v change in each situation?

a. A larger hose is found. Then the pool is filled at a rate of 1360 gallons per hour.

b. Before filling up the pool with a hose, a water truck adds 2000 gallons of water to the pool.

61. MAKING AN ARGUMENT (4 MTR) Is it true that for all linear functions, a horizontal stretch by a factor of c produces the same result as a vertical shrink by a factor of $\frac{1}{c}$? Explain.

62. THOUGHT PROVOKING When is the graph of $y = f(x) + w$ the same as the graph of $y = f(x + w)$ for linear functions? Explain your reasoning.

REVIEW & REFRESH

WATCH

63. The red figure is similar to the blue figure. Describe a similarity transformation between the figures.

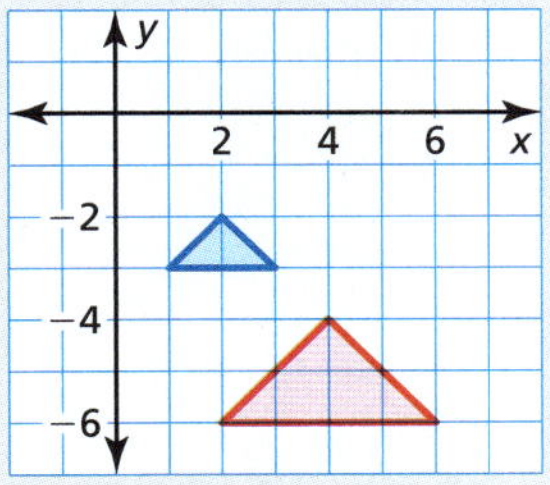

In Exercises 64 and 65, solve the inequality. Graph the solution, if possible.

64. $5|x + 7| < 25$

65. $-2|x + 1| \geq 18$

66. **REASONING** Complete the inequality $-\frac{1}{6}n$ ▭ $\frac{2}{3}$ with <, ≤, >, or ≥ so that the solution is $n \leq -4$.

67. Evaluate $g(x) = \frac{1}{4}x - 5$ when $x = 12$ and when $x = -2$.

7 MTR **68.** **MODELING REAL LIFE** An elevator on the top floor of a building begins to descend to the ground floor. The function $h(t) = -8t + 250$ models the situation, where $h(t)$ is the height (in meters) of the elevator t seconds after it begins to descend.

a. Graph the function, and find its domain and range.

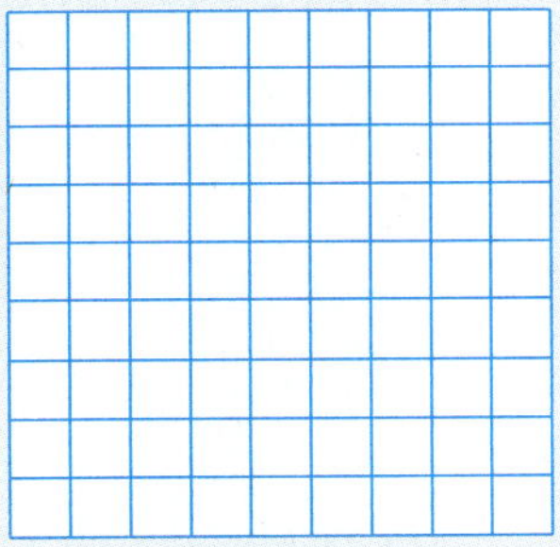

b. Interpret the terms and coefficient in the equation, and the x-intercept of its graph.

In Exercises 69–72, solve the equation. Check your solution.

69. $2.5b = 10$

70. $\frac{c}{5} + 1 = -2$

71. $14 - 3q = 4q - 14 + q$

72. $|-4r + 6| - 5 = 13$

7 MTR

73. **MODELING REAL LIFE** The linear function $m = 55 - 8.5b$ represents the amount m (in dollars) of money that you have after buying b books.

a. Find the domain of the function. Is the domain discrete or continuous? Explain.

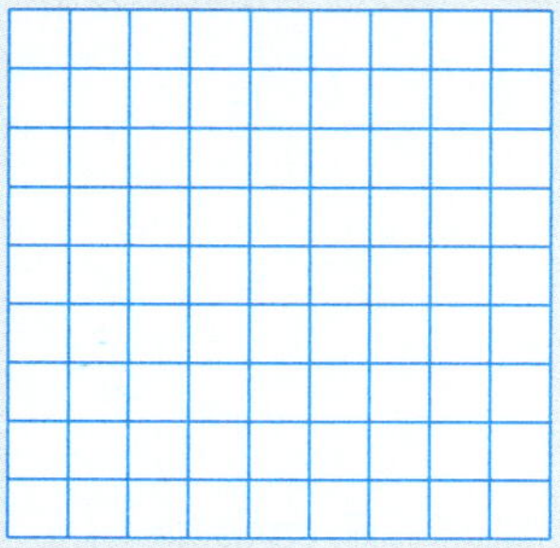

b. Graph the function using its domain.

In Exercises 74 and 75, graph *f* and *h*. Describe the transformation from the graph of *f* to the graph of *h*.

74. $f(x) = x;\ h(x) = \frac{1}{3}x$

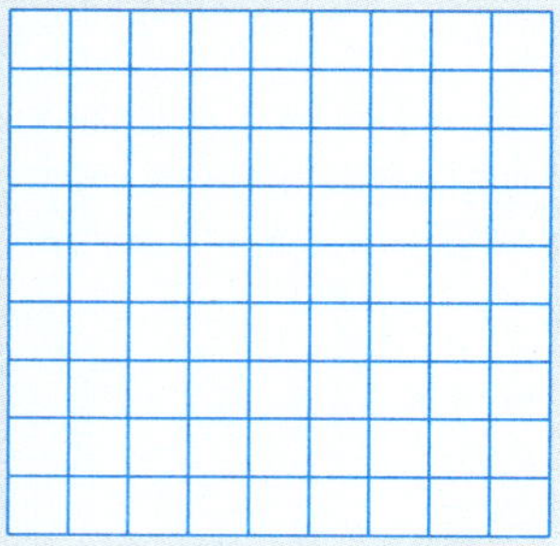

75. $f(x) = x;\ h(x) = x - 4$

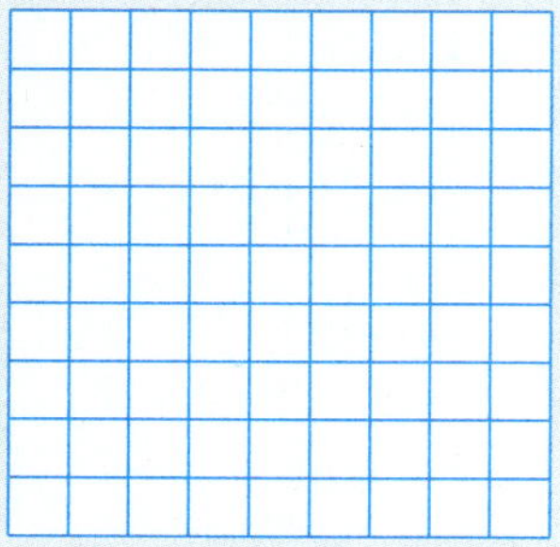

5 MTR

76. **STRUCTURE** The graph of the equation $Ax + By = 15$ is shown. Find the values of A and B.

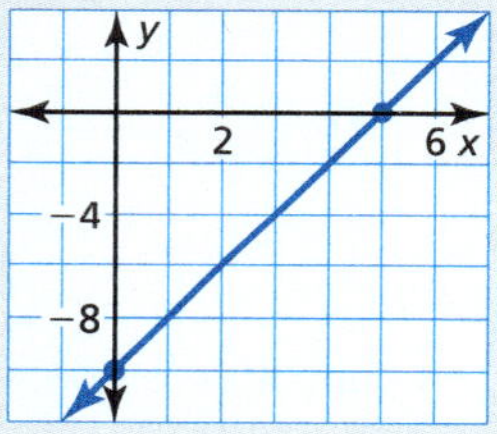

77. Determine whether the relation is a function. Explain.

$(-10, 2), (-8, 3), (-6, 5), (-8, 8), (-10, 6)$

78. Solve the formula for h.

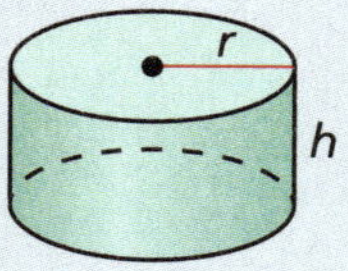

$V = \pi r^2 h$

79. Write an inequality that represents the graph.

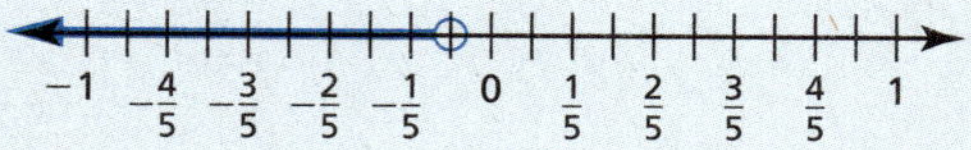

3.8 Graphing Absolute Value Functions

Learning Target: Graph absolute value functions.

Success Criteria:
- I can identify characteristics of absolute value functions.
- I can graph absolute value functions.
- I can describe transformations of graphs of absolute value functions.

Algebraic Reasoning
MA.912.AR.4.3 Given a table, equation or written description of an absolute value function, graph that function and determine its key features.
Functions
MA.912.F.2.1 Identify the effect on the graph or table of a given function after replacing $f(x)$ by $f(x) + k$, $kf(x)$, $f(kx)$ and $f(x + k)$ for specific values of k.
H **Also MA.912.F.2.3**

EXPLORE IT! Understanding Graphs of Absolute Value Functions

Work with a partner.

a. Think about the absolute value of a number. What characteristics might you observe in the graph of an *absolute value function*?

b. Graph $y = |x|$. Make several observations about the graph.

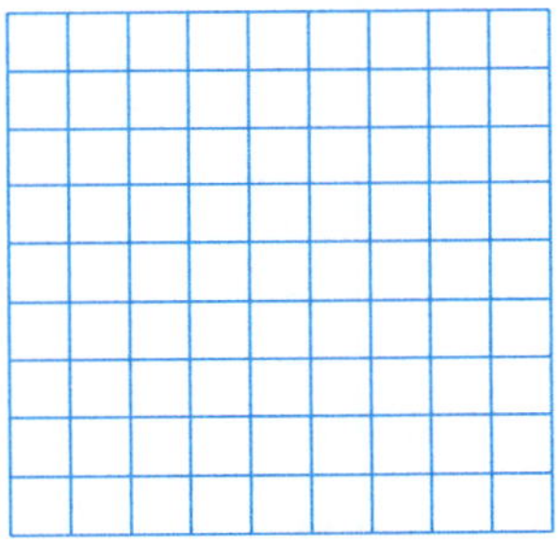

c. Let f be the parent absolute value function $f(x) = |x|$. Which of the following functions have a graph with one x-intercept? two x-intercepts? no x-intercept? Explain your reasoning.

$g(x) = f(x) - 1$ $\quad$ $h(x) = f(x - 1)$ $\quad$ $p(x) = -f(x)$ $\quad$ $q(x) = f(x) + 1$

RELATE CONCEPTS 5 MTR
How can you use what you know about transformations of linear functions to make conclusions about transformations of absolute value functions?

d. Match each absolute value function with its graph. Explain your reasoning. Then use technology to check your answers.

i. $g(x) = -|x - 2|$

ii. $g(x) = |x - 2| + 2$

iii. $g(x) = |x - 2| - 2$

iv. $g(x) = 2|x - 2|$

A.

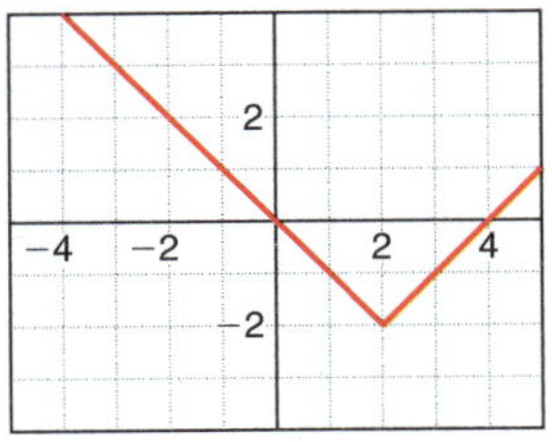

B.

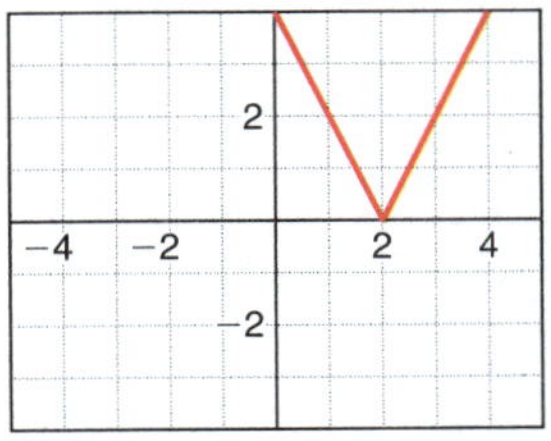

C.

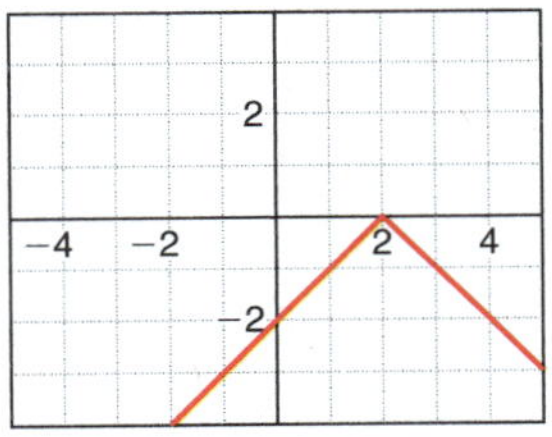

D.

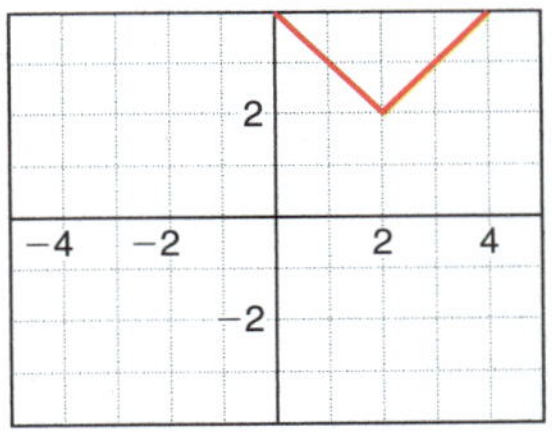

GO DIGITAL

Characteristics of Absolute Value Functions

Vocabulary

absolute value function, *p. 268*
vertex, *p. 268*
vertex form, *p. 273*

WORDS AND MATH

In geometry, a *vertex* is the point where the sides meet for an angle, polygon, or solid.

KEY IDEA

Absolute Value Function

An **absolute value function** is a function that contains an absolute value expression. The parent absolute value function is $f(x) = |x|$. The graph of $f(x) = |x|$ is V-shaped and symmetric about the y-axis. The **vertex** is the point where the graph changes direction. The vertex of the graph of $f(x) = |x|$ is $(0, 0)$.

The domain of $f(x) = |x|$ is all real numbers. The range is $y \geq 0$.

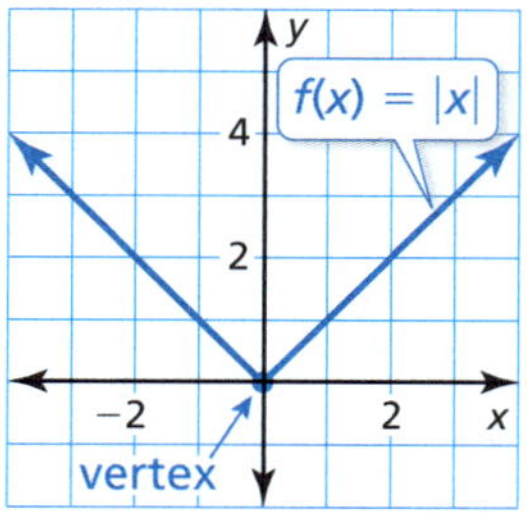

EXAMPLE 1 Describing Characteristics

Determine when the function $y = -|x| + 2$ is positive, negative, increasing, or decreasing. Then describe the end behavior of the function.

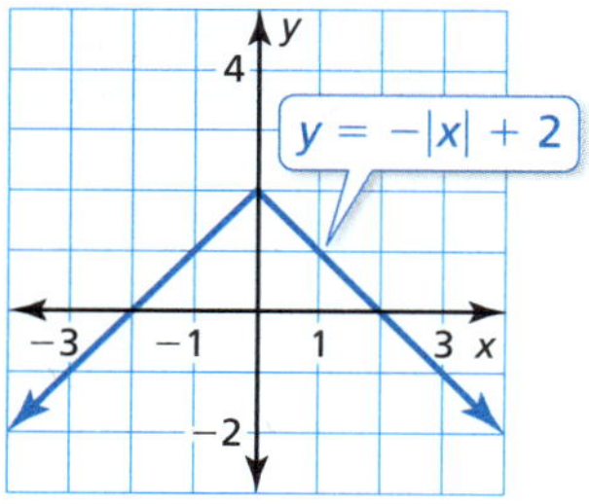

SOLUTION

Positive and Negative:

The x-intercepts are ± 2. The function is negative when $x < -2$, positive when $-2 < x < 2$, and negative when $x > 2$.

Increasing and Decreasing:

The vertex is $(0, 2)$. The function is increasing when $x < 0$ and decreasing when $x > 0$.

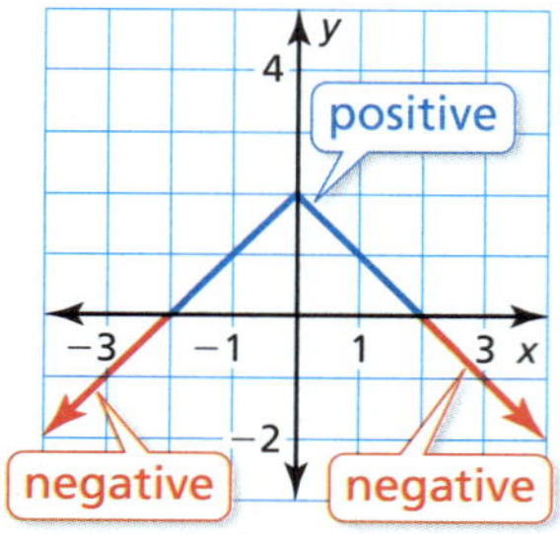

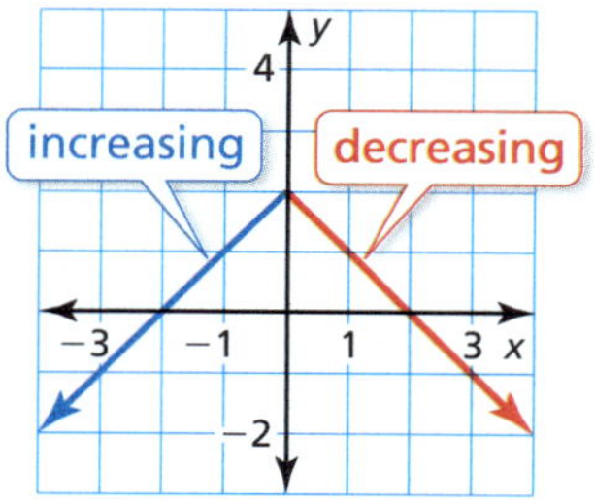

End behavior: The graph shows that the function values decrease as x approaches both positive and negative infinity. So, $y \to -\infty$ as $x \to -\infty$ and $y \to -\infty$ as $x \to +\infty$.

GO DIGITAL

Transforming Graphs of Absolute Value Functions

The graphs of all other absolute value functions are transformations of the graph of the parent function $f(x) = |x|$. The transformations presented in the previous section also apply to absolute value functions.

EXAMPLE 2 Graphing Absolute Value Functions

WATCH

Graph each function. Compare each graph to the graph of $f(x) = |x|$. Find the domain and range.

a. $q(x) = 2|x|$ **b.** $m(x) = |x - 2|$

STUDY TIP

A vertical stretch of the graph of $f(x) = |x|$ is *narrower* than the graph of $f(x) = |x|$.

A vertical shrink of the graph of $f(x) = |x|$ is *wider* than the graph of $f(x) = |x|$.

SOLUTION

a. Step 1 Make a table of values.

x	-2	-1	0	1	2
$q(x)$	4	2	0	2	4

Step 2 Plot the ordered pairs.

Step 3 Draw the graph.

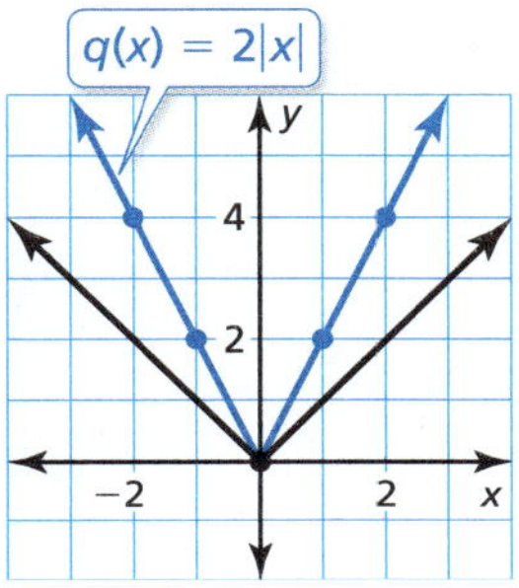

▶ The function q is of the form $y = a \cdot f(x)$, where $a = 2$. So, the graph of q is a vertical stretch of the graph of f by a factor of 2. The domain is all real numbers. The range is $y \geq 0$.

HELP A CLASSMATE (1 MTR)

Explain to a classmate why you can also describe the transformation in part (a) as a horizontal shrink.

b. Step 1 Make a table of values.

x	0	1	2	3	4
$m(x)$	2	1	0	1	2

Step 2 Plot the ordered pairs.

Step 3 Draw the graph.

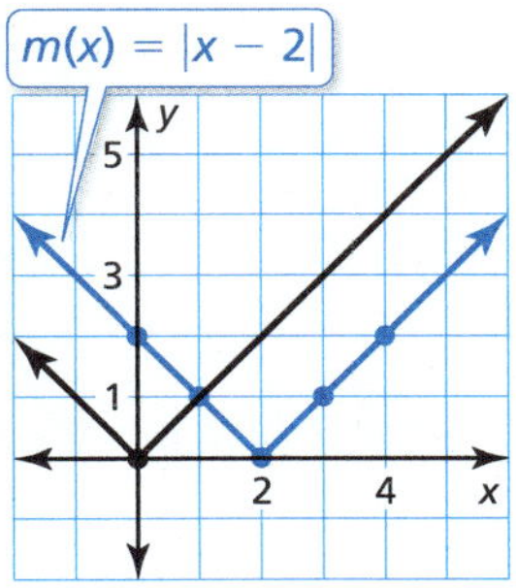

▶ The function m is of the form $y = f(x - h)$, where $h = 2$. So, the graph of m is a horizontal translation 2 units right of the graph of f. The domain is all real numbers. The range is $y \geq 0$.

GO DIGITAL

SELF-ASSESSMENT

1 I don't understand yet. 2 I can do it with help. 3 I can do it on my own. 4 I can teach someone else.

Determine when the function is positive, negative, increasing, or decreasing. Then describe the end behavior of the function.

1.

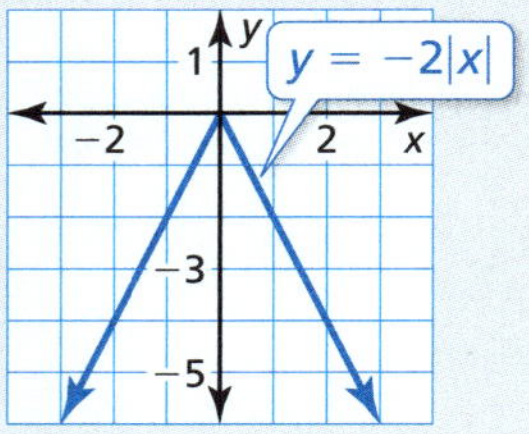

2.

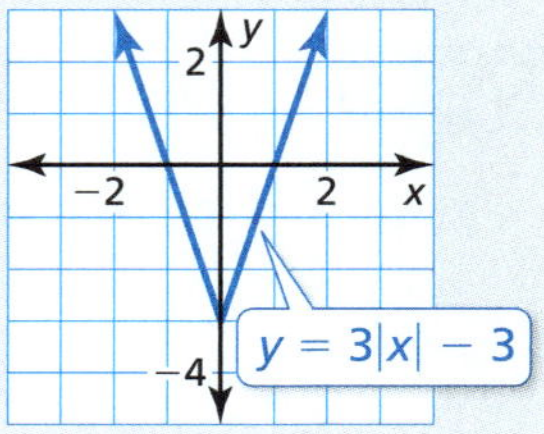

3.

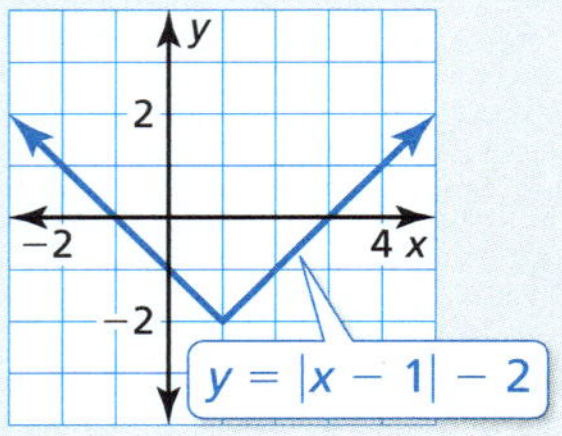

1 MTR **4.** **HELP A CLASSMATE** Explain to a classmate how to use the vertex and x-intercepts to determine when an absolute value function is positive, negative, increasing, or decreasing.

Graph the function. Compare the graph to the graph of $f(x) = |x|$. Find the domain and range.

5. $h(x) = |x| - 1$

6. $n(x) = |x + 4|$

7. $t(x) = -3|x|$

8. $v(x) = \frac{1}{4}|x|$

9. **REASONING** Without graphing, explain how the graph of $g(x) = |x| + 5$ compares to the graph of $f(x) = |x|$.

5 MTR **10.** **USE STRUCTURE** How do you know whether the graph of $g(x) = a|x|$ is a vertical stretch or a vertical shrink of the graph of $f(x) = b|x|$?

Describing Transformations

EXAMPLE 3 **Describing a Transformation** WATCH

Let $f(x) = |3x| - 1$. Graph $g(x) = -f(x)$. Describe the transformation from the graph of f to the graph of g.

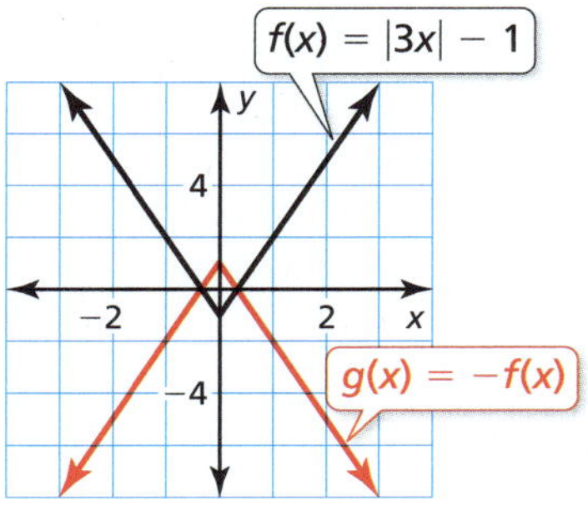

SOLUTION

To find the outputs of g, multiply the outputs of f by -1. The graph of g consists of the points $(x, -f(x))$.

x	−2	−1	0	1	2
f(x)	5	2	−1	2	5
−f(x)	−5	−2	1	−2	−5

▶ The graph of g is a reflection in the x-axis of the graph of f.

EXAMPLE 4 **Describing a Transformation** WATCH H

Describe the transformation from the graph of f to the graph of g.

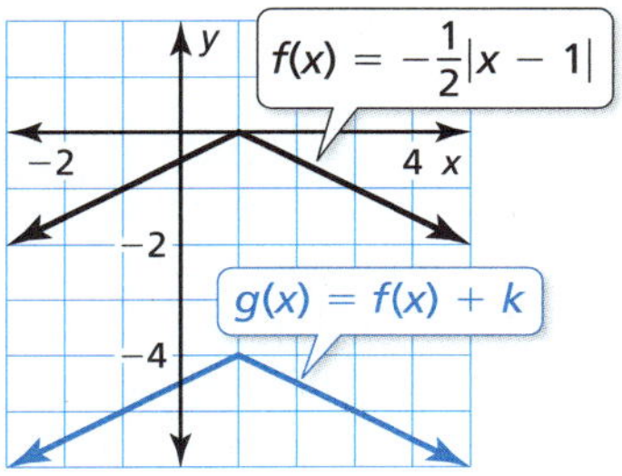

SOLUTION

Compare f and g to find the value of k. The function $g(x) = f(x) + k$ indicates that the graph of g is a vertical translation of the graph of f. The graphs of f and g show that for any input, the output of g is 4 less than the output of f. For example, $g(1) = -4$ and $f(1) = 0$. So, $k = -4$.

▶ The graph of g is a translation 4 units down of the graph of f.

GO DIGITAL

SELF-ASSESSMENT

1 I don't understand yet. **2** I can do it with help. **3** I can do it on my own. **4** I can teach someone else.

Using *f*, graph (a) *g* and (b) *h*. Describe the transformations from the graph of *f* to the graphs of *g* and *h*.

11. $f(x) = |x + 3|$; $g(x) = f(x) - 4$; $h(x) = f(x - 4)$

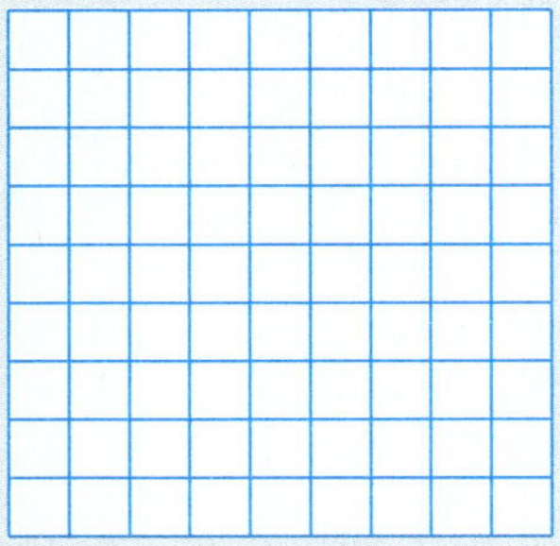

12. $f(x) = -|x|$; $g(x) = 2f(x)$; $h(x) = f(2x)$

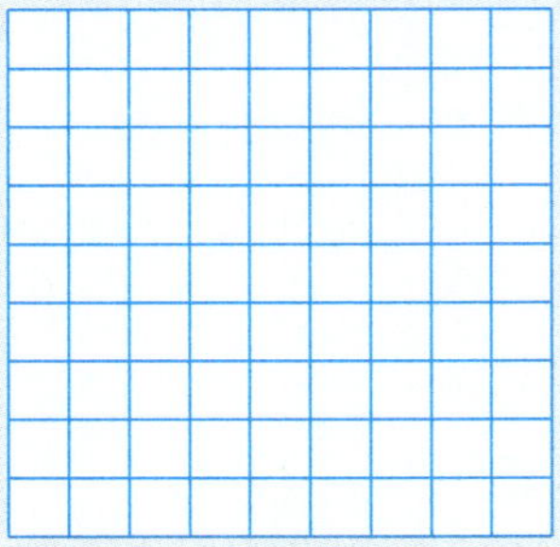

Describe the transformation from the graph of *f* to the graph of *g*.

13.

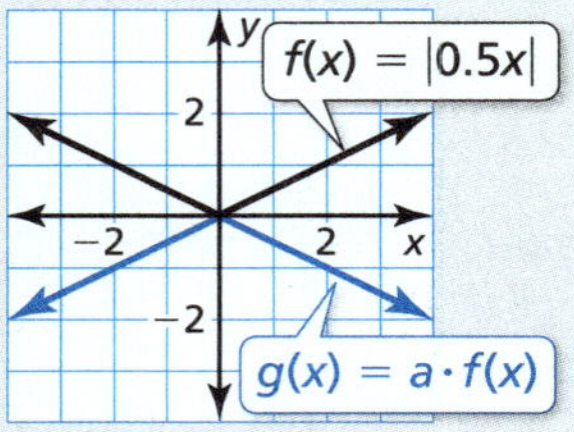

14.

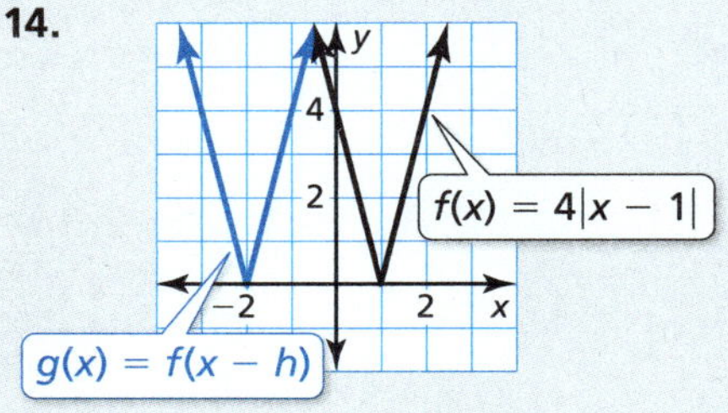

15.

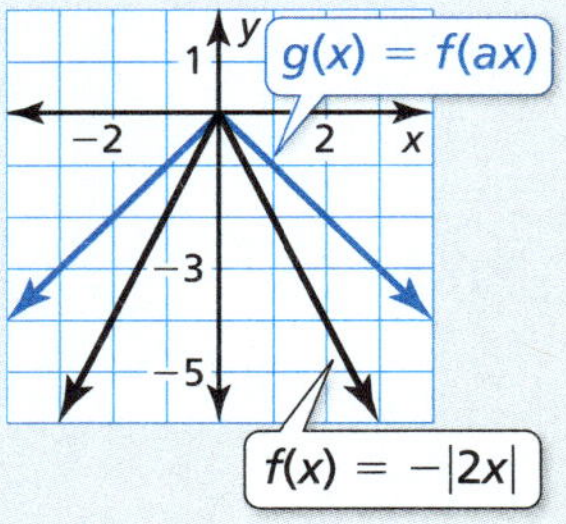

16. Graph the absolute value functions *f* and *g* represented by the table. Describe the transformation from the graph of *f* to the graph of *g*.

x	-2	-1	1	2
$f(x)$	2	4	4	2
$g(x)$	1	2	2	1

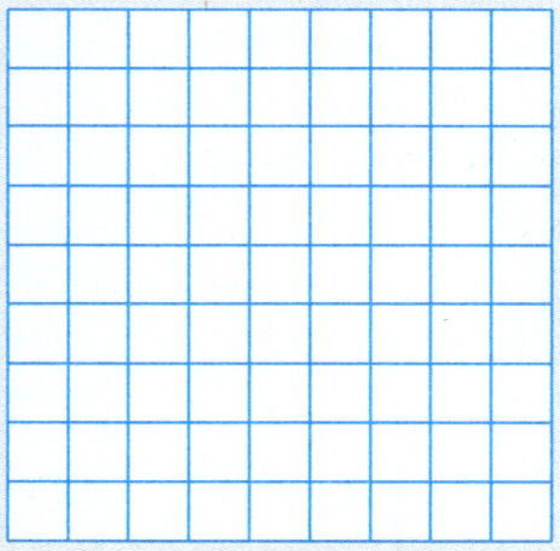

17. OPEN-ENDED Write an absolute value function that is a transformation of the parent absolute value function. Describe the end behavior of the function.

Using Vertex Form

KEY IDEA

Vertex Form of an Absolute Value Function

An absolute value function written in the form $g(x) = a|x - h| + k$, where $a \neq 0$, is in **vertex form**. The vertex of the graph of g is (h, k).

Any absolute value function can be written in vertex form, and its graph is symmetric about the line $x = h$.

7 MTR **EXAMPLE 5** **Modeling Real Life** WATCH

You ride your bicycle around a circular trail one time. The function $f(x) = -\frac{1}{3}|x - 4.5| + 1.5$ represents the shortest distance (in miles) along the trail between you and your starting point after x minutes. (a) Graph the function. Find the domain and range in this context. (b) Interpret the intercepts and the vertex.

SOLUTION

a. The function is in vertex form, $g(x) = a|x - h| + k$, where $h = 4.5$ and $k = 1.5$. So, the vertex is $(h, k) = (4.5, 1.5)$. Substitute 0 for $f(x)$ to find any x-intercepts.

$$0 = -\tfrac{1}{3}|x - 4.5| + 1.5$$
$$4.5 = |x - 4.5|$$
$$x - 4.5 = 4.5 \quad \text{or} \quad x - 4.5 = -4.5$$
$$x = 9 \qquad\qquad x = 0$$

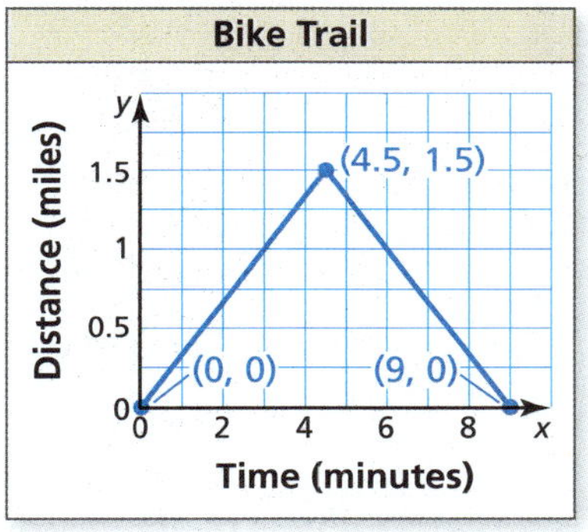

Graph the function using the points (0, 0), (4.5, 1.5), and (9, 0). The time x and distance $f(x)$ must be greater than or equal to 0 in this context. So, the domain is $\{x \mid 0 \leq x \leq 9\}$ and the range is $\{f(x) \mid 0 \leq f(x) \leq 1.5\}$.

b. The intercepts 0 and 9 indicate that it takes you $9 - 0 = 9$ minutes to ride around the trail. The vertex (4.5, 1.5) indicates that you are 1.5 miles from your starting point after 4.5 minutes. You can also determine that you are halfway around the trail at that time.

1 MTR **ANALYZE A PROBLEM**

Explain why it makes sense that the graph begins at (0, 0). How can you use symmetry to find the other intercept?

GO DIGITAL

SELF-ASSESSMENT
1 I don't understand yet. 2 I can do it with help. 3 I can do it on my own. 4 I can teach someone else.

18. The function $d(x) = \frac{1}{3}|x - 15| - 5$ represents the elevation (in meters) of a scuba diver x seconds after descending from the surface.

a. Graph the function. Find the domain and range in this context.

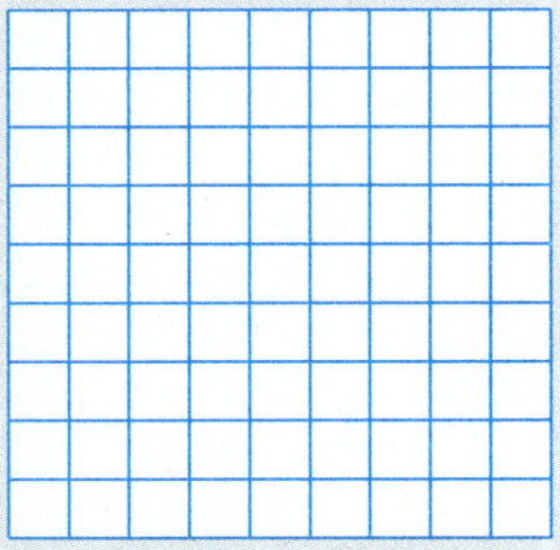

b. Interpret the intercepts and the vertex.

19. WHAT IF? The function $f(x) = -0.25|x - 8| + 2$ models the situation in Example 5. What is the radius of the trail? At what speed did you ride your bicycle? Explain your reasoning.

3.8 Practice WITH CalcChat® AND CalcView®

In Exercises 1–6, determine when the function is positive, negative, increasing, or decreasing. Then describe the end behavior of the function. *(See Example 1.)*

▶ **1.**

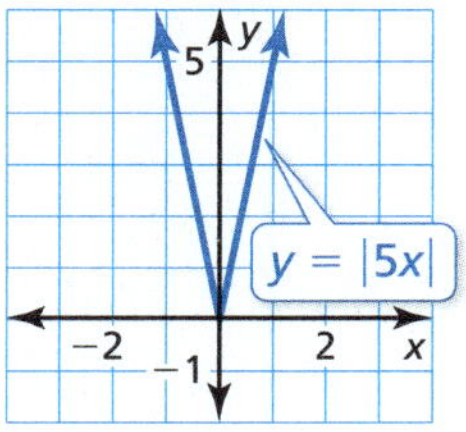

2.

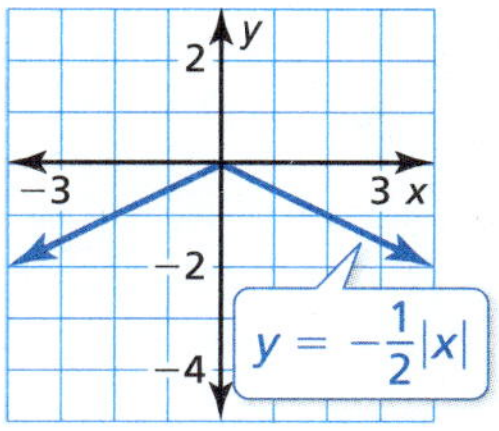

3.

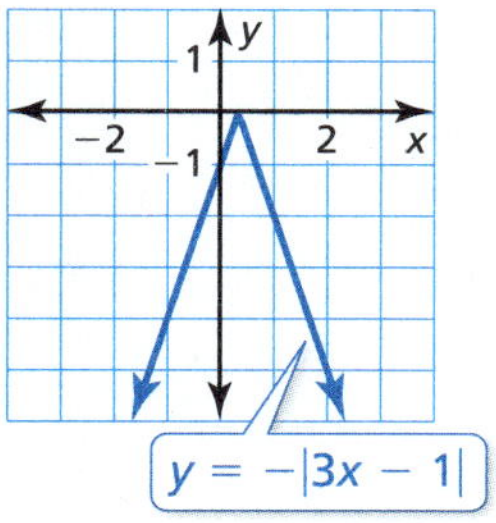

4.

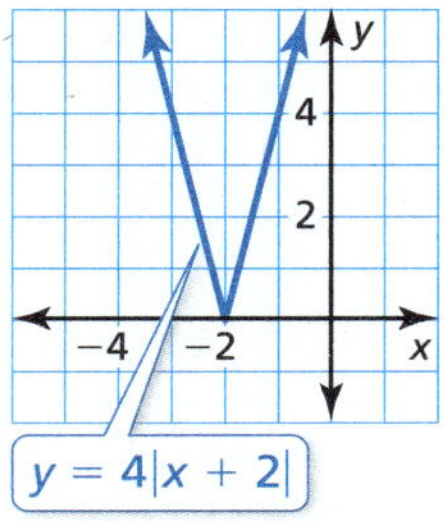

5.

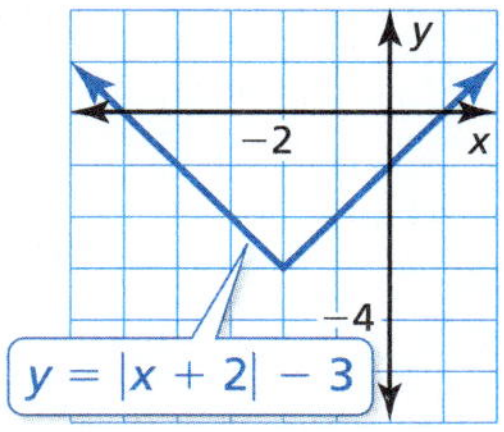

6.

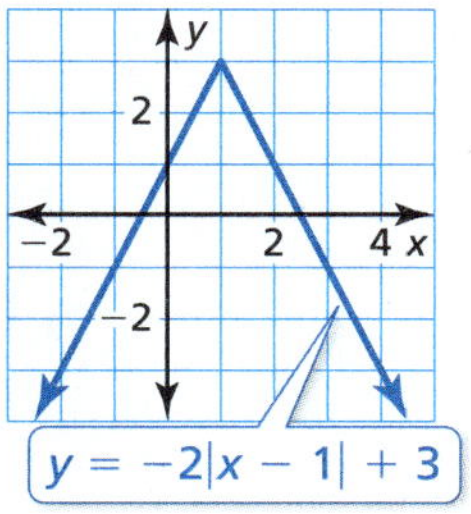

In Exercises 7–10, use the graphs of *f* and *h* to describe the transformation from the graph of *f* to the graph of *h*.

7. $f(x) = |x - 6|;\ h(x) = f(x) - 2$

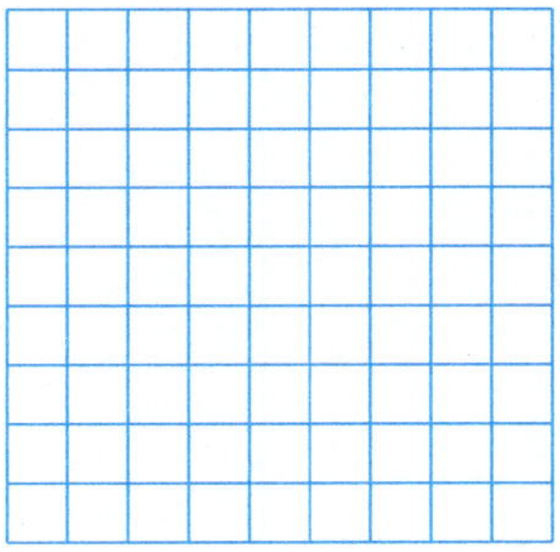

8. $f(x) = -2|x + 4|;\ h(x) = f(-x)$

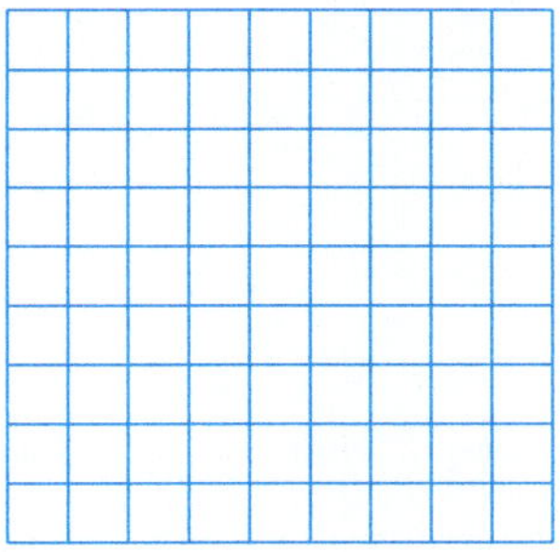

9. $f(x) = -8x;\ h(x) = f\left(\frac{3}{4}x\right)$

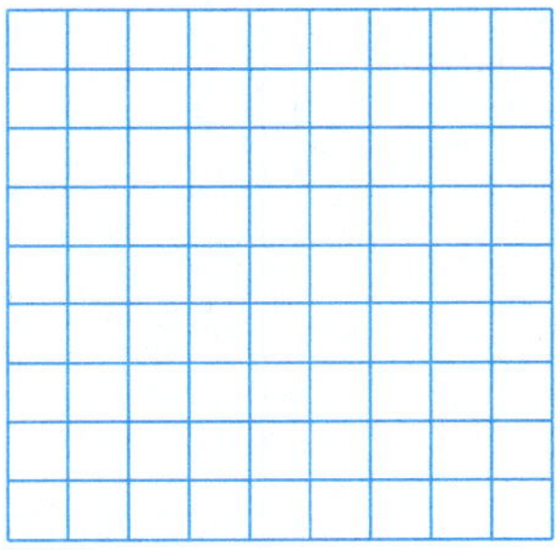

10. $f(x) = \frac{1}{7}|x| + 1;\ h(x) = f(6x)$

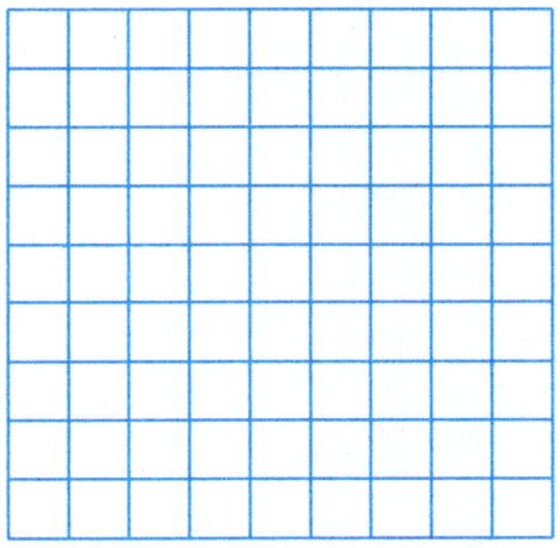

GO DIGITAL

In Exercises 11–20, graph the function. Compare the graph to the graph of $f(x) = |x|$. Find the domain and range. *(See Example 2.)*

▶ **11.** $d(x) = |x| - 4$

12. $r(x) = |x| + 5$

13. $m(x) = |x + 1|$

14. $v(x) = |x - 3|$

15. $m(x) = -|x|$

16. $v(x) = |-x|$

17. $p(x) = \frac{1}{3}|x|$

18. $j(x) = 3|x|$

▶ **19.** $a(x) = |5x|$

20. $q(x) = \left|\frac{3}{2}x\right|$

4 MTR ERROR ANALYSIS **In Exercises 21 and 22, describe and correct the error in graphing the function.**

21.

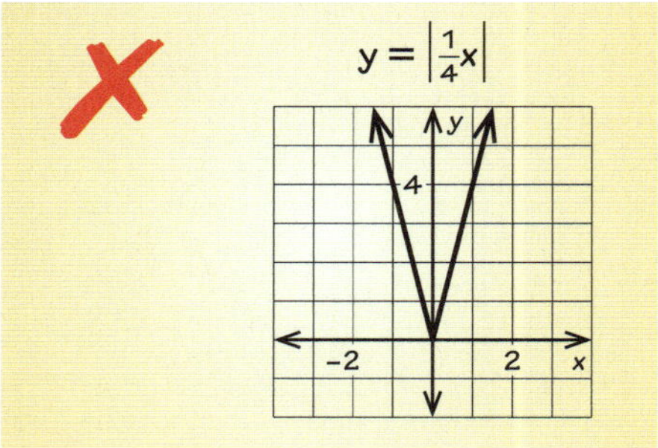

22.

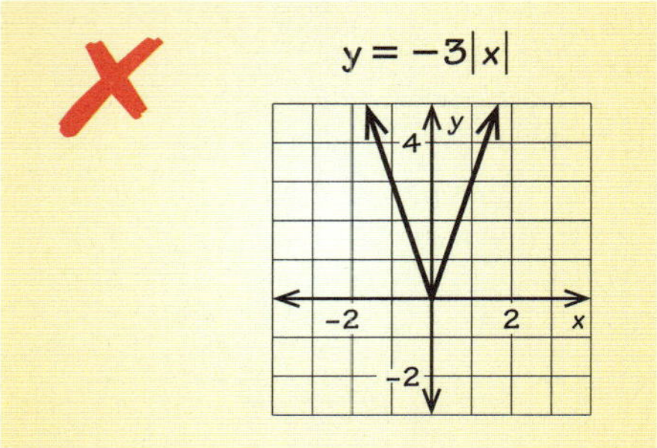

In Exercises 23–28, write an equation that represents the given transformation(s) of the graph of $g(x) = |x|$.

23. vertical translation 7 units down

24. horizontal translation 10 units left

25. reflection in the x-axis

26. reflection in the y-axis

27. vertical shrink by a factor of $\frac{1}{4}$

28. horizontal stretch by a factor of 3

In Exercises 29–32, using f, graph (a) g and (b) h. Describe the transformations from the graph of f to the graphs of g and h. *(See Example 3.)*

▶29. $f(x) = -|x + 7|$; $g(x) = f(x) + 4$; $h(x) = f(x + 4)$

30. $f(x) = 2|x| + 11$; $g(x) = -f(x)$; $h(x) = f(-x)$

31. $f(x) = \frac{1}{6}|x + 5|$; $g(x) = 3f(x)$; $h(x) = f(3x)$

32. $f(x) = 3|x| - 4$; $g(x) = \frac{1}{5}f(x)$; $h(x) = f\left(\frac{1}{5}x\right)$

In Exercises 33–42, describe the transformation from the graph of f to the graph of g. *(See Example 4.)*

33.

x	−4	−3	−2	−1	0
$f(x)$	−1	0	−1	−2	−3
$g(x) = f(x) + k$	−6	−5	−6	−7	−8

34.

x	−5	−3	−1	1	3
$f(x)$	2	0	−2	0	2
$g(x) = a \cdot f(x)$	1	0	−1	0	1

35.

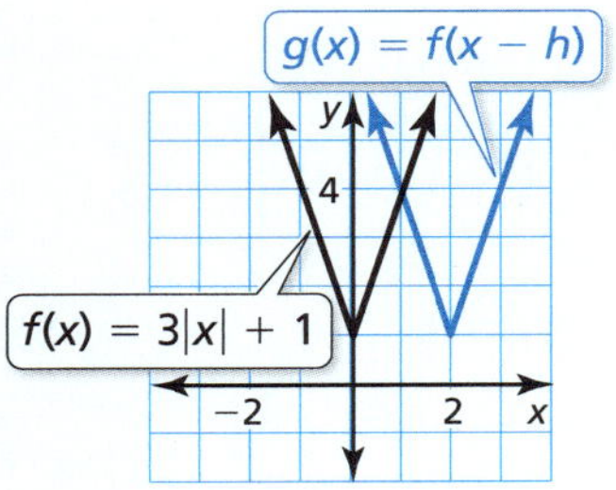

36.

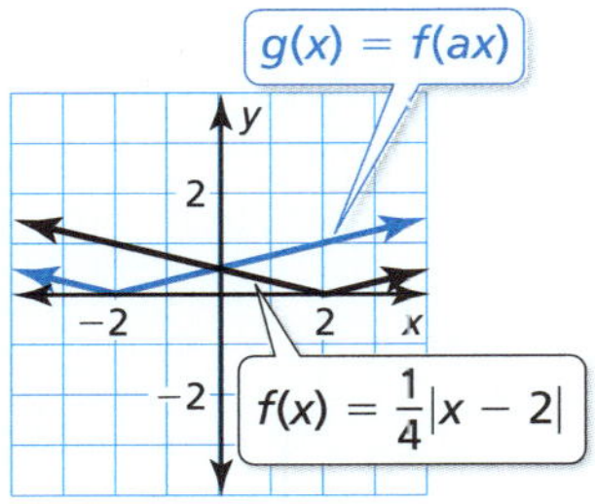

37.

x	1	2	3	4	5
$f(x)$	3	2	1	0	1
$g(x)$	9	6	3	0	3

38.

x	−4	−3	−2	−1	0
$f(x)$	−5	−6	−7	−6	−5
$g(x)$	5	6	7	6	5

39.

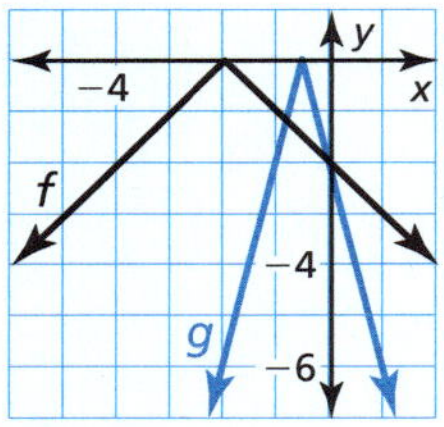

40.

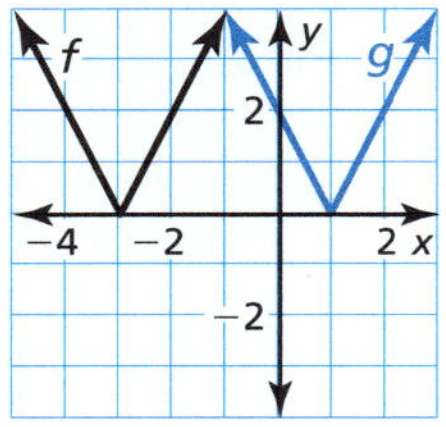

41.

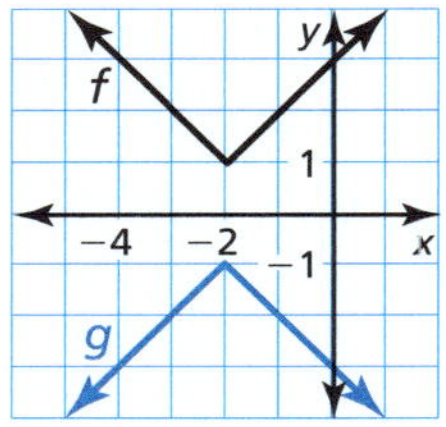

42.

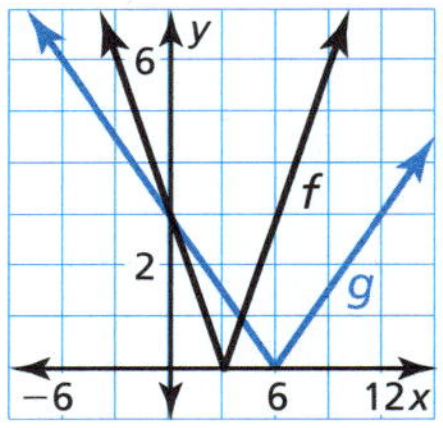

43. MODELING REAL LIFE You are running a ten-mile race. The function $d(t) = \frac{1}{8}|t - 40|$ represents the distance (in miles) you are from a water stop after t minutes. *(See Example 5.)*

7 MTR

a. Graph the function. Find the domain and range in this context.

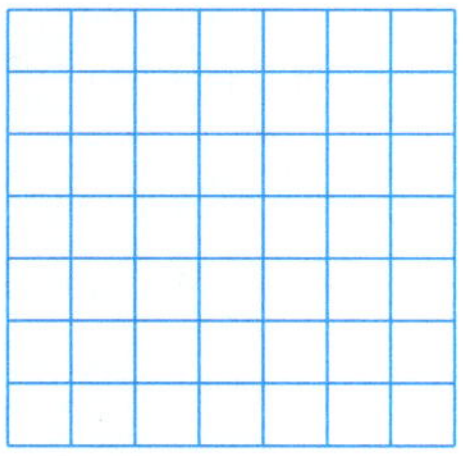

b. Interpret the intercepts and the vertex. When is the function decreasing? increasing? Explain what each represents in this context.

7 MTR

44. MODELING REAL LIFE A traveler is driving from Georgia to Florida. The function $d(t) = 60|t - 2.5|$ represents the distance (in miles) the car is from the state line after t hours.

a. Graph the function. Find the domain and range in this context.

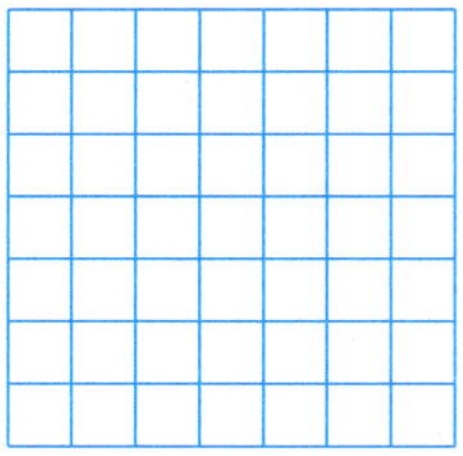

b. Interpret the intercepts and the vertex. When is the function decreasing? increasing? Explain what each represents in this context.

45. REASONING Is it possible for an absolute value function to always be increasing? decreasing? Explain your reasoning.

46. HOW DO YOU SEE IT?
The object of a computer game is to break bricks by deflecting a ball toward them using a paddle. The graph shows the current path of the ball and the location of the last brick.

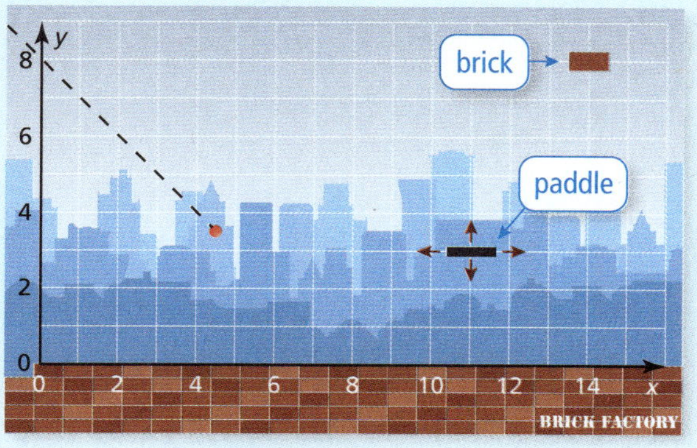

a. You can move the paddle up, down, left, and right. At what coordinates should you place the paddle to break the last brick? Assume the ball deflects at a right angle.

b. You move the paddle to the coordinates in part (a), and the ball is deflected. How can you write an absolute value function that describes the path of the ball?

47. B.E.S.T. TEST PREP Which of the following functions have the same end behavior?

Ⓐ $a(x) = 4|x - 2| + 3$

Ⓑ $b(x) = -\frac{3}{2}|x + 5|$

Ⓒ $c(x) = |-2x - 6| - 1$

Ⓓ $d(x) = \left|9 - \frac{1}{2}x\right|$

48. THOUGHT PROVOKING
Graph an absolute value function f that represents the route a wide receiver runs in a football game. Let the x-axis represent distance (in yards) across the field horizontally. Let the y-axis represent distance (in yards) down the field. Limit the domain so the route is realistic.

49. USING TOOLS Graph $y = 2|x + 2| - 6$ and $y = -2$ in the same coordinate plane. Use the graph to solve the equation $2|x + 2| - 6 = -2$. Use technology to check your solutions.

50. DIG DEEPER Write the vertex of the absolute value function $f(x) = |ax - h| + k$ in terms of a, h, and k.

4 MTR **51. MAKING AN ARGUMENT** Let p be a positive constant, where the graph of $y = |x| + p$ is a vertical translation in the positive direction of the graph of $y = |x|$. Does this mean that the graph of $y = |x + p|$ is a horizontal translation in the positive direction of the graph of $y = |x|$? Explain.

REVIEW & REFRESH

In Exercises 52 and 53, solve the equation.

52. $-4|2x - 3| + 12 = -8$

53. $|x + 4| = |5x + 2|$

54. Describe the transformation from the graph of f to the graph of g.

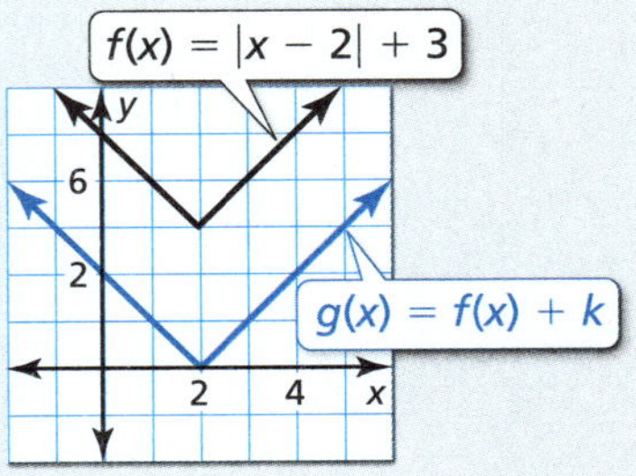

In Exercises 55–58, solve the inequality. Graph the solution, if possible.

55. $2a - 7 \leq -2$

56. $-3(2p + 4) > -6p - 5$

57. $4(3h + 1.5) \geq 6(2h - 2)$

58. $-4(x + 6) < 2(2x - 9)$

In Exercises 59 and 60, use the graphs of f and g to describe the transformation from the graph of f to the graph of g.

59. $f(x) = -\frac{1}{2}x$; $g(x) = f(x + 2)$

60. $f(x) = 3x - 1$; $g(x) = -f(x)$

7 MTR **61. MODELING REAL LIFE** You have \$15 to purchase pecans and walnuts. The equation $12x + 7.5y = 15$ models this situation, where x is the number of pounds of pecans and y is the number of pounds of walnuts.

a. Interpret the terms and coefficients in the equation.

b. Graph the equation. Interpret the intercepts.

62. Let $f(t)$ be the outside temperature (in degrees Celsius) t hours after 9 A.M. Explain the meaning of each statement.

a. $f(4) = 30$ **b.** $f(m) = 28.9$ **c.** $f(2) = f(9)$ **d.** $f(6.5) > f(0)$

63. Solve $y = 3x - 7$ for x.

64. OPEN-ENDED Draw a graph that does *not* represent a function.

65. Find the slope of the line.

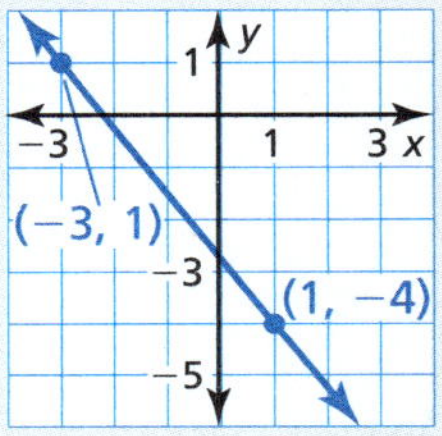

3 Chapter Review WITH CalcChat®

Chapter Learning Target: Understand graphing linear functions.

Chapter Success Criteria:
- ◆ I can identify the graph of a linear function.
- ◆ I can graph linear functions written in different forms.
- ■ I can describe the characteristics of a function.
- ■ I can explain how a transformation affects the graph of a linear function.

◆ Surface
■ Deep

SELF-ASSESSMENT 1 I don't understand yet. 2 I can do it with help. 3 I can do it on my own. 4 I can teach someone else.

3.1 Functions (pp. 173–186)

WATCH

Learning Target: Understand the concept of a function.

Vocabulary (AZ VOCAB)
relation
function
domain
range
independent variable
dependent variable

Determine whether the relation is a function. Explain.

1. (0, 1), (5, 6), (7, 9), (8, 9)

2.

Input, x	Output, y
5	11
7	19
9	3

Determine whether the graph represents a function. Then find the domain and range.

3.

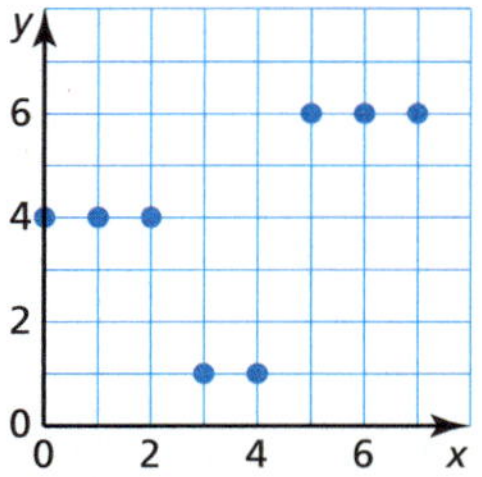

4.

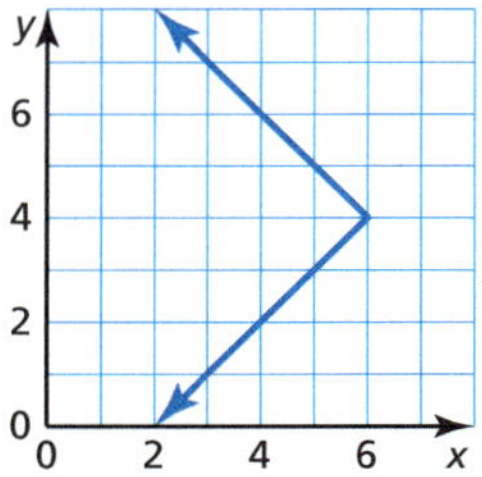

5.

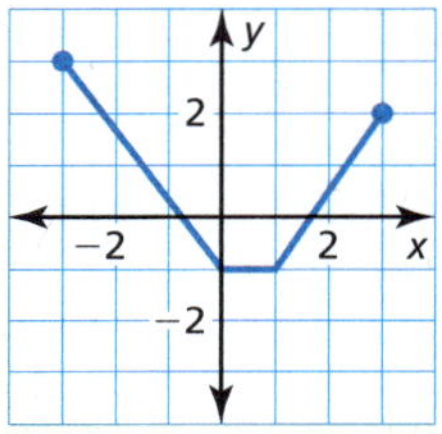

6.

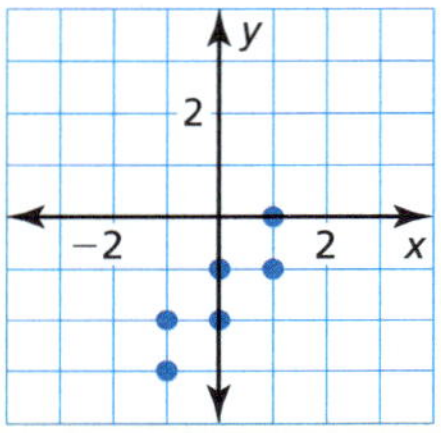

GO DIGITAL

7. You have $170. You start a part-time job that pays $8.50 per hour.

a. Does the situation represent a function? If so, identify the independent and dependent variables.

b. You work no more than 4 hours. Find the domain and range.

8. Write a relation consisting of five ordered pairs that satisfies the following conditions.

- The relation is a function.
- Switching the x- and y-coordinates of each ordered pair results in a relation that is *not* a function.

3.2 Characteristics of Functions *(pp. 187–196)* WATCH

Learning Target: Describe characteristics of functions.

Vocabulary AZ VOCAB
- x-intercept
- y-intercept
- increasing
- decreasing
- end behavior

Approximate when the function is positive, negative, increasing, or decreasing. Then describe the end behavior of the function.

9.

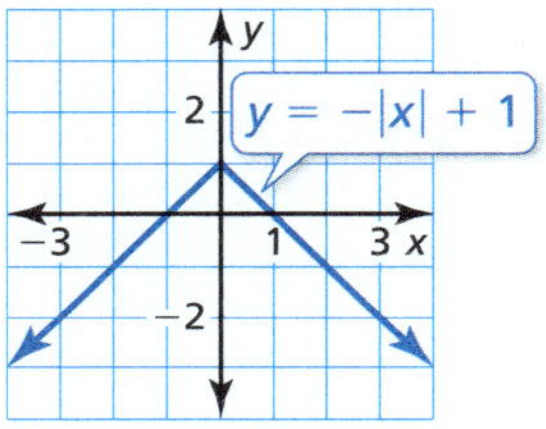

10.

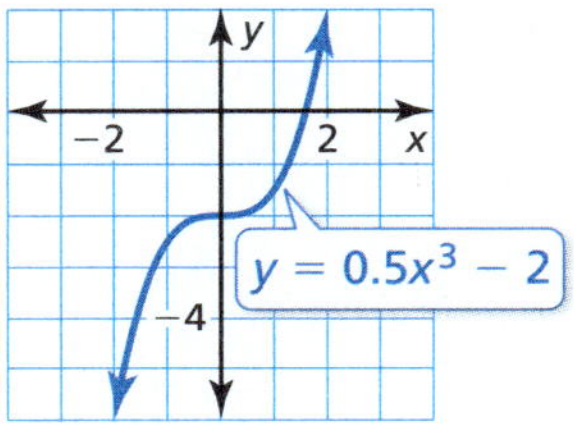

11. A goalie kicks a soccer ball so that it lands about 60 meters away, reaching a maximum height of about 15 meters after traveling a horizontal distance of about 30 meters. The graph shows the path of the second kick. Compare the two kicks.

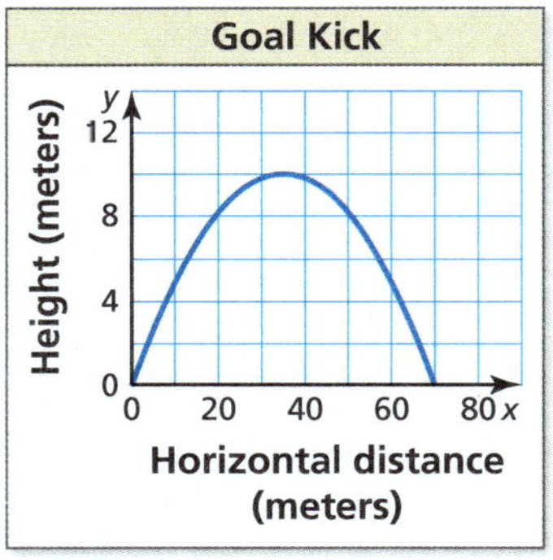

12. Sketch a graph of a function with the given characteristics.

- The x-intercepts are $-\frac{7}{2}$, $-\frac{1}{2}$, and $\frac{5}{2}$.
- The function is increasing when $x < -\frac{3}{2}$, decreasing when $-\frac{3}{2} < x < 1$, and increasing when $x > 1$.

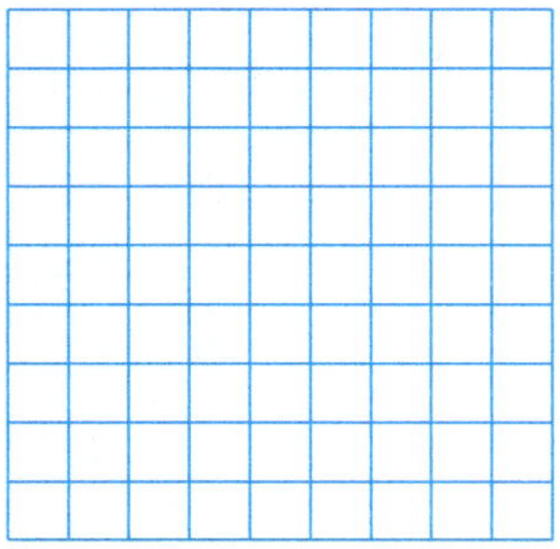

3.3 Linear Functions (pp. 197–212) WATCH

Learning Target: Identify and graph linear functions.

Vocabulary (AZ VOCAB)

linear equation in two variables
linear function
nonlinear function
solution of a linear equation in two variables
discrete domain
continuous domain

Determine whether the table, graph, or equation represents a *linear* or *nonlinear* function. Explain.

13.

x	2	7	12	17
y	2	−1	−4	−7

14.

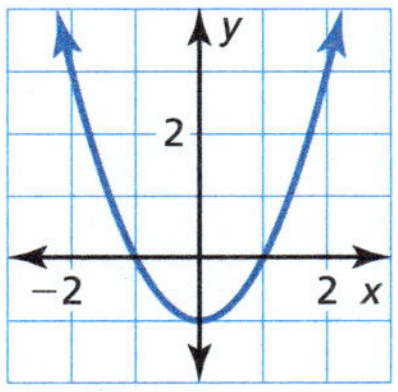

15. $y - 3 = 3x + 2$

16. $y = 2\sqrt{x}$

Graph the function using its domain. Explain your reasoning.

17.

Games, x	1	2	3	4	5
Tokens, y	8	6	4	2	0

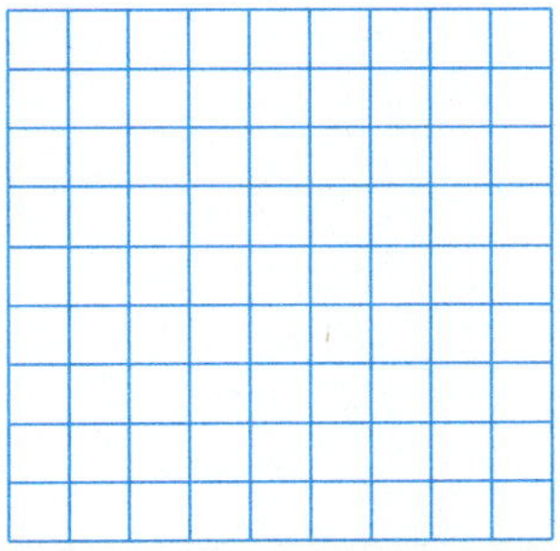

18.

Time (minutes), x	1.5	3.0	4.5
Elevation (feet), y	1500	3000	4500

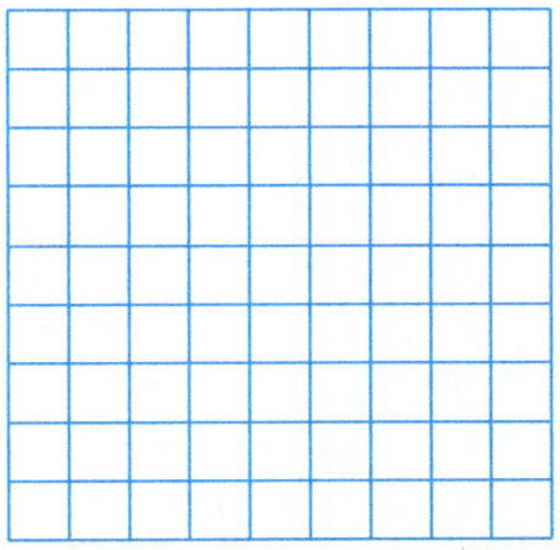

19. The function $y = 60 - 8x$ represents the amount y (in dollars) of money you have after buying x movie tickets. (a) Find the domain of the function. Is the domain *discrete* or *continuous*? Explain. (b) Graph the function using its domain.

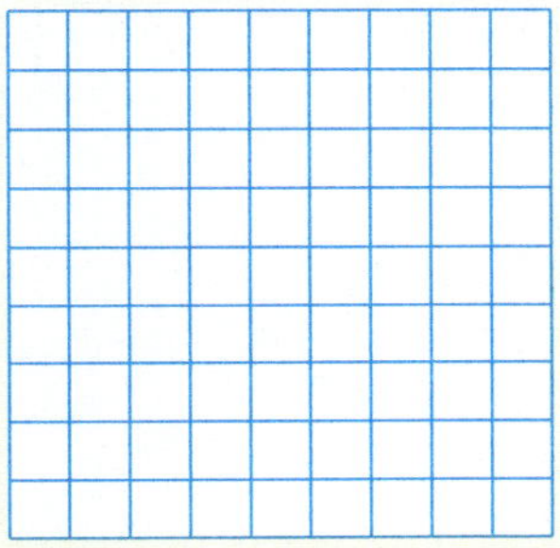

3.4 Function Notation (pp. 213–222)

Learning Target: Understand and use function notation.

Vocabulary

function notation

Evaluate the function when $x = -3$, 0, and 5.

20. $f(x) = x + 8$

21. $h(x) = 3x - 9$

22. Let $p(t)$ be the number of people in a stadium t hours after 11:00 A.M. Explain the meaning of each statement.

a. $p(3) = p(5)$

b. $p(6) < p(2.5)$

Find the value of x so that the function has the given value.

23. $k(x) = 7x$; $k(x) = 49$

24. $r(x) = -5x - 1$; $r(x) = 19$

Graph the linear function.

25. $g(x) = -2x - 3$

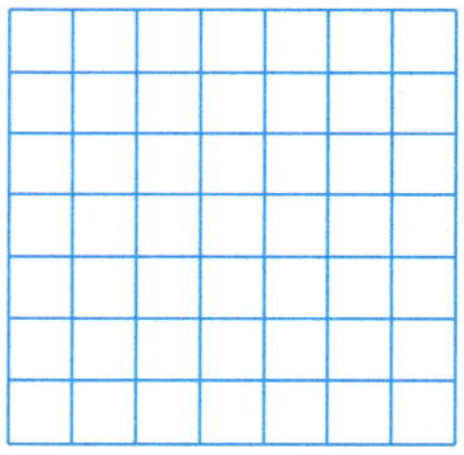

26. $h(x) = \frac{2}{3}x + 4$

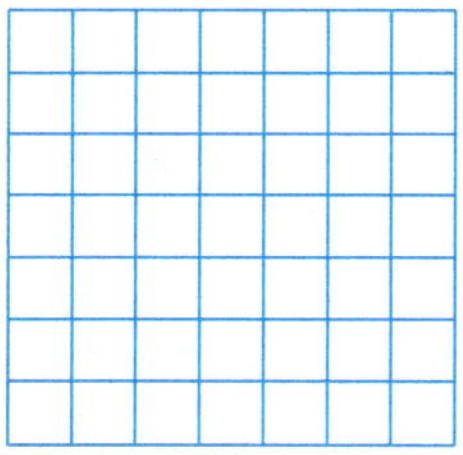

27. The function $d(x) = 1375 - 110x$ represents the distance (in miles) a high-speed train is from its destination after x hours.

a. How far is the train from its destination after 8 hours?

b. How long does the train travel before reaching its destination?

3.5 Graphing Linear Equations in Standard Form (pp. 223–232) WATCH

Learning Target: Graph and interpret linear equations written in standard form.

Vocabulary
standard form

Graph the linear equation.

28. $x = 6$

29. $y = \frac{3}{2}$

Use intercepts to graph the linear equation. Label the points corresponding to the intercepts.

30. $2x + 3y = 6$

31. $8x - 4y = 16$

32. $-12x - 3y = 36$

33. $\frac{1}{2}x - y = -2$

34. Graph the equations $x = -2$, $y = 2$, and $-x + y = 2$. Find the area of the enclosed figure.

35. You lose track of how many 2-point baskets and 3-point baskets a team makes in a basketball game. The team misses all the 1-point baskets and still scores 54 points. The equation $2x + 3y = 54$ models the total points scored.

a. What do the terms and coefficients of the equation represent?

b. Can the number of 3-point baskets made be odd? Explain your reasoning.

c. Graph the equation. Interpret the intercepts.

d. Find four possible solutions in the context of the problem.

3.6 Graphing Linear Equations in Slope-Intercept Form (pp. 233–250)

WATCH

Learning Target: Find the slope of a line and use slope-intercept form.

Vocabulary AZ VOCAB

slope
rise
run
slope-intercept form
constant function

36. Describe the slope of the line. Then find the slope.

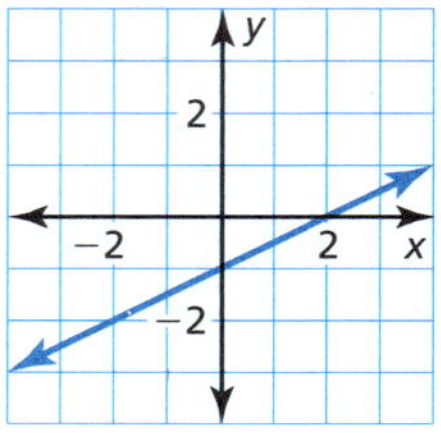

The points represented by the table lie on a line. Find the slope of the line.

37.

x	*y*
6	9
11	15
16	21
21	27

38.

x	*y*
3	−5
3	−2
3	5
3	8

39.

x	*y*
−4	−1.6
−3	−1.6
1	−1.6
9	−1.6

Graph the linear equation. Identify the *x*-intercept.

40. $y = 2x + 4$

41. $-5x + y = -10$

42. $-\frac{1}{2}x + y = 1$

43. $x + 3y = 9$

44. A linear function h models a relationship in which the dependent variable decreases 2 units for every 3 units the independent variable increases. The value of the function at 0 is 2. Graph h. Identify the slope and the intercepts of the graph.

3.7 Transformations of Linear Functions (pp. 251–266) WATCH

Learning Target: Graph transformations of linear functions.

Let $f(x) = 3x + 4$. Graph f and h. Describe the transformation from the graph of f to the graph of h.

45. $h(x) = f(x + 3)$

46. $h(x) = f(x) + 1$

47. $h(x) = f(-x)$

48. $h(x) = -f(x)$

49. $h(x) = 3f(x)$

50. $h(x) = f(6x)$

Vocabulary AZ VOCAB

family of functions
parent function
transformation
translation
reflection
horizontal shrink
horizontal stretch
vertical stretch
vertical shrink

51. Graph $f(x) = -5x - 1$ and $g(x) = 5x + 1$. Describe the transformation from the graph of f to the graph of g.

52. The table represents two linear functions f and g. Describe the transformation from the graph of f to the graph of g.

x	−1	0	1	2	3
f(x)	−1	2	5	8	11
g(x)	1	2	3	4	5

53. The regular cost (in dollars) of a streaming service for x months is represented by $R(x) = 14x + 3$. The function $D(x) = R(n \cdot x)$ represents the cost of the deluxe plan for the same streaming service. The cost of the deluxe plan for 4 months is \$93. Find the value of n.

3.8 Graphing Absolute Value Functions (pp. 267–280) WATCH

Learning Target: Graph absolute value functions.

Vocabulary AZ VOCAB

absolute value function
vertex
vertex form

Determine when the function is positive, negative, increasing, or decreasing. Then describe the end behavior of the function.

54.

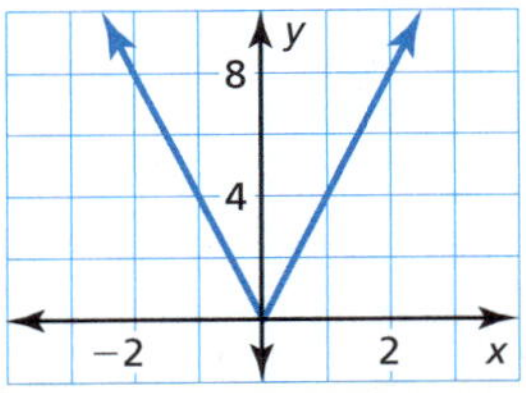

55.

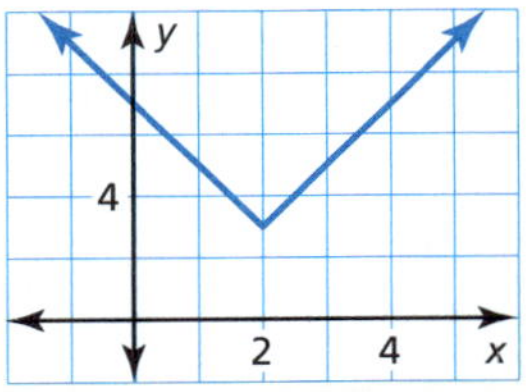

Graph the function. Compare the graph to the graph of $f(x) = |x|$. Find the domain and range.

56. $m(x) = |x| + 6$

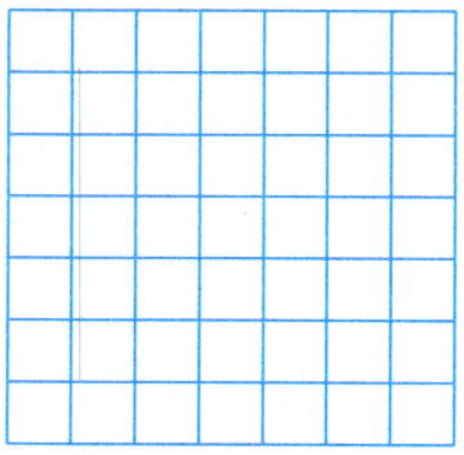

57. $p(x) = |x - 4|$

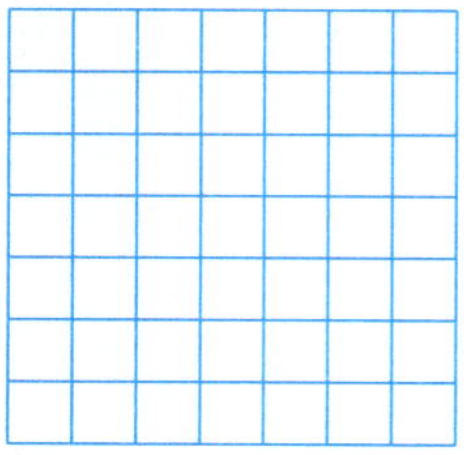

58. $q(x) = 4|x|$

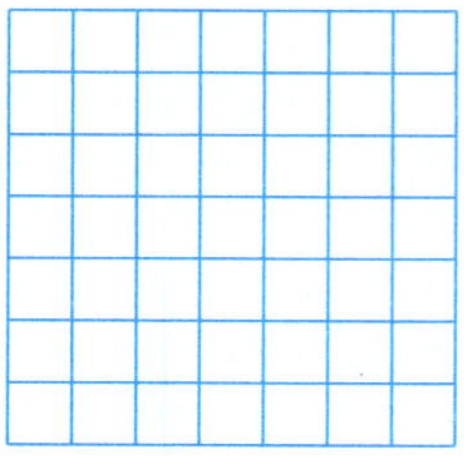

59. $r(x) = -\frac{1}{4}|x|$

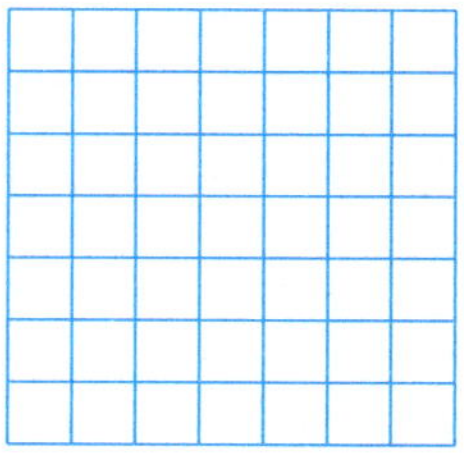

Write an equation that represents the given transformation(s) of the graph of $g(x) = |x|$.

60. horizontal translation 9 units right

61. vertical shrink by a factor of $\frac{1}{6}$

Describe the transformation from the graph of f to the graph of g.

62.

x	−3	−2	−1	0	1
$f(x)$	2	0	2	4	6
$g(x)$	4	0	4	8	12

63.

x	−4	−3	−2	−1	0
$f(x)$	−1.5	−1	−0.5	0	−0.5
$g(x)$	−0.5	0	−0.5	−1	−1.5

64. Write a function g whose graph is a horizontal shrink by a factor of $\frac{1}{3}$ of the graph of f shown.

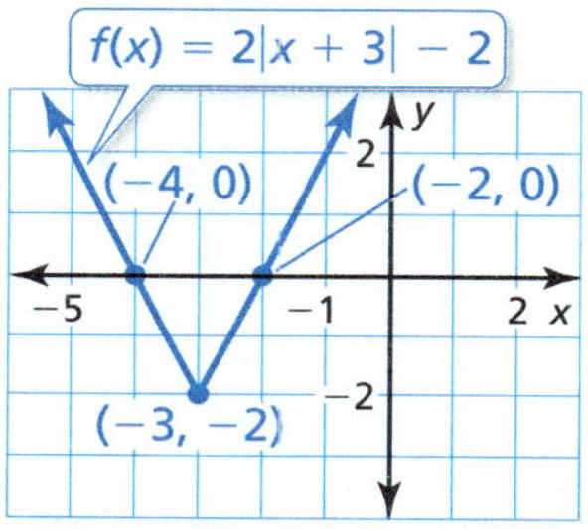

65. Your distance (in miles) from an exit after t hours on a highway is represented by $d(t) = |65t - 13|$.

a. Graph the function and interpret the intercepts.

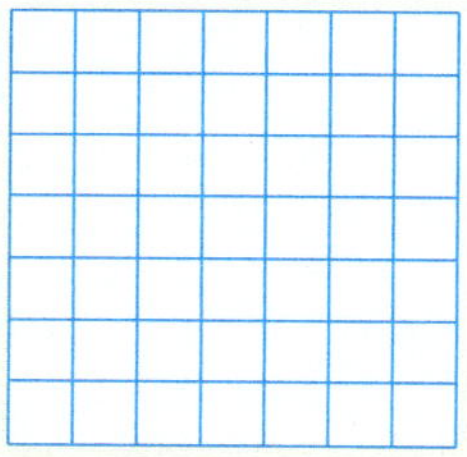

b. A sign says that after this exit, you will need to travel an additional 52 miles before reaching a second exit. How long does it take to reach the second exit?

Mathematical Thinking and Reasoning

3 MTR COMPLETE TASKS WITH MATHEMATICAL FLUENCY

Mathematicians who complete tasks with mathematical fluency select efficient and appropriate methods for solving problems within the given context.

1. In Exercise 24(c) on page 230, explain why using a graph may not be the most appropriate method to solve the problem. Then describe a more appropriate method.

2. Your friend graphs a linear equation to find the x-intercept. What is a possible method your friend could have used? Explain how your friend could find the x-intercept without graphing.

3 Practice Test WITH CalcChat®

Determine whether the relation is a function. If the relation is a function, determine whether the function is *linear* or *nonlinear*. Explain.

1.

x	−1	0	1	2
y	6	5	9	14

2. $y = -2x + 3$

3. $x = -2$

Graph the equation and identify the intercept(s). If the equation is linear, find the slope.

4. $2x - 3y = 6$

5. $y = 4.5$

6. $y = \frac{4}{5}x + 3$

7. $y = |x - 1| - 2$

Use the graph of the function shown.

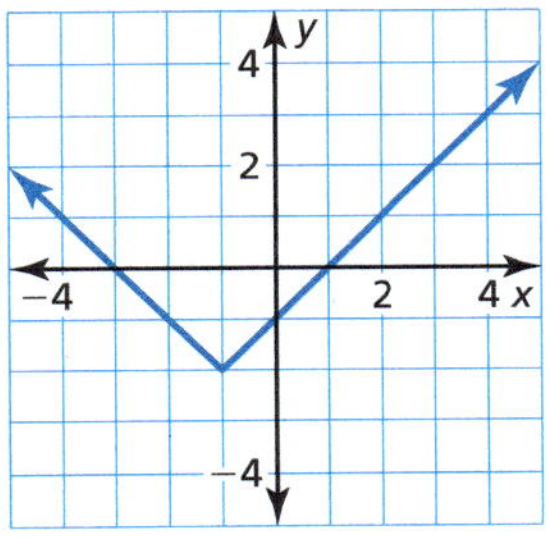

8. Find the domain and range. Is the domain *discrete* or *continuous*? Explain.

9. Approximate when the function is positive, negative, increasing, or decreasing. Then describe the end behavior of the function.

Graph *f* and *g*. Describe the transformations from the graph of *f* to the graph of *g*.

10. $f(x) = x$; $g(x) = -x + 3$

11. $f(x) = 5x$; $g(x) = 5x + 3$

GO DIGITAL

12. Describe the transformation from the graph of f to the graph of g.

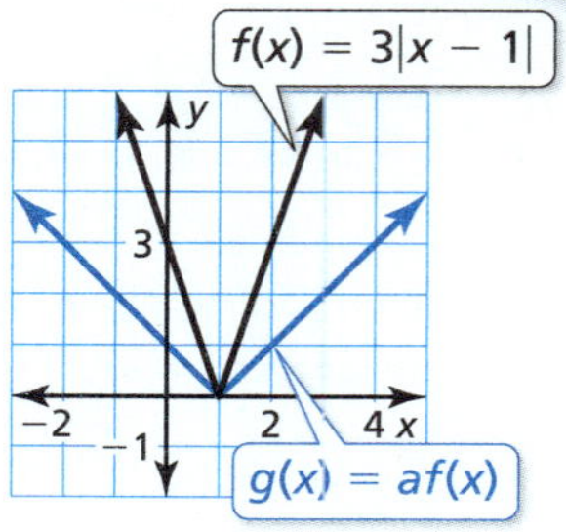

13. The function $m = 30 - 3r$ represents the amount m (in dollars) of money you have after renting r video games.

a. Identify the independent and dependent variables.

b. Find the domain and range of the function. Is the domain *discrete* or *continuous*? Explain.

c. Graph the function using its domain.

14. A mountain climber is scaling a cliff that is 500 feet above sea level. The graph shows the elevation of the climber over time.

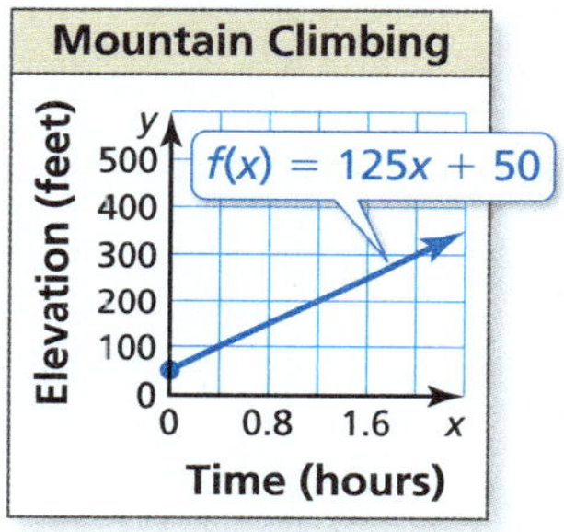

a. Interpret the slope and the y-intercept.

b. How long does it take the climber to reach the top of the cliff? Explain.

15. Graph the equations $y = 2$, $y = -3$, $y = -\frac{5}{2}x + 12$, and $-5x + 2y = -6$ in the same coordinate plane. What is the area of the enclosed shape?

16. A rock band releases a new single. The number (in thousands) of times the song is downloaded at an online store increases and then decreases as described by the function $n(t) = -2|t - 20| + 40$, where t is time (in weeks).

a. Identify the independent and dependent variables.

b. Graph n. Describe the transformation from the graph of $f(t) = -\frac{1}{2}|t - 20| + 10$ to the graph of n.

3 Performance Task
Into the Deep!

A 12-liter tank compressed to 200 bar can hold 2400 liters of air, which lasts a beginner scuba diver about 1 hour when diving at a depth of 10 meters.

Scuba tanks come in several sizes and are filled with compressed air. The table shows the capacities of several tanks compressed to a pressure of 200 bar or 300 bar.

		TANK SIZE			
		10 L	12 L	15 L	18 L
COMPRESSION	200 bar	2000 L	**2400 L**	3000 L	3600 L
	300 bar	3000 L	3600 L	4500 L	5400 L

Pressure increases 1 atmosphere (atm) for every 10-meter increase in depth.

As pressure doubles, the amount of air that you inhale with each breath also doubles.

1 atm	0 m
2 atm	10 m
3 atm	20 m
4 atm	30 m
5 atm	40 m

The maximum depth for recreational divers is about 40 meters.

GO DIGITAL

Scuba stands for:
Self
Contained
Underwater
Breathing
Apparatus.

DIVE PLANNING

Plan a dive. Make sure to choose a tank size, a depth that you will dive to, and the amount of time that you will spend underwater. Include a graph of the amount of oxygen you will have remaining over time.

Explain how you can increase the duration of your dive. Describe how to model this change using transformations.

3 B.E.S.T. Test Prep WITH CalcChat®
Cumulative Practice

WATCH Tutorial videos are available for each exercise.

1. A car rental company charges an initial fee of \$42 and a daily fee of \$12. A customer pays a total of \$138. How many days did the customer rent the car?

GRIDDED RESPONSE

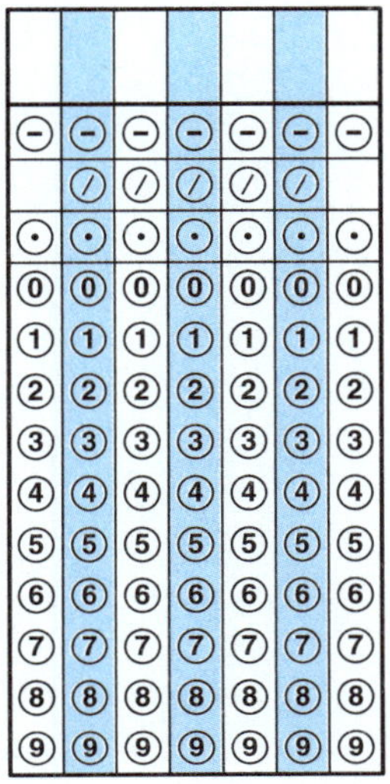

2. Which of the following numbers is *not* a solution of $6x - 11 \geq 4x - 13$?

Ⓐ -2 Ⓑ -1 Ⓒ 0 Ⓓ 1

3. Solve $8x - 7 = 4(x + 1) + 7$.

GRIDDED RESPONSE

$x =$ ▭

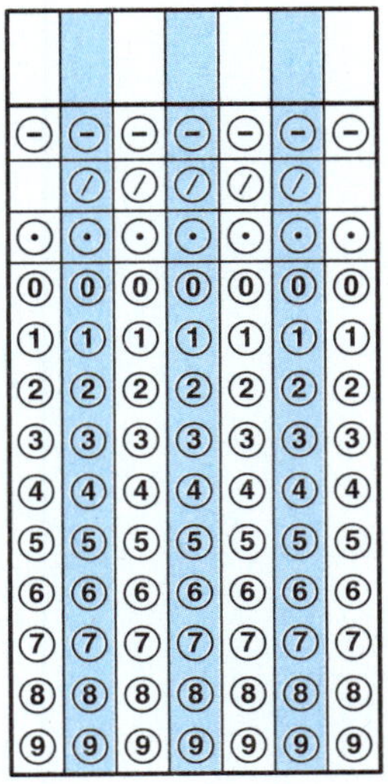

GO DIGITAL

4. Which ordered pair is a solution of the equation represented by the graph?

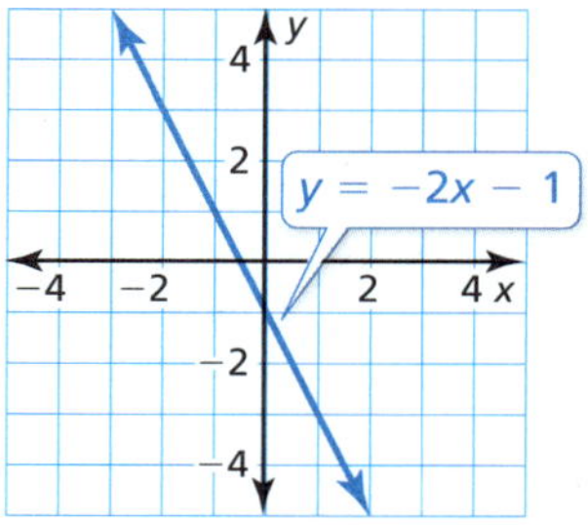

Ⓐ $(-1.5, 4)$ Ⓒ $(2, 3)$

Ⓑ $(-1, 0)$ Ⓓ $(0, -1)$

5. Determine whether each function is *linear* or *nonlinear*.

Function	Linear	Nonlinear
x: 1, 2, 3, 4; y: 18, 15, 11, 6	Ⓐ	Ⓑ
$-x + y = 12$	Ⓒ	Ⓓ
x: 3, 6, 9, 12; y: 4, 11, 18, 25	Ⓔ	Ⓕ
$y = \frac{6}{x}$	Ⓖ	Ⓗ

6. The expression $18 + 1.5x$ is 8 less than 36.5. What is the value of $4x$?

GRIDDED RESPONSE

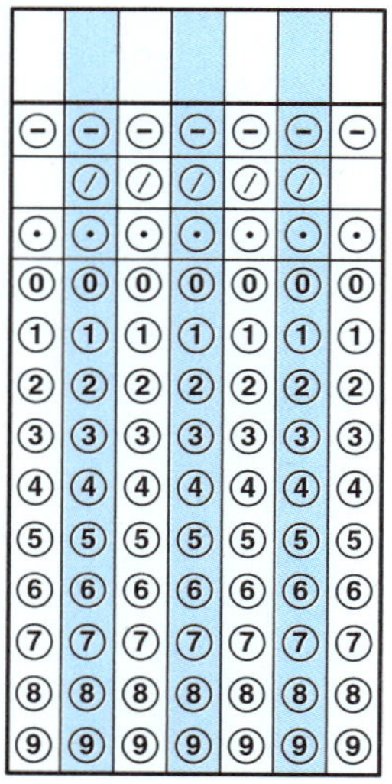

7. Which inequality symbol completes the inequality so that its solution is represented by the graph?

$$-3(x + 7) \;\square\; -24$$

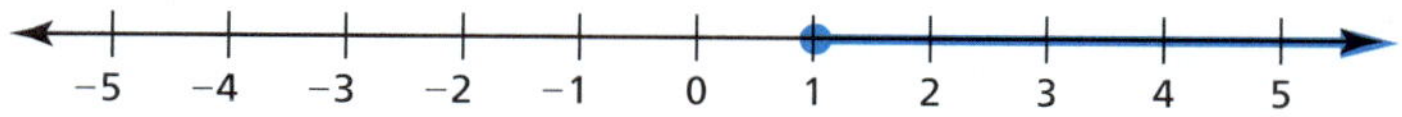

Ⓐ $<$ Ⓑ $\leq$ Ⓒ $>$ Ⓓ $\geq$

8. The table shows the cost (in dollars) of shrimp at a seafood market. Is this situation represented by a *linear* or *nonlinear* function? Is the domain *discrete* or *continuous*?

Pounds, x	0.5	1	1.5	2
Cost, y	6	12	18	24

	Discrete	**Continuous**
Linear	Ⓐ	Ⓑ
Nonlinear	Ⓒ	Ⓓ

9. Which equations have exactly one solution? Select all that apply.

Ⓐ $2x - 9 = 5x - 33$

Ⓑ $5x - 6 = 10x + 10$

Ⓒ $2(8x - 3) = 4(4x + 7)$

Ⓓ $-7x + 5 = 2(x - 10.1)$

Ⓔ $6(2x + 4) = 4(4x + 10)$

Ⓕ $8(3x + 4) = 2(12x + 16)$

10. The graph of which function g is a vertical shrink by a factor of $\frac{1}{4}$ of the graph of f?

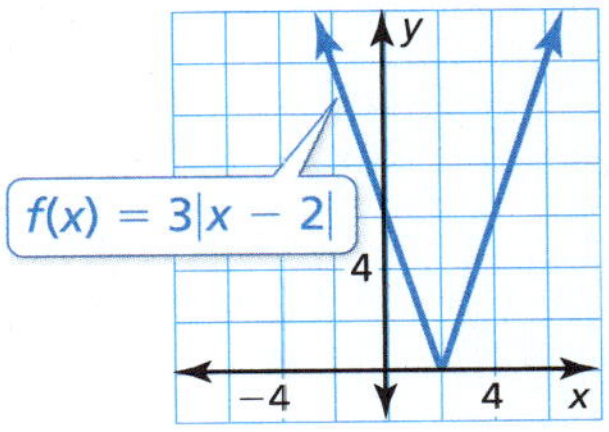

Ⓐ $g(x) = 3|x - 2| + \frac{1}{4}$

Ⓑ $g(x) = 12|x - 2|$

Ⓒ $g(x) = 3\left|\frac{1}{4}x - 2\right|$

Ⓓ $g(x) = \frac{3}{4}|x - 2|$

11. What is the sum of the integer solutions of $2|x - 5| < 16$??

GRIDDED RESPONSE

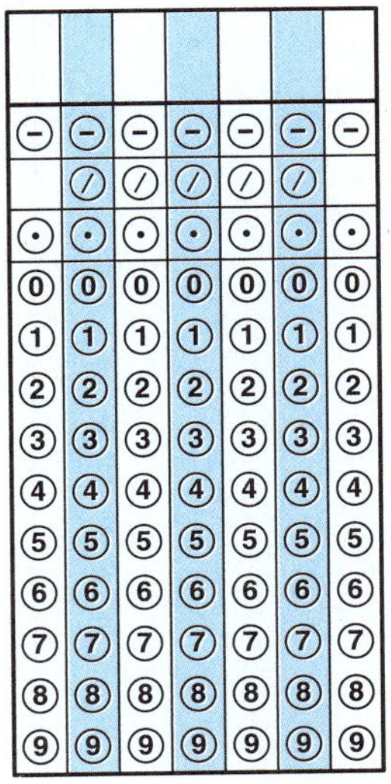

12. The graph of the function f is shown. Which of the following equal 2?

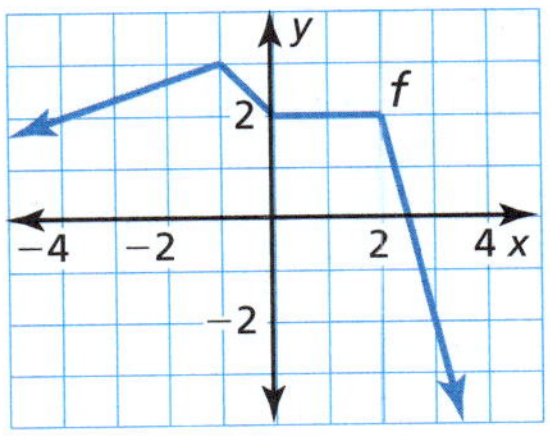

I. $f(-4)$ II. $f\left(\frac{5}{4}\right)$ III. $f(2)$

Ⓐ I only

Ⓑ I and III only

Ⓒ II and III only

Ⓓ I, II, and III

4 Writing Linear Functions

NATIONAL GEOGRAPHIC EXPLORER

Katey Walter Anthony

WATCH

Dr. Katey Walter Anthony measures the rate at which the permafrost in Alaskan lakes is thawing, causing a release of methane. Her data feed into mathematical models that predict global warming, which inspire ideas to reduce it. One of the primary ideas for reducing global warming is to implement the use of renewable energy.

- What are the main ways that electricity is generated? Of these, which are classified as *renewable energy*?
- On a wind farm, how much electricity is produced per day by each turbine?
- How many homes does a typical wind turbine power?

Renewable Energy

STEM

Wind is one example of a renewable energy resource that can provide long-lasting benefits. In the Performance Task, you will write a proposal for a new wind farm in your community, detailing the size, cost, and energy production of the farm.

GO DIGITAL

Preparing for Chapter 4

Chapter Learning Target: Understand writing linear functions.

Chapter Success Criteria:
- ◆ I can determine the slope of a line given ordered pairs, a graph, a table, or a context.
- ◆ I can write the equation of a line in different forms.
- ■ I can write equations to model and solve real-life problems.
- ■ I can interpret scatter plots and analyze lines of fit.

◆ Surface
■ Deep

Chapter Vocabulary

AZ VOCAB

Work with a partner. Discuss each of the vocabulary terms.

linear model

perpendicular lines

point-slope form

correlation

scatter plot

causation

parallel lines

interpolation

extrapolation

GO DIGITAL

Mathematical Thinking and Reasoning

6 MTR

ASSESS THE REASONABLENESS OF SOLUTIONS

Mathematicians who assess the reasonableness of solutions use benchmark quantities to determine if a solution makes sense.

Work with a partner. A wind farm contains 250 wind turbines that produce varying amounts of energy each day.

1. A particular turbine on the wind farm produces 545 kilowatt hours (kWh) of energy every half hour that it runs. The turbine runs for 4 hours and 55 minutes. What is the total amount of energy produced by the turbine?

Your friend solves a simpler form of the problem, as shown.

$$\text{Energy production} \approx \frac{550 \text{ kWh}}{1/2 \text{ h}} \bullet 5 \text{ h}$$

$$= \frac{1100 \text{ kWh}}{1 \cancel{\text{h}}} \bullet 5 \cancel{\text{h}}$$

$$= 5500 \text{ kWh}$$

a. Your friend solves the original problem and determines that the turbine produces 5600 kilowatt hours of energy. Without solving, determine whether this solution is reasonable. Explain your reasoning.

b. Solve the original problem. Is your answer reasonable? Explain.

2. The owner of the wind farm wants to know the annual energy output of the entire farm. How could you use a simpler form of the problem to find a reasonable solution?

4 Prepare WITH CalcChat®

Using a Coordinate Plane

WATCH

Example 1 **What ordered pair corresponds to point *A*?**

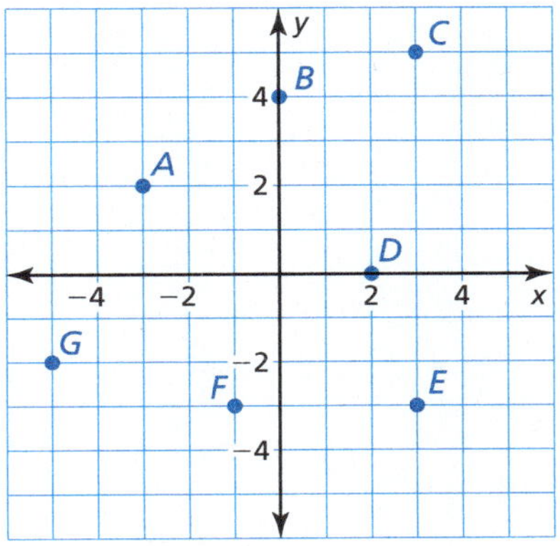

Point A is 3 units to the left of the origin and 2 units up. So, the x-coordinate is -3 and the y-coordinate is 2.

▶ The ordered pair $(-3, 2)$ corresponds to point A.

Use the graph to answer the question.

1. What ordered pair corresponds to point G?

2. What ordered pair corresponds to point D?

3. Which point is located in Quadrant I?

4. Which point is located in Quadrant IV?

GO DIGITAL

Rewriting Equations

WATCH

Example 2 **Solve the equation $3x - 2y = 8$ for y.**

$$3x - 2y = 8$$ Write the equation.

$$3x - 2y - 3x = 8 - 3x$$ Subtraction Property of Equality

$$-2y = 8 - 3x$$ Simplify.

$$\frac{-2y}{-2} = \frac{8 - 3x}{-2}$$ Division Property of Equality

$$y = -4 + \frac{3}{2}x$$ Simplify.

Solve the equation for *y*.

5. $x - y = 5$

6. $6x + 3y = -1$

7. $0 = 2y - 8x + 10$

8. $-x + 4y - 28 = 0$

9. $2y + 1 - x = 7x$

10. $y - 4 = 3x + 5y$

5 MTR **11.** **STRUCTURE** Both coordinates of a point (x, y) are multiplied by the same negative number. How does this change the location of the point? (*Hint:* Consider every possible location of the original point.)

4.1 Writing Equations in Slope-Intercept Form

Learning Target: Write equations of lines in slope-intercept form.

Success Criteria:
- I can find the slope and the y-intercept of a line.
- I can use the slope and the y-intercept to write an equation of a line.
- I can explain the relationship between simple interest and linear growth.
- I can write equations in slope-intercept form to solve real-life problems.

Algebraic Reasoning
MA.912.AR.2.2 Write a linear two-variable equation to represent the relationship between two quantities from a graph, a written description or a table of values within a mathematical or real-world context.
Financial Literacy
MA.912.FL.3.2 Solve real-world problems involving simple, compound and continuously compounded interest.
Also MA.912.AR.2.5, MA.912.FL.3.4

EXPLORE IT! Interpreting a Real-Life Graph

Work with a partner. You find the following graph online.

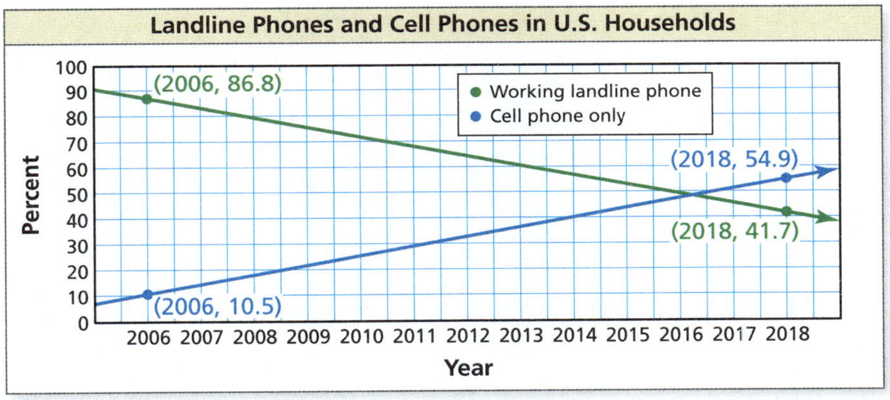

a. Explain what the graph represents. Make several observations from the graph.

b. Your friend thinks something is wrong with the graph because for a given year, the two percents do not add up to 100%. Is your friend's reasoning valid? Explain.

c. You want to write an equation that represents each line. What do you need to consider to write the equations? What do you need to calculate?

d. Approximate the slope of each line. Interpret each slope in the context of the problem.

e. When do you expect the percent of U.S. households with only cell phone service will exceed 70%? Explain how you made your prediction.

ANALYZE A PROBLEM 1 MTR

What would you let the independent variable represent in your equations in part (c)? Why?

GO DIGITAL

Writing Equations in Slope-Intercept Form

Vocabulary AZ VOCAB

linear model, *p. 305*

EXAMPLE 1 Using Slopes and y-Intercepts to Write Equations

WATCH

Write an equation of each line with the given slope and y-intercept.

a. slope = −3; y-intercept = $\frac{1}{2}$ **b.** slope = 0; y-intercept = −2

SOLUTION

a. $y = mx + b$ Write the slope-intercept form.

$y = -3x + \frac{1}{2}$ Substitute −3 for *m* and $\frac{1}{2}$ for *b*.

▶ An equation is $y = -3x + \frac{1}{2}$.

b. $y = mx + b$ Write the slope-intercept form.

$y = 0x + (-2)$ Substitute 0 for *m* and −2 for *b*.

$y = -2$ Simplify.

▶ An equation is $y = -2$.

SELF-ASSESSMENT 1 I don't understand yet. 2 I can do it with help. 3 I can do it on my own. 4 I can teach someone else.

Write an equation of the line with the given slope and y-intercept.

1. slope = 7; y-intercept = 2

2. slope = $\frac{1}{3}$; y-intercept = −1

3. REASONING Write equations that represent the x-axis and the y-axis. Are the equations in slope-intercept form? Explain your reasoning.

EXAMPLE 2 Using Graphs to Write Equations

WATCH

Write an equation of each line in slope-intercept form.

a.

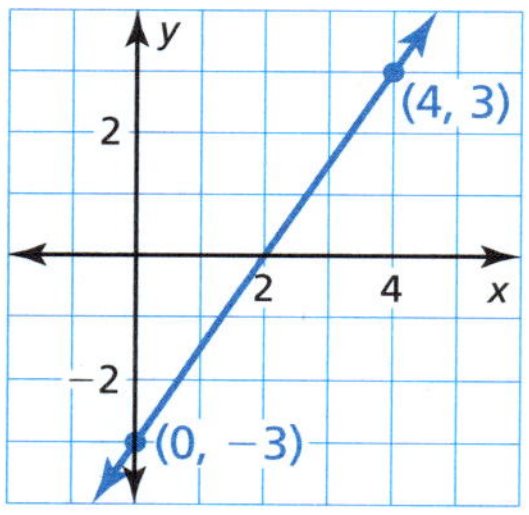

b.

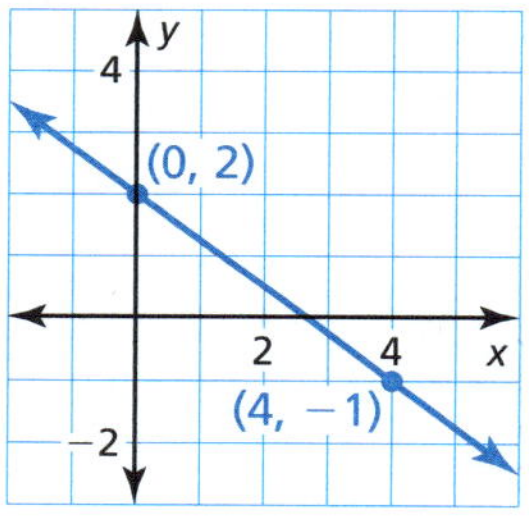

STUDY TIP

You can use any two points on a line to find the slope.

STUDY TIP

After writing an equation, check that the given points are solutions of the equation.

SOLUTION

a. Find the slope and y-intercept.

Let $(x_1, y_1) = (0, -3)$ and $(x_2, y_2) = (4, 3)$.

$$m = \frac{y_2 - y_1}{x_2 - x_1}$$

$$= \frac{3 - (-3)}{4 - 0} = \frac{6}{4}, \text{ or } \frac{3}{2}$$

Because the line crosses the y-axis at (0, −3), the y-intercept is −3.

▶ So, the equation is $y = \frac{3}{2}x - 3$.

b. Find the slope and y-intercept.

Let $(x_1, y_1) = (0, 2)$ and $(x_2, y_2) = (4, -1)$.

$$m = \frac{y_2 - y_1}{x_2 - x_1}$$

$$= \frac{-1 - 2}{4 - 0} = \frac{-3}{4}, \text{ or } -\frac{3}{4}$$

Because the line crosses the y-axis at (0, 2), the y-intercept is 2.

▶ So, the equation is $y = -\frac{3}{4}x + 2$.

GO DIGITAL

HELP A CLASSMATE

1 MTR

In part (b), help a classmate understand how to write the equation without performing any calculations.

EXAMPLE 3 Using Points to Write Equations

WATCH

Write an equation of the line that passes through the points in the table.

a.

x	-3	0	3	6
y	5	-1	-7	-13

b.

x	0	4	8	12
y	-5.8	-5.8	-5.8	-5.8

SOLUTION

a. Use the points $(-3, 5)$ and $(0, -1)$ to find the slope.

$$m = \frac{-1 - 5}{0 - (-3)} = \frac{-6}{3} = -2$$

Because the line crosses the y-axis at $(0, -1)$, the y-intercept is -1.

▶ So, an equation is $y = -2x - 1$.

b. Use the points $(0, -5.8)$ and $(8, -5.8)$ to find the slope.

$$m = \frac{-5.8 - (-5.8)}{8 - 0} = \frac{0}{8} = 0$$

Because the line crosses the y-axis at $(0, -5.8)$, the y-intercept is -5.8.

▶ So, an equation is $y = -5.8$.

EXAMPLE 4 Writing a Linear Function

WATCH

REMEMBER

If f is a function and x is in its domain, then $f(x)$ represents the output of f corresponding to the input x.

Write a linear function f with the values $f(0) = 10$ and $f(6) = 34$.

SOLUTION

Step 1 Interpret the function values. The values $f(0) = 10$ and $f(6) = 34$ indicate that $(0, 10)$ and $(6, 34)$ are on the graph of f.

Step 2 Find the slope of the line that passes through $(0, 10)$ and $(6, 34)$.

$$m = \frac{34 - 10}{6 - 0} = \frac{24}{6} = 4$$

Step 3 Write an equation of the line. Because the line crosses the y-axis at $(0, 10)$, the y-intercept is 10. Use the slope and y-intercept to write an equation of the line.

$y = mx + b$ Write the slope-intercept form.

$y = 4x + 10$ Substitute 4 for m and 10 for b.

▶ A function is $f(x) = 4x + 10$.

SELF-ASSESSMENT

1 I don't understand yet. 2 I can do it with help. 3 I can do it on my own. 4 I can teach someone else.

4. Write an equation of each line shown at the right in slope-intercept form.

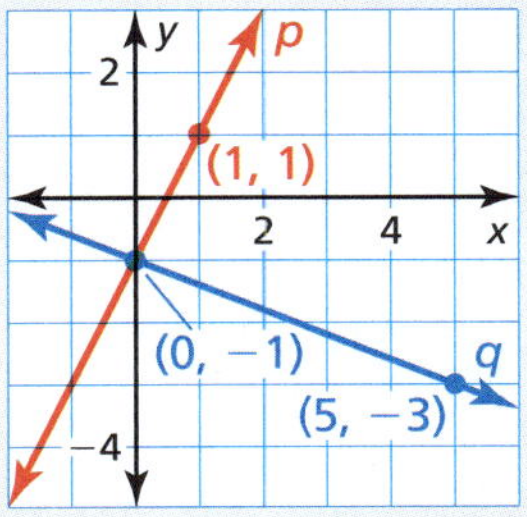

5. Write an equation of the line that passes through the points in the table.

x	0	2	4	6
y	2	6	10	14

GO DIGITAL

SELF-ASSESSMENT 1 I don't understand yet. 2 I can do it with help. 3 I can do it on my own. 4 I can teach someone else.

Write a linear function g with the given values.

6. $g(0) = 9, g(8) = 7$

7. $g(-2.5) = -5, g(0) = -4$

5 MTR **8.** **CONNECTING CONCEPTS** A function f represents a proportional relationship where $f(1) = \frac{2}{3}$. Write the function.

Using the Simple Interest Formula

Linear functions are used in situations involving simple interest. Recall that the amount I (in dollars) of simple interest earned is represented by $I = Prt$, where P is the principal (in dollars), r is the annual interest rate (in decimal form), and t is time (in years).

EXAMPLE 5 Finding Simple Interest

WATCH

You deposit \$250 in an account that earns simple interest at an annual rate of 6%.

a. Write and graph a function that represents the amount (in dollars) of interest earned after t years. Interpret the slope of the graph.

b. Is there enough money in the account after 4 years to buy a bicycle that costs \$300?

SOLUTION

a. $I = Prt$ — Write the simple interest formula.

$I = 250(0.06)t$ — Substitute 250 for P and 0.06 for r.

$I = 15t$ — Simplify.

▶ The function $I = 15t$ represents the amount of interest earned. The slope is 15. So, the amount of interest earned each year is \$15.

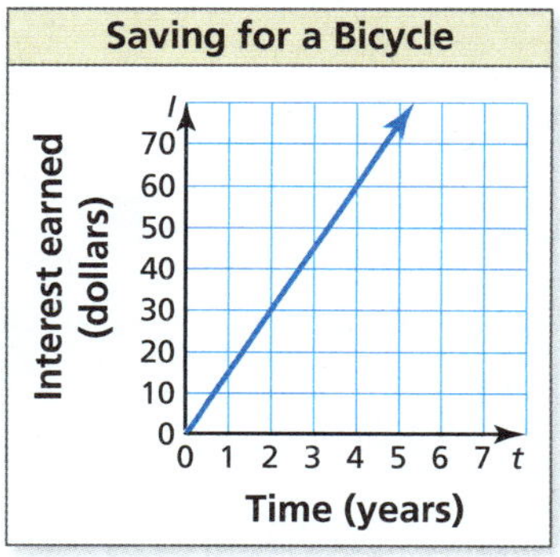

b. To determine whether you have enough money to buy the bicycle after 4 years, evaluate the function when $t = 4$. Then add the interest earned to the principal.

$I = 15t$ — Write the function.

$I = 15(4)$ — Substitute 4 for t.

$I = 60$ — Multiply.

▶ The balance of the account after 4 years is \$250 + \$60 = \$310. So, you have enough money in the account to buy the bicycle after 4 years.

USE ANOTHER METHOD 2 MTR

Write a function that represents the total account balance after t years. Interpret the slope and y-intercept. Then use this function to answer part (b).

GO DIGITAL

SELF-ASSESSMENT

1 I don't understand yet. 2 I can do it with help. 3 I can do it on my own. 4 I can teach someone else.

Write and graph a function that represents the amount of simple interest earned by the account after *t* years.

9. principal = \$500; annual interest rate = 2%

10. principal = \$750; annual interest rate = 5%

2 MTR **11. MULTIPLE REPRESENTATIONS** Accounts A and B both earn simple interest. The graph shows the balance of Account A over time. Account B has a principal of \$1500 and an annual interest rate of 2%. Compare the principals and interest rates of the accounts. Which account has a greater balance after 5 years? after 10 years? Justify your answers.

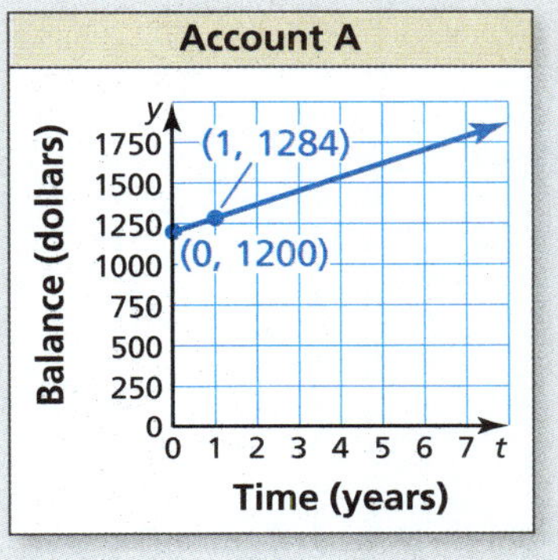

5 MTR **12. CONNECTING CONCEPTS** Explain the relationship between simple interest and linear growth.

Solving Real-Life Problems

A **linear model** is a linear function that models a real-life situation. When a quantity y changes at a constant rate with respect to a quantity x, you can use the equation $y = mx + b$ to model the relationship. The value of m is the constant rate of change, and the value of b is the initial, or starting, value of y.

7 MTR EXAMPLE 6 Modeling Real Life

WATCH STEM

Excluding hydroelectric and solar, renewable energy sources in the U.S. generated 143.4 million megawatt hours of electricity in 2009. This quantity increased at an approximately constant rate and reached 333.0 million megawatt hours by 2017. Estimate the amount of electricity generated from these sources in 2021.

SOLUTION

1. **Understand the Problem** You know the amounts of electricity generated in two distinct years and that it increased at a constant rate. You are asked to estimate the amount generated in a later year.
2. **Make a Plan** Find the initial value and the rate of change. Use these values to write a linear model and estimate the amount generated in 2021.
3. **Solve and Check** Let x represent the number of years since 2009, and let y represent the number of megawatt hours (in millions). Because 2009 corresponds to $x = 0$ and 2017 corresponds to $x = 8$, the linear model representing the situation passes through the points (0, 143.4) and (8, 333).

Let $(x_1, y_1) = (0, 143.4)$ and $(x_2, y_2) = (8, 333)$. The initial value is the y-intercept b, which is 143.4. The rate of change is the slope m.

$$m = \frac{y_2 - y_1}{x_2 - x_1} = \frac{333 - 143.4}{8 - 0} = \frac{189.6}{8} = 23.7$$

Megawatt hours (millions)	=	Initial value	+	Rate of change	•	Years since 2009
y	=	143.4	+	23.7	•	x

$y = 143.4 + 23.7x$ Write the equation.

2021 corresponds to $x = 12$. → $y = 143.4 + 23.7(12)$ Substitute 12 for x.

$y = 427.8$ Simplify.

▶ The linear model is $y = 23.7x + 143.4$. The model estimates that renewable energy sources generated about 427.8 million megawatt hours in 2021.

Another Way Use the slope to find amounts of electricity generated in later years.

x	2017	2018	2019	2020	2021
y	333.0	356.7	380.4	404.1	427.8

+ 23.7 + 23.7 + 23.7 + 23.7

SELF-ASSESSMENT

1 I don't understand yet. 2 I can do it with help. 3 I can do it on my own. 4 I can teach someone else.

13. Wind energy in the U.S. generated about 74 million megawatt hours of electricity in 2009. This quantity increased at an approximately constant rate and reached about 254 million megawatt hours by 2017. Estimate how many more megawatt hours were generated from wind in 2020 than in 2016. Explain your reasoning.

GO DIGITAL

4.1 Practice WITH CalcChat® AND CalcView®

In Exercises 1–6, write an equation of the line with the given slope and *y*-intercept. *(See Example 1.)*

▶ **1.** slope: 2
y-intercept: 9

2. slope: 0
y-intercept: 5

3. slope: -3
y-intercept: 0

4. slope: -7.5
y-intercept: 1.5

5. slope: $\frac{2}{3}$
y-intercept: -8

6. slope: $-\frac{3}{4}$
y-intercept: $-\frac{1}{4}$

In Exercises 7–10, write an equation of the line in slope-intercept form. *(See Example 2.)*

▶ **7.**

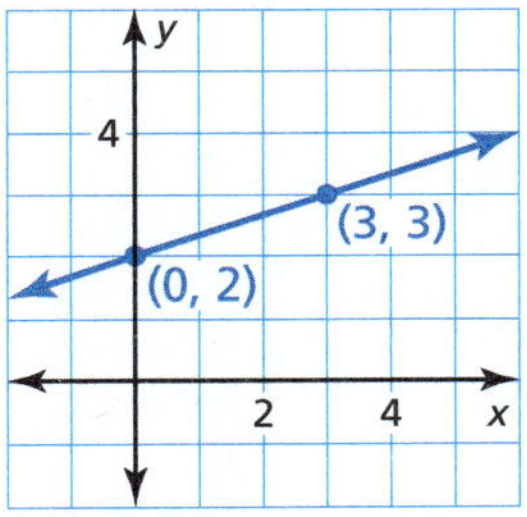

8.

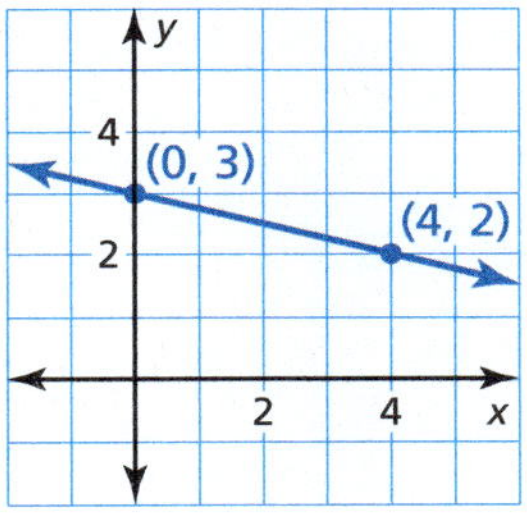

9.

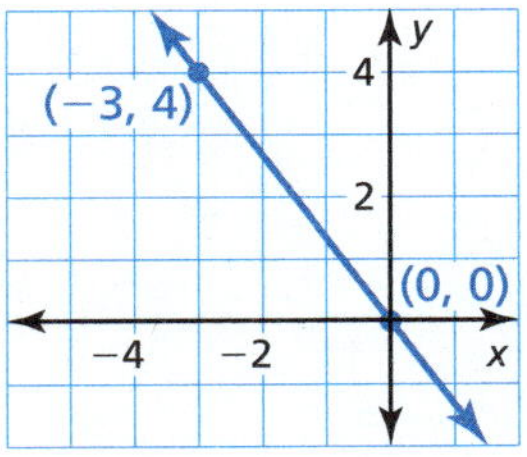

10.

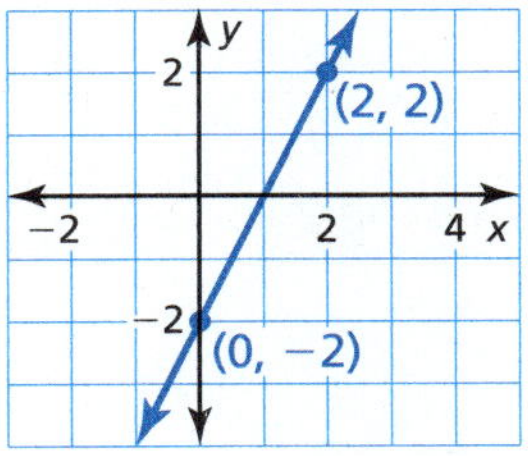

GO DIGITAL

In Exercises 11–14, write an equation of the line that passes through the points in the table. *(See Example 3.)*

11.

x	0	1	2	3
y	10	7	4	1

12.

x	-2	0	2	3
y	-17	-5	7	13

13.

x	-6	-4	-2	0	2
y	0	-8	-16	-24	-32

14.

x	-2	-1.5	-1	-0.5	0	0.5	1
y	-0.4	1	2.4	3.8	5.2	6.6	8

In Exercises 15–20, write a linear function f with the given values. *(See Example 4.)*

15. $f(0) = 2, f(2) = 4$

16. $f(0) = 7, f(3) = 1$

17. $f(4) = -3, f(0) = -2$

18. $f(5) = -1, f(0) = -5$

19. $f\left(-\frac{1}{2}\right) = 1, f(0) = -4$

20. $f(0) = 3.75, f(-6) = 3.75$

In Exercises 21 and 22, write a linear function f with the given values.

21.

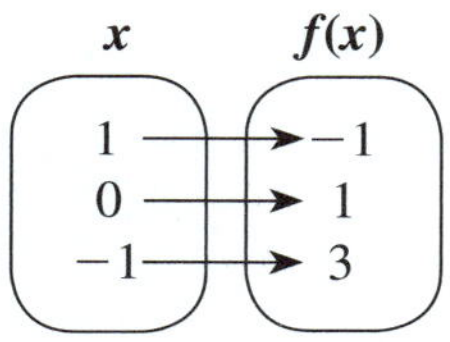

22.

x	$f(x)$
-4	-2
-2	-1
0	0

23. 4 MTR **ERROR ANALYSIS** Describe and correct the error in writing an equation of the line with a slope of 2 and a y-intercept of 7.

✗ $y = 7x + 2$

24. 4 MTR **ERROR ANALYSIS** Describe and correct the error in writing an equation of the line shown.

✗

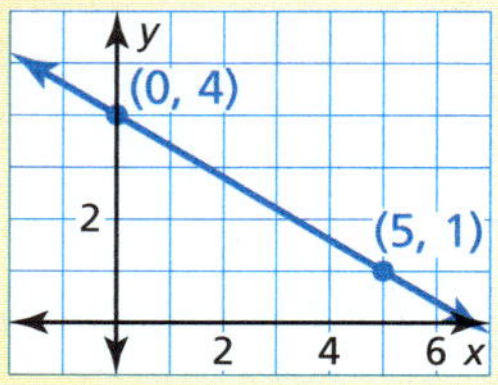

$$\text{slope} = \frac{1-4}{0-5} = \frac{-3}{-5} = \frac{3}{5}$$

$$y = \frac{3}{5}x + 4$$

25. PROBLEM SOLVING You deposit $320 in an account that earns simple interest at an annual rate of 7.5%. *(See Example 5.)*

a. Write and graph a function that represents the amount (in dollars) of interest earned after t years. Interpret the slope of the graph.

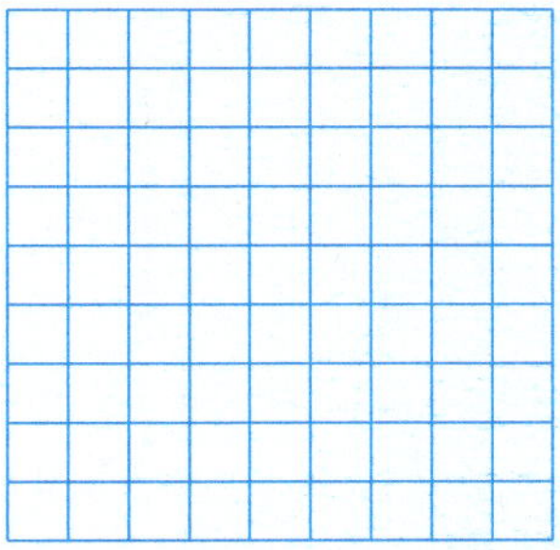

b. Is there enough money in the account after 3 years to buy a game console that costs $400?

26. B.E.S.T. TEST PREP You deposit $735 in an account that earns simple interest at an annual rate of 6.4%. How much money is in the account after 8 years?

(A) $782.04 (C) $1205.40

(B) $1111.32 (D) $4498.20

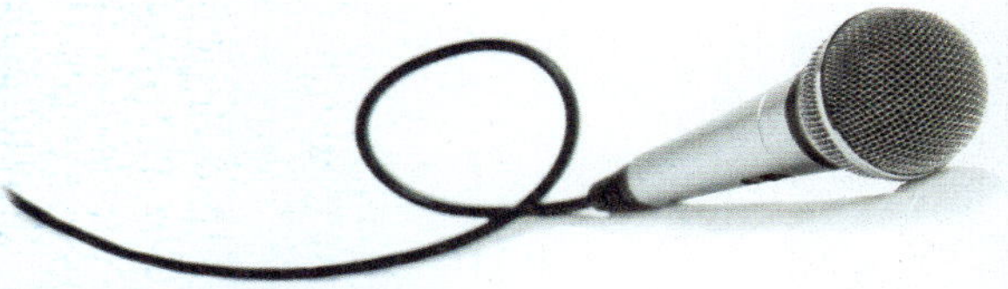

27. MODELING REAL LIFE A public university charged $9500 for tuition and fees in the 2015–2016 academic year. This cost increased at a constant rate and reached $10,500 in the 2020–2021 academic year. Estimate the cost of tuition and fees in the 2024–2025 academic year. *(See Example 6.)*

28. MODELING REAL LIFE A recording studio charges musicians an initial fee of $50 to record an album. Studio time costs an additional $75 per hour. Is it less expensive to purchase 12 hours of recording time at the studio or a $795 music software program that you can use to record on your own computer? Use a linear model to justify your answer.

29. MODELING REAL LIFE You want to save money for a trip to the Cocoa Beach Pier. You deposit $920 in an account that earns simple interest at an annual rate of 10%. Travel and entertainment will cost $600, and lodging will cost $800.

a. How many years will it take for you to save enough money for the trip? Explain.

b. Another bank advertises an annual interest rate of 15.7%. How much sooner can you go on the trip if you open an account at this bank instead? Explain your reasoning.

30. ASSESS REASONABLENESS Your friend says that if you deposit $940 in the account in Exercise 29, you'll have enough money to go on the trip two years earlier. Is your friend's claim reasonable? Explain.

31. REASONING A vendor sells paintings at the Zora! Festival in Eatonville, Florida. The table shows the profit $P(x)$ (in dollars) the vendor earns from selling x paintings at the festival.

x	0	10	20	30
$P(x)$	-800	-250	300	850

a. Write and graph a linear function P from the values. Interpret the slope and y-intercept.

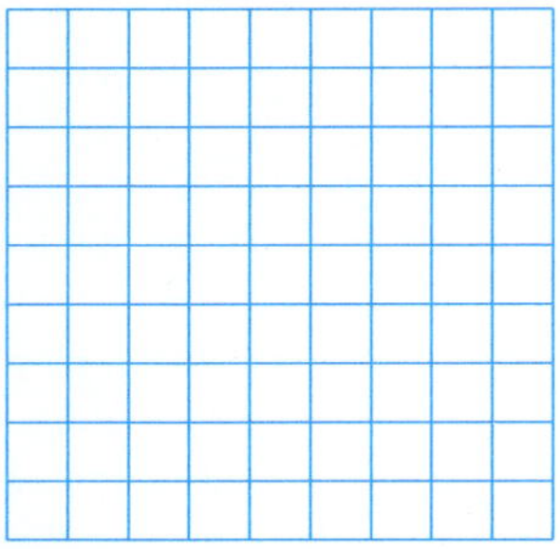

b. How many paintings must the vendor sell for the booth to be profitable? Explain your reasoning.

32. PROBLEM SOLVING The graph shows how much you are paid p (in dollars) for h hours of cleaning yards. How long does it take you to earn \$200? Justify your answer.

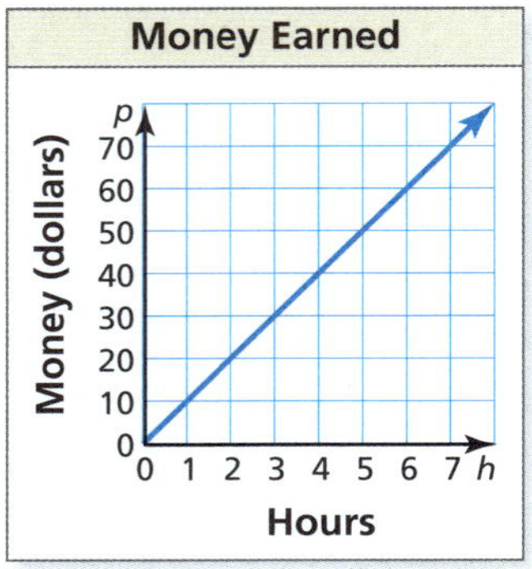

33. 7 MTR **MODELING REAL LIFE** You want to take a ride sharing service to the movies. Service A charges a \$5 initial fee and an additional 20 cents per mile, and Service B charges no initial fee and 60 cents per mile.

a. When would you use Service A? Service B? Explain.

b. You have a coupon for Service A that reduces the initial fee per ride to \$1. How does this change your answer in part (a)? Explain.

3 MTR **34. CHOOSE A METHOD** Describe a real-life situation that can be modeled by a linear function. Write and graph a function that represents the situation. Would you use an equation or a graph to analyze the situation? Justify your answer.

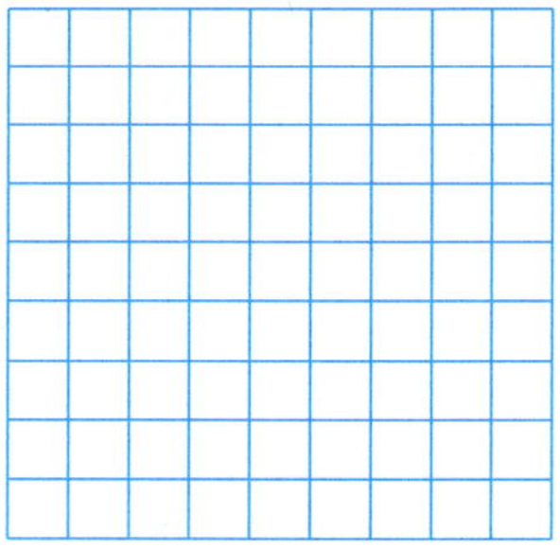

Cocoa Beach is known as the Surfing Capital of the East Coast. Cocoa Beach Pier is the center of surfing activity.

4 MTR **35. MAKING AN ARGUMENT** Your friend claims that given $f(0)$ and any other value of a linear function f, you can write an equation in slope-intercept form that represents the function. Your cousin disagrees, claiming that the two points could lie on a vertical line. Who is correct? Explain.

36. THOUGHT PROVOKING
A linear function f has values $f(-9) = -2$ and $f(-3) = -6$. The y-intercept of a linear function g is six greater than the y-intercept of f, and the x-intercept of g is the same as the x-intercept of f. Write equations that represent f and g.

5 MTR **37. CONNECTING CONCEPTS** Line ℓ is a reflection in the x-axis of line k. Write an equation that represents line k.

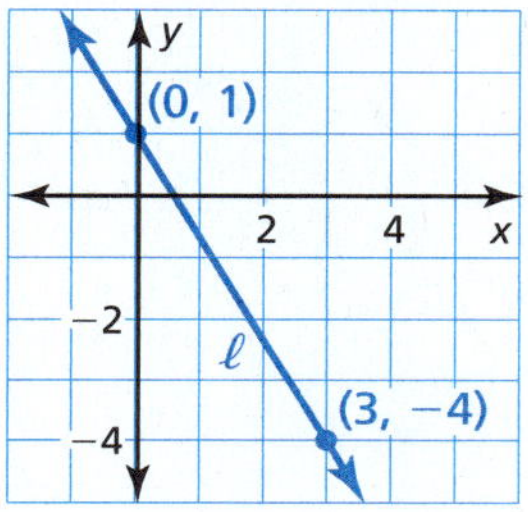

38. HOW DO YOU SEE IT?
The profits of Company A and Company B x years since 2016 can be modeled by $f(x) = ax + b$ and $g(x) = cx + d$, respectively.

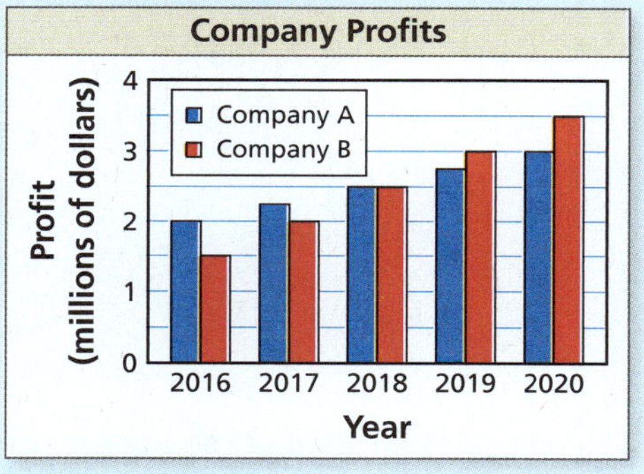

a. Compare the values of b and d. Explain your reasoning.

b. Compare the values of a and c. Explain your reasoning.

39. DIG DEEPER Write a linear function with the values $f(0) = b$ and $f(1) = b + m$. What can you conclude?

REVIEW & REFRESH

WATCH

In Exercises 40–42, solve the equation.

40. $-4y - 10 = 4(y - 3)$

41. $2(3d + 3) = 7 + 6d$

42. $-5(-4 + 2n) = -10(n - 2)$

43. Write an equation of the line in slope-intercept form.

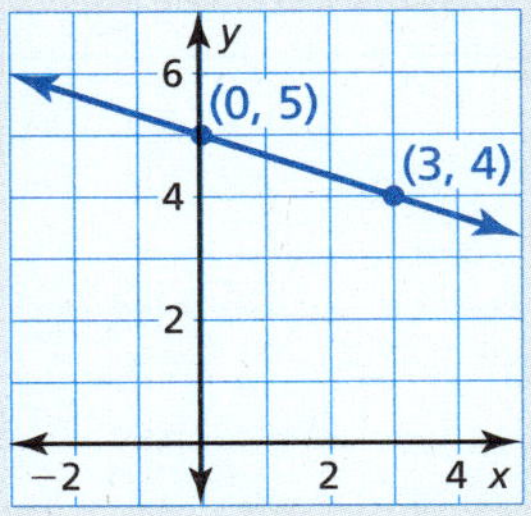

44. Use intercepts to graph the linear equation $-4x + 2y = 16$. Label the points corresponding to the intercepts.

45. Let $g(x) = -\frac{1}{2}|x + 2| - 4$. (a) Describe the transformations from the graph of $f(x) = -|x + 2| - 8$ to the graph of g. (b) Graph g.

46. REASONING What is the least value of $4x - 5$ when $-\frac{1}{5} \leq x - \frac{7}{10}$?

In Exercises 47 and 48, find the slope and y-intercept of the graph of the linear equation.

47. $y = 9.5$

48. $10x + y = -7$

49. Tell whether 18 is a solution of $-13 < 5 - x$.

7 MTR **50. MODELING REAL LIFE** Your total earnings (in dollars) after working x weeks are represented by the function f. You get a promotion, and your weekly earnings are multiplied by a factor of a. Use the graph to find and interpret the value of a.

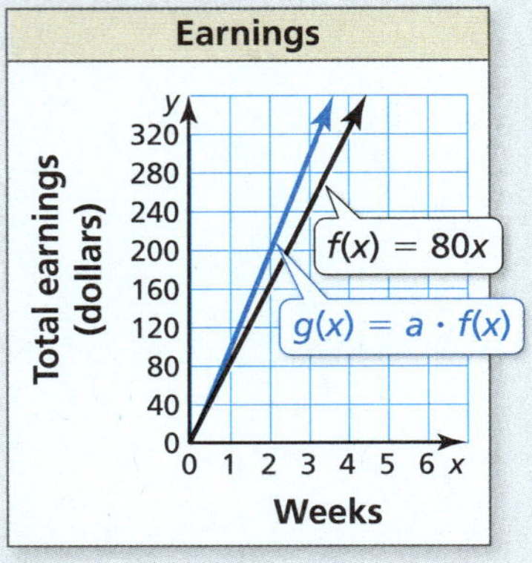

4.2 Writing Equations in Point-Slope Form

Learning Target: Write and graph equations of lines in point-slope form.

Success Criteria:
- I can graph linear equations written in point-slope form.
- I can use a point on a line and the slope to write an equation of the line.
- I can use any two points to write an equation of a line.
- I can write a linear function using any two function values.

Algebraic Reasoning
MA.912.AR.2.2 Write a linear two-variable equation to represent the relationship between two quantities from a graph, a written description or a table of values within a mathematical or real-world context.
MA.912.AR.2.4 Given a table, equation or written description of a linear function, graph that function, and determine and interpret its key features.
Also MA.912.AR.2.5

EXPLORE IT! Writing Equations

Work with a partner.

a. For each graph, find the y-intercept of the line that has the given slope and passes through the given point. Then write an equation of the line.

$m = \frac{1}{2}$

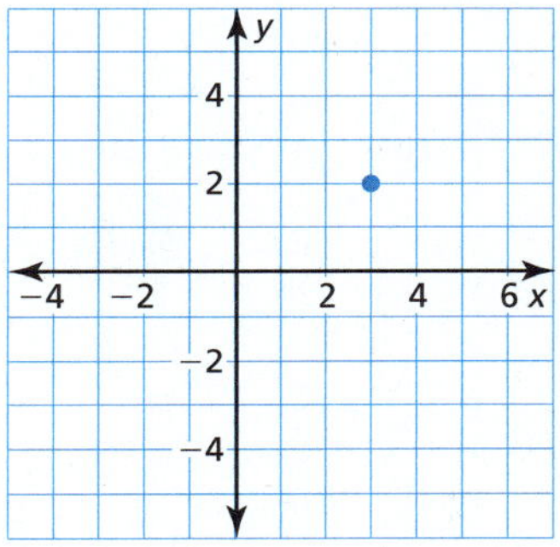

$m = -2$

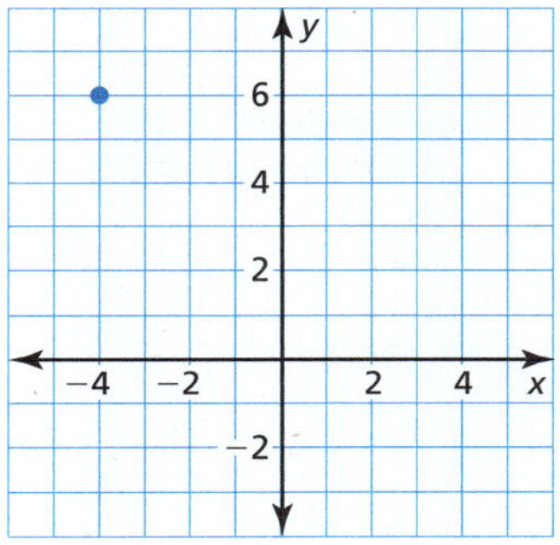

b. The point (x_1, y_1) is a given point on a nonvertical line. The point (x, y) is any other point on the line. Write an equation that represents the slope m. Then solve your equation for $(y - y_1)$. What does the resulting equation represent? Explain your reasoning.

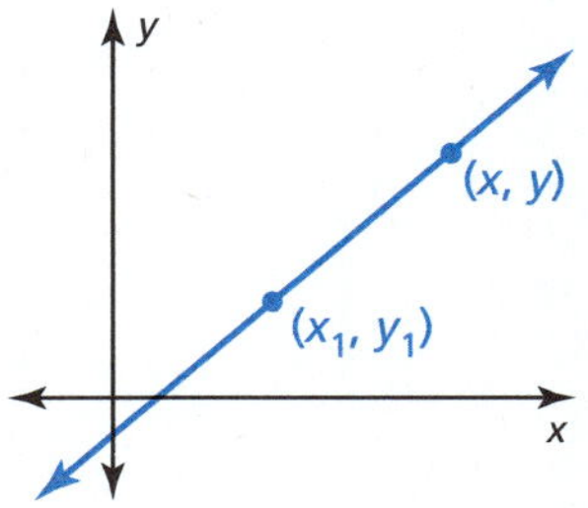

MAKE A CONNECTION 2 MTR

What information do you need in order to write an equation of a line using your equation in part (b)?

c. Justify your equations in part (a) using the results of part (b). Which method do you prefer? Explain your reasoning.

GO DIGITAL

Vocabulary

point-slope form, *p. 314*

Using Point-Slope Form

Given a point on a line and the slope of the line, you can write an equation of the line. Consider the line that passes through (2, 3) and has a slope of $\frac{1}{2}$. Let (x, y) be another point on the line where $x \neq 2$. You can write an equation relating x and y using the slope formula with $(x_1, y_1) = (2, 3)$ and $(x_2, y_2) = (x, y)$.

$$m = \frac{y_2 - y_1}{x_2 - x_1} \quad \text{Write the slope formula.}$$

$$\frac{1}{2} = \frac{y - 3}{x - 2} \quad \text{Substitute values.}$$

$$\frac{1}{2}(x - 2) = y - 3 \quad \text{Multiply each side by } (x - 2).$$

The equation in *point-slope form* is $y - 3 = \frac{1}{2}(x - 2)$.

KEY IDEA

Point-Slope Form

Words A linear equation written in the form $y - y_1 = m(x - x_1)$ is in **point-slope form**. The line passes through the point (x_1, y_1), and the slope of the line is m.

Algebra $y - y_1 = m(x - x_1)$

slope (m)

passes through (x_1, y_1)

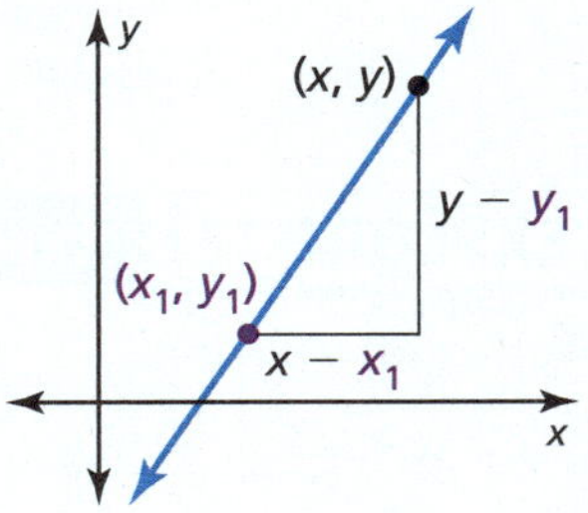

JUSTIFY A RESULT 4 MTR

Show how to use slope-intercept form to justify the value of the *y*-intercept.

EXAMPLE 1 Using Point-Slope Form to Graph an Equation

WATCH

Graph $y + 3 = -\frac{1}{2}(x - 2)$. Identify the intercepts.

SOLUTION

Step 1 Write the equation in the form $y - y_1 = m(x - x_1)$.

$$y - (-3) = -\frac{1}{2}(x - 2)$$

Step 2 Identify the slope and a point on the line.

$$m = -\frac{1}{2} \text{ and } (x_1, y_1) = (2, -3)$$

Step 3 Plot the point (2, −3).

Step 4 Use the slope to find another point on the line

$$\text{slope} = \frac{\text{rise}}{\text{run}} = \frac{-1}{2}$$

Plot the point that is 2 units right and 1 unit down from (2, −3). Draw a line through the two points.

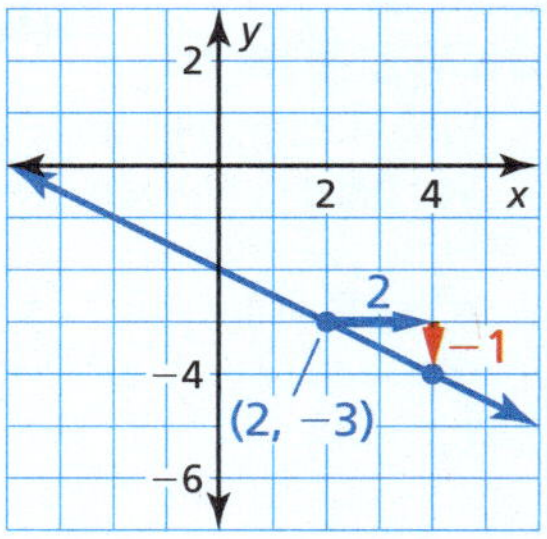

▶ The line appears to intersect the x-axis at (−4, 0) and the y-axis at (0, −2). So, the x-intercept is about −4 and the y-intercept is about −2.

GO DIGITAL

EXAMPLE 2 Using a Slope and a Point to Write an Equation

WATCH

Write an equation in point-slope form of the line that passes through the given point and has the given slope. Then graph the line.

a. $(1, -4)$; $m = -2$ **b.** $(-8, 3)$; $m = \frac{1}{4}$

SOLUTION

a. $y - y_1 = m(x - x_1)$ Write the point-slope form.

$y - (-4) = -2(x - 1)$ Substitute -2 for m, 1 for x_1, and -4 for y_1.

$y + 4 = -2(x - 1)$ Simplify.

Check

$y + 4 = -2(x - 1)$

$-4 + 4 \stackrel{?}{=} -2(1 - 1)$

$0 = 0$ ✓

▶ An equation is $y + 4 = -2(x - 1)$. Use the point $(1, -4)$ and the slope $m = -2$ to graph the line.

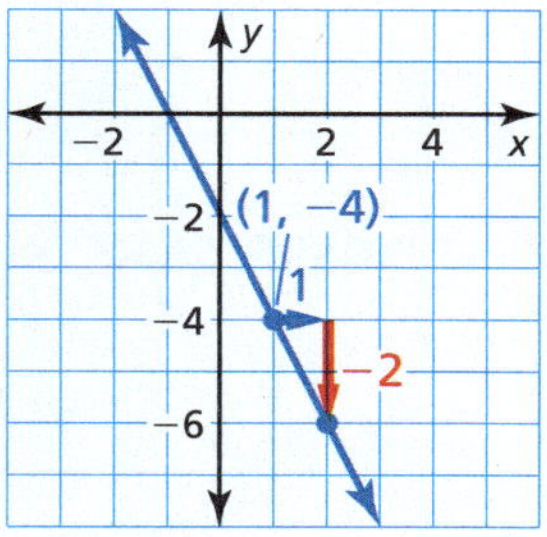

b. $y - y_1 = m(x - x_1)$ Write the point-slope form.

$y - 3 = \frac{1}{4}[x - (-8)]$ Substitute $\frac{1}{4}$ for m, -8 for x_1, and 3 for y_1.

$y - 3 = \frac{1}{4}(x + 8)$ Simplify.

Check

$y - 3 = \frac{1}{4}(x + 8)$

$3 - 3 \stackrel{?}{=} \frac{1}{4}(-8 + 8)$

$0 = 0$ ✓

▶ An equation is $y - 3 = \frac{1}{4}(x + 8)$. Use the point $(-8, 3)$ and the slope $m = \frac{1}{4}$ to graph the line.

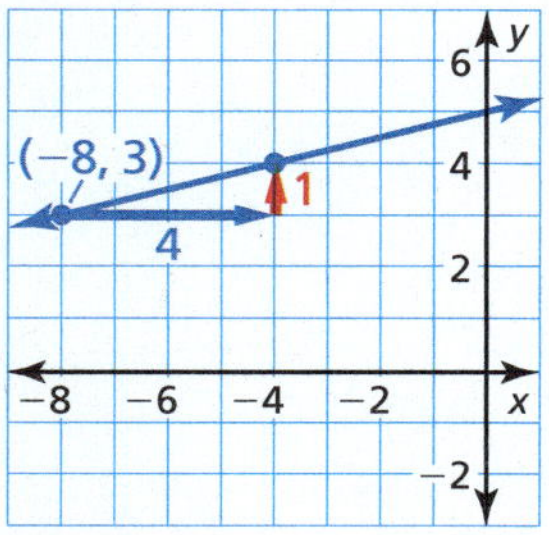

SELF-ASSESSMENT

1 I don't understand yet. 2 I can do it with help. 3 I can do it on my own. 4 I can teach someone else.

1. Graph $y + 3 = \frac{1}{4}(x + 4)$. Identify the intercepts.

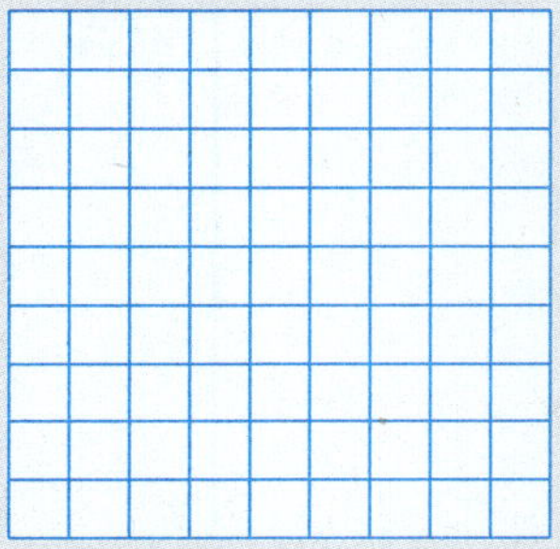

GO DIGITAL

SELF-ASSESSMENT

1 I don't understand yet. 2 I can do it with help. 3 I can do it on my own. 4 I can teach someone else.

Write an equation in point-slope form of the line that passes through the given point and has the given slope. Then graph the line.

2. $(3, -1)$; $m = -2$

3. $\left(-\frac{2}{5}, \frac{4}{5}\right)$; $m = \frac{3}{4}$

4 MTR **4. DIFFERENT WORDS, SAME QUESTION** Which is different? Find "both" answers.

Graph $y = 2x - 6$.	Graph $y - 2 = 2(x - 5)$.
Graph $y + 4 = 2(x - 2)$.	Graph $2x - y = 8$.

Writing Equations of Lines Given Two Points

When you are given two points on a line, you can write an equation of the line using the following steps.

Step 1 Find the slope of the line.

Step 2 Use the slope and one of the points to write an equation of the line in point-slope form.

ANOTHER WAY

You can use either of the given points to write an equation of the line.

Use $m = -2$ and $(3, -2)$.

$$y - (-2) = -2(x - 3)$$
$$y + 2 = -2x + 6$$
$$y = -2x + 4$$

EXAMPLE 3 Using Two Points to Write an Equation

WATCH

Write an equation in slope-intercept form of the line shown.

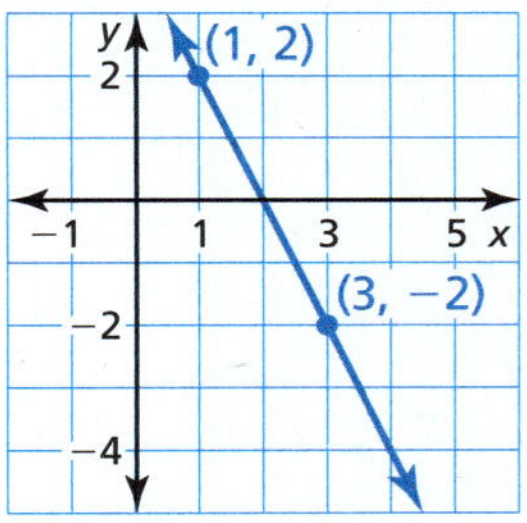

SOLUTION

Step 1 Find the slope of the line.

$$m = \frac{-2 - 2}{3 - 1} = \frac{-4}{2} = -2$$

Step 2 Use the slope $m = -2$ and the point $(1, 2)$ to write an equation of the line.

$y - y_1 = m(x - x_1)$	Write the point-slope form.
$y - 2 = -2(x - 1)$	Substitute -2 for m, 1 for x_1, and 2 for y_1.
$y - 2 = -2x + 2$	Distributive Property
$y = -2x + 4$	Write in slope-intercept form.

An equation is $y = -2x + 4$.

GO DIGITAL

EXAMPLE 4 Writing a Linear Function

WATCH

Write a linear function f with the values $f(4) = -2$ and $f(8) = 4$.

SOLUTION

The function values $f(4) = -2$ and $f(8) = 4$ indicate that $(4, -2)$ and $(8, 4)$ are on the graph of f.

Step 1 Find the slope of the line that passes through $(4, -2)$ and $(8, 4)$.

$$m = \frac{4 - (-2)}{8 - 4} = \frac{6}{4} = 1.5$$

Step 2 Use the slope $m = 1.5$ and the point $(8, 4)$ to write an equation of the line.

$y - y_1 = m(x - x_1)$	Write the point-slope form.
$y - 4 = 1.5(x - 8)$	Substitute 1.5 for m, 8 for x_1, and 4 for y_1.
$y - 4 = 1.5x - 12$	Distributive Property
$y = 1.5x - 8$	Write in slope-intercept form.

▶ A function is $f(x) = 1.5x - 8$.

SELF-ASSESSMENT

1 I don't understand yet. 2 I can do it with help. 3 I can do it on my own. 4 I can teach someone else.

Write an equation in slope-intercept form of the line that passes through the given points.

5. $(1, 4), (3, 10)$

6. $(-4, -1), (8, -4)$

7. Write a linear function g with the values $g(2) = 3$ and $g(6) = 5$.

Solving Real-Life Problems

7 MTR **EXAMPLE 5** **Modeling Real Life** WATCH

The Kennedy Space Center sells patches to commemorate NASA missions. A school administrator is ordering patches online to give to students as souvenirs. The table shows the total costs of ordering different numbers of patches. Determine the cost of ordering 25 patches.

Number of patches	4	6	8	10
Total cost (dollars)	42.96	56.94	70.92	84.90

SOLUTION

1. **Understand the Problem** You know the total costs for four different orders of patches. You are asked to determine the total cost of ordering 25 patches.
2. **Make a Plan** Find the rate of change for consecutive data pairs in the table. If the rate of change is constant, you can use the point-slope form to write a linear model. Use the model to find the total cost of 25 patches.
3. **Solve and Check**

Step 1 Find the rate of change for consecutive data pairs in the table.

$$\frac{56.94 - 42.96}{6 - 4} = 6.99, \frac{70.92 - 56.94}{8 - 6} = 6.99, \frac{84.90 - 70.92}{10 - 8} = 6.99$$

Because the rate of change is constant, the data are linear.

Step 2 Use the constant rate of change (slope) $m = 6.99$ and the data pair (4, 42.96) to write a linear model. Let C represent the total cost (in dollars), and let n represent the number of patches.

$C - C_1 = m(n - n_1)$ Write the point-slope form.

$C - 42.96 = 6.99(n - 4)$ Substitute 6.99 for m, 4 for n_1, and 42.96 for C_1.

$C - 42.96 = 6.99n - 27.96$ Distributive Property

$C = 6.99n + 15$ Write in slope-intercept form.

To find the total cost of ordering 25 patches, find C when $n = 25$.

$$C = 6.99(25) + 15 = 189.75$$

▶ The total cost of ordering 25 patches is $189.75.

Check To check that your model is correct, verify that the other data pairs are solutions of the equation.

$56.94 = 6.99(6) + 15$ ✓

$70.92 = 6.99(8) + 15$ ✓

$84.90 = 6.99(10) + 15$ ✓

SELF-ASSESSMENT

1 I don't understand yet. 2 I can do it with help. 3 I can do it on my own. 4 I can teach someone else.

8. A political campaign manager orders bumper stickers online. The company charges a shipping fee in addition to the cost per sticker. Customers who order more than 100 stickers receive a 25% discount on the price of each bumper sticker. The table shows the total costs of ordering different numbers of stickers. What is the total cost of ordering 275 bumper stickers?

Number of stickers	Total cost (dollars)
25	53.25
50	98.25
75	143.25
100	188.25

GO DIGITAL

4.2 Practice WITH CalcChat® AND CalcView®

In Exercises 1–4, graph the equation. Identify the intercepts. *(See Example 1.)*

▶ **1.** $y - 2 = 2(x - 2)$

2. $y - 12 = 4(x - (-3))$

3. $y - (-9) = -3(x - (-1))$

4. $y - (-5) = -\frac{5}{7}(x - 14)$

In Exercises 5–12, write an equation in point-slope form of the line that passes through the given point and has the given slope. Then graph the line. *(See Example 2.)*

5. $(2, 1)$; $m = 2$

6. $(3, 5)$; $m = -1$

▶ **7.** $(7, -4)$; $m = -6$

8. $(-8, -2)$; $m = 5$

9. $\left(\frac{5}{6}, 0\right)$; $m = -3$

10. $\left(0, -\frac{1}{2}\right)$; $m = \frac{3}{4}$

11. $(5, -12)$; $m = -\frac{2}{5}$

12. $(-6, 8.2)$; $m = 1.5$

GO DIGITAL

In Exercises 13–16, write an equation in slope-intercept form of the line shown. *(See Example 3.)*

13.

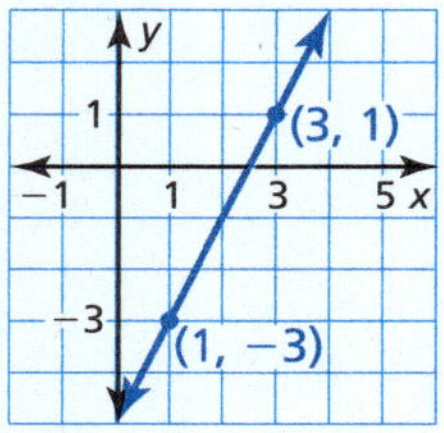

14.

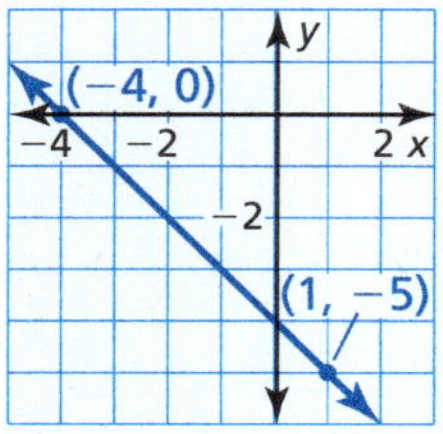

15.

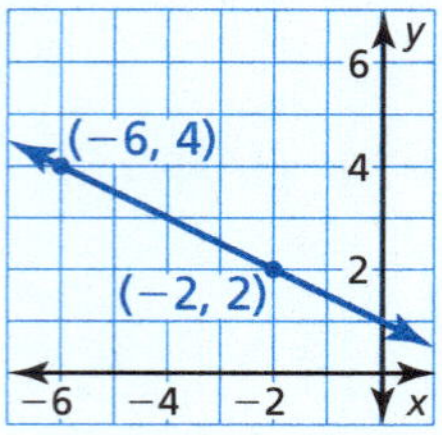

16.

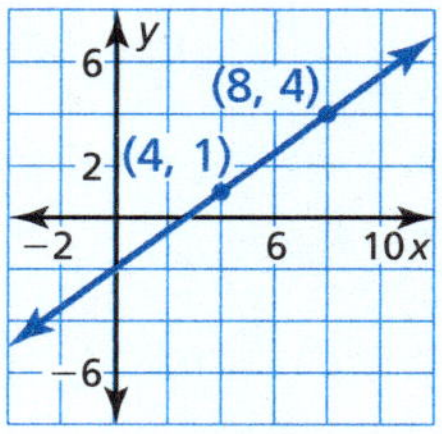

In Exercises 17–22, write an equation in slope-intercept form of the line that passes through the given points.

17. $(7, 2), (2, 12)$

18. $(6, -2), (12, 1)$

19. $(1, -9), (-3, -9)$

20. $(-5, 19), (5, 13)$

21. $(6, 11), \left(2, \frac{25}{3}\right)$

22. $(2, -3), \left(-\frac{1}{2}, \frac{1}{8}\right)$

In Exercises 23–28, write a linear function *f* with the given values. *(See Example 4.)*

23. $f(2) = -2, f(1) = 1$

24. $f(5) = 7, f(-2) = 0$

25. $f(-4) = 2, f(6) = -3$

26. $f(-10) = 4.5, f(-2) = 4.5$

27. $f(-3) = 1, f(13) = 5$

28. $f(-9) = 10, f(-1) = -2$

In Exercises 29 and 30, tell whether the data in the table can be modeled by a linear equation. Explain. If possible, write a linear equation that represents *y* as a function of *x*.

29.

x	2	4	6	8	10
y	−1	5	15	29	47

30.

x	0	1	2	4	5
y	1.2	1.4	1.6	2	2.2

7 MTR **31.** **MODELING REAL LIFE** A homeowner charges a processing fee and a daily fee to rent a house. The table shows the total costs of renting the house for different numbers of days. *(See Example 5.)*

Days	2	4	6	8
Total cost (dollars)	258	467	676	885

a. Can the situation be modeled by a linear equation? Explain.

b. What is the processing fee? the daily fee?

c. A guest can spend no more than $1200 on the house rental. What is the maximum number of days the guest can rent the house?

7 MTR **32.** **MODELING REAL LIFE** You want to order posters to advertise your band. A company charges $109.95 for the first 100 posters and $65 for each additional 100 posters.

a. Write an equation that represents the total cost (in dollars) of the posters as a function of the number (in hundreds) of posters ordered.

b. Interpret the slope and y-intercept.

c. Find the total cost of 1000 posters.

4 MTR **33.** **ERROR ANALYSIS** Describe and correct the error in writing an equation of the line that passes through the point $(4, -5)$ and has slope $m = -2$.

✗
$$y + (-5) = -2(x - 4)$$
$$y - 5 = -2(x - 4)$$

4 MTR **34.** **ERROR ANALYSIS** Describe and correct the error in writing an equation of the line that passes through the points $(1, 2)$ and $(4, 3)$.

✗
$$m = \frac{3 - 2}{4 - 1} = \frac{1}{3} \qquad y - 2 = \frac{1}{3}(x - 4)$$

7 MTR **35.** **MODELING REAL LIFE** The table represents the time x (in minutes) and the distance y (in miles) you bike.

Time, x	30	40	50	60
Distance, y	6	8	10	12

a. Write an equation in point-slope form that represents distance as a function of time. Then graph the line.

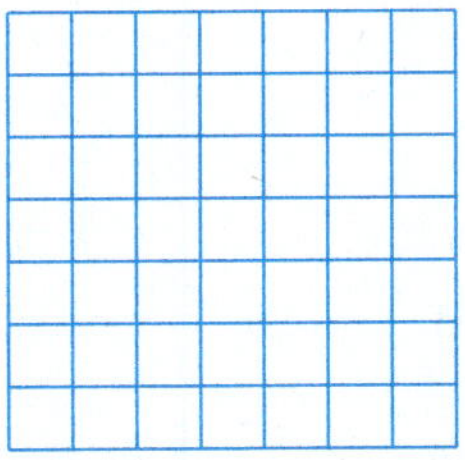

b. Interpret the slope and the y-intercept.

c. How far can you bike in 4 hours? Justify your answer.

36. **PROBLEM SOLVING** Volunteers work for six hours to clean up litter in a park. The graph represents the time x (in hours) and the number y of garbage bags filled.

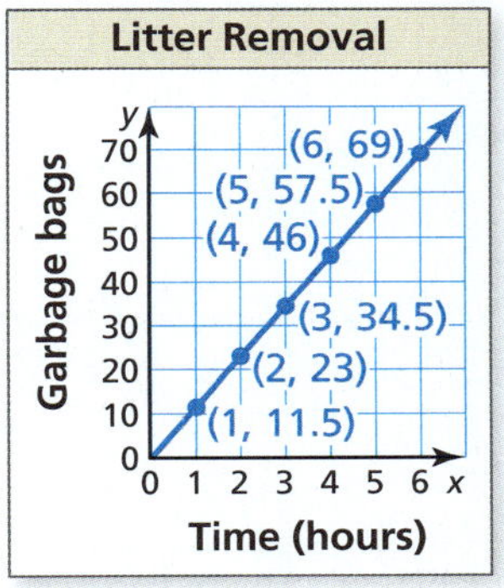

a. Write an equation in point-slope form that represents the garbage bags filled as a function of time. Interpret the slope and the y-intercept.

b. Interpret the domain and range of the equation.

c. How many garbage bags could the volunteers fill in 12 hours? Explain.

37. REASONING For a class project, you reduce your electricity use by 3 kilowatt hours (kWh) each day for 7 days. Find the amount of electricity you save during the project. How much electricity could you save in 14 days? Explain your reasoning.

38. CHOOSE A METHOD The Tampa Bay Buccaneers begin a play on their 5-yard line. They advance 10 yards each of the next 3 plays.

3 MTR

a. Write an equation in point-slope form that represents the yards from their goal line as a function of the number of plays. Then graph the line.

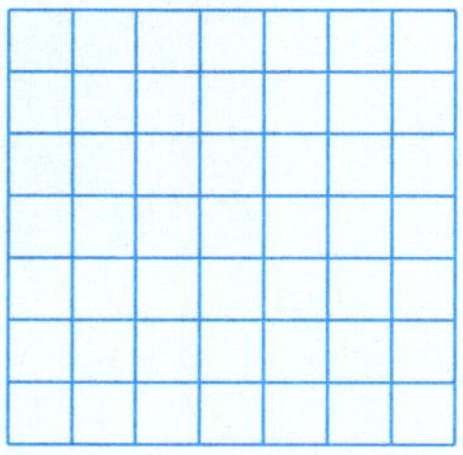

b. How many plays does it take the team to reach the 50-yard line at this rate?

c. Did you use the equation or the graph to find your answer in part (b)? Why did you use this method?

39. OPEN-ENDED Write an equation of the line. Describe a real-life situation that the line could represent. Does your situation affect the domain? Explain your reasoning.

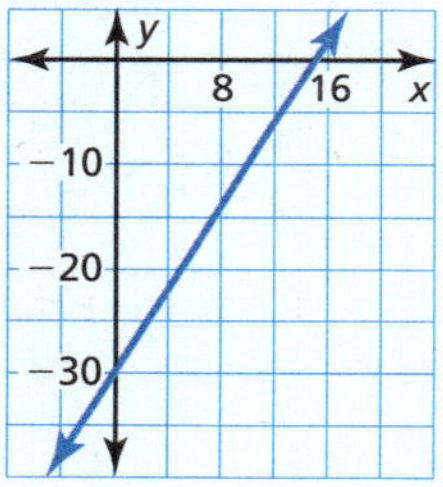

5 MTR **40. STRUCTURE** Write an equation in point-slope form and slope-intercept form of a line that passes through (0, 0) and has a slope of 2. What do you notice?

41. COMPARE METHODS Consider point-slope form and slope-intercept form.

4 MTR

a. When would you prefer to write an equation in point-slope form? in slope-intercept form? Explain.

b. Which form do you prefer to use when graphing a line? Explain your reasoning.

4 MTR **42. MAKING AN ARGUMENT** Your friend says she can write a linear function g with the values $g(4) = -2$ and $g(-1) = -2$. Is your friend correct? Explain.

5 MTR **43.** **CONNECTING CONCEPTS** Compare the graph of $y = 2x$ to the graph of $y - 1 = 2(x + 3)$. Make a conjecture about the graphs of $y = mx$ and $y - k = m(x - h)$.

44. **HOW DO YOU SEE IT?**
The graph shows two points that lie on the graph of a linear function.

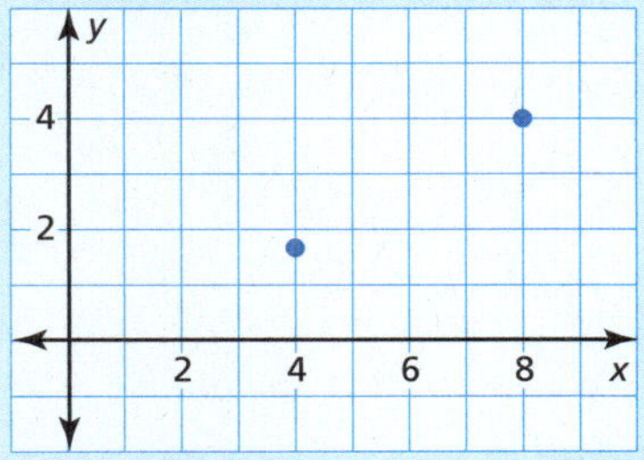

a. Does the y-intercept of the graph of the linear function appear to be positive or negative? Explain.

b. Estimate the coordinates of the two points. How can you use your estimates to confirm your answer in part (a)?

2 MTR **45.** **MULTIPLE REPRESENTATIONS** Three bank accounts are opened and then have fixed amounts of money withdrawn each month. The graph shows Account A, the table represents Account B, and the equation $y = -22.5x + 90$ represents Account C, where y represents the amount of money (in dollars) left after x months.

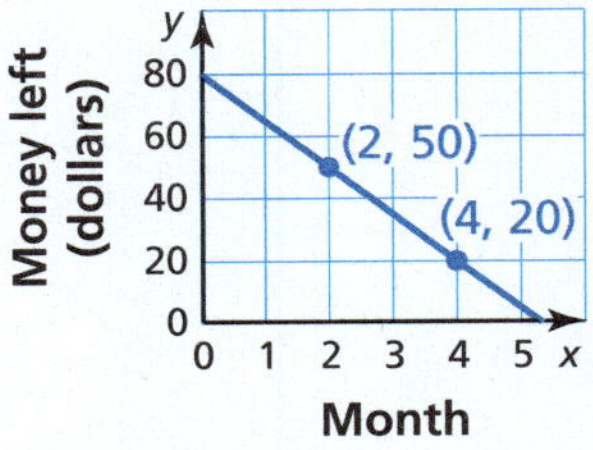

Month, x	Money left, y
1	\$100
2	\$75
3	\$50
4	\$25

a. Interpret the domains of each account. Which account has the greatest initial value? the least initial value?

b. Which account has the most amount of money withdrawn each month? the least amount?

c. Which account runs out of money first? last?

46. **THOUGHT PROVOKING**
A line passing through $\left(p, \frac{1}{2}\right)$ and $(-8, q)$ has a slope of $\frac{3}{4}$. Find two possible values for each of p and q, and write the corresponding equations of the lines in slope-intercept form.

REVIEW & REFRESH

In Exercises 47–50, write the reciprocal of the number.

47. 5

48. -8

49. $-\frac{2}{7}$

50. $\frac{3}{2}$

51. Write an equation in point-slope form of the line that passes through the point $(-9, 1)$ and has a slope of $\frac{2}{3}$.

52. WRITING Compare the graphs of $p(x) = |x - 6|$ and $q(x) = |x| - 6$.

53. Determine whether the domain is *discrete* or *continuous*. Explain.

Input Years, *x*	1	2	3
Output Height of tree (feet), *y*	6	9	12

54. Write a linear function f with the values $f(0) = 2$ and $f(5) = -3$.

7 MTR **55. MODELING REAL LIFE** The total cost (in dollars) to cater an event with p people is represented by $C(p) = 18p + 50$. The set-up fee increases by \$25. The new total cost is represented by $T(p) = C(p) + 25$. Describe the transformation from the graph of C to the graph of T.

56. Solve the inequality $2r + 3 < 7$ *or* $-r + 9 \leq 2$. Graph the solution.

In Exercises 57 and 58, graph the linear equation and identify the intercepts.

57. $4x + 5y = 20$

58. $y = \frac{1}{2}x - 3$

4.3 Writing Equations in Standard Form

Learning Target: Write equations of lines in standard form.

Success Criteria:
- I can convert between different forms of linear equations.
- I can use points to write an equation of a line in standard form.
- I can find a missing coefficient of an equation in standard form.

Algebraic Reasoning

MA.912.AR.2.2 Write a linear two-variable equation to represent the relationship between two quantities from a graph, a written description or a table of values within a mathematical or real-world context.

MA.912.AR.2.5 Solve and graph mathematical and real-world problems that are modeled with linear functions. Interpret key features and determine constraints in terms of the context.

Also MA.912.AR.2.4

EXPLORE IT! Using Intercepts

Work with a partner. You spend $150 on fruit trays and vegetable trays for a party.

APPLY MATHEMATICS (7 MTR)
Describe another real-life situation where you might choose to write a linear equation in standard form.

Fruit Tray: $50

Vegetable Tray: $25

a. Complete the verbal model that represents this situation.

$\dfrac{\square}{\text{1 fruit tray}}$ • Number of fruit trays + $\dfrac{\square}{\text{1 vegetable tray}}$ • Number of vegetable trays = $\square$

b. You buy x fruit trays and y vegetable trays. Write and graph an equation in standard form that represents this situation.

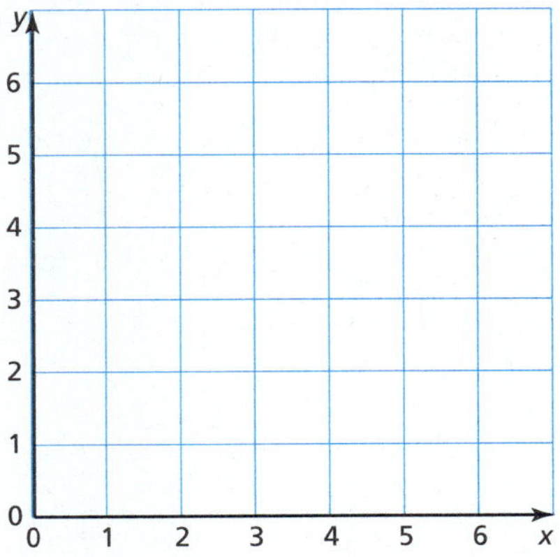

c. Find and interpret the domain, range, x-intercept, y-intercept, and the slope of the line in this context.

GO DIGITAL

Writing Equations in Standard Form

Recall that the linear equation $Ax + By = C$ is in standard form, where A, B, and C are real numbers, and A and B are not both zero. All linear equations can be written in standard form.

STUDY TIP

It is common to use integer values for A, B, and C. You can write an equivalent equation by multiplying each side by 4.

$$\frac{1}{4}x + y = -2$$

$$4 \cdot \left(\frac{1}{4}x + y\right) = 4 \cdot (-2)$$

$$x + 4y = -8$$

EXAMPLE 1 Writing a Linear Equation in Standard Form

WATCH

Write the linear equation $y = -\frac{1}{4}x - 2$ in standard form.

SOLUTION

$y = -\frac{1}{4}x - 2$ Write the equation.

$\frac{1}{4}x + y = -2$ Add $\frac{1}{4}x$ to each side.

▶ An equation in standard form is $\frac{1}{4}x + y = -2$.

EXAMPLE 2 Using Points to Write an Equation

WATCH

Write an equation in standard form of the line shown.

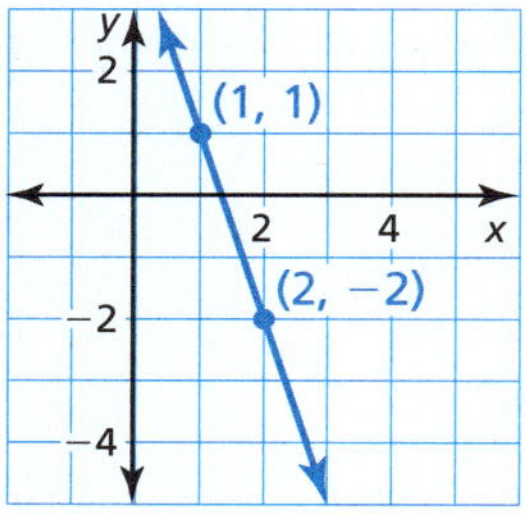

SOLUTION

Step 1 Find the slope of the line.

$$m = \frac{1 - (-2)}{1 - 2} = \frac{3}{-1}, \text{ or } -3$$

Step 2 Use the slope $m = -3$ and the point $(1, 1)$ to write an equation in point-slope form.

$y - y_1 = m(x - x_1)$ Write the point-slope form.

$y - 1 = -3(x - 1)$ Substitute -3 for m, 1 for x_1, and 1 for y_1.

Step 3 Write the equation in standard form.

$y - 1 = -3(x - 1)$ Write the equation.

$y - 1 = -3x + 3$ Distributive Property

$3x + y - 1 = 3$ Add $3x$ to each side.

$3x + y = 4$ Add 1 to each side.

▶ An equation is $3x + y = 4$.

ANOTHER WAY

You can use either of the given points to write an equation of the line.

Use $m = -3$ and $(2, -2)$.

$$y - (-2) = -3(x - 2)$$

$$y + 2 = -3x + 6$$

$$3x + y + 2 = 6$$

$$3x + y = 4$$

GO DIGITAL

SELF-ASSESSMENT

1 I don't understand yet. **2** I can do it with help. **3** I can do it on my own. **4** I can teach someone else.

Write the linear equation in standard form.

1. $y = \frac{2}{5}x + 1$

2. $y + 1 = -\frac{1}{4}(x - 3)$

Write an equation in standard form of the line that passes through the given points.

3.

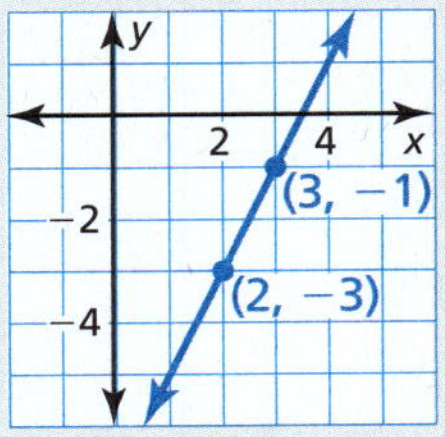

4.

x	−4	−1	2	5
y	5	1	−3	−7

Recall that equations of horizontal lines have the form $y = b$ and equations of vertical lines have the form $x = a$. You cannot write an equation of a vertical line in slope-intercept form or point-slope form because the slope of a vertical line is undefined. However, you can write an equation of a vertical line in standard form.

EXAMPLE 3 B.E.S.T. Test Prep: Horizontal and Vertical Lines

WATCH

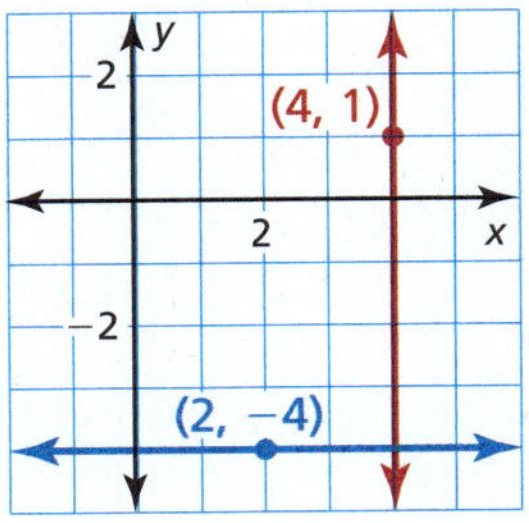

The graphs of two lines are shown. An equation of the blue line is

Ⓐ $x = -4$
Ⓑ $x = 4$
Ⓒ $y = -4$
Ⓓ $y = 4$

and an equation of the red line is

Ⓐ $x = -4$
Ⓑ $x = 4$
Ⓒ $y = -4$
Ⓓ $y = 4$

.

SOLUTION

The y-coordinate of the given point on the blue line is −4. This means that all points on the line have a y-coordinate of −4. So, an equation of the line is $y = -4$.

The x-coordinate of the given point on the red line is 4. This means that all points on the line have an x-coordinate of 4. So, an equation of the line is $x = 4$.

▶ So, the first correct answer is Ⓒ and the second correct answer is Ⓑ.

ANOTHER WAY

Using the slope-intercept form to find an equation of the horizontal line gives you $y = 0x - 4$, or $y = -4$.

GO DIGITAL

EXAMPLE 4 Completing an Equation in Standard Form

WATCH

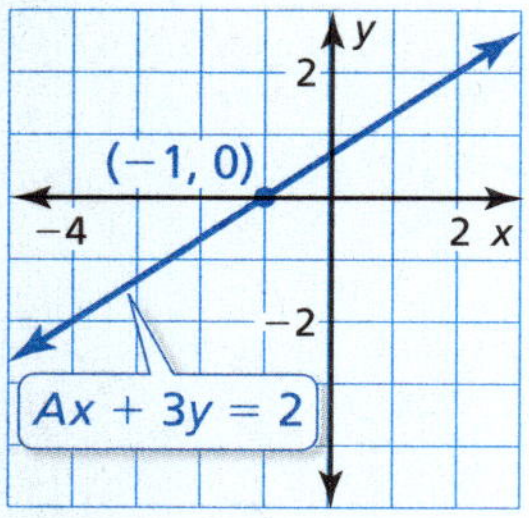

Find the missing coefficient in the equation of the line shown. Write the completed equation.

SOLUTION

Step 1 Find the value of A. Substitute the coordinates of the given point for x and y in the equation. Then solve for A.

$$A + 3y = 2$$ Write the equation.

$$A(-1) + 3(0) = 2$$ Substitute −1 for x and 0 for y.

$$-A = 2$$ Simplify.

$$A = -2$$ Divide each side by −1.

Step 2 Complete the equation.

$$-2x + 3y = 2$$ Substitute −2 for A.

▶ An equation is $-2x + 3y = 2$.

SELF-ASSESSMENT

1 I don't understand yet. 2 I can do it with help. 3 I can do it on my own. 4 I can teach someone else.

Write equations of the horizontal and vertical lines that pass through the given point.

5. $(-8, -9)$

6. $(13, -5)$

Find the missing coefficient in the equation of the line that passes through the given point. Write the completed equation.

7. $-4x + By = 7$; $(-1, 1)$

8. $Ax + y = -3$; $(2, 11)$

Solving Real-Life Problems

7 MTR **EXAMPLE 5** **Modeling Real Life** WATCH

Your class is taking a trip to the public library. You can travel in small and large vans. A small van holds 8 people, and a large van holds 12 people. Your class can fill 15 small vans and 2 large vans.

a. Write an equation in standard form that models the possible combinations of small and large vans that your class can fill.

b. Graph the equation from part (a).

c. Find four possible combinations.

SOLUTION

a. Write a verbal model. Then write an equation.

Capacity of small van	•	Number of small vans	+	Capacity of large van	•	Number of large vans	=	People on trip
8	•	s	+	12	•	ℓ	=	p

Because your class can fill 15 small vans and 2 large vans, use (15, 2) to find the value of p.

$8s + 12\ell = p$ Write the equation.

$8(15) + 12(2) = p$ Substitute 15 for s and 2 for ℓ.

$144 = p$ Simplify.

▶ So, the equation $8s + 12\ell = 144$ models the possible combinations.

b. Use intercepts to graph the equation.

Find the intercepts.

Substitute 0 for s.

$8(0) + 12\ell = 144$

$\ell = 12$

Substitute 0 for ℓ.

$8s + 12(0) = 144$

$s = 18$

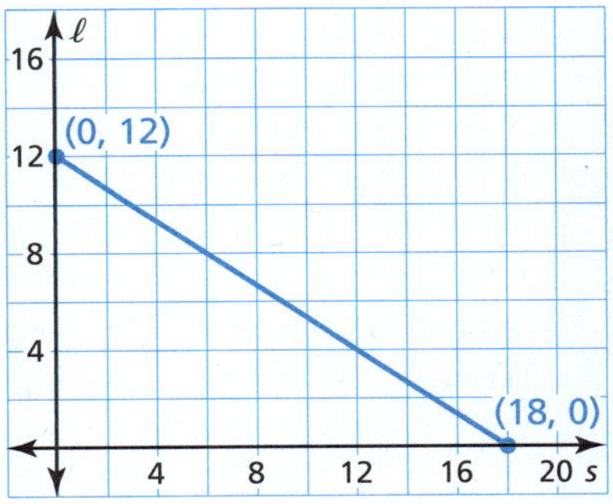

Plot the points (0, 12) and (18, 0). Connect them with a line segment. For this problem, only whole-number values of s and ℓ make sense.

ANOTHER WAY

Another way to find possible combinations is to substitute values for s or ℓ in the equation and solve for the other variable.

c. The graph passes through (0, 12), (6, 8), (12, 4), and (18, 0). So, four possible combinations are 0 small and 12 large, 6 small and 8 large, 12 small and 4 large, and 18 small and 0 large.

GO DIGITAL

SELF-ASSESSMENT 1 I don't understand yet. 2 I can do it with help. 3 I can do it on my own. 4 I can teach someone else.

9. **WHAT IF?** Eight students decide not to go on the class trip. Write an equation in standard form that models the possible combinations of small and large vans that your class can fill. Find four possible combinations.

4.3 Practice WITH CalcChat® AND CalcView®

In Exercises 1–6, write the linear equation in standard form. *(See Example 1.)*

1. $y = 5x + 4$

2. $y = -3x - 10$

3. $y + 4 = 2(x - 7)$

4. $y - 2 = \frac{1}{3}(x + 6)$

5. $y - \frac{2}{3} = \frac{4}{3}(x + 2)$

6. $y + \frac{5}{2} = \frac{1}{2}(x - 1)$

In Exercises 7–12, write an equation in standard form of the line that passes through the given point and has the given slope.

7. $(-3, 2)$; $m = 1$

8. $(4, -1)$; $m = 3$

9. $(0, 5)$; $m = -2$

10. $(-8, 0)$; $m = -4$

11. $(-4, -4)$; $m = -\frac{3}{2}$

12. $(-6, -10)$; $m = \frac{1}{6}$

In Exercises 13–16, write an equation in standard form of the line that passes through the given points. *(See Example 2.)*

13.

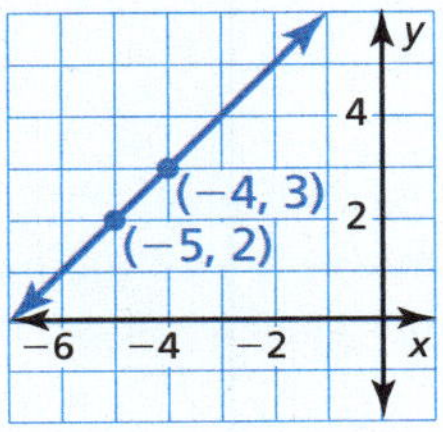

14.

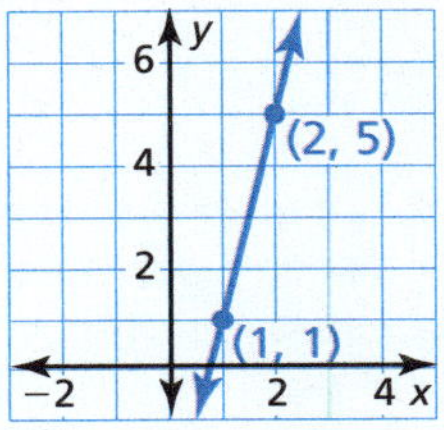

15.

x	y
−6	6
−3	2
0	−2
3	−6

16.

x	y
−4	4
−3	2
−2	0
−1	−2

In Exercises 17–20, find the slope and *y*-intercept of the line. Justify your answer.

17. $-x + y = -10$

18. $5x + 10y = 15$

19. $9x - 3y = -12$

20. $-2x + 4y = -5$

In Exercises 21–24, write equations of the horizontal and vertical lines that pass through the given point. *(See Example 3.)*

21. $(2, 3)$

22. $(-5, -4)$

23. $(8, -1)$

24. $(-6, 2)$

In Exercises 25–28, find the missing coefficient in the equation of the line shown. Write the completed equation. *(See Example 4.)*

25.

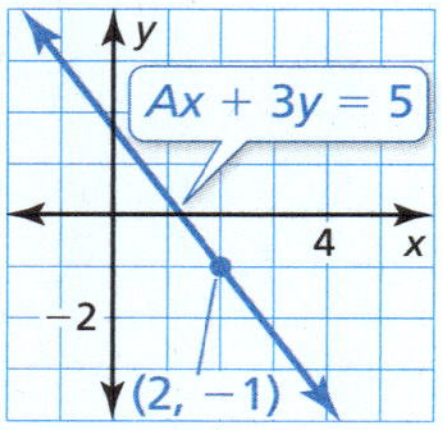

26.

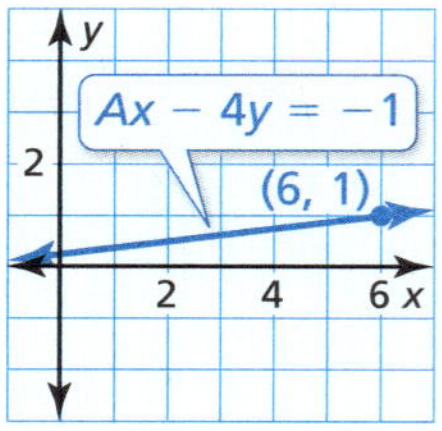

27.

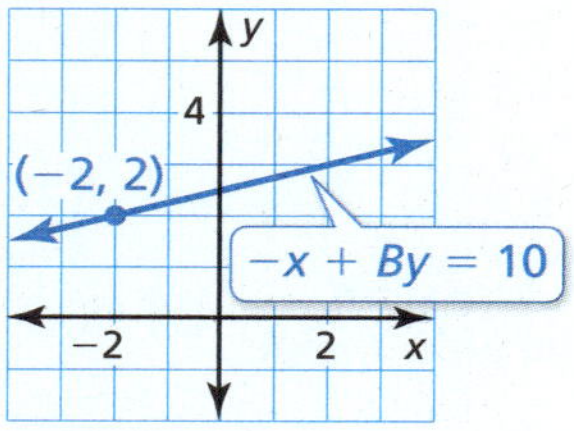

28.

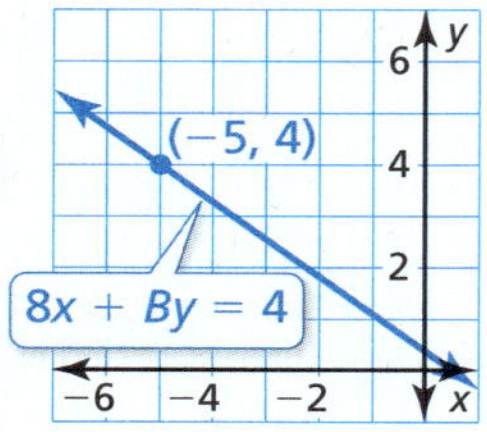

29. **MODELING REAL LIFE** The diagram shows the prices of two types of ground-cover plants. A gardener can afford to buy 125 vinca plants and 60 phlox plants. *(See Example 5.)*

a. Write an equation in standard form that models the possible combinations of vinca and phlox plants the gardener can afford to buy.

b. Graph the equation from part (a).

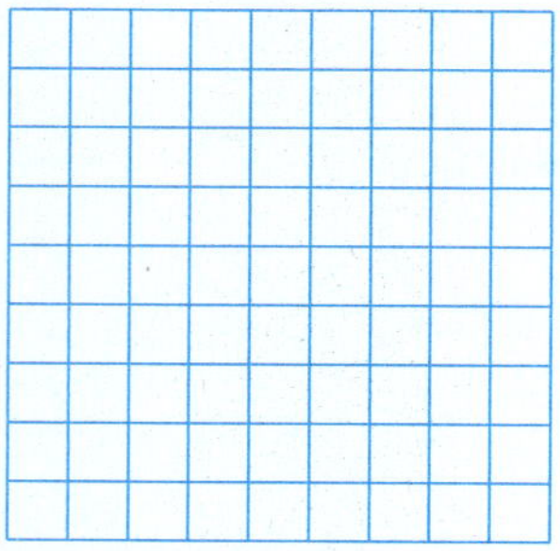

c. Find four possible combinations.

30. **MODELING REAL LIFE** One bus ride costs $0.75. One subway ride costs $1. A monthly pass for unlimited bus and subway rides costs the same as 36 bus rides plus 36 subway rides.

a. Write an equation in standard form that models the possible combinations of bus and subway rides with the same total cost as the pass.

b. Graph the equation from part (a).

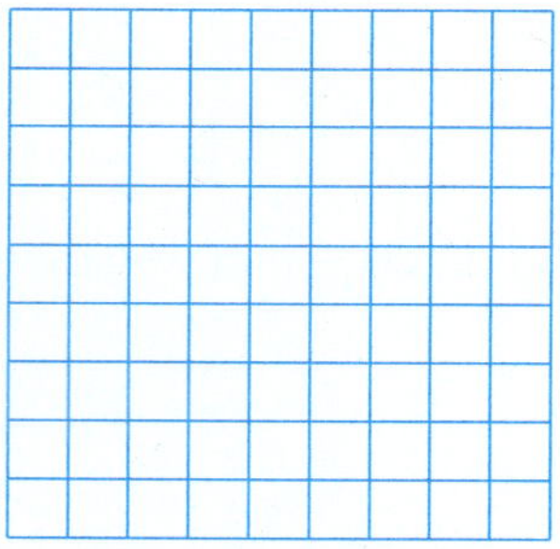

c. You ride the bus 60 times in one month. How many times must you ride the subway for the total cost of the rides to equal the cost of the pass? Explain your reasoning.

4 MTR **31. MAKING AN ARGUMENT** Your friend says that you can write an equation of a horizontal line in standard form but not in slope-intercept form or point-slope form. Is your friend correct? Explain.

32. HOW DO YOU SEE IT?
A dog kennel charges \$25 per night to board your dog. The kennel also sells dog treats for \$5 each. The graph shows the possible combinations of nights at the kennel and treats that you can buy for \$100.

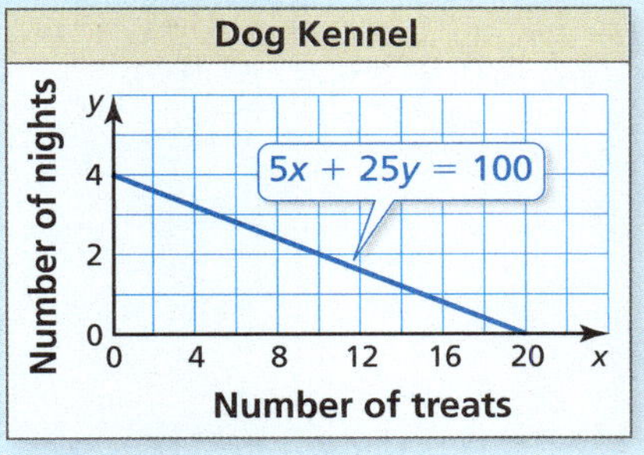

a. List two possible combinations.

b. Interpret the intercepts of the graph.

5 MTR **33. STRUCTURE** Write an equation in standard form of the line that passes through $(a, 0)$ and $(0, b)$, where $a \neq 0$ and $b \neq 0$.

34. THOUGHT PROVOKING
Use the graph shown.

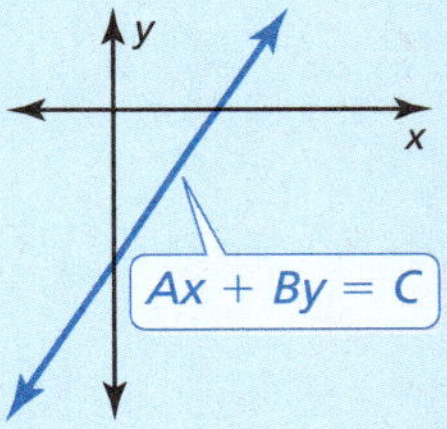

a. What are the signs of B and C when A is positive? when A is negative?

b. Explain how to change the equation so that the graph is reflected in the x-axis.

c. Explain how to change the equation so that the graph is translated horizontally.

5 MTR **35. CONNECTING CONCEPTS** Write an equation in standard form that models the possible lengths and widths (in feet) of a rectangle with the same perimeter as a rectangle that is 10 feet wide and 20 feet long. Make a table that shows five possible lengths and widths of the rectangle.

WATCH

REVIEW & REFRESH

36. Write an equation of the line in slope-intercept form.

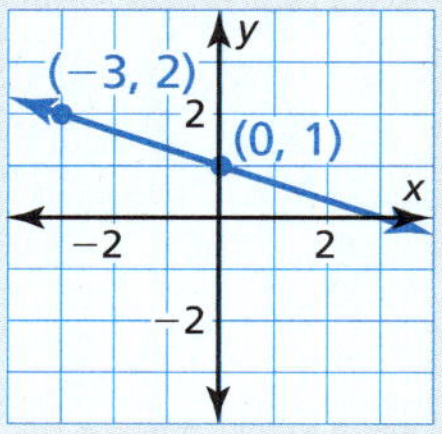

37. Graph $f(x) = |x + 7|$. Compare the graph to the graph of $f(x) = |x|$. Find the domain and range.

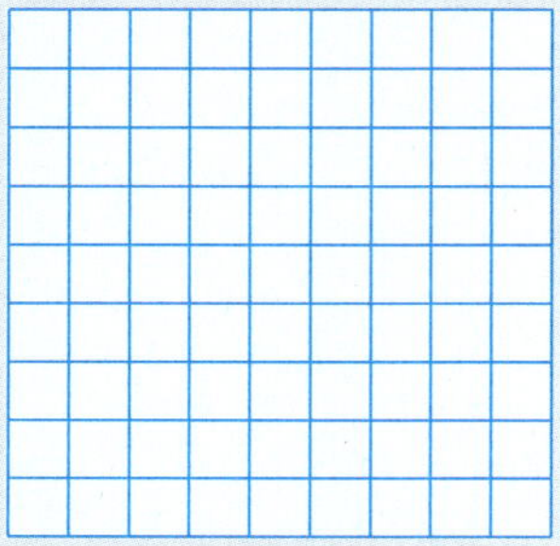

38. Write an equation in standard form of a line that passes through the given points.

x	y
−4	−2
0	1
4	4
8	7

39. Write a linear function f with values $f(-3) = 5$ and $f(6) = 11$.

In Exercises 40–43, graph f and g. Describe the transformation from the graph of f to the graph of g.

40. $f(x) = -x + 6;\ g(x) = f(-5x)$

41. $f(x) = -\frac{1}{4}x + 2;\ g(x) = -f(x)$

42. $f(x) = 3x - 1;\ g(x) = f(x + 2)$

43. $f(x) = 4x - 6;\ g(x) = \frac{1}{2}f(x)$

7 MTR **44.** **MODELING REAL LIFE** You are sponsored by a company to participate in a walk for charity. Participants can walk any distance up to 15 miles. The function $d(m) = 50m + 100$ represents the amount the company donates where m represents the number of miles you walk. Find the domain and range in this context. Then graph the function. Interpret the slope and the intercepts of the graph.

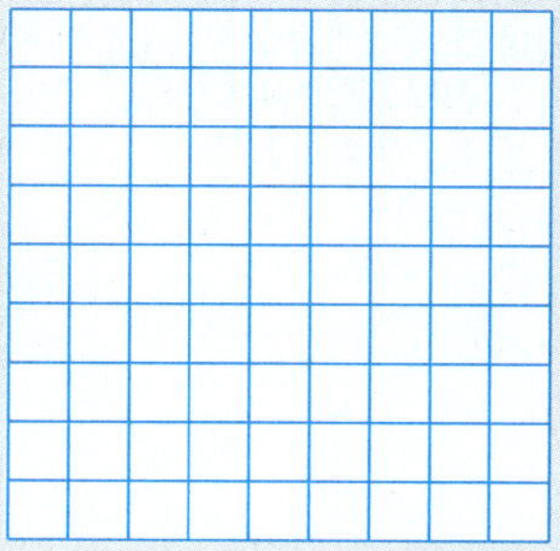

45. Solve $-4x < 16$. Graph the solution.

46. Solve $5x - 2y = 14$ for y.

4.4 Writing Equations of Parallel and Perpendicular Lines

Learning Target: Recognize and write equations of parallel and perpendicular lines.

Success Criteria:
- I can identify parallel and perpendicular lines from their equations.
- I can write equations of parallel lines.
- I can write equations of perpendicular lines.

Algebraic Reasoning

MA.912.AR.2.2 Write a linear two-variable equation to represent the relationship between two quantities from a graph, a written description or a table of values within a mathematical or real-world context.

MA.912.AR.2.3 Write a linear two-variable equation for a line that is parallel or perpendicular to a given line and goes through a given point.

Also MA.912.AR.2.5

EXPLORE IT! Recognizing Parallel and Perpendicular Lines

Work with a partner. Consider the graph of the linear function *f*.

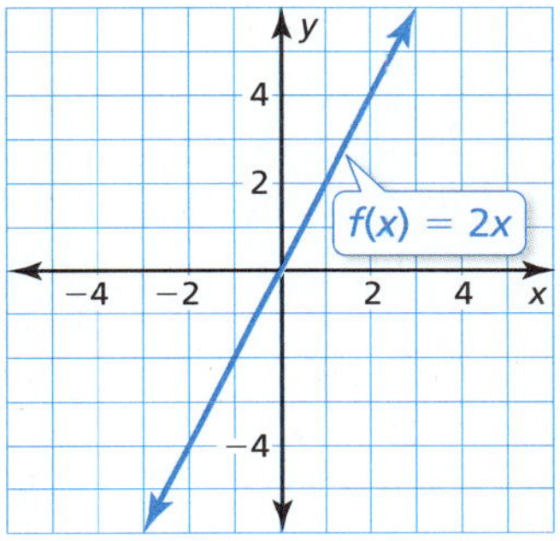

a. Write and graph a function *g* that is a horizontal or vertical translation of the graph of *f*. Do the graphs ever intersect? How do you know?

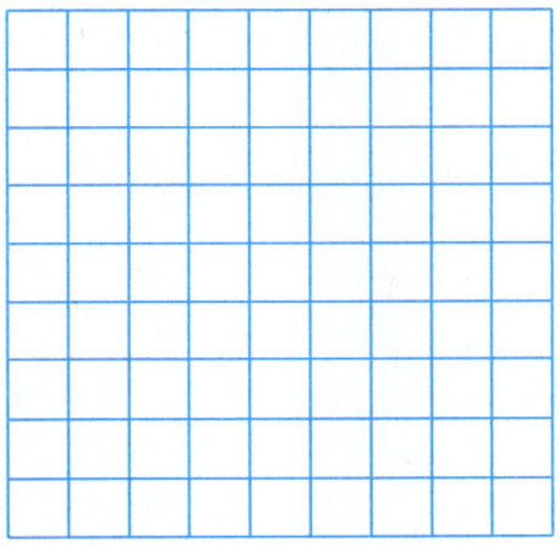

b. Write and graph a function *h* that is a 90° clockwise rotation of the graph of *f*. Do the graphs ever intersect? If so, what are the measures of the angles created by the intersection? How do you know?

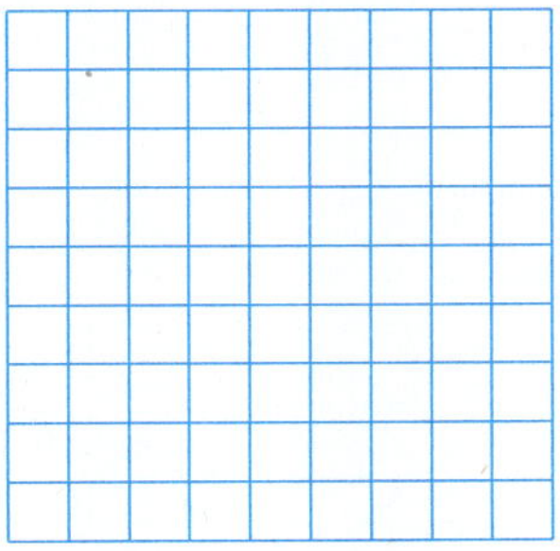

GO DIGITAL

Two lines in the same plane that never intersect are **parallel lines**. Two lines in the same plane that intersect to form right angles are **perpendicular lines**.

c. Compare your equations and graphs with other students. Make a conjecture about how you can use equations to determine whether two lines are parallel or perpendicular.

d. Write a linear function that has a different slope than the graph of f. Repeat parts (a) and (b) using this function. Do the results support your conjecture in part (c)?

e. Without graphing, determine whether any of the following are equations of parallel or perpendicular lines. Explain your reasoning.

$3x + 4y = 6$ Equation 1

$3x + 4y = 12$ Equation 2

$4x - 3y = 12$ Equation 3

6 MTR

ASSESS REASONABLENESS

Use a graph to show that your answers in part (e) are reasonable.

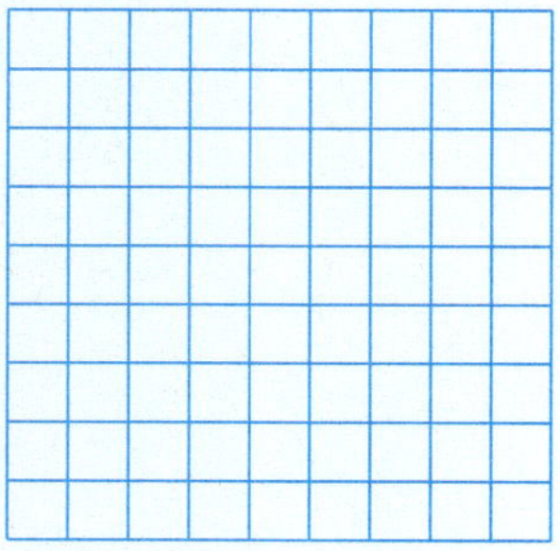

Identifying and Writing Equations of Parallel Lines

Vocabulary AZ VOCAB

parallel lines, *p. 337*
perpendicular lines, *p. 338*

READING

The phrase "*A if and only if B*" is a way of writing two conditional statements at once. It means that if *A* is true, then *B* is true. It also means that if *B* is true, then *A* is true.

KEY IDEA

Parallel Lines and Slopes

Two lines in the same plane that never intersect are **parallel lines**. Two distinct nonvertical lines are parallel if and only if they have the same slope.

All distinct vertical lines are parallel.

EXAMPLE 1 Identifying Parallel Lines

WATCH

Determine which of the lines are parallel.

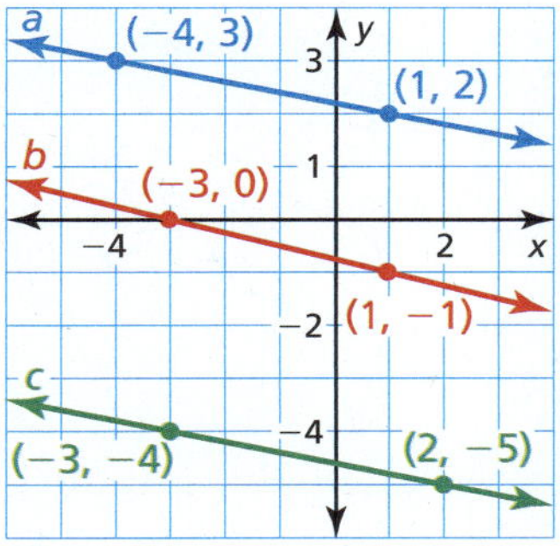

SOLUTION

Find the slope of each line.

Line a: $m = \dfrac{2 - 3}{1 - (-4)} = -\dfrac{1}{5}$

Line b: $m = \dfrac{-1 - 0}{1 - (-3)} = -\dfrac{1}{4}$

Line c: $m = \dfrac{-5 - (-4)}{2 - (-3)} = -\dfrac{1}{5}$

▶ Lines a and c have the same slope, so they are parallel.

EXAMPLE 2 Writing an Equation of a Parallel Line

WATCH

Write an equation of the line that passes through $(5, -4)$ and is parallel to the line $y = 2x + 3$.

SOLUTION

Step 1 Find the slope of the parallel line. The graph of the given equation has a slope of 2. So, the parallel line that passes through $(5, -4)$ also has a slope of 2.

Step 2 Use the slope-intercept form to find the y-intercept of the parallel line.

$y = mx + b$	Write the slope-intercept form.
$-4 = 2(5) + b$	Substitute 2 for m, 5 for x, and -4 for y.
$-14 = b$	Solve for b.

▶ Using $m = 2$ and $b = -14$, an equation of the parallel line is $y = 2x - 14$.

GO DIGITAL

SELF-ASSESSMENT

1 I don't understand yet. 2 I can do it with help. 3 I can do it on my own. 4 I can teach someone else.

1. Line *a* passes through $(-5, 3)$ and $(-6, -1)$. Line *b* passes through $(3, -2)$ and $(2, -7)$. Are the lines parallel? Explain.

2. Write an equation of the line that passes through $(-4, 2)$ and is parallel to the line $y = \frac{1}{4}x + 1$.

4 MTR **3.** **WHICH ONE DOESN'T BELONG?** Which equation does *not* belong with the other three? Explain your reasoning.

$-4y = x - 8$ $\quad\frac{1}{4}y = x - 1$ $\quad y = 4x - 1$ $\quad -4x + y = 3$

Identifying and Writing Equations of Perpendicular Lines

STUDY TIP

The product of a nonzero number *m* and its negative reciprocal is -1.

$$m\left(-\frac{1}{m}\right) = -1$$

KEY IDEA

Perpendicular Lines and Slopes

Two lines in the same plane that intersect to form right angles are **perpendicular lines**. Nonvertical lines are perpendicular if and only if their slopes are negative reciprocals.

Vertical lines are perpendicular to horizontal lines.

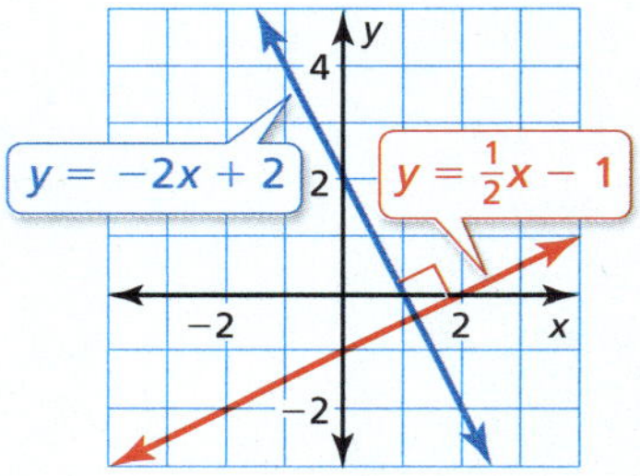

EXAMPLE 3 **Identifying Parallel and Perpendicular Lines** WATCH

Determine which of the lines, if any, are parallel or perpendicular.

Line *a*: $y = 4x + 2$ Line *b*: $x + 4y = 3$ Line *c*: $-8y - 2x = 16$

SOLUTION

Write the equations in slope-intercept form. Then compare the slopes.

Line *a*: $y = 4x + 2$ Line *b*: $y = -\frac{1}{4}x + \frac{3}{4}$ Line *c*: $y = -\frac{1}{4}x - 2$

▶ Lines *b* and *c* have slopes of $-\frac{1}{4}$, so they are parallel. Line *a* has a slope of 4, the negative reciprocal of $-\frac{1}{4}$, so it is perpendicular to lines *b* and *c*.

GO DIGITAL

EXAMPLE 4 Writing an Equation of a Perpendicular Line

Write an equation of the line that passes through $(-3, 1)$ and is perpendicular to the line $y = \frac{1}{2}x + 3$.

WATCH

SOLUTION

Step 1 Find the slope of the perpendicular line. The graph of the given equation has a slope of $\frac{1}{2}$. Because the slopes of perpendicular lines are negative reciprocals, the slope of the perpendicular line that passes through $(-3, 1)$ is -2.

Step 2 Use the slope $m = -2$ and the point-slope form to write an equation of the perpendicular line that passes through $(-3, 1)$.

$$y - y_1 = m(x - x_1)$$ Write the point-slope form.

$$y - 1 = -2[x - (-3)]$$ Substitute -2 for m, -3 for x_1, and 1 for y_1.

$$y - 1 = -2x - 6$$ Simplify.

$$y = -2x - 5$$ Write in slope-intercept form.

▶ An equation of the perpendicular line is $y = -2x - 5$.

SELF-ASSESSMENT

1 I don't understand yet. 2 I can do it with help. 3 I can do it on my own. 4 I can teach someone else.

4. Determine which of the lines, if any, are parallel or perpendicular. Explain.

Line a: $2x + 6y = -3$ Line b: $y = 3x - 8$ Line c: $-6y + 18x = 9$

5. Write an equation of the line that passes through $(-3, 5)$ and is perpendicular to the line $y = -3x - 1$.

Writing Equations for Real-Life Problems

7 MTR **EXAMPLE 5** **Modeling Real Life** WATCH

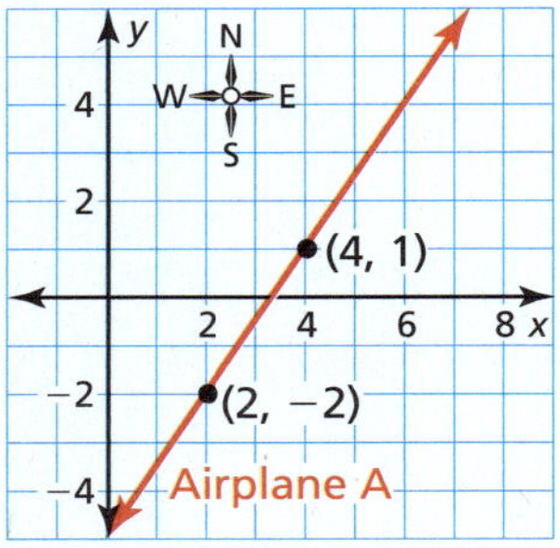

The planned path of Airplane A is shown in the graph. Each grid square represents 1 square mile. Airplane B will fly along a path parallel to Airplane A, passing through the point (14, 4). Airplane C will fly along a path perpendicular to each of these paths, passing through the point (7, −1). An air traffic controller is in charge of the region represented by the fourth quadrant. Do any of the paths intersect in the air traffic controller's region?

SOLUTION

Use the slope of the path of Airplane A to write equations that represent the paths of Airplanes B and C. Then graph the equations to determine whether any paths intersect in the air traffic controller's region, the fourth quadrant.

Airplane A Find the slope of the path of Airplane A. The line passes through the points (2, −2) and (4, 1). So, the slope is $m = \frac{1 - (-2)}{4 - 2} = \frac{3}{2}$.

Airplane B

Because the paths of Airplanes A and B are parallel, the slopes of their graphs are the same.

Use the slope $m = \frac{3}{2}$ and the point (14, 4) to write an equation.

$$y - y_1 = m(x - x_1)$$

$$y - 4 = \frac{3}{2}(x - 14)$$

$$y - 4 = \frac{3}{2}x - 21$$

$$y = \frac{3}{2}x - 17$$

Airplane C

Because the paths of Airplanes A and C are perpendicular, the slopes of their graphs are negative reciprocals. So, the slope of the path of Airplane C is $-\frac{2}{3}$.

Use the slope $m = -\frac{2}{3}$ and the point (7, −1) to write an equation.

$$y - y_1 = m(x - x_1)$$

$$y - (-1) = -\frac{2}{3}(x - 7)$$

$$y + 1 = -\frac{2}{3}x + \frac{14}{3}$$

$$y = -\frac{2}{3}x + \frac{11}{3}$$

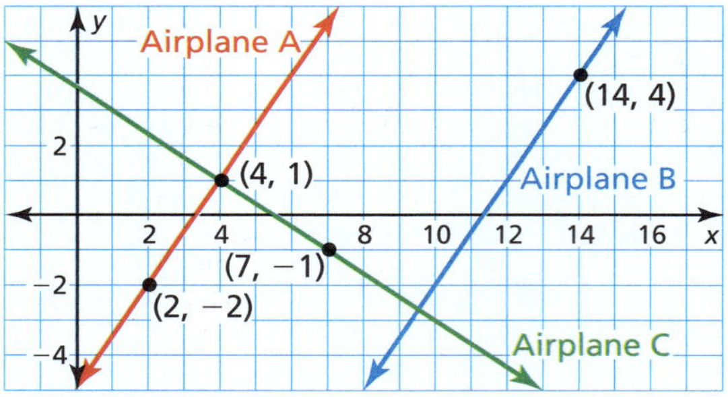

► The graph shows that the paths of Airplanes B and C intersect in the air traffic controller's region.

SELF-ASSESSMENT

1 I don't understand yet. 2 I can do it with help. 3 I can do it on my own. 4 I can teach someone else.

6. In Example 5, the pilot of Airplane C submits a new flight plan, which indicates a path that is a translation of the original path. Do any of the paths intersect in the air traffic controller's region when the translation is (a) 3 miles north or (b) 3 miles west? Explain your reasoning.

GO DIGITAL

4.4 Practice WITH CalcChat® AND CalcView®

In Exercises 1–6, determine which of the lines, if any, are parallel. Explain. *(See Example 1.)*

1. 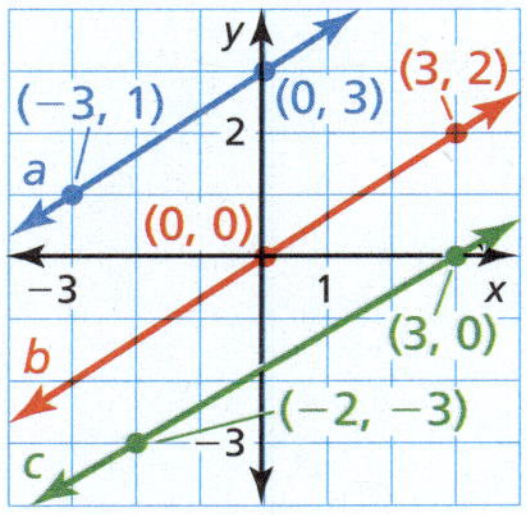

2. 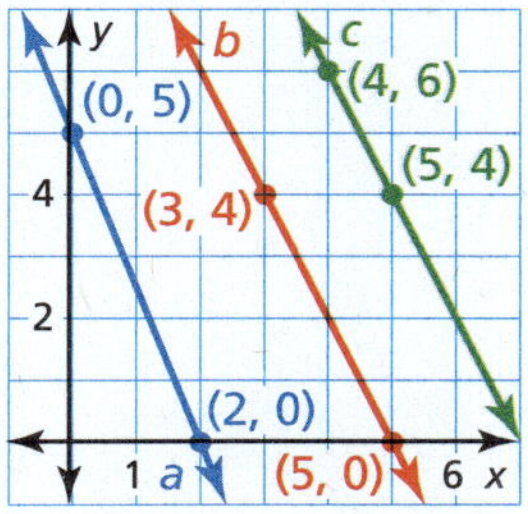

▶ 3. Line a passes through $(-1, -2)$ and $(1, 0)$.
Line b passes through $(4, 2)$ and $(2, -2)$.
Line c passes through $(0, 2)$ and $(-1, 1)$.

4. Line a passes through $(-1, 3)$ and $(1, 9)$.
Line b passes through $(-2, 12)$ and $(-1, 14)$.
Line c passes through $(3, 8.5)$ and $(6, 10.5)$.

5. Line a: $4y + x = 8$
Line b: $2y + x = 4$
Line c: $2y = -3x + 6$

6. Line a: $3y - x = 6$
Line b: $3y = x + 18$
Line c: $3y - 2x = 9$

In Exercises 7–12, write an equation of the line that passes through the given point and is parallel to the given line. *(See Example 2.)*

7. $(0, 2)$; $x = 9$

8. $(-2, -7)$; $y = -2$

9. $(-1, 3)$; $y = -3x + 2$

10. $(1, 2)$; $y = -5x + 4$

▶ 11. $(6, 4)$; $3y - x = -12$

12. $(2, -5)$; $2y = 3x + 10$

In Exercises 13–18, determine which of the lines, if any, are parallel or perpendicular. Explain. *(See Example 3.)*

13. 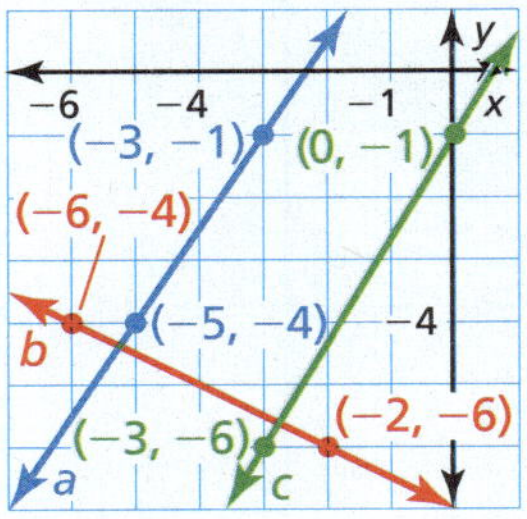

14. 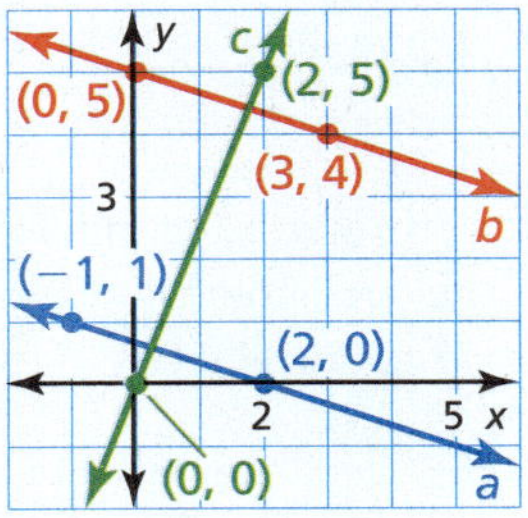

GO DIGITAL

15. Line a passes through $(-2, 1)$ and $(0, 3)$.
Line b passes through $(4, 1)$ and $(6, 4)$.
Line c passes through $(1, 3)$ and $(4, 1)$.

16. Line a passes through $(2, 10)$ and $(4, 13)$.
Line b passes through $(4, 9)$ and $(6, 12)$.
Line c passes through $(2, 10)$ and $(4, 9)$.

17. Line a: $4x - 3y = 2$
Line b: $y = \frac{4}{3}x + 2$
Line c: $4y + 3x = 4$

18. Line a: $y = 6x - 2$
Line b: $6y = -x$
Line c: $y + 6x = 1$

In Exercises 19–24, write an equation of the line that passes through the given point and is perpendicular to the given line. *(See Example 4.)*

19. $(2, 5)$; $x = -6$

20. $(-8, 4)$; $y = 7$

21. $(7, 10)$; $y = -\frac{1}{5}x - 9$

22. $(-4, -1)$; $y = \frac{4}{3}x + 6$

23. $(-3, 3)$; $2y = 8x - 6$

24. $(8, 1)$; $2y + 4x = 12$

25. 7 MTR **MODELING REAL LIFE** A city water department is proposing the construction of a new water pipe. The new pipe will be perpendicular to the existing pipe shown, passing through the point $(1, 0)$. The two pipes will be connected at their intersection. At what point will the two pipes intersect? *(See Example 5.)*

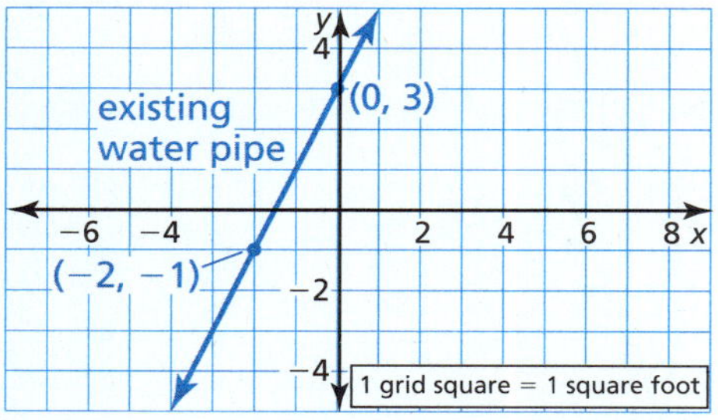

26. 7 MTR **MODELING REAL LIFE** A parks and recreation department wants to construct a new bike path that is parallel to the railroad tracks and does not intersect the trees shown. Will the department be able to build the path so that it passes through the parking area at the point $(4, 5)$? Justify your answer.

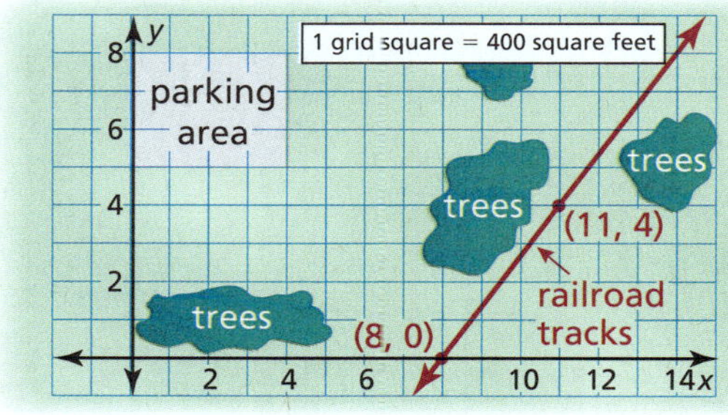

4 MTR **27. ERROR ANALYSIS** Describe and correct the error in writing an equation of the line that passes through $(4, -5)$ and is perpendicular to the line $y = \frac{1}{3}x + 5$.

✗

$$y - y_1 = m(x - x_1)$$
$$y - (-5) = 3(x - 4)$$
$$y + 5 = 3x - 12$$
$$y = 3x - 17$$

28. HOW DO YOU SEE IT?
A softball academy charges students an initial registration fee plus a monthly fee. The graph shows the total amounts paid by two students over a 4-month period. The lines are parallel. Did one of the students pay a greater registration fee? a greater monthly fee? Explain.

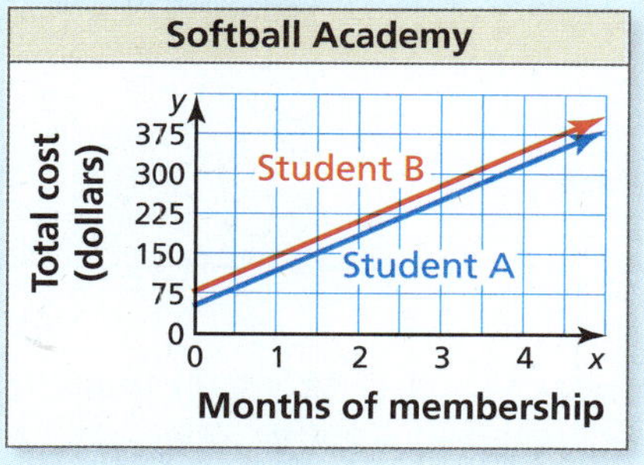

5 MTR **29. CONNECTING CONCEPTS** The vertices of a quadrilateral are $A(2, 2)$, $B(6, 4)$, $C(8, 10)$, and $D(4, 8)$. Is quadrilateral $ABCD$ a parallelogram? a rectangle? Explain.

30. REASONING Lines a and b are perpendicular. Lines b and c are perpendicular. The slope of line a is m. What are the slopes of lines b and c? What can you conclude?

4 MTR **DISCUSS MATHEMATICAL THINKING** **In Exercises 31–33, determine whether the statement is *always*, *sometimes*, or *never* true. Explain your reasoning.**

31. Two lines with positive slopes are perpendicular.

32. A vertical line is parallel to the y-axis.

33. Two lines with the same y-intercept are perpendicular.

34. THOUGHT PROVOKING
You are designing a new logo for your math club. Your teacher asks you to include at least one pair of parallel lines and at least one pair of perpendicular lines. Sketch your logo in a coordinate plane. Write the equations of the parallel and perpendicular lines.

4 MTR **35. MAKING AN ARGUMENT**
A hockey puck leaves the blade of a hockey stick, bounces off a wall, and travels in a new direction, as shown. Your friend claims the path of the puck forms a right angle. Is your friend correct? Explain.

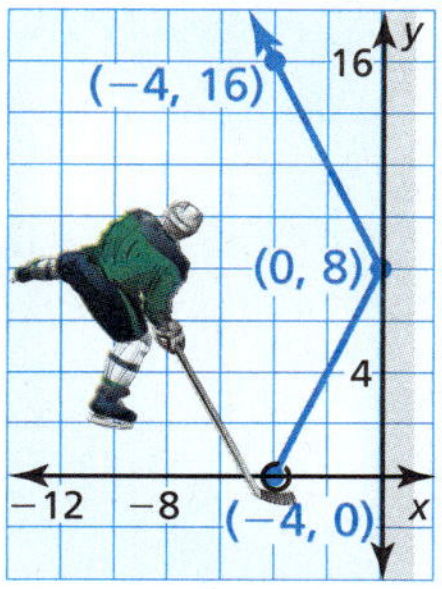

REVIEW & REFRESH

36. Determine whether the relation is a function. Explain.

$(-1, 6), (1, 4), (-1, 2), (1, 6), (-1, 5)$

37. **MODELING REAL LIFE** The table shows the amounts of water remaining in a water tank as it drains. How much water remains in the tank after 30 minutes?

Time (minutes)	8	10	12	14	16
Water (gallons)	155	150	145	140	135

38. Graph $x > \frac{3}{4}$.

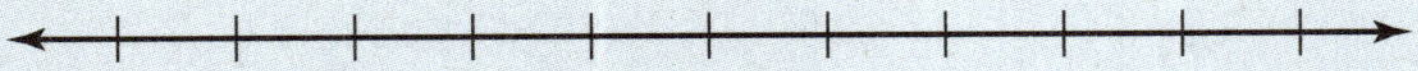

In Exercises 39 and 40, graph the function. Compare the graph to the graph of $f(x) = |x|$. Find the domain and range.

39. $g(x) = |x| + 7$

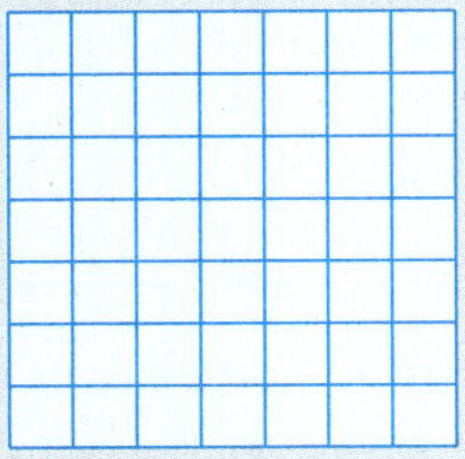

40. $h(x) = -4|x|$

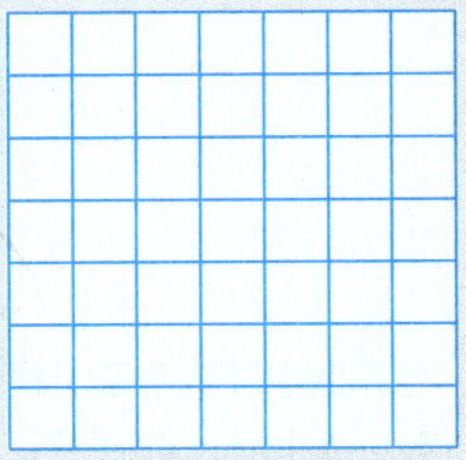

In Exercises 41 and 42, graph the linear equation.

41. $x = 6$

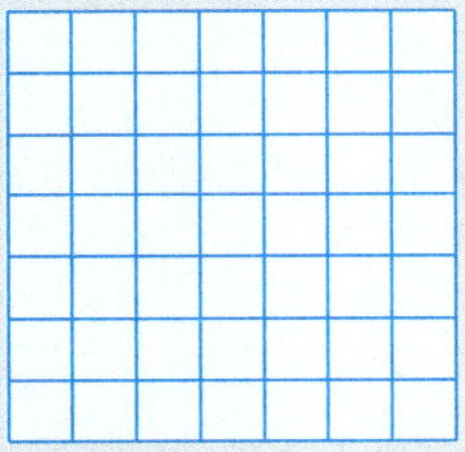

42. $y = -\frac{3}{2}$

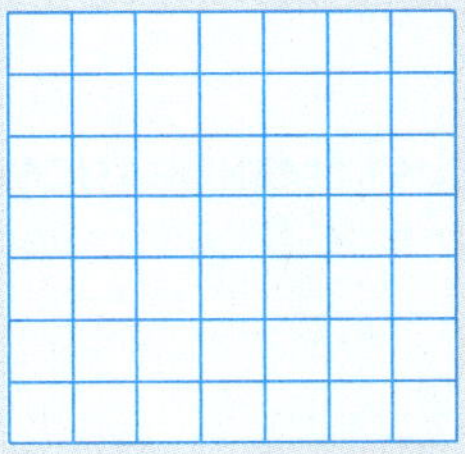

43. Convert 50.2 ounces to kilograms. Round to the nearest hundredth.

44. Write an equation of the line that passes through (4, 3) and is (a) parallel and (b) perpendicular to the line shown.

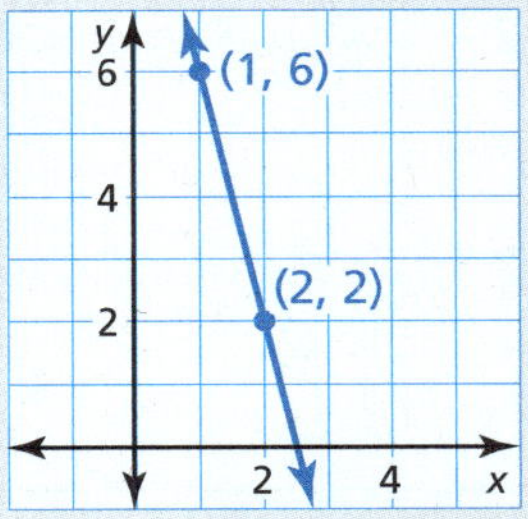

45. Write the linear equation $y = -\frac{5}{2}x + 4$ in standard form.

46. **STRUCTURE** For what value of a are the graphs of $6y = -2x + 4$ and $2y = ax - 5$ parallel? perpendicular?

47. Find the surface area of the square pyramid.

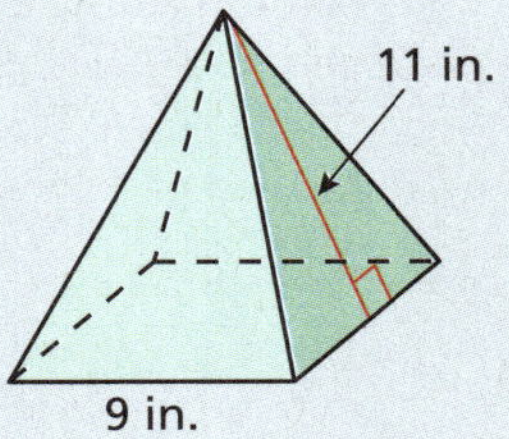

4.5 Scatter Plots and Lines of Fit

Learning Target: Use scatter plots and lines of fit to describe relationships between data.

Success Criteria:
- I can read and interpret scatter plots.
- I can identify correlations between data.
- I can write and interpret an equation of a line of fit.

Algebraic Reasoning
MA.912.AR.2.5 Solve and graph mathematical and real-world problems that are modeled with linear functions. Interpret key features and determine constraints in terms of the context.
Data Analysis and Probability
MA.912.DP.2.4 Fit a linear function to bivariate numerical data that suggests a linear association and interpret the slope and *y*-intercept of the model. Use the model to solve real-world problems in terms of the context of the data.

EXPLORE IT! Examining Scatter Plots

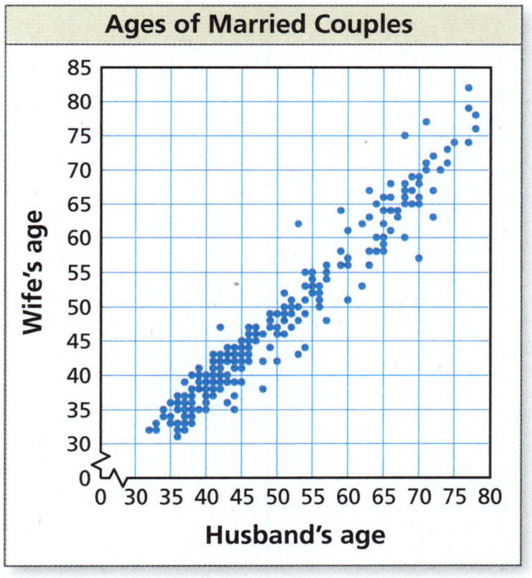

Work with a partner. A survey was taken of 179 married couples. Each person was asked his or her age. The graph shows the results.

a. Make several observations about the data in the graph. What do the data show? What might be some reasons for the patterns in the data?

b. Is the relationship positive or negative? Describe what that means in this context.

c. Do the data have a linear relationship? If so, explain how you can use a linear equation to represent the data.

GO DIGITAL

d. The graph at the right shows the median ages of American men and women at their first marriage for selected years from 1960 to 2015. Make several observations about the data in the graph. Why do you think the ages are increasing over time?

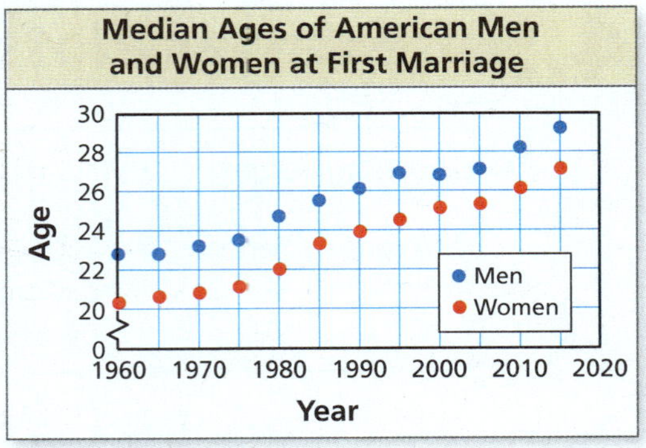

e. Explain how you can use a linear equation to represent each set of data. Then write each equation. Let x represent the number of years since 1960. Explain the method you used.

f. Find and interpret the slope and y-intercept of the graph of each equation in part (e).

g. Explain how you can use your equation from part (e) to predict when the median age of American women at their first marriage will be 30.

6 MTR **ASSESS REASONABLENESS**

Is it reasonable to use your equation from part (e) to predict the median ages in the year 2075? in the year 2500? Explain your reasoning.

Interpreting Scatter Plots

Vocabulary

scatter plot, *p. 347*
correlation, *p. 348*
line of fit, *p. 349*

KEY IDEA

Scatter Plot

A **scatter plot** is a graph that shows the relationship between two data sets. The two data sets are graphed as ordered pairs in a coordinate plane. Scatter plots can show trends in the data.

EXAMPLE 1 Interpreting a Scatter Plot

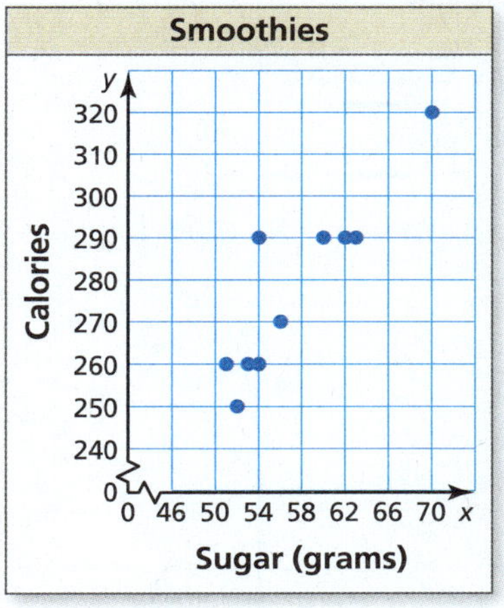

The scatter plot shows the amounts x (in grams) of sugar and the numbers y of calories in 10 smoothies.

a. How many calories are in the smoothie that contains 56 grams of sugar?

b. How many grams of sugar are in the smoothie that contains 320 calories?

c. What tends to happen to the number of calories as the number of grams of sugar increases?

SOLUTION

a. Draw a horizontal line from the point that has an x-value of 56. It intersects the y-axis at 270.

▶ So, the smoothie has 270 calories.

b. Draw a vertical line from the point that has a y-value of 320. It intersects the x-axis at 70.

▶ So, the smoothie has 70 grams of sugar.

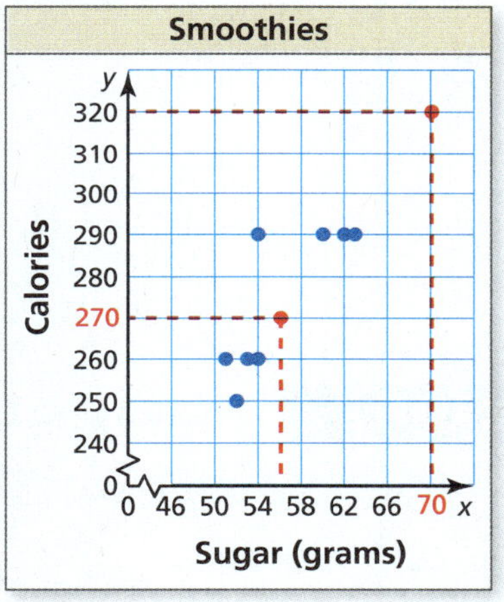

c. Looking at the graph, the plotted points go up from left to right.

▶ So, as the number of grams of sugar increases, the number of calories increases.

SELF-ASSESSMENT

1 I don't understand yet. 2 I can do it with help. 3 I can do it on my own. 4 I can teach someone else.

1. How many calories are in the smoothie that contains 51 grams of sugar?

2. How many grams of sugar are in the smoothie that contains 250 calories?

3. Another point, (55, 280), is plotted on the graph. Explain the meaning of this point.

4. **ASSESS REASONABLENESS** Do you think it is possible for a smoothie to be represented by a point on the y-axis? on the x-axis? Explain your reasoning.

GO DIGITAL

SELF-ASSESSMENT

1 I don't understand yet. 2 I can do it with help. 3 I can do it on my own. 4 I can teach someone else.

5. **REASONING** From the graph, find the number of smoothies for each description. Explain your reasoning.

   a. smoothies with at least 270 calories

   b. smoothies with less than 50 grams of sugar

   c. smoothies with more than 275 calories and less than 62 grams of sugar

Identifying Correlations between Data Sets

A **correlation** is a relationship between data sets. You can use a scatter plot to describe the correlation between data.

READING

Whether a correlation is positive or negative is sometimes referred to as the *direction* of the correlation.

Positive Linear Correlation

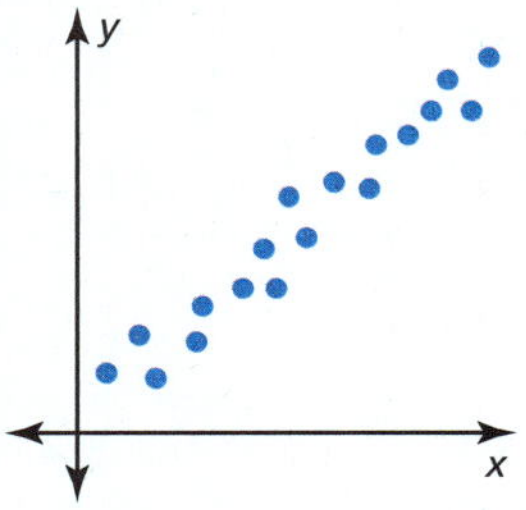

The points lie close to a line. As *x* increases, *y* increases.

Negative Linear Correlation

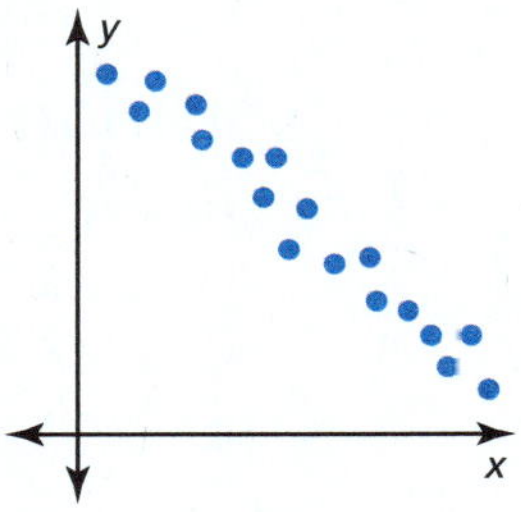

The points lie close to a line. As *x* increases, *y* decreases.

No Correlation

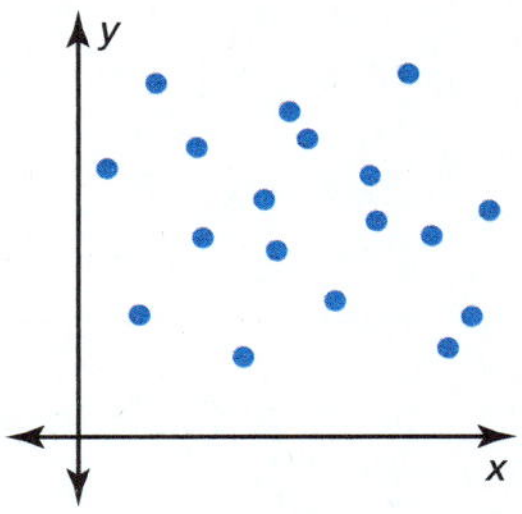

The points show no pattern.

EXAMPLE 2 Identifying Correlations

Describe the relationship between the data in each scatter plot.

a. age and vehicles owned

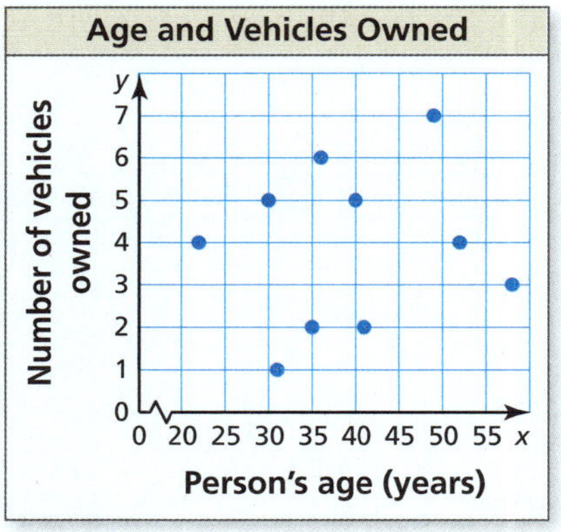

b. temperature and coat sales at a store

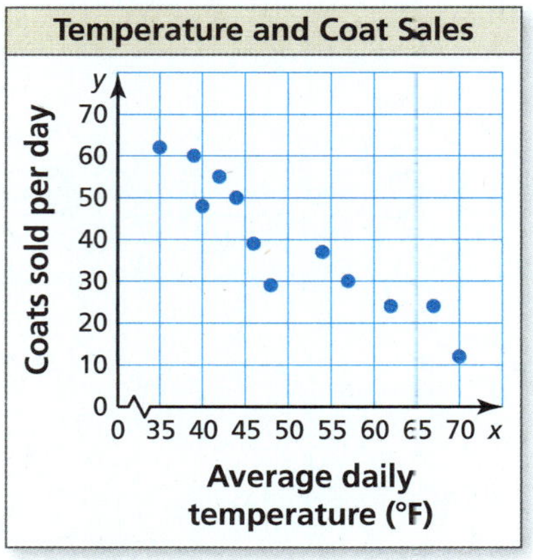

SOLUTION

a. The points show no pattern. The number of vehicles owned does not depend on a person's age. So, the scatter plot shows no correlation.

b. The points appear to lie close to a line with a negative slope. As the average temperature increases, the number of coats sold decreases. So, the scatter plot shows a negative linear correlation.

GO DIGITAL

SELF-ASSESSMENT
1 I don't understand yet. **2** I can do it with help. **3** I can do it on my own. **4** I can teach someone else.

Make a scatter plot of the data. Then describe the relationship between the data.

6.

Temperature (°F), x	82	78	68	87	75	71	92	84
Attendees (thousands), y	4.5	4.0	1.7	5.5	3.8	2.9	4.7	5.3

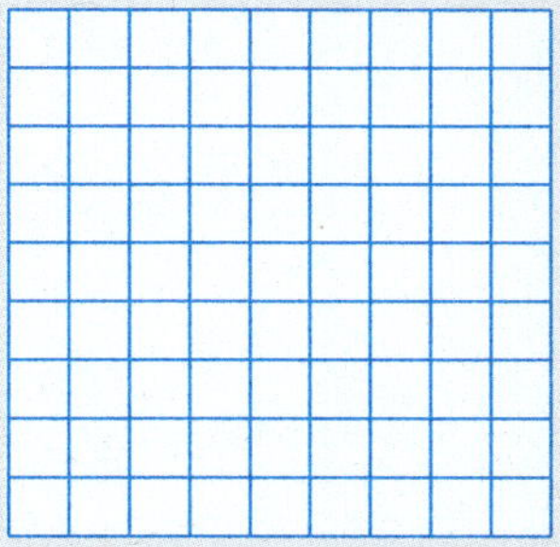

7.

Age of a car (years), x	1	2	3	4	5	6	7	8
Value (thousands), y	\$24	\$21	\$19	\$18	\$15	\$12	\$8	\$7

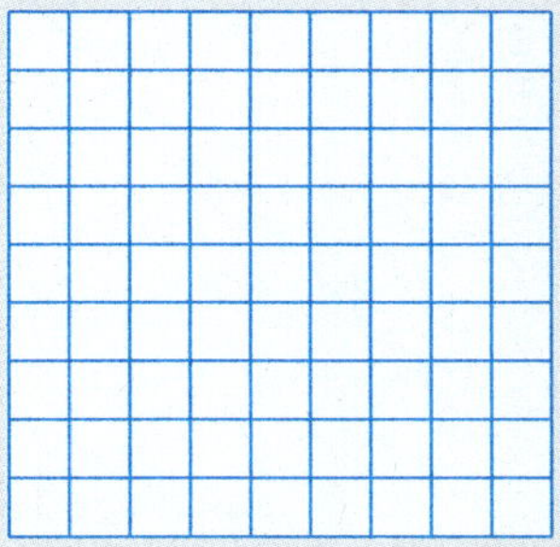

8. OPEN-ENDED Give an example of a real-life data set that has no correlation.

Using Lines of Fit to Model Data

When data show a positive or negative linear correlation, you can model the *trend* in the data using a line of fit. A **line of fit** is a line drawn on a scatter plot that is close to most of the data points.

STUDY TIP
A line of fit is also called a *trend line*.

KEY IDEA
Using a Line of Fit to Model Data

Step 1 Make a scatter plot of the data.

Step 2 Decide whether the data can be modeled by a line.

Step 3 Draw a line that appears to fit the data closely. There should be about as many points above the line as below it.

Step 4 Write an equation using two points on the line. The points do not have to represent actual data pairs, but they must lie on the line of fit.

EXAMPLE 3 Finding a Line of Fit

The table shows the total numbers y (in millions) of subscribers to a video-sharing website x years since 2010. Write an equation that models the total number of subscribers as a function of the number of years since 2010. Interpret the slope and y-intercept of the line of fit.

Year, x	Subscribers (millions), y
0	9
1	21
2	26
3	33
4	43
5	53
6	71
7	76
8	89

SOLUTION

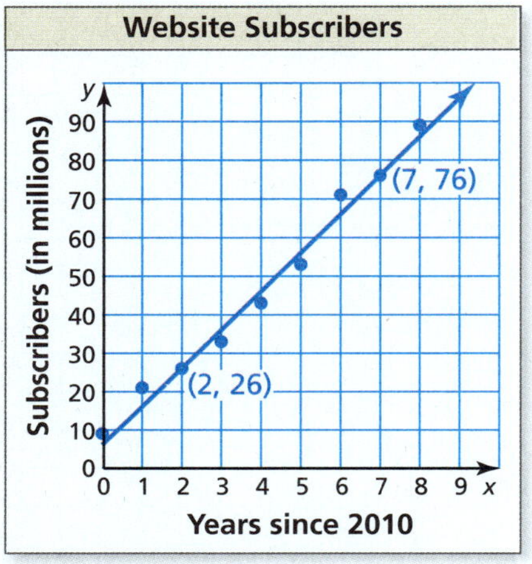

Step 1 Make a scatter plot of the data.

Step 2 Decide whether the data can be modeled by a line. Because the scatter plot shows a positive linear correlation, you can fit a line to the data.

Step 3 Draw a line that appears to fit the data closely. Try to have as many points above the line as below it. One possibility is shown.

Step 4 Write an equation using two points on the line. The line passes through (2, 26) and (7, 76). The slope of the line is $m = \frac{76 - 26}{7 - 2} = 10$.

Use the slope $m = 10$ and the point (2, 26) to write an equation of the line.

$y - y_1 = m(x - x_1)$ Write the point-slope form.

$y - 26 = 10(x - 2)$ Substitute 10 for m, 2 for x_1, and 26 for y_1.

$y = 10x + 6$ Solve for y.

An equation of a line of fit is $y = 10x + 6$. The slope is 10 and the y-intercept is 6. So, in 2010 there were about 6 million subscribers, and the number of subscribers increased by about 10 million each year.

2 MTR MODEL A PROBLEM

Does a line of fit always need to pass through one or more of the data points? Explain.

SELF-ASSESSMENT

1 I don't understand yet. 2 I can do it with help. 3 I can do it on my own. 4 I can teach someone else.

9. The table shows the gross revenue y (in millions of dollars) for a movie each week for x weeks since its release. Write an equation that models the gross revenue as a function of the number of weeks since its release. Interpret the slope and intercepts of the line of fit.

Week, x	1	2	3	4	5	6	7	8
Gross revenue (millions), y	\$135	\$110	\$77	\$65	\$34	\$21	\$14	\$8

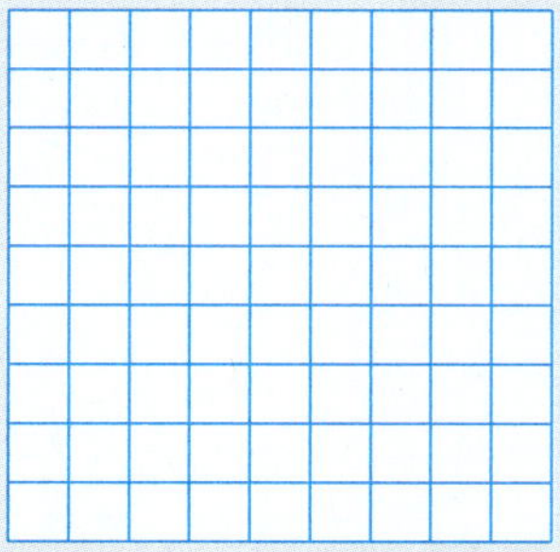

GO DIGITAL

4.5 Practice WITH CalcChat® AND CalcView®

1. INTERPRETING A SCATTER PLOT The scatter plot shows the amounts x (in gigabytes) of random-access memory (RAM) and the prices y (in dollars) of 10 laptops. *(See Example 1.)*

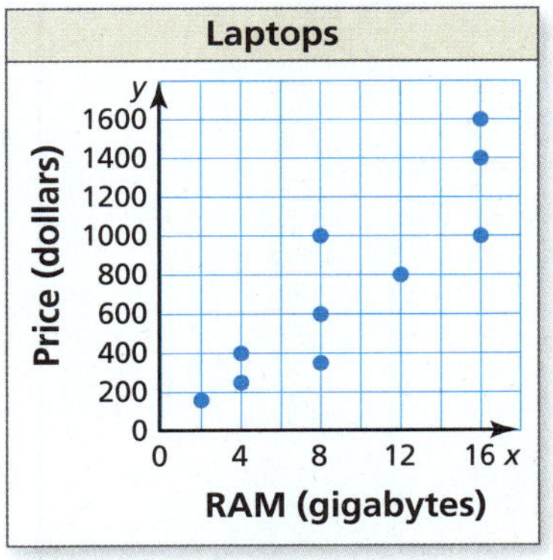

a. What is the price of the laptop with a RAM of 12 gigabytes?

b. What is the RAM of the $1400 laptop?

c. What tends to happen to the price as the RAM increases?

2. INTERPRETING A SCATTER PLOT The scatter plot shows the earned run averages and the winning percentages of eight pitchers on a baseball team.

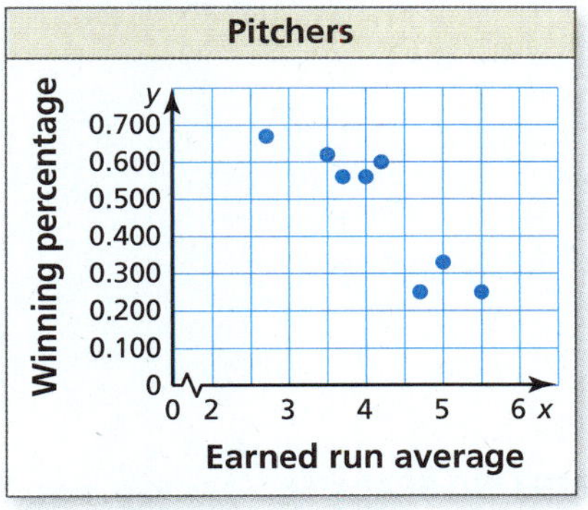

a. What is the winning percentage of the pitcher with an earned run average of 4.20?

b. What is the earned run average of the pitcher with a winning percentage of 0.333?

c. What tends to happen to the winning percentage as the earned run average increases?

In Exercises 3–6, describe the relationship between the data in the scatter plot. *(See Example 2.)*

3.

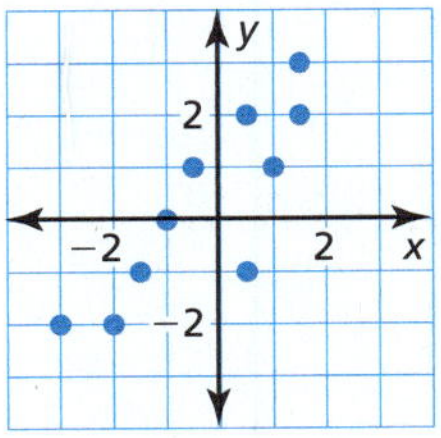

4.

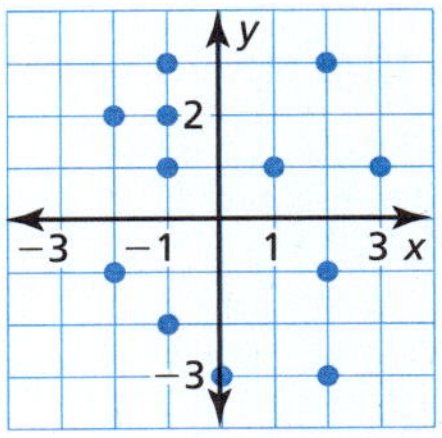

5.

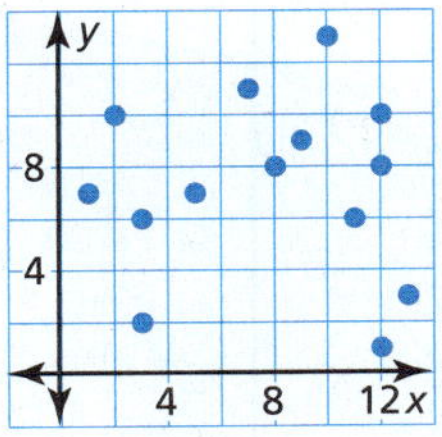

6.

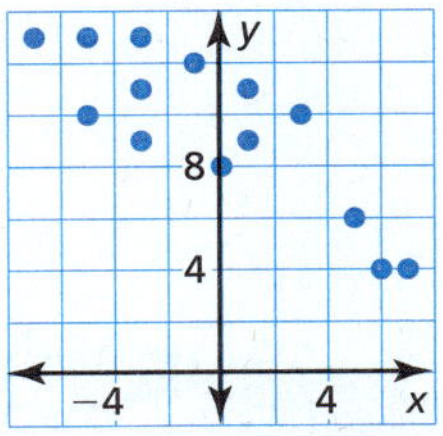

GO DIGITAL

In Exercises 7 and 8, make a scatter plot of the data. Then describe the relationship between the data.

7.

x	3.1	2.2	2.5	3.7	3.9	1.5	2.7	2.0
y	1	0	1	2	0	2	3	2

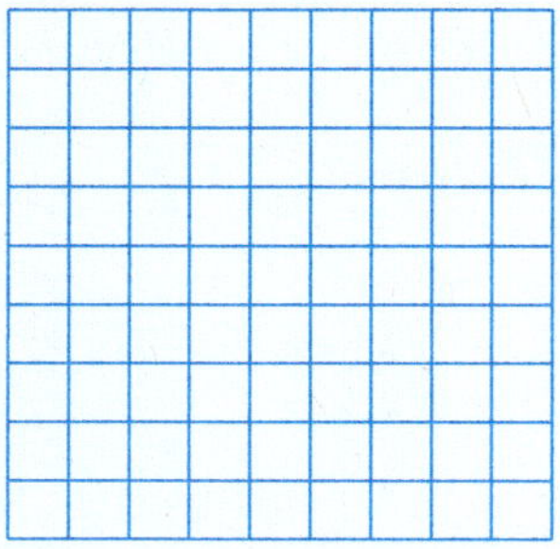

8.

x	3	4	5	6	7	8	9	10
y	67	67	50	33	25	21	19	4

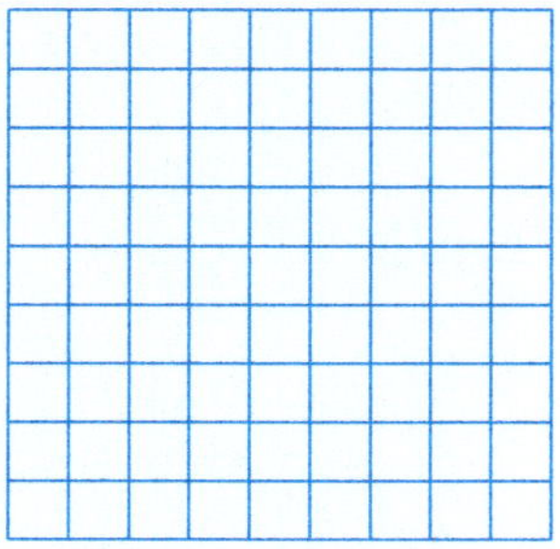

9. **MODELING REAL LIFE** The table shows the total amounts y (in thousands of dollars) of money a homeowner saves on electric bills x years after installing solar panels. *(See Example 3.)*

x	0	5	10	15	20	25
y	−12	−5.2	3.8	10.5	20	28.4

a. Write an equation that models the total amount of money saved as a function of the number of years after the solar panels were installed.

b. Interpret the slope and y-intercept of the line of fit.

10. **MODELING REAL LIFE** The table shows the amounts of storage left y (in gigabytes) on a music-playing device when there are x songs on the device.

x	0	242	519	698	825	1009
y	16	14.3	14.1	13.5	12.7	11.6

a. Write an equation that models the amount of storage left as a function of the number of songs.

b. Interpret the slope and y-intercept of the line of fit.

11. ASSESS REASONABLENESS Your friend says that a line of fit must pass through at least one of the data points. Is your friend correct? Explain.

12. HOW DO YOU SEE IT?
The graph shows part of a data set and a line of fit for the data set. Four data points are missing. Choose possible coordinates for these data points.

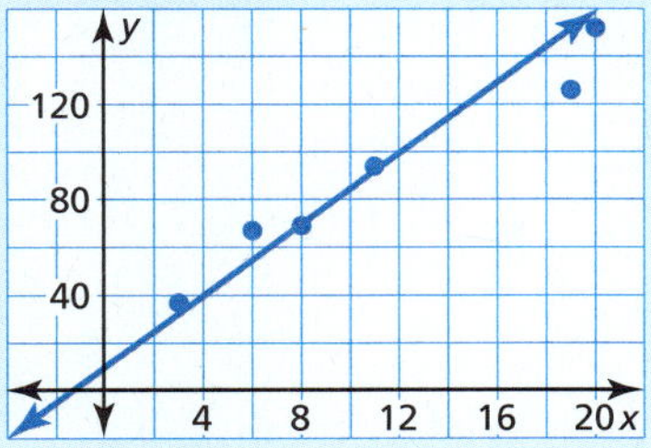

13. INVESTIGATE Measure the heights and arm spans of five people.

a. Make a scatter plot using the data you collected. Then draw a line of fit for the data.

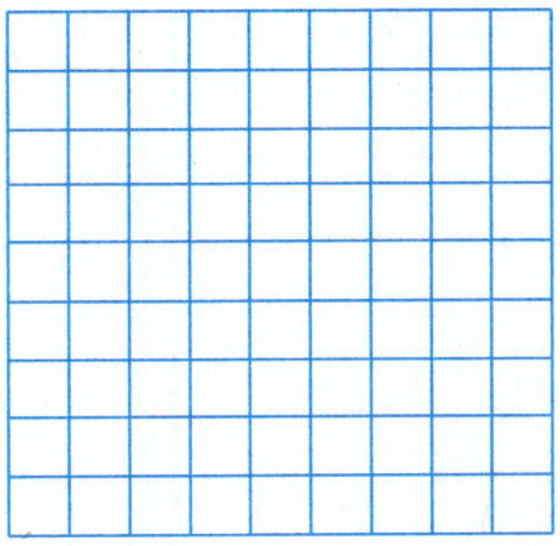

b. Interpret the terms and coefficient in the equation of the line of fit.

14. WRITING When is data best displayed in a scatter plot rather than in another type of display, such as a bar graph or circle graph?

15. DISCUSS MATHEMATICAL THINKING Is it possible to fit a line to the data in the tables? If so, write an equation of the line. If not, explain why.

x	−12	−9	−7	−4	−3	−1
y	150	76	50	15	10	1

x	2	5	6	7	9	15
y	5	22	37	52	90	226

16. THOUGHT PROVOKING
Describe a situation in which a line is a good fit for a set of data, but the data do *not* show a positive or a negative linear correlation.

REVIEW & REFRESH

17. REASONING A data set has no correlation. Does it make sense to find a line of fit for the data? Explain.

18. Write an equation of the line that passes through the given point and is (a) parallel and (b) perpendicular to the given line.

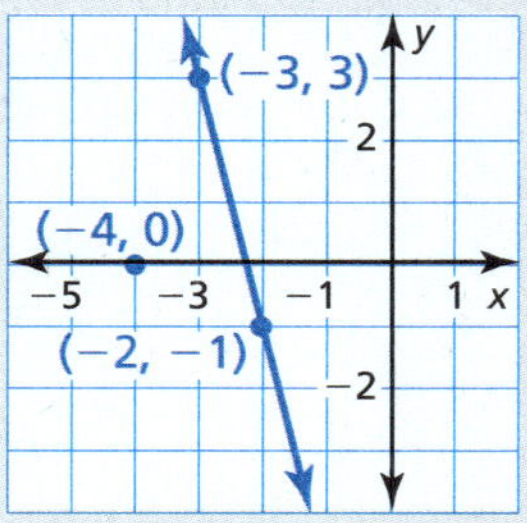

19. Make a scatter plot of the data. Then describe the relationship between the data.

x	14	12	10	8	6	4	2
y	4	1	0	−1	−2	−4	−5

In Exercises 20 and 21, graph the function. Compare the graph to the graph of $f(x) = |x|$.

20. $h(x) = |x| + 2$

21. $g(x) = |x - 1|$

22. MODELING REAL LIFE The costs for setting up and maintaining a website at two different website hosting companies are shown. You have \$620. At which company can you set up and maintain a website for the greatest amount of time? Explain.

Company A

Set-up fee: **\$48**
Maintenance fee: **\$44** per month

Company B

NO SET-UP FEE!!!
Maintenance fee: \$62 per month

23. Tell whether the data can be modeled by a linear equation. Explain. If possible, write a linear equation that represents y as a function of x.

x	−3	−1	1	3	5
y	16	11.5	7	2.5	−2

24. Solve $P = 2\ell + 2w$ for w.

25. Write the linear equation $y = 9.5x + 1.2$ in standard form.

4.6 Analyzing Lines of Fit

Learning Target: Use residuals to analyze linear relationships.

Success Criteria:
- I can use residuals to interpret a linear correlation.
- I can use residuals to determine how well lines of fit model data.
- I can distinguish between correlation and causation.

Data Analysis and Probability
MA.912.DP.1.3 Explain the difference between correlation and causation in the contexts of both numerical and categorical data.
MA.912.DP.2.6 Given a scatter plot with a line of fit and residuals, determine the strength and direction of the correlation. Interpret strength and direction within a real-world context.
Also MA.912.AR.2.5, H MA.912.DP.2.5

EXPLORE IT! Analyzing Residuals

Work with a partner. Consider the scatter plots shown below.

Scatter Plot A

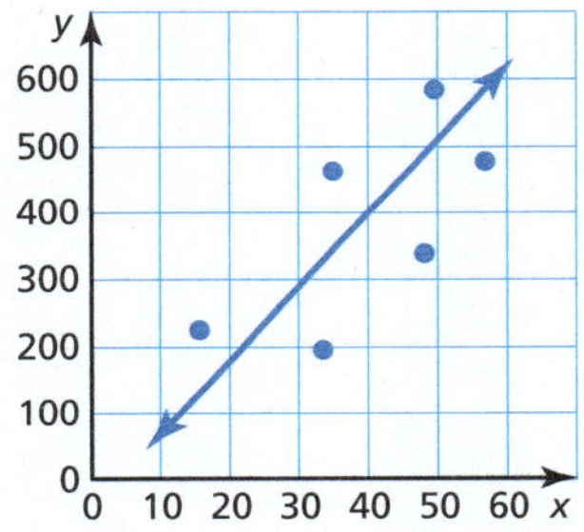

Scatter Plot B

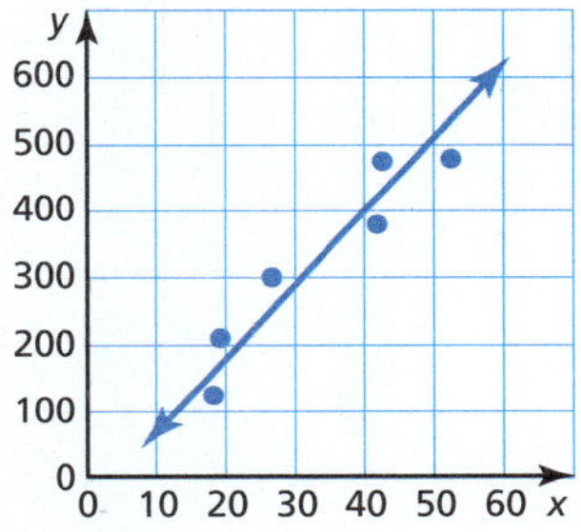

a. Make several observations about each scatter plot.

b. Estimate the y-value of each point, y_{point}. Then use the x-value of the point to estimate the corresponding y-value of the line of fit, y_{line}. Use these values to complete each table.

Scatter Plot A		
y_{point}	y_{line}	$y_{\text{point}} - y_{\text{line}}$

Scatter Plot B		
y_{point}	y_{line}	$y_{\text{point}} - y_{\text{line}}$

GO DIGITAL

c. The differences in part (b) are called *residuals*. What do the values of the residuals tell you about the correlation between x and y in each scatter plot?

d. Draw a scatter plot that shows a *strong* negative linear relationship. Then draw a scatter plot that shows a *weak* negative linear relationship. Explain how to use lines of fit and residuals to justify your answers.

4 MTR **CONSTRUCT AN ARGUMENT**

Does a strong correlation indicate that a change in x *causes* a change in y? Describe a real-life situation to justify your answer.

Vocabulary VOCAB

residual, *p. 357*
causation, *p. 359*

Analyzing Residuals

One way to determine how well a line of fit models a data set is to analyze *residuals*.

KEY IDEA

Residuals

A **residual** is the difference of the y-value of a data point and the corresponding y-value found using the line of fit. A residual can be positive, negative, or zero.

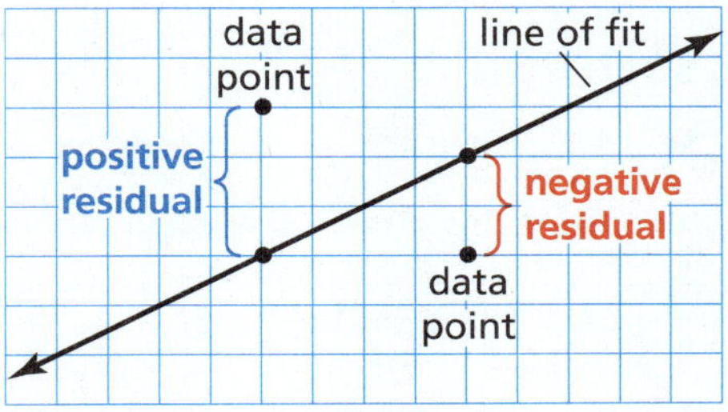

A scatter plot of the residuals shows how well a model fits a data set. If the model is a good fit, then the absolute values of the residuals are relatively small, and the residual points will be more or less evenly dispersed about the horizontal axis. Small absolute values indicate a strong correlation, and large absolute values indicate a weak correlation.

EXAMPLE 1 Using Residuals

WATCH

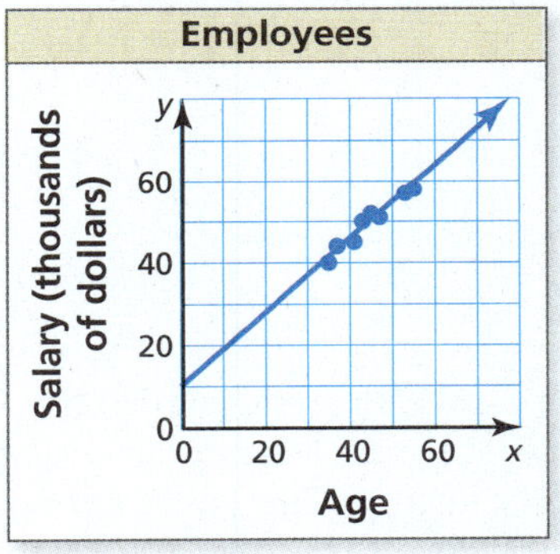

The scatter plot shows the ages x and salaries y (in thousands of dollars) of eight employees at a company. The equation $y = 0.9x + 10$ models the data. The residuals are shown in the table. Interpret the strength and direction of the correlation.

x	35	37	41	43	45	47	53	55
y	40	44	45	50	52	51	57	58
Residual	-1.5	0.7	-1.9	1.3	1.5	-1.3	-0.7	-1.5

SOLUTION

Because the absolute values of the residuals are relatively small and the slope of the line of fit is positive, you can conclude that there is a strong positive correlation between age and salary. So, as age increases, salary also increases.

SELF-ASSESSMENT

1 I don't understand yet. 2 I can do it with help. 3 I can do it on my own. 4 I can teach someone else.

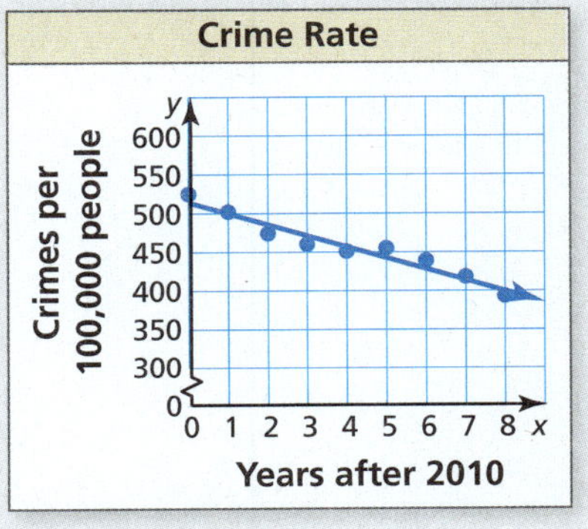

1. The scatter plot shows the violent crime rate y (in crimes per 100,000 people) in Florida x years after 2010. The equation $y = -14.3x + 514$ models the data. The residuals are shown in the table. Interpret the strength and direction of the correlation.

x	0	1	2	3	4	5	6	7	8
y	525	502	474	460	451	455	439	418	393
Residual	11	2.3	-11.4	11.1	-5.8	12.5	10.8	4.1	-6.6

GO DIGITAL

EXAMPLE 2 Using Residuals

WATCH H

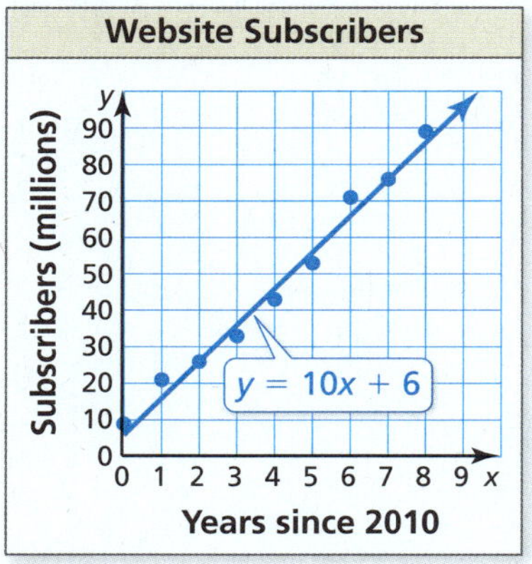

In Example 3 in Section 4.5, the equation $y = 10x + 6$ models the data in the table shown. Identify the number of positive and negative residuals, the residual with the greatest absolute value, and the residual with the least absolute value. Is the model a good fit?

Year, *x*	0	1	2	3	4	5	6	7	8
Subscribers (millions), *y*	9	21	26	33	43	53	71	76	89

SOLUTION

Step 1 Calculate the residuals and organize your results in a table.

Step 2 Use the points (x, residual) to make a scatter plot.

x	*y*	*y*-Value from model	Residual
0	9	6	$9 - 6 = 3$
1	21	16	$21 - 16 = 5$
2	26	26	$26 - 26 = 0$
3	33	36	$33 - 36 = -3$
4	43	46	$43 - 46 = -3$
5	53	56	$53 - 56 = -3$
6	71	66	$71 - 66 = 5$
7	76	76	$76 - 76 = 0$
8	89	86	$89 - 86 = 3$

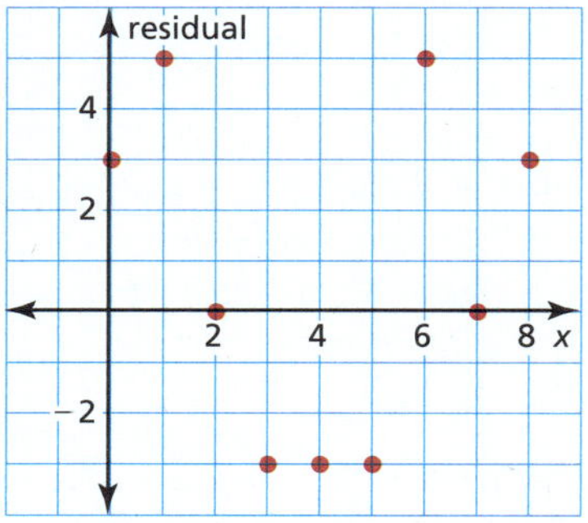

▶ There are 4 positive residuals and 3 negative residuals. The residuals of 5 have the greatest absolute values, and the residuals of 0 have the least absolute values. The absolute values of the residuals are relatively small, and the points are more or less evenly dispersed about the horizontal axis. So, the equation $y = 10x + 6$ is a good fit.

5 MTR **RELATE CONCEPTS**

Suppose the set of y-values contained an outlier. What would you expect to be true about the value of the corresponding residual?

GO DIGITAL

SELF-ASSESSMENT

1 I don't understand yet. 2 I can do it with help. 3 I can do it on my own. 4 I can teach someone else.

2. The table shows the attendances y (in thousands) at an amusement park from 2011 to 2021, where $x = 0$ represents the year 2011. The equation $y = -9.2x + 850$ models the data. Identify the number of positive and negative residuals, the residual with the greatest absolute value, and the residual with the least absolute value. Is the model a good fit? Explain your reasoning.

Year, x	0	1	2	3	4	5	6	7	8	9	10
Attendance, y	850	845	828	798	800	792	785	781	775	760	760

3. WRITING Describe when a residual is positive, negative, and zero.

Correlation and Causation

When a change in one variable causes a change in another variable, it is called **causation**. Causation produces a strong correlation between the two variables. The converse is *not* true. In other words, correlation does not imply causation.

EXAMPLE 3 Identifying Correlation and Causation

WATCH

Tell whether a correlation is likely in the situation. If so, tell whether there is a causal relationship. Explain your reasoning.

READING

A causal relationship exists when one variable *causes* a change in another variable.

a. time spent exercising and the number of calories burned

▶ There is a positive correlation and a causal relationship because the more time you spend exercising, the more calories you burn.

b. state of residence and political party affiliation

▶ There may be a correlation but no causal relationship. Living in a certain state will not cause you to have a certain political party affiliation.

GO DIGITAL

7 MTR

EXAMPLE 4 Modeling Real Life

WATCH

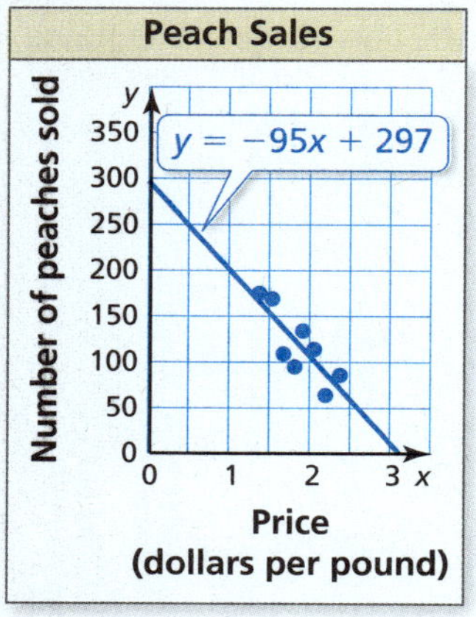

The scatter plot shows the price x (in dollars per pound) of peaches at a store and the weekly number y of peaches sold. The equation $y = -95x + 297$ models the data. The residuals are shown in the table. (a) Interpret the strength and direction of the correlation. (b) Interpret the slope and y-intercept of the line of fit in this situation. (c) Determine whether there is a causal relationship. Explain your reasoning.

x	1.92	2.06	1.38	1.54	1.82	2.38	1.68	2.20
y	134	114	175	169	95	86	109	64
Residual	19.4	12.7	9.1	18.3	−29.1	15.1	−28.4	−24

SOLUTION

a. Because the absolute values of the residuals are relatively large and the slope of the line of fit is negative, you can conclude that there is a weak negative correlation between price and the number of peaches sold. So, as price increases, the number of peaches sold generally decreases.

b. The slope of −95 indicates that for every \$1 increase in price, about 95 fewer peaches are sold. The y-intercept of 297 indicates that the store can expect to sell about 297 peaches when the price is \$0 per pound.

c. There is a causal relationship because as price increases, fewer people are willing to buy the peaches.

SELF-ASSESSMENT

1 I don't understand yet. 2 I can do it with help. 3 I can do it on my own. 4 I can teach someone else.

4. Is there a correlation between time spent playing video games and grade point average? If so, is there a causal relationship? Explain your reasoning.

5. WRITING In your own words, explain why correlation does not imply causation.

6. Is there a causal relationship between age and salary in Example 1? Explain your reasoning.

4.6 Practice WITH CalcChat® AND CalcView®

In Exercises 1 and 2, use the line of fit and the residuals to interpret the strength and direction of the correlation. *(See Example 1.)*

1. The table shows the total cost y (in dollars) to buy x 8-by-10 photos. The equation $y = 4x$ models the data.

Photos, x	0	1	2	3	4	5
Total cost, y	1	10	18	21	19	16
Residual	1	6	10	9	3	−4

2. The table shows the growth y (in inches) of an elk's antlers during week x. The equation $y = -0.7x + 6.8$ models the data.

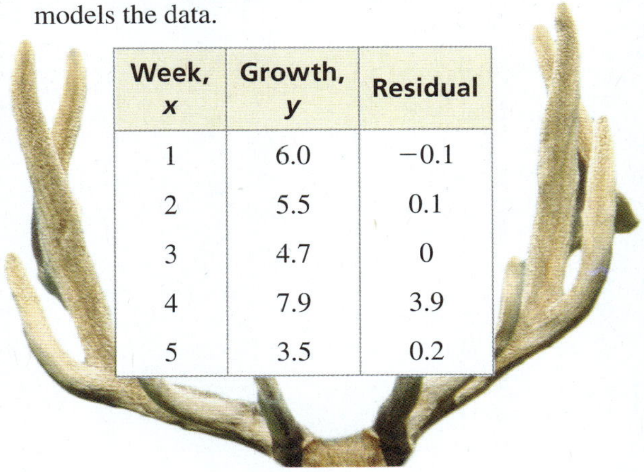

Week, x	Growth, y	Residual
1	6.0	−0.1
2	5.5	0.1
3	4.7	0
4	7.9	3.9
5	3.5	0.2

In Exercises 3 and 4, identify the number of positive and negative residuals, the residual with the greatest absolute value, and the residual with the least absolute value. Is the model a good fit? *(See Example 2.)*

3. The table shows the number y of trees sold at a nursery from February to July. In the table, $x = 1$ represents February. The equation $y = 60x + 4$ models the data.

Month, x	1	2	3	4	5	6
Trees sold, y	68	135	172	245	300	370

4. The table shows the approximate numbers y (in thousands) of movie tickets sold from January to June for a theater. In the table, $x = 1$ represents January. The equation $y = 1.3x + 27$ models the data.

Month, x	1	2	3	4	5	6
Ticket sales, y	27	28	36	28	32	35

In Exercises 5–8, tell whether a correlation is likely in the situation. If so, tell whether there is a causal relationship. Explain your reasoning. *(See Example 3.)*

5. time spent talking on a cell phone and the remaining battery life

6. favorite color and color of shoes

7. the number of hats you own and the size of your head

8. a person's hair color and job

GO DIGITAL

9. MODELING REAL LIFE The table shows the number y (in billions) of text messages sent each year from 2015 to 2019 in the United States. In the table, $x = 1$ represents 2015. The equation $y = 75x + 1602$ models the data. The residuals are shown in the table. *(See Example 4.)*

7 MTR

Year, x	1	2	3	4	5
Text messages (billions), y	1889	1661	1500	2000	2098
Residual	212	−91	−327	98	121

a. Interpret the strength and direction of the correlation.

b. Interpret the slope and y-intercept of the line of fit in this situation.

c. Determine whether there is a causal relationship. Explain your reasoning.

10. OPEN-ENDED Describe a data set that has an outlier. How does the outlier affect the residual? Explain.

11. HOW DO YOU SEE IT?
Match each correlation with its strength and direction. Explain your reasoning.

a.

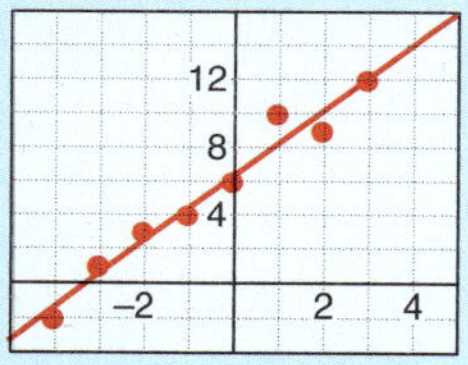

c.

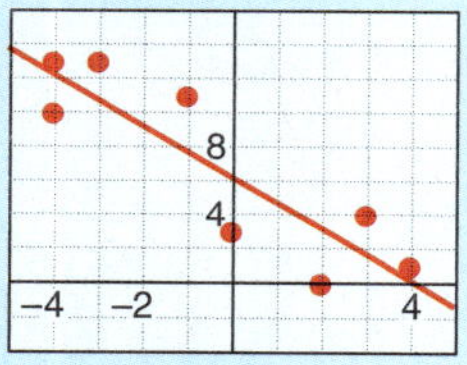

b.

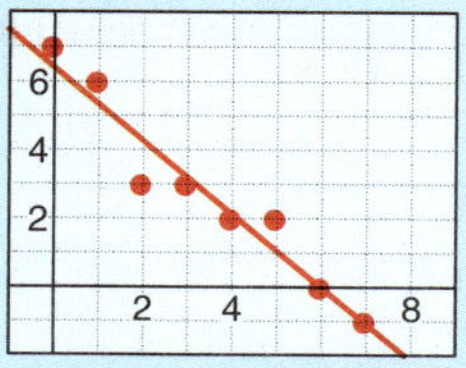

d.

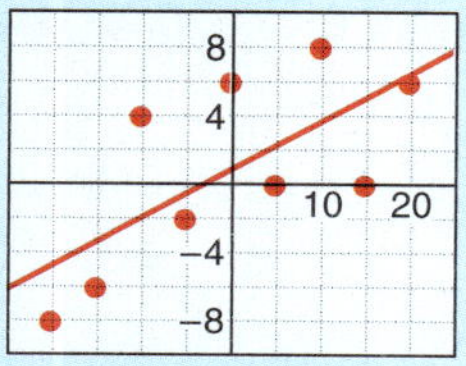

A. strong positive

B. strong negative

C. weak positive

D. weak negative

12. OPEN-ENDED A data set consists of the number x of people at Park A and the number y of people at Park B recorded daily for 1 week. Sketch a possible graph of the data set. Describe the relationship shown in the graph and determine whether there is a causal relationship. Explain.

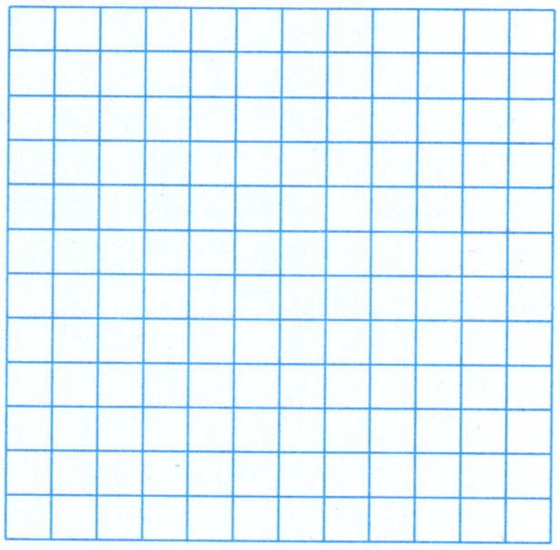

13. MAKING AN ARGUMENT Your friend says that the line $y = 1.7x$ is a good fit for the data below because the absolute values of the residuals are relatively small. Your cousin makes a scatter plot of the data and says the model is not a good fit because the data do not appear to be linear. Who is correct? Explain.

x	1.0	0.8	1.5	0.5	5.0	1.2	0.75
y	1.25	1.5	1.0	0.8	8.5	2.0	2.5

14. THOUGHT PROVOKING The time line shows the amounts of electricity (in millions of megawatt hours) generated by nuclear power in the United States from 2012 to 2019.

U.S. Nuclear Power Generation

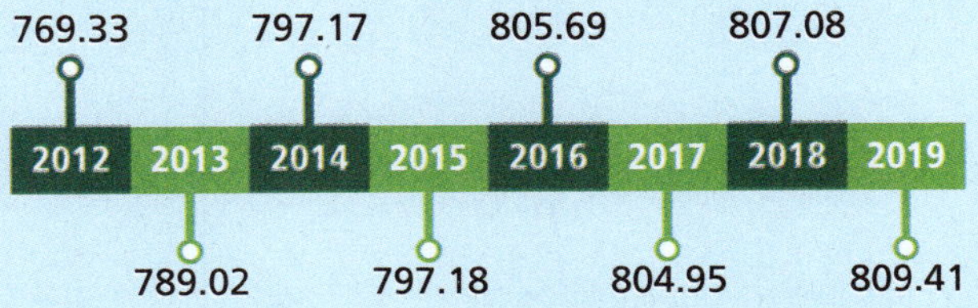

a. Analyze the data. Is a linear model a good fit? Explain.

b. Estimate the amount of electricity generated by nuclear power in 2023. Explain your method.

REVIEW & REFRESH

In Exercises 15 and 16, solve the inequality. Graph the solution.

15. $20 \geq \frac{4}{5}w$

16. $-9y < 24$

17. Is there a correlation between the outdoor temperature and the number of reported illnesses? If so, is there a causal relationship? Explain your reasoning.

18. MODELING REAL LIFE You buy two tickets to an escape room using a coupon for \$5 off your entire purchase. You pay a total of \$48.15, which includes 7% sales tax. What is the original price of one ticket?

19. Determine whether the table represents a *linear* or *nonlinear* function. Explain.

x	2	4	6	8
y	13	8	3	−2

20. Write equations of the horizontal and vertical lines that pass through $(-3, 12)$.

21. Describe the relationship between the data in the scatter plot.

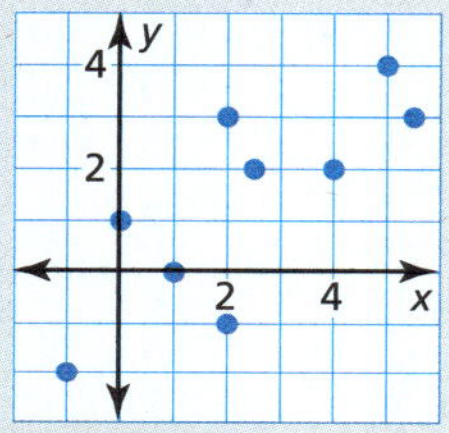

22. Write an equation in slope-intercept form of the line shown.

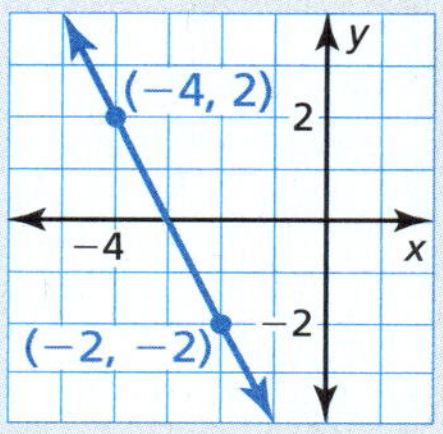

23. Determine which of the lines, if any, are parallel or perpendicular. Explain.

Line a passes through $(-2, 2)$ and $(2, 1)$.

Line b passes through $(1, -8)$ and $(3, 0)$.

Line c passes through $(-4, -3)$ and $(0, -2)$.

In Exercises 24 and 25, solve the equation. Check your solutions.

24. $|-3d| = 15$

25. $|b - 8| = |b + \frac{1}{4}|$

26. The table shows the approximate depth y (in feet) of an ascending diver after x minutes. The equation $y = 1.6x - 12.7$ models the data. Use the line of fit and the residuals to interpret the strength and direction of the correlation.

Minute, x	0	1	2	3	4	5	6
Depth, y	−15	−10	−9	−6	−6	−5	−2
Residual	−2.3	1.1	0.5	1.9	0.3	−0.3	−1.1

4.7 Modeling with Linear Functions

Learning Target: Use lines of fit to solve real-life problems.

Success Criteria:
- I can use technology to find lines of best fit.
- I can interpret slopes and y-intercepts of lines of best fit.
- I can use lines of best fit to approximate or predict values in a real-life situation.

Algebraic Reasoning

MA.912.AR.2.5 Solve and graph mathematical and real-world problems that are modeled with linear functions. Interpret key features and determine constraints in terms of the context.

Data Analysis and Probability

MA.912.DP.2.4 Fit a linear function to bivariate numerical data that suggests a linear association and interpret the slope and y-intercept of the model. Use the model to solve real-world problems in terms of the context of the data.

EXPLORE IT! Comparing Lines of Fit

CONSTRUCT AN ARGUMENT (4 MTR)

What are some characteristics of a line of fit that might make it more reliable than other lines of fit?

Work with a partner. Two different lines of fit are drawn for the same scatter plot.

Line A

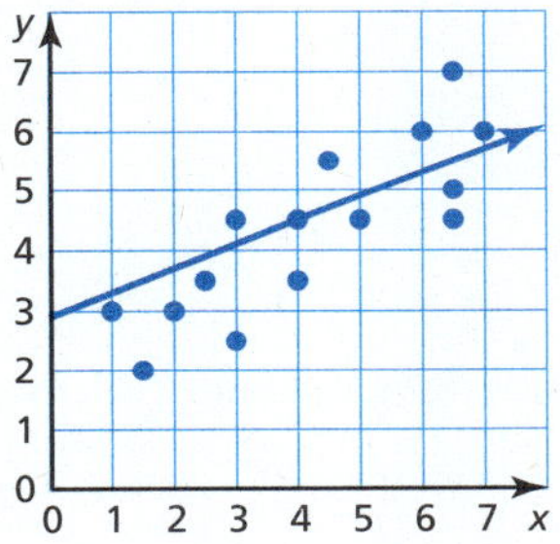

Line B

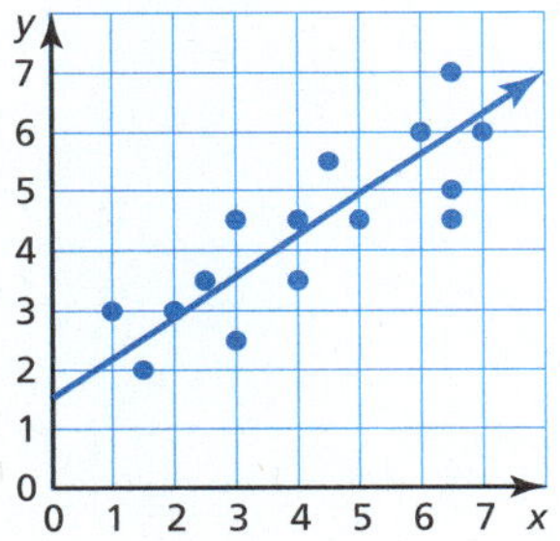

a. Which line is a better fit? Explain your reasoning.

b. How would you define a *line of best fit*? How can you *analytically* find a line of best fit for a data set?

GO DIGITAL

The table shows the temperatures x (in degrees Fahrenheit) and numbers y of people at a beach.

Temperature (°F), x	Number of people, y
68	105
70	210
73	290
76	240
80	300
81	385
86	380
90	490
92	430
95	570
97	510
99	560

c. Make a scatter plot of the data. Then write an equation that models the data. Compare your equation with those of other classmates.

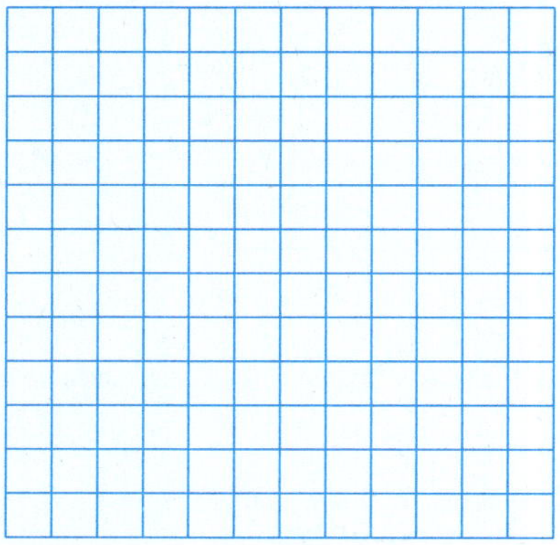

d. Choose an equation from part (c) that you think best represents the data. Do you think this equation is the equation of the line of best fit? Explain.

e. How can you predict the number of people who will be at the beach if the temperature is expected to reach 85°F? Explain.

Finding Lines of Best Fit

You can use technology to perform a method called **linear regression** to find a precise line of fit called a **line of best fit**. This line best models a set of data.

Vocabulary
AZ VOCAB

linear regression, *p. 367*
line of best fit, *p. 367*
interpolation, *p. 370*
extrapolation, *p. 370*

EXAMPLE 1 Finding a Line of Best Fit Using Technology

WATCH

Use technology to find an equation of the line of best fit for the data. Then graph the equation with the data.

x	12	8	9	5	7	15	11	9
y	18	25	23	32	27	11	20	21

SOLUTION

STUDY TIP

You know how to use two points to find an equation of a line of fit. When finding an equation of the line of best fit, every point in the data set is used.

Step 1 Enter the data from the table into a technology table.

x	y
12	18
8	25
9	23
5	32
7	27
15	11
11	20
9	21

Step 2 Use *linear regression*. The values in the equation can be rounded to obtain $y = -2.0x + 41$.

$y = mx + b$

PARAMETERS

$m = -1.99265$ (slope) $b = 41.0551$ (y-intercept)

STATISTICS

$r^2 = 0.9752$

$r = -0.9875$

Step 3 Graph the equation $y = -2.0x + 41$ with the data.

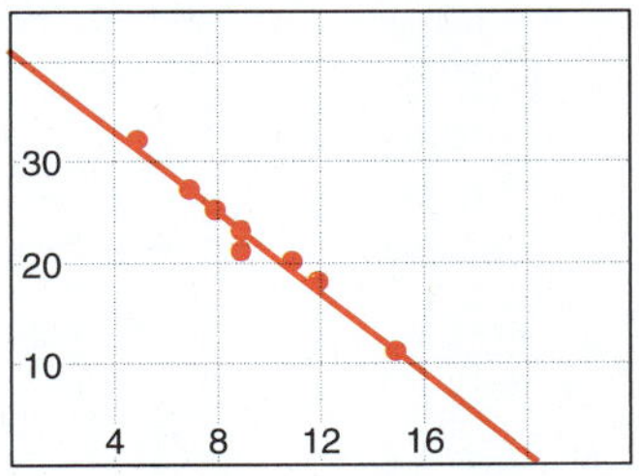

SELF-ASSESSMENT

1 I don't understand yet. 2 I can do it with help. 3 I can do it on my own. 4 I can teach someone else.

Use technology to find an equation of the line of best fit for the data. Then graph the equation with the data.

1.

x	*y*
6	13
13	25
2	4
5	10
7	12
1	2

2.

x	*y*
31	81
46	54
24	102
50	43
28	93
33	67

3.

x	*y*
4	0
7	2
−3	−4
−9	−6
0	−2
−6	−6

GO DIGITAL

7 MTR

EXAMPLE 2 Modeling Real Life

WATCH

The table shows the durations x (in minutes) of several eruptions of the geyser Old Faithful and the times y (in minutes) until the next eruption.

Duration, x	2.0	3.7	4.2	1.9	3.1	2.5	4.4	3.9
Time, y	60	83	84	58	72	62	85	85

a. Use technology to find an equation of the line of best fit. Then graph the equation with the data.

b. Interpret the slope and y-intercept of the line of best fit.

SOLUTION

a. Step 1 Enter the data from the table into a technology table.

x	y
2.0	60
3.7	83
4.2	84
1.9	58
3.1	72
2.5	62
4.4	85
3.9	85

Step 2 Use *linear regression*. The values in the equation can be rounded to obtain $y = 12.0x + 35$.

$y = mx + b$

PARAMETERS

$m = 11.9901$ ← slope $\quad b = 35.1068$ ← y-intercept

STATISTICS

$r^2 = 0.9579$

$r = 0.9787$

Step 3 Graph the equation $y = 12.0x + 35$ with the data.

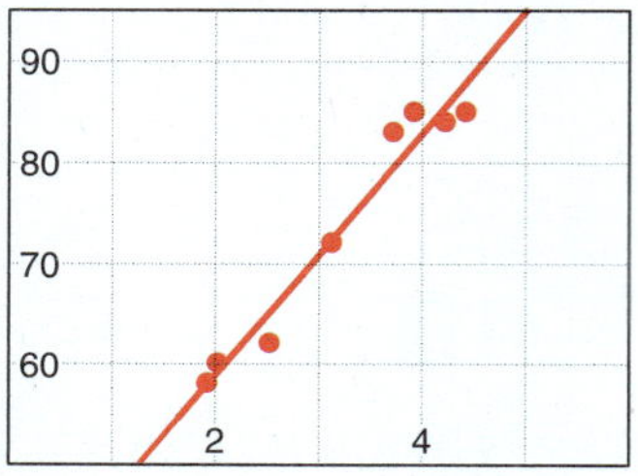

b. The slope of the line is about 12. This means the time until the next eruption increases by about 12 minutes for each minute the duration increases. The y-intercept is about 35, but it has no meaning in this context because the duration cannot be 0 minutes.

GO DIGITAL

1 MTR ANALYZE A PROBLEM

How can you determine appropriate scales for your graph?

SELF-ASSESSMENT

1 I don't understand yet. 2 I can do it with help. 3 I can do it on my own. 4 I can teach someone else.

4. The table shows the monthly numbers x of social media advertisements purchased by a company and the monthly revenue y (in thousands of dollars) of the company.

Number of advertisements, x	50	125	75	100	125	150	75	175
Monthly revenue, y	42	58	48	51	54	59	45	63

a. Use technology to find an equation of the line of best fit. Then graph the equation with the data.

b. Interpret the slope and y-intercept of the line of best fit.

Using a graph or its equation to *approximate* a value between two known values is called **interpolation**. Using a graph or its equation to *predict* a value outside the range of known values is called **extrapolation**. In general, the farther removed a value is from the known values, the less confidence you can have in the accuracy of the prediction.

WORDS AND MATH

How can the prefixes *inter-* and *extra-* help you remember the meanings of *interpolation* and *extrapolation*?

EXAMPLE 3 Interpolating and Extrapolating Data

WATCH

Refer to Example 2. Use the equation of the line of best fit.

a. Approximate the time until the next eruption after an eruption lasting $3\frac{1}{2}$ minutes.

b. Predict the time until the next eruption after an eruption lasting 5.0 minutes.

SOLUTION

a. $y = 12.0x + 35$ — Write the equation.

$= 12.0\left(3\frac{1}{2}\right) + 35$ — Substitute $3\frac{1}{2}$ for x.

$= 77$ — Evaluate.

▶ The next eruption will occur about 77 minutes after an eruption lasting $3\frac{1}{2}$ minutes.

b. Use technology to graph the equation and find the value of y when $x \approx 5.0$.

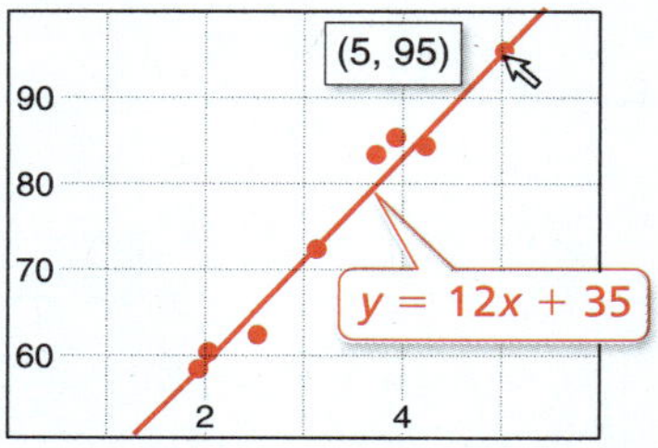

▶ The next eruption will occur about 95 minutes after an eruption lasting 5.0 minutes.

Another Method Find the value of y for which $x = 5.0$ algebraically.

$y = 12.0x + 35$ — Write the equation.

$y = 12.0(5) + 35$ — Substitute 5 for x.

$= 95$ ✓ — Evaluate.

APPLY MATHEMATICS 7 MTR

You arrive at Old Faithful at 10:43 A.M. About how long do you have to wait to see an eruption when the last eruption occurred at 10:06 A.M. and lasted 2 minutes and 15 seconds?

SELF-ASSESSMENT

1 I don't understand yet. 2 I can do it with help. 3 I can do it on my own. 4 I can teach someone else.

5. Refer to Exercise 4 on the previous page. Predict the monthly revenue of the company when 250 advertisements are purchased.

4 MTR **6.** **DISCUSS MATHEMATICAL THINKING** Why do you think extrapolating a value to make a prediction is likely to result in a less accurate prediction than interpolating a value to find an estimate?

GO DIGITAL

4.7 Practice WITH CalcChat® AND CalcView®

In Exercises 1–4, use technology to find an equation of the line of best fit for the data. Then graph the equation with the data. *(See Example 1.)*

1.

x	-15	-10	-5	0	5	10	15	20
y	-4	2	7	16	22	30	37	43

2.

x	5.4	6.8	7.2	8.6	9.0	10.4	11.8
y	12	-2	8	3	-1	-4	6

3.

x	10	12	14	15	16	16	17
y	104	109	120	126	126	128	144

4.

x	-14	-12	-10	-6	-2	0	4
y	74	52	68	43	50	34	42

7 MTR **5. MODELING REAL LIFE** The table shows the numbers y of people who volunteer at an animal shelter on day x. *(See Example 2.)*

Day, x	1	2	3	4	5	6	7	8
People, y	9	5	13	11	10	11	19	12

a. Use technology to find an equation of the line of best fit. Then plot the data and graph the equation in the same viewing window.

b. Interpret the slope and y-intercept of the line of best fit.

7 MTR **6. MODELING REAL LIFE** The table shows the total numbers y of people who reported an earthquake x minutes after it ended.

Minutes, x	**People, y**
1	12
2	97
3	408
4	915
5	1420
6	1786
7	2092

a. Use technology to find an equation of the line of best fit. Then plot the data and graph the equation in the same viewing window.

b. Interpret the slope and y-intercept of the line of best fit.

GO DIGITAL

7. **MODELING REAL LIFE** The table shows the mileages x (in thousands of miles) and the selling prices y (in thousands of dollars) of several used automobiles of the same year and model. *(See Example 3.)*

Mileage, *x*	22	14	18	30	8	24
Price, *y*	16	17	17	14	18	15

a. Use technology to find an equation of the line of best fit. Then interpret the slope and y-intercept.

b. Approximate the price of an automobile with 25,000 miles.

c. Predict the price of an automobile with 6000 miles.

8. **MODELING REAL LIFE** The table shows the grade point averages y of several students and the numbers x of hours they spend watching television each week.

Hours, *x*	5	3	12	20	15	8	4
GPA, *y*	3.4	3.5	2.7	2.1	2.8	3.0	3.7

a. Use technology to find an equation of the line of best fit. Then interpret the slope and y-intercept.

b. Approximate the GPA of a student who watches 14 hours of television each week.

c. Predict the GPA of a student who watches 1 hour of television each week.

9. **WRITING** Describe how the values of the slope and y-intercept of the line of best fit of a set of data are related to the data being modeled.

10. **HOW DO YOU SEE IT?**
The graph shows a set of data. Which line is the line of best fit?

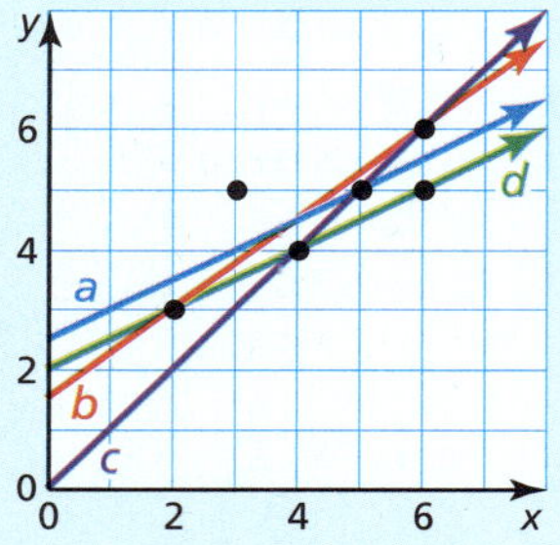

11. **REASONING** You are given the line of best fit of a data set. Can you identify any points in the data set? Explain your reasoning.

12. THOUGHT PROVOKING The graph shows four points from a set of data.

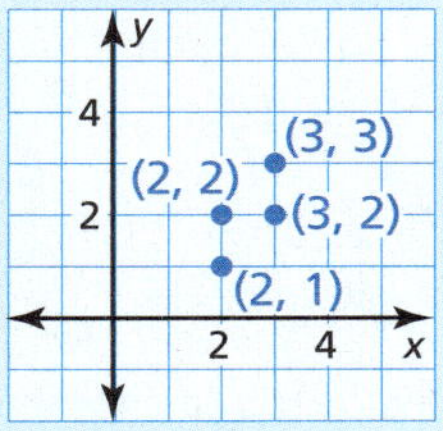

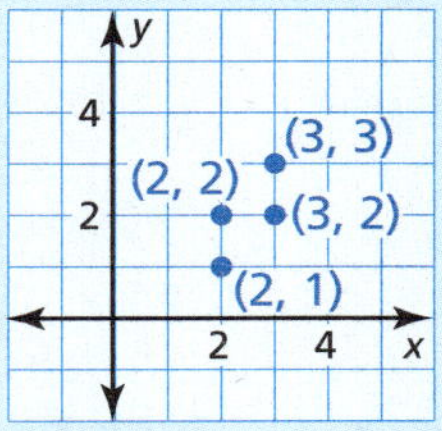

a. Plot four additional points on the graph so that the slope of the line of best fit is positive and the y-intercept is negative. Justify your answer.

b. Plot four additional points on the original graph so that the slope of the line of best fit is negative and the y-intercept is positive. Justify your answer.

7 MTR **13. PERFORMANCE TASK** Research the number of registered voters in your town for the past ten years. Make a scatter plot for each political party to show how the number of registered voters in each party changes over time. Explain how you can make predictions for the next election. List any factors that could affect the accuracy of your predictions. Repeat this process for registered voters nationwide. Compare your results. What conclusions can you make from the data?

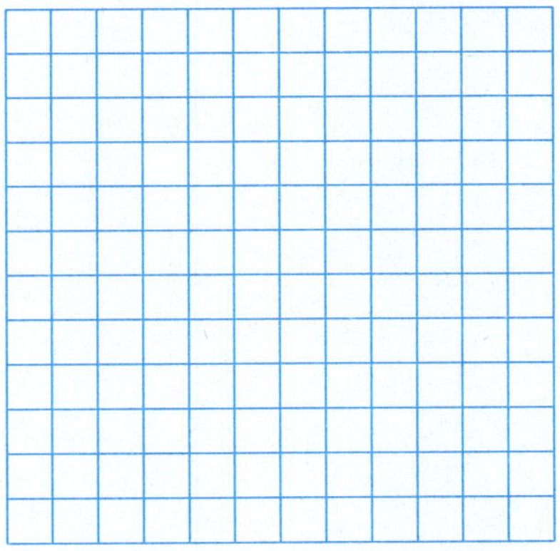

REVIEW & REFRESH

In Exercises 14 and 15, find the slope and the y-intercept of the linear equation.

14. $y = -5x + 3$

15. $y = 4.5$

16. Determine whether the relation is a function. Explain.

Input, x	Output, y
-1	14
0	15
1	19
2	14
3	16

17. Find the missing coefficient in the equation of the line shown. Write the completed equation.

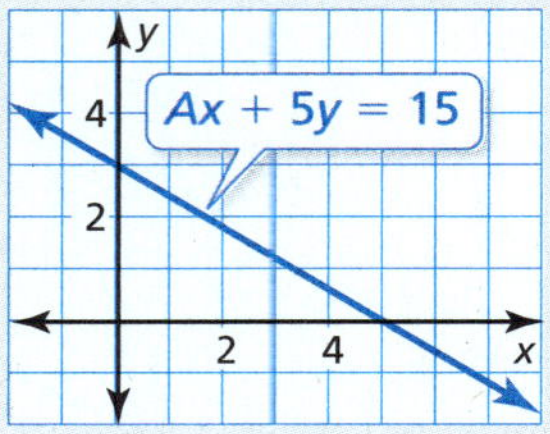

18. WRITING Compare interpolation and extrapolation.

19. Write an equation of the line that passes through (2, 1) and is parallel to the line $y = -3x - 9$.

20. Make a scatter plot of the data. Then describe the relationship between the data.

Year, x	1	2	3	4	5	6
Tickets sold, y	56	78	102	108	125	129

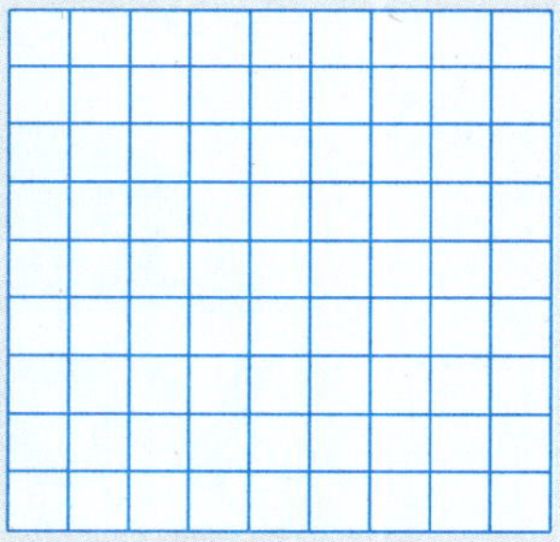

21. Is a correlation likely between the amount of time an athlete spends exercising each day and the number of daily calories the athlete consumes? If so, tell whether there is a causal relationship. If not, explain why not.

22. MODELING REAL LIFE The table shows the temperatures x (in degrees Fahrenheit) and the numbers y of shoppers at a mall.

Temperature, x	53	76	64	61	78	58
Number of shoppers, y	422	331	384	390	326	409

a. Approximate the number of shoppers when the temperature is 70°F.

b. Predict the number of shoppers when the temperature is 85°F.

23. Solve $5x - 1 > 2x + 8$.

4 Chapter Review WITH CalcChat®

Chapter Learning Target: Understand writing linear functions.

Chapter Success Criteria:

- ◆ I can determine the slope of a line given ordered pairs, a graph, a table, or a context.
- ◆ I can write the equation of a line in different forms.
- ■ I can write equations to model and solve real-life problems.
- ■ I can interpret scatter plots and analyze lines of fit.

◆ Surface
■ Deep

SELF-ASSESSMENT 1 I don't understand yet. 2 I can do it with help. 3 I can do it on my own. 4 I can teach someone else.

4.1 Writing Equations in Slope-Intercept Form (pp. 301–312)

WATCH

Learning Target: Write equations of lines in slope-intercept form.

Vocabulary AZ VOCAB
linear model

Write an equation of the line in slope-intercept form.

1.

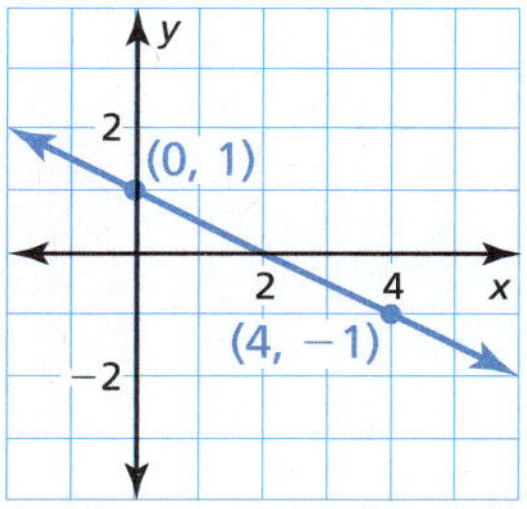

2.

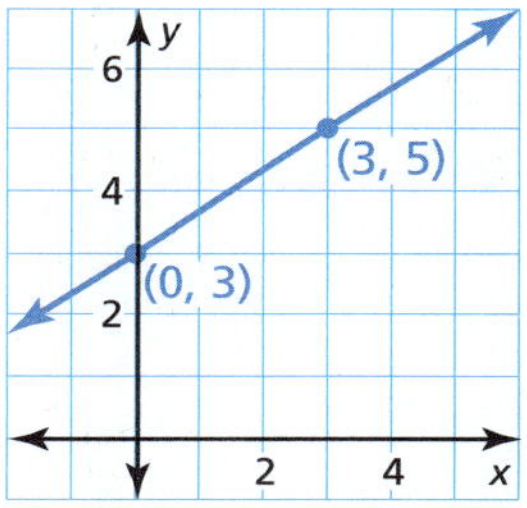

3. A landlord charged \$865 per month to rent an apartment in 2010. The rent increased at a constant rate and reached \$1065 per month in 2018. Estimate the monthly rent in 2021.

GO DIGITAL

4.2 Writing Equations in Point-Slope Form (pp. 313–324) WATCH

Learning Target: Write and graph equations of lines in point-slope form.

Vocabulary AZ VOCAB

point-slope form

4. Write an equation in point-slope form of the line that passes through the point (4, 7) and has a slope of -1. Then graph the line and identify the intercepts.

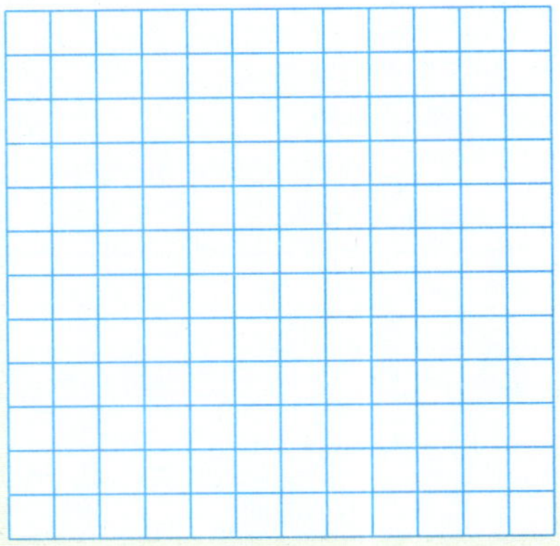

Write a linear function f with the given values.

5. $f(10) = 5, f(2) = -3$

6. $f(3) = -4, f(5) = -4$

7. $f(6) = 8, f(9) = 3$

8. Write $Ax + By = C$ in point-slope form, where A and B are nonzero constants.

9. You are ordering party hats for New Year's Eve. The table shows the total costs of ordering different numbers of party hats. Determine the total cost of ordering 25 party hats.

Number of party hats	3	6	9	12
Total cost (dollars)	2.67	5.34	8.01	10.68

4.3 Writing Equations in Standard Form (pp. 325–334)

Learning Target: Write equations of lines in standard form.

Write the linear equation in standard form.

10. $y = -6 - 2x$

11. $y - 3 = \frac{1}{4}(x + 8)$

Write an equation in standard form of the line that passes through the given points and has the given slope.

12. $(-2, 0)$; $m = -2$

13. $(1, 6)$; $m = \frac{3}{2}$

14. A dog kennel charges \$30 per night to board your dog and \$6 for each hour of playtime. The amount of money you spend is given by $30x + 6y = 180$, where x is the number of nights and y is the number of hours of playtime. Graph the equation and interpret the intercepts.

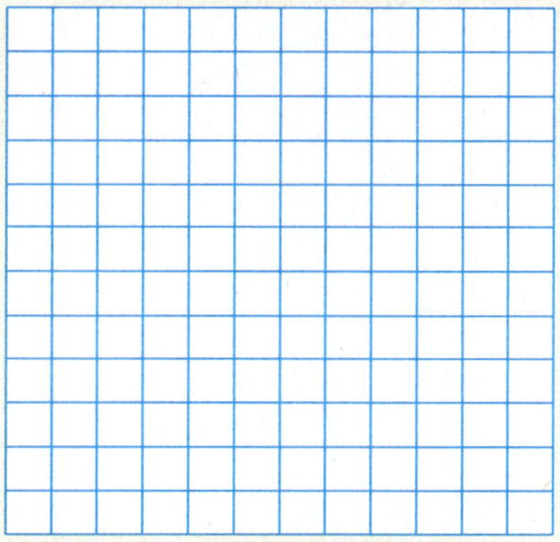

4.4 Writing Equations of Parallel and Perpendicular Lines (pp. 335–344)

Learning Target: Recognize and write equations of parallel and perpendicular lines.

Vocabulary

parallel lines
perpendicular lines

Determine which of the lines, if any, are parallel or perpendicular. Explain.

15. Line a passes through (0, 4) and (4, 3).

Line b passes through (0, 1) and (4, 0).

Line c passes through (2, 0) and (4, 4).

16. Line a: $2x - 7y = 14$

Line b: $y = \frac{7}{2}x - 8$

Line c: $2x + 7y = -21$

17. Write an equation of the line that passes through (1, 5) and is parallel to the line $y = -4x + 2$.

18. Write an equation of the line that passes through $(2, -3)$ and is perpendicular to the line $y = -2x - 3$.

4.5 Scatter Plots and Lines of Fit (pp. 345–354) WATCH

Learning Target: Use scatter plots and lines of fit to describe relationships between data.

Vocabulary
- scatter plot
- correlation
- line of fit

The scatter plot shows the roasting times y (in hours) and weights x (in pounds) of seven turkeys.

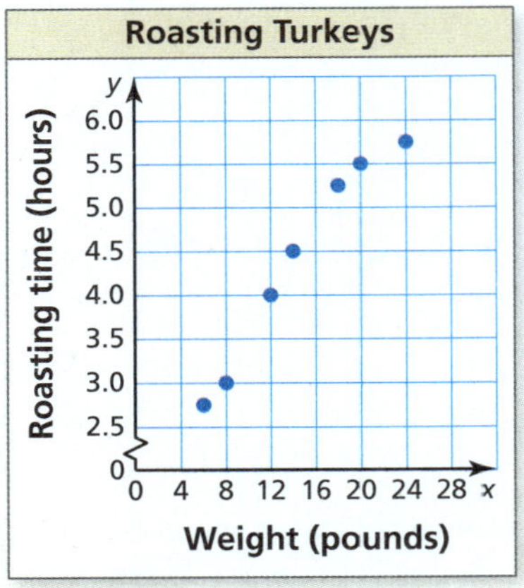

19. What is the roasting time for a 12-pound turkey?

20. Describe the relationship between the data.

21. The table shows the salary caps y (in millions of dollars) in the NBA x years since the beginning of the season in 2013. Write an equation that models the salary cap as a function of time. Interpret the slope and y-intercept of the line of fit.

Year, x	0	1	2	3	4
Salary cap (millions of dollars), y	58.68	63.07	70.00	91.14	99.09

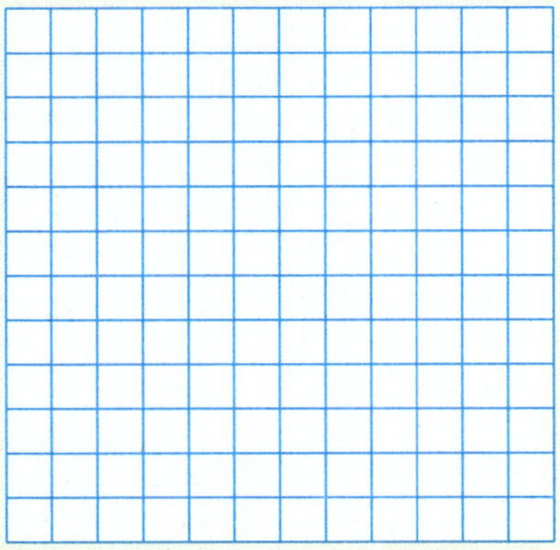

4.6 Analyzing Lines of Fit *(pp. 355–364)* WATCH

Learning Target: Use residuals to analyze linear relationships.

22. The table shows the heights x (in inches) and shoe sizes y of several students. The equation $y = \frac{1}{2}x - 21.5$ models the data. The residuals are shown in the table.

Height, x	64	62	70	63	72	68	66	74	68	59
Shoe size, y	9	7	12	8	13	9.5	9	13.5	10	6.5
Residual	−1.5	−2.5	−1.5	−2	−1.5	−3	−2.5	−2	−2.5	−1.5

Vocabulary AZ VOCAB

residual
causation

a. Make a scatter plot of the data. Interpret the strength and direction of the correlation.

b. Interpret the slope and y-intercept of the line of fit in this situation.

c. Determine whether there is a causal relationship. Explain your reasoning.

4.7 Modeling with Linear Functions (pp. 365–374)

WATCH

Learning Target: Use lines of best fit to solve real-life problems.

Vocabulary
linear regression
line of best fit
interpolation
extrapolation

23. Use technology to find an equation of the line of best fit for the data. Then graph the equation with the data.

x	1	5	-4	0	-2	3	-7
y	2	-3	16	8	12	-1	21

24. The table shows the monthly numbers x of flyers a nonprofit distributes and the monthly numbers of people y who donate to the nonprofit.

Number of Flyers, x	104	34	92	22	48	62	55	87
Number of People who Donated, y	84	14	79	8	26	46	32	60

a. Use technology to find an equation of the line of best fit. Then graph the equation with the data.

b. Interpret the slope and y-intercept of the line of best fit.

c. Predict the number of people who will donate when the nonprofit distributes 120 flyers.

Mathematical Thinking and Reasoning

6 MTR **ASSESS THE REASONABLENESS OF SOLUTIONS**
Mathematicians who assess the reasonableness of solutions use benchmark quantities to determine if a solution makes sense.

1. Refer to Exercise 26 on page 309. Your friend says after 8 more years, the account will have at least \$2000. Without calculating, determine if your friend's statement is reasonable. Explain your reasoning.

2. The scatter plot shows the height y (in feet) and the number of months x since a sapling was planted. Is it reasonable to estimate that after one year the sapling will be at least 18 feet tall? Explain your reasoning.

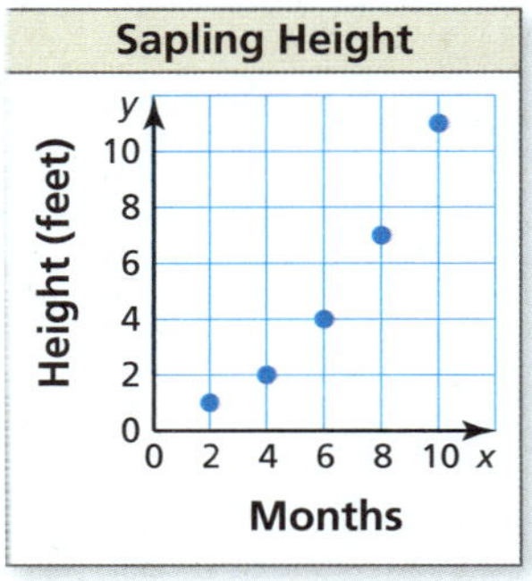

4 Practice Test WITH CalcChat®

Write an equation in slope-intercept form of the line with the given characteristics.

1. passes through $(0, 6)$ and $(3, -3)$

2. parallel to the line $y = 3x - 1$; passes through $(-2, -8)$

3. Write an equation in point-slope form that is perpendicular to the line $y = \frac{1}{4}x - 9$ and passes through $(1, 1)$.

4. Write a linear function f with the values $f(0) = 6$ and $f(7) = 27$.

Write an equation in standard form of the line with the given characteristics.

5. passes through $(2, 8)$ and has a slope of $\frac{3}{2}$

6. passes through $(-4, 2)$ and $(1, -3)$

7. A school cafeteria charges \$1.50 for breakfast and \$3.00 for lunch. At the beginning of the school year, a student adds exactly enough money to their meal account to pay for both breakfast and lunch for ten days. (a) Write an equation in standard form that models the possible combinations of breakfasts and lunches the student can afford to buy. (b) Graph the equation. (c) The student eats breakfast for four days and then decides to start eating breakfast before coming to school in the morning. How many total lunches can the student buy before having to add more money to their meal account?

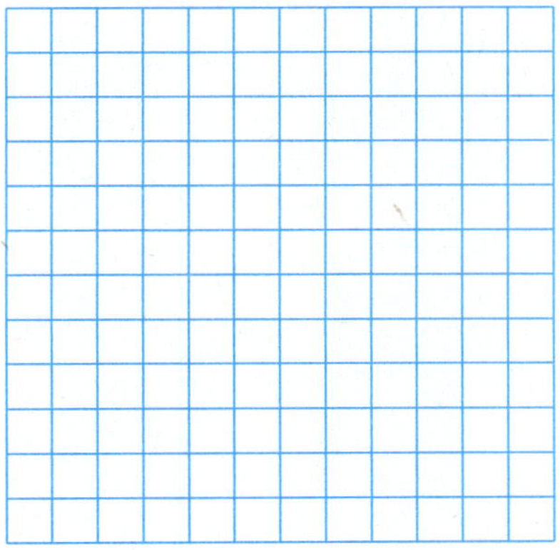

GO DIGITAL

8. Let a, b, c, and d be constants. Determine which of the lines, if any, are parallel or perpendicular. Explain.

Line 1: $y - c = ax$ Line 2: $ay = -x - b$ Line 3: $ax + y = d$

9. The graph of f is a line that passes through the points $(-7, 11)$ and $(3, 5)$. Write an equation of a line that is a horizontal shrink by a factor of $\frac{1}{2}$ of the graph of f.

10. A survey asks participants how many people are in their household and the number of pets they own. The table shows the results.

People, x	5	1	4	4	2	6	5	1	3
Pets, y	2	1	3	0	1	3	3	0	2

a. Make a scatter plot of the data. Interpret the strength and direction of the correlation.

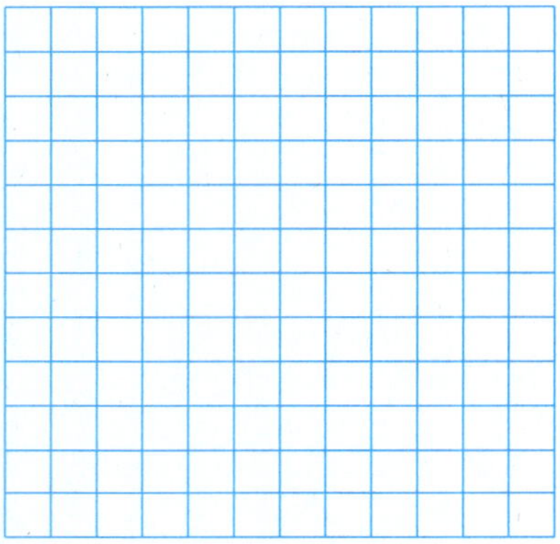

b. Use technology to find an equation of the line of best fit. Interpret the slope and y-intercept.

c. Predict how many pets a household with 8 people will have.

11. The table shows the amounts x (in dollars) spent on advertising for a festival and the attendances y of the festival for several years.

a. Use technology to find an equation of the line of best fit. Interpret the slope and y-intercept.

b. What would you expect a scatter plot of the residuals to look like? Explain your reasoning.

c. Is there a causal relationship in the data? Explain.

d. Predict the attendance when the advertising cost is $8900.

Advertising (dollars), x	**Yearly attendance, y**
500	400
1000	550
1500	550
2000	800
2500	650
3000	800
3500	1050
4000	1100

4 Performance Task
This One's a Breeze!

The capacity of a wind turbine is the maximum amount of power it can generate. Most wind farms have turbines with capacities of 2 to 3 megawatts (MW), which is equivalent to 2000 to 3000 kilowatts (kW).

In optimal conditions, the actual amount of power generated by a wind turbine is typically about 35% of its capacity.

In the United States, installing commercial wind turbines costs about $1.65 million per megawatt.

The average American household uses about 10,400 kilowatt hours (kWh) of energy each year.

Wind turbines require about $\frac{3}{4}$ acre of land per megawatt of power.

Kern County, California, has more than 4500 wind turbines.

GO DIGITAL

DESIGN A WIND FARM

Write a proposal to government officials for a new wind farm in your county. Choose the amount of land that will be occupied by your farm and the power of the turbines. Use functions and graphs to show the cost of the turbines and the total power generated. Relate the energy output of the wind farm to the amount of energy used in a typical household.

Energy (kWh) = Power (kW) × Time (h)

4 B.E.S.T. Test Prep WITH CalcChat®
Cumulative Practice

WATCH Tutorial videos are available for each exercise.

1. Consider the function $f(x) = x - 1$. Select each function shown in the graph.

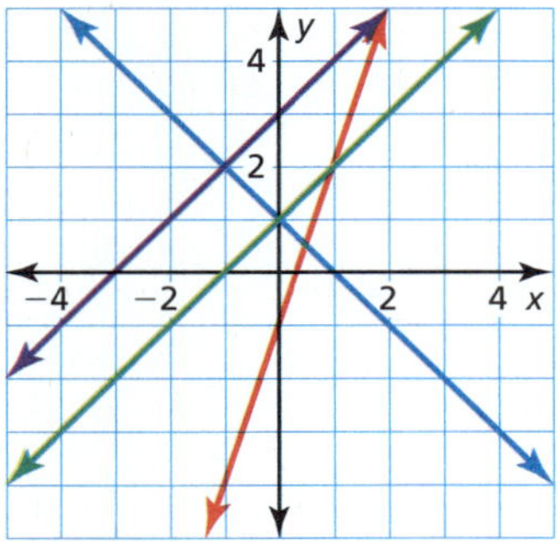

Ⓐ $f(x + 2)$

Ⓑ $f(3x)$

Ⓒ $f(x) + 4$

Ⓓ $f(-x)$

Ⓔ $3f(x)$

Ⓕ $-f(x)$

2. What is the minimum value of x for which the inequality $-2.4x + 6 \leq -23.76$ is true?

GRIDDED RESPONSE

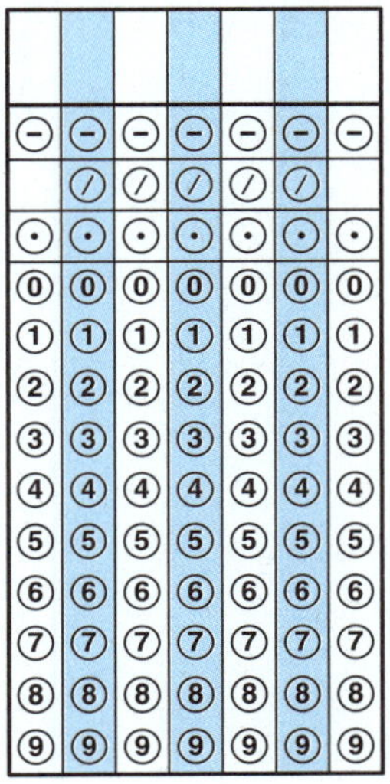

3. Which equation is equivalent to $\frac{3}{4}x - \frac{5}{2}y = -2x$?

Ⓐ $y = \frac{1}{2}x$

Ⓑ $3x - \frac{5}{2}y = -8x$

Ⓒ $\frac{3}{4}x = -2x - \frac{5}{2}y$

Ⓓ $y = \frac{11}{10}x$

4. You download a digital soccer game for \$2.50. You can add new players for \$1.50 each to upgrade your team. The total cost c is a function of the number n of new players that you add. Which of the following statements about the domain and the graph of the function is correct?

Ⓐ The domain is discrete, and the point (4, 6) lies on the graph.

Ⓑ The domain is continuous, and the point (4, 6) lies on the graph.

Ⓒ The domain is discrete, and the point (5, 10) lies on the graph.

Ⓓ The domain is continuous, and the point (5, 10) lies on the graph.

GO DIGITAL

5. The table shows the daily high temperatures x (in degrees Fahrenheit) and the numbers y of frozen fruit bars sold on eight randomly selected days. The equation $y = 3x - 50$ models the data.

Temperature (°F), x	54	60	68	72	78	84	92	98
Frozen fruit bars, y	40	120	180	260	280	260	220	180

Which points appear on a scatter plot of the residuals? Select all that apply.

(A) (96, 78)

(B) (78, 96)

(C) (60, −10)

(D) (60, 10)

(E) (−98, 64)

(F) (98, −64)

6. Find the value of y so that the equation $8x - 13y = 5y + 30$ is true when $x = 2$.

GRIDDED RESPONSE

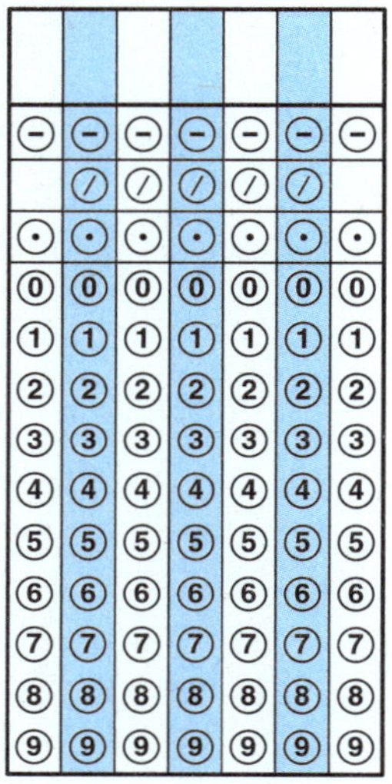

7. Which graph represents the solution to the inequality $-\frac{2}{3}x \geq 2$?

(A)
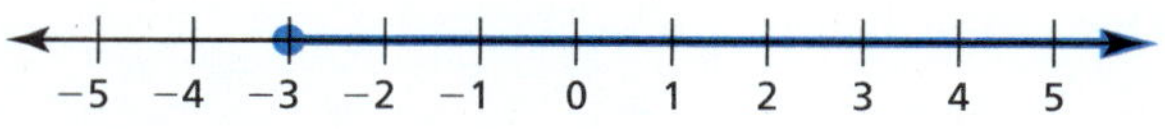

(B)
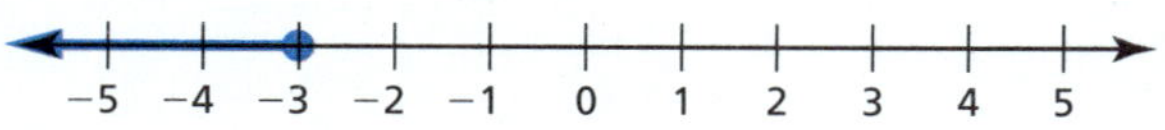

(C)
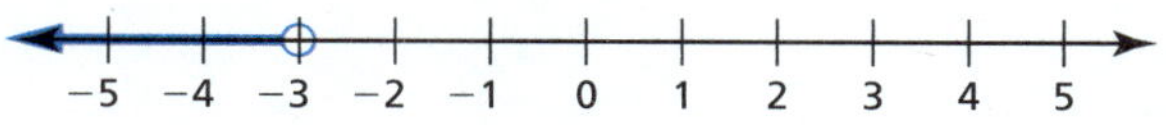

(D)
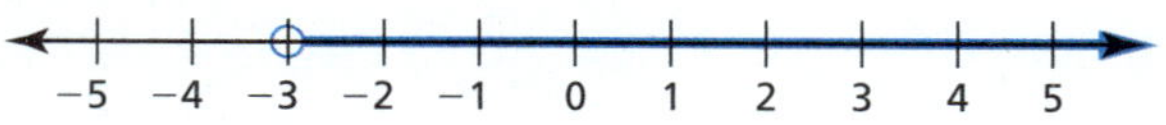

8. Find values for m and b so that the graph of $y = mx + b$ passes through the points $(6, 1)$ and $(-2, -3)$.

Ⓐ $m = \frac{1}{2}, b = -2$

Ⓑ $m = \frac{1}{2}, b = 2$

Ⓒ $m = -\frac{1}{2}, b = 4$

Ⓓ $m = -\frac{1}{2}, b = -4$

9. Which function g is a translation 3 units to the left of the graph of f?

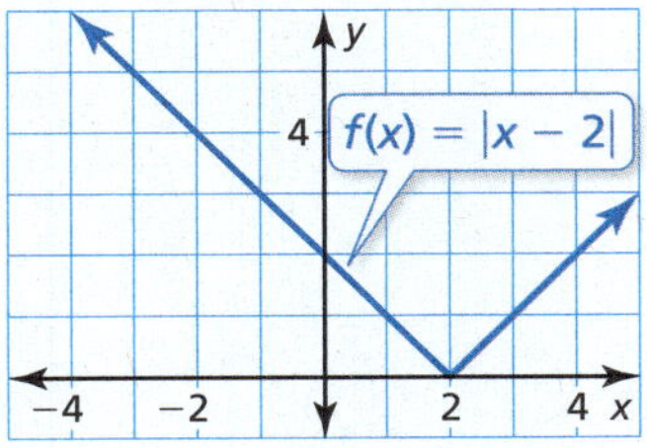

Ⓐ $g(x) = |x + 1|$

Ⓑ $g(x) = |x - 2| + 3$

Ⓒ $g(x) = |x - 2| - 3$

Ⓓ $g(x) = |x - 5|$

10. Use the characteristics of the given lines to determine which of the statements are true. Select all that apply.

Line g passes through the points $(0, 1)$ and $(2, -5)$.

Line h passes through the points $(-3, 3)$ and $(3, 1)$.

Line k passes through the points $(6, -2)$ and $(0, -4)$.

Line m passes through the points $(0, -1)$ and $(1, -4)$.

Line n passes through the points $(-1, 0)$ and $(1, 6)$.

Ⓐ Line g and line h are perpendicular.

Ⓑ Line g and line m are parallel.

Ⓒ Line k and line m are parallel.

Ⓓ Line h and line n are perpendicular.

Ⓔ Line g and line k are perpendicular.

Ⓕ Line h and line k are parallel.

5 Solving Systems of Linear Equations

NATIONAL GEOGRAPHIC EXPLORER

Corey J. Jaskolski

WATCH

Corey Jaskolski is an engineer with degrees in physics and mathematics. He led a team that developed the world's first pressure-tolerant lithium-polymer battery pack used by underwater vehicles. The battery can withstand the crushing pressure of deep-ocean deployments without needing to be protected inside a pressure vessel.

- What is the deepest that a human has been outside of an underwater vehicle? inside an underwater vehicle?
- What is the pressure of seawater at a depth of 1000 feet? 2000 feet? 3000 feet? 4000 feet? Graph your results. Is pressure a linear function of depth?

STEM

The deepest location on Earth, the Challenger Deep, is located in the Pacific Ocean. In the Performance Task, you will plan an expedition to the Challenger Deep, including a dive schedule and goals that you hope to accomplish.

GO DIGITAL

Deep Ocean Exploration

Preparing for Chapter 5

Chapter Learning Target: Understand solving systems of linear equations.

Chapter Success Criteria:

- ◆ I can identify a system of linear equations.
- ◆ I can describe different methods for solving systems of linear equations.
- ■ I can analyze systems of linear equations and decide what solution method is most efficient.
- ■ I can predict whether a system of linear equations has one solution, no solution, or infinitely many solutions.

◆ Surface
■ Deep

Chapter Vocabulary

Work with a partner. Discuss each of the vocabulary terms.

system of linear equations

half-planes

linear inequality in two variables

system of linear inequalities

GO DIGITAL

Mathematical Thinking and Reasoning

3 MTR **COMPLETE TASKS WITH MATHEMATICAL FLUENCY**

Mathematicians who complete tasks with mathematical fluency select efficient and appropriate methods for solving problems within the given context.

Work with a partner. A dive center earns $9550 by selling tickets for deep-sea dives to tourists. The dive center sells a total of 14 tickets: x Basic Adventure tickets and y Extreme Adventure tickets.

1. Write two equations to represent this situation. Explain your reasoning.

2. Use technology to graph both equations. Explain how you determined an appropriate viewing window for this situation.

3. Without using technology, find the point of intersection of the graphs of the equations. Explain your method. Check your answer using technology.

4. Interpret the point of intersection.

5. When does it make sense to use technology to find the point of intersection? Explain your reasoning.

5 Prepare WITH CalcChat®

Graphing Linear Functions

WATCH

Example 1 **Graph $3 + y = \frac{1}{2}x$.**

Step 1 Rewrite the equation in slope-intercept form.

$$y = \frac{1}{2}x - 3$$

Step 2 Find the slope and the y-intercept.

$$m = \frac{1}{2} \text{ and } b = -3$$

Step 3 The y-intercept is -3. So, plot $(0, -3)$.

Step 4 Use the slope to find another point on the line.

$$\text{slope} = \frac{\text{rise}}{\text{run}} = \frac{1}{2}$$

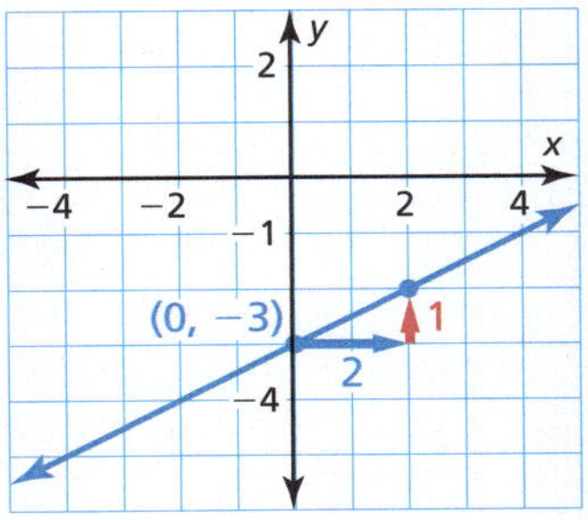

Plot the point that is 2 units right and 1 unit up from $(0, -3)$. Draw a line through the two points.

Graph the equation.

1. $y + 4 = x$

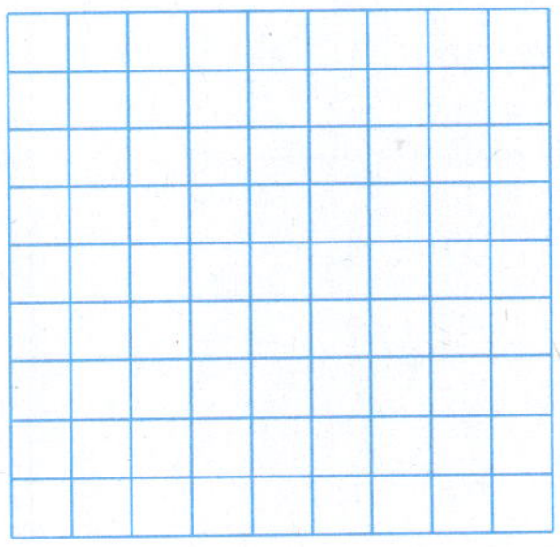

2. $6x - y = -1$

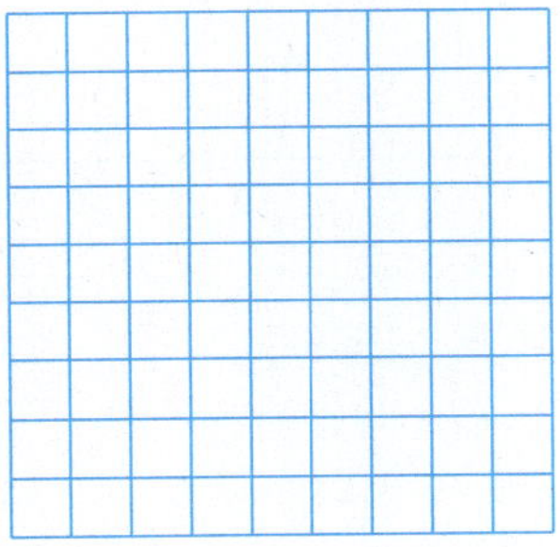

3. $4x + 5y = 20$

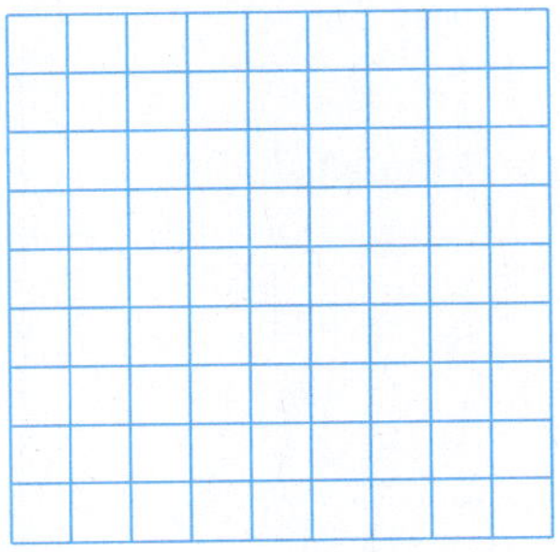

4. $-2y + 12 = -3x$

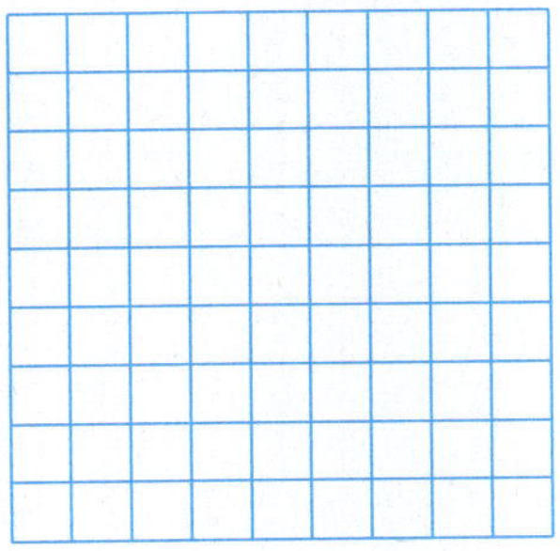

GO DIGITAL

Solving and Graphing Linear Inequalities

WATCH

Example 2 **Solve $2x - 17 \le 8x - 5$. Graph the solution.**

$$2x - 17 \le 8x - 5$$ Write the inequality.

$$+5 \qquad +5$$ Addition Property of Inequality

$$2x - 12 \le 8x$$ Simplify.

$$-2x \qquad -2x$$ Subtraction Property of Inequality

$$-12 \le 6x$$ Simplify.

$$\frac{-12}{6} \le \frac{6x}{6}$$ Division Property of Inequality

$$-2 \le x$$ Simplify.

▶ The solution is $x \ge -2$.

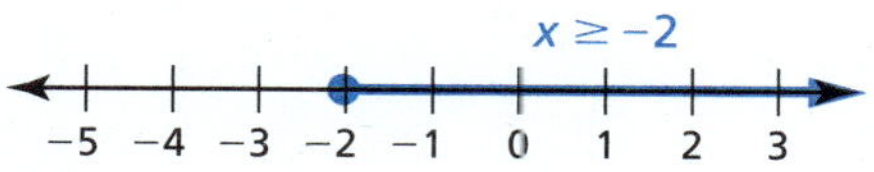

Solve the inequality. Graph the solution.

5. $m + 4 > 9$

6. $24 \le -6t$

7. $2a - 5 \le 13$

8. $-1.25z + 1 < -14$

9. $4k - 16 < \frac{1}{2}k + 5$

10. $7w + 9 \ge 2w - 3$

1 MTR **11. ANALYZE A PROBLEM** The graphs of the linear functions g and h have different slopes. The value of both functions when $x = a$ is b. When you graph g and h in the same coordinate plane, what happens at the point (a, b)?

5.1 Solving Systems of Linear Equations by Graphing

Learning Target: Solve linear systems by graphing.

Success Criteria:
- I can determine whether an ordered pair is a solution of a system.
- I can graph a linear system.
- I can approximate the solution of a linear system using a graph.

Algebraic Reasoning

MA.912.AR.9.1 Given a mathematical or real-world context, write and solve a system of two-variable linear equations algebraically or graphically.

MA.912.AR.9.6 Given a real-world context, represent constraints as systems of linear equations or inequalities. Interpret solutions to problems as viable or non-viable options.

Also MA.912.AR.2.2

EXPLORE IT! Using a System of Linear Equations

Work with a partner. You have a bag of dimes and quarters. You put the coins in a coin-counting machine and see the following display.

a. You want to know how many dimes and how many quarters you had. Do you have enough information to find these quantities? Explain your reasoning.

b. Your friend tries to find the numbers of dimes and quarters by creating the table shown. Did your friend find the solution? If not, find the solution.

Dimes	80	60	50	40	43
Quarters	6	26	36	46	46
Total value (dollars)	9.50	12.50	14.00	15.50	15.80

ANALYZE A PROBLEM (1 MTR)

Describe your friend's approach to creating the table. What mistake did your friend make?

c. Write an equation in two variables that represents the number of coins you had. Then write an equation in two variables that represents the total value of the coins you had.

d. In the same coordinate plane, graph your equations from part (c). How can you use the graph to find the numbers of dimes and quarters you had? Explain.

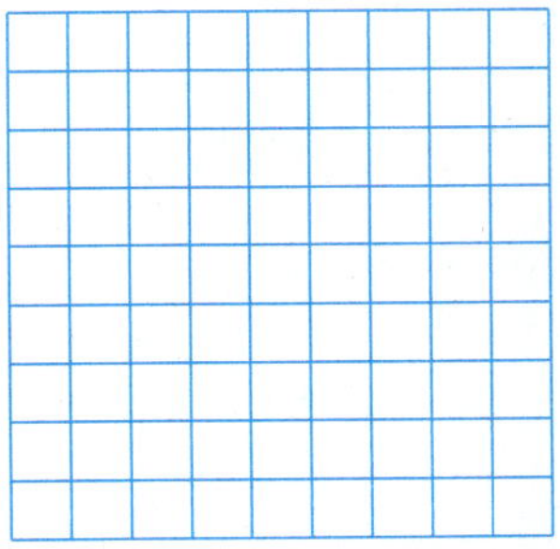

GO DIGITAL

Systems of Linear Equations

Vocabulary

system of linear equations, *p. 394*
solution of a system of linear equations, *p. 394*

A **system of linear equations** is a set of two or more linear equations in the same variables. An example is shown.

$x + y = 7$ Equation 1

$2x - 3y = -11$ Equation 2

A **solution of a system of linear equations** in two variables is an ordered pair that is a solution of each equation in the system.

EXAMPLE 1 Checking Solutions

Tell whether the ordered pair is a solution of the system of linear equations.

a. (2, 5); $x + y = 7$ Equation 1
$2x - 3y = -11$ Equation 2

b. (−2, 0); $y = -2x - 4$ Equation 1
$y = x + 4$ Equation 2

SOLUTION

a. Substitute 2 for x and 5 for y in each equation.

Equation 1	Equation 2
$x + y = 7$	$2x - 3y = -11$
$2 + 5 \stackrel{?}{=} 7$	$2(2) - 3(5) \stackrel{?}{=} -11$
$7 = 7$ ✓	$-11 = -11$ ✓

▶ Because the ordered pair (2, 5) is a solution of each equation, it is a solution of the linear system.

READING

A system of linear equations is also called a *linear system*.

b. Substitute −2 for x and 0 for y in each equation.

Equation 1	Equation 2
$y = -2x - 4$	$y = x + 4$
$0 \stackrel{?}{=} -2(-2) - 4$	$0 \stackrel{?}{=} -2 + 4$
$0 = 0$ ✓	$0 \neq 2$ ✗

▶ The ordered pair (−2, 0) is a solution of the first equation, but it is not a solution of the second equation. So, (−2, 0) is *not* a solution of the linear system.

GO DIGITAL

SELF-ASSESSMENT
1 I don't understand yet. 2 I can do it with help. 3 I can do it on my own. 4 I can teach someone else.

Tell whether the ordered pair is a solution of the system of linear equations.

1. (0, 0); $2x + y = 0$
$-x + 2y = 5$

2. (1, 4); $y = 3x + 1$
$y = -x + 5$

3. (4, −10); $y = -2.5x$
$3x + y = 2$

4. (−2, −0.5); $y + x = -3$
$x = 2y - 1$

5. REASONING One equation in a linear system is $\frac{1}{2}x + y = 1$. Is it possible for the system to have a solution of (0, 0)? (100, −49)? Explain your reasoning.

6. OPEN-ENDED Write a system of linear equations that has a solution of (−1, −3).

Solving Systems of Linear Equations by Graphing

A solution of a system of linear equations is a point of intersection of the graphs of the equations.

KEY IDEA

Solving a System of Linear Equations by Graphing

Step 1 Graph each equation in the same coordinate plane.

Step 2 Estimate the point of intersection.

Step 3 Check the point from Step 2 by substituting for x and y in each equation of the original system.

EXAMPLE 2 Solving a System of Linear Equations by Graphing

WATCH

Solve the system by graphing.

$y = -2x + 5$ Equation 1

$y = 4x - 1$ Equation 2

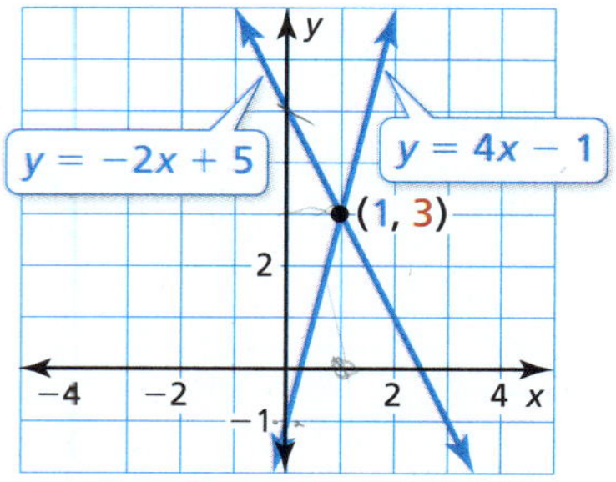

SOLUTION

Step 1 Graph each equation.

Step 2 Estimate the point of intersection. The graphs appear to intersect at (1, 3).

Step 3 Check that (1, 3) is a solution of each equation.

STUDY TIP

Always check that the estimated intersection point is a solution of each equation in the system.

Equation 1	Equation 2
$y = -2x + 5$	$y = 4x - 1$
$3 \stackrel{?}{=} -2(1) + 5$	$3 \stackrel{?}{=} 4(1) - 1$
$3 = 3$ ✓	$3 = 3$ ✓

▶ The solution is (1, 3).

Another Way Use technology to solve the system.

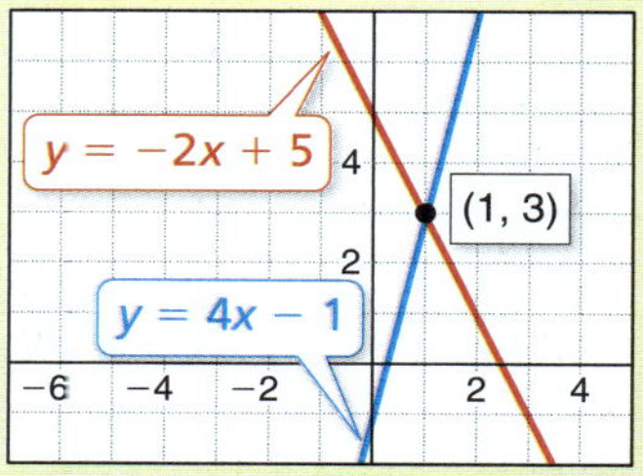

SELF-ASSESSMENT

1 I don't understand yet. 2 I can do it with help. 3 I can do it on my own. 4 I can teach someone else.

Solve the system by graphing.

7. $y = x - 2$
$y = -x + 4$

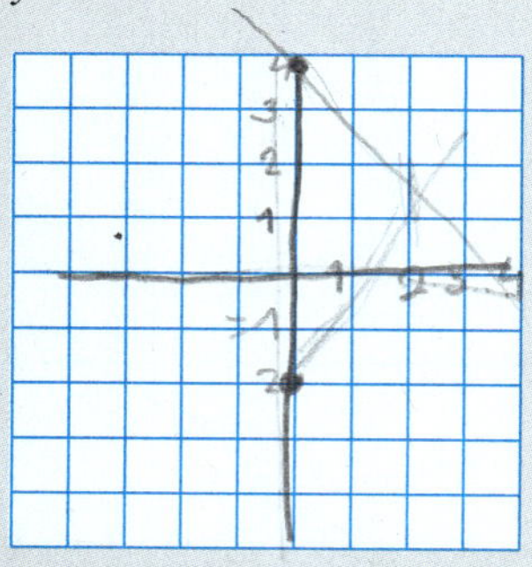

8. $y = \frac{1}{2}x + 3$
$y = -\frac{3}{2}x - 5$

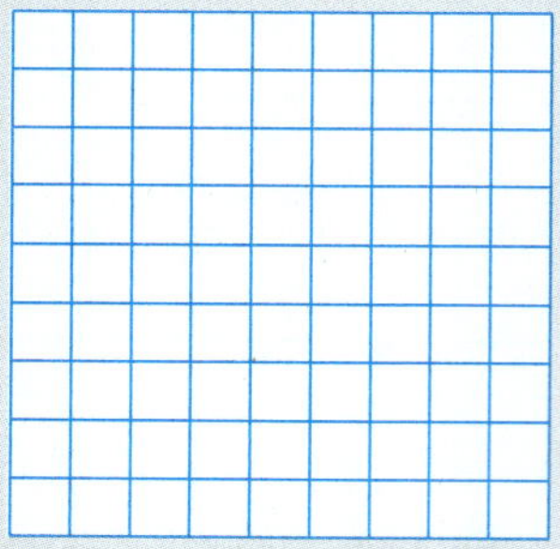

9. $2x + y = -6$
$3x - 0.5y = -7$

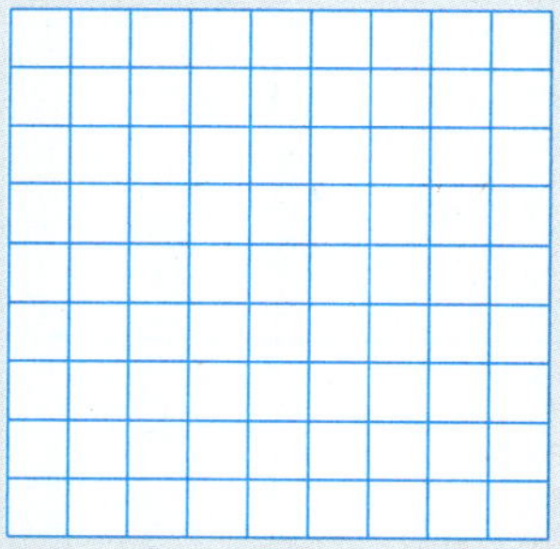

10. OPEN-ENDED Draw a graph that represents a system of linear equations with a solution of (0, −2).

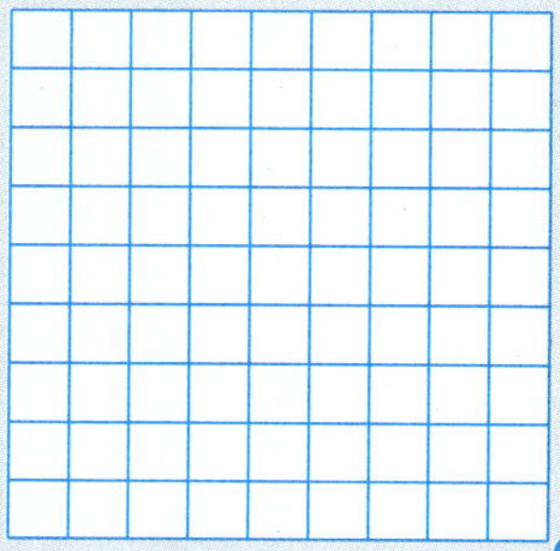

GO DIGITAL

Solving Real-Life Problems

7 MTR **EXAMPLE 3** **Modeling Real Life** WATCH

A roofing contractor buys 15 bundles of shingles and 8 rolls of roofing paper for \$640. In a second purchase, the contractor buys 8 bundles of shingles and 2 rolls of roofing paper for \$296. Find the price per bundle of shingles and the price per roll of roofing paper.

SOLUTION

1. **Understand the Problem** You know the total price of each purchase and how many of each item were purchased. You are asked to find the price of each item.

2. **Make a Plan** Use a verbal model to write a system that represents the problem. Then solve the system.

3. **Solve and Check**

Verbal Model Number of bundles • Price per bundle + Number of rolls • Price per roll = Total cost of purchase

Variables Let x be the price (in dollars) per bundle, and let y be the price (in dollars) per roll.

System $15x + 8y = 640$ Equation 1 (first purchase)

$8x + 2y = 296$ Equation 2 (second purchase)

Graph each equation. Note that only the first quadrant is shown because x and y must be positive.

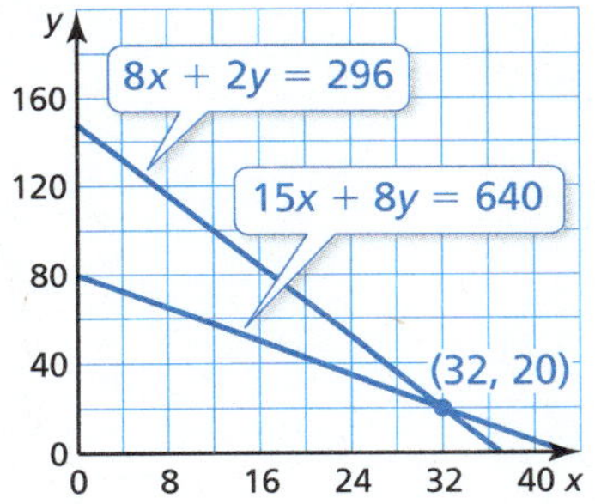

The graphs appear to intersect at (32, 20). Check that (32, 20) is a solution of each equation.

Equation 1

$$15x + 8y = 640$$
$$15(32) + 8(20) \stackrel{?}{=} 640$$
$$640 = 640 \checkmark$$

Equation 2

$$8x + 2y = 296$$
$$8(32) + 2(20) \stackrel{?}{=} 296$$
$$296 = 296 \checkmark$$

▶ The solution is (32, 20). So, the price per bundle of shingles is \$32, and the price per roll of roofing paper is \$20.

Another Way Assume the contractor buys 4 times the amounts in the second purchase, so that each purchase contains 8 rolls of roofing paper. The 32 bundles and 8 rolls would cost \$1184. The extra 17 bundles of shingles cost \$1184 − \$640 = \$544. So, the price for shingles is \$544 ÷ 17 bundles = \$32 per bundle.

GO DIGITAL

SELF-ASSESSMENT

1 I don't understand yet. **2** I can do it with help. **3** I can do it on my own. **4** I can teach someone else.

11. You have a total of 18 science and history questions for homework. You have six more science questions than history questions. How many questions do you have in each subject?

12. You order 3 strings of white LED lights and 2 strings of colored LED lights for \$66. In a second order, you buy one string of each type for \$27.

a. Which type of LED light is more expensive?

b. Which type of LED light do you spend more money buying? How much more?

5.1 Practice WITH CalcChat® AND CalcView®

In Exercises 1–6, tell whether the ordered pair is a solution of the system of linear equations. *(See Example 1.)*

1. (2, 6); $x + y = 8$, $3x - y = 0$

2. (8, 2); $x - y = 6$, $2x - 10y = 4$

3. (−1, 3); $y = -7x - 4$, $y = 8x + 5$

4. (5, −6); $6x + 3y = 12$, $4x + y = 14$

5. $\left(\frac{1}{2}, -2\right)$; $6x + 5y = -7$, $2x - 4y = -8$

6. (−2.5, −4); $y = 6x + 11$, $2x + y = -9$

In Exercises 7 and 8, use the graph to solve the system. Check your solution.

7. $x - y = 4$
$4x + y = 1$

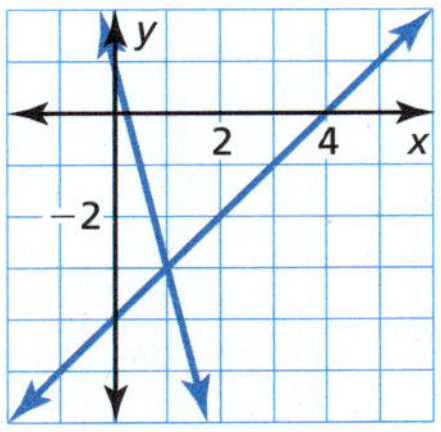

8. $6y + 3x = 18$
$-x + 4y = 24$

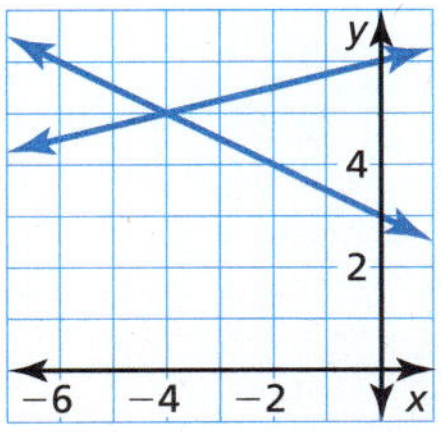

In Exercises 9–16, solve the system by graphing. *(See Example 2.)*

9. $y = -x + 7$
$y = x + 1$

10. $y = -x + 4$
$y = 2x - 8$

11. $y = \frac{1}{3}x + 2$
$y = \frac{2}{3}x + 5$

12. $y = \frac{3}{4}x - 4$
$y = -\frac{1}{2}x + 11$

13. $9x + 3y = -3$
$2x - y = -4$

14. $3y - 9x = 9$
$x + 3y = -6$

15. $4x - 4y = 22$
$y = -5.5$

16. $x - 2y = -\frac{1}{2}$
$-4x - 8y = 2$

GO DIGITAL

USING TOOLS **In Exercises 17–20, use technology to solve the system.**

17. $0.2x + 0.4y = 4$
$-0.6x + 0.6y = -3$

18. $-1.6x - 3.2y = -24$
$2.6x + 2.6y = 26$

19. $-7x + 6y = 0$
$0.5x + y = 2$

20. $4x - y = 1.5$
$2x + y = 1.5$

21. **ERROR ANALYSIS** Describe and correct the error in solving the linear system.

4 MTR

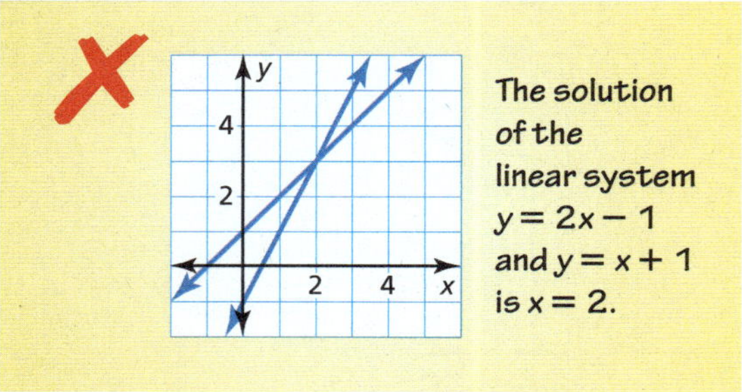

22. **B.E.S.T. TEST PREP** You make a total of 16 two-point and three-point shots in a basketball game. You score a total of 35 points. Which system can be used to find the number p of two-point shots and the number q of three-point shots you make? Explain your reasoning.

Ⓐ $p + q = 35$
$2p + 3q = 16$

Ⓑ $p + q = 16$
$2p + 3q = 35$

Ⓒ $p + q = 16$
$3p + 2q = 35$

Ⓓ $p + q = 35$
$16p + 16q = 35$

23. **MODELING REAL LIFE** You have 40 minutes to exercise at the gym, and you want to burn a total of 300 calories using both machines. How much time should you spend on each machine? *(See Example 3.)*

7 MTR

Elliptical Trainer

8 calories per minute

Stationary Bike

6 calories per minute

7 MTR **24.** **MODELING REAL LIFE** You collect \$234 selling small and large smoothies. You sell a total of 46 smoothies. How many of each size did you sell?

5 MTR **25.** **CONNECTING CONCEPTS** Angle X and angle Y are complementary angles. The measure of angle Y is 6 less than twice the measure of angle X. What is the measure of each angle?

26. **HOW DO YOU SEE IT?** The graph shows the total costs of ordering x key chains from three different websites.

a. For what numbers of key chains are the costs the same at two different websites? Explain.

b. How do your answers in part (a) relate to systems of linear equations?

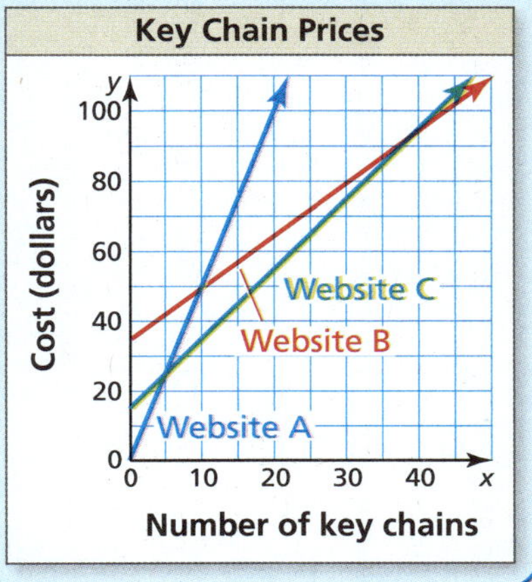

4 MTR **27.** **MAKING AN ARGUMENT** You and your friend start at different locations on an 18-mile hiking trail. You start at the trailhead and walk 4.5 miles per hour. Your friend starts 1.5 miles from the trailhead and walks 3 miles per hour.

a. Your friend says that you will be at the same location on the trail after one hour of hiking. Is your friend correct? Explain.

b. Who will reach the end of the trail first? How much longer will it take the other person to reach the end of the trail? Explain.

28. **THOUGHT PROVOKING** Without graphing, use slopes and intercepts to determine which quadrant contains the solution of the system below. Explain your reasoning.

$5x + 13y = 72$

$4x + 7y = 65$

REVIEW & REFRESH

In Exercises 29 and 30, solve the literal equation for *y*.

29. $9x + 18 = 6y - 3x$

30. $\frac{3}{4}x + \frac{1}{4}y = 5$

31. MULTIPLE REPRESENTATIONS The graph of a linear function passes through the point $(12, -5)$ and has a slope of $\frac{2}{5}$. Represent this function in two other forms.

In Exercises 32–35, solve the equation.

32. $n + 6 = 11$

33. $\frac{r}{3} = -4$

34. $2p - 7 = 9$

35. $\frac{k+1}{8} = 3$

36. Describe the relationship between the data in the scatter plot.

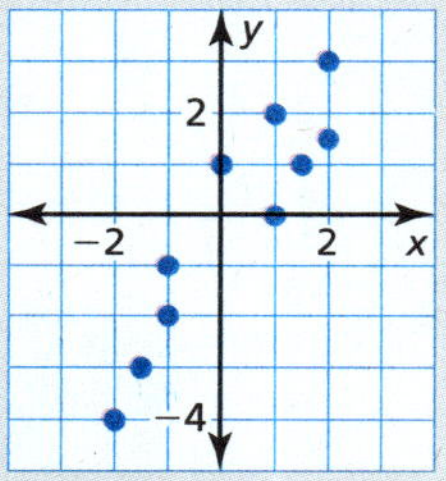

37. Solve the system $x - 4y = -4$ and $-3x - 4y = 12$ by graphing.

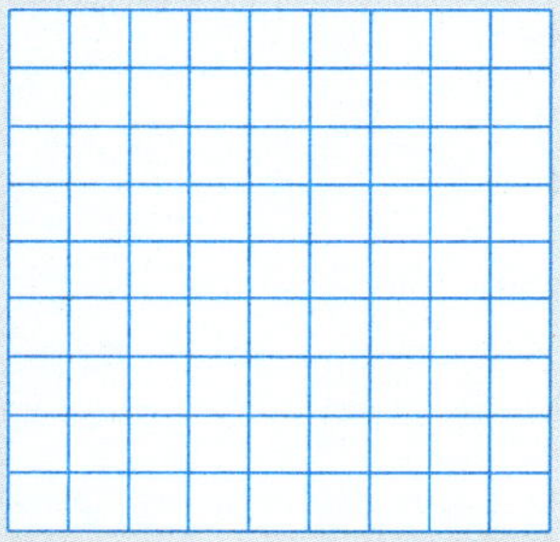

38. Use residuals to determine whether $y = 7x - 2.5$ is a good fit for the data in the table. Explain.

x	0.5	1.0	1.5	2.0	2.5	3.0	3.5	4.0
y	2.5	5	7	14	15	17	21	27.5

39. Estimate the intercepts of the graph of the function.

40. MODELING REAL LIFE The table shows the times *x* (in minutes) you run and distances *y* (in miles) you travel.

Time, *x*	7	10	15	18	19	22	25	30
Distance, *y*	0.8	1	1.5	1.9	2	2.4	2.7	3

a. Use technology to find an equation of the line of best fit. Then interpret the slope and *y*-intercept.

b. Approximate the distance you run in 12 minutes.

5.2 Solving Systems of Linear Equations by Substitution

Learning Target: Solve linear systems by substitution.

Success Criteria:

- I can solve a system of linear equations by substitution.
- I can solve a linear equation in two variables for either variable.
- I can solve real-life problems using substitution.

Algebraic Reasoning

MA.912.AR.9.1 Given a mathematical or real-world context, write and solve a system of two-variable linear equations algebraically or graphically.

MA.912.AR.9.6 Given a real-world context, represent constraints as systems of linear equations or inequalities. Interpret solutions to problems as viable or non-viable options.

Also MA.912.AR.2.2

EXPLORE IT! Solving Systems of Linear Equations

Work with a partner.

a. Two students are solving the linear system below. The first portions of their solutions are shown. Justify each solution step and describe their methods. Are the methods valid? Explain.

$x - 6y = -11$ Equation 1

$3x + y = 5$ Equation 2

Student 1

$x - 6y = -11$ Equation 1

$x - 6(-3x + 5) = -11$ __________

$x + 18x - 30 = -11$ __________

$19x - 30 = -11$ __________

$19x = 19$ __________

$x = 1$ __________

Student 2

$3x + y = 5$ Equation 2

$3(6y - 11) + y = 5$ __________

$18y - 33 + y = 5$ __________

$19y - 33 = 5$ __________

$19y = 38$ __________

$y = 2$ __________

GO DIGITAL

b. What is the solution of the linear system in part (a)?

c. Explain how to solve a linear system using one of the methods above. Then choose one of the methods to solve each system. Check your solutions.

i. $x + 2y = -7$
$2x - y = -9$

ii. $x - 2y = -6$
$2x + y = -2$

iii. $3x - y = -6$
$4x + 5y = 11$

4 MTR **COMPARE METHODS**

How can understanding different solution methods help you solve systems of linear equations?

Solving Linear Systems by Substitution

Another way to solve a system of linear equations is to use substitution to obtain an equation in one variable.

KEY IDEA

Solving a System of Linear Equations by Substitution

Step 1 Solve one of the equations for one of the variables or terms.

Step 2 Substitute the expression from Step 1 into the other equation and solve for the other variable.

Step 3 Substitute the value from Step 2 into one of the original equations and solve to find the value of the other variable.

WORDS AND MATH

When someone makes a substitution, they replace one thing with another. When you solve a system of linear equations by substitution, you make two substitutions.

EXAMPLE 1 **Solving a System of Linear Equations by Substitution**

WATCH

Solve the system by substitution.

$y = -2x - 9$ Equation 1

$6x - 5y = -19$ Equation 2

SOLUTION

Step 1 Equation 1 is already solved for y.

Step 2 Substitute $-2x - 9$ for y in Equation 2 to obtain an equation in one variable, x. Then solve the equation to find the value of x.

$6x - 5y = -19$	Equation 2
$6x - 5(-2x - 9) = -19$	Substitute $-2x - 9$ for y.
$6x + 10x + 45 = -19$	Distributive Property
$16x + 45 = -19$	Combine like terms.
$16x = -64$	Subtract 45 from each side.
$x = -4$	Divide each side by 16.

Step 3 Substitute -4 for x in Equation 1 and solve for y.

$y = -2x - 9$	Equation 1
$= -2(-4) - 9$	Substitute -4 for x.
$= 8 - 9$	Multiply.
$= -1$	Subtract.

▶ The solution is $(-4, -1)$.

Check

Equation 1

$y = -2x - 9$

$-1 \stackrel{?}{=} -2(-4) - 9$

$-1 = -1$ ✓

Equation 2

$6x - 5y = -19$

$6(-4) - 5(-1) \stackrel{?}{=} -19$

$-19 = -19$ ✓

GO DIGITAL

SELF-ASSESSMENT

1 I don't understand yet. 2 I can do it with help. 3 I can do it on my own. 4 I can teach someone else.

1. **WRITING** Explain how you can use two equations in a system of linear equations to find the value of one of the variables.

Solve the system by substitution. Check your solution.

2. $y = 3x + 14$
   $y = -4x$

3. $3x + 2y = 0$
   $y = \frac{1}{2}x - 1$

4. $x = 6y - 7$
   $4x + y = -3$

USE ANOTHER METHOD 2 MTR

Describe another way to solve the system by substitution.

EXAMPLE 2 Solving a System of Linear Equations by Substitution

WATCH

Solve the system by substitution.

$3x = y + 8$ Equation 1

$3x + 2y = -1$ Equation 2

SOLUTION

Step 1 Notice that both equations have a term of $3x$, and Equation 1 is already solved for $3x$.

Step 2 Substitute $y + 8$ for $3x$ in Equation 2 and solve to find the value of y.

$3x + 2y = -1$ Equation 2

$y + 8 + 2y = -1$ Substitute $y + 8$ for $3x$.

$3y + 8 = -1$ Combine like terms.

$3y = -9$ Subtract 8 from each side.

$y = -3$ Divide each side by 3.

Step 3 Substitute -3 for y in Equation 1 and solve for x.

$3x = y + 8$ Equation 1

$3x = -3 + 8$ Substitute -3 for y.

$3x = 5$ Add.

$x = \frac{5}{3}$ Divide each side by 3.

▶ The solution is $\left(\frac{5}{3}, -3\right)$.

Graphical Check

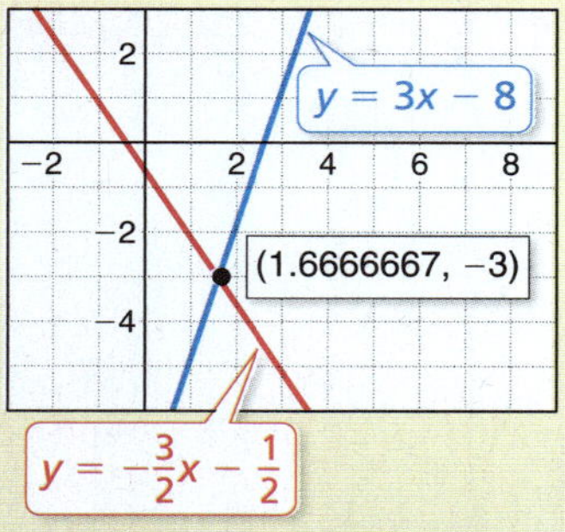

Algebraic Check

Equation 1

$3x = y + 8$

$3\left(\frac{5}{3}\right) \stackrel{?}{=} -3 + 8$

$5 = 5$ ✓

Equation 2

$3x + 2y = -1$

$3\left(\frac{5}{3}\right) + 2(-3) \stackrel{?}{=} -1$

$-1 = -1$ ✓

GO DIGITAL

SELF-ASSESSMENT

1 I don't understand yet. 2 I can do it with help. 3 I can do it on my own. 4 I can teach someone else.

5 MTR **5. STRUCTURE** A system has two equations that are both written in slope-intercept form. Which method would you use to solve this system, graphing or substitution? Explain your reasoning.

Solve the system by substitution. Check your solution.

6. $4x + 5y = 7$
$5y = 2x + 19$

7. $2x = 4y - 5$
$2x - 3y = 1$

8. $x - 2y = 7$
$3x - 2y = 3$

9. $-x + y = -4.5$
$4x - y = 16.5$

Solving Real-Life Problems

7 MTR **EXAMPLE 3** **Modeling Real Life** WATCH

A comedy club earns \$1088 from an opening night performance and \$1183 from a second performance. On opening night, the club sells 68 adult tickets and 136 student tickets. For the second performance, the club sells 79 adult tickets and 140 student tickets. What is the price of each type of ticket?

SOLUTION

1. **Understand the Problem** You know the amounts earned for each performance, and the total numbers of adult and student tickets sold for each. You are asked to find the price of each type of ticket.
2. **Make a Plan** Use a verbal model to write a system that represents the problem. Then solve the system.
3. **Solve and Check**

Verbal Model Number of adult tickets • Adult ticket price + Number of student tickets • Student ticket price = Total amount earned

Variables Let x be the price (in dollars) of an adult ticket, and let y be the price (in dollars) of a student ticket.

System $68x + 136y = 1088$ Equation 1 (first performance)

$79x + 140y = 1183$ Equation 2 (second performance)

Step 1 Solve for y in Equation 1.

$68x + 136y = 1088$ Equation 1

$y = 8 - \frac{1}{2}x$ Solve for y.

Step 2 Substitute $8 - \frac{1}{2}x$ for y in Equation 2 and solve for x.

$79x + 140y = 1183$ Equation 2

$79x + 140\left(8 - \frac{1}{2}x\right) = 1183$ Substitute $8 - \frac{1}{2}x$ for y.

$79x + 1120 - 70x = 1183$ Distributive Property

$x = 7$ Solve for x.

Step 3 Substitute 7 for x in Equation 1 and solve for y.

$68x + 136y = 1088$ Equation 1

$68(7) + 136y = 1088$ Substitute 7 for x.

$y = 4.5$ Solve for y.

▶ The solution is (7, 4.5). So, an adult ticket costs \$7, and a student ticket costs \$4.50.

Check

Equation 1

$68(7) + 136(4.5) \stackrel{?}{=} 1088$

$1088 = 1088$ ✓

Equation 2

$79(7) + 140(4.5) \stackrel{?}{=} 1183$

$1183 = 1183$ ✓

SELF-ASSESSMENT

1 I don't understand yet. 2 I can do it with help. 3 I can do it on my own. 4 I can teach someone else.

10. REASONING You are selling tickets at a dance. Individual tickets cost \$6, and 2 tickets for a couple cost \$10. After the dance, you count \$1075 and 195 tickets. Your friend finds \$1 near your table and asks if it belongs with the ticket money. Do you think it does? How many couples bought tickets for the dance? Explain your reasoning.

GO DIGITAL

5.2 Practice WITH CalcChat® AND CalcView®

In Exercises 1–6, describe how you would obtain an equation in one variable to solve the system by substitution.

1. $x + 4y = 30$
$x = 2y$

2. $y = -8x + 2$
$2x + y = -10$

3. $12y = x - 15$
$-3x + 12y = 3$

4. $5x + 3y = 11$
$5x = y + 5$

5. $x - y = -3$
$4x + 3y = -5$

6. $3x + 5y = 25$
$x - 2y = -6$

In Exercises 7–16, solve the system by substitution. Check your solution. *(See Examples 1 and 2.)*

7. $x = 17 - 4y$
$y = x - 2$

8. $6x - 9 = y$
$y = -3x$

▶ **9.** $x = 16 - 4y$
$3x + 4y = 8$

10. $-5x + 3y = 51$
$y = 10x - 8$

▶ **11.** $-5x + 6y = -11$
$6y = x + 5$

12. $8x = 5y + 24$
$-9y = 40 - 8x$

13. $2x - 3y = -9$
$x - 5y = -29$

14. $2x - y = 23$
$x + 4y = -20$

15. $\frac{1}{3}x + y = -1$
$\frac{1}{3}x + 8y = 13$

16. $5x + 2y = 9$
$-0.5x - y = 7.5$

GO DIGITAL

17. ERROR ANALYSIS Describe and correct the error in solving the linear system $2y = 3x + 4$ and $7x - 2y = 12$.

4 MTR

✗

$$7x - 2y = 12$$
$$7x - 3x + 4 = 12$$
$$4x + 4 = 12$$
$$4x = 8$$
$$x = 2$$

$$2y = 3x + 4$$
$$2y = 3(2) + 4$$
$$2y = 10$$
$$y = 5$$

The solution is (2, 5).

18. ERROR ANALYSIS Describe and correct the error in solving for one of the variables in the linear system $8x + 2y = -12$ and $5x - y = 4$.

4 MTR

✗

$$5x - y = 4$$
$$-y = -5x + 4$$
$$y = 5x - 4$$

$$5x - (5x - 4) = 4$$
$$5x - 5x + 4 = 4$$
$$4 = 4$$

19. MODELING REAL LIFE A test is worth 100 points. Each problem is worth either 2 points or 5 points. The number of 5-point problems is 22 fewer than the number of 2-point problems. How many problems of each type are on the test? *(See Example 3.)*

7 MTR

20. MODELING REAL LIFE A group spends \$277.50 to rent 15 tubes for a float down the Ichetucknee River. How many of each type of tube does the group rent?

7 MTR

21. OPEN-ENDED Write a linear system that has the ordered pair (15, −25) as its solution. Then solve the system by substitution to justify your answer.

22. HOW DO YOU SEE IT?

The graphs of two linear equations are shown.

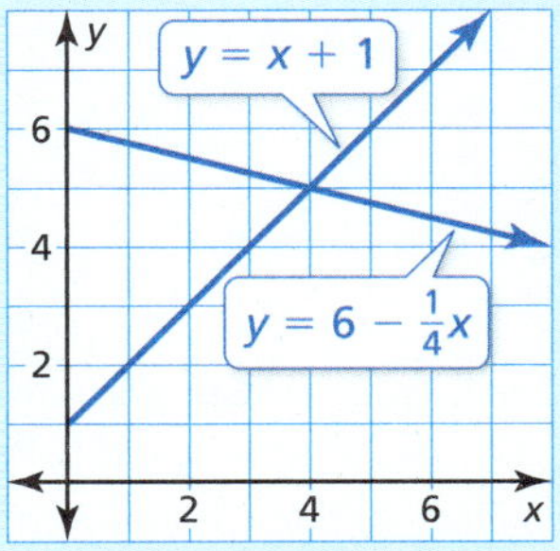

a. At what point do the lines appear to intersect?

b. Can you solve a system of linear equations by substitution to check your answer in part (a)? Explain.

4 MTR **23. MAKING AN ARGUMENT** To solve the system $-7x - 2y = 21$ and $-7x = 42 - y$ by substitution, you begin by solving for y in the second equation. Your friend says that this step is not necessary. Is your friend correct? Explain.

24. B.E.S.T. TEST PREP For the system shown, what is the value of $y - x$?

$$x + \frac{3}{4}y = -14$$
$$-4x + 3y = -16$$

Ⓐ -17 Ⓒ 7

Ⓑ -7 Ⓓ 17

5 MTR **CONNECTING CONCEPTS In Exercises 25 and 26, find the values of *x* and *y*.**

25. $x + 2 = 3y$

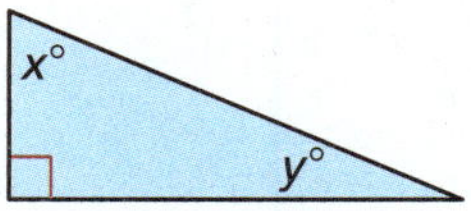

26. $-2x + y = -35$

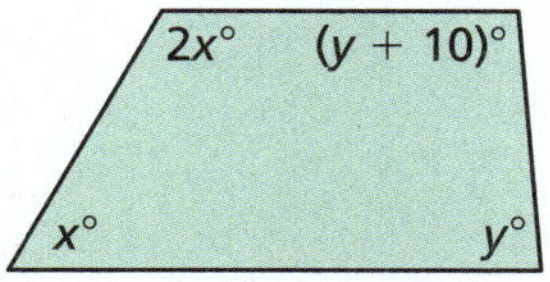

27. REASONING Find the values of a and b so that the solution of the linear system is $(-9, 1)$.

$ax + by = -31$ Equation 1

$ax - by = -41$ Equation 2

28. THOUGHT PROVOKING
Write a system of linear equations in which $(3, -5)$ is a solution of Equation 1 but not a solution of Equation 2, and $(-1, 7)$ is the solution of the system. Then solve the system by substitution to verify that $(-1, 7)$ is the solution.

29. NUMBER SENSE The sum of the digits of a two-digit number is 11. When the digits are reversed, the number increases by 27. Find the original number.

30. DIG DEEPER You withdraw \$375 from your bank account. You receive a stack of 24 bills consisting of \$5, \$10, and \$20 bills. The number of \$5 bills is one-half the number of \$10 bills. How many of each type of bill do you receive?

REVIEW & REFRESH

WATCH

In Exercises 31–33, find the sum or difference.

31. $(x - 4) + (2x - 7)$

32. $(6d + 2) - (3d - 3)$

33. $2(5v + 6) - 6(-9v + 2)$

34. Solve the system by substitution.

$$x - 8y = 7$$
$$5x + 6y = 12$$

35. The theoretical probability of drawing a red marble from a bag is $\frac{2}{5}$. The bag contains 60 marbles.

a. How many red marbles are in the bag?

b. A marble is drawn from the bag and replaced 80 times. How many times do you expect a red marble to be drawn?

36. Use technology to find an equation of the line of best fit for the data. Then graph the equation with the data.

x	*y*
20	65
21	42
15	25
33	87
28	76
30	79

37. REASONING Find the value of a so that the line that passes through $(-5, a)$ and $(1, -10)$ has a slope of $-\frac{4}{3}$.

38. Tell whether a correlation is likely for the number of car accidents and the weather. If so, tell whether there is a causal relationship. Explain your reasoning.

In Exercises 39 and 40, graph the function. Compare the graph to the graph of $f(x) = |x|$. Find the domain and range.

39. $g(x) = |x + 5|$

40. $p(x) = |x| - 8$

41. Solve the system by graphing.

$$y = \frac{2}{3}x + 4$$
$$y = -2x - 4$$

42. Solve $3|2x - 7| > 18$. Graph the solution.

43. MODELING REAL LIFE An investor owns shares of Stock A and Stock B. The investor owns a total of 200 shares with a total value of $4000. How many shares of each stock does the investor own?

Stock	Price
A	$9.50
B	$27.00

5.3 Solving Systems of Linear Equations by Elimination

Learning Target: Solve linear systems by elimination.

Success Criteria:

- I can add or subtract linear equations.
- I can solve a system of linear equations by elimination.
- I can explain why the elimination method produces a valid solution.
- I can solve real-life problems using elimination.

Algebraic Reasoning

MA.912.AR.9.1 Given a mathematical or real-world context, write and solve a system of two-variable linear equations algebraically or graphically.

MA.912.AR.9.6 Given a real-world context, represent constraints as systems of linear equations or inequalities. Interpret solutions to problems as viable or non-viable options.

Also MA.912.AR.2.2

EXPLORE IT! Solving Systems of Linear Equations

A medianoche is a sandwich that originated in Cuba.

Work with a partner. You, your friend, and your cousin buy drinks and medianoches at a food truck. Each drink is the same price, and each medianoche is the same price.

- You purchase a drink and a medianoche for $7.50.
- Your cousin purchases a drink and three medianoches for $19.50.

a. How can you use variables to write an equation that represents each purchase?

b. Your cousin uses a system to determine the price of a drink and the price of a medianoche. Describe the solution method shown. Is the method valid? Explain your reasoning.

$x + 3y = 19.50$ Your cousin

$x + y = 7.50$ You

$2y = 12$

So, $y = 6$ and each medianoche is $6.

Each drink is $7.50 − $6 = $1.50.

GO DIGITAL

c. Your friend purchases two drinks and four medianoches for \$27.00 and writes the system below to check the answer in part (b). What can you do to one or both equations so that you can use an approach similar to the approach in part (b)? Solve the system.

$2x + 4y = 27.00$	Your friend
$x + y = 7.50$	You

d. Explain how to solve a system of linear equations algebraically without using substitution.

5 MTR **MAKE A PLAN**

How can you use the coefficients of the variable terms to decide on a strategy for solving the system in part (c)?

Solving Linear Systems by Elimination

KEY IDEA

Solving a System of Linear Equations by Elimination

Step 1 Multiply, if necessary, one or both equations by a constant so at least one pair of like terms has the same or opposite coefficients.

Step 2 Add or subtract the equations to eliminate one of the variables.

Step 3 Solve the resulting equation.

Step 4 Substitute the value from Step 3 into one of the original equations and solve for the other variable.

WORDS AND MATH

Elimination is the process of removing something. When you solve a system of linear equations by elimination, you add or subtract equations to remove one of the variables.

When at least one pair of like terms in a linear system has the same or opposite coefficients, you can add or subtract the equations to *eliminate* one of the variables. Then use the resulting equation to solve the system.

System 1

$a = b$ Equation 1

$c = d$ Equation 2

System 2

$a + c = b + d$ Equation 3

$c = d$ Equation 2

To justify this approach, consider System 1. In this system, a and c are algebraic expressions, and b and d are constants. You can rewrite Equation 1 as Equation 3 by adding c on the left and d on the right by the Addition Property of Equality. You can rewrite Equation 3 as Equation 1 by subtracting c on the left and d on the right by the Subtraction Property of Equality. Because you can rewrite either system as the other, System 1 and System 2 have the same solution.

EXAMPLE 1 Solving a System of Linear Equations by Elimination

WATCH

Solve the system by elimination.

$3x + 2y = 4$ Equation 1

$3x - 2y = -4$ Equation 2

SOLUTION

Step 1 Because the coefficients of the x-terms are the same, you do not need to multiply either equation by a constant.

Step 2 Subtract the equations to eliminate the x-terms.

$3x + 2y = 4$ Equation 1

$\underline{3x - 2y = -4}$ Equation 2

$4y = 8$ Subtract the equations.

Step 3 Solve for y.

$4y = 8$ Resulting equation from Step 2

$y = 2$ Divide each side by 4.

Step 4 Substitute 2 for y in one of the original equations and solve for x.

$3x + 2y = 4$ Equation 1

$3x + 2(2) = 4$ Substitute 2 for y.

$3x = 0$ Simplify.

$x = 0$ Divide each side by 3.

▶ The solution is (0, 2).

ANOTHER WAY

Because the coefficients of the y-terms are opposites, you can add the equations to eliminate the y-terms.

$$\begin{aligned} 3x + 2y &= 4 \\ \underline{3x - 2y} &\underline{= -4} \\ 6x \quad &= 0 \end{aligned}$$

Check

Equation 1

$3(0) + 2(2) \stackrel{?}{=} 4$

$4 = 4$ ✓

Equation 2

$3(0) - 2(2) \stackrel{?}{=} -4$

$-4 = -4$ ✓

GO DIGITAL

EXAMPLE 2 Solving a System of Linear Equations by Elimination

WATCH

Solve the system by elimination.

$-10x + 3y = 1$ Equation 1

$-5x - 6y = 23$ Equation 2

ANOTHER WAY

To use subtraction to eliminate one of the variables, multiply Equation 2 by 2 and subtract the equations.

$$\begin{aligned} -10x + 3y &= 1 \\ -10x - 12y &= 46 \\ \hline 15y &= -45 \end{aligned}$$

SOLUTION

Step 1 Notice that no pairs of like terms have the same or opposite coefficients. One way to solve by elimination is to multiply Equation 2 by -2 so that the coefficients of the x-terms are opposites.

$-10x + 3y = 1$ → $-10x + 3y = 1$ Equation 1

$-5x - 6y = 23$ Multiply by -2. → $10x + 12y = -46$ Revised Equation 2

Step 2 Add the equations to eliminate the x-terms.

$-10x + 3y = 1$ Equation 1

$10x + 12y = -46$ Revised Equation 2

$15y = -45$ Add the equations.

Step 3 Solve for y.

$15y = -45$ Resulting equation from Step 2

$y = -3$ Divide each side by 15.

Step 4 Substitute -3 for y in one of the original equations and solve for x.

$-5x - 6y = 23$ Equation 2

$-5x - 6(-3) = 23$ Substitute -3 for y.

$-5x + 18 = 23$ Multiply.

$-5x = 5$ Subtract 18 from each side.

$x = -1$ Divide each side by -5.

▶ The solution is $(-1, -3)$.

Check

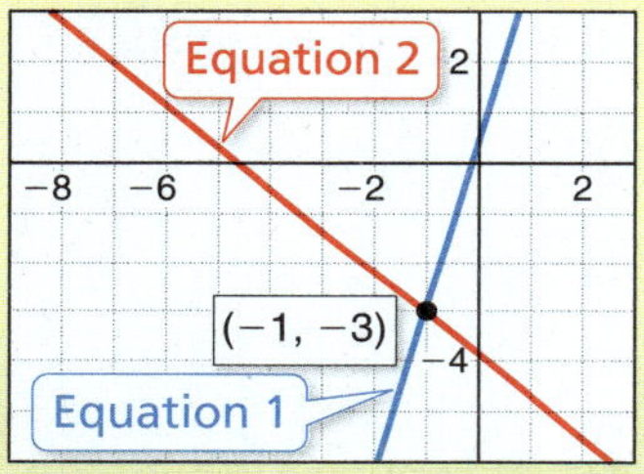

SELF-ASSESSMENT

1 I don't understand yet. 2 I can do it with help. 3 I can do it on my own. 4 I can teach someone else.

Solve the system by elimination. Check your solution.

1. $2x + y = -4$
$x + y = 9$

2. $3x + 2y = 7$
$-3x + 4y = 5$

3. $4x - 3y = 15$
$-3y - 4x = 6$

GO DIGITAL

SELF-ASSESSMENT

1 I don't understand yet. 2 I can do it with help. 3 I can do it on my own. 4 I can teach someone else.

5 MTR **4. STRUCTURE** In the system at the right, for what value of a can you eliminate a variable by adding the equations? For what value of b can you eliminate a variable by subtracting the equations?

$\frac{1}{2}x + ay = -15$ Equation 1

$bx - \frac{7}{5}y = 1$ Equation 2

Solve the system by elimination. Check your solution.

5. $x - 3y = 24$
$3x + y = 12$

6. $x + 4y = 22$
$4x + y = 13$

7. $-5x + \frac{1}{2}y = 3$
$4x - 2y = -8$

8. REASONING Your friend says that replacing one equation in a system with the sum of that equation and a multiple of the other produces a system with the same solution. Use properties of equality to show that your friend is correct.

Solving Real-Life Problems

EXAMPLE 3 **Modeling Real Life** WATCH

A business with locations in Orlando and Tampa buys seven large delivery vans and five small delivery vans. Orlando receives five large vans and two small vans for a total cost of \$235,000. Tampa receives two large vans and three small vans for a total cost of \$160,000. What is the cost of each type of van?

SOLUTION

Use a verbal model to write and solve a linear system that represents the problem.

Verbal Model Number of large vans • Cost of large van + Number of small vans • Cost of small van = Total cost of vans

Variables Let x be the cost (in dollars) of a large van, and let y be the cost (in dollars) of a small van.

System $5x + 2y = 235{,}000$ Equation 1 (Orlando)

$2x + 3y = 160{,}000$ Equation 2 (Tampa)

GO DIGITAL

STUDY TIP

In Example 3, both equations are multiplied by a constant so that the coefficients of the y-terms are the same.

Step 1 One way to find the cost of each type of van is to first eliminate the y-terms and solve for x. Multiply Equation 1 by 3 and Equation 2 by 2.

$5x + 2y = 235{,}000$ → Multiply by 3. → $15x + 6y = 705{,}000$ Revised Equation 1

$2x + 3y = 160{,}000$ → Multiply by 2. → $4x + 6y = 320{,}000$ Revised Equation 2

Step 2 Subtract the equations to obtain $11x = 385{,}000$.

Step 3 Solving the equation $11x = 385{,}000$ gives $x = 35{,}000$.

Step 4 Substitute 35,000 for x in one of the original equations and solve for y.

$5(35{,}000) + 2y = 235{,}000$ Substitute 35,000 for x in Equation 1.

$y = 30{,}000$ Solve for y.

▶ The solution is (35,000, 30,000). So, a large van costs \$35,000, and a small van costs \$30,000.

SELF-ASSESSMENT

1 I don't understand yet. 2 I can do it with help. 3 I can do it on my own. 4 I can teach someone else.

9. WHAT IF? The total cost of the vans for Orlando is \$228,500. The total cost for Tampa is \$153,000. What is the cost of each type of van?

CONCEPT SUMMARY

Methods for Solving Linear Systems

Method	When to Use
Graphing *(Lesson 5.1)*	To estimate solutions
Substitution *(Lesson 5.2)*	When one of the variable terms in one of the equations has a coefficient of 1 or −1
Elimination *(Lesson 5.3)*	When at least one pair of like terms has the same or opposite coefficients
Elimination (Multiply First) *(Lesson 5.3)*	When one of the variables cannot be eliminated by adding or subtracting the equations

5.3 Practice WITH CalcChat® AND CalcView®

In Exercises 1–8, solve the system by elimination. Check your solution. *(See Example 1.)*

1. $x + 2y = 13$
$-x + y = 5$

2. $9x + y = 2$
$-4x - y = -17$

▶3. $5x + 6y = 50$
$x - 6y = -26$

4. $-x + y = 4$
$x + 3y = 4$

5. $-3x - 5y = -7$
$-4x + 5y = 14$

6. $1.5x - 9y = -21$
$-1.5x - 3y = 9$

7. $-y - 10 = 6x$
$5x + y = -10$

8. $3x - 30 = y$
$7y - 6 = 3x$

In Exercises 9–16, solve the system by elimination. Check your solution. *(See Example 2.)*

9. $x + y = 2$
$2x + 7y = 9$

10. $8x - 5y = 11$
$4x - 3y = 5$

▶11. $11x - 20y = 28$
$3x + 4y = 36$

12. $10x - 9y = 46$
$-2x + 3y = 10$

13. $4x - 3y = 8$
$5x - 2y = -11$

14. $-2x - 5y = 9$
$3x + 11y = 4$

15. $9x + 2y = 39$
$6x + 13y = -9$

16. $12x - 7y = -2$
$8x + 11y = 30$

7 MTR **17.** **MODELING REAL LIFE** A service center charges a fee of x dollars for an oil change plus y dollars per quart of oil used. Customer A receives 5 quarts of oil and pays a total of \$37.45. Customer B receives 7 quarts of oil and pays a total of \$46.45. Find the fee and cost per quart of oil. *(See Example 3.)*

7 MTR **18.** **MODELING REAL LIFE** A music website charges x dollars for individual songs and y dollars for entire albums. Person A pays \$25.92 to download 6 individual songs and 2 albums. Person B pays \$33.93 to download 4 individual songs and 3 albums. How much does the website charge to download a song? an entire album?

GO DIGITAL

19. ERROR ANALYSIS Describe and correct the error in solving for one of the variables in the linear system $5x - 7y = 16$ and $x + 7y = 8$.

4 MTR

20. WRITING For what values of a can you solve the linear system $ax + 3y = 2$ and $4x + 5y = 6$ by elimination without multiplying first? Explain.

3 MTR

CHOOSE A METHOD **In Exercises 21–26, solve the system using any method. Explain your choice of method.**

21. $3x + 2y = 4$
$2y = 8 - 5x$

22. $-6y + 2 = -4x$
$y - 2 = x$

23. $y - x = 2$
$y = -\frac{1}{4}x + 7$

24. $3x + y = \frac{1}{3}$
$2x - 3y = \frac{8}{3}$

25. $0.3x - 0.2y = -2.1$
$0.6x + 1.3y = 0.9$

26. $\frac{1}{3}x + \frac{2}{3}y = 2$
$\frac{1}{2}x - \frac{1}{4}y = -\frac{3}{4}$

27. OPEN-ENDED Write a linear system for which you can add *or* subtract to eliminate a variable.

28. HOW DO YOU SEE IT? The circle graph shows the results of a survey in which 50 students were asked about their favorite meal.

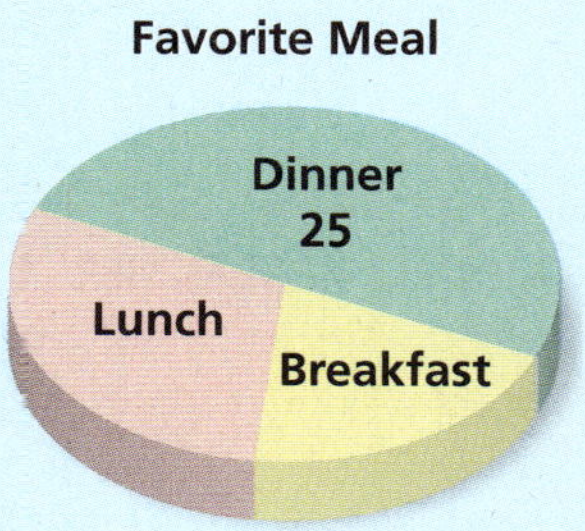

a. Estimate the numbers of students who chose breakfast and lunch.

b. The number of students who chose lunch is 5 more than the number of students who chose breakfast. Write a linear system that represents the numbers of students who chose breakfast and lunch.

c. Explain how you can solve the linear system in part (b) to check your answers in part (a).

29. B.E.S.T. TEST PREP Which of the following approaches result in an equation in one variable? Select all that apply. Explain your reasoning.

$3x + y = 7$ Equation 1
$-x - 2y = 16$ Equation 2

(A) Add the equations.

(B) Multiply Equation 2 by 3 and subtract the equations.

(C) Multiply Equation 1 by 2 and add the equations.

(D) Solve Equation 1 for y and substitute the result in Equation 2.

4 MTR **30. MAKING AN ARGUMENT** Your friend says that any system of equations that can be solved by elimination can be solved by substitution in an equal or fewer number of steps. Is your friend correct? Explain.

31. PROBLEM SOLVING You use bottles of 100% fruit juice and 20% fruit juice to make fruit punch for a party. How many quarts of each type of juice should you mix to make 6 quarts of 80% fruit juice?

32. PROBLEM SOLVING A motorboat takes 40 minutes to travel 20 miles downstream. The return trip takes 60 minutes. For both trips, the boat travels through the water at a constant speed. What is the speed of the current?

4 MTR **33. DISCUSS MATHEMATICAL THINKING** Refer to the discussion of System 1 and System 2 on page 415. Without solving, explain why the systems shown have the same solution.

System 1		System 2	
$3x - 2y = 8$	Equation 1	$5x = 20$	Equation 3
$x + y = 6$	Equation 2	$x + y = 6$	Equation 2

34. THOUGHT PROVOKING
There are three integers. The sums of each distinct pair of integers are -13, -4, and 3. What is the greatest integer?

35. DIG DEEPER Solve the system of equations for x, y, and z. Explain your steps.

$x + 7y + 3z = 29$ Equation 1
$3z + x - 2y = -7$ Equation 2
$5y = 10 - 2x$ Equation 3

REVIEW & REFRESH

In Exercises 36 and 37, solve the equation.

36. $5d - 8 = 1 + 5d$

37. $9 + 4t = 12 - 4t$

38. WRITING Explain how to solve the system shown by elimination.

$2x - 3y = -4$ Equation 1

$-5x + 9y = 7$ Equation 2

39. Write an equation of the line that passes through $(-5, -2)$ and is (a) parallel and (b) perpendicular to $y = \frac{2}{3}x + 1$.

In Exercises 40 and 41, solve the system by elimination. Check your solution.

40. $2x - y = 14$
$-3x + y = -6$

41. $x + 3y = -6$
$3x - 4y = 8$

42. Determine whether the graph represents a function. Explain.

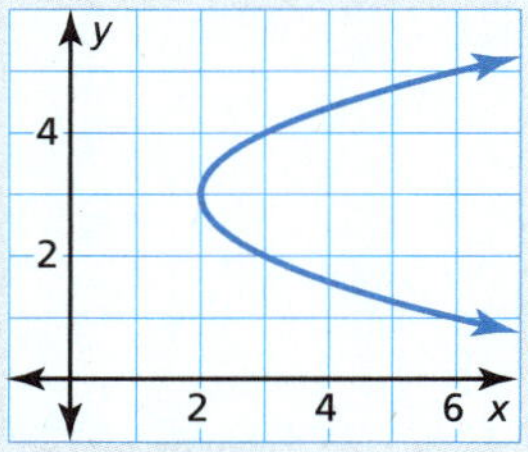

43. Tell whether $(-2, 3)$ is a solution of the system $y = \frac{1}{2}x + 4$ and $3x - y = 6$.

44. Use intercepts to graph $7x - 3y = 21$. Label the points corresponding to the intercepts.

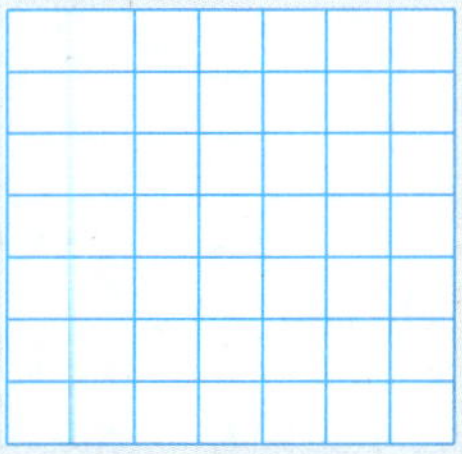

45. REASONING Find the value of each symbol in the system.

★ − ■ = −5 Equation 1

★ + ★ = 11 − ■ Equation 2

46. Evaluate the function $d(x) = -2x + 9$ when $x = 5$.

In Exercises 47–52, solve the inequality. Graph the solution.

47. $c + 15 \leq -7$

48. $9 > -6y$

49. $8 - 3z < 5z - 16$

50. $|7d + 23| \geq -10$

51. $-1 < \frac{1}{2}(g - 8) < 9$

52. $0 \geq r + 1$ *or* $\frac{2}{3}r \geq 4$

53. Graph $f(x) = |x - 4| + 2$. Compare the graph to the graph of $g(x) = |x - 4| + 3$.

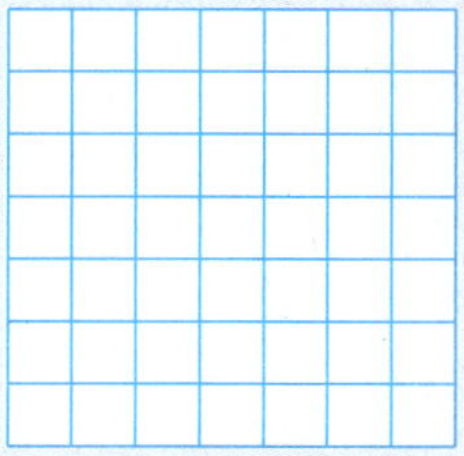

5.4 Solving Special Systems of Linear Equations

Learning Target: Solve linear systems with different numbers of solutions.

Success Criteria:
- I can determine the number of solutions of a system.
- I can solve a system of linear equations with any number of solutions.

Algebraic Reasoning

MA.912.AR.9.1 Given a mathematical or real-world context, write and solve a system of two-variable linear equations algebraically or graphically.

MA.912.AR.9.6 Given a real-world context, represent constraints as systems of linear equations or inequalities. Interpret solutions to problems as viable or non-viable options.

Also MA.912.AR.2.2

EXPLORE IT! Solving Linear Systems

Work with a partner. You invest \$30 in equipment to make skateboards. The materials for each skateboard cost \$20. You have three plans for how to sell the skateboards.

Plan 1: Sell each skateboard for \$20.

Plan 2: Sell each skateboard for \$25.

Plan 3: Sell the first skateboard for \$50 to make up for your initial costs, and then sell every other skateboard for \$20.

a. Match each plan with one of the following systems. Explain your reasoning.

System 1: $y = 20x + 30$ Equation 1 (cost)
$y = 25x$ Equation 2 (revenue)

System 2: $y = 20x + 30$ Equation 1 (cost)
$y = 20x + 30$ Equation 2 (revenue)

System 3: $y = 20x + 30$ Equation 1 (cost)
$y = 20x + 50$ Equation 2 (revenue)

System 4: $y = 20x + 30$ Equation 1 (cost)
$y = 20x$ Equation 2 (revenue)

b. What does the solution of each system represent?

GO DIGITAL

c. Solve the system for each plan by graphing. Then solve the systems algebraically. What do you notice?

d. Which plan makes the most sense? Explain your reasoning.

e. Explain how you can use slopes and y-intercepts to determine the number of solutions of a system.

1 MTR **ANALYZE A PROBLEM**

For the system that has one solution, what does the vertical distance between the lines represent to the left of the intersection point? to the right?

The Numbers of Solutions of Linear Systems

KEY IDEA

Solutions of Systems of Linear Equations

A system of linear equations can have *one solution*, *no solution*, or *infinitely many solutions*.

One solution

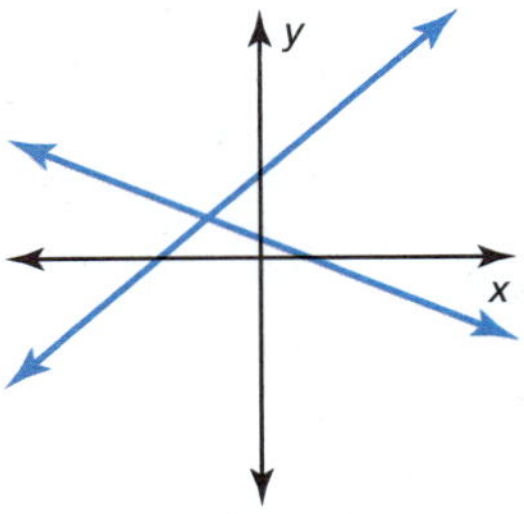

The lines intersect.
- different slopes

No solution

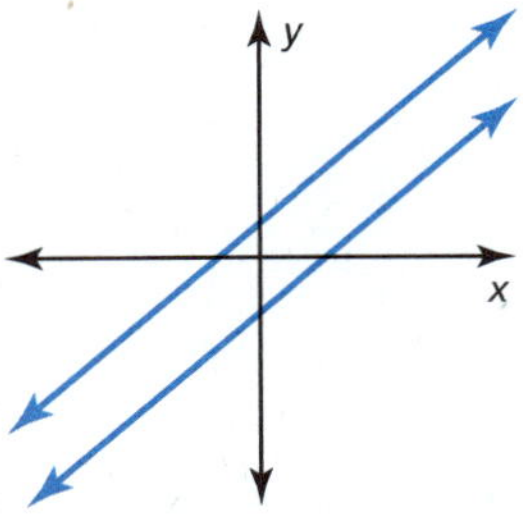

The lines are parallel.
- same slope
- different y-intercepts

Infinitely many solutions

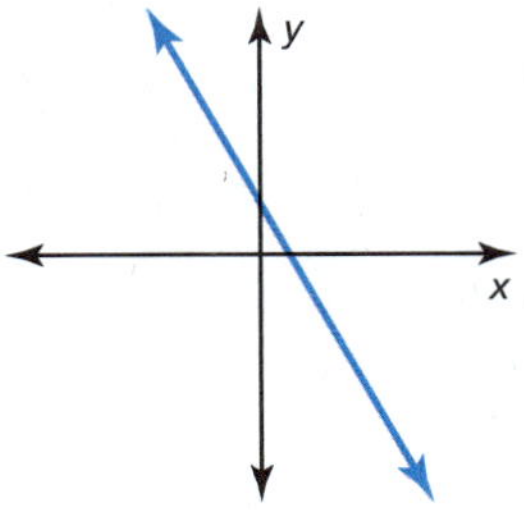

The lines are the same.
- same slope
- same y-intercept

STUDY TIP

A linear system with no solution is called an *inconsistent system*.

A linear system with infinitely many solutions is called a *consistent dependent system*.

EXAMPLE 1 Solving a System: No Solution

WATCH

Solve the system using any method.

$y = 2x + 1$ Equation 1

$y = 2x - 5$ Equation 2

SOLUTION

Method 1 Solve by graphing.

Graph each equation.

The lines have the same slope, 2, and different y-intercepts, 1 and -5. So, the lines are parallel.

Because parallel lines do not intersect, there is no point that is a solution of both equations.

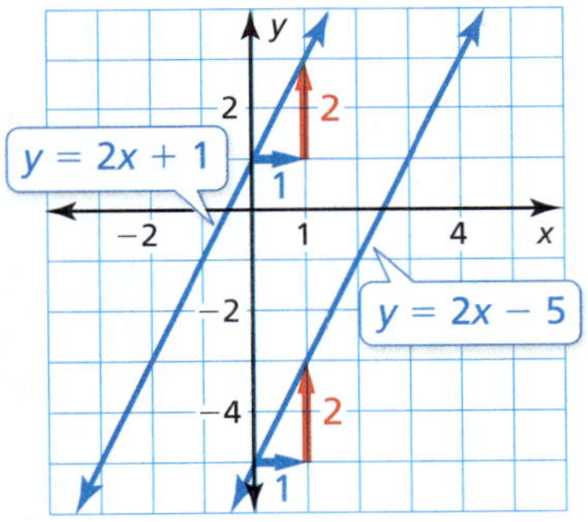

▶ So, the system has no solution.

Method 2 Because the equations are solved for y, another way to solve is by substitution.

Substitute $2x - 5$ for y in Equation 1.

$$y = 2x + 1 \quad \text{Equation 1}$$

$$2x - 5 = 2x + 1 \quad \text{Substitute } 2x - 5 \text{ for } y.$$

$$-5 = 1 \ ✗ \quad \text{Subtract } 2x \text{ from each side.}$$

▶ The equation $-5 = 1$ is never true. So, the system has no solution.

ANOTHER WAY

You can solve some linear systems by inspection. In Example 1, notice you can rewrite the system as

$-2x + y = 1$

$-2x + y = -5.$

This system has no solution because $-2x + y$ cannot be equal to both 1 and -5.

GO DIGITAL

EXAMPLE 2 Solving a System: Infinitely Many Solutions

WATCH

Solve the system using any method.

$-2x + y = 3$ Equation 1

$-4x + 2y = 6$ Equation 2

SOLUTION

Method 1 Solve by graphing.

Graph each equation.

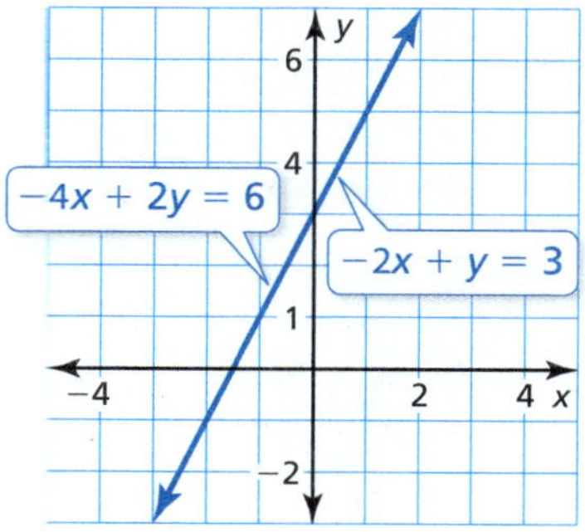

The lines have the same slope, 2, and the same y-intercept, 3. So, the lines are the same.

▶ Because the lines are the same, the system has infinitely many solutions. The solutions are all the points on the line $-2x + y = 3$.

Method 2 Another way to solve is by elimination. Multiply Equation 1 by -2 so that the coefficients of the x-terms are opposites.

USE ANOTHER METHOD (2 MTR)

Explain how you can solve the system by inspection.

Step 1 Multiply Equation 1 by -2.

$-2x + y = 3$ → Multiply by -2. → $4x - 2y = -6$ Revised Equation 1

$-4x + 2y = 6$ → $-4x + 2y = 6$ Equation 2

Step 2 Add the equations.

$4x - 2y = -6$ Revised Equation 1

$\underline{-4x + 2y = 6}$ Equation 2

$0 = 0$ Add the equations.

▶ The equation $0 = 0$ is always true. So, the system has infinitely many solutions. The solutions are all the points on the line $-2x + y = 3$.

SELF-ASSESSMENT

1 I don't understand yet. 2 I can do it with help. 3 I can do it on my own. 4 I can teach someone else.

Solve the system. Explain your choice of method.

1. $x + y = 3$
$2x + 2y = 6$

2. $y = -x + 3$
$2x + 2y = 4$

3. $5x + y = 4$
$x + 6y = 9.5$

4. $y = -10x + 2$
$10x + y = 10$

5. $\frac{5}{2}x + y = -10$
$\frac{5}{2}x = -10 - y$

6. $x + y = 3$
$x + 2y = 4$

GO DIGITAL

SELF-ASSESSMENT

1 I don't understand yet. 2 I can do it with help. 3 I can do it on my own. 4 I can teach someone else.

7. **REASONING** Is it possible for a system of linear equations to have exactly two solutions? Explain.

5 MTR 8. **STRUCTURE** For what value(s) of a does the system have no solution? infinitely many solutions? Is it possible for the system to have exactly one solution?

$3x - 9y = a$ Equation 1
$-x + 3y = 2$ Equation 2

Solving Real-Life Problems

7 MTR **EXAMPLE 3** **Modeling Real Life** WATCH

You buy 1 bag of dog food and 2 bags of treats online for a total of \$48. A few weeks later, you buy 2 bags of the same dog food and 4 bags of the same treats for a total of \$96. Find the price of each bag of food and each bag of treats.

SOLUTION

1. **Understand the Problem** You know the numbers of bags of dog food and treats you buy in two separate purchases as well as the total cost of each purchase. You are asked to find the price of each bag of food and each bag of treats.
2. **Make a Plan** Use a verbal model to write a system that represents the problem. Then solve the system.
3. **Solve and Check**

Verbal Model Number of bags of food $\cdot$ Cost of bag of food $+$ Number of bags of treats $\cdot$ Cost of bag of treats $=$ Total cost

Variables Let x be the cost (in dollars) of a bag of food, and let y be the cost (in dollars) of a bag of treats.

System $x + 2y = 48$ Equation 1
$2x + 4y = 96$ Equation 2

GO DIGITAL

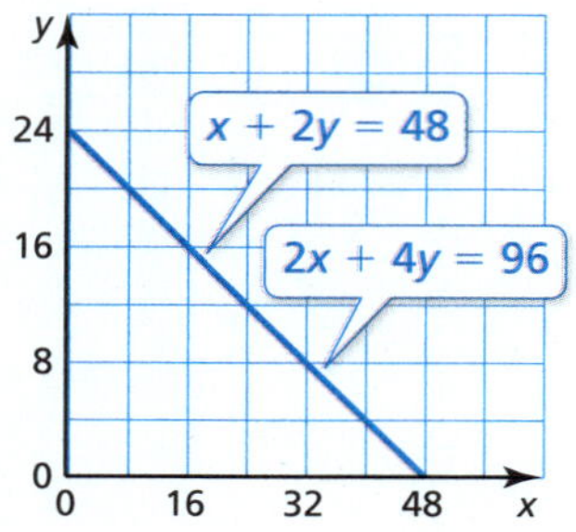

One way to find the costs per bag is to first eliminate the x-terms and solve for y. Multiply Equation 1 by 2 and subtract the equations.

$x + 2y = 48$	Multiply by 2.	$2x + 4y = 96$	Revised Equation 1
$2x + 4y = 96$		$2x + 4y = 96$	Equation 2
		$0 = 0$	Subtract the equations.

▶ The equation $0 = 0$ is always true. So, the solutions are all the points on the line $x + 2y = 48$. In this context, x and y must be positive numbers. There are many points with positive number coordinates on the line, so there is not enough information to determine the price of each bag.

Look Back Find ordered pairs (x, y) that are solutions of Equation 1. You should find that they are also solutions of Equation 2.

Equation 1: Let $x = 30$.

$30 + 2y = 48$

$y = 9$

Equation 2: Test (30, 9).

$2(30) + 4(9) \stackrel{?}{=} 96$

$96 = 96$ ✓

Equation 1: Let $x = 40$.

$40 + 2y = 48$

$y = 4$

Equation 2: Test (40, 4).

$2(40) + 4(4) \stackrel{?}{=} 96$

$96 = 96$ ✓

SELF-ASSESSMENT 1 I don't understand yet. 2 I can do it with help. 3 I can do it on my own. 4 I can teach someone else.

9. WHAT IF? In Example 3, you purchase 2 bags of the same dog food and 1 bag of the same treats for a total of \$81. Do you now have enough information to find the prices? If so, find the prices and explain why this new information is sufficient to do so. If not, explain why not.

5.4 Practice WITH CalcChat® AND CalcView®

In Exercises 1–10, solve the system. Explain your choice of method. *(See Examples 1 and 2.)*

1. $y = -2x - 4$
$y = 2x - 4$

2. $y = -6x - 8$
$y = -6x + 8$

3. $3x - y = 6$
$-3x + y = -6$

4. $-x + 2y = 7$
$x - 2y = 7$

5. $4x + 4y = -8$
$-2x - 2y = 4$

6. $15x - 5y = -20$
$-3x + y = 4$

7. $9x - 15y = 24$
$6x - 10y = -16$

8. $3x - 2y = -5$
$4x + 5y = 47$

9. $\frac{4}{3}y = 3x - 14$
$3x + \frac{4}{3}y = -10$

10. $-\frac{1}{4}x + 3y = 6$
$-2x + 24y = 48$

In Exercises 11–16, use only the slopes and *y*-intercepts of the graphs of the equations to determine the number of solutions of the system. Explain your reasoning.

11. $y = 7x + 13$
$-21x + 3y = 39$

12. $y = -6x - 3$
$12x + 2y = -6$

13. $4x + 3y = 27$
$4x - 3y = -27$

14. $-7x + 7y = 1$
$2x - 2y = -18$

15. $-18x + 6y = 24$
$3x - y = -2$

16. $2x - 2y = 16$
$3x - 6y = 30$

GO DIGITAL

4 MTR **ERROR ANALYSIS** **In Exercises 17 and 18, describe and correct the error in determining the number of solutions of the system.**

17. ✗

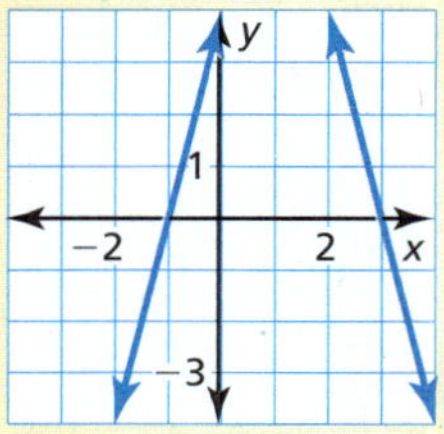

$-4x + y = 4$

$4x + y = 12$

The lines do not intersect. So, the system has no solution.

18. ✗

$y = 3x - 8$

$y = 3x - 12$

The lines have the same slope. So, the system has infinitely many solutions.

19. **7 MTR** **MODELING REAL LIFE** A small bag of trail mix contains 3 cups of dried fruit and 4 cups of almonds. A large bag contains $4\frac{1}{2}$ cups of dried fruit and 6 cups of almonds. Find the price of 1 cup of dried fruit and 1 cup of almonds. *(See Example 3.)*

$9 $6

20. **7 MTR** **MODELING REAL LIFE** In a canoe race, the distance y (in miles) that Team A travels in x hours is represented by $y = 6x$. Team B travels 6 miles per hour and is 2.25 miles ahead of Team A. The teams continue traveling at their current rates for the remainder of the race. Will Team A catch up to Team B? Use a system to justify your answer.

21. **PROBLEM SOLVING** A train travels from Orlando to Miami, and then back to Orlando. The table shows the numbers of tickets purchased for each leg of the trip. The cost per ticket is the same for each leg of the trip. Is there enough information to determine the cost of one coach ticket? Explain.

Destination	Coach tickets	Business class tickets	Money collected (dollars)
Orlando	60	90	1950
Miami	66	100	2160

22. **4 MTR** **MAKING AN ARGUMENT** One admission to an ice-skating rink costs x dollars, and renting a pair of ice skates costs y dollars. Your friend says she can determine the exact cost of one admission and one skate rental. Is your friend correct? Explain.

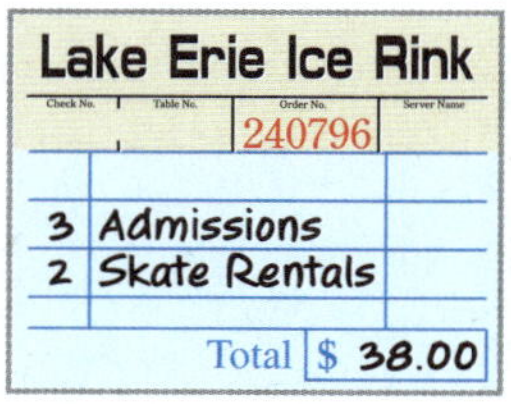

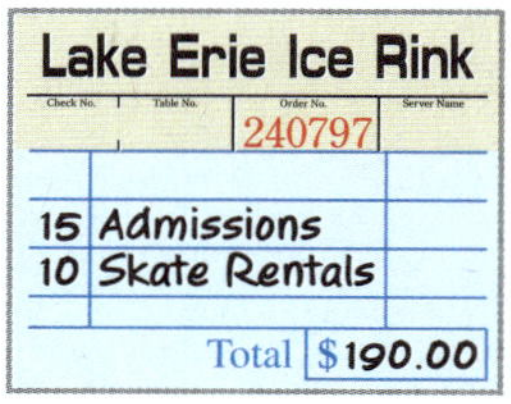

23. REASONING In a system of linear equations, one equation has a slope of 2 and the other equation has a slope of $-\frac{1}{3}$. How many solutions does the system have? Explain.

24. HOW DO YOU SEE IT? The graphs of three linear equations are shown.

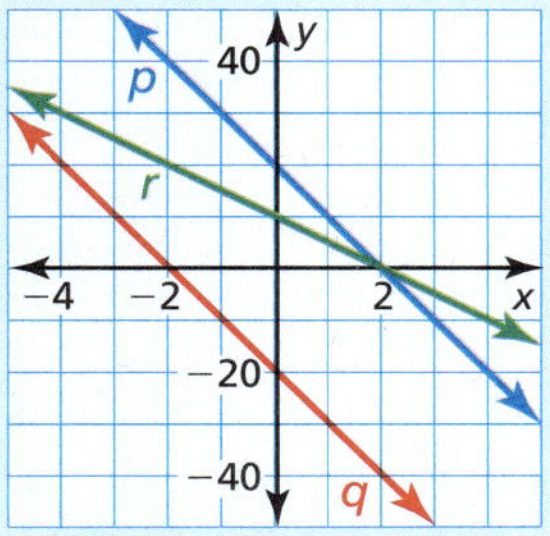

a. Name a pair of lines whose equations form a system that has one solution.

b. Name a pair of lines whose equations form a system that has no solution.

5 MTR **25. STRUCTURE** Write a system that contains $3x - 8y = 7$ and has (a) one solution, (b) no solution, and (c) infinitely many solutions.

26. B.E.S.T. TEST PREP Which system has no solution?

Ⓐ $y = -\frac{1}{5}x + 2$
$y = -\frac{3}{5}x + 2$

Ⓑ $y = -\frac{3}{5}x + 5$
$-\frac{3}{5}x + y = 6$

Ⓒ $-3x - 5y = -15$
$12x + 20y = 60$

Ⓓ $-\frac{3}{5}x = y - 4$
$-6x - 10y = 40$

4 MTR **27. DISCUSS MATHEMATICAL THINKING** Consider the system $y = ax + 4$ and $y = bx - 2$, where a and b are real numbers. Determine whether each statement is *always*, *sometimes*, or *never* true. Explain your reasoning.

a. The system has infinitely many solutions.

b. The system has no solution.

c. When $a > b$, the system has one solution.

28. THOUGHT PROVOKING
Write a system of three linear equations in two variables so that any two of the equations form a system that has exactly one solution, but the entire system has no solution.

REVIEW & REFRESH

WATCH

29. Use the graph to solve the system. Check your solution.

$y = \frac{1}{2}x - 1$
$y = 4x + 6$

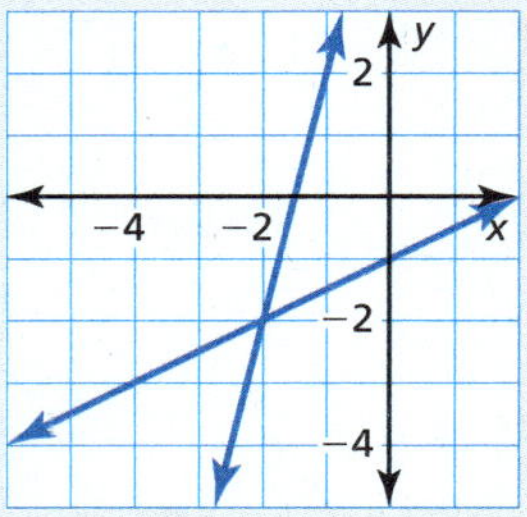

In Exercises 30 and 31, solve the equation. Check your solutions.

30. $|3x - 45| = 12x$

31. $|2x + 1| = |3x - 11|$

32. Solve the system by elimination. Check your solution.

$x + 3y = 1$
$5x + 6y = 14$

33. Solve the literal equation $y = 7x + 5xz - 8$ for x.

In Exercises 34 and 35, determine whether the equation represents a *linear* or *nonlinear* function. Explain.

34. $y = \frac{3}{x} + 7$

35. $y = 9x - \sqrt{16}$

In Exercises 36 and 37, use only the slopes and *y*-intercepts of the graphs of the equations to determine the number of solutions of the system. Explain your reasoning.

36. $y = -4x + 11$
$4x + y = -11$

37. $2x - 3y = -15$
$-\frac{2}{3}x + y = 5$

5 MTR **38.** **STRUCTURE** Without simplifying, identify the slope of the line given by the equation $y + 10 = -\frac{1}{4}(x - 8)$. Then identify one point on the line.

39. Evaluate $g(x) = 3 - \frac{5}{6}x$ when $x = 12$.

40. Solve the system by substitution. Check your solution.

$y = x - 4$
$-2x + y = 18$

7 MTR **41.** **MODELING REAL LIFE** The graph shows the distances d (in feet) that would break the women's long-jump record at your school. Write and interpret an inequality that represents the distances.

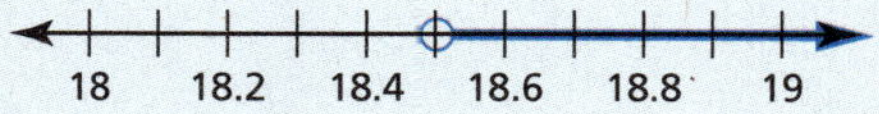

5.5 Solving Equations by Graphing

Learning Target: Solve equations by graphing.

Success Criteria:
- I can solve a linear equation by graphing.
- I can explain why the x-coordinate of a point where $y = f(x)$ and $y = g(x)$ intersect is a solution of $f(x) = g(x)$.

Algebraic Reasoning

MA.912.AR.2.1 Given a real-world context, write and solve one-variable multi-step linear equations.

MA.912.AR.2.2 Write a linear two-variable equation to represent the relationship between two quantities from a graph, a written description or a table of values within a mathematical or real-world context.

EXPLORE IT! Solving a Real-Life Problem

Work with a partner. Two autonomous underwater vehicles (AUVs) are mapping the ocean floor. One begins an ascent to the surface while the other begins a descent from the surface. The graph shows the depth of each AUV over time.

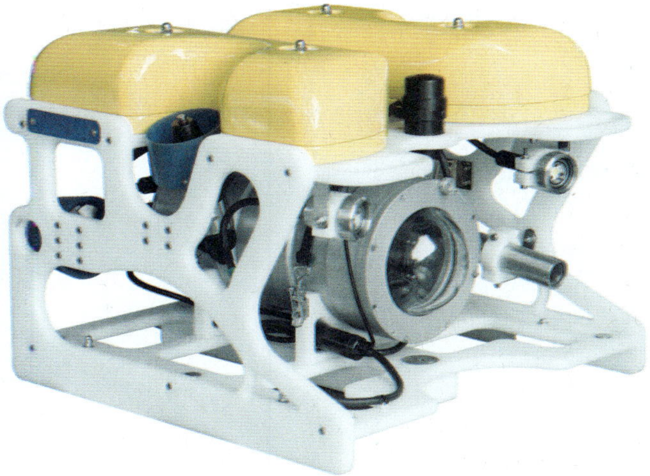

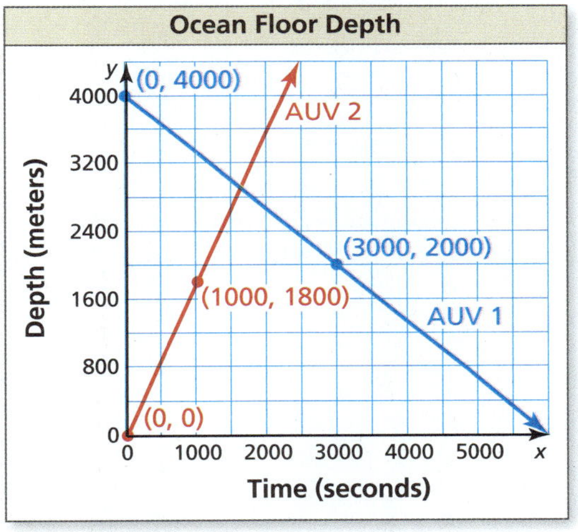

a. In the graph, does the line with a positive slope indicate that the AUV is ascending or descending? Why?

b. Approximate the intersection point and explain what it represents.

GO DIGITAL

c. What does each expression below represent in this situation? Explain your reasoning.

Expression 1: $-\frac{2}{3}x + 4000$

Expression 2: $\frac{9}{5}x$

d. What does the solution of $-\frac{2}{3}x + 4000 = \frac{9}{5}x$ represent? Solve the equation.

e. How can you find the solution of an equation in one variable using a graph? Explain why your method works.

1 MTR **ANALYZE A PROBLEM**

How does determining the number scales for the axes of the graph affect the approximation of the intersection point?

Solving Linear Equations by Graphing

STUDY TIP

You can think of this as solving the system of equations

$y = f(x)$

$y = g(x)$

by graphing.

KEY IDEA

Solving Equations by Graphing

Step 1 To solve the equation $f(x) = g(x)$, first write functions to represent each side of the equation.

$$f(x) = g(x)$$

$y = f(x)$ $y = g(x)$

Step 2 Graph the functions. The x-value of an intersection point of the graphs of the functions is a solution of the equation $f(x) = g(x)$.

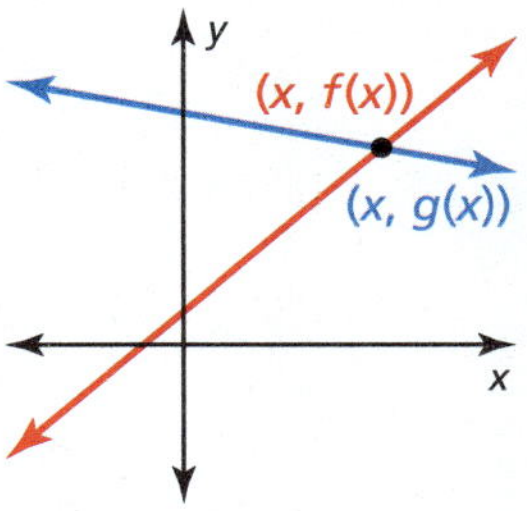

EXAMPLE 1 **Solving a Linear Equation by Graphing**

WATCH

Solve $-x + 1 = 2x - 5$ by graphing. Check your solution.

SOLUTION

Step 1 Write functions to represent each side of the original equation.

$$-x + 1 = 2x - 5$$

$y = -x + 1$ $y = 2x - 5$

Step 2 Graph the functions and find the intersection point.

The graphs intersect at $(2, -1)$.

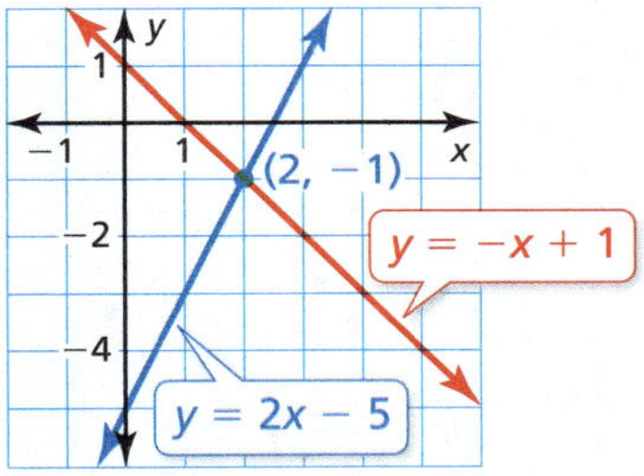

Check

$-x + 1 = 2x - 5$

$-(2) + 1 \stackrel{?}{=} 2(2) - 5$

$-1 = -1$ ✓

▶ So, the solution of the equation is $x = 2$.

SELF-ASSESSMENT

1 I don't understand yet. 2 I can do it with help. 3 I can do it on my own. 4 I can teach someone else.

Solve the equation by graphing. Check your solution.

1. $\frac{1}{2}x - 3 = 2x$

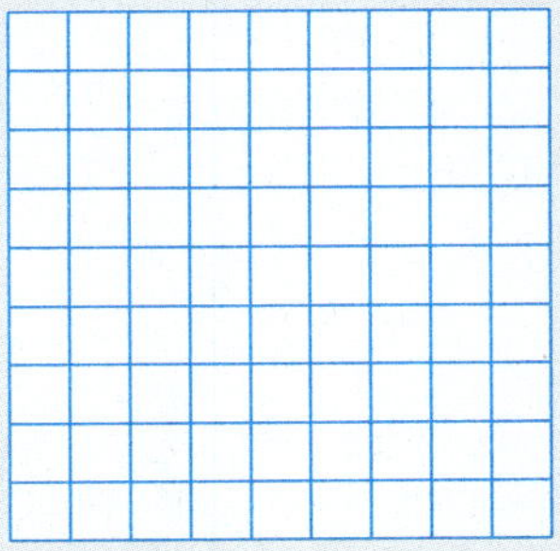

2. $-4 + 9x = -3x + 2$

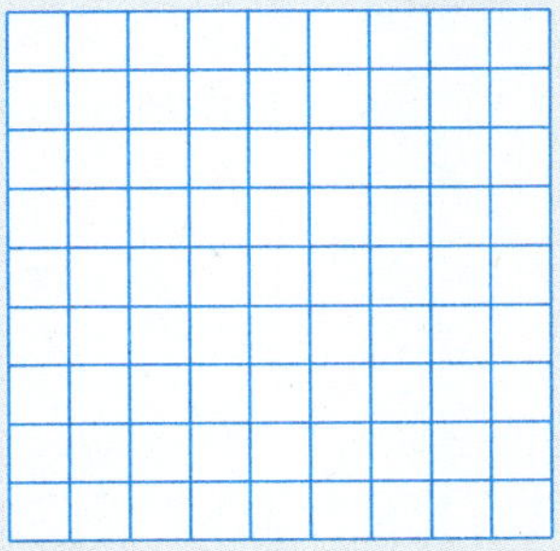

3. $-3x - 2.5 = x - 2.5$

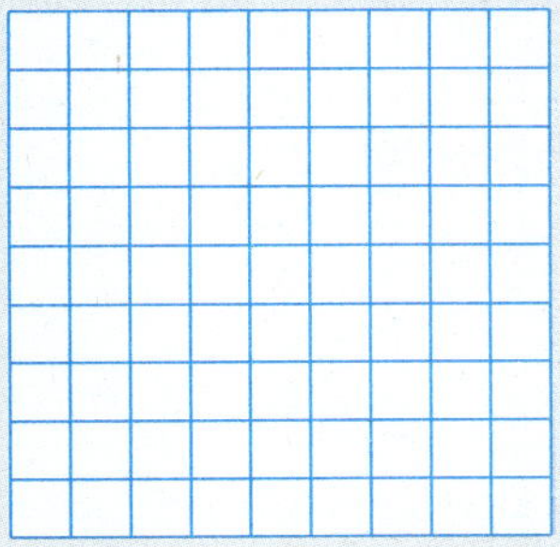

GO DIGITAL

SELF-ASSESSMENT

1 I don't understand yet. 2 I can do it with help. 3 I can do it on my own. 4 I can teach someone else.

4. **WRITING** Explain why the x-coordinates of the points where the graphs of the equations $y = f(x)$ and $y = g(x)$ intersect are the solutions of the equation $f(x) = g(x)$.

4 MTR 5. **DIFFERENT WORDS, SAME QUESTION** Which is different? Find "both" answers.

What is the solution of $x + 1 = 2x - 2$?	When are the values of $x + 1$ and $2x - 2$ equal?
At what point do the graphs of $y = x + 1$ and $y = 2x - 2$ intersect?	What is the x-value of the intersection point of the graphs of $y = x + 1$ and $y = 2x - 2$?

EXAMPLE 2 B.E.S.T. Test Prep: Determining the Number of Solutions by Graphing

WATCH

What is the solution of $x + 1 = \frac{1}{2}(2x + 8)$?

Ⓐ no solution

Ⓑ $x = 1$

Ⓒ $x = 4$

Ⓓ infinitely many solutions

SOLUTION

Step 1 Write functions to represent each side of the original equation.

$$x + 1 = \frac{1}{2}(2x + 8)$$

$y = x + 1$ $\quad$ $y = \frac{1}{2}(2x + 8)$

Step 2 Graph the functions.

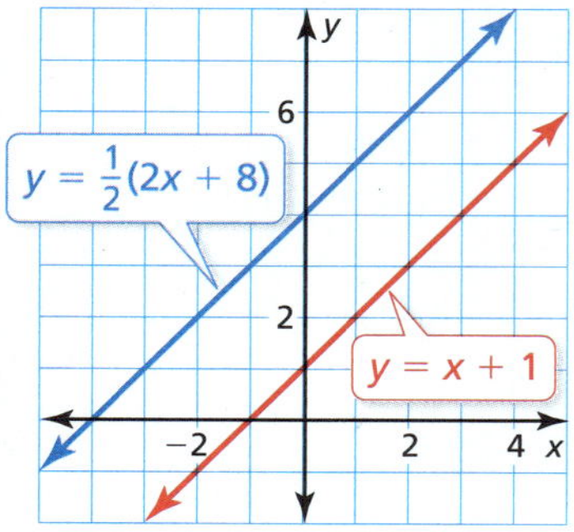

The lines have the same slope and different y-intercepts. So, the lines are parallel. Because parallel lines do not intersect, there is no point that is a solution of both linear equations. So, the original equation has no solution.

Check

$x + 1 = \frac{1}{2}(2x + 8)$

$x + 1 = x + 4$

$1 = 4$ ✗

The equation $1 = 4$ is never true.

So, the system has no solution. ✓

▶ So, the correct answer is Ⓐ.

GO DIGITAL

SELF-ASSESSMENT 1 I don't understand yet. 2 I can do it with help. 3 I can do it on my own. 4 I can teach someone else.

Solve the equation by graphing. Determine whether the equation has *one solution*, *no solution*, or *infinitely many solutions*.

6. $-\frac{1}{2}x + 1 = \frac{1}{2}(x - 2)$

7. $x + 3 = \frac{1}{3}(3x + 9)$

8. $-\frac{1}{4}(12x - 8) = -3x - 1$

4 MTR **9. WHICH ONE DOESN'T BELONG?** Which equation does not belong with the other three? Explain your reasoning.

$3(x + 1) = 3x + 3$ | $\frac{1}{3}(9x + 3) = \frac{1}{6}(18x + 6)$ | $\frac{1}{2}x + 1 = \frac{1}{2}(x + 4)$ | $2x + 1 = \frac{1}{2}(4x + 2)$

Solving Real-Life Problems

7 MTR **EXAMPLE 3** **Modeling Real Life** WATCH

You are studying two glaciers. In 2020, Glacier A had an area of about 40 square miles and Glacier B had an area of about 32 square miles. You estimate that Glacier A will melt at a rate of 2 square miles per decade and Glacier B will melt at a rate of 0.25 square mile per decade. In what year will the areas of the glaciers be the same?

SOLUTION

Step 1 Use a verbal model to write an equation that represents the problem. Let x be the number of decades after 2020. Then write functions to represent each side of the equation.

Glacier A: Area of Glacier A in 2020 − Area lost per decade after 2020 • Number of decades after 2020

=

Glacier B: Area of Glacier B in 2020 − Area lost per decade after 2020 • Number of decades after 2020

$$40 - 2x = 32 - 0.25x$$

$y = 40 - 2x$ $\qquad$ $y = 32 - 0.25x$

GO DIGITAL

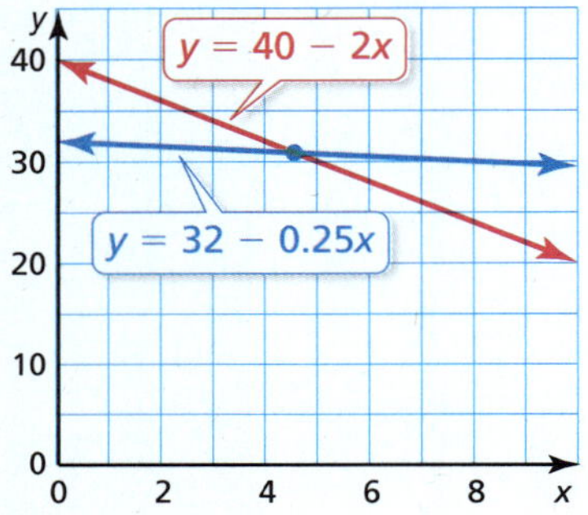

Step 2 Graph the functions. The graphs intersect between $x = 4$ and $x = 5$. Make a table using x-values between 4 and 5. Use an increment of 0.1.

x	4.1	4.2	4.3	4.4	4.5	4.6	4.7
$y = 40 - 2x$	31.8	31.6	31.4	31.2	31	30.8	30.6
$y = 32 - 0.25x$	30.98	30.95	30.93	30.9	30.88	30.85	30.83

Notice when $x = 4.5$, the area of Glacier A is greater than the area of Glacier B. When $x = 4.6$, the area of Glacier A is less than the area of Glacier B. So, the solution must be between $x = 4.5$ and $x = 4.6$. Make another table using x-values between 4.5 and 4.6. Use an increment of 0.01.

x	4.51	4.52	4.53	4.54	4.55	4.56	4.57	4.58
$y = 40 - 2x$	30.98	30.96	30.94	30.92	30.9	30.88	30.86	30.84
$y = 32 - 0.25x$	30.87	30.87	30.87	30.87	30.86	30.86	30.86	30.86

When $x = 4.57$, the corresponding y-values are about the same. So, the graphs intersect at about (4.57, 30.86).

▶ So, the areas of the glaciers will be the same after about 4.57 decades, or around the year 2066.

SELF-ASSESSMENT

1 I don't understand yet. 2 I can do it with help. 3 I can do it on my own. 4 I can teach someone else.

10. WHAT IF? In 2020, Glacier C had an area of about 30 square miles. You estimate that it will melt at a rate of 0.45 square mile per decade. In what year will the areas of Glacier A and Glacier C be the same?

5.5 Practice WITH CalcChat® AND CalcView®

In Exercises 1 and 2, use the graph to solve the equation. Check your solution.

1. $-3 = 4x + 1$

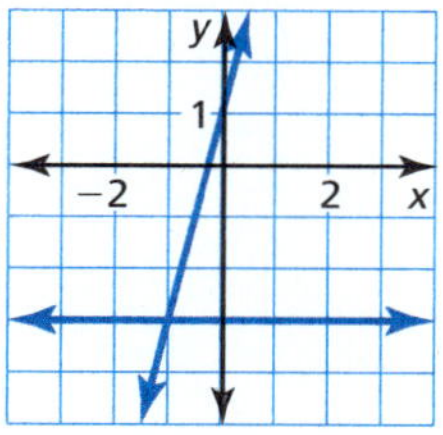

2. $-\frac{3}{2}x - 2 = -4x + 3$

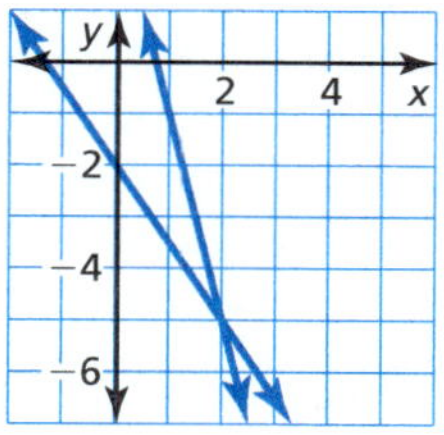

In Exercises 3–10, solve the equation by graphing. Check your solution. *(See Example 1.)*

3. $x + 4 = -x$

4. $-2x + 6 = 5x - 1$

▶ **5.** $\frac{1}{2}x - 2 = 9 - 5x$

6. $-5 + \frac{1}{4}x = 3x + 6$

7. $5x - 7 = 2(x + 1)$

8. $-6(x + 4) = -3x - 6$

9. $\frac{4}{5}x + \frac{7}{5} = 3x - 3$

10. $-x + 2.5 = 2x - 0.5$

In Exercises 11–18, solve the equation by graphing. Determine whether the equation has *one solution*, *no solution*, or *infinitely many solutions*. *(See Example 2.)*

▶ **11.** $-2x - 3 = 2(x - 2)$

12. $-4(2 - x) = 4x - 8$

13. $\frac{1}{2}(8x + 3) = 4x + \frac{3}{2}$

14. $-x - 5 = -\frac{1}{3}(3x + 5)$

15. $5(2x - 4) = -2x - 8$

16. $-3(x - 1) = \frac{1}{4}(x + 12)$

17. $-x + 5 - 2x = -(3x - 5)$

18. $2.2x - 6 = 0.55(4x + 6)$

GO DIGITAL

19. MTR 7 **MODELING REAL LIFE** You and your friend race underwater remote control vehicles to the bottom of a pool. You have a 2-foot head start, and your vehicle descends at a rate of 1.5 feet per second. Your friend's vehicle descends at a rate of 2 feet per second. Solve $-2x = -1.5x - 2$ by graphing to determine when you and your friend's vehicles are at the same depth. Justify your answer.

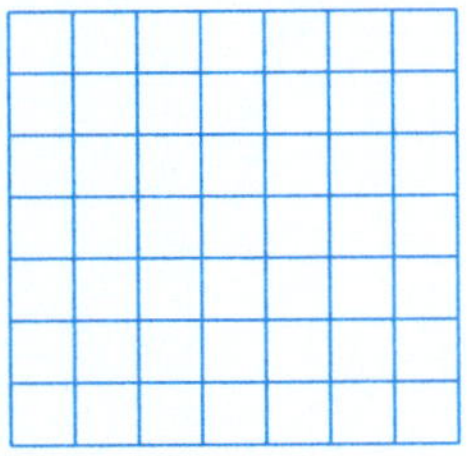

20. MTR 6 **ASSESS REASONABLENESS** Your friend says that when the pool in Exercise 19 is more than 8 feet deep, you will win the race. Is your friend's claim reasonable? Explain your reasoning.

21. MTR 5 **STRUCTURE** Use the graph to solve $2x + 4 = x - 1$. Check your solutions.

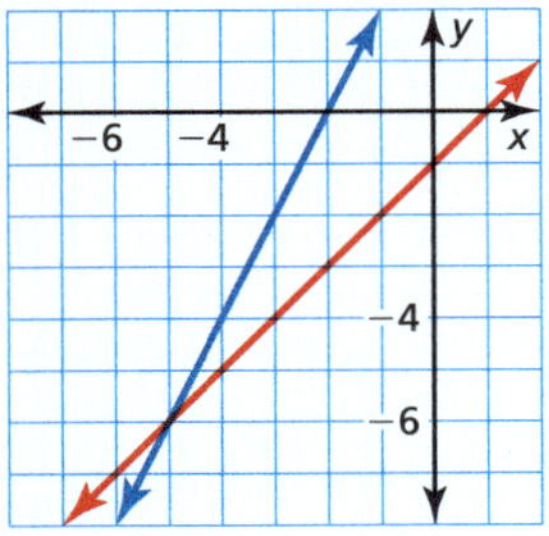

22. MTR 4 **ERROR ANALYSIS** Describe and correct the error in solving $-\frac{1}{3}x + 2 = \frac{2}{3}x + 5$ by graphing.

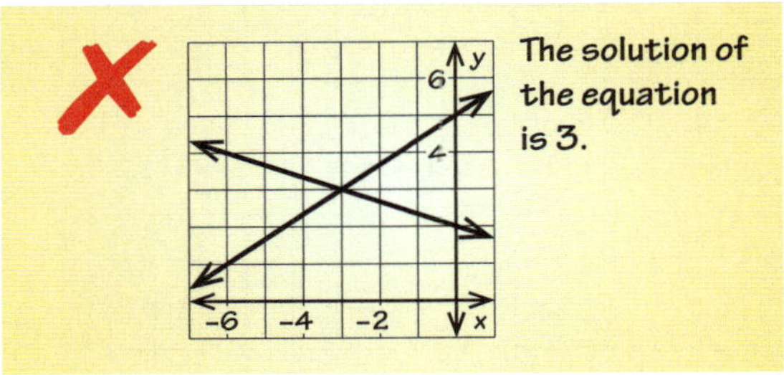

USING TOOLS **In Exercises 23 and 24, use technology to solve the equation.**

23. $0.7x + 0.5 = -0.2x - 1.3$

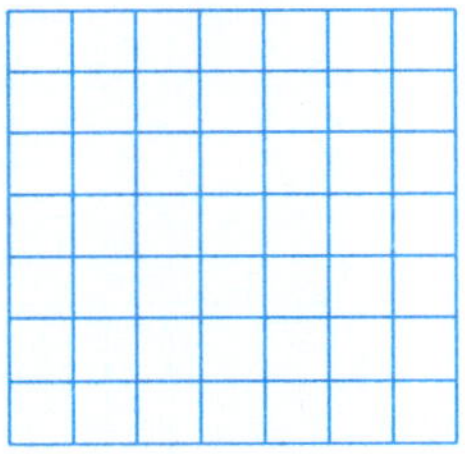

24. $2.1x + 0.6 = -1.4x + 6.9$

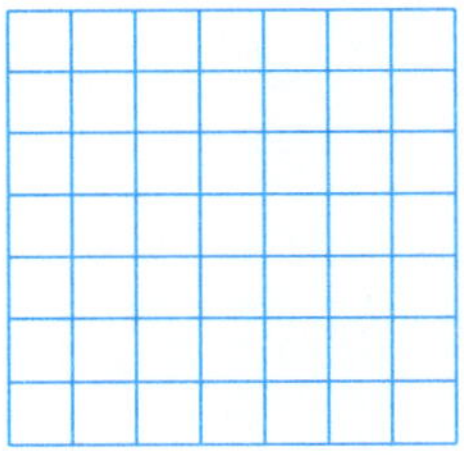

25. MTR 7 **MODELING REAL LIFE** There are about 34 million gallons of water in Reservoir A and about 38 million gallons in Reservoir B. During a drought, Reservoir A loses about 0.8 million gallons per month and Reservoir B loses about 1.1 million gallons per month. After how many months will the reservoirs contain the same amount of water? *(See Example 3.)*

26. MTR 7 **MODELING REAL LIFE** Your dog is 16 years old in dog years. Your cat is 28 years old in cat years. For every human year, your dog ages by 7 dog years and your cat ages by 4 cat years. In how many human years will both pets be the same age in their respective types of years?

27. **MAKING AN ARGUMENT** The graphs of $y = -x + 4$ and $y = 2x - 8$ intersect at (4, 0). Your friend says the solution of the equation $-x + 4 = 2x - 8$ is (4, 0). Is your friend correct? Explain.

28. **HOW DO YOU SEE IT?** The graph shows the total revenue and expenses of a company x years after it opens for business.

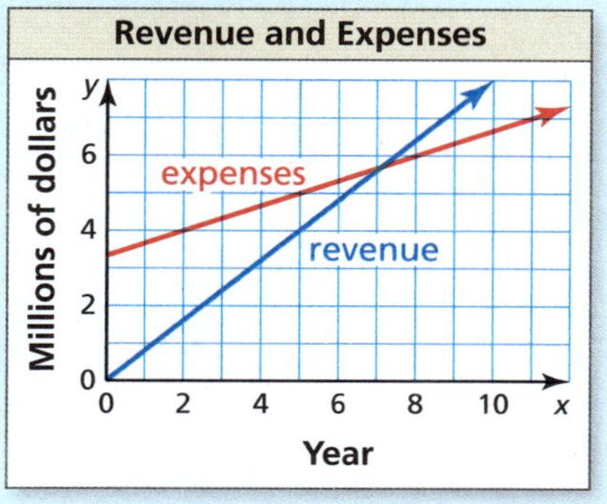

a. Estimate the point of intersection of the graphs.

b. Interpret your answer in part (a).

29. **OPEN-ENDED** Find values for m and b so that the solution of $mx + b = -2x - 1$ is $x = -3$.

30. **REASONING** Determine the sign of the solution of $ax + b = cx + d$ in each situation. Justify your reasoning with a graph.

a. $0 < b < d$ and $a < c$

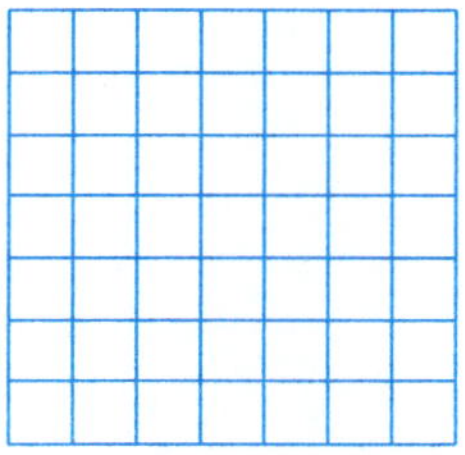

b. $d < b < 0$ and $a < c$

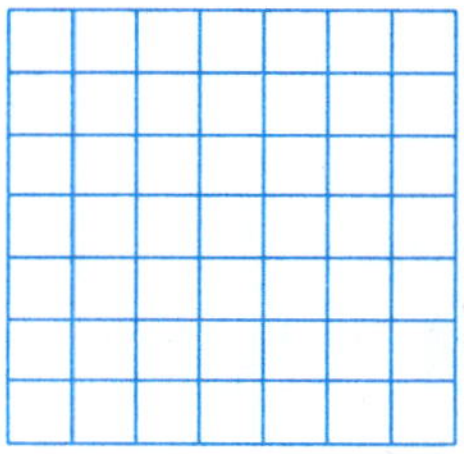

31. **DIG DEEPER** You and your friend race across a 200-meter field. Your friend has a 50-meter head start. The equations shown represent you and your friend's distances d (in meters) from the starting line after t seconds.

You: $d = 5t$

Your friend: $d = \frac{10}{3}t + 50$

a. How long does it take you to catch up to your friend?

b. Who finishes the race first? How much sooner does this person finish? Explain.

32. **THOUGHT PROVOKING** Explain how you can use a graph to solve $\frac{1}{2}x + 4 \leq -\frac{1}{4}x + 1$.

REVIEW & REFRESH

WATCH

In Exercises 33 and 34, use the graphs of *f* and *g* to describe the transformation from the graph of *f* to the graph of *g*.

33. $f(x) = x - 5;\ g(x) = f(x) + 2$

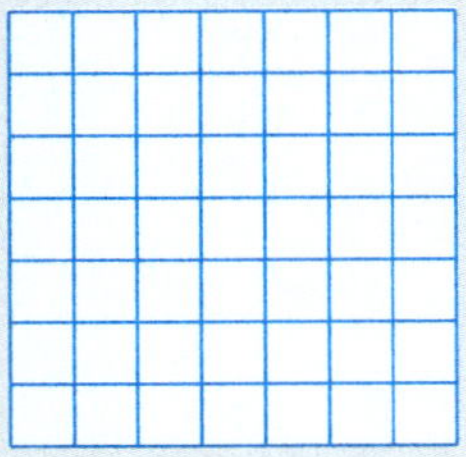

34. $f(x) = \frac{1}{2}x - 2;\ g(x) = f(x - 1)$

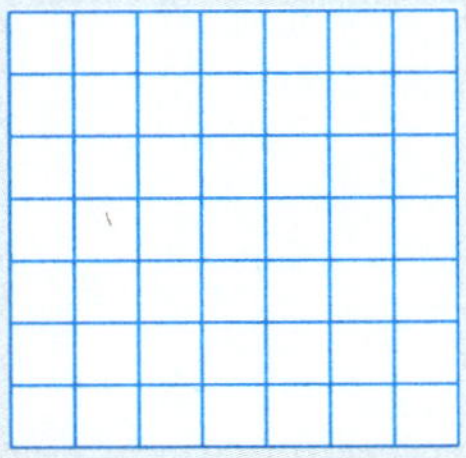

35. OPEN-ENDED Give an example of a real-life data set that shows a negative correlation.

36. Use the graph to solve $3x + 8 = x - 4$. Check your solutions.

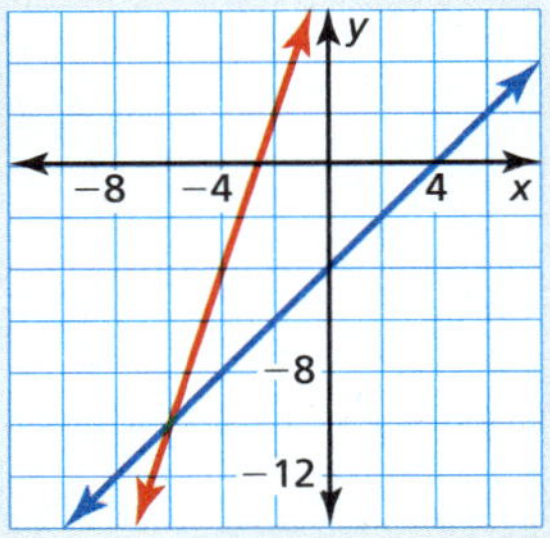

37. Tell whether $n = -5$ is a solution of the inequality $14 \geq -2n + 4$.

In Exercises 38 and 39, graph the inequality.

38. $n \geq 9$

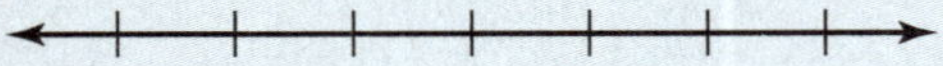

39. $c < -6$

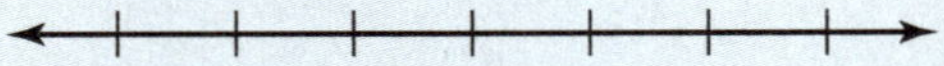

7 MTR **40. MODELING REAL LIFE** You sell small and large candles at a crafts fair. You collect \$144 selling a total of 28 candles. How many of each type of candle did you sell?

In Exercises 41–44, solve the system using any method. Explain your choice of method.

41. $y = -x + 8$
$6x - 2y = 16$

42. $-3x - 3y = 4$
$1.5x + 1.5y = -2$

43. $2x + 5y = -9$
$-2x - y = 17$

44. $y = \frac{3}{2}x + 1$
$y = -\frac{1}{4}x + 8$

45. Solve $3x - 1 = -x + 7$ by graphing. Determine whether the equation has *one solution*, *no solution*, or *infinitely many solutions*.

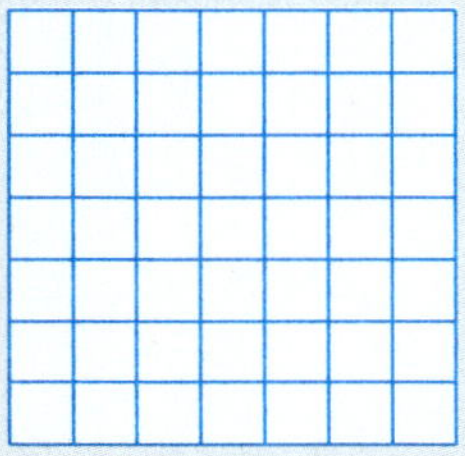

46. Write an equation in point-slope form of the line that passes through $(9, -2)$ and has a slope of $-\frac{2}{3}$.

47. Determine whether the equation $y = 2x(x - 5)$ represents a *linear* or *nonlinear* function. Explain.

5.6 Graphing Linear Inequalities in Two Variables

Learning Target: Graph linear inequalities in two variables.

Success Criteria:
- I can determine whether an ordered pair is a solution of a linear inequality in two variables.
- I can graph linear inequalities in two variables.
- I can interpret solutions of a linear inequality in two variables in a real-life situation.

Algebraic Reasoning

MA.912.AR.2.7 Write two-variable linear inequalities to represent relationships between quantities from a graph or a written description within a mathematical or real-world context.

MA.912.AR.2.8 Given a mathematical or real-world context, graph the solution set to a two-variable linear inequality.

EXPLORE IT! Graphing a Linear Inequality in Two Variables

ANALYZE A PROBLEM (1 MTR)

If you used only sand, about how much could you purchase? If you used only gravel, about how much could you purchase? What are the advantages and disadvantages of each for a dog pen?

Work with a partner. You have \$60 to spend on sand and gravel to make a pen for your dog.

a. Use an inequality to represent the situation.

b. Identify several solutions (x, y) of the inequality. Plot your solutions in the coordinate plane.

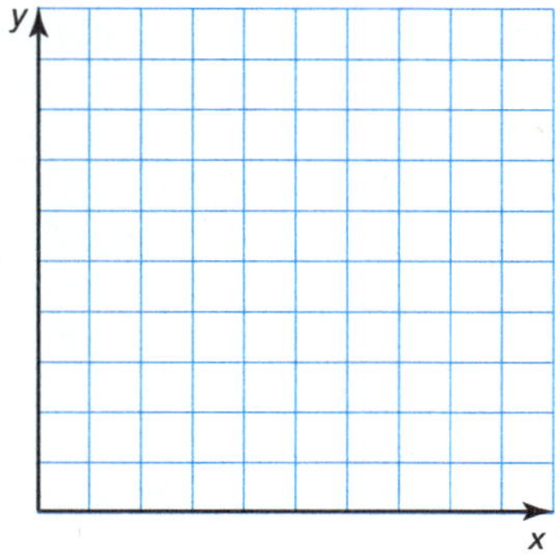

c. Graph every possible solution of the inequality in the coordinate plane. Explain your method.

d. Use technology to graph the inequality. Compare the result with your graph in part (b).

e. Use technology to graph each inequality.

i. $y < x + 1.5$ **ii.** $y \geq \frac{1}{4}x - 3$ **iii.** $x + y > 7$ **iv.** $4x + 2y \leq 9$

f. Explain how to graph a linear inequality in two variables without using technology.

GO DIGITAL

Vocabulary

AZ VOCAB

linear inequality in two variables, *p. 444*
solution of a linear inequality in two variables, *p. 444*
graph of a linear inequality, *p. 445*
half-planes, *p. 445*

Linear Inequalities

A **linear inequality in two variables**, x and y, can be written in one of the following forms where a, b, and c are real numbers.

$$ax + by < c \qquad ax + by \le c$$

$$ax + by > c \qquad ax + by \ge c$$

A **solution of a linear inequality in two variables** is an ordered pair (x, y) that makes the inequality true.

EXAMPLE 1 Checking Solutions

WATCH

Tell whether the ordered pair is a solution of the inequality.

a. $2x + y < -3;\ (-1, 9)$

b. $x - 3y \ge 8;\ (2, -2)$

SOLUTION

a. $2x + y < -3$ — Write the inequality.

$2(-1) + 9 \overset{?}{<} -3$ — Substitute -1 for x and 9 for y.

$7 \not< -3$ ✗ — Simplify. 7 is *not* less than -3.

▶ So, $(-1, 9)$ is *not* a solution of the inequality.

b. $x - 3y \ge 8$ — Write the inequality.

$2 - 3(-2) \overset{?}{\ge} 8$ — Substitute 2 for x and -2 for y.

$8 \ge 8$ ✓ — Simplify. 8 is equal to 8.

▶ So, $(2, -2)$ is a solution of the inequality.

SELF-ASSESSMENT

1 I don't understand yet. 2 I can do it with help. 3 I can do it on my own. 4 I can teach someone else.

Tell whether the ordered pair is a solution of the inequality.

1. $x + y > 0;\ (-2, 2)$

2. $4x - y \ge 5;\ (0, 0)$

3. $5x - 2y \le -1;\ (-4, -1)$

4. $-2x - 3y < 15;\ (5.5, -7)$

GO DIGITAL

Graphing Linear Inequalities in Two Variables

The **graph of a linear inequality** in two variables shows all the solutions of the inequality in a coordinate plane. A dashed boundary line means that points on the line are *not* solutions. A solid boundary line means that points on the line are solutions.

All solutions of $y < 2x$ lie on one side of the boundary line $y = 2x$.

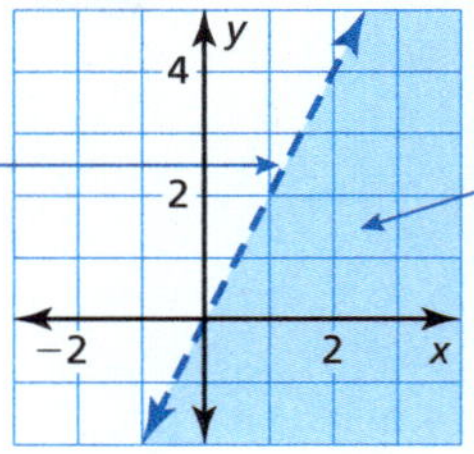

The boundary line divides the coordinate plane into two **half-planes**. The shaded half-plane is the graph of $y < 2x$.

KEY IDEA

Graphing a Linear Inequality in Two Variables

Step 1 Graph the boundary line for the inequality. Use a dashed line for < or >. Use a solid line for ≤ or ≥.

Step 2 Test a point that is not on the boundary line to determine whether it is a solution of the inequality.

Step 3 When the test point is a solution, shade the half-plane that contains the point. When the test point is *not* a solution, shade the half-plane that does *not* contain the point.

EXAMPLE 2 Graphing a Linear Inequality in Two Variables

Graph $y \leq 2$ in a coordinate plane.

WATCH

SOLUTION

Step 1 Graph $y = 2$. Use a solid line because the inequality symbol is ≤.

Step 2 Test (0, 0).

$y \leq 2$ Write the inequality.

$0 \leq 2$ ✓ Substitute.

Step 3 Because (0, 0) is a solution, shade the half-plane that contains (0, 0).

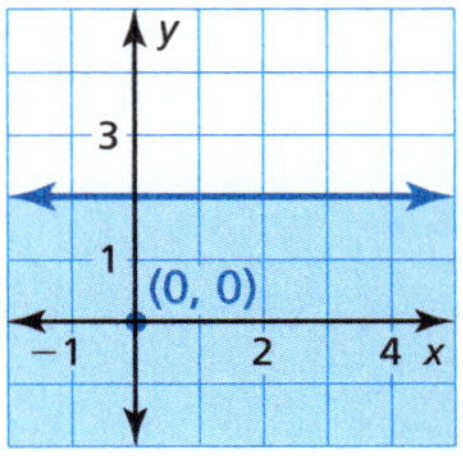

STUDY TIP

It is often convenient to use the origin as a test point. However, you must choose a different test point when the origin is on the boundary line.

GO DIGITAL

EXAMPLE 3 Graphing a Linear Inequality in Two Variables

WATCH

Graph $-x + 2y > 2$ in a coordinate plane.

SOLUTION

Step 1 Graph $-x + 2y = 2$, or $y = \frac{1}{2}x + 1$. Use a dashed line because the inequality symbol is >.

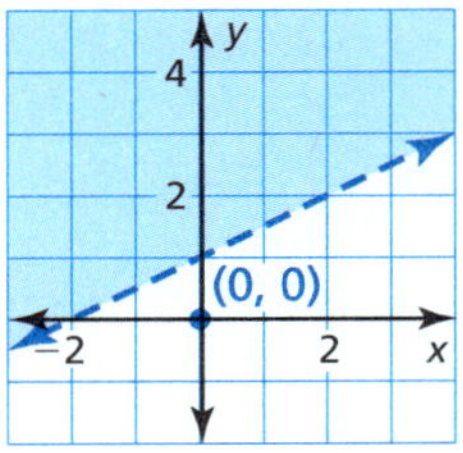

Step 2 Test (0, 0).

$$-x + 2y > 2 \qquad \text{Write the inequality.}$$

$$-(0) + 2(0) \stackrel{?}{>} 2 \qquad \text{Substitute.}$$

$$0 \not> 2 \ ✗ \qquad \text{Simplify.}$$

Step 3 Because (0, 0) is *not* a solution, shade the half-plane that does *not* contain (0, 0).

Check

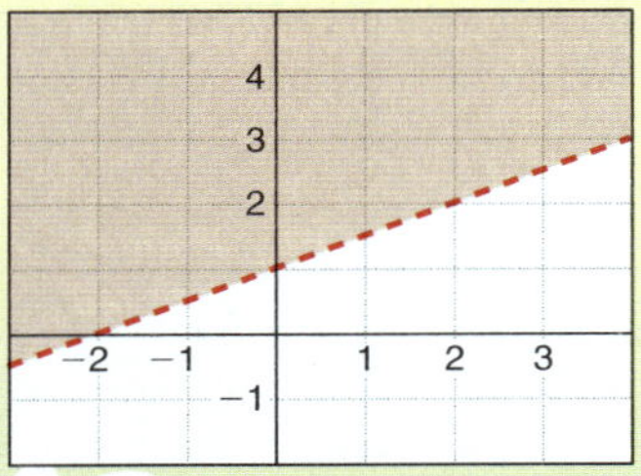

SELF-ASSESSMENT

1 I don't understand yet. 2 I can do it with help. 3 I can do it on my own. 4 I can teach someone else.

Graph the inequality in a coordinate plane.

5. $y > -1$

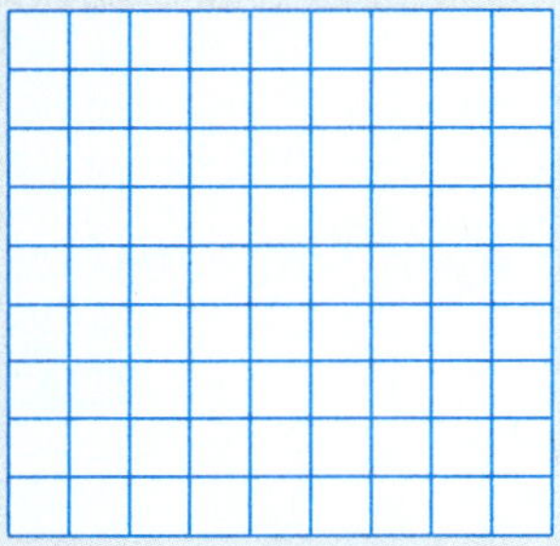

6. $x \leq -4$

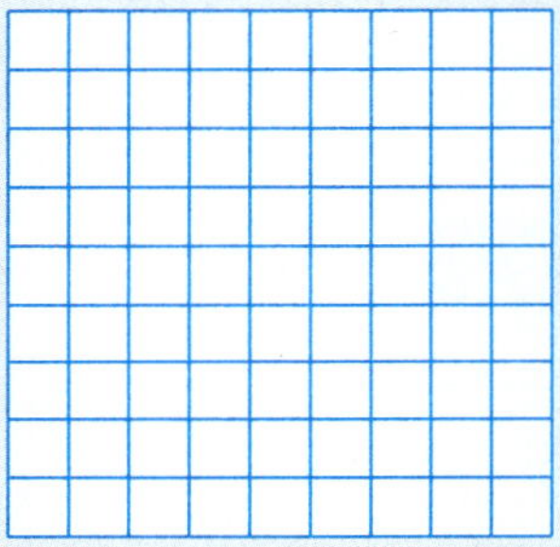

7. $x + y \leq -4$

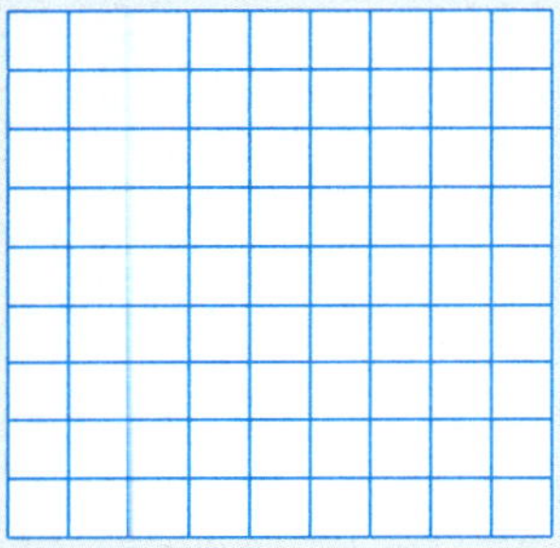

8. $x - 2y < 0$

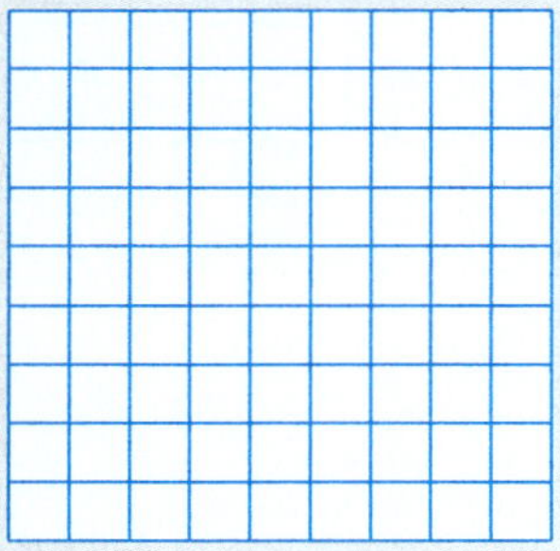

9. $x \leq 0.75y - 3$

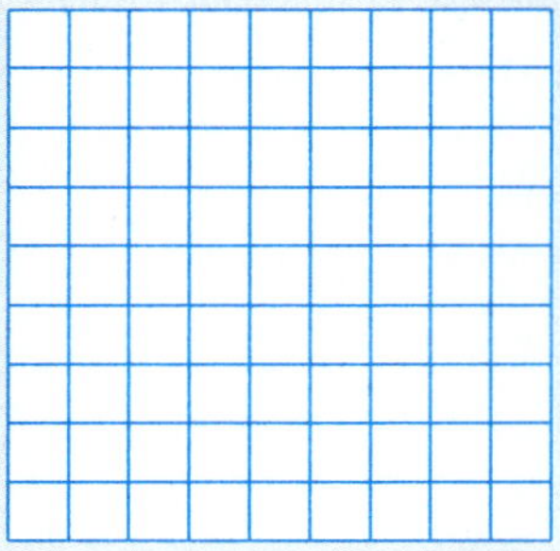

10. $\frac{3}{4} \geq -2x + \frac{1}{2}y$

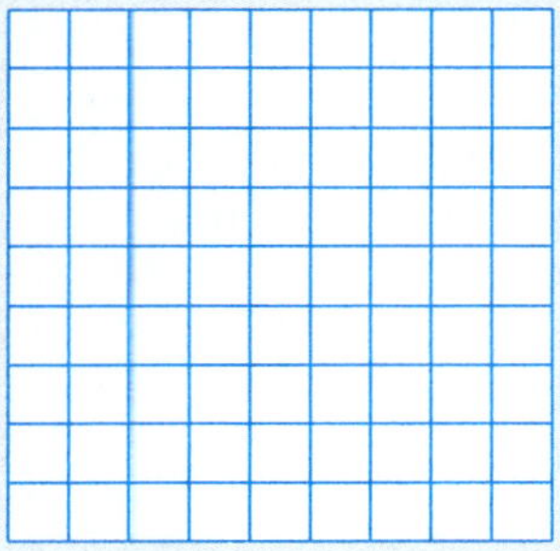

11. WRITING When determining which half-plane to shade in the graph of an inequality in two variables, why is it important to test a point that is not on the boundary line?

Solving Real-Life Problems

7 MTR **EXAMPLE 4** **Modeling Real Life** WATCH

You can spend at most \$10 on grapes and apples for a fruit salad. Grapes cost \$2.50 per pound, and apples cost \$1 per pound. Write and graph an inequality that represents the amounts of grapes and apples you can buy. Identify and interpret two solutions of the inequality.

SOLUTION

1. **Understand the Problem** You know the most that you can spend and the prices per pound for grapes and apples. You are asked to write and graph an inequality and then identify and interpret two solutions.
2. **Make a Plan** Use a verbal model to write an inequality that represents the problem. Then graph the inequality. Use the graph to identify two solutions. Then interpret the solutions.
3. **Solve and Check**

Verbal Model Cost per pound of grapes • Pounds of grapes + Cost per pound of apples • Pounds of apples ≤ Amount you can spend

Variables Let x be pounds of grapes and y be pounds of apples.

Inequality $2.50 \cdot x + 1 \cdot y \leq 10$

Step 1 Graph $2.5x + y = 10$, or $y = -2.5x + 10$. Use a solid line because the inequality symbol is ≤. Restrict the graph to the first quadrant because negative values do not make sense in this real-life context.

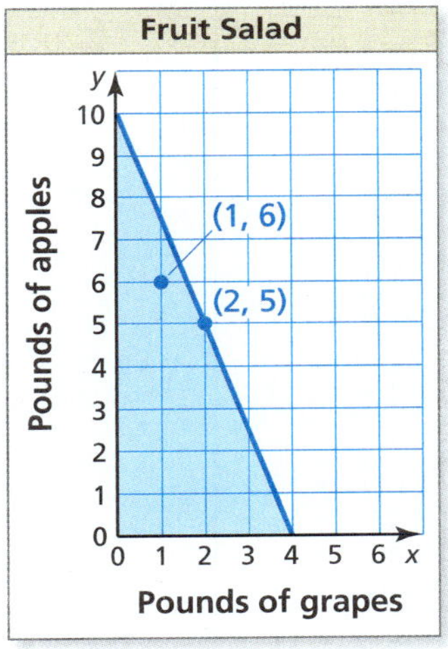

Step 2 Test (0, 0).

$2.5x + y \leq 10$ Write the inequality.

$2.5(0) + 0 \stackrel{?}{\leq} 10$ Substitute.

$0 \leq 10$ ✓ Simplify.

Step 3 Because (0, 0) is a solution, shade the half-plane that contains (0, 0).

▶ One possible solution is (1, 6) because it lies in the shaded half-plane. Another possible solution is (2, 5) because it lies on the solid line. So, two possible combinations of grapes and apples that you can buy are 1 pound of grapes and 6 pounds of apples, or 2 pounds of grapes and 5 pounds of apples.

Check Check your solutions by substituting them into the original inequality.

$2.5x + y \leq 10$	$2.5x + y \leq 10$
$2.5(1) + 6 \stackrel{?}{\leq} 10$	$2.5(2) + 5 \stackrel{?}{\leq} 10$
$8.5 \leq 10$ ✓	$10 \leq 10$ ✓

GO DIGITAL

SELF-ASSESSMENT

1 I don't understand yet. 2 I can do it with help. 3 I can do it on my own. 4 I can teach someone else.

12. You can spend at most \$12 on red peppers and tomatoes for salsa. Red peppers cost \$4 per pound, and tomatoes cost \$3 per pound. Write and graph an inequality that represents the amounts of red peppers and tomatoes you can buy. Identify and interpret two solutions of the inequality.

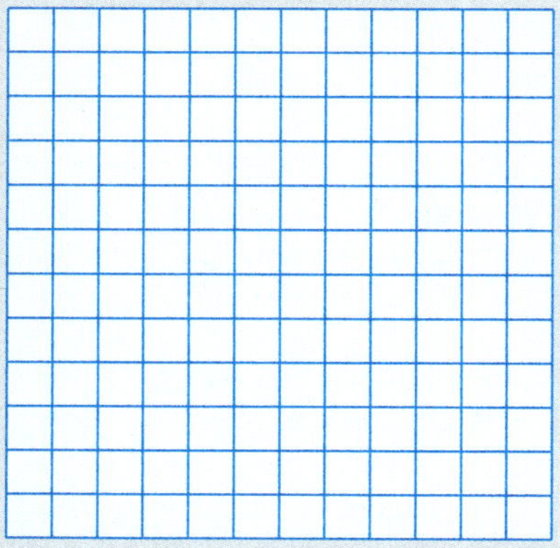

5.6 Practice WITH CalcChat® AND CalcView®

In Exercises 1–8, tell whether the ordered pair is a solution of the inequality. *(See Example 1.)*

1. $x + y < 7$; $(2, 3)$

2. $x - y \leq 0$; $(5, 4)$

▶**3.** $x + 3y \geq -2$; $(-9, 1)$

4. $8x + y > -6$; $(-1, 2)$

5. $-6x + 4y \leq 6$; $(-3, -3)$

6. $3x - 5y \geq 0.5$; $(-1.5, -1)$

7. $y + 1 < -\frac{1}{6}(x + 6)$; $\left(-8, -\frac{2}{3}\right)$

8. $y + 2 < 2(4x - 2)$; $\left(\frac{1}{4}, -5\right)$

In Exercises 9–14, tell whether the ordered pair is a solution of the inequality whose graph is shown.

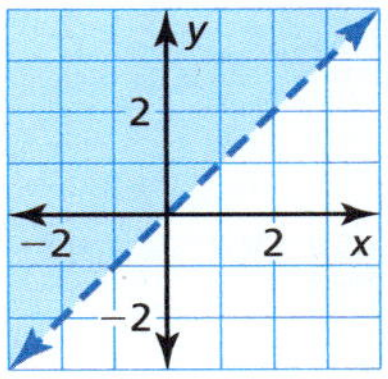

9. $(0, -1)$

10. $(-1, 3)$

11. $(1, 4)$

12. $(0, 0)$

13. $(3, 3)$

14. $\left(2, 1\frac{1}{2}\right)$

In Exercises 15–20, graph the inequality in a coordinate plane. *(See Example 2.)*

15. $y \leq 5$

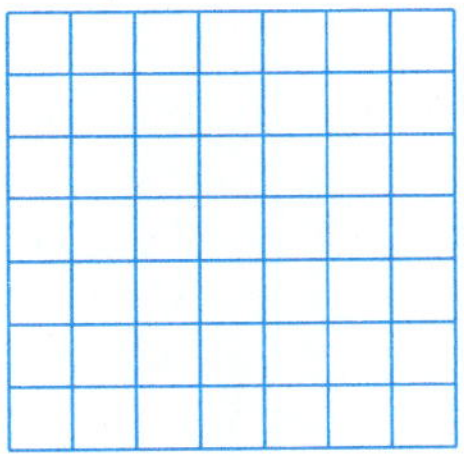

16. $y > 6$

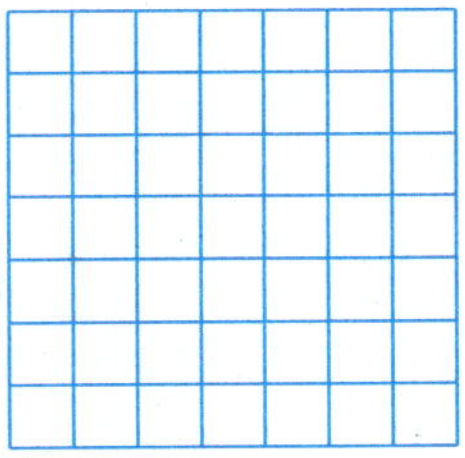

▶**17.** $x < 2$

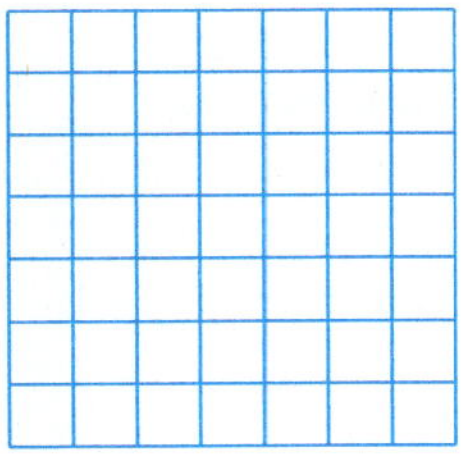

18. $x \geq -3$

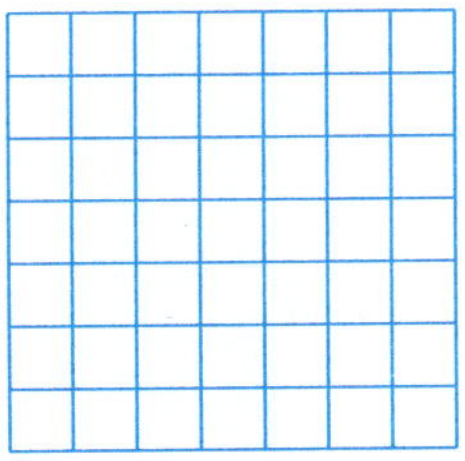

19. $y > -3\frac{1}{2}$

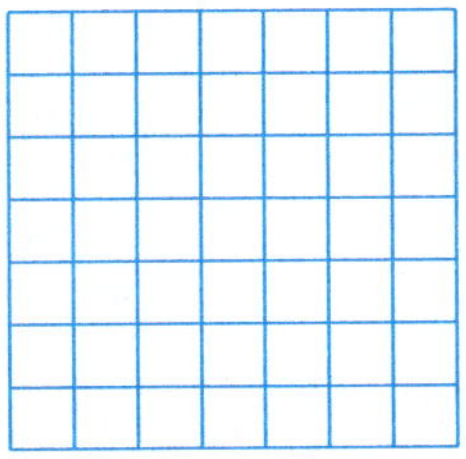

20. $x < 7.5$

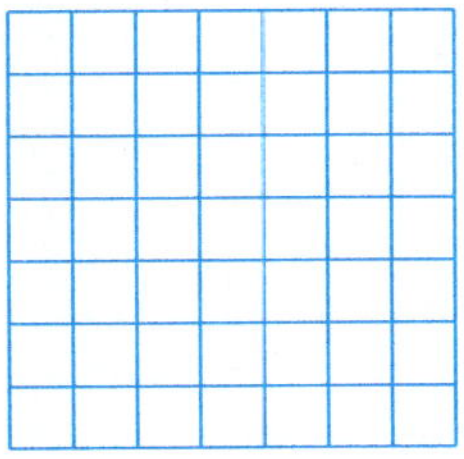

GO DIGITAL

In Exercises 21–28, graph the inequality in a coordinate plane. *(See Example 3.)*

21. $y > -2x - 4$

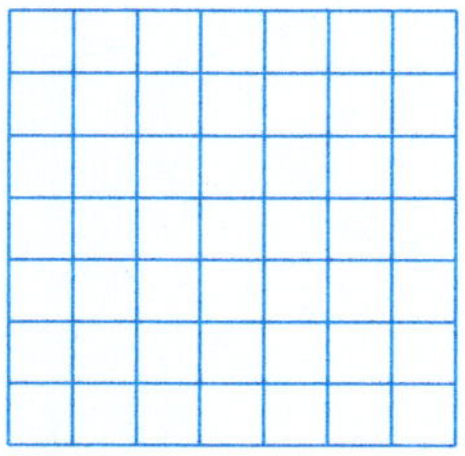

22. $y \geq -x - 1$

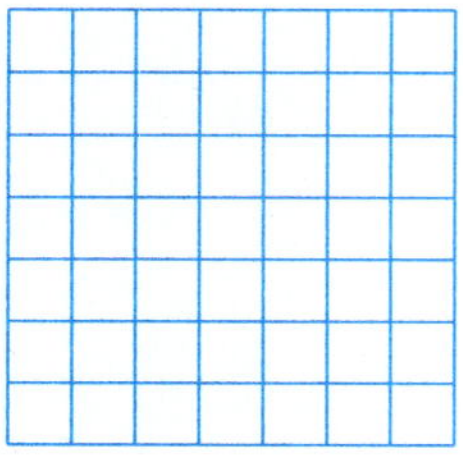

23. $y - 1 < 4(x - 2)$

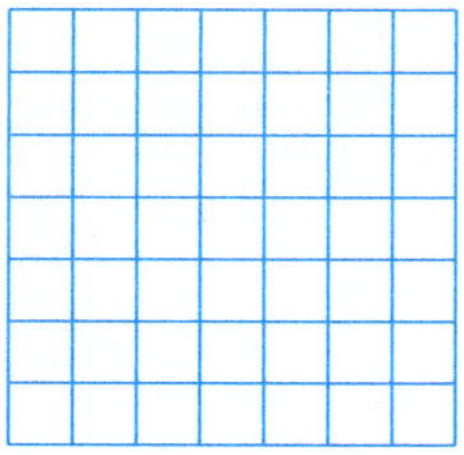

24. $y + 11 \leq 3(x + 2)$

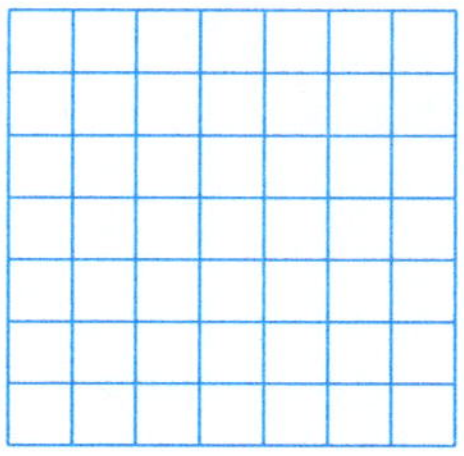

▶**25.** $5x - 2y \leq 6$

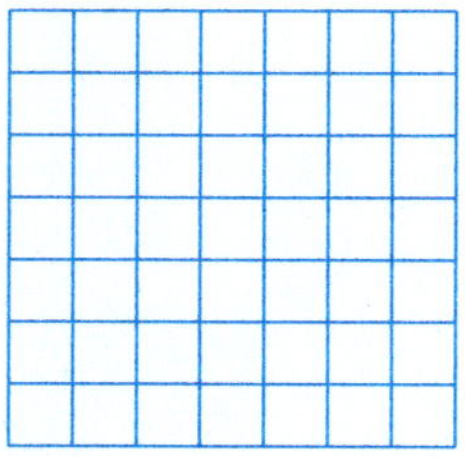

26. $-x + 4y > -12$

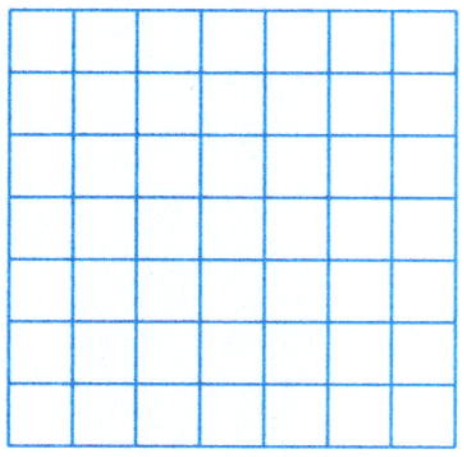

27. $-4.5y \geq 27x$

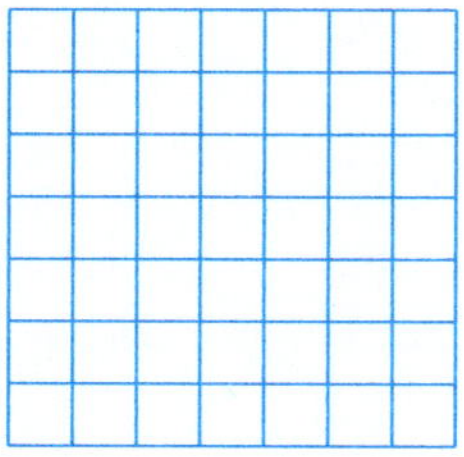

28. $\frac{4}{3}x + y < 0$

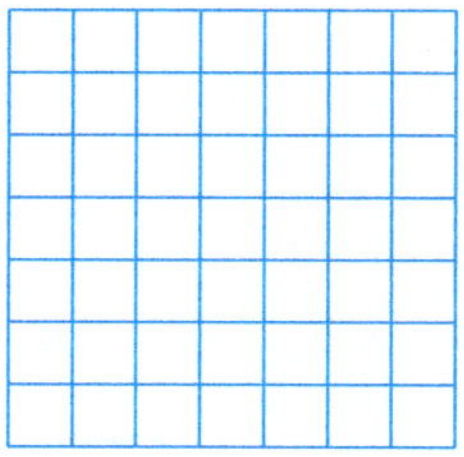

4 MTR **ERROR ANALYSIS** **In Exercises 29 and 30, describe and correct the error in graphing the inequality.**

29. $y < -x + 1$

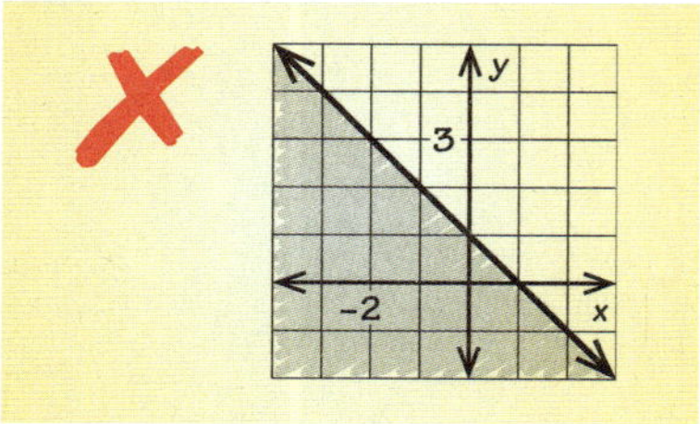

30. $y \leq 3x - 2$

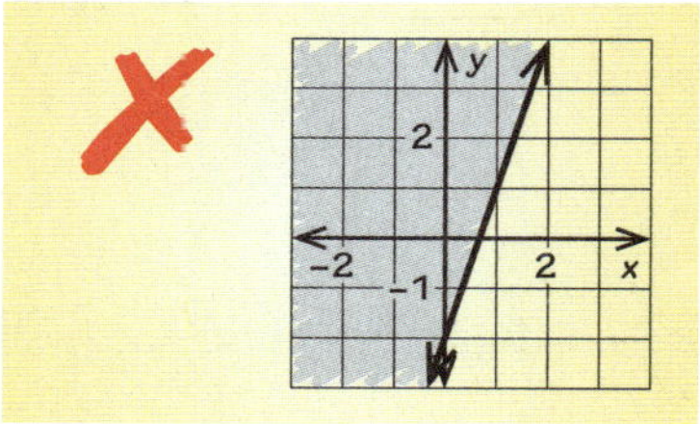

31. 7 MTR **MODELING REAL LIFE** A carpenter has at most \$250 to spend on lumber. The inequality $8x + 12y \leq 250$ represents the numbers x of 2-by-8 boards and the numbers y of 4-by-4 boards the carpenter can buy. Can the carpenter buy twelve 2-by-8 boards and fourteen 4-by-4 boards? Explain.

7 MTR **32.** **MODELING REAL LIFE** The inequality $3x + 2y \geq 93$ represents the numbers x of multiple-choice questions and the numbers y of matching questions you can answer correctly to receive an A on a test. You answer 20 multiple-choice questions and 18 matching questions correctly. Do you receive an A on the test? Explain.

In Exercises 33 and 34, write an inequality that represents the graph.

33.

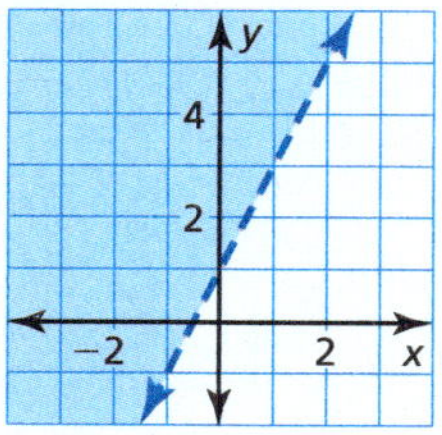

34.

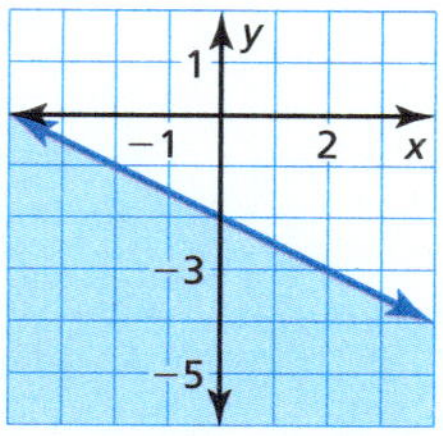

35. 7 MTR **MODELING REAL LIFE** You have at most \$25 to spend on in-app purchases for a game. Sets of extra lives cost \$1 each, and bags of gold cost \$5 each. Write and graph an inequality that represents the numbers of each item you can buy. Identify and interpret two solutions of the inequality. *(See Example 4.)*

36. **MODELING REAL LIFE** The total ticket sales from a school play must be at least \$1500 to cover the expenses of producing the play. Student tickets cost \$6, and adult tickets cost \$10. Write and graph an inequality that represents how many adult and student tickets the club must sell. Identify and interpret two solutions of the inequality.

37. **STRUCTURE** Complete the inequality y ____ $mx + b$, where $b > 0$, so that the graph of the inequality has a dashed boundary line and $(0, 0)$ is a solution.

38. **HOW DO YOU SEE IT?**
Match each inequality with its graph.

a. $3x - 2y \leq 6$ **c.** $3x - 2y > 6$

b. $3x - 2y < 6$ **d.** $3x - 2y \geq 6$

A.

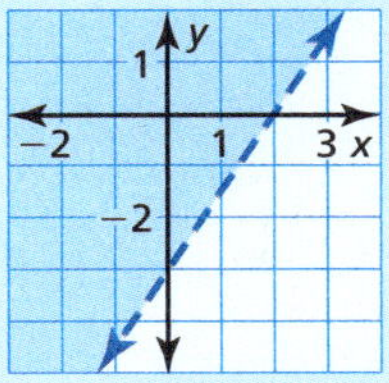

C.

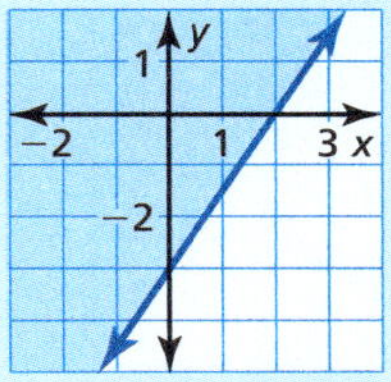

B.

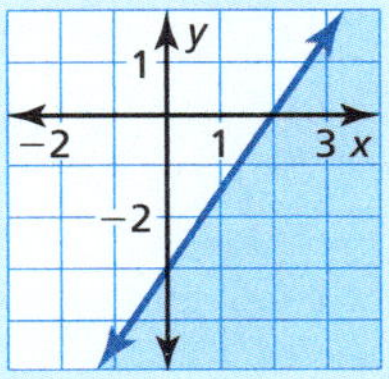

D.

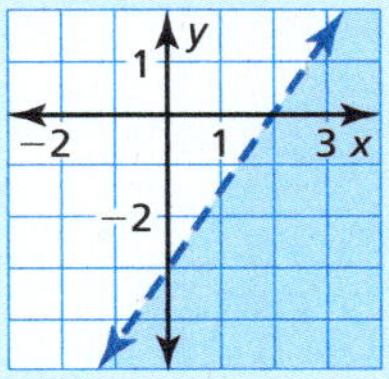

39. **MAKING AN ARGUMENT** Your friend says you cannot use $(0, 0)$ as the test point when graphing an inequality whose boundary line represents a proportional relationship. Is your friend correct? Explain.

40. **THOUGHT PROVOKING**
Write a linear inequality in two variables that has the following properties.

- $(0, 0)$, $(0, -1)$, and $(0, 1)$ are *not* solutions.
- $(1, 1)$, $(3, -1)$, and $(-1, 3)$ are solutions.

REASONING In Exercises 41 and 42, write and graph an inequality whose graph is described by the given information.

41.
- $(2, 5)$ and $(-3, -5)$ lie on the boundary line.
- $(6, 5)$ and $(-2, -3)$ are solutions.

42.
- $(-7, -16)$ and $(1, 8)$ lie on the boundary line.
- $(-7, 0)$ and $(3, 14)$ are *not* solutions.

43. **DIG DEEPER** Two large boxes and three small boxes weigh 270 pounds. One large box and four small boxes weigh 235 pounds.

a. The weight limit on an elevator is 2000 pounds. Write and graph an inequality that represents the numbers of large and small boxes a 200-pound delivery person can take on the elevator.

b. Explain why some solutions of the inequality may not be practical in real life.

REVIEW & REFRESH

44. Solve the system using any method. Explain your choice of method.

$y = \frac{4}{5}x - 2$

$-8x + 10y = -20$

45. Approximate when the function is positive, negative, increasing, or decreasing. Then describe the end behavior of the function.

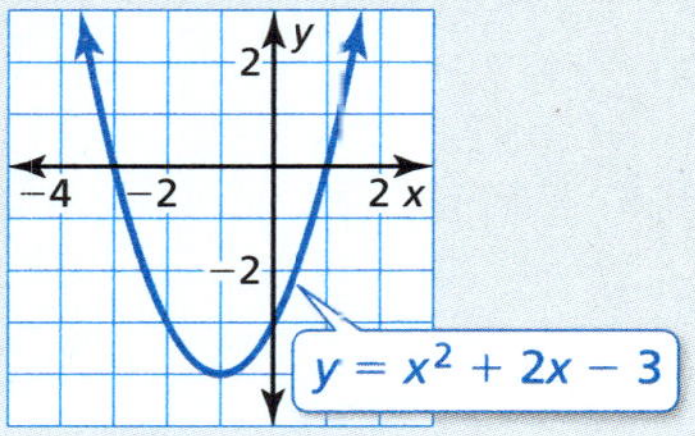

46. Graph $x - 5y > -10$ in a coordinate plane.

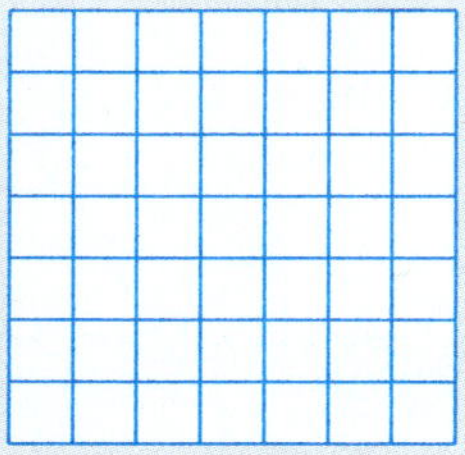

In Exercises 47 and 48, write the linear equation in standard form.

47. $y = -6x + 13$

48. $y - 3 = \frac{1}{4}(x + 12)$

49. **WRITING** For what values of b can you solve the linear system $7x + 3y = -1$ and $9x + by = -15$ by elimination without multiplying first? Explain.

50. Write 3.26×10^7 in standard form.

In Exercises 51 and 52, solve the equation by graphing. Check your solution(s).

51. $\frac{1}{3}x - 4 = -3x + 6$

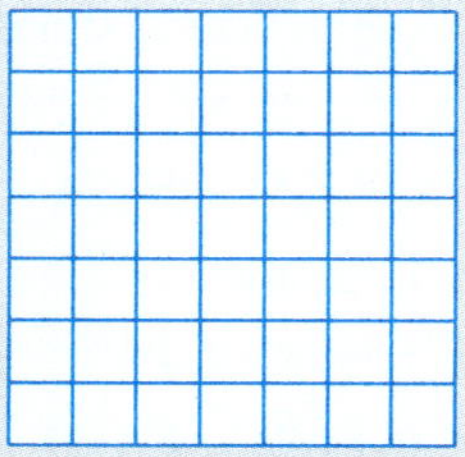

52. $x + 5 = 2x + 1$

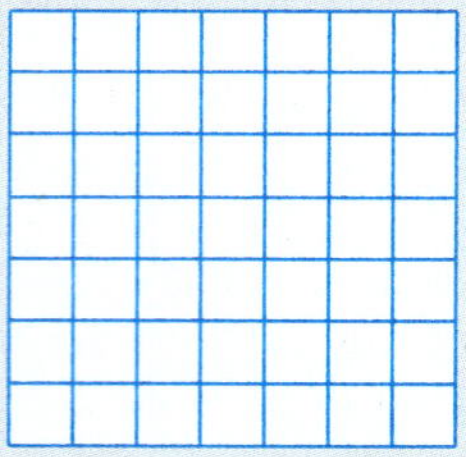

In Exercises 53 and 54, write an inequality that represents the graph.

53.

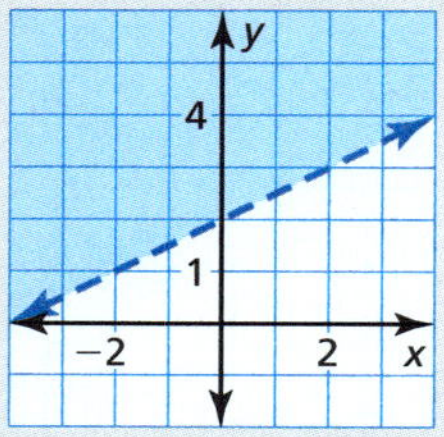

54.

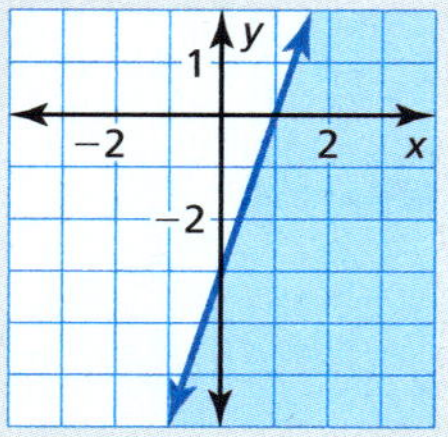

55. Determine whether the relation is a function. Explain.

$(-5, 2), (-7, 4), (-3, 0), (-4, 3), (-5, 4)$

5.7 Systems of Linear Inequalities

Learning Target: Graph and write systems of linear inequalities.

Success Criteria:
- I can determine whether an ordered pair is a solution of a system of linear inequalities.
- I can graph systems of linear inequalities.
- I can write systems of linear inequalities from a graph.
- I can solve real-life problems using systems of linear inequalities.

Algebraic Reasoning
MA.912.AR.9.4 Graph the solution set of a system of two-variable linear inequalities.
MA.912.AR.9.6 Given a real-world context, represent constraints as systems of linear equations or inequalities. Interpret solutions to problems as viable or non-viable options.
Also MA.912.AR.2.7, MA.912.AR.2.8

EXPLORE IT! Writing Systems of Linear Inequalities

Work with a partner.

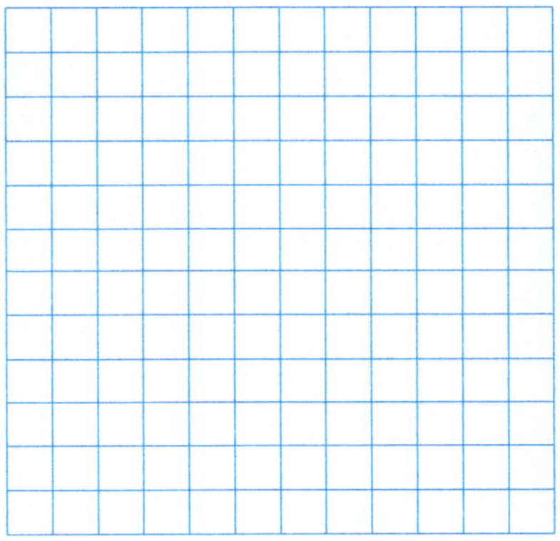

a. Write two linear equations: one with a positive slope and a nonzero y-intercept, and one with a negative slope and a nonzero y-intercept. Graph the equations in the same coordinate plane.

b. How many regions are formed by the graphs of the equations? Shade and label each region a different color.

c. How can you represent a region algebraically? Use your method to represent each region in part (b).

d. Use your method to represent the shaded region of each graph algebraically.

i.

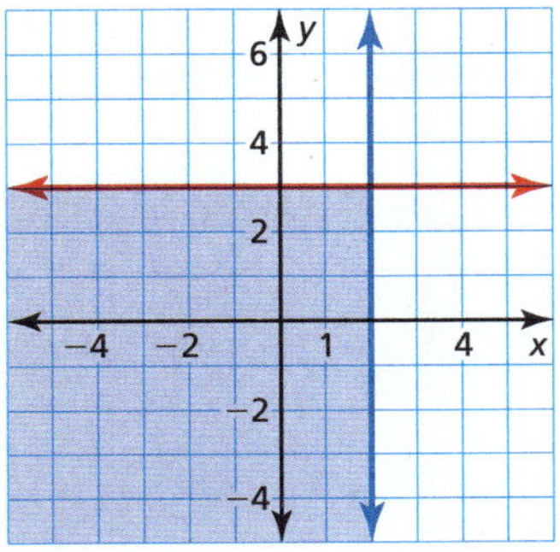

ii.

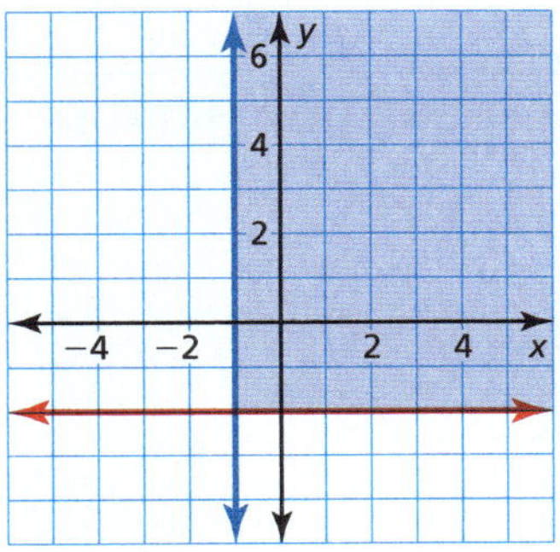

ANALYZE A PROBLEM 1 MTR

How can you use technology to check your results in part (c)?

GO DIGITAL

Systems of Linear Inequalities

Vocabulary AZ VOCAB

system of linear inequalities, *p. 454*
solution of a system of linear inequalities, *p. 454*
graph of a system of linear inequalities, *p. 456*

A **system of linear inequalities** is a set of two or more linear inequalities in the same variables. An example is shown below.

$y < x + 2$ Inequality 1

$y \geq 2x - 1$ Inequality 2

A **solution of a system of linear inequalities** in two variables is an ordered pair that is a solution of each inequality in the system.

EXAMPLE 1 Checking Solutions

WATCH

Tell whether each ordered pair is a solution of the system of linear inequalities.

$y < 2x$ ✓   Inequality 1

$y \geq x + 1$ Inequality 2

$5 < 6$ ✓

$5 \geq 3 + 1$

$5 \geq 4$ ✓

a. (3, 5)   **b.** (−2, 0)

SOLUTION

a. Substitute 3 for x and 5 for y in each inequality.

Inequality 1	Inequality 2
$y < 2x$	$y \geq x + 1$
$5 \stackrel{?}{<} 2(3)$	$5 \stackrel{?}{\geq} 3 + 1$
$5 < 6$ ✓	$5 \geq 4$ ✓

▶ Because the ordered pair (3, 5) is a solution of each inequality, it is a solution of the system.

b. Substitute −2 for x and 0 for y in each inequality.

Inequality 1	Inequality 2
$y < 2x$	$y \geq x + 1$
$0 \stackrel{?}{<} 2(-2)$	$0 \stackrel{?}{\geq} -2 + 1$
$0 \not< -4$ ✗	$0 \geq -1$ ✓

▶ Because (−2, 0) is not a solution of each inequality, it is *not* a solution of the system.

3 MTR REFLECT ON YOUR METHOD

In part (b), do you need to substitute the ordered pair into the second inequality? Explain.

GO DIGITAL

SELF-ASSESSMENT

1 I don't understand yet. 2 I can do it with help. 3 I can do it on my own. 4 I can teach someone else.

1. **VOCABULARY** How many linear inequalities are in a system of linear inequalities?

2. **WRITING** How can you verify that an ordered pair is a solution of a system of linear inequalities?

Tell whether the ordered pair is a solution of the system of linear inequalities.

3. $(-1, 5)$; $y < 5$
   $y > x - 4$

4. $(1, 4)$; $y \geq 3x + 1$
   $y > x - 1$

5. $\left(0, -\frac{5}{2}\right)$; $y > \frac{1}{2}x - 8$
   $y < 6 - x$

6. **OPEN-ENDED** One inequality in a system is $y \geq 2x + 3$. Write another possible inequality in the system so that $(-2, 6)$ is a solution of the system.

Graphing Systems of Linear Inequalities

The **graph of a system of linear inequalities** is the graph of all the solutions of the system.

KEY IDEA

Graphing a System of Linear Inequalities

Graph each inequality in the same coordinate plane. Then find the intersection of the half-planes that are solutions of the inequalities. This intersection is the graph of the system.

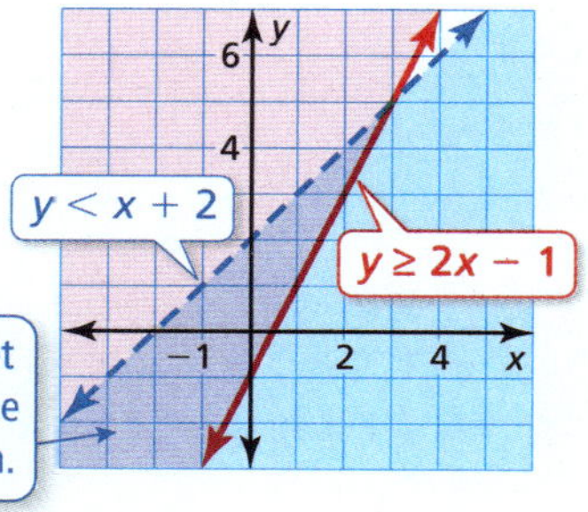

EXAMPLE 2 Graphing a System of Linear Inequalities

WATCH

Graph the system. Identify a solution.

$y \leq 3$ Inequality 1

$y > x + 2$ Inequality 2

SOLUTION

Graph each inequality. Then find the intersection of the half-planes.

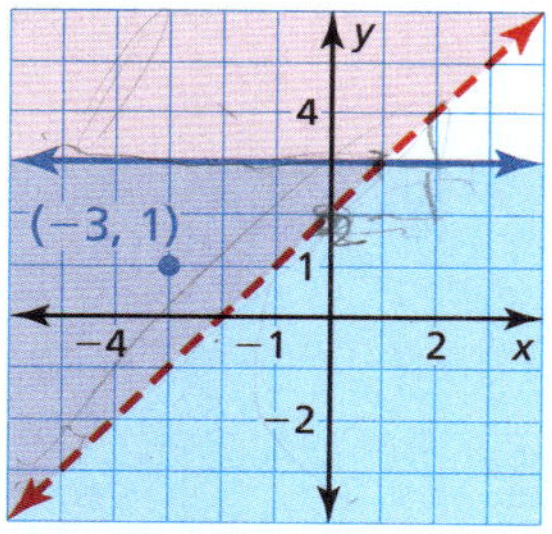

▶ One solution is $(-3, 1)$.

Check

Verify that $(-3, 1)$ is a solution of each inequality.

Inequality 1	Inequality 2
$y \leq 3$	$y > x + 2$
$1 \leq 3$ ✓	$1 \overset{?}{>} -3 + 2$
	$1 > -1$ ✓

GO DIGITAL

EXAMPLE 3

Graphing a System of Linear Inequalities: No Solution

WATCH

Graph the system.

$2x + y < -1$ Inequality 1

$2x + y > 3$ Inequality 2

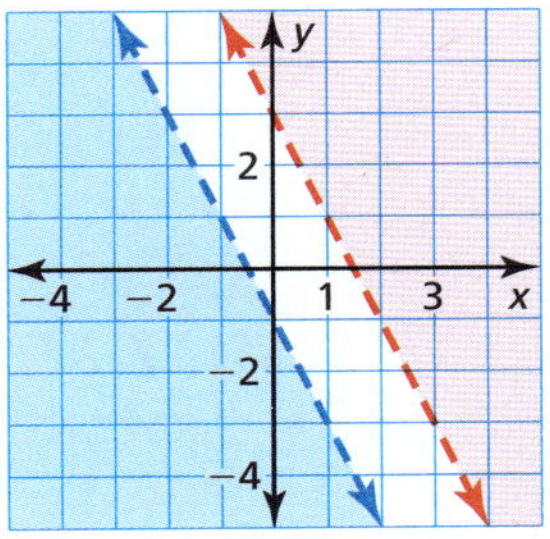

SOLUTION

Graph each inequality. Then find the intersection of the half-planes. Notice that the lines are parallel, and the half-planes do not intersect.

▶ So, the system has no solution.

SELF-ASSESSMENT

1 I don't understand yet. 2 I can do it with help. 3 I can do it on my own. 4 I can teach someone else.

Graph the system. Identify a solution, if possible.

7. $y \geq -x + 4$
$x + y \leq 0$

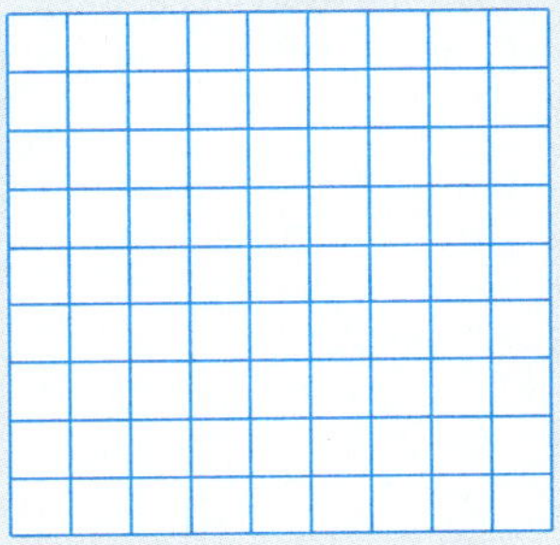

8. $y > 2x - 3$
$y \geq \frac{1}{2}x + 1$

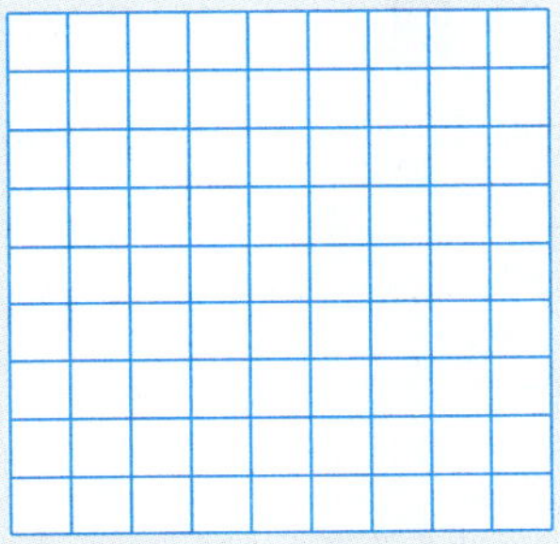

9. $-2x + y < 4$
$2x + y > 4$

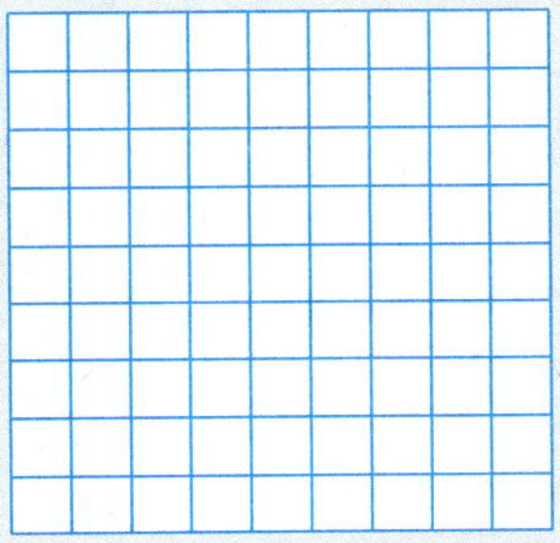

Writing Systems of Linear Inequalities

EXAMPLE 4

Writing a System of Linear Inequalities

WATCH

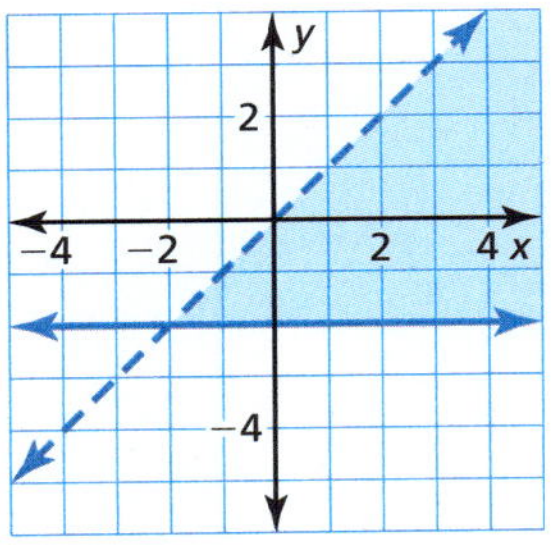

Write a system of linear inequalities represented by the graph.

SOLUTION

Inequality 1 The horizontal boundary line passes through $(0, -2)$. So, an equation of the line is $y = -2$. The shaded region is *above* the *solid* boundary line, so the inequality is $y \geq -2$.

Inequality 2 The slope of the other boundary line is 1, and the y-intercept is 0. So, an equation of the line is $y = x$. The shaded region is *below* the *dashed* boundary line, so the inequality is $y < x$.

▶ The system of linear inequalities represented by the graph is

$y \geq -2$ Inequality 1

$y < x.$ Inequality 2

GO DIGITAL

EXAMPLE 5 Writing a System of Linear Inequalities

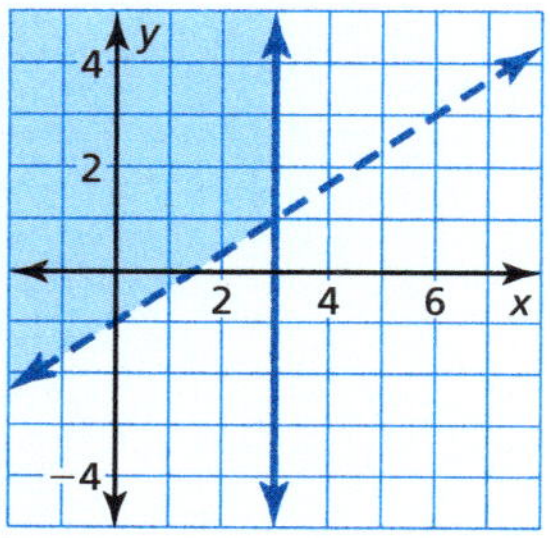

Write a system of linear inequalities represented by the graph.

SOLUTION

Inequality 1 The vertical boundary line passes through (3, 0). So, an equation of the line is $x = 3$. The shaded region is to the *left* of the *solid* boundary line, so the inequality is $x \leq 3$.

Inequality 2 The slope of the other boundary line is $\frac{2}{3}$, and the y-intercept is -1. So, an equation of the line is $y = \frac{2}{3}x - 1$. The shaded region is *above* the *dashed* boundary line, so the inequality is $y > \frac{2}{3}x - 1$.

▶ The system of linear inequalities represented by the graph is

$x \leq 3$ Inequality 1

$y > \frac{2}{3}x - 1.$ Inequality 2

SELF-ASSESSMENT

1 I don't understand yet. 2 I can do it with help. 3 I can do it on my own. 4 I can teach someone else.

Write a system of linear inequalities represented by the graph.

10.

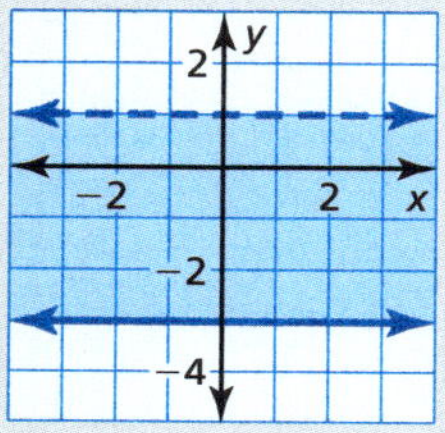

11.

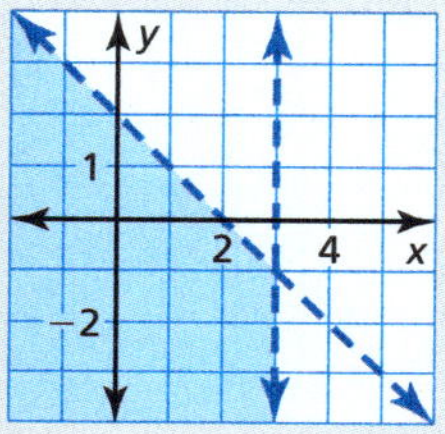

12.

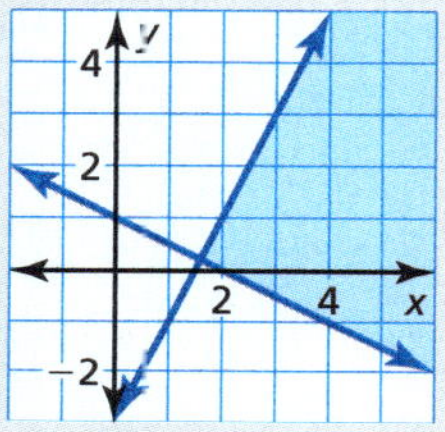

13. OPEN-ENDED Write a system of linear inequalities whose graph can be represented by a rectangular region.

14. REASONING Is it possible to write a system of three linear inequalities that has no solution? If so, give an example. If not, explain why not.

Solving Real-Life Problems

7 MTR **EXAMPLE 6** **Modeling Real Life** WATCH

A company is loading recliners and sofas onto a trailer that has a volume of about 3800 cubic feet. Each recliner takes up about 40 cubic feet, and each sofa takes up about 80 cubic feet. The company wants the shipment to have at least 30 recliners and more than 25 sofas. Write and graph a system that represents the situation. Give one example of the numbers of recliners and sofas the company can have in the shipment.

SOLUTION

1. **Understand the Problem** You know the volume of the trailer and the volume of each recliner and sofa. You also know how many recliners and sofas the company wants in the shipment. You are asked to give an example of the numbers of recliners and sofas the company can have in the shipment.

2. **Make a Plan** Use the given information to write a system of linear inequalities. Then graph the system and identify and interpret an ordered pair in the solution region.

3. **Solve and Check** Let r be the number of recliners, and let s be the number of sofas in the shipment.

$40r + 80s \leq 3800$ at most 3800 cubic feet is available in the shipment

$r \geq 30$ at least 30 recliners in the shipment

$s > 25$ more than 25 sofas in the shipment

Graph the system.

Numbers of Recliners and Sofas in Shipment

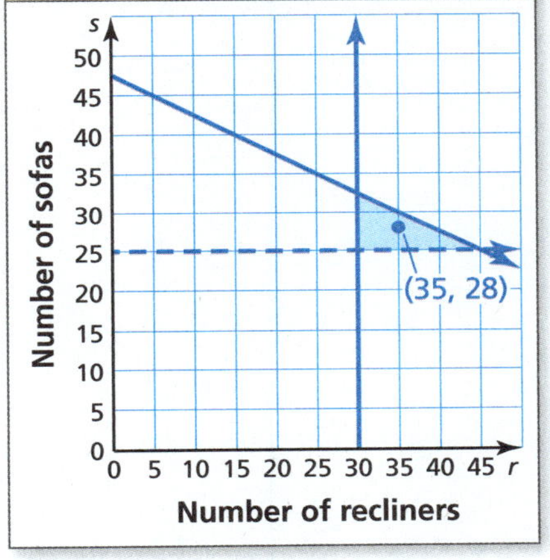

One ordered pair in the solution region is (35, 28).

▶ So, the company can have 35 recliners and 28 sofas in the shipment.

Check Check your solution by substituting it into the inequalities in the system.

$40r + 80s \leq 3800$ $\quad$ $r \geq 30$ $\quad$ $s > 25$

$40(35) + 80(28) \overset{?}{\leq} 3800$ $\quad$ $35 \geq 30$ ✓ $\quad$ $28 > 25$ ✓

$3640 \leq 3800$ ✓

GO DIGITAL

SELF-ASSESSMENT

1 I don't understand yet. 2 I can do it with help. 3 I can do it on my own. 4 I can teach someone else.

15. Identify and interpret another ordered pair in the solution region in Example 6.

16. You have at most 8 hours to spend at the mall and at the beach. You want to spend more than 2 hours at the mall and more than 4 hours at the beach.

a. Write and graph a system that represents the situation. Give one example of the amount of time you can spend at each location.

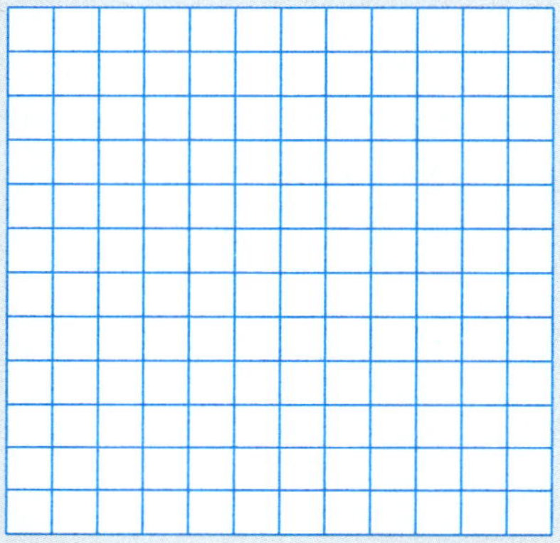

b. You want to spend at least 45 more minutes at the mall. How does this change the system in part (a)? Is your example still valid? Explain.

5.7 Practice WITH CalcChat® AND CalcView®

In Exercises 1–4, tell whether the ordered pair is a solution of the system of linear inequalities. *(See Example 1.)*

1. $(-5, 2)$; $y < 4$, $y > x + 3$

2. $(1, -1)$; $y > -2$, $y > x - 5$

3. $(0, 0)$; $y \le x + 7$, $y \ge 2x + 3$

4. $(4, -3)$; $y \le -x + 1$, $y \le 5x - 2$

In Exercises 5–8, tell whether the ordered pair is a solution of the system of linear inequalities.

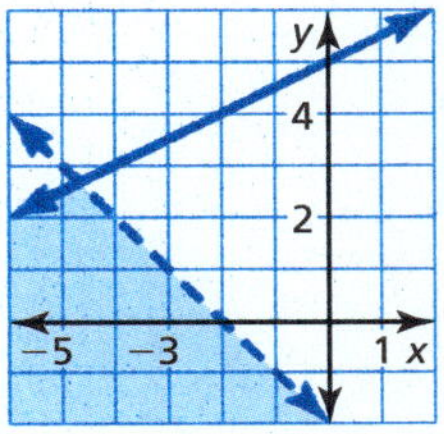

5. $(-4, 3)$

6. $(-3, -1)$

7. $(-2, 0)$

8. $(1, 0.5)$

In Exercises 9–18, graph the system. Identify a solution, if possible. *(See Examples 2 and 3.)*

9. $y > -3$
$y \ge 5x$

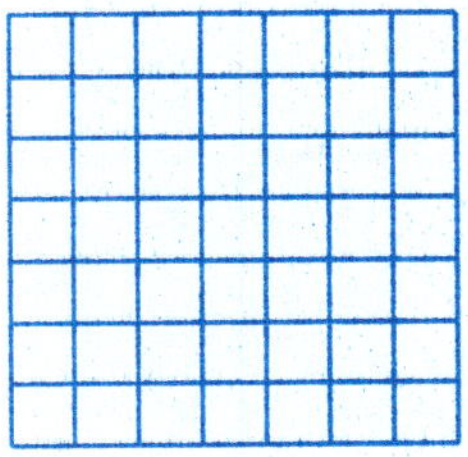

10. $y < -1$
$x > 4$

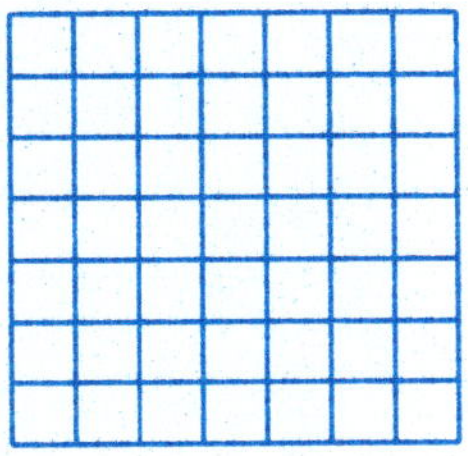

11. $y < -2$
$y > 2$

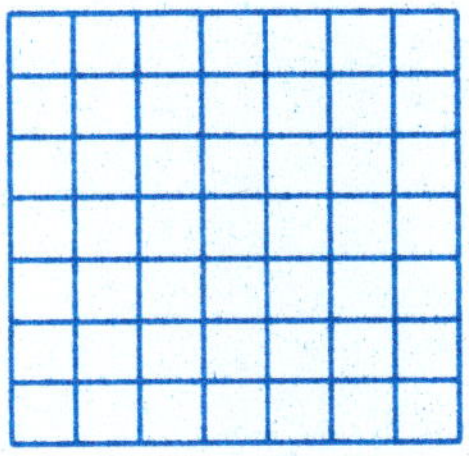

12. $y < x - 1$
$y \ge x + 1$

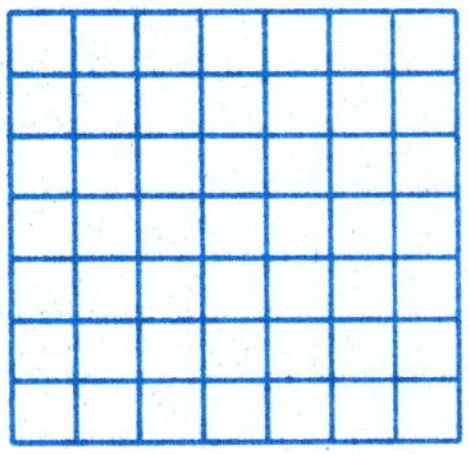

13. $y \ge -5$
$y - 1 < 3x$

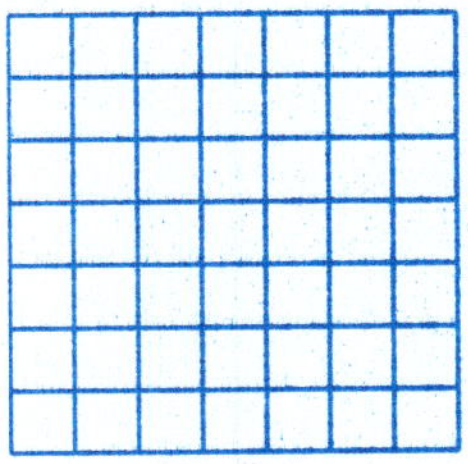

14. $x + y > 4$
$y \ge \frac{3}{2}x - 9$

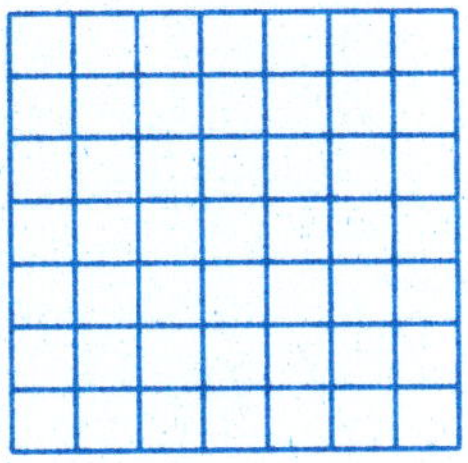

15. $x + y > 1$
$-x - y < -3$

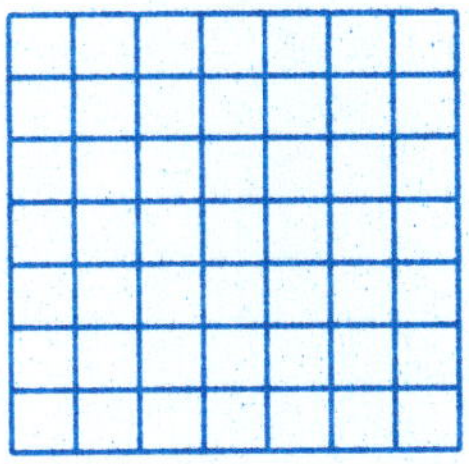

16. $2x + y \le 5$
$y + 2 \ge -2x$

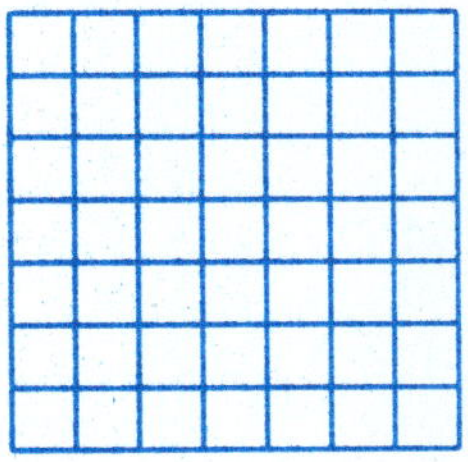

17. $x < 3.5$
$y > 1$
$y \ge -x + 1$

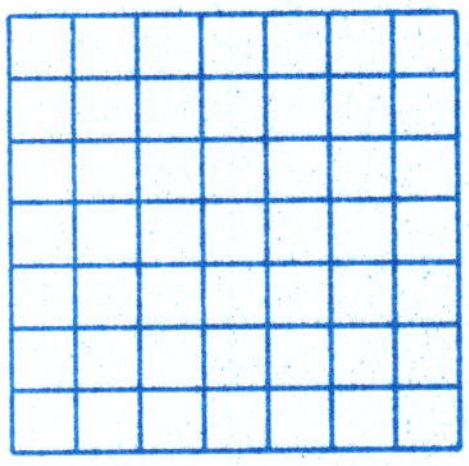

18. $\frac{3}{4}x + y \le 3$
$\frac{3}{4}x - y \ge 1$
$y > -1\frac{1}{2}$

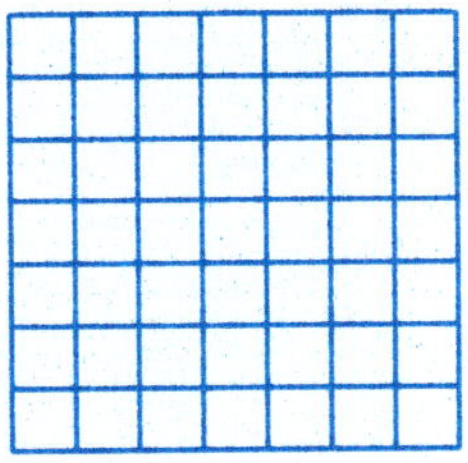

GO DIGITAL

In Exercises 19–24, write a system of linear inequalities represented by the graph. *(See Examples 4 and 5.)*

19. 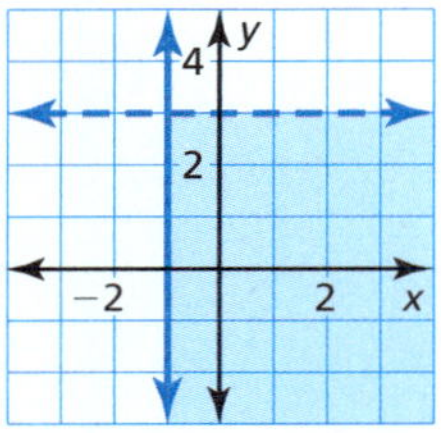

20. 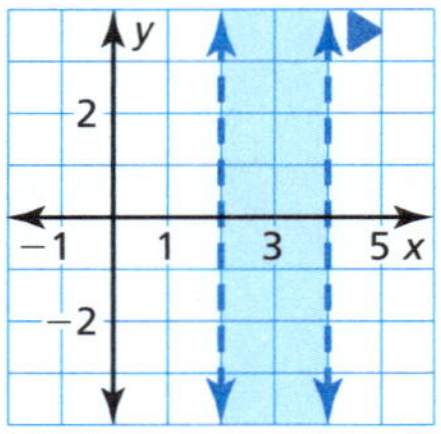

21. 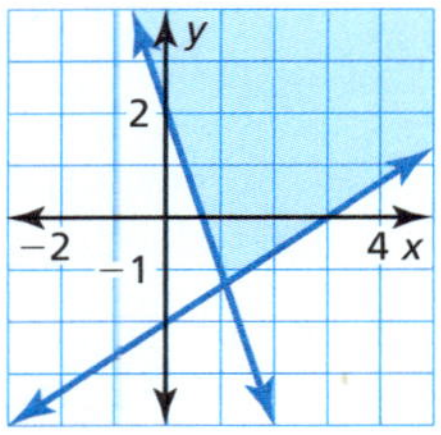

22. 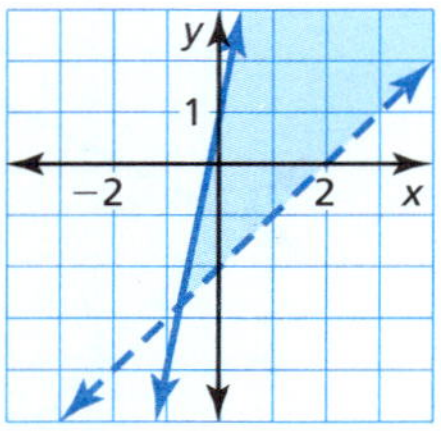

23. 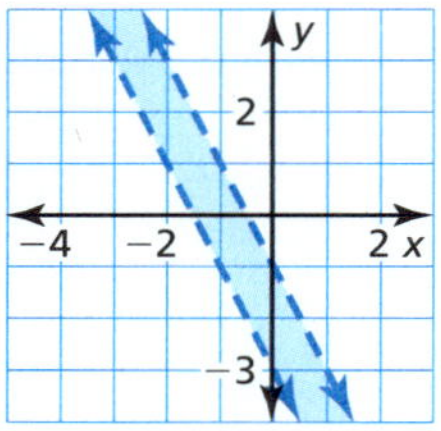

24. 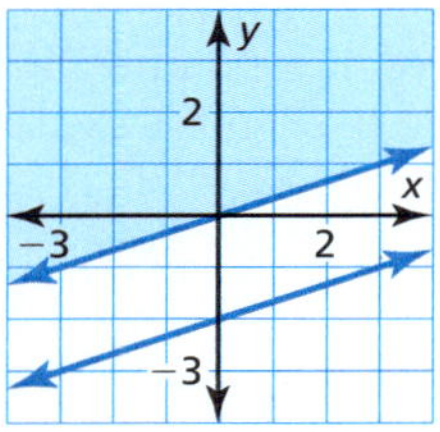

25. ERROR ANALYSIS Describe and correct the error in graphing the system $y \leq 3x + 4$ and $y > \frac{1}{2}x + 2$.

4 MTR

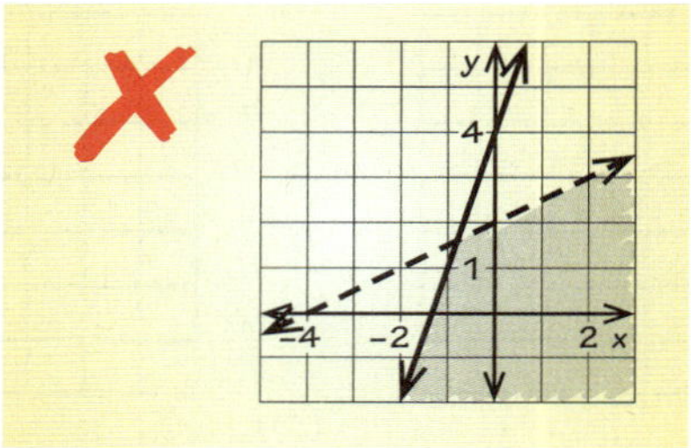

26. B.E.S.T. TEST PREP Which of the following systems is represented by the graph?

Ⓐ $y \leq -\frac{1}{2}x - 2$
$y > 4x + 1$

Ⓑ $y \leq -\frac{1}{2}x - 2$
$y < 4x + 1$

Ⓒ $y < -\frac{1}{2}x - 2$
$y \geq 4x + 1$

Ⓓ $y < -\frac{1}{2}x - 2$
$y \leq 4x + 1$

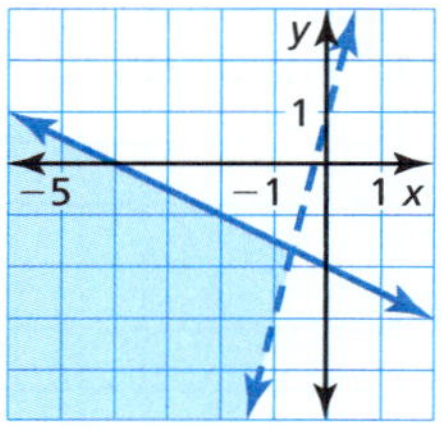

27. MODELING REAL LIFE A group of scientists have at most 7 hours to spend on an expedition to one of the deepest areas of the ocean. They expect the total travel time to be more than 3 hours and want to spend at least $2\frac{1}{2}$ hours exploring. Write and graph a system that represents the situation. Give one example of the amount of time they can spend on each part of the expedition. *(See Example 6.)*

7 MTR

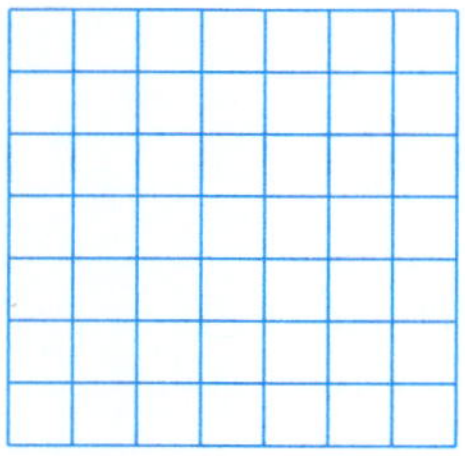

7 MTR

28. MODELING REAL LIFE You earn \$10 per hour working at a grocery store and must work there at least 8 hours per week. You also teach music lessons for \$15 per hour. Between the two jobs, you need to earn at least \$120 per week and work no more than 20 hours per week. Write and graph a system that represents the situation. Give one example of the number of hours you can work at each job.

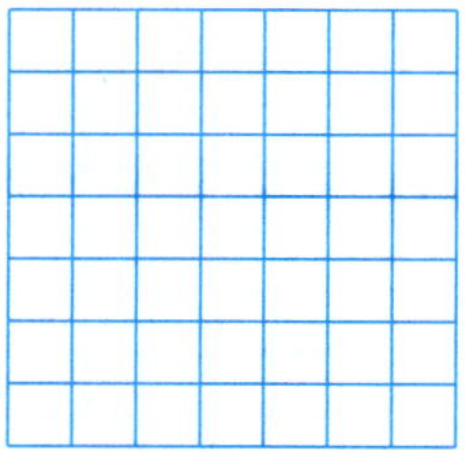

29. **MODELING REAL LIFE** You are fishing for surfperch and rockfish. The graph shows limits on the numbers of fish you are allowed to catch per day.

Rockfish

a. Write and interpret a system of linear inequalities that represents the situation.

b. Can you catch 11 surfperch and 9 rockfish in 1 day? Explain.

30. **REASONING** Describe the graph of the system shown.

$$x - y \leq 4$$
$$x - y \geq 4$$

31. **PROBLEM SOLVING** Your cousin plans to spend less than half of her monthly \$2000 paycheck on housing and savings. She wants to spend at least 10% of her paycheck on savings and at most 30% of it on housing. Give one example of the amount of money your cousin can spend on savings and housing. Justify your answer using a system of linear inequalities.

32. **PROBLEM SOLVING** A travel club can spend at most 10 nights in two cities on a trip. The club needs to reserve four rooms each night and wants to spend no more than \$4200 on hotels and fuel. The estimated fuel cost is \$200. Can the club spend 3 nights in City A and 6 nights in City B? 7 nights in City A and 3 nights in City B? Justify your answers using a system of linear inequalities.

Nightly Hotel Rates	
City A hotel	**City B hotel**
\$85 per room	\$130 per room

33. **CONNECTING CONCEPTS** The vertices of a shaded rectangle are $(-1, 1)$, $(6, 1)$, $(6, -3)$, and $(-1, -3)$.

a. Write a system of linear inequalities with a graph that can be represented by the shaded rectangle.

b. Find the area of the rectangle.

34. **CONNECTING CONCEPTS** The vertices of a shaded triangle are $(2, 5)$, $(6, -3)$, and $(-2, -3)$.

a. Write a system of linear inequalities with a graph that can be represented by the shaded triangle.

b. Find the area of the triangle.

35. **STRUCTURE** Write a system of linear inequalities that has the same solutions as $|y| < x$, where $x > 0$. Graph the system.

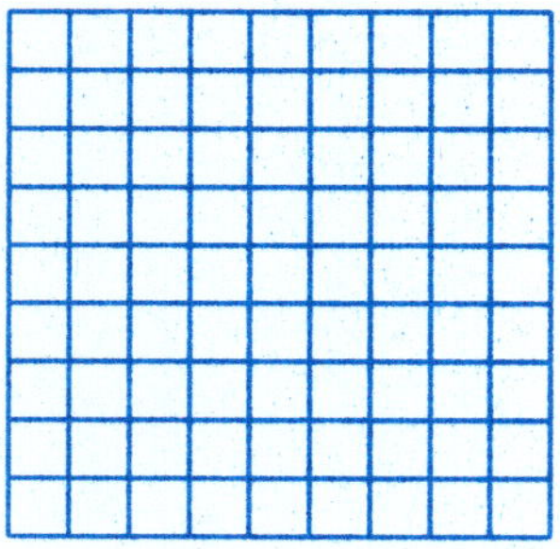

36. **HOW DO YOU SEE IT?**
The graphs of two linear equations are shown.

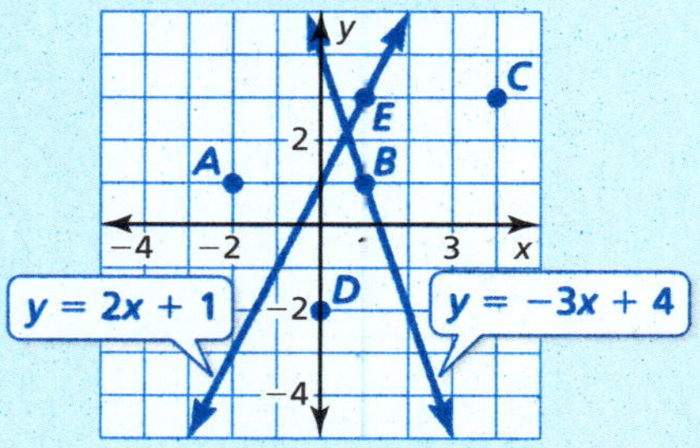

Replace the equal signs with inequality symbols to create a system of linear inequalities that has points *C* and *E* as solutions, but not points *A*, *B*, and *D*. Explain your reasoning.

$y \;\square\; -3x + 4$

$y \;\square\; 2x + 1$

37. **MAKING AN ARGUMENT** Your friend says that a system of linear inequalities in which the boundary lines are parallel must have no solution. Is your friend correct? Explain.

38. **REASONING** Is it possible for the solution set of a system of linear inequalities to be all points in the coordinate plane? Explain your reasoning.

OPEN-ENDED **In Exercises 39–41, write a system of linear inequalities with the given characteristic.**

39. All solutions are in Quadrant I.

40. All solutions have one positive coordinate and one negative coordinate.

41. There are no solutions.

42. **OPEN-ENDED** One inequality in a system is $-4x + 2y > 6$. Write another possible inequality in the system so that the system has no solution.

7 MTR **43. PERFORMANCE TASK** The table shows three systems.

System A	System B	System C
$y \geq x$	$y > x + 4$	$y < x$
$y \leq x + 4$	$x \geq -6$	$x \leq 6$
$y \geq -2$	$y \leq 6$	$y \geq -2$
$y \leq 6$		

a. Graph each system in the same coordinate plane. Color the solutions of System A yellow, the solutions of System B green, and the solutions of System C red. Erase all other shading.

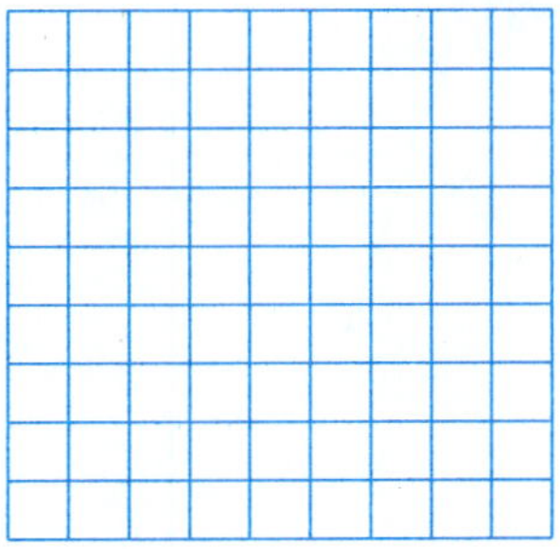

b. The directions in part (a) produce the flag of a country. Determine which country the flag represents.

c. Choose the flag of a different country, or design your own flag. Describe how to draw the flag using systems of linear inequalities.

44. THOUGHT PROVOKING
Write a system of linear inequalities that has exactly one solution.

45. DIG DEEPER You make necklaces and key chains to sell at a crafts fair. The table shows the amounts of time and money it takes to make a necklace and a key chain, and the amounts of time and money you have available for making them.

	Necklace	Key chain	Available
Time (hours)	0.5	0.25	20
Cost (dollars)	2	3	120

a. Give three examples of the number of each item you can make. Justify your answers using a system of linear inequalities.

b. You sell each necklace for \$10 and each key chain for \$8. How many necklaces and key chains should you sell to maximize your revenue? What is the maximum revenue? (*Hint:* The maximum revenue occurs at one of the vertices of the graph of the system in part (a).)

REVIEW & REFRESH

46. Graph $-\frac{3}{4}x - y < 6$ in a coordinate plane.

In Exercises 47 and 48, write the product as a power.

47. $(-13) \cdot (-13) \cdot (-13)$

48. $x \cdot x \cdot x \cdot x \cdot x \cdot x$

49. Write a system of linear inequalities represented by the graph.

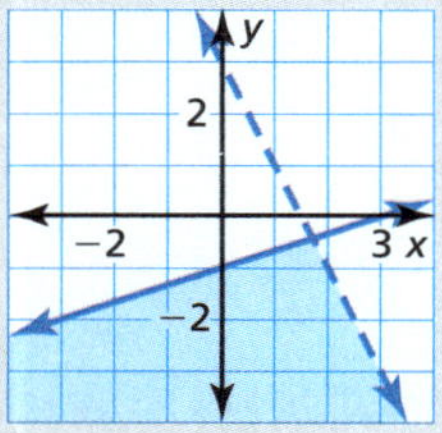

50. Write an equation of the line with a slope of $-\frac{1}{4}$ and a y-intercept of -1.

In Exercises 51 and 52, solve the equation.

51. $\frac{2}{3}(x - 6) = 4$

52. $6x - 7 = -2x - 9$

In Exercises 53 and 54, solve the system using any method. Explain your choice of method.

53. $5x + 10y = 8$
$3x + 6y = 4$

54. $-11x + 2y = 12$
$y = 4x + 3$

7 MTR **55.** **MODELING REAL LIFE** Slitsnails are large mollusks that live in deep waters. They have been found in the range of elevations shown. Write and graph a compound inequality that represents this range.

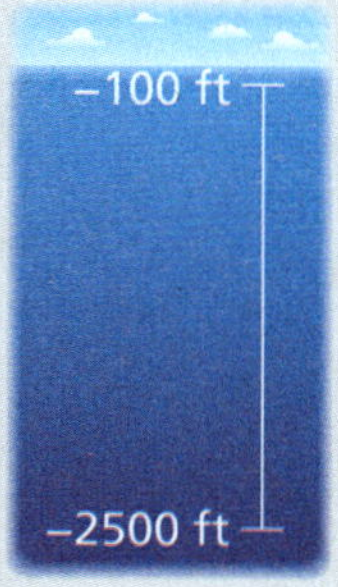

56. Solve $x + 5 = -2x - 4$ by graphing. Check your solution.

57. **OPEN-ENDED** Write an absolute value equation that has exactly one solution.

58. Use intercepts to graph the equation $-3x + 6y = 24$. Label the points corresponding to the intercepts.

59. Make a scatter plot of the data. Then describe the relationship between the data.

x	4	8	1	9	3	6	2	5
y	−2	0	−5	−1	−5	−2	−7	−4

60. Graph $f(x) = |x - 3|$ and $g(x) = |x - 3| + 1$. Describe the transformation from the graph of f to the graph of g.

5 Chapter Review WITH CalcChat®

Chapter Learning Target: Understand solving systems of linear equations.

Chapter Success Criteria:

- ◆ I can identify a system of linear equations.
- ◆ I can describe different methods for solving systems of linear equations.
- ■ I can analyze systems of linear equations and decide what solution method is most efficient.
- ■ I can predict whether a system of linear equations has one solution, no solution, or infinitely many solutions.

◆ Surface
■ Deep

SELF-ASSESSMENT 1 I don't understand yet. 2 I can do it with help. 3 I can do it on my own. 4 I can teach someone else.

5.1 Solving Systems of Linear Equations by Graphing (pp. 393–402)

WATCH

Learning Target: Solve linear systems by graphing.

Vocabulary VOCAB

system of linear equations
solution of a system of linear equations

Solve the system by graphing.

1. $y = -3x + 1$
$y = x - 7$

2. $y = -4x + 3$
$4x - 2y = 6$

3. $5x + 5y = 15$
$2x - 2y = 10$

4. $-\frac{2}{3}x + y = 2$
$y + 8 = 4x$

5. Write a system of linear equations in two variables that has a solution of $(4.2, -2.5)$. Use a graph to justify your answer.

GO DIGITAL

6. The graphs of two equations in a linear system have the same x-intercept. One equation in the system is $\frac{1}{5}x + 4y = a$. What is the solution of the system?

7. You plant a spruce tree that grows 4 inches per year and a hemlock tree that grows 6 inches per year. The initial heights of the trees are shown. After how many years will the trees be the same height?

5.2 Solving Systems of Linear Equations by Substitution (pp. 403–412) WATCH

Learning Target: Solve linear systems by substitution.

Solve the system by substitution. Check your solution.

8. $3x + y = -9$
$y = 5x + 7$

9. $x + 4y = 6$
$x - y = 1$

10. $2x + 3y = 4$
$y + 3x = 6$

11. You spend \$20 total on tubes of paint and disposable brushes for an art project. Tubes of paint cost \$4.00 each, and brushes cost \$0.50 each. You purchase twice as many brushes as tubes of paint. How many brushes and tubes of paint do you purchase?

5.3 Solving Systems of Linear Equations by Elimination (pp. 413–422)

WATCH

Learning Target: Solve linear systems by elimination.

Solve the system by elimination. Check your solution.

12. $9x - 2y = 34$
$5x + 2y = -6$

13. $x + 6y = 28$
$2x - 3y = -19$

14. $8x - 6y = -3$
$6x - 5y = -1$

15. In a football game, all of the home team's points are from 7-point touchdowns and 3-point field goals. The team scores six times. Find the numbers of touchdowns and field goals that the home team scores.

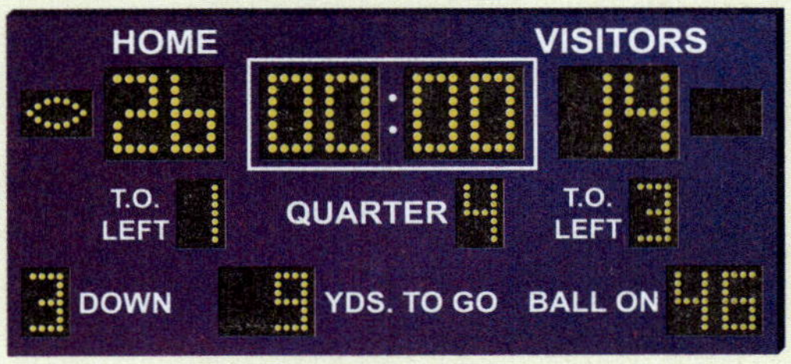

5.4 Solving Special Systems of Linear Equations *(pp. 423–432)*

WATCH

Learning Target: Solve linear systems with different numbers of solutions.

Use the graph to determine whether the system has *no solution*, *one solution*, or *infinitely many solutions*. Justify your answer algebraically.

16.

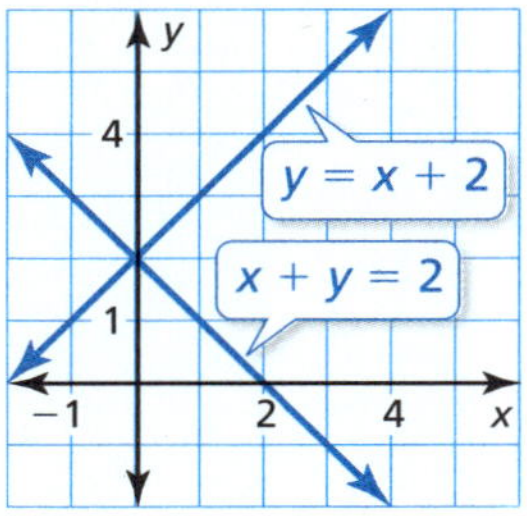

17.

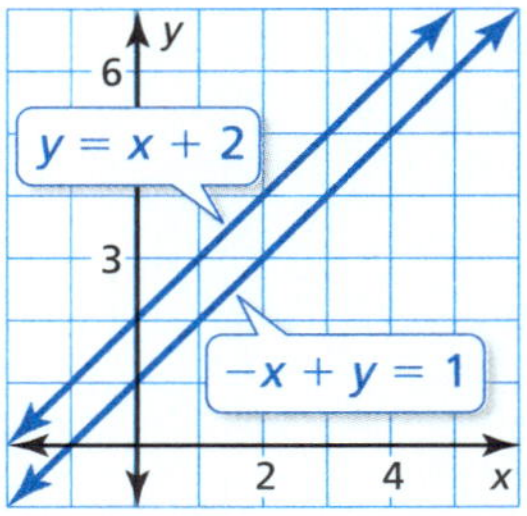

18.

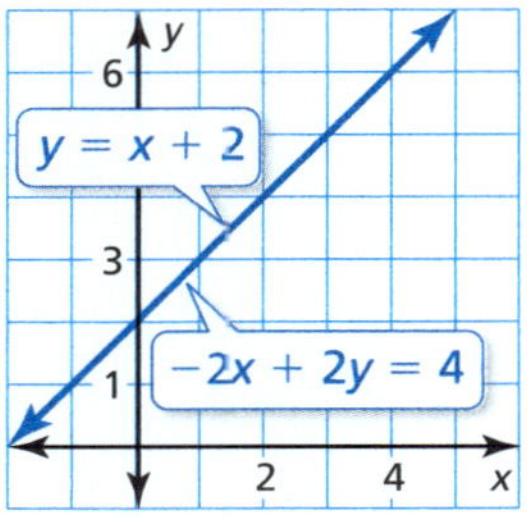

Solve the system using any method. Explain your choice of method.

19. $x = y + 2$
$-3x + 3y = 6$

20. $0.25x - 6y = -6$
$-5x + 10y = 10$

21. $-4x + 4y = 32$
$3x + 24 = 3y$

5.5 Solving Equations by Graphing (pp. 433–442) WATCH

Learning Target: Solve equations by graphing.

Solve the equation by graphing. Check your solution(s).

22. $\frac{1}{3}x + 5 = -2x - 2$

23. $x - 1 = \frac{1}{2}(4x + 6)$

24. $\frac{1}{5}(x - 2) = \frac{1}{5}(2x + 7)$

25. In 2020, Forest A had an area of about 4000 acres and Forest B had an area of about 3600 acres. Researchers expect deforestation to cause the area of Forest A to decrease at a rate of 105 acres per decade and the area of Forest B to decrease at a rate of 30 acres per decade. In what year do they expect the areas of the forests to be the same?

5.6 Graphing Linear Inequalities in Two Variables (pp. 443–452) WATCH

Learning Target: Graph linear inequalities in two variables.

Graph the inequality in a coordinate plane.

26. $y > -4$

27. $-9x + 3y \geq 3$

28. $5x + 10y < 40$

Vocabulary AZ VOCAB

linear inequality in two variables
solution of a linear inequality in two variables
graph of a linear inequality
half-planes

Write an inequality that represents the graph.

29.

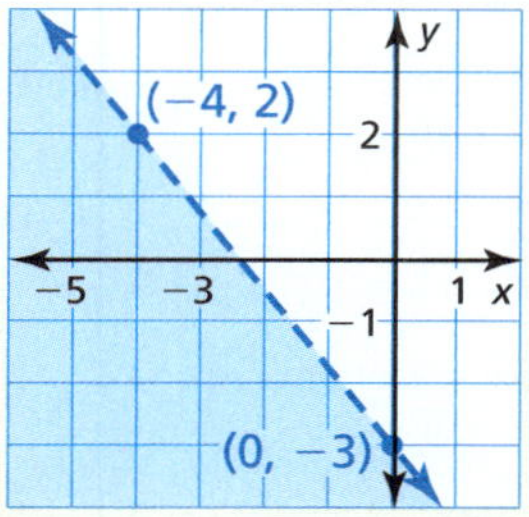

30.

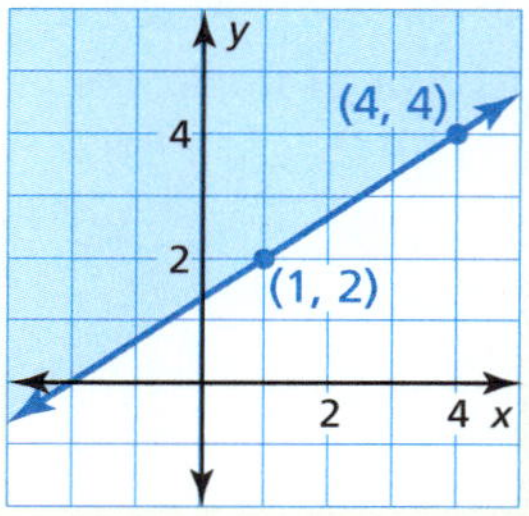

5.7 Systems of Linear Inequalities (pp. 453–466) WATCH

Learning Target: Graph and write systems of linear inequalities.

Vocabulary AZ VOCAB
system of linear inequalities
solution of a system of linear inequalities
graph of a system of linear inequalities

Graph the system.

31. $y \leq x - 3$
$y \geq x + 1$

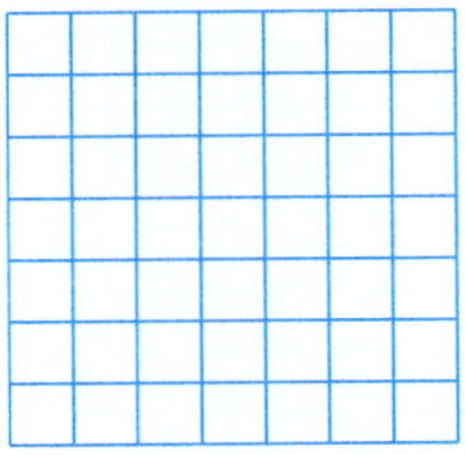

32. $y > -2x + 3$
$y \geq \frac{1}{4}x - 1$

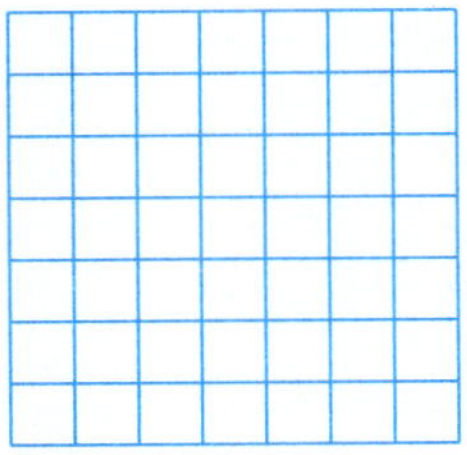

33. $x + 3y > 6$
$2x + y < 7$

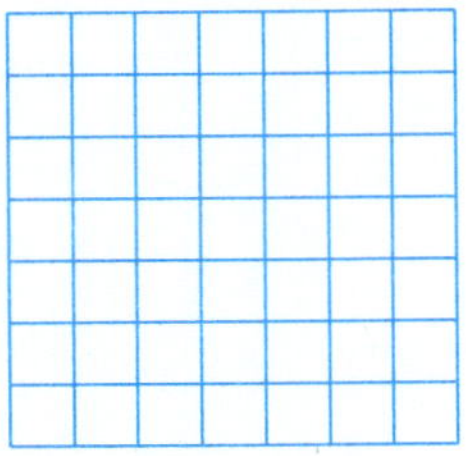

Match the system of linear inequalities with its graph, where *a* and *b* are positive numbers. Explain your reasoning.

34. $y \leq ax + b$
$y > ax - b$

35. $y \geq ax + b$
$y < ax - b$

36. $y < ax + b$
$y \geq ax - b$

A.

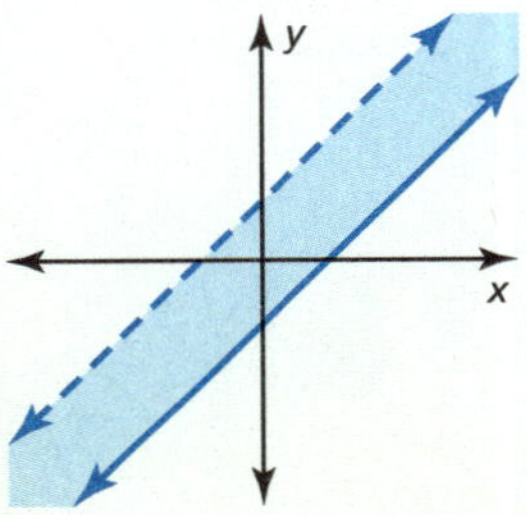

B.

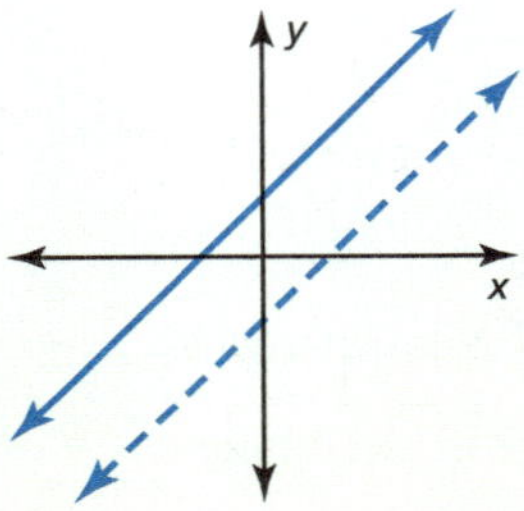

C.

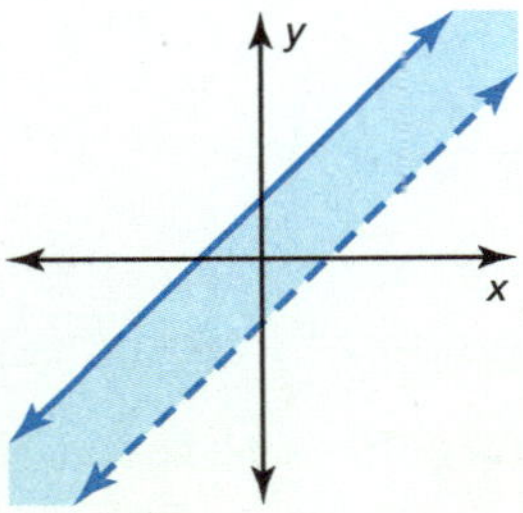

Mathematical Thinking and Reasoning

3 MTR **COMPLETE TASKS WITH MATHEMATICAL FLUENCY**
Mathematicians who complete tasks with mathematical fluency select efficient and appropriate methods for solving problems within the given context.

1. Describe a situation in this chapter where you could use more than one method to solve a problem.

2. When is it most helpful to use elimination to solve a linear system? Explain your reasoning.

5 Practice Test WITH CalcChat®

Solve the system using any method. Explain your choice of method.

1. $8x + 3y = -9$
$-8x + y = 29$

2. $\frac{1}{2}x + y = -6$
$y = \frac{3}{5}x + 5$

3. $y = 4x + 4$
$-8x + 2y = 8$

4. $x = y - 11$
$x - 3y = 1$

5. $6x - 4y = 9$
$9x - 6y = 15$

6. $y = 5x - 7$
$-4x + y = -1$

Write an inequality that represents the graph.

7.

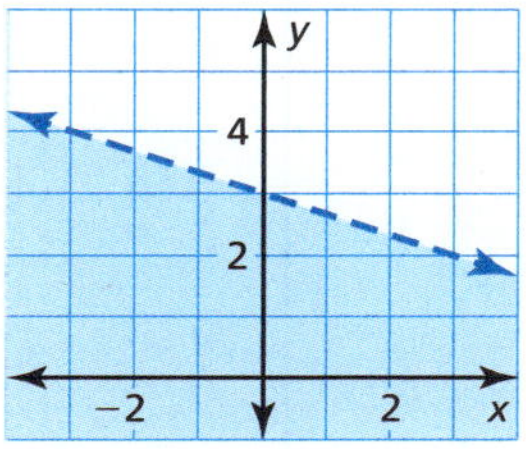

8.

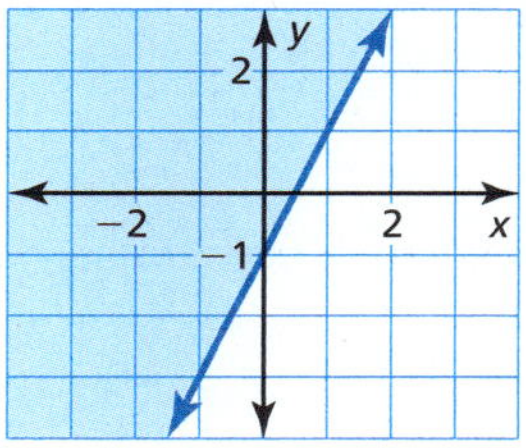

Graph the system. Identify a solution, if possible.

9. $y > \frac{1}{2}x + 4$
$2y \leq x + 4$

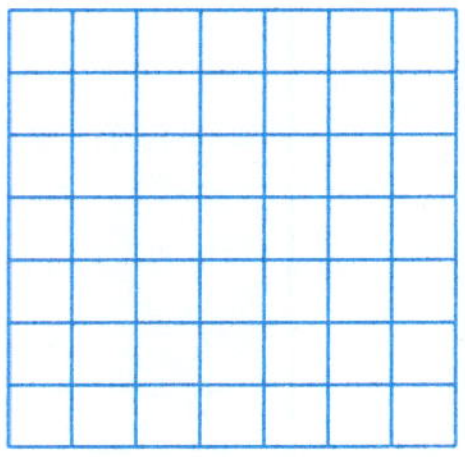

10. $x + y < 1$
$5x + y > 4$

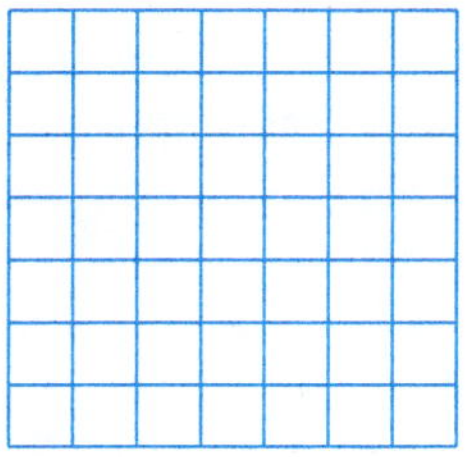

11. $y \geq -\frac{2}{3}x + 1$
$-3x + y > -2$

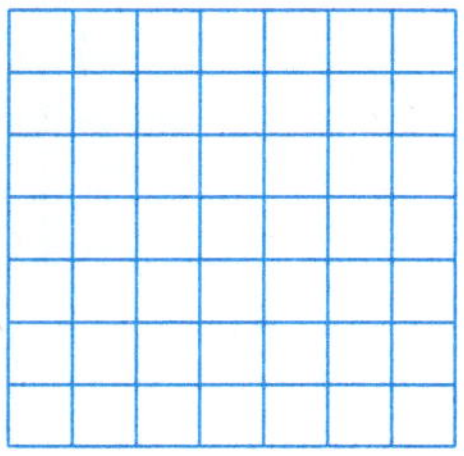

GO DIGITAL

12. Solve $\frac{1}{2}(6x - 8) = -x + 2$ by graphing. Check your solutions.

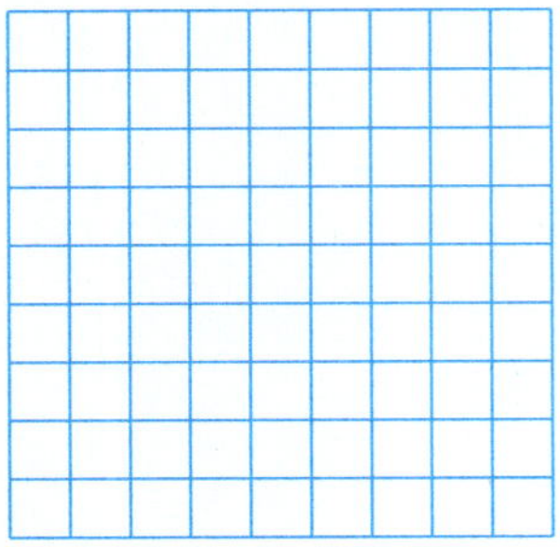

13. You pay \$45.50 for 10 gallons of gasoline and 2 quarts of oil at a gas station. Your friend pays \$22.75 for 5 gallons of the same type of gasoline and 1 quart of the same type of oil.

a. Is there enough information to determine the cost of 1 gallon of gasoline and 1 quart of oil? Justify your answer.

b. The receipt shown is for buying the same type of gasoline and same type of oil. Is there now enough information to determine the cost of 1 gallon of gasoline and 1 quart of oil? Justify your answer.

14. Graph the system. Then write a compound inequality represented by the graph. Explain your reasoning.

$y \geq 2x + 1$

$5x > y - 3$

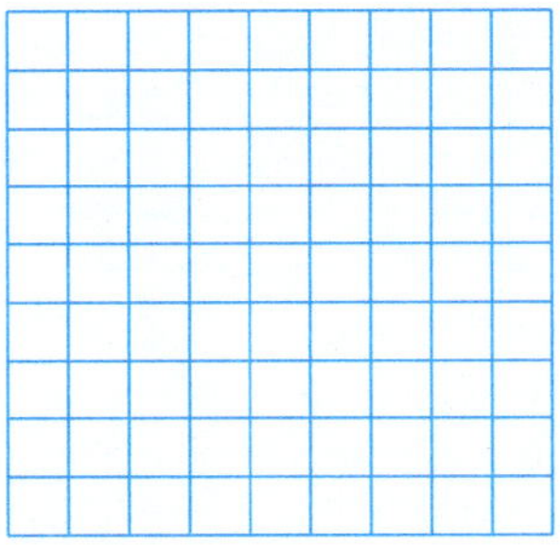

15. You have at most \$60 to spend on trophies and medals to give as prizes for a contest.

a. Write and graph an inequality that represents the numbers of trophies and medals you can buy. Identify and interpret a solution of the inequality.

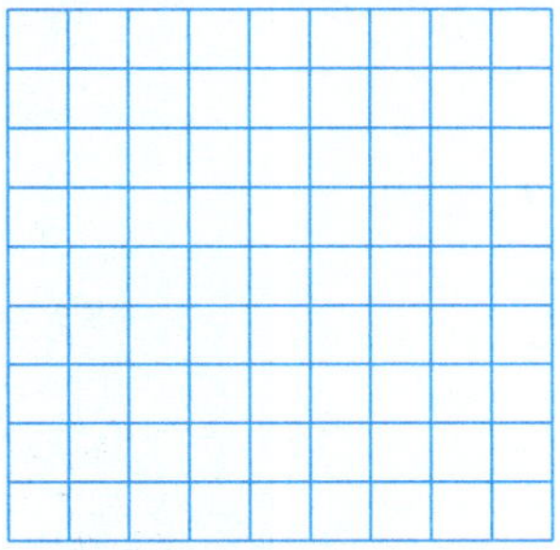

b. You want to purchase at least 6 items. Write and graph a system that represents the situation. How many of each item can you buy?

5 Performance Task

A Challenging Descent

Mariana Trench

The Mariana Trench in the Pacific Ocean is home to the deepest location on Earth, the **Challenger Deep**.

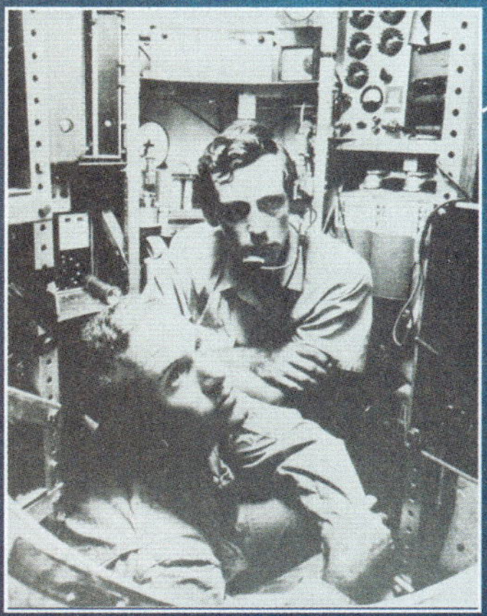

January 23, 1960

Aboard the bathyscaphe *Trieste*, Jacques Piccard and Don Walsh became the first people to explore the Challenger Deep. The expedition lasted **8 hours and 22 minutes**, with only **20 minutes** on the ocean floor.

March 26, 2012

Film director James Cameron piloted the *Deepsea Challenger* on the second manned dive to the Challenger Deep. The expedition lasted **6 hours and 40 minutes**, with **2 hours and 34 minutes** on the ocean floor.

Submersibles can ascend more rapidly than they can descend because of the buoyancy of the air inside a submersible's *ballasts*. For Piccard and Walsh, the descent took about **1.5 times as long** as the ascent. For Cameron, the descent took about **1.75 times as long** as the ascent.

Mount Everest

29,035 ft

Challenger Deep

36,201 ft

GO DIGITAL

PLAN AN EXPEDITION

You pilot a manned dive to the Challenger Deep. Use the ascent times and the descent times for the 1960 and 2012 expeditions to write a plan for your dive, including

- *how long you will spend descending,*
- *how long you will spend on the ocean floor,*
- *how long you will spend ascending,* and
- *goals you hope to accomplish.*

Dive schedules must be flexible to allow for unexpected circumstances. Determine the maximum total amount of time for your expedition and the minimum and maximum amounts of time you want to spend on the ocean floor. Use a graph to show the amounts of time that you can spend on the ocean floor and the amounts of time that you can spend traveling.

5 B.E.S.T. Test Prep WITH CalcChat®
Cumulative Practice

WATCH Tutorial videos are available for each exercise.

1. Which equation is represented by the graph?

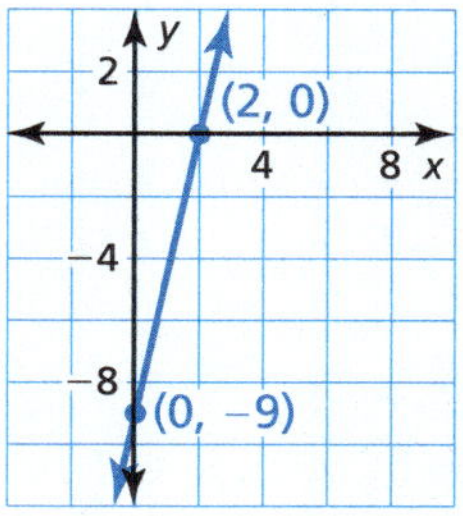

Ⓐ $9x - 2y = -18$

Ⓑ $-9x - 2y = 18$

Ⓒ $9x + 2y = 18$

Ⓓ $-9x + 2y = -18$

2. A company rents out 6-, 8-, 12-, and 16-passenger vans. The function $C(x) = 100 + 5x$ represents the cost C (in dollars) of renting an x-passenger van for a day. Which numbers are in the range of the function? Select all that apply.

Ⓐ 130

Ⓑ 140

Ⓒ 150

Ⓓ 160

Ⓔ 170

Ⓕ 180

Ⓖ 190

Ⓗ 200

3. Determine which inequality signs complete the system of linear inequalities so that the graph represents the system.

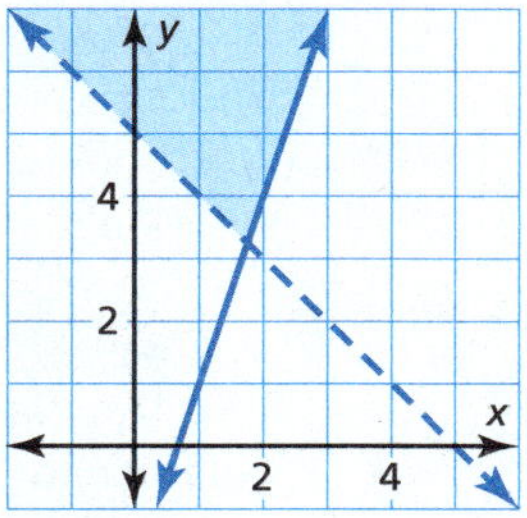

Inequality	≥	>	≤	<
y ☐ $3x - 2$	Ⓐ	Ⓑ	Ⓒ	Ⓓ
y ☐ $-x + 5$	Ⓔ	Ⓕ	Ⓖ	Ⓗ

GO DIGITAL

4. **GRIDDED RESPONSE** You are ordering T-shirts for a concert. The table shows the costs of ordering different numbers of shirts. Determine the total cost of ordering 55 T-shirts.

Number of T-shirts	15	25	30	35
Total cost (dollars)	147.60	246	295.20	344.40

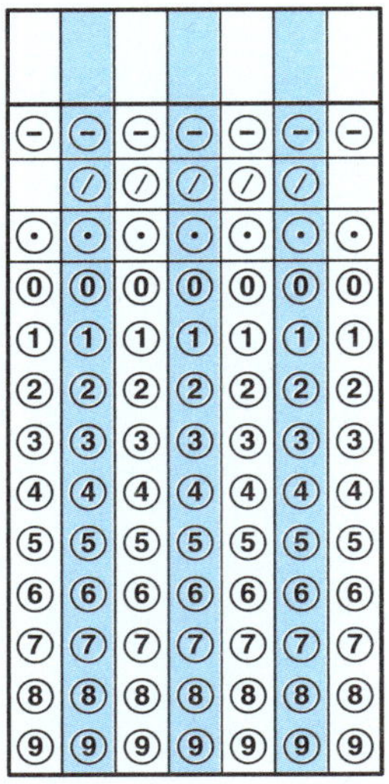

5. The graph of a function g is a translation 4 units right of the graph of $f(x) = |x + 2|$. What are the coordinates of the vertex of the graph of g?

Ⓐ $(-6, 0)$

Ⓑ $(-2, 4)$

Ⓒ $(2, 0)$

Ⓓ $(-2, -4)$

6. Which two equations form a system of linear equations that has no solution?

1: $y = 3x + 2$

2: $y = \frac{1}{3}x + 2$

3: $y = 3x + \frac{1}{2}$

Ⓐ Equation 1 and Equation 2

Ⓑ Equation 1 and Equation 3

Ⓒ Equation 2 and Equation 3

Ⓓ Each pair of equations has a solution.

7. Consider the equation $ax - 8 = 4 - x$.

When a is equal to [Ⓐ -12 / Ⓑ -7 / Ⓒ 1 / Ⓓ 5], the solution is $x = -2$. When a is equal to [Ⓐ -1 / Ⓑ 0 / Ⓒ 1 / Ⓓ 4], the equation has no solution.

8. Which inequality is represented by the graph?

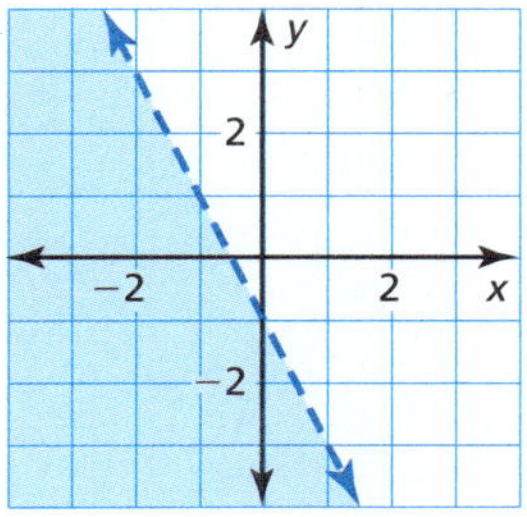

Ⓐ $y + 2x \le -1$

Ⓑ $y + 1 < -2x$

Ⓒ $-2x < y + 1$

Ⓓ $-2x - y \le 1$

9. Solve the equation by graphing.

GRIDDED RESPONSE

$6x - 2 = \frac{2}{3}(12x + 3)$

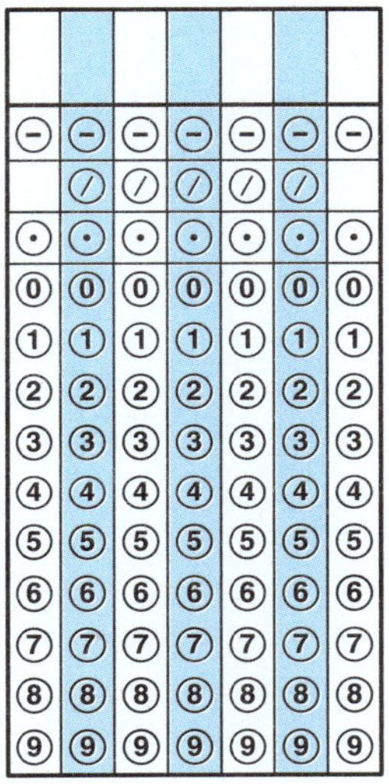

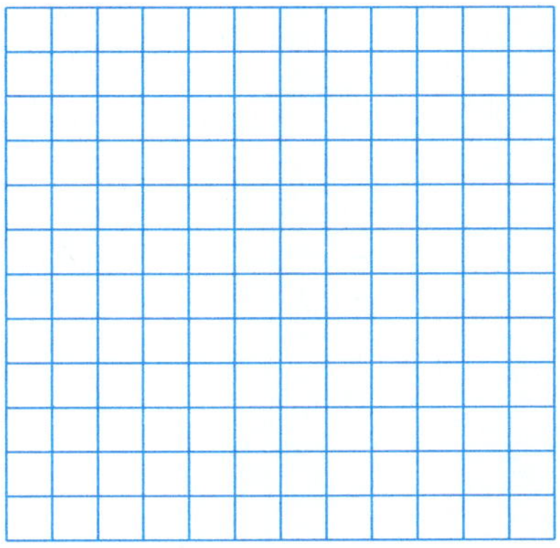

10. Determine whether the equation is written in *point-slope form* or *standard form.*

Equation	Point-Slope Form	Standard Form
$-6x + y = -1$	Ⓐ	Ⓑ
$\frac{1}{4}y + 3x = -24$	Ⓒ	Ⓓ
$\frac{1}{2}(x - 2) = y - 3$	Ⓔ	Ⓕ

11. Which is a solution to the equation $|5x - 8| - 4 = -2$? Select all that apply.

Ⓐ $x = 2$

Ⓑ $x = -2$

Ⓒ $x = \frac{5}{6}$

Ⓓ $x = \frac{6}{5}$

Ⓔ $x = -\frac{6}{5}$

Ⓕ no solution

Selected Answers

Chapter 1

Prepare with CalcChat

1. -7 2. -13 3. 8 4. 4.9
5. -2 6. 1.6 7. $\frac{11}{10}$ 8. $\frac{7}{3}$
9. 6 10. -24 11. 63 12. -28
13. $\frac{1}{24}$ 14. -0.8 15. -0.4 16. $\frac{3}{8}$
17. 3 18. 14.875
19. a. Both numbers are positive or the number with the greater absolute value is positive; *Sample answer:* 2 and 5, or 6 and -2
b. Both numbers have the same sign; *Sample answer:* 3 and 5, or -2 and -7
c. Both numbers have the same sign; *Sample answer:* 10 and 2, or -8 and -4

Section 1.1

1.1 Practice

1. $x = 3$; Subtract 5 from each side.
3. $y = 7$; Add 4 to each side.
5. $w = -7$; Subtract 3 from each side.
7. $a = 5.6$; Add 0.4 to each side.
9. $t = -1$; Subtract $\frac{3}{2}$ from each side.
11. $p - 12.95 = 44$; \$56.95
13. $g = 4$; Divide each side by 5.
15. $p = 15$; Multiply each side by 5.
17. $s = -6$; Divide each side by 9.
19. $x = -8.4$; Multiply each side by -6.
21. $r = -12$; Divide each side by 9π.
23. $p = -3$ 25. $r = -8$
27. $m = 14$ 29. $d = -5.7$ 31. $f = 4\pi$
33. Subtract -0.8 from each side, not add; $r = 12.6 - (-0.8)$; $r = 13.4$
35. $x + 100 + 120 + 100 = 360$; $x = 40$
37. C
39. $24.76s = 50$; 2.02 yd/sec 41. $-5 = 20 - T$; 25°F
43. no; 12 cans cost $8.64 \div 0.80 = \$10.80$ and $\$10.80 > \$10$.
45. $h = 4$ ft 47. $r = 3$ in.
49. a. 5; 10
b. -2; 9
51. 71; Because $\frac{1}{6}$ of the girls is 6, there are 36 girls. Because $\frac{2}{7}$ of the boys is 10, there are 35 boys; $36 + 35 = 71$
53. $x = -\frac{7}{b}$; $b < 0$ 55. $x = -6.5c$; $c < 0$
57. a. 132 hits
b. no; Player B has $132 - 33 = 99$ hits. $\frac{99}{x} > 0.296$, $x < 334$ at-bats

1.1 Review & Refresh

59. $\frac{4}{15}$ 60. $1\frac{5}{12}$
61. $\frac{5}{6}$ 62. $3\frac{2}{21}$
63. 7
64. 150, 2, $\frac{1}{4}$; $50 : \frac{1}{2}$, $150 : \frac{3}{2}$, $200 : 2$, $25 : \frac{1}{4}$
65. $-3.6x - 10$ 66. $-24m + 28$ 67. $2y + 4$
68. 9 arrangements 69. $0.\overline{7}$, $77.\overline{7}\%$
70. $10.99 + 1.5n$; \$15.49 71. $4x + 5$
72. $x = -12$; Subtract 7 from each side.
73. $b = -27$; Multiply each side by -9.
74. $t = 2.5$; Divide each side by -1.8.
75. $w = -\frac{7}{12}$; Add $\frac{1}{4}$ to each side.
76. 3.2

Section 1.2

1.2 Practice

1. $w = 4$ 3. $q = 1$ 5. $z = -32$ 7. $h = 4$
9. $v = 3$ 11. $y = 0.5$ 13. 6 min 15. $z = 3$
17. $m = 3$ 19. $x = -\frac{27}{2}$ 21. $c = 5.5$
23. $2n + 13 = 75$; $n = 31$ 25. $8 + \frac{n}{3} = -2$; $n = -30$
27. $6(n + 15) = -42$; $n = -22$
29. $x = 125$; 120°, 100°, 120°, 135°, 120°, 125°
31. When using the Distributive Property in the second step, the second term should be positive; $-14 + 2y + 4 = -4$; $-10 + 2y = -4$; $2y = 6$; $y = 3$
33. $30(8.75) + 11t = 400$; 12.5 h
35. $983.5 - 1.4 - 2s = 974.9$; 3.6 MB
37. 30 in. by 45 in.
39. Add 1 to each side; Multiply each side by -2; Add 8 to each side; Divide each side by 5.
41. $x = \frac{15}{16}$; *Sample answer:* Distributive Property; There are no fractions until the last step.
43. 3 people
45. $x = \frac{12.5 + b}{a}$; $a < 0$ and $b > -12.5$, or $a > 0$ and $b < -12.5$
47. $x = -\frac{8}{b}$; $b > 0$
49. 16, 18, 20; The next consecutive even integers after $2n$ are $2n + 2$ and $2n + 4$. Solve the equation $2n + (2n + 2) + (2n + 4) = 54$. Then substitute the solution into the expressions for the integers.

1.2 Review & Refresh

51. 0.765 52. $\frac{1}{2}$ 53. 27.4 54. $-\frac{11}{4}$
55. 77.6 times 56. 49%, 0.5, $\frac{11}{20}$ 57. 30 m; 54 m^2
58. $n = \frac{15}{2}$ 59. $x = -2$ 60. $z = 12.4$
61. $r = \frac{4}{3}$ 62. $p = 4$
63. $A'(-2, 1)$, $B'(0, 3)$, $C'(1, -1)$
64. \$162.50 65. $8(3x + 4)$

Section 1.3

1.3 Practice

1. $x = 3$ 3. $p = 7$ 5. $t = -1$ 7. $x = \frac{1}{2}$
9. $g = -4$ 11. $x = -3$ 13. $y = 1.2$
15. no solution 17. $h = 3$ 19. $w = \frac{1}{4}$
21. all real numbers 23. 2 h 25. 4 sec

27. **a.** 3 h; The cost at Studio A is $10.49 + 8h$ and the cost at Studio B is $14.99 + 6.5h$. To find when the costs are the same, set these two expressions equal and solve for the time.

b. The costs will never be the same; *Sample answer:* The cost for Studio B changes to $14.99 + 8h$, and the new equation has no solution.

29. $a = 5$; Both sides simplify to $10x + 15$.

31. 11, 12

33. no solution; 5 more than a number will never be equal to 5 less than the same number.

35. C, D

1.3 Review & Refresh

37. 2.25π cm³ or about 7.069 cm³

38. $v = 5$ 39. $k = -9$ 40. $x = -\frac{3}{5}$

41. $n = 31.5$ 42. $t = -2$ 43. $c = \frac{1}{3}$

44. 105 cm² 45. 48 words per minute

46. $-|21|, -16, |-10|, 22, |-32|$

47. 140 ft

Section 1.4

1.4 Practice

1. 9 3. 0 5. -35 7. 9

9. no solution

11. $m = -10, m = 4$

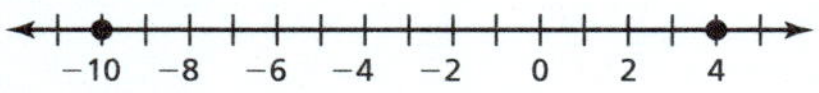

13. $t = -12, t = 12$

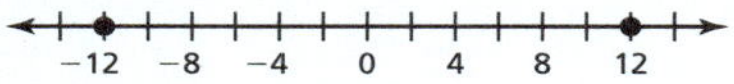

15. $b = -3.5, b = 6$

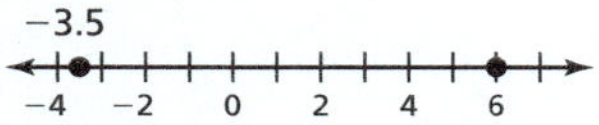

17. $w = -4, w = 5.5$

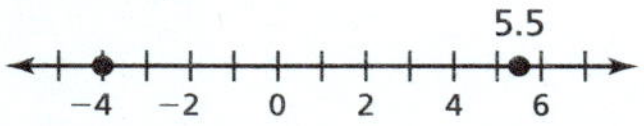

19. no solution 21. $s = 20$

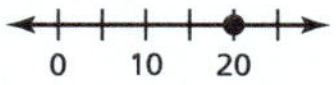

23. $|d - 92.95| = 1.55$; 91.4 million mi, 94.5 million mi

25. B 27. C 29. $n = 3, n = 5$

31. $k = -0.4, k = 6$ 33. $p = \frac{2}{3}, p = 10$

35. $h = 0.25$ 37. $f = \frac{7}{12}$ 39. $|x - 13| = 5$

41. $|x - 5| = 3.5$

43. The absolute value cannot be negative. So, there is no solution.

45. **a.** the distance the car travels after t seconds

b. 5 sec, 7.5 sec

47. no; The absolute value has to be isolated first, which makes the constant on the right positive.

49. always; Square roots of the same number have the same absolute value.

51. sometimes; The equation will only have two solutions if p is positive.

53. Absolute value equations will have no solution when the absolute value is equal to a negative number, one solution when the absolute value is equal to zero, and two solutions when the absolute value is equal to a positive number; *Sample answer:* $|x + 12| = -2$ has no solution, $|x + 12| = 0$ has one solution, and $|x + 12| = 2$ has two solutions.

55. A, E

57. *Sample answer:* In a round of a trivia game, you lose 5 points for an incorrect answer and win 5 points for a correct answer. You have 67 points. x represents your score after your next answer.

59. $|x - 84.5| = 14.5$

1.4 Review & Refresh

61. $c = 0$ 62. no solution

63. all real numbers 64. $y = -3$

65.

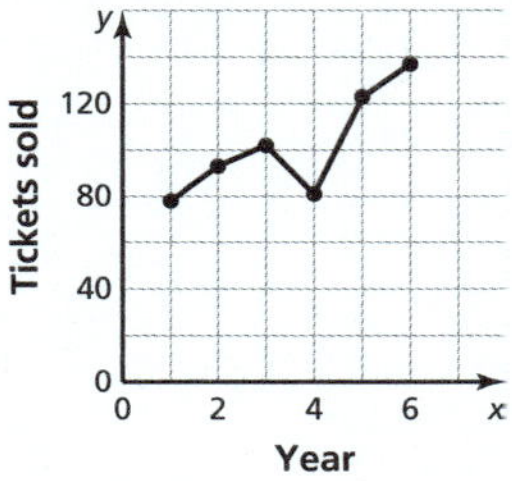

66. $13h + 8.5$ 67. 0.00000007

68. 2590 69. 90 cm³ 70. 1900.7 ft³

71. Addition Property of Equality

72. Division Property of Equality

73. 6 in. 74. 12 ft 75. 27 min, 33 min

76. $2\frac{3}{4}$ 77. 8000

78. 10,849.06, or 10,925 79. 1.61, 1.63, or 1.65

Section 1.5

1.5 Practice

1. $y = 13 + 3x$ 3. $y = -13 + 9x$ 5. $y = 9x - 45$

7. $y = x - 3$ 9. $y = 18x + 12$ 11. $x = \frac{1}{12}y$

13. $x = \dfrac{a}{2 + 6z}$ 15. $x = \dfrac{y - 6}{4 + r}$

17. $x = \dfrac{r}{s + t}$ 19. $x = \dfrac{y - 12}{-5 - 4k}$

21. **a.** $x = \dfrac{C - 60}{85}$

b. 3 trips; 5 trips

23. The equation is not solved for x because there is still a term with x on both sides; $x = y - x + 6$; $2x = y + 6$; $x = \dfrac{y + 6}{2}$

25. $C = R - P$ 27. $b_2 = \dfrac{2A}{h} - b_1$

29. $C = A\left(\dfrac{R}{5} + 0.3\right)$

31. **a.** $r = \dfrac{L - S}{L}$

b. 20%

33. 6.25 yr 35. \$75

37. a. $d = 55t$; $d = 20g$

b. $55t = 20g$; $g = \frac{11t}{4}$

c. 16.5 gal; 330 mi; The amount of gasoline used can be found using the formula from part (b). Either of the original formulas can be used to find the distance.

39. $a = \frac{b + c}{bx - 1}$

41. a. P = pressure, V = volume, n = amount, R = ideal gas constant, T = temperature

b. about 2133.5 L

43. a. 1.1 ft; 1.3 ft; 1.4 ft

b. *Sample answer:* It is easier to find the radius when the circumference formula is rewritten for r.

45. $A = \frac{5}{2}bh$; $h = \frac{2A}{5b}$

1.5 Review & Refresh

47. 37
48. 14
49. $\frac{7}{4}$
50. 93
51. $y = 6x - 12$
52. 90π in.^{2}
53. no

54. a. $h = \frac{231G}{\ell w}$

b. about 16 in.

55. $x = 8, x = -2$

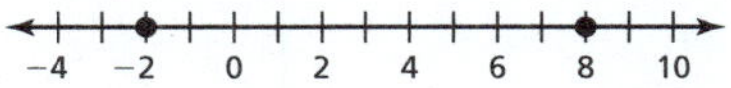

56. $y = 1, y = 7$

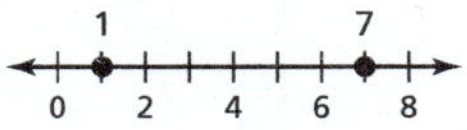

57. no solution

58. $s = -15$; $s = -3$

59. yes
60. 3 h
61. $z = 30$
62. $t = -3$
63. $y = -\frac{3}{2}$

Chapter 1 Review

1. $z = -9$; Subtract 3 from each side.
2. $t = -13$; Divide each side by -0.2.
3. $n = 10$; Multiply each side by -5.
4. $y = 8.6$; Add 2.7 to each side.
5. $b = -\frac{1}{9\pi}$; Divide each side by π.
6. $w = 1\frac{1}{2}$; Subtract $1\frac{4}{5}$ from each side.
7. Subtraction Property of Equality; Because a and b are negative numbers, $\frac{a}{b}$ is positive and the inverse operation is subtraction.
8. \$25.95
9. $y = -9$
10. $b = -5$
11. $n = 6$
12. $z = -5$
13. $x = 18$
14. $w = \frac{25}{4}$
15. decreases; The equation can be rewritten as $x = 7b$, so when the value of b decreases, the value of $7b$ also decreases.
16. 23, 25, 27
17. $n = -4$
18. $m = -24$
19. $y = 9$
20. all real numbers
21. $z = -\frac{4}{15}$
22. no solution

23. *Sample answer:*

$7(2 + 3x) = 77x$ $7(2 + 3x) = 77x$

$14 + 21x = 77x$ $2 + 3x = 11x$

$14 = 56x$ or $2 = 8x$

$\frac{14}{56} = x$ $\frac{2}{8} = x$

$\frac{1}{4} = x$ $\frac{1}{4} = x$

In the first method, I used the Distributive Property to eliminate the parentheses, subtracted $21x$ from each side, divided both sides by 56, and simplified the fraction. In the second method, I divided each side by 7, subtracted $3x$ from both sides, divided both sides by 8, and simplified the fraction.

24. 2475 mi

25. *Sample answer:* Change $4d$ to $2d$; $6(3 + 2d) = 24d$; $\frac{3}{2} = d$

26. a. sometimes

b. sometimes

c. always

27. $y = 14, y = -20$
28. $k = 12, k = -6$
29. $g = \frac{5}{2}$
30. no solution
31. $w = 3, w = -\frac{1}{5}$
32. $x = -1$
33. *Sample answer:* $|x| = 7$
34. *Sample answer:* $|x + 3| = 7$
35. *Sample answer:* $|x - 6.4| = 3$
36. *Sample answer:* $|x| = -8$
37. $|v - 84.5| = 10.5$
38. Minimum: 10.5 hours; maximum: 13.5 hours
39. $y = \frac{1}{2}x - 5$
40. $y = 2x - 2$
41. $y = -\frac{5}{2}x$
42. $y = \frac{a}{9 + 3x}$
43. $x = \frac{-7 - 3y}{9}$
44. $x = \frac{3y - 9}{5}$
45. $x = \frac{6y}{2b}$
46. $x = 3by$
47. \$750

48. a. $s = \frac{12 + 3h}{5}$; $h = \frac{5s - 12}{3}$

b. 51.6 mi/h

c. 76 ft

49. a. $K = \frac{5}{9}(F - 32) + 273.15$

b. 355.37 K

Chapter 1 Practice Test

1. $x = 22$
2. $x = -3$
3. $x = -3, x = 9$
4. $x = 3$
5. all real numbers
6. no solution
7. $c \neq 5$; If c is 5, then the equation is an identity. For all other values of c, subtracting $3x$ from each side will give a statement that is always false.
8. $c < 0$; An absolute value cannot be negative.
9. $y = -\frac{17}{3}x$
10. $y = \frac{x - 3}{3}$
11. $y = \frac{2x}{4x - 1}$
12. $y = \frac{3x}{a - 3}$
13. $|h - 34| = 4$

14. a. $w = \frac{P - 2\ell}{2}$

b. 65 yd

c. 4.8%

15. It will give a negative value on the right and absolute value cannot be negative.

16. **a.** $M = 130 + 10\ell - \frac{5}{2}g$

b. amount of money in your account before mowing lawns

c. $171.25

17. 8.3 min

Chapter 1 B.E.S.T. Test Prep

1. D **2.** B **3.** 15 expert trails

4. A, C, E, F **5.** D **6.** $4 **7.** A

8. C; B **9.** B **10.** C, D, F **11.** B

Chapter 2

Prepare with CalcChat

1.
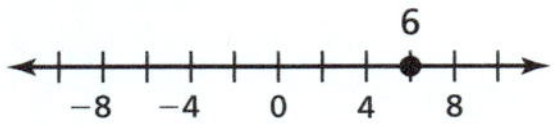

2.
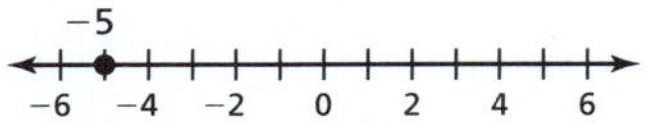

3.
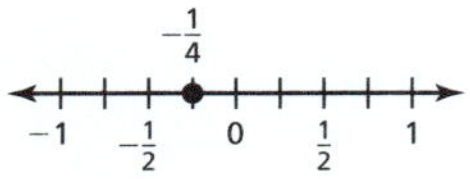

4.
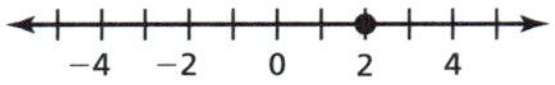

5.

6.
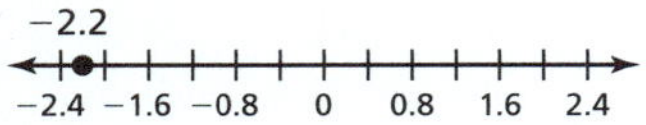

7. $<$ **8.** $<$ **9.** $>$ **10.** $>$

11. $=$ **12.** $<$ **13.** $-b < -a$

Section 2.1

2.1 Practice

1. $x > 3$ **3.** $15 \le \frac{t}{5}$ **5.** $v + 6.2 \ge -4.7$

7. $3k - \frac{5}{3} \le \frac{4}{9}$ **9.** no **11.** yes

13. yes **15.** yes **17.** yes

19. $\ell < 4800$

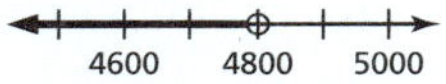

21. *Sample answer:* You ride your bike 12 miles each day for x days, and you ride at least 60 miles.

23.
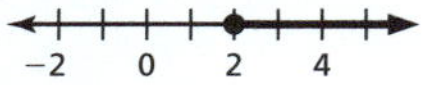

25.
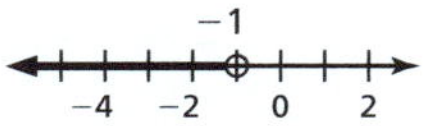

27.
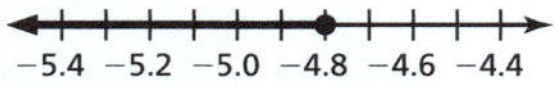

29.
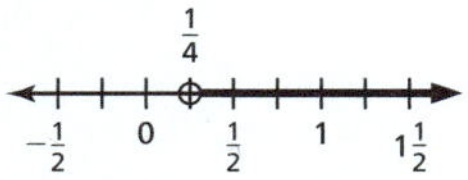

31. The arrow should point to the left.

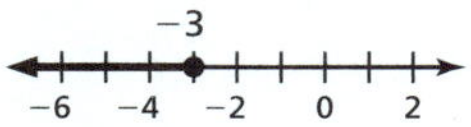

33. $h < 450$

35. $x \le 4$

37. $m \ge 9.25$; The state requires that employees earn at least $9.25 per hour.

39. C

41. Because $Y < X$, $2Y < X + Y$; not true

43. Because $X > Y$, $\frac{Y}{X+Y} < 1$ and $\frac{X}{Y} > 1$, so $\frac{Y}{X+Y} < \frac{X}{Y}$; true

45. $\le$ **47.** $x < 3$

49. yes; You ride the bus about $2 \times 5 \times 4 = 40$ times per month and spend $40(1.65) = \$66 > \$52$.

51. a. $r > 5.71$

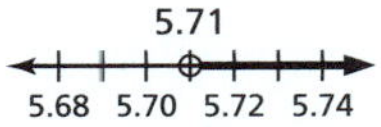

b. The graph includes speeds that are faster than a runner can run.

c. *Sample answer:* $r > 5.71$ and $r < 10$

2.1 Review & Refresh

52. $x = 1$ **53.** $y = -1$ **54.** $z = 8$ **55.** $w = 4$

56. $v = 3$ **57.** $s = -8$

58. The triangles are similar; $x = 45$ and $y = 112$, making the corresponding angle pairs of the triangle congruent.

59. *Sample answer:* (a) $5x - 3 = 7$ (b) $2(2x - 3) = 4x - 8$ (c) $2x + 6 = 2(x + 3)$

60. $a = -6, a = 9$ **61.** no solution

62. $g = 4$ **63.** $h = -1$ **64.** $118.75 **65.** 5.25

66. 3600 **67.** $x = \frac{v}{yz}$

68. $x = \frac{s - 2r}{3}$ **69.** $x = \frac{w - 2}{3}$ **70.** $x = n - \frac{1}{2}$

71. 11.989 ft, 12.01 ft, 12.1 ft; 12.01 ft

72.

73.
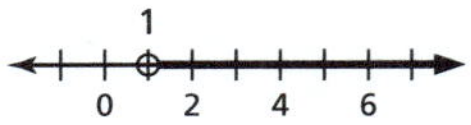

74. a. $h < 107.1$ in.

b. no; A height of 9 feet is equal to 108 inches, which is not less than 107.1 inches.

75. 24, 18, 36; 12 : 3, 24 : 6, 72 : 18, 36 : 9

76. $8 \le z$ **77.** $p - 1 > 6$

Section 2.2

2.2 Practice

1. $x < -1$

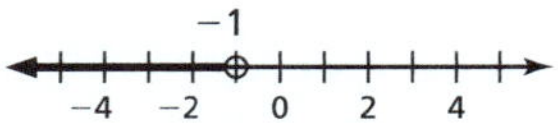

3. $m \le 7$

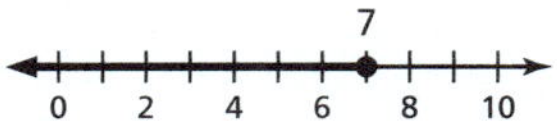

5. $r < 1$

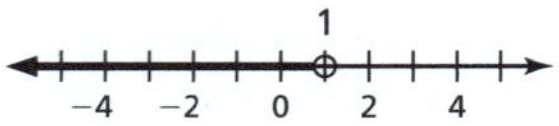

7. $w > -2$

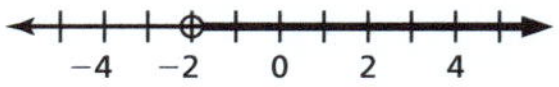

9. $h \ge 8$

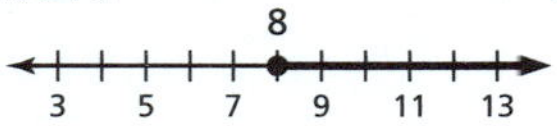

11. $j < -3.8$

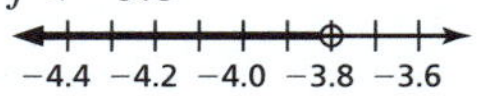

13. $p \le -\frac{2}{5}$

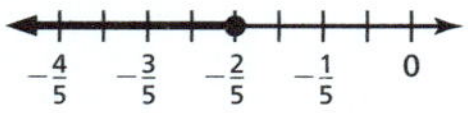

15. $n + 8 > 11; n > 3$

17. $n - 9 < 4; n < 13$ **19.** more than 33 goals

21. 10 should have been added to each side of the inequality, not just the left.

$$-10 + x \geq -9$$
$$-10 + 10 + x \geq -9 + 10$$
$$x \geq 1$$

23. hair dryer and souvenir, or souvenir and boots

25. $14.2 + 14.2 + x < 51.3$; $x < 22.9$

27. **a.** score greater than 117.4 points

b. they both are; Both scores are greater than 117.4 points.

29. **a.** $x \geq 6$

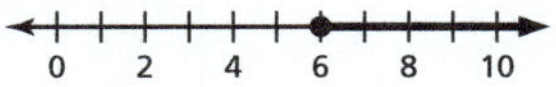

b. $x < 17.7$

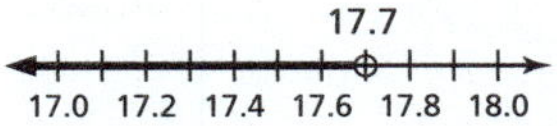

31. A, D

33. *Sample answer:* $x + 33.2 \leq 50$; A shelf can safely support up to 50 pounds. The combined weight of items on the shelf is 33.2 pounds. x represents the possible weights of items that can be put on the shelf safely.

2.2 Review & Refresh

34. -63 **35.** 132 **36.** 9 **37.** -4

38. $y = 6$ **39.** $n = -29.2$

40. $x \geq 16$; You must be 16 years or older to obtain a driver's license.

41. $x = -\frac{8}{5}, x = 12$ **42.** $a < -10$ **43.** $\frac{3}{7}$, or 42.9%

44. $w \leq -5$

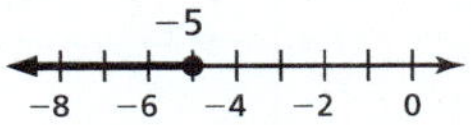

45. $x > 2.7$

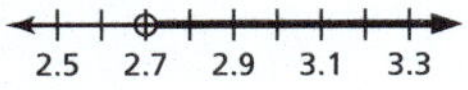

46. 2 h 30 min there, 2 h 45 min back

47. 11 **48.** $-\frac{2}{9}$

Section 2.3

2.3 Practice

1. $y \leq -3$

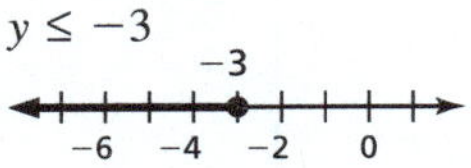

3. $c \leq 5$

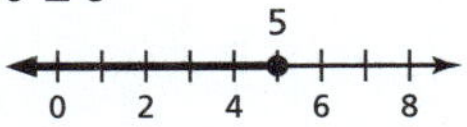

5. $n \geq -2$

7. $t > 4$

9. $x > -4$

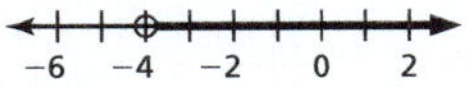

11. $t \geq -6$

13. $w \leq \frac{55}{2}$

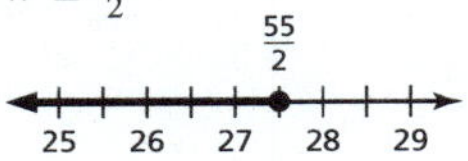

15. $n \leq -2.25$

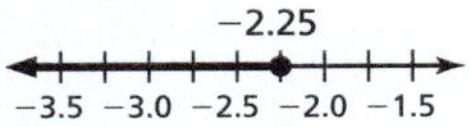

17. 4.5 h

19. The inequality should not be reversed when multiplying each side by $\frac{3}{2}$; $\frac{3}{2} \cdot (-6) > \frac{3}{2} \cdot \frac{2}{3}x$; $-\frac{18}{2} > x$; $-9 > x$; $x < -9$; The solution is $x < -9$.

21. $y > 12$ **23.** $n > -16$

25. more than 50 million bills

27. **a.** at least 2000 glass bottles

b. at least 1000 plastic bottles

c. $0.05g + 0.10p \geq 100$

29. no; The distance you run in 4 hours would be no more than 25.2 miles, which is less than the distance required for a marathon.

31. Because x may represent a positive or negative number, the inequality may need to be reversed when multiplying by x.

33. less than 13.5 mi

2.3 Review & Refresh

35. $x = 2$ **36.** $y = -4$ **37.** no solution

38. $x = -3$ **39.** $x = 5.5$ **40.** 2.5 years

41. $d > -4.5$

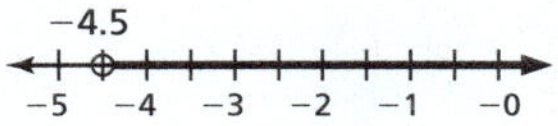

42. $c \leq 21$

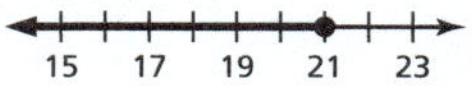

43. $2^3 \cdot 3^2$ **44.** 85% **45.** 25% **46.** 120%

47. $\frac{2}{3}$ **48.** at most \$8.01

49. $A'(-1, -4), B'(-3, -1), C'(4, -1), D'(3, -4)$

50. 24, 25

51.

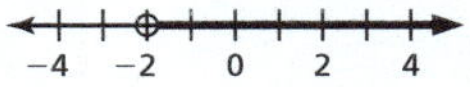

52.

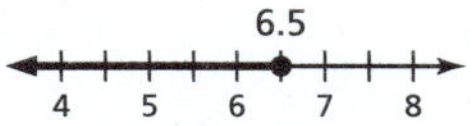

53.

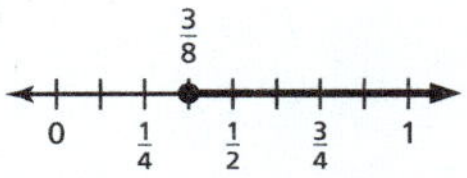

54.

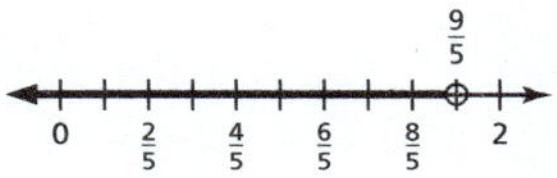

55. **a.** $\frac{1}{20}$, or 5%; 1 face with a 20 out of 20 faces

b. $\frac{9}{20}$, or 45%; 9 faces with a single digit (1–9) out of 20 faces

c. $\frac{1}{4}$, or 25%; 5 faces with a multiple of 4 (4, 8, 12, 16, 20) out of 20 faces.

Section 2.4

2.4 Practice

1. $x > 5$

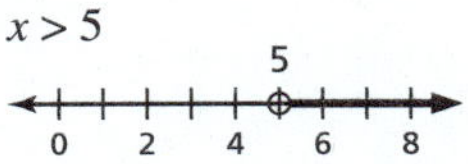

3. $v \leq \frac{1}{2}$

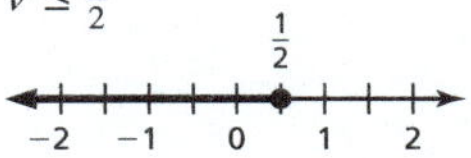

5. $w > 2$

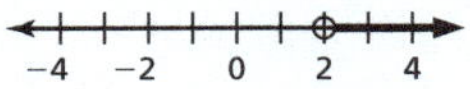

7. $p < -16$

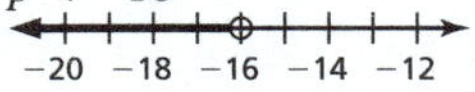

9. $a \geq -4.1$

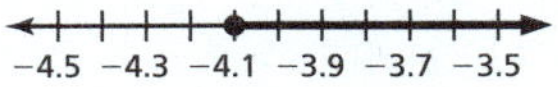

11. $m > 3$

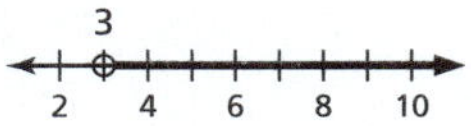

13. $d > -2$

15. all real numbers

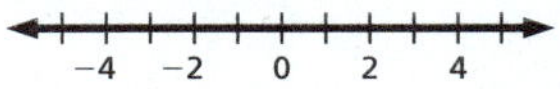

17. no solution **19.** no solution

21. all real numbers

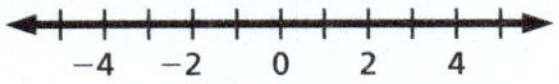

23. In the first step, you need to use the Distributive Property on the left side; $x + 24 \geq 12$; $x \geq -12$

25. at least 40 active min

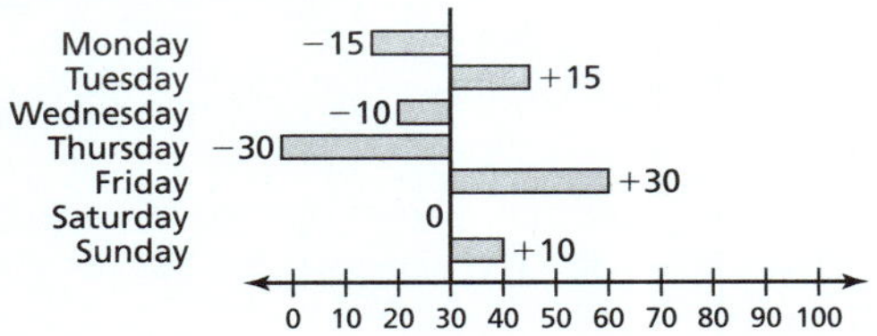

27. $x > 4$

29. $a = 4$

31. *Sample answer:* $-2, -4, -3$

33. 7 stories; Using the Pythagorean Theorem, the 74-foot ladder can reach at most 70 feet. Solving the inequality $10n - 8 \leq 70$ gives $n \leq 7.8$, so the ladder cannot quite reach the 8th story.

2.4 Review & Refresh

35. $y = -3x - 1$

36. $x = 8$

37. $n \geq -7$

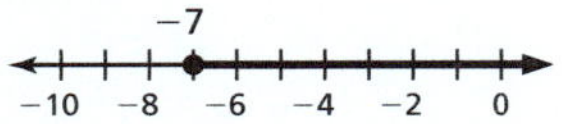

38. $b < -15.2$

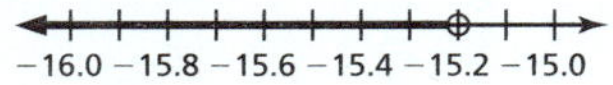

39. $x < -\frac{1}{7}$

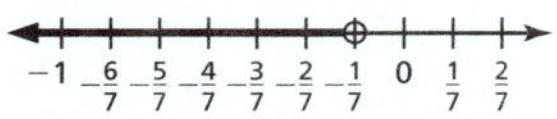

40. all real numbers

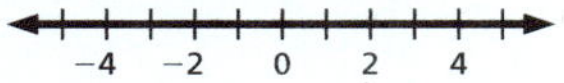

41. a. 3 months

b. The number of weeks is reduced; $20w + 50 \geq 229.95$, $w \geq 9$ weeks

42. yes

43. $6y \leq 10$

44. $p + 7 > 24.8$

45. $z = -1$

46. no solution

47. 25 students; 40%

Section 2.5

2.5 Practice

1. $2 < p < 6$

3. $m > -7\frac{2}{3}$ *or* $m \leq -10$

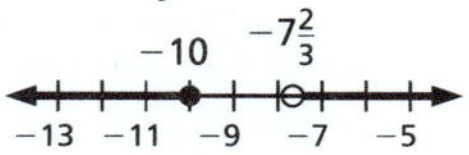

5. $1 < x \leq 6$

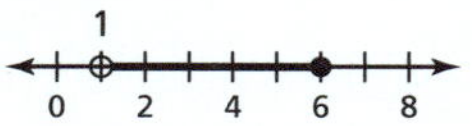

7. $v < -5$ *or* $v > 5$

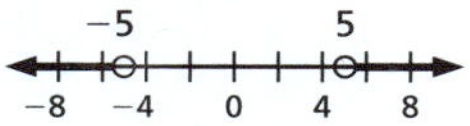

9. $r < -\frac{5}{2}$ *or* $r \geq \frac{3}{8}$

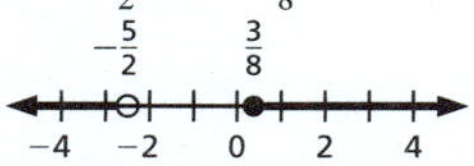

11. $-10 < x < 5$

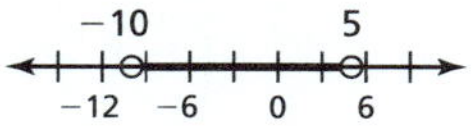

13. a. *Sample answer:* $1700 < h \leq 2500$

b. *Sample answer:* $4000 < h \leq 14{,}410$

15.

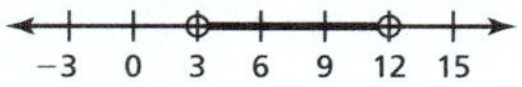

17.

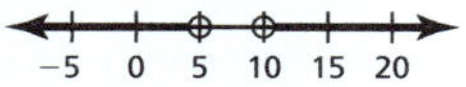

19. $\{x \mid x < -8 \text{ or } x \geq -4\}$

21. $\{x \mid x \neq 100\}$

23. $\{x \mid 4 \leq x < 12\}$

25. $\{w \mid w \leq -4 \text{ or } w > 8\}$

27. $\{m \mid m \text{ is a real number}\}$

29. $\{x \mid x = -1\}$

31. $-4 \leq F \leq 5$

33. no solution

35. $y > 7$

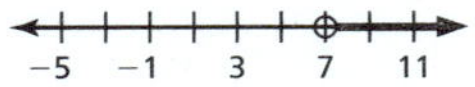

37. all real numbers

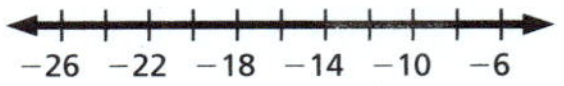

39. at least 3 and no more than 15

41. $h < 50.4$ in. *or* $h > 74.0$ in., **or** $h < 50.9$ in. *or* $h > 74.7$ in.

43. $36 \leq x \leq 96$

45. $k = 8.5$

47. $7.3 + 5.5 > x$, $7.3 + x > 5.5$, $5.5 + x > 7.3$; no; $5.5 + 1.5 \not> 7.3$

2.5 Review & Refresh

48. $A'(1, 4)$; $B'(-2, -2)$; $C'(-5, 1)$

49. $d = 54, d = -54$

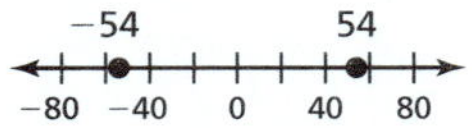

50. no solution

51. $r = -11.4, r = 7.4$

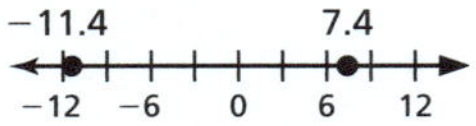

52. $w = -26, w = -\frac{2}{3}$

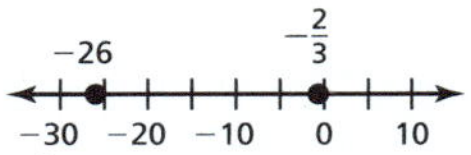

53. strong positive correlation

54. 5 quarters, 3 dimes, 6 nickels

55. $-3 < x \leq 2$

56. $x \leq \frac{1}{3}$ *or* $x > \frac{5}{3}$

57. 64%

58. *Sample answer:* The probability of spinning a 4 is about $\frac{1}{6}$, so you can predict you will spin a 4 about $\frac{1}{6} \cdot 50 = 8\frac{1}{3}$, or about 8 times.

59. 83% or higher

60. $q \leq 5.8$

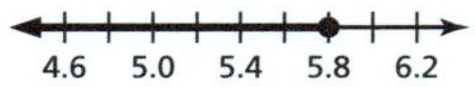

61. $z > -\frac{1}{4}$

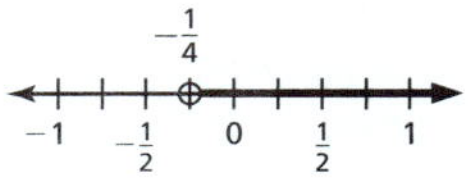

62. $x \leq -9$

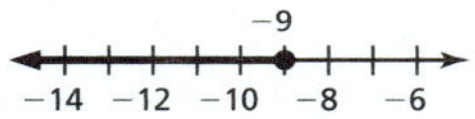

63. $x \geq \frac{3}{8}$

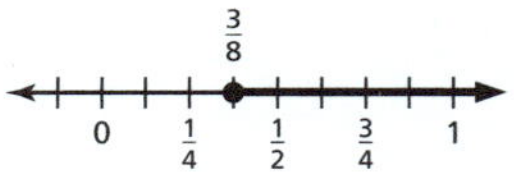

64. $\frac{2 \text{ mi}}{3 \text{ h}}, \frac{3 \text{ h}}{2 \text{ mi}}$

Miles	$\frac{4}{3}$	$\frac{8}{3}$	4
Hours	2	4	6

65. $A = 18.49\pi \text{ cm}^2$ or about 58.1 cm^2

Section 2.6

2.6 Practice

1. $-3 < x < 3$

3. $d < -12$ *or* $d > -6$

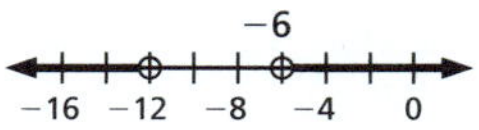

5. all real numbers

7. no solution

9. $t \leq -\frac{2}{3}$ *or* $t \geq 3$

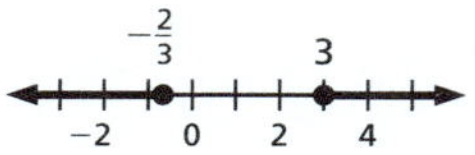

11. $m > 20$ *or* $m < 8$

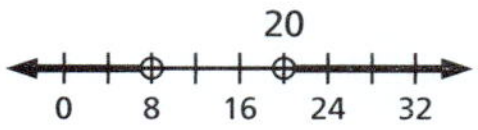

13. $-4 \leq w \leq -\frac{4}{3}$

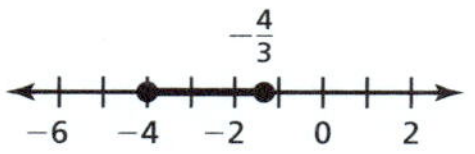

15. $f < 12$ *or* $f > 12$

17. $|n| < 6$; $-6 < n < 6$

19. $|w - 500| \le 30$; 470 to 530 words

21. The absolute value inequality should be written as a compound inequality; $-20 < x - 5 < 20$; $-15 < x < 25$

23. the gasket with a weight of 0.53 lb; $|0.6 - w| > 0.06$, $w < 0.54$ *or* $w > 0.66$

25. $\left|\frac{1}{2} \cdot 4(x + 6) - 2 \cdot 6\right| < 2$; $-1 < x < 1$

27. $d = 0.86$

29. true

31. false; It has to be a solution of $x + 3 \le -8$ *or* $x + 3 \ge 8$.

33. yes; The solution is $n > 0$ *or* $n < 0$ which includes all real numbers except 0.

35. $6 < x < 7$; *Sample answer:* Solve each inequality, then draw a sketch of the 2 solutions on the same number line to see where they intersect.

2.6 Review & Refresh

36–39.

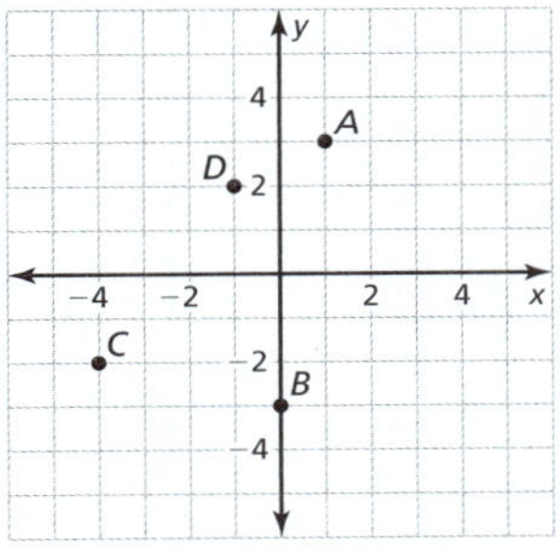

36. Quadrant I

37. y-axis

38. Quadrant III

39. Quadrant II

40. yes; Because the absolute value must be positive, all values will be greater than -6.

41. 1, 6, 11, 16, 21

42. $m = -\frac{3}{4}$

43. $x = -5, x = -2$

44. all real numbers

45. $x < -4$

46. $x > -7c$

47. $x \le -\frac{10.5}{c}$

48. -6

49. $\frac{2}{5}$

50. you bike faster

51. $t \le -18.5$

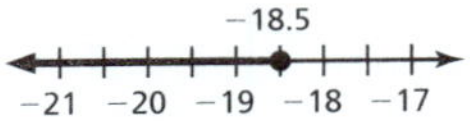

52. $x > -3$

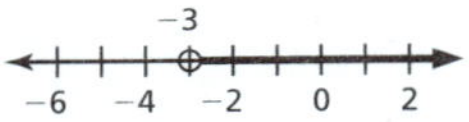

53. $-2 < y \le 1$

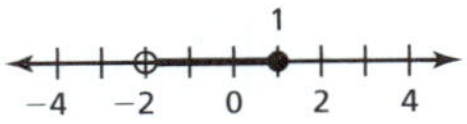

54. $x < -4$ *or* $x > \frac{8}{3}$

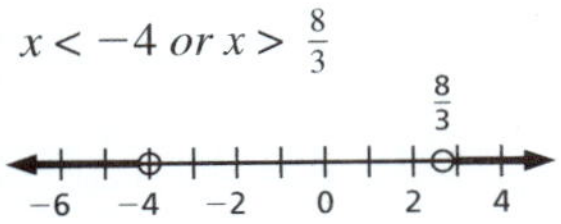

55. $b \le \frac{4}{3}$ *or* $b \ge 2$

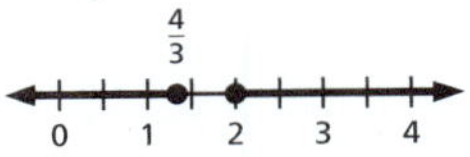

56. 81

57. -100

Chapter 2 Review

1. $d - 2 < -1$

2. $5h \le 10$

3. no

4. yes

5. yes

6.

7.

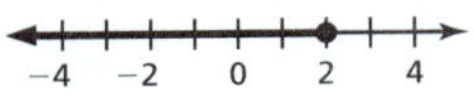

8.

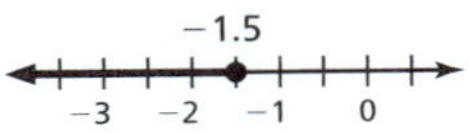

9.

10. $y > 2$

11. $y \le -0.06$

12. a. $s \ge 350$

$t \ge 2$

$u \ge 5$

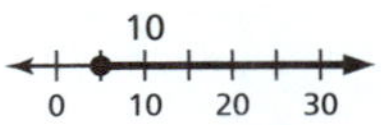

b. no; One of the requirements is to swim 350 yards, which is equal to 1050 feet. If you only swim 915 feet you do not meet this requirement.

13. sometimes; If $M > 0$ and $N > 0$, then $\frac{M}{N} > 1$ and $\frac{N}{M} < 1$, so $\frac{M}{N} > \frac{N}{M}$. If $M < 0$ and $N < 0$, then $\frac{M}{N} < 1$ and $\frac{N}{M} > 1$, so $\frac{M}{N} < \frac{N}{M}$.

14. $p < 6$

15. $r > -2$

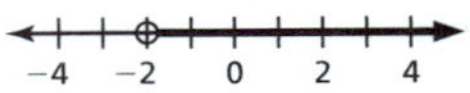

16. $m \le 8.8$

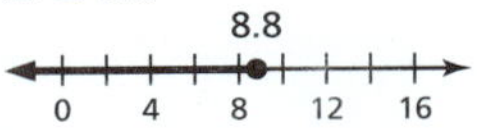

17. $x \le -10.5$

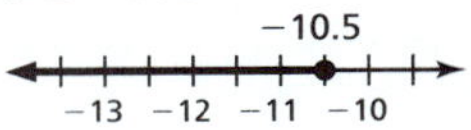

18. *Sample answer:* $-1 > b - \frac{1}{3}$

19. more than 1.18 m

20. $x > -7$

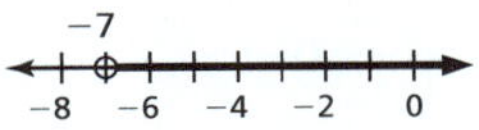

21. $g \ge -20$

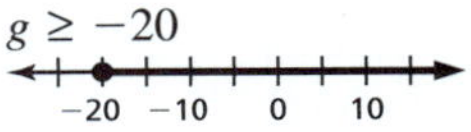

22. $n \ge -4$

23. $s \le -88$

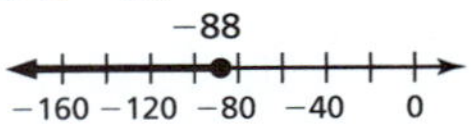

24. $q > 18$

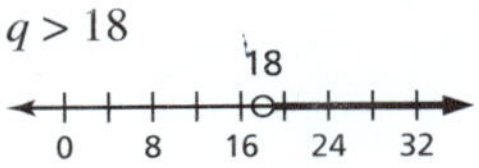

25. $k < -5$

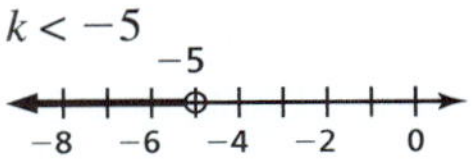

26. *Sample answer:* $3h \ge 9.75$

27. $x > 5$

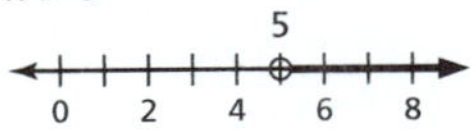

28. $b > -26$

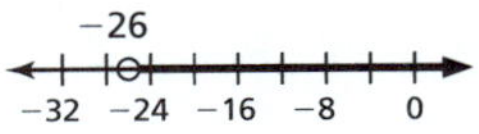

29. $n \ge 2.25$

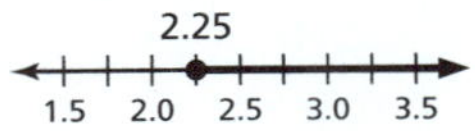

30. $s \le \frac{14}{3}$

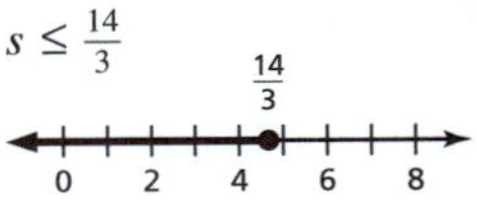

31. no solution

32. $r > 2.8$

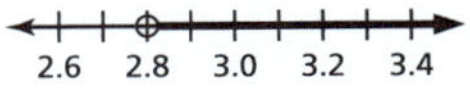

33. 16 or more months

34. $-6 < x \le 8$

35. $\{z \mid -2 \le z \le 6\}$

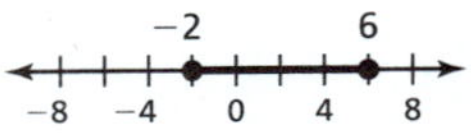

36. $\{p \mid p \le 2$ *or* $p > 3\}$

37. $\{r \mid r < -20$ *or* $r \ge -5\}$

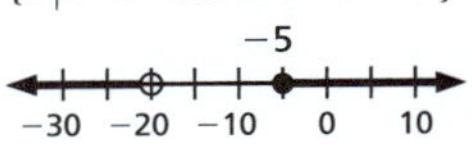

38. $\left\{d \,\middle|\, -\frac{3}{2} < d \le 4\right\}$

39. $8000 < x \le 8850$

40. $45 \le \dfrac{s}{1.61} \le 70$ and $\{s \mid 72.45 \le s \le 112.70\}$, or $45 \le 0.62s \le 70$ and $\{s \mid 72.58 \le s \le 112.90\}$

41. $m \ge 10$ *or* $m \le -10$

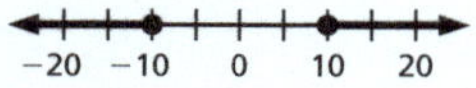

42. no solution

43. $-\frac{14}{3} < g < 2$

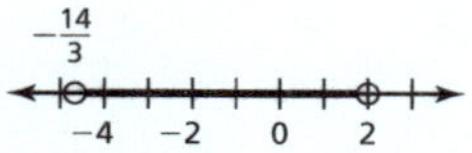

44. all real numbers

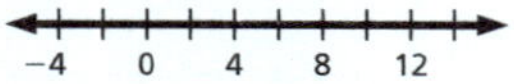

45. $|h - 106| \le 7$; 99 cm to 113 cm

Chapter 2 Practice Test

1. $y + 9 \ge -1$
2. $|k - 10| < 3$
3. $m \le -7$

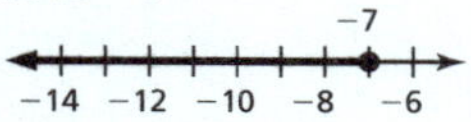

4. $x \ge -8$

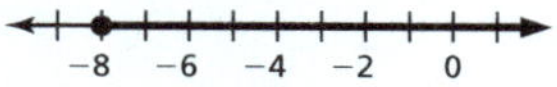

5. all real numbers

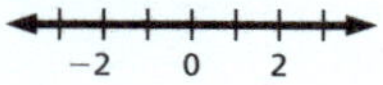

6. $-3 \le a \le 2$

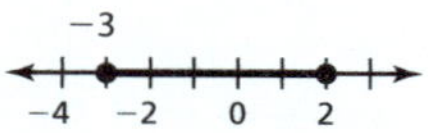

7. $h < 9.5$ *or* $h > 11$

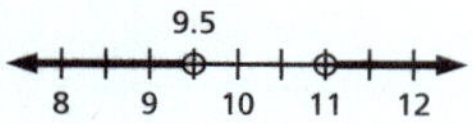

8. $\frac{1}{3} < b < 3$

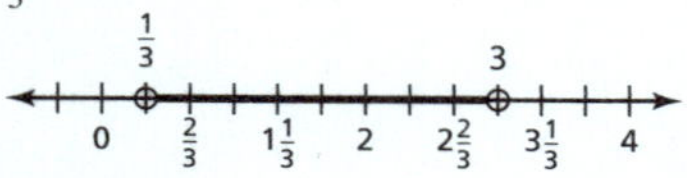

9. at least \$405
10. $|w - 0.3| \le 0.0003$; between 0.2997 in. and 0.3003 in.
11. $-3 < x \le 2$

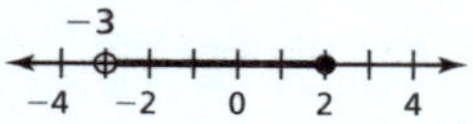

The values between −3 and 2, including 2, are not solutions.

12. scores greater than 6
13. $8.8t < 6.6t + 55$, $t < 25$ sec
14. a. 6.25%
    b. $175 + 1.0625(p - 175) \le 430$; $p \le 415$
    c. any item of clothing that costs more than \$875; Solve the inequality $1.05p < 175 + 1.0625(p - 175)$.

Chapter 2 B.E.S.T. Test Prep

1. A
2. 10.4
3. D
4. B, E
5. −15
6. C
7. −2
8. A, B, C, D
9. D
10. A, D, E

Chapter 3

Prepare with CalcChat

1–6.

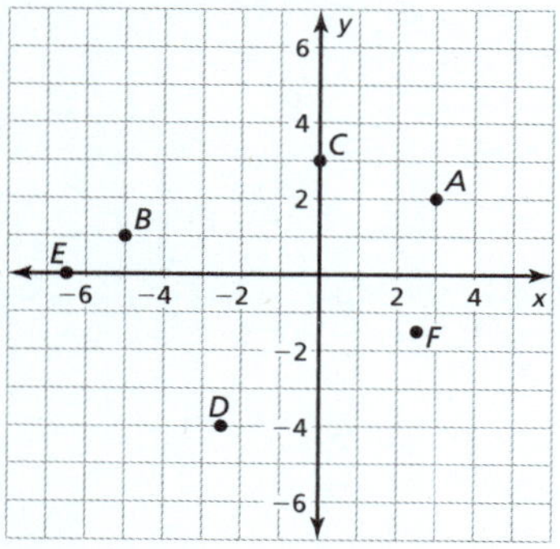

1. in Quadrant I
2. in Quadrant II
3. on positive y-axis
4. in Quadrant III
5. on negative x-axis
6. in Quadrant IV
7. 17
8. −7
9. 20
10. 34
11. 42
12. $\frac{15}{2}$
13. Start at the origin. Move a units right and b units up. Plot the point; Start at the origin. Move a units left and b units up. Plot the point; Start at the origin. Move a units right and b units down. Plot the point; Start at the origin. Move a units left and b units down. Plot the point.

Section 3.1

3.1 Practice

1. function; Every input has exactly one output.
3. not a function; The input 2 has two outputs, 3 and 2.
5. not a function; The input 16 has two outputs, −2 and 2, and the input 1 has two outputs, −1 and 1.
7. function; No vertical line can be drawn through more than one point on the graph.
9. not a function; A vertical line can be drawn through more than one point on the graph in many places, such as (4, 0) and (4, 6).
11. domain: −2, −1, 0, 1, 2; range: −2, 0, 2
13. domain: $-4 \le x \le 2$; range: $2 \le y \le 6$
15. The amount of time is the dependent variable and the number of quarters is the independent variable.
17. a. yes; The total cost of the cell phone plan is the dependent variable and the number of cell phone lines is the independent variable.
    b. domain: 1, 2, 3, 4; range: 30, 60, 90, 120
19. A function can have one output paired with two inputs, but cannot have one input paired with more than one output; The relation is a function. No input is paired with more than one output.
21. *Sample answer:* The balance of the savings account is \$100 in month 0 and increases by \$25 per month through month 4.

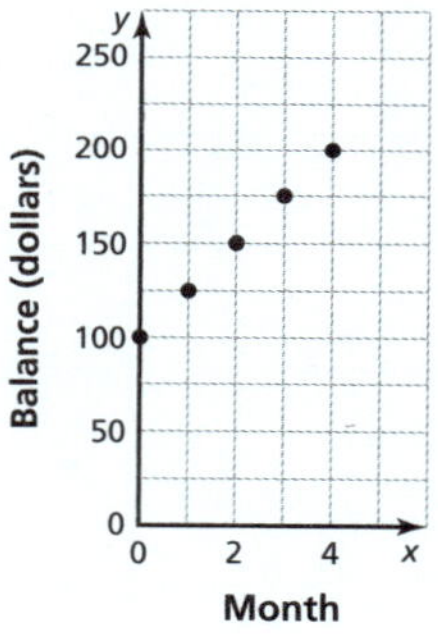

yes; No vertical line can be drawn through more than one point on the graph.

23. −2
25. no; A vertical line does not represent a function.
27. no; Items that cost the same to make could be sold for different prices.
29. yes; Each student has exactly one homeroom teacher.
31. true
33. false; More than one input can have the same output in a function, so reversing the values may not produce a function.
35. A, C, D
37. domain: all real numbers; range: $y \ge 0$
39. domain: all real numbers; range: $y \ge -6$

41. domain: $3 < h < 23$; range: $26 < P < 46$

3.1 Review & Refresh

42. no
43. 21
44. 36%
45. $n = -2.1$
46. $x = 5$
47. $c = 7$
48. $h = -10$
49. function; Every input has exactly one output.
50. $7 \leq \frac{d}{-5}$
51. \$31.80
52. $z < -4$

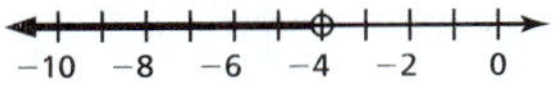

53. $y \leq 5.5$

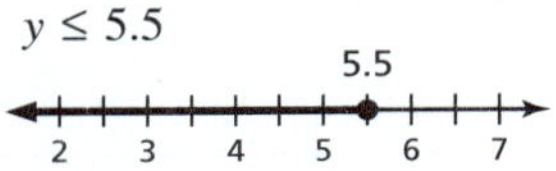

54. $x \geq -14$

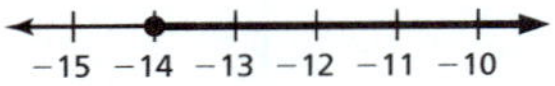

55. $w > -3$

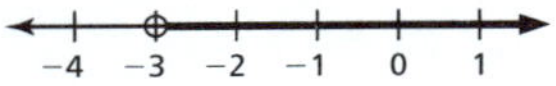

56. $t \leq 2$ *or* $t \geq 8$

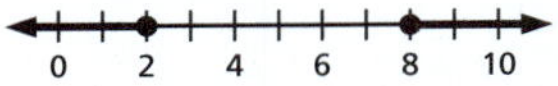

57. $-10 \leq m < -2$

58. domain: $-3 \leq x \leq 2$; range: $-2 \leq y \leq 1$
59. $a = -3$
60. $x < -1$ *or* $x \geq 2$
61. 12 points
62. $y = \frac{1}{2}x - 3$
63. 1278 ft^2

Section 3.2

3.2 Practice

1. x-intercept: about -3, y-intercept: about 1
3. x-intercept: about 5, y-intercept: about -10
5. positive: $x < -2$; negative: $x > -2$; decreasing: for all real numbers; $y \to -\infty$ as $x \to +\infty$ and $y \to +\infty$ as $x \to -\infty$
7. positive: $1 < x < 5$, negative: $x < 1$ and $x > 5$, increasing: $x < 3$, decreasing: $x > 3$; $y \to -\infty$ as $x \to +\infty$ and $y \to -\infty$ as $x \to -\infty$
9. *Sample answer:*

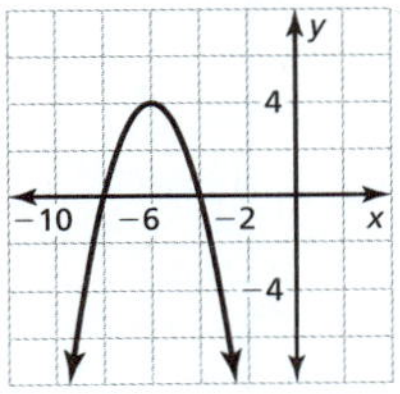

11. The initial speed of the blue car is 5 mi/h greater. The stopping time for the red car is about 1 second longer.
13. The function is not positive when $x = 3$; The function is positive when $x < 3$ and $x > 3$.
15. B, C
17. *Sample answer:*

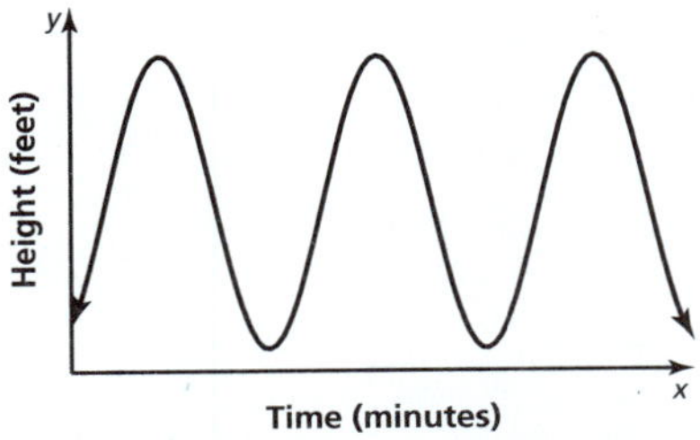

As time increases, your height will oscillate between the maximum height at the top of the Ferris wheel to the minimum height at the bottom of the Ferris wheel.

3.2 Review & Refresh

19. $-5 \leq n < -1$

20. $k \leq -\frac{1}{2}$ *or* $k \geq 2\frac{1}{2}$

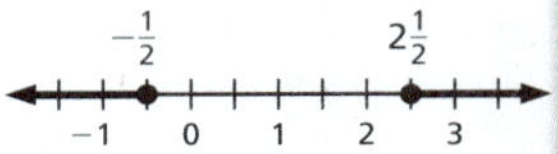

21. $b = -28$
22. $x = -5$
23. $t = \frac{1}{3}$
24. $m = -3$
25. coffee and muffin, coffee and bagel
26. 6
27. x-intercepts: about -3.5 and -1.5, y-intercept: about -3
28. $a > 4$

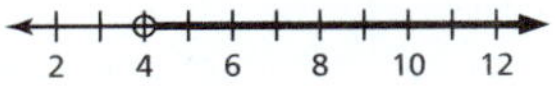

29. $r \geq -10$

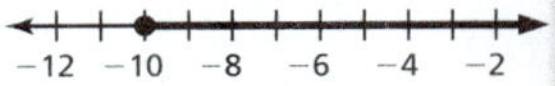

30. $x < -8$

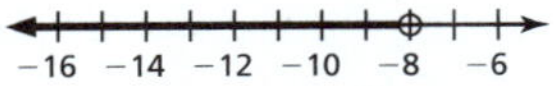

31. $x < -21$ *or* $x > -15$

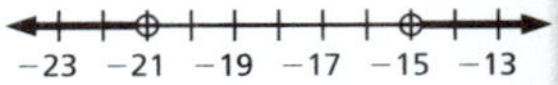

32. (a) *Sample answer:* (4, 3); Each input has exactly one output. (b) *Sample answer:* (2, 3); The input 2 has two outputs, 2 and 3.

Section 3.3

3.3 Practice

1. nonlinear; The graph is not a line.
3. linear; The graph is a line.
5. nonlinear; The graph is not a line.
7. linear; As x increases by 1, y increases by 5. The rate of change is constant.
9. nonlinear; As x increases by 4, y decreases by different amounts. The rate of change is not constant.
11. The graph is not a line.
13. The increase in y needs to be done by adding or subtracting the same amount to be linear, not multiplying; As x increases by 2, y increases by different amounts. The rate of change is not constant. So, the function is nonlinear.
15. nonlinear; It cannot be rewritten in the form $y = mx + b$.
17. linear; It can be rewritten as $y = -1x + 2$.
19. linear; It can be rewritten as $y = 1x + 2$.
21. linear; It can be rewritten as $y = 1x - 54$.
23. A, C, E, F
25.

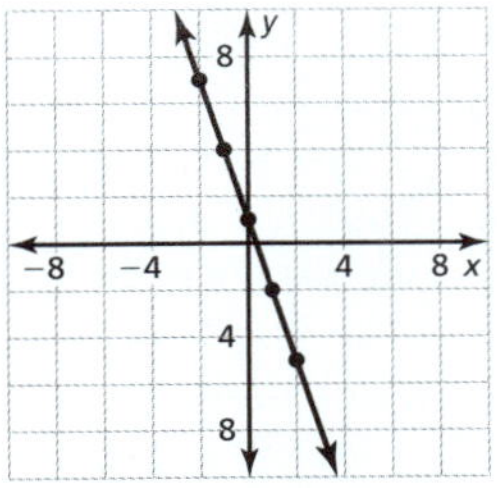

27.

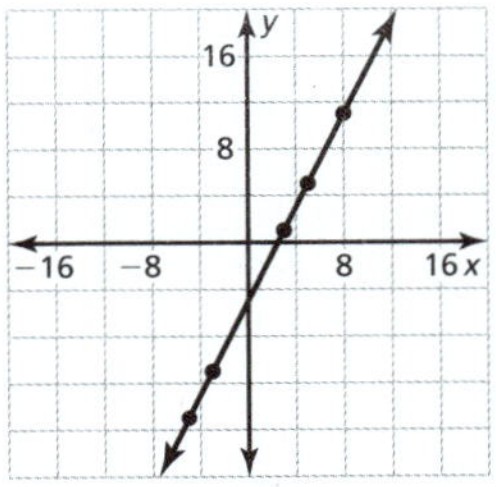

29. 2, 4, 6; discrete; The graph consists of individual points.
31. continuous; The time can be any value greater that or equal to 0.
33. **a.** 10 represents the amount of money you can spend, $1.44p$ represents the cost of printing photographs, and 1.44 represents the price per photograph.
b. the set of all integers between 0 and 6; discrete; The number of photographs must be a whole number.

c.

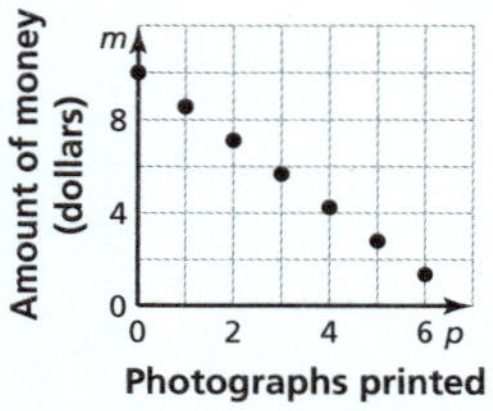

35. a. yes; As the number of minutes increase by 1, the number of gallons increase by 17. The rate of change is constant, so the situation represents a linear function.

b. $m \geq 0$; continuous; Because it is possible to have a portion of a minute, the number of minutes can be any value greater than or equal to 0.

c.

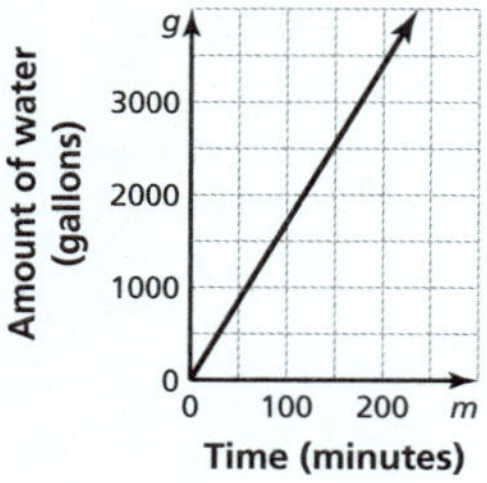

37. 2, 5, 8

39. *Sample answer:* the distance traveled y when driving 65 miles per hour for x hours; The domain for the function that represents the distance traveled is $x \geq 0$ which is continuous.

41. linear; As x increases by 1, y increases by 4. The rate of change is constant.

43. a. \$10.20

b. domain: $0 \leq x \leq 18$; range: $0 \leq y \leq 183.60$

45. a. the total gallons of water in one jug of each type; continuous

b. the total number of jugs of both types; discrete

c. the total gallons of water in all the jugs of the first types; continuous

d. the total gallons of water in all the jugs of both types; continuous

47. Check students' work. Simple Tees when $x \leq 26$ and T-shirts Unlimited when $27 \leq x \leq 200$

49. no; A linear function can be constant.

51. The range is discrete because each value of the domain maps to exactly one value of the range; The range is discrete or continuous because each value of the domain maps to either certain values or all of the values in the range.

53. *Sample answer:* profit (or loss) on the sale of x units at \$1 each that cost \$0.75 to make, plus \$50 in fixed costs

3.3 Review & Refresh

54. $h = -13$

55. $y = 3$

56. $g = 4$

57. $w = -12, w = 6$

58. $\frac{6}{7}$

59. $8\frac{3}{4}$

60. 14

61. $\frac{2}{9}$

62. no; The graph does not pass through the origin.

63. $n + 12 \geq 35$

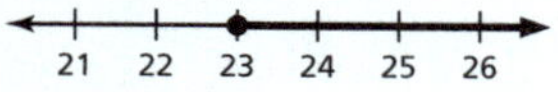

64. not a function

65. function

66. discrete; The number of stories must be a whole number.

67. *Sample answer:* $-5x \geq 25$

68. a. yes; Profit is the dependent variable, and the number of tickets sold is the independent variable.

b. domain: the set of integers between 0 and 9350; range: $0 \leq p \leq 560{,}532.50$; discrete; You cannot buy part of a ticket.

69. positive: $0.7 < x < 4.3$, negative: $x < 0.7$ and $x > 4.3$, increasing: $x < 2.5$, decreasing: $x > 2.5$; $y \to -\infty$ as $x \to +\infty$; $y \to -\infty$ as $x \to -\infty$

70. $-\frac{23}{2} \leq x < \frac{13}{2}$

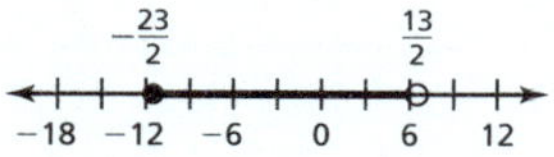

71. $q < -6$ *or* $q \geq 5$

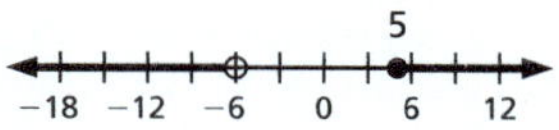

72. all real numbers

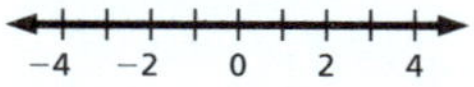

73. $0 \leq z \leq 3$

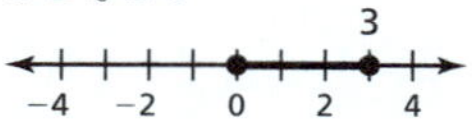

74. linear; The rate of change is constant.

75. 1.07×10^8

76. 2.0×10^{-6}

Section 3.4

3.4 Practice

1. 4; 6; 11

3. 13; 9; −1

5. $-\frac{7}{2}$; -3; $-\frac{7}{4}$

7. 10.2; 6.2; −3.8

9. a. There are no customers in the restaurant at 8 A.M.

b. There are the same number of customers in the restaurant at 11 A.M. as there are at 4 P.M.

c. There are 29 customers in the restaurant n hours after 8 A.M.

d. There are fewer customers in the restaurant at 9:30 P.M. than there are at 8 P.M.

11. $x = -9$

13. $x = -2$

15. $x = -2$

17. $x = 5$

19. \$77.50

21.

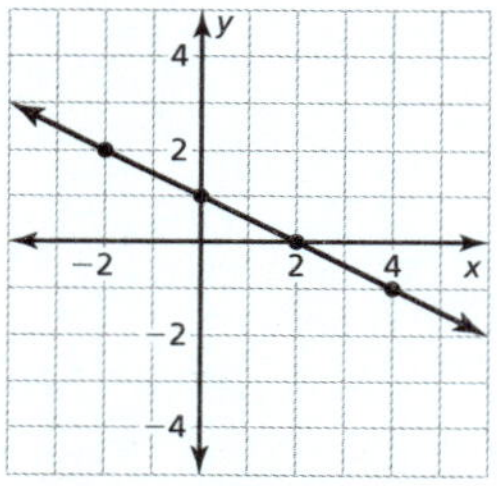

23.

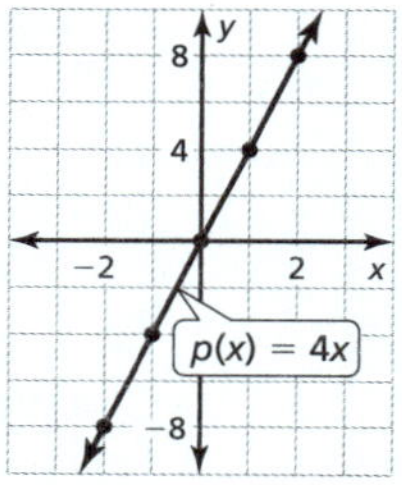

25.

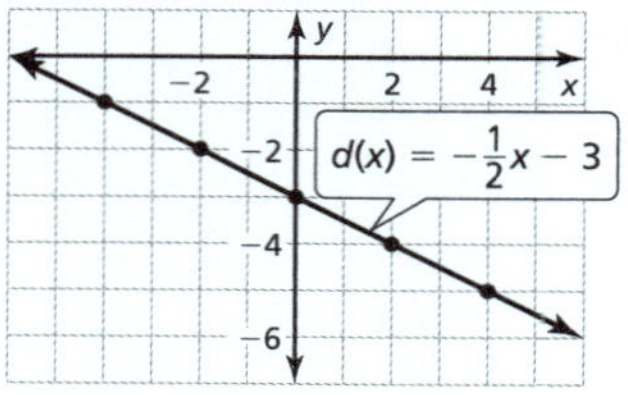

27.

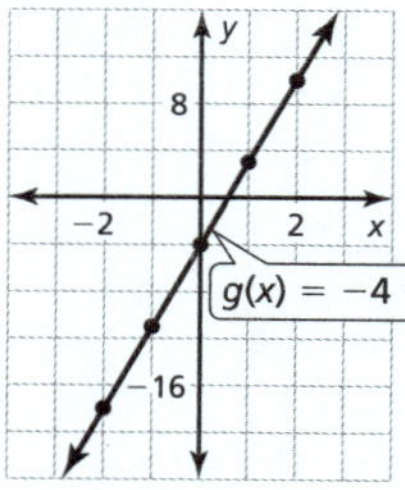

29. Contractor B; Using the function, the cost for Contractor A is \$250. The table shows an increase of \$30 for every increase of 2 hours, so the cost for Contractor B is \$220.

31. 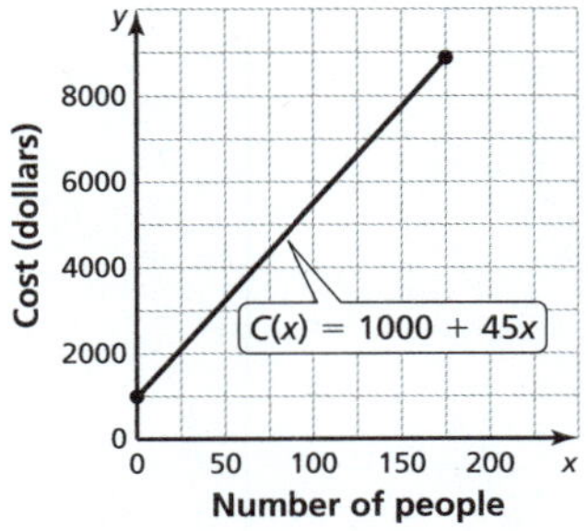

The domain, $0 \le x \le 175$, represents the possible number of people who can attend. The range, $0 \le y \le 8875$, represents the possible total cost of the venue.

33. **a.** the student's height at age 14; no; The units for height are not given.

b. The height of the student is 58 inches at age 15; The only reasonable units are inches.

35. false; The function could include operations that would not give the same result. For example, if $f(x) = x^2$, $f(3 + 4) \neq f(3) + f(4)$.

3.4 Review & Refresh

37. *Sample answer:*

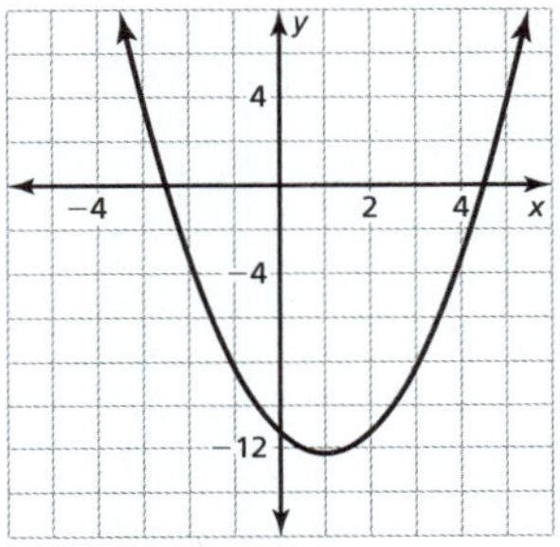

38. $a < -7$ *or* $a > 15$

39. $-3 \le k < -\frac{1}{3}$

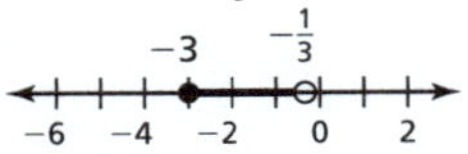

40. function; Each input has exactly one output.

41. $4n - 10.5 \ge -1.5$

42. $x = -4$

43. $x = \dfrac{m}{5 + 6y}$

44. \$2.00

45. nonlinear; The graph is not a line.

46. −9 and −7

47. $1.\overline{27}$

48. 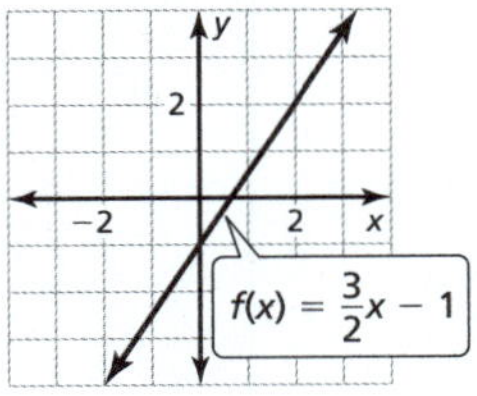

Section 3.5

3.5 Practice

1. 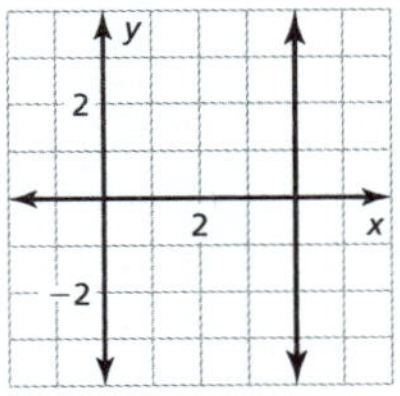

3. 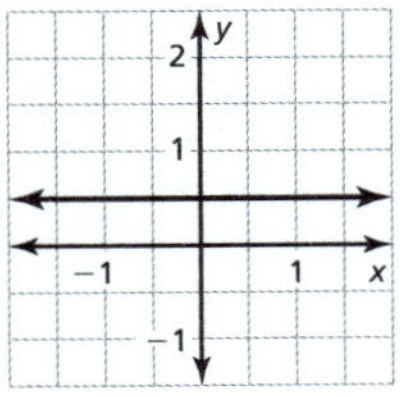

5. 6; 4

7. $\frac{2}{3}$; $-\frac{1}{3}$

9. 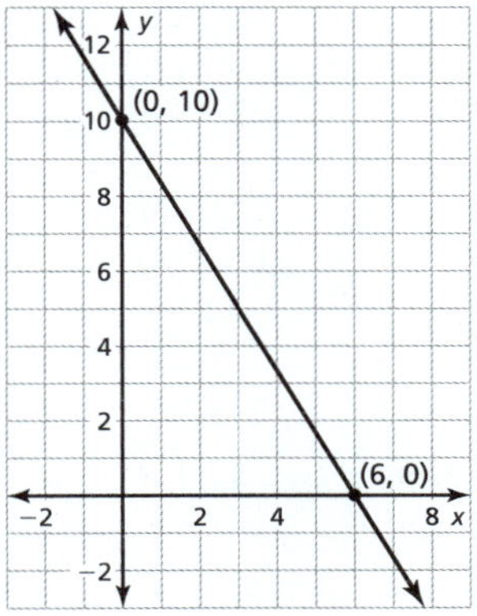

11. 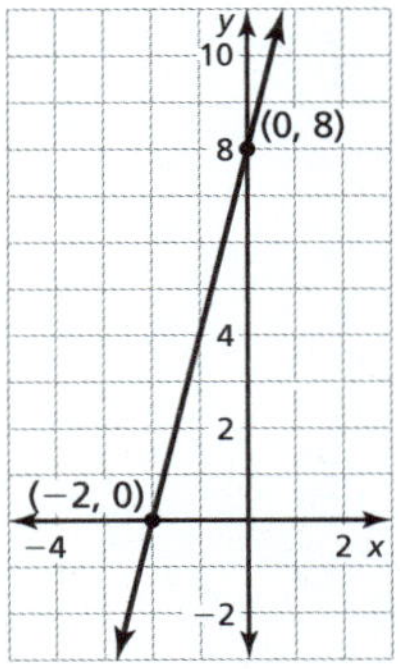

13. 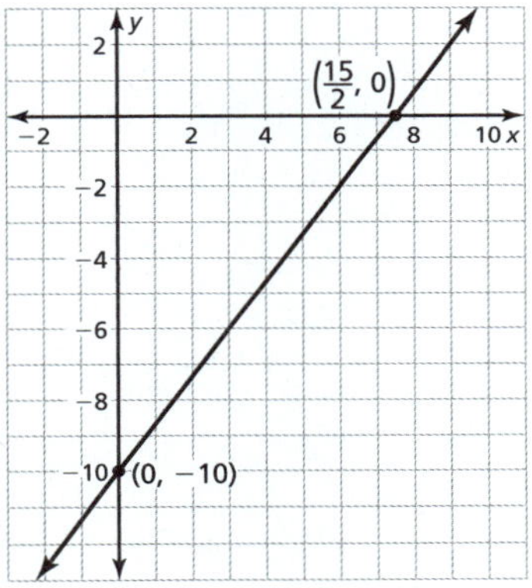

15. 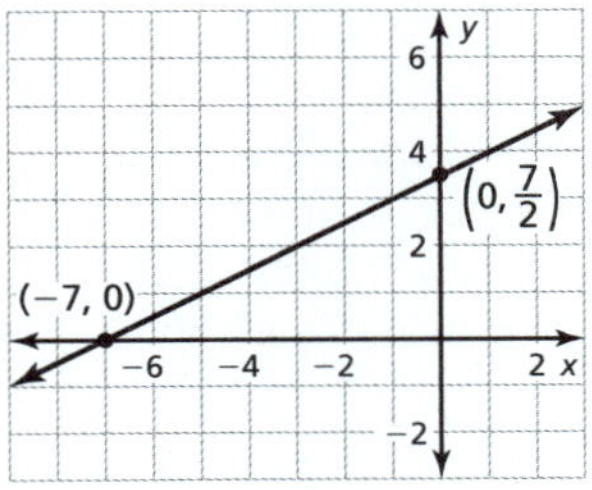

17. 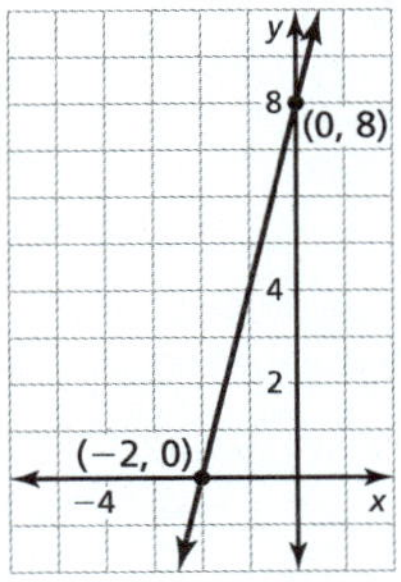

19. A

21. D

23. a. $10x$ represents the total cost of short-sleeved shirts at \$10 a shirt. $12y$ represents the total cost of long-sleeved shirts at \$12 a shirt. 300 represents the total amount you can spend on shirts.

b. 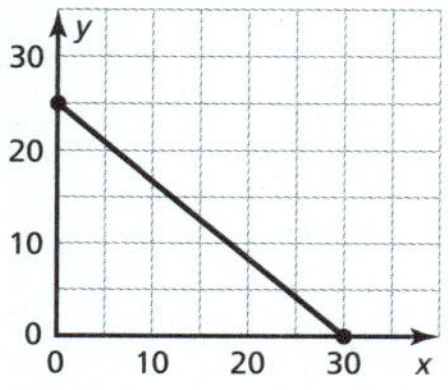

The x-intercept shows that you can buy 30 short-sleeved shirts and 0 long-sleeved shirts. The y-intercept shows that you can buy 25 long-sleeved shirts and 0 short-sleeved shirts.

c. 30 short-sleeved and 0 long-sleeved, 0 short-sleeved and 25 long-sleeved, 18 short-sleeved and 10 long-sleeved

25. The x- and y-intercepts are switched.

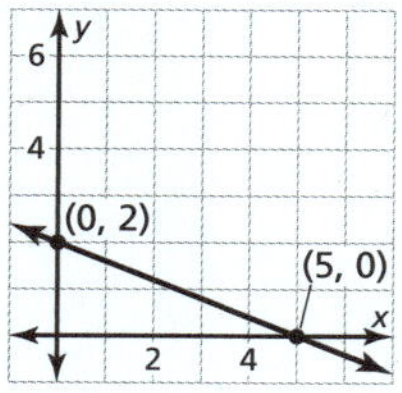

27. *Sample answer:* $x = -1, y = 5, x = 2, y = 1$

29. *Sample answer:* $x = 2, y = 1, y = -\frac{3}{2}x + 7$

31. yes; $x = a$ can be written as $1x + 0y = a$, and $y = b$ can be written as $0x + 1y = b$.

33. B

35. a. $11x + 7.5y = 99$; no; You need to buy both stamps and envelopes. The intercepts represent when you do not buy either stamps or envelopes.

b. no; When $x = 5$ and $y = 2$, the number of stamps and envelopes are the same, but you only spend \$70.

3.5 Review & Refresh

36. a. 48

b. 250 min, or 4 h 10 min

37. x-intercept: 1, y-intercept: -1

38. The graph of a linear function is a line, a nonlinear function does not form a line.

39. nonlinear; It cannot be written in the form $y = mx + b$.

40. $b \leq -17$

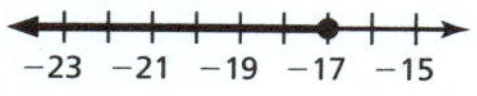

41. $c < 45$

42. $-3; 6$ **43.** $g = 7.3$ **44.** $h = 4$

45. all real numbers **46.** $n = \frac{2}{3}, n = \frac{7}{3}$

47. 45 **48.** $x = -12$ **49.** 4, -2

Section 3.6

3.6 Practice

1. negative; $-\frac{3}{5}$ **3.** positive; 3

5. -5 **7.** $\frac{1}{2}$ **9.** undefined

11. $m = 60$; The bus is traveling at a speed of 60 miles per hour.

13. slope: -3; y-intercept: 2 **15.** slope: 6; y-intercept: 0

17. slope: 0.75; y-intercept: 4 **19.** slope: $-\frac{1}{6}$; y-intercept: $\frac{1}{3}$

21. To be in slope-intercept form, the equation needs to be solved for y, not x; $y = -\frac{1}{4}x$; The slope is $-\frac{1}{4}$ and the y-intercept is 0.

23.

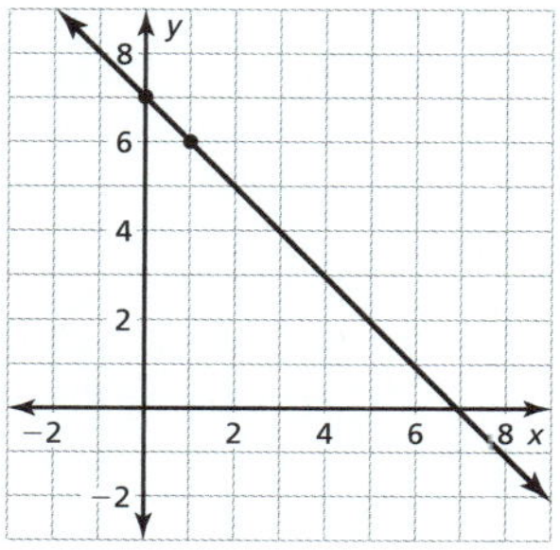

x-intercept: 7

25.

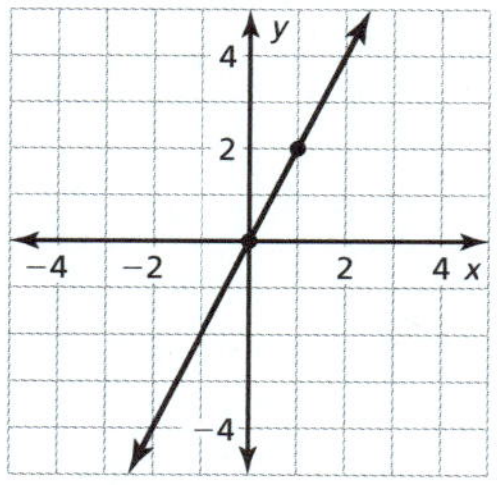

x-intercept: 0

27.

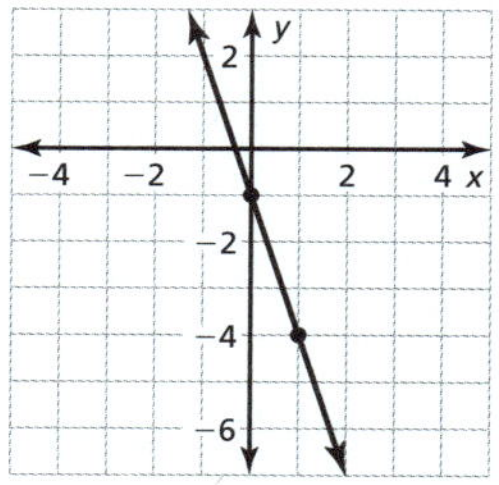

x-intercept: $-\frac{1}{3}$

29.

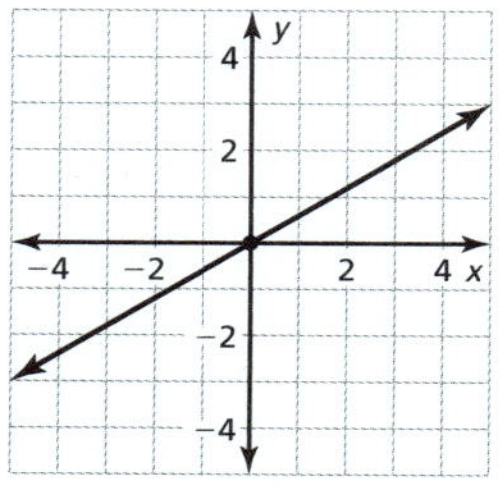

x-intercept: 0

31.

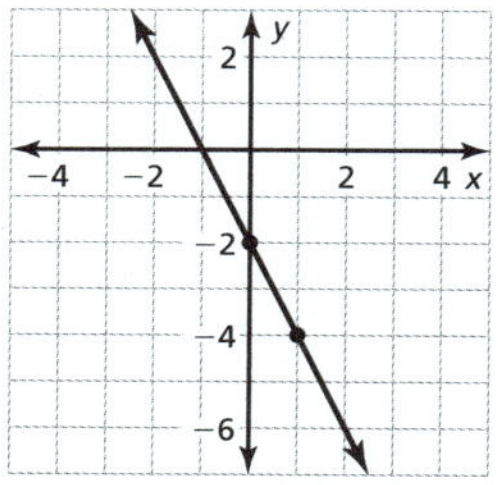

slope: -2; y-intercept: -2; x-intercept: -1

33.

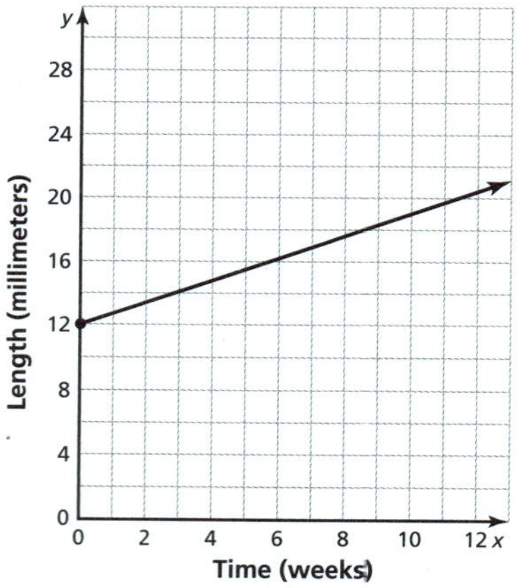

slope: $\frac{7}{10}$; y-intercept: 12; So, the right index fingernail is initially 12 millimeters long.

35. The slope is 3, but the graph shows a slope of $\frac{1}{3}$.

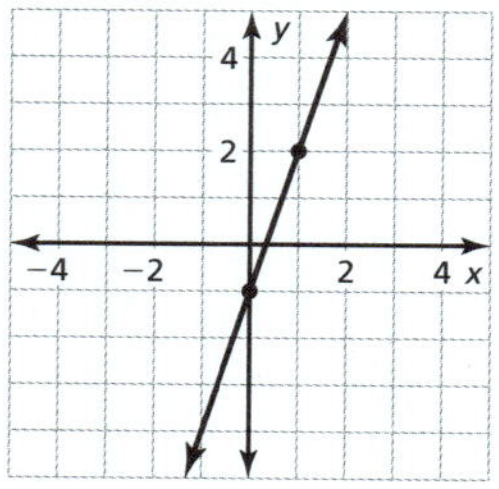

37. a. domain: $0 \le t \le 6$; range: $2 \le y \le 5$

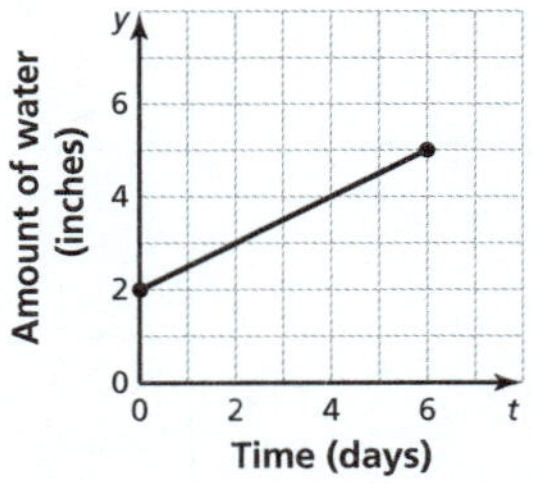

b. The slope is $\frac{1}{2}$. So, the water amount in the rain barrel changes at a rate of $\frac{1}{2}$ inch per day. The y-intercept is 2. So, the amount of water in the rain barrel before the rain began was 2 inches. There is no t-intercept in this context.

39. Find and plot the intercepts, then draw a line through the intercepts. Or, rewrite the equation in slope-intercept form, plot the slope and the y-intercept, then draw a line through the points; *Sample answer:* standard form; It requires less steps.

41. A, D

43. a.

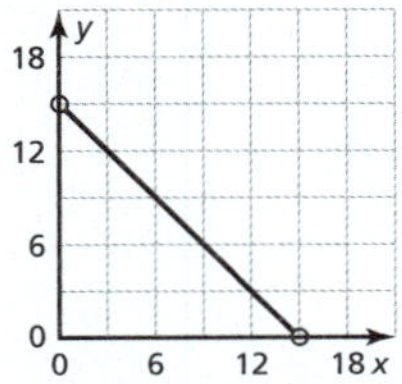

b. The slope of each graph is the same. The open circles in the graph in part (a) are closer to the origin.

45.

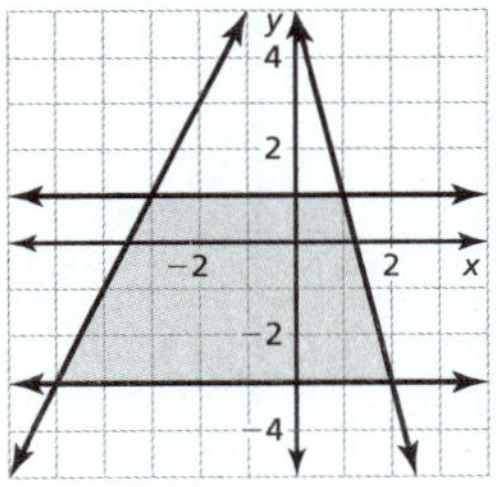

22 units^2

47. a. $y = \frac{1}{3}x + 5$

b. $y = \frac{7}{4}x - \frac{1}{4}$; $y = 2x - 4$

c. $y = -3x + 8$

d. $y = -4x - 9$; $y = -x - \frac{4}{3}$

49. $k = \frac{1}{8}$

51.
$$\begin{aligned}\frac{y_2 - y_1}{x_2 - x_1} &= \frac{(mx_2 + b) - (mx_1 + b)}{x_2 - x_1} \\ &= \frac{mx_2 + b - mx_1 - b}{x_2 - x_1} \\ &= \frac{mx_2 - mx_1}{x_2 - x_1} \\ &= \frac{m(x_2 - x_1)}{x_2 - x_1} \\ &= m\end{aligned}$$

53. $g(p + 2)$; 8 units greater; The value of $g(x)$ will increase 12 units when moving 2 units right, the value of $h(x)$ will increase 4 units when moving 2 units right, and $12 - 4 = 8$.

3.6 Review & Refresh

54. $Q'(-1, 4)$, $R'(1, 2)$, $S'(1, -1)$, $T'(-1, -3)$

55. $Q'(-2, 2)$, $R'(-1, 1)$, $S'\left(-1, -\frac{1}{2}\right)$, $T'\left(-2, -\frac{3}{2}\right)$

56. $Q'(4, 4)$, $R'(2, 2)$, $S'(2, -1)$, $T'(4, -3)$

57. $x = -17.5$

58. all real numbers

59. $a = \frac{3}{2}$

60. $q = -1$

61. slope: $\frac{7}{4}$; y-intercept: $-\frac{5}{2}$

62. $r \ge 7$

63. a. $(3, -8)$

b. $\left(-1, \frac{3}{4}\right)$

64.

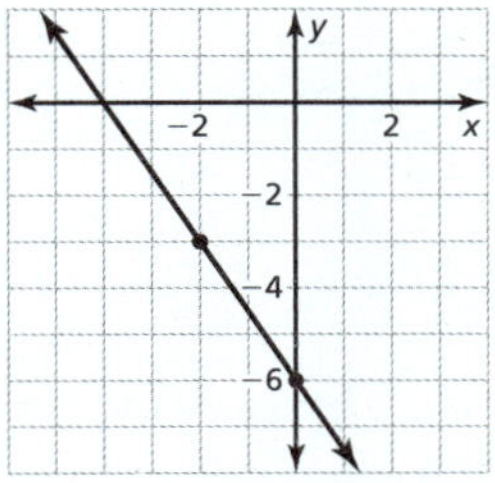

x-intercept: -4

65. nonlinear; The rate of change is not constant.

66. linear; It can be rewritten as $y = -3x + 12$.

67. B or D; $|0.80p - 30| \le 5$, $31.25 \le p \le 43.75$

68.

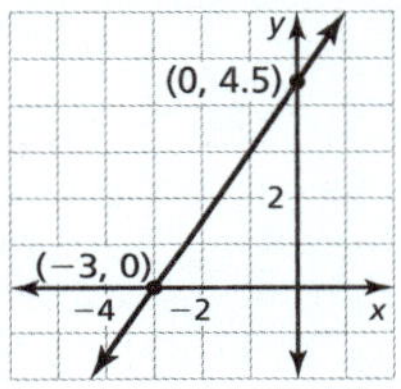

69.

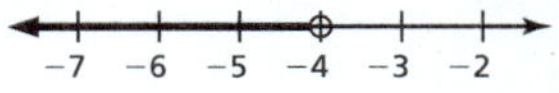

70.

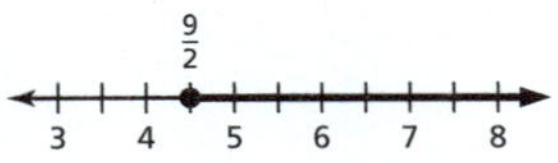

Section 3.7

3.7 Practice

1. The graph of g is a vertical translation 2 units up of the graph of f.

3. The graph of g is a vertical translation 3 units down of the graph of f.

5. The graph of g is a horizontal translation 5 units left of the graph of f.

7. The graph of f is a horizontal translation 5 units right of the graph of d.

9. The graph of h is reflection in the x-axis of the graph of f.

11. The graph of h is reflection in the y-axis of the graph of f.

13. The graph of r is a vertical stretch of the graph of f by a factor of 2.

15. The graph of r is a horizontal stretch of the graph of f by a factor of 2.

17. The graph of r is a vertical stretch of the graph of f by a factor of 3.

19. The graph of h is a horizontal shrink of the graph of f by a factor of $\frac{1}{3}$.

21. The graph of h is a vertical shrink of the graph of f by a factor of $\frac{1}{6}$.

23. The graph of h is a horizontal shrink of the graph of f by a factor of $\frac{1}{5}$.

25. The graph of d is reflection in the y-axis of the graph of t.

27. The graph of g is a horizontal translation 4 units left of the graph of f.

29. The graph of g is a horizontal translation 2 units right of the graph of f.

31. The graph of g is a vertical stretch of the graph of f by a factor of 6.

33. $g(x) = f(x - 2)$ **35.** $g(x) = f(x) + 4$

37. $f(x - 2)$ is a translation to the right, not to the left.

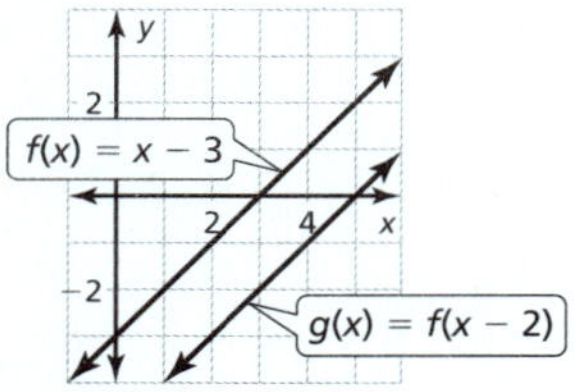

39. The graph of g is a horizontal translation 1 unit left of the graph of f.

41. The graph of g is a horizontal stretch by a factor of 3 of the graph of f.

43. The graph of g is a reflection in the x-axis of the graph of f.

45. The graph of g is a horizontal shrink by a factor of $\frac{1}{2}$ of the graph of f.

47. $a = \frac{2}{3}$; In January, the gym's monthly fee is reduced by a factor of two-thirds.

49. B and C, A and F; Adding 4 to the y-coordinate of each point on B gives the corresponding y-coordinate on C. Adding 2 to the y-coordinate of each point of F gives you the corresponding y-coordinate on A. D would require a vertical shrink of A; E would require a vertical shrink and a reflection in the x-axis of A.

51. **a.** stretch

b. 1

c. x-axis

53. *Sample answer:* $g(x) = \frac{1}{2}f(x)$

55.

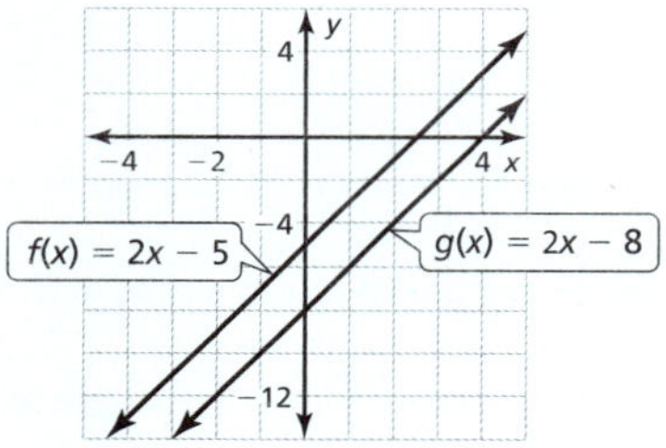

$g(x) = f(x) - 3$; The graph of g is a vertical translation 3 units down of the graph of f.

57.

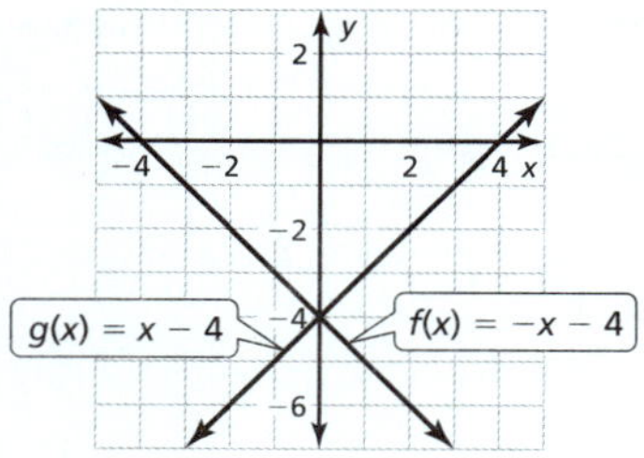

$g(x) = f(-x)$; The graph of g is a reflection in the y-axis of the graph of f.

59. Translate the graph of $f(x) = x$ horizontally 5 units left.

61. no; Let $f(x) = 2x + 4$. $f\left(\frac{1}{2}x\right) = x + 4$ is a horizontal stretch by a factor of 2. $\frac{1}{2} \cdot f(x) = x + 2$ is a vertical shrink by a factor of $\frac{1}{2}$. Because $x + 4 \neq x + 2$, $f\left(\frac{1}{2}x\right) \neq \frac{1}{2} \cdot f(x)$. So, $f(cx) \neq \frac{1}{c} \cdot f(x)$.

3.7 Review & Refresh

63. Dilate the blue triangle by a factor of 2.

64. $-12 < x < -2$

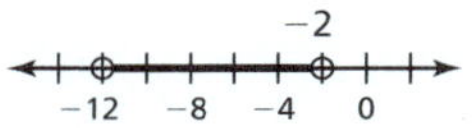

65. no solution **66.** $\geq$ **67.** -2; $-\frac{11}{2}$

68. **a.**

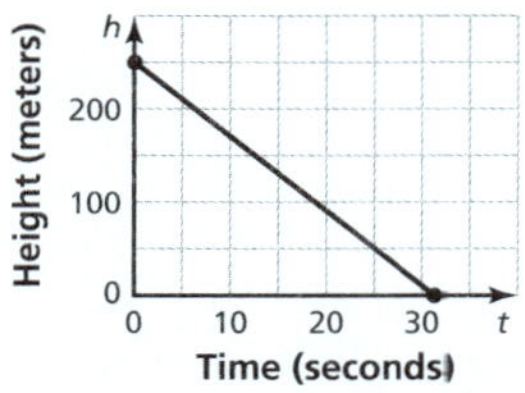

domain: $0 \leq t \leq 31.25$; range: $0 \leq h(t) \leq 250$

b. $-8t$ represents the distance the elevator descends after t seconds at a rate of 8 m/sec. 250 represents the height at the top floor. The t-intercept shows it takes 31.25 seconds to reach the ground floor.

69. $b = 4$ **70.** $c = -15$

71. $q = \frac{7}{2}$ **72.** $r = -3, r = 6$

73. **a.** 0, 1, 2, 3, 4, 5, 6; discrete; The number of books must be a whole number.

b.

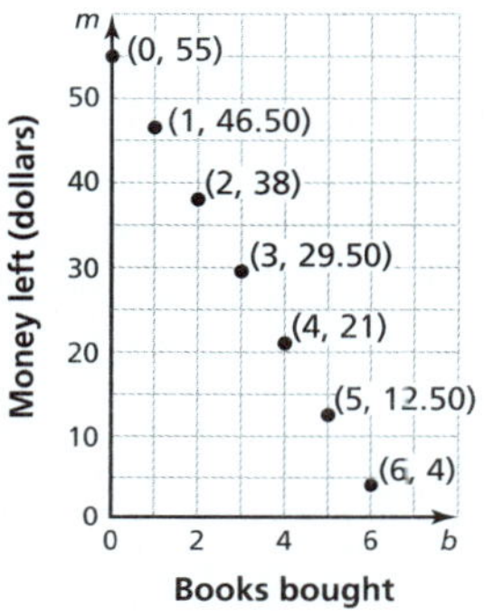

74.

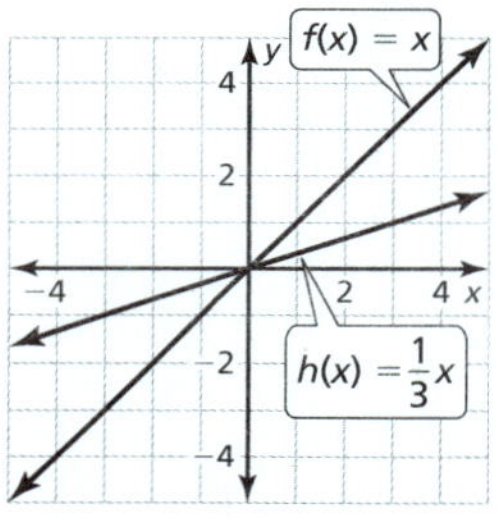

The graph of h is a vertical shrink by a factor of $\frac{1}{3}$ of the graph of f.

75.

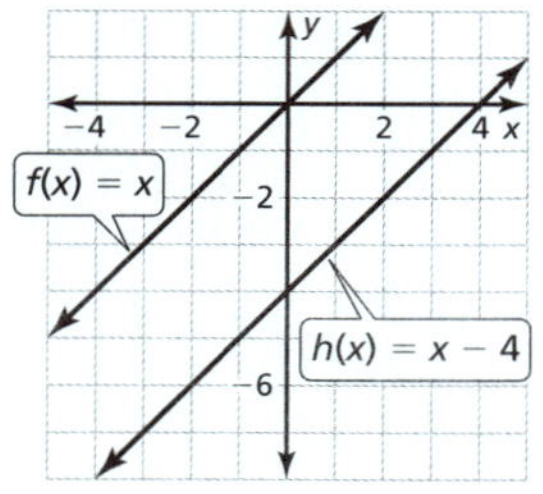

The graph of h is a vertical translation 4 units down of the graph of f.

76. $A = 3$, $B = -\frac{3}{2}$

77. not a function; The input -10 has two outputs, 2 and 6, and the input -8 has two outputs, 3 and 8.

78. $h = \dfrac{V}{\pi r^2}$ **79.** $x < -\dfrac{1}{10}$

Section 3.8

3.8 Practice

1. positive: $x < 0$ and $x > 0$; negative: none; decreasing: $x < 0$; increasing $x > 0$; $y \to +\infty$ as $x \to -\infty$ and $y \to +\infty$ as $x \to +\infty$

3. positive: none; negative: $x < \frac{1}{3}$ and $x > \frac{1}{3}$; decreasing: $x > \frac{1}{3}$; increasing $x < \frac{1}{3}$; $y \to -\infty$ as $x \to -\infty$ and $y \to -\infty$ as $x \to +\infty$

5. positive: $x < -5$ and $x > 1$; negative: $-5 < x < 1$; decreasing: $x < -2$; increasing $x > -2$; $y \to +\infty$ as $x \to -\infty$ and $y \to +\infty$ as $x \to +\infty$

7. The graph of h is a vertical translation 2 units down of the graph of f.

9. The graph of h is a horizontal stretch of the graph of f by a factor of $\frac{4}{3}$.

11.

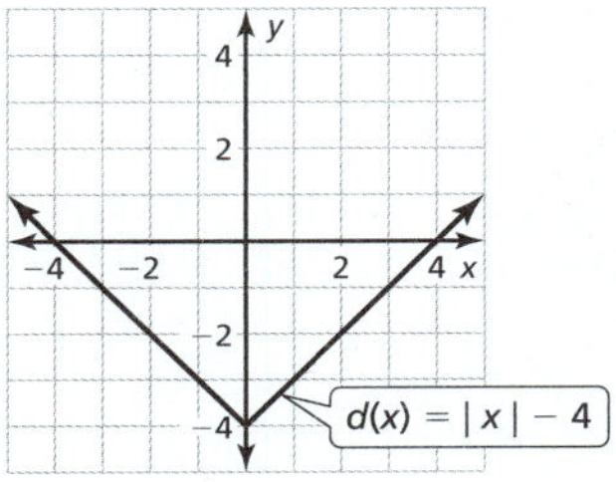

The graph of d is a vertical translation 4 units down of the graph of f; domain: all real numbers; range $y \geq -4$

13.

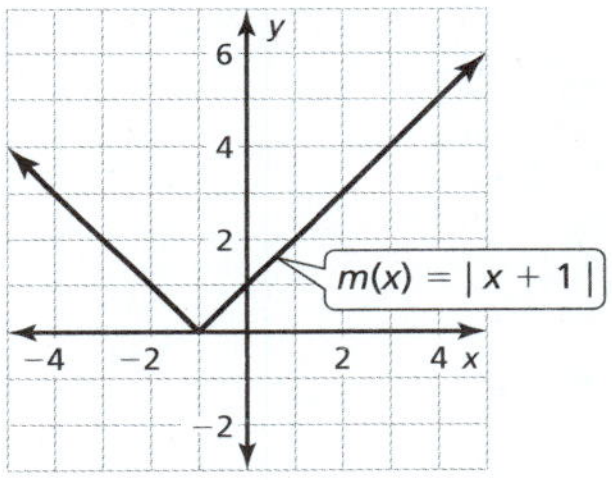

The graph of m is a horizontal translation 1 unit left of the graph of f; domain: all real numbers; range $y \geq 0$

15.

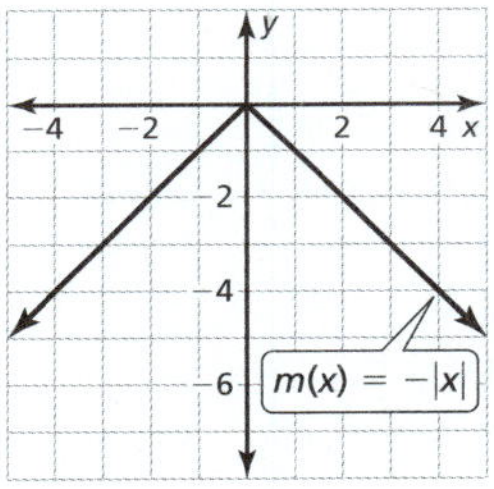

The graph of m is a reflection in the x-axis of the graph of f; domain: all real numbers; range $y \leq 0$

17.

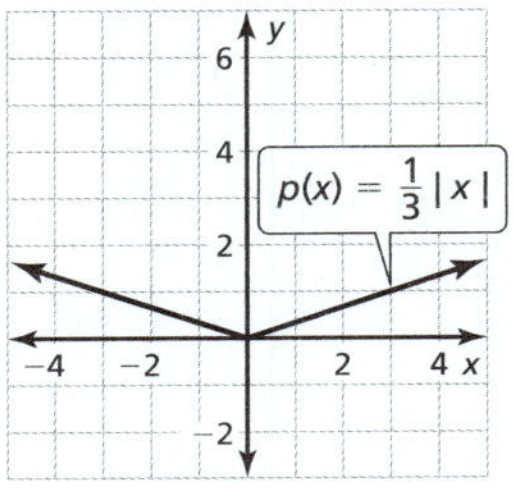

The graph of p is a vertical shrink of the graph of f by a factor of $\frac{1}{3}$; domain: all real numbers; range $y \geq 0$

19.

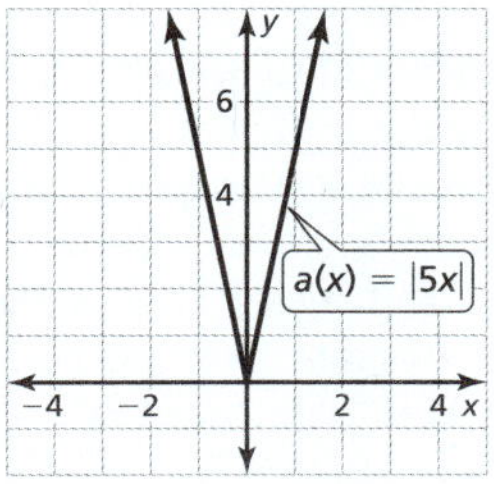

The graph of a is a horizontal shrink of the graph of f by a factor of $\frac{1}{5}$; domain: all real numbers; range $y \geq 0$

21. The graph should be a horizontal stretch by a factor of 4, not a horizontal shrink by a factor of $\frac{1}{4}$.

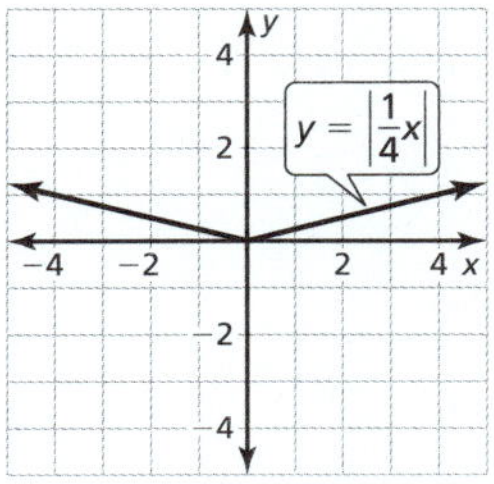

23. $h(x) = |x| - 7$ **25.** $h(x) = -|x|$ **27.** $h(x) = \frac{1}{4}|x|$

29.

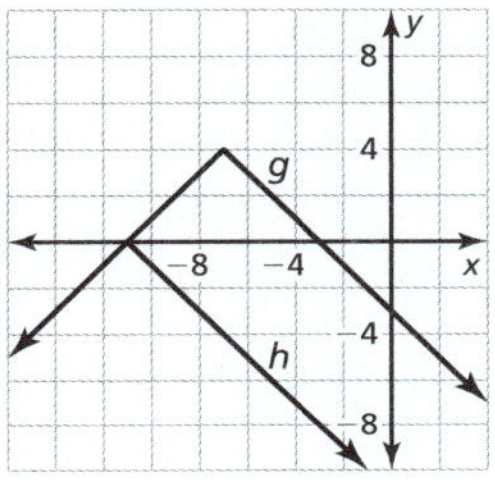

The graph of g is a vertical translation 4 units up of the graph of f. The graph of h is a horizontal translation 4 units left of the graph of f.

31.

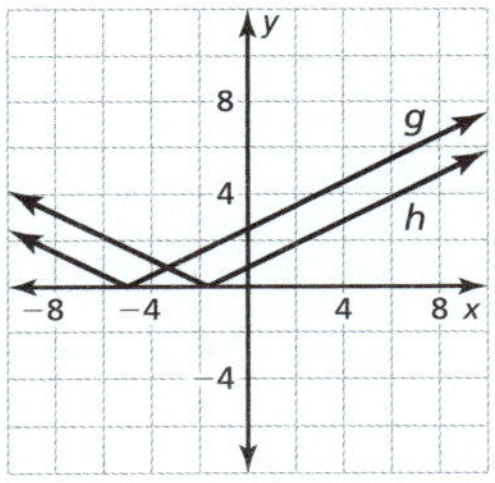

The graph of g is vertical stretch of the graph of f by a factor of 3. The graph of h is a horizontal shrink of the graph of f by a factor of $\frac{1}{3}$.

33. The graph of g is a vertical translation 5 units down of the graph of f.

35. The graph of g is a horizontal translation 2 units right of the graph of f.

37. The graph of g is a vertical stretch of the graph of f by a factor of 3.

39. The graph of g is a horizontal shrink of the graph of f by a factor of $\frac{1}{4}$.

41. The graph of g is a reflection in the x-axis of the graph of f.

43. a.

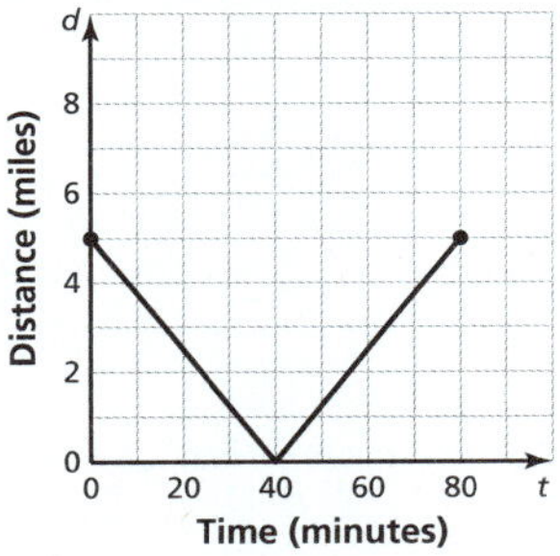

domain: $0 \leq t \leq 80$; range: $0 \leq d(t) \leq 5$

b. The *d*-intercept 5 means you start the race 5 miles away from the water stop. The *t*-intercept and vertex is (40,0). So, you reach the water stop 40 minutes after starting the 10-mile race. You can also determine you are halfway through the race at that time. The function is decreasing when $0 < t < 40$ which means you are getting closer to the water stop. The function is increasing when $40 < t < 80$ which means you are getting farther from the water stop.

45. no; no; Because the graph is V-shaped, half of the graph is decreasing and the other half is increasing.

47. A, C, D

49.

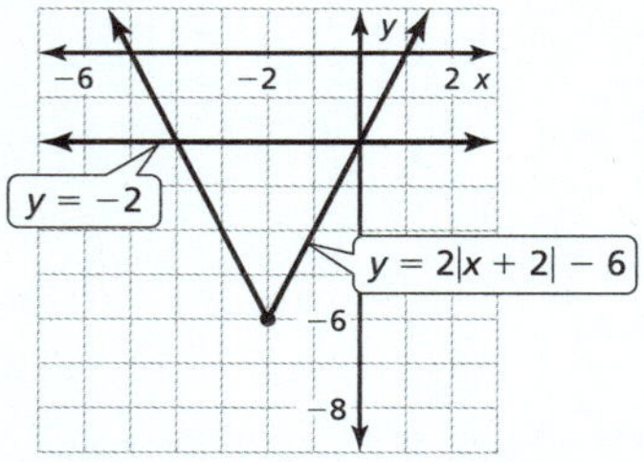

$x = 0, x = -4$

51. no; The form of a horizontal translation of $y = f(x)$ is $y = f(x - h)$. So, if *p* is positive, the graph of $y = |x + p|$ is a horizontal translation in the negative direction.

3.8 Review & Refresh

52. $x = -1, x = 4$

53. $x = -1, x = \frac{1}{2}$

54. The graph of *g* is a vertical translation 3 units down of the graph of *f*.

55. $a \leq \frac{5}{2}$

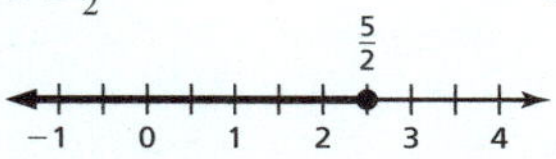

56. no solution

57. all real numbers

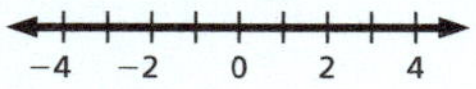

58. $x > -\frac{3}{4}$

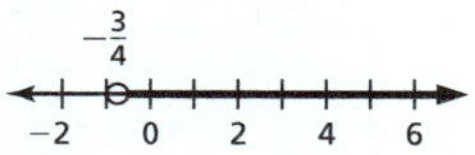

59. The graph of *g* is a horizontal translation 2 units left of the graph of *f*.

60. The graph of *g* is a reflection in the *x*-axis of the graph of *f*.

61. a. $12x$ represents the total you spend on pecans at $12/lb; $7.5y$ represents the total you spend on walnuts at $7.50/lb.

b.

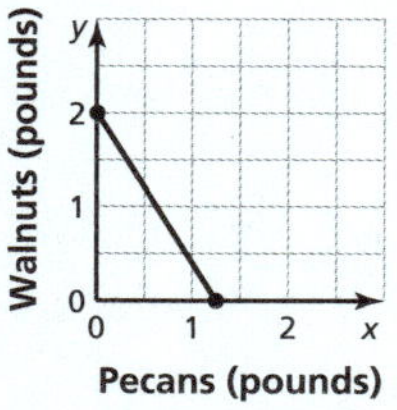

The *y*-intercept shows you can buy 2 pounds of walnuts when you do not buy any pecans. The *x*-intercept shows you can buy 1.25 pounds of pecans when you do not buy any walnuts.

62. a. At 1 P.M., the temperature is 30°C.

b. *m* hours after 9 A.M., the temperature is 28.9°C.

c. The temperature is the same at 11 A.M. and 6 P.M.

d. The temperature is higher at 3:30 P.M. than at 9 A.M.

63. $x = \frac{y + 7}{3}$

64. *Sample answer:*

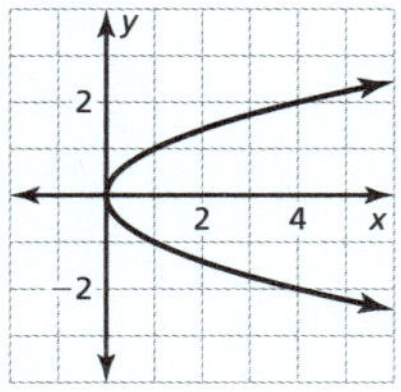

65. $-\frac{5}{4}$

Chapter 3 Review

1. function; Every input has exactly one output.
2. function; Every input has exactly one output.
3. function; domain: 0, 1, 2, 3, 4, 5, 6, 7; range: 1, 4, 6
4. not a function; domain: $x \leq 6$; range: all real numbers
5. function; domain: $-3 \leq x \leq 3$; range: $-1 \leq y \leq 3$
6. not a function; domain: $-1, 0, 1$; range: $-3, -2, -1, 0$
7. **a.** yes; The amount of money you have is the dependent variable, and the number of hours you work is the independent variable.

   b. domain: $0 \leq x \leq 4$; range: $170 \leq y \leq 204$
8. *Sample answer:* (1, 3), (2, −1), (3, 3), (4, −2), (5, 3)
9. positive: $-1 < x < 1$; negative: $x < -1$ and $x > 1$; increasing: $x < 0$; decreasing: $x > 0$; $y \to -\infty$ as $x \to +\infty$ and $y \to -\infty$ as $x \to -\infty$
10. positive: $x > 1.6$; negative: $x < 1.6$; increasing: for all real numbers; $y \to +\infty$ as $x \to +\infty$ and $y \to -\infty$ as $x \to -\infty$
11. The second kick has a greater horizontal distance and the first kick has a greater maximum height.
12. *Sample answer:*

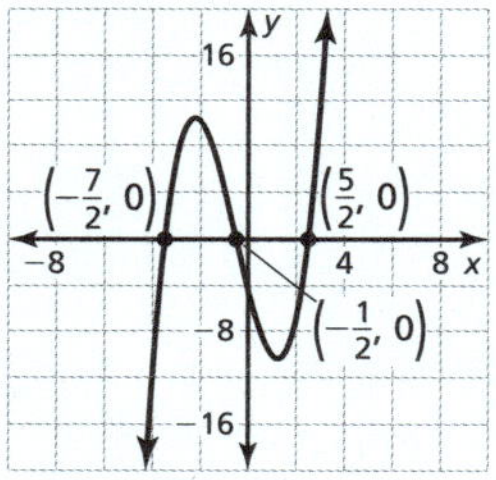

13. linear; As *x* increases by 5, *y* decreases by 3. The rate of change is constant.
14. nonlinear; The graph is not a line.
15. linear; It can be rewritten as $y = 3x + 5$.
16. nonlinear; It cannot be rewritten as $y = mx + b$.
17.

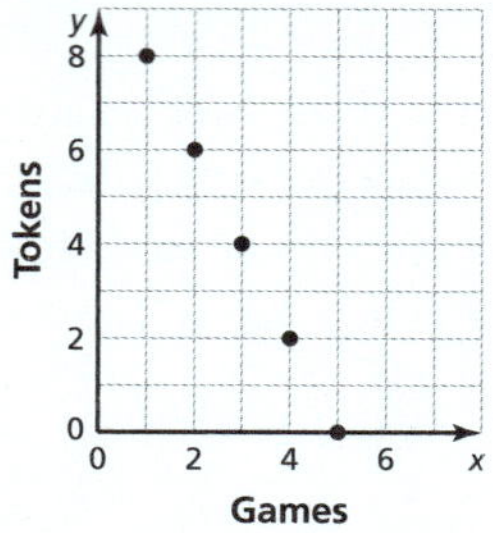

Because it is not possible to play part of a game, the domain is discrete.

18.

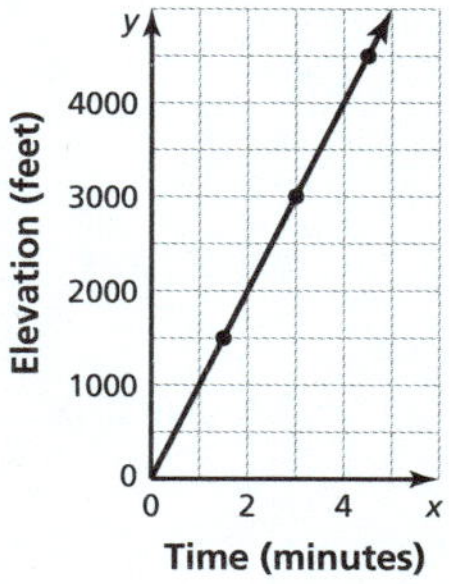

19. **a.** 0, 1, 2, 3, 4, 5, 6, 7; discrete; The number of tickets bought must be a whole number.

b. 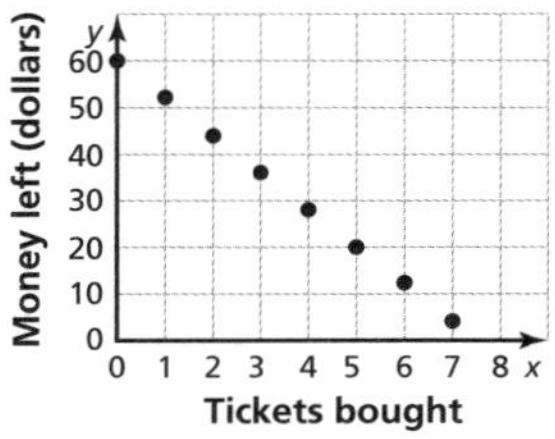

20. 5, 8, 13

21. $-18, -9, 6$

22. **a.** There is the same number of people in the stadium at 2:00 P.M. and 4:00 P.M.

b. There are less people in the stadium at 5:00 P.M. than at 1:30 P.M.

23. $x = 7$

24. $x = -4$

25. 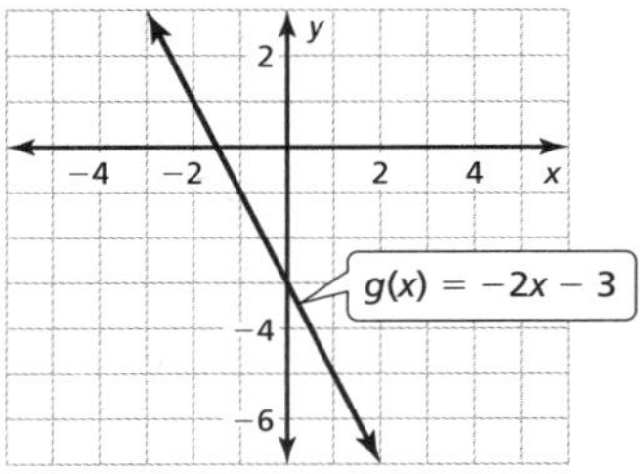

26. 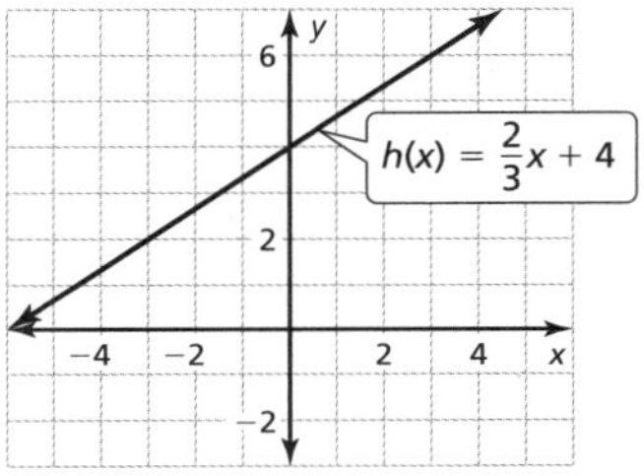

27. **a.** 495 mi

b. 12.5 h

28. 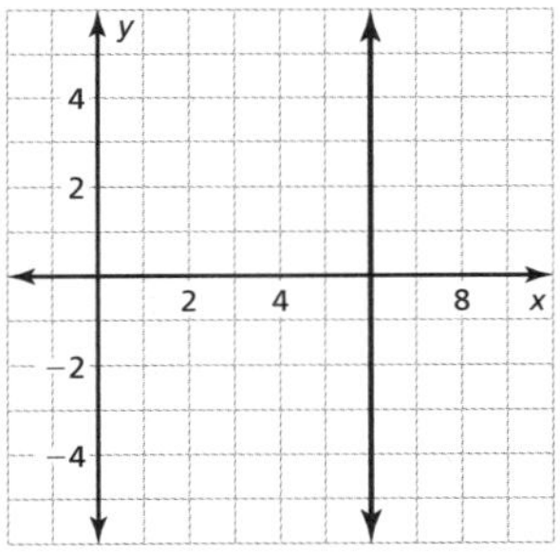

29. 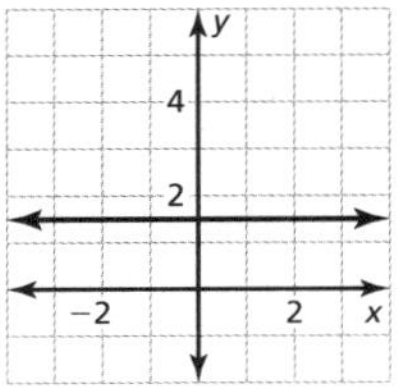

30. 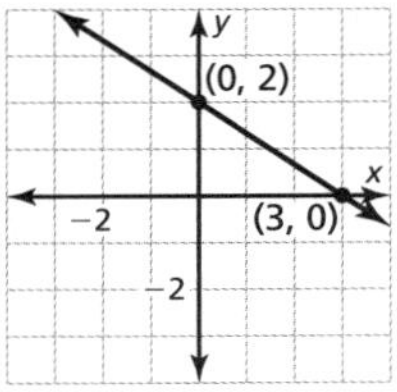

31. 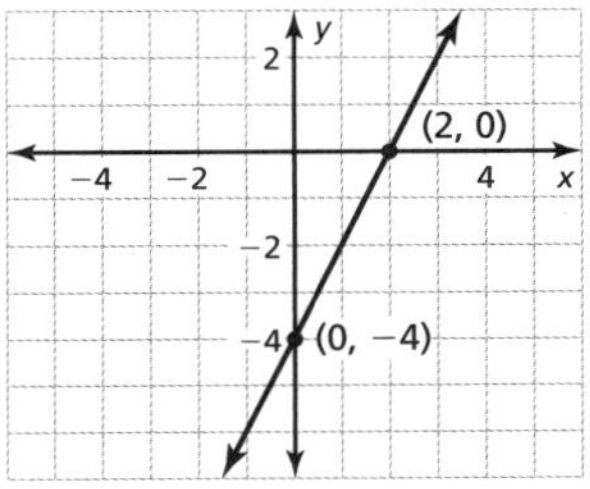

32. 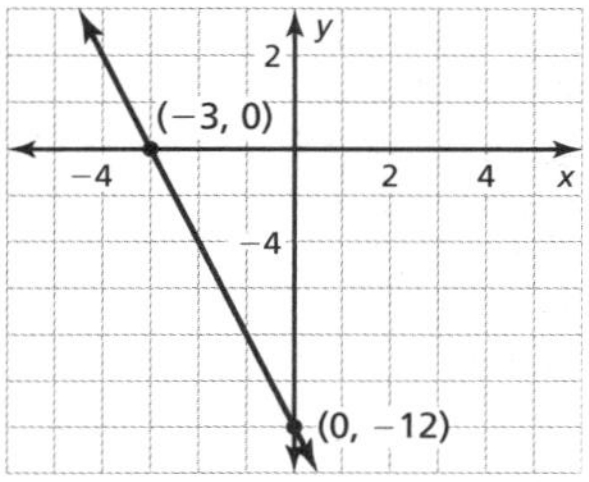

33. 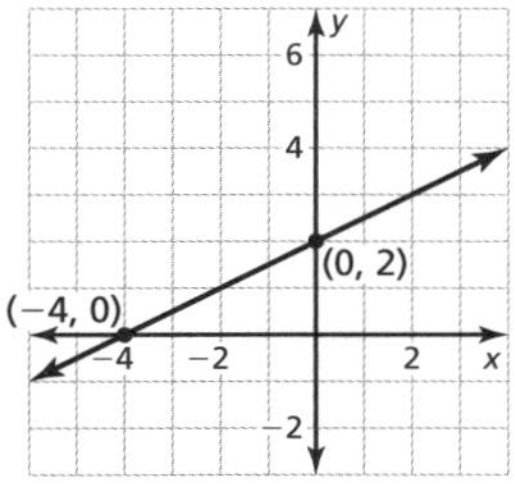

34. 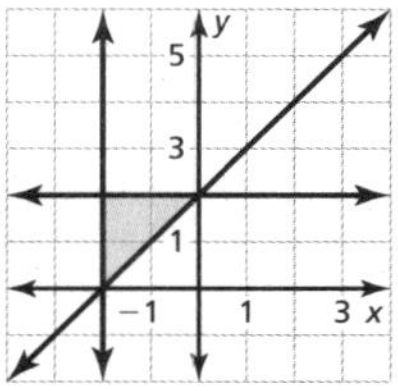

2 units^2

35. **a.** $2x$ represents the total points scored by 2-point baskets; $3y$ represents the total points scored by 3-point baskets. The x-intercept indicates 27 two-point baskets were made if there were no three-point baskets. The y-intercept indicates 18 three-point baskets were made if there were no two-point baskets.

b. no; If y is odd, then $3y$ will also be odd. Subtracting an odd number from 54 will also be odd, so dividing this result by 2 to find x will never give a whole number.

c. 

d. *Sample answer:* 24 two-point baskets and 2 three-point baskets; 9 two-point baskets and 12 three-point baskets; 6 two-point baskets and 14 three-point baskets; 12 two-point baskets and 10 three-point baskets

36. positive; $\frac{1}{2}$

37. $\frac{6}{5}$

38. undefined

39. 0

40. 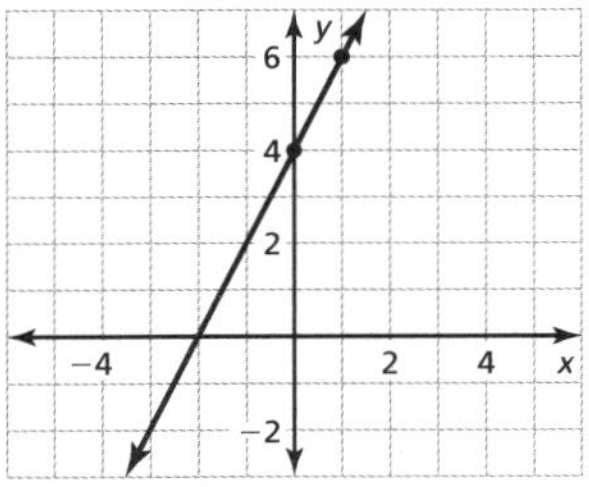

x-intercept: -2

41. 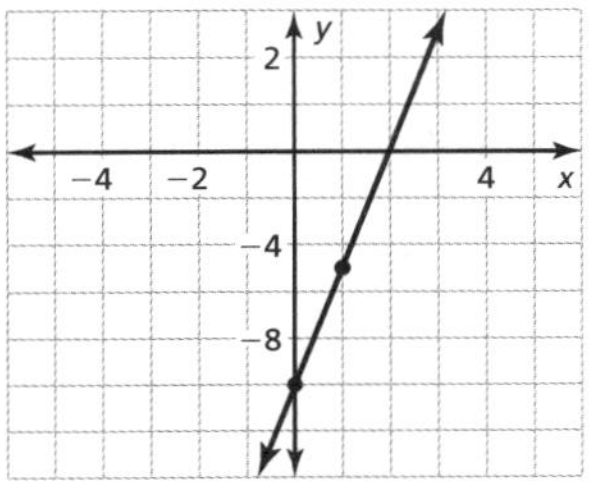

x-intercept: 2

42.

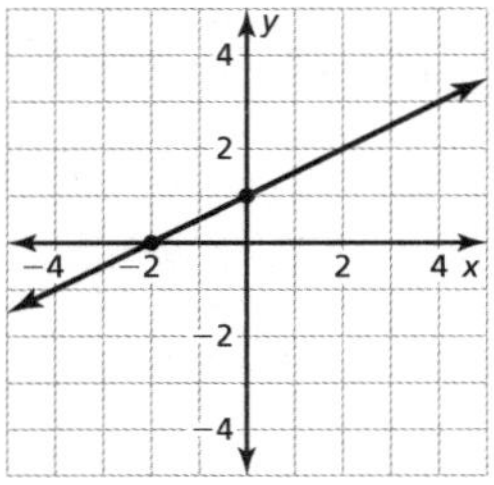

x-intercept: -2

43.

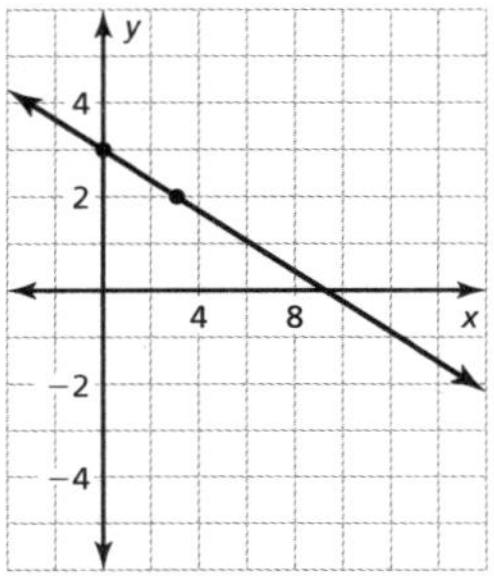

x-intercept: 9

44.

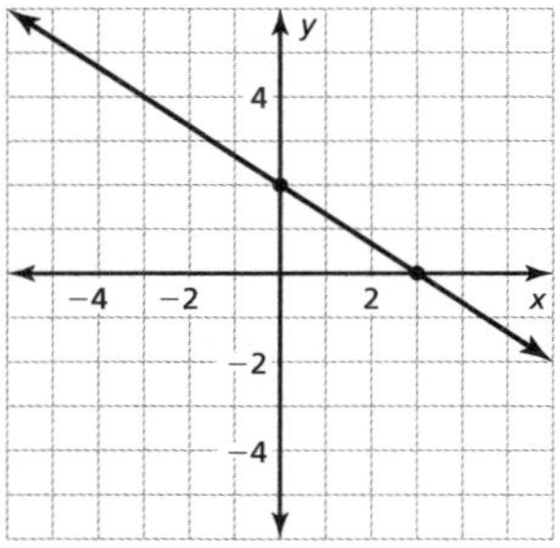

slope: $-\frac{2}{3}$; y-intercept: 2; x-intercept: 3

45.

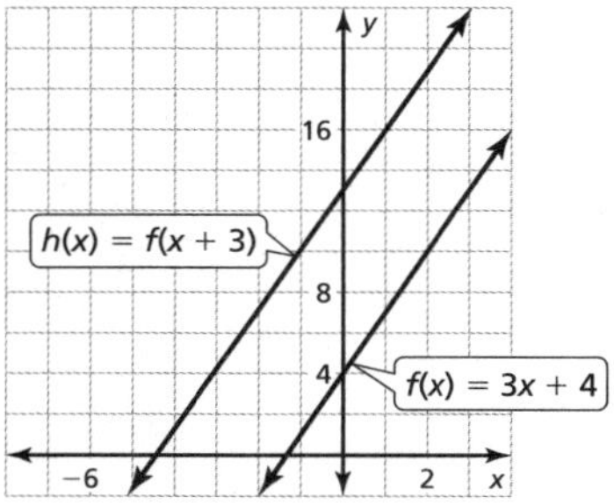

The graph of h is a horizontal translation 3 units left of the graph of f.

46.

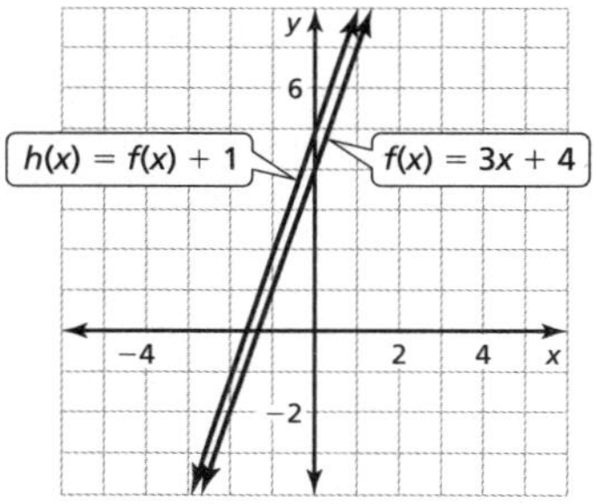

The graph of h is a vertical translation 1 unit up of the graph of f.

47.

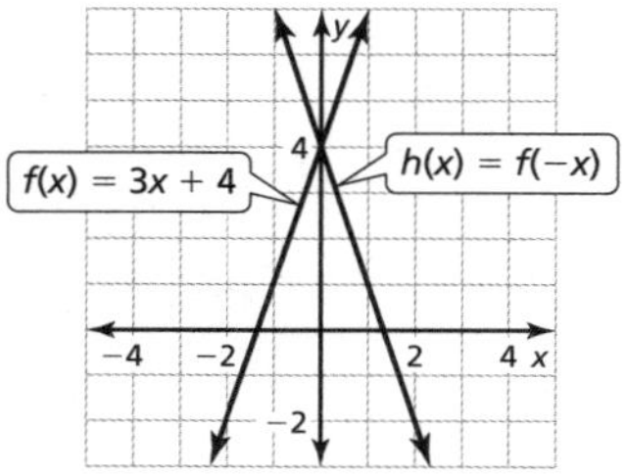

The graph of h is a reflection in the y-axis of the graph of f.

48.

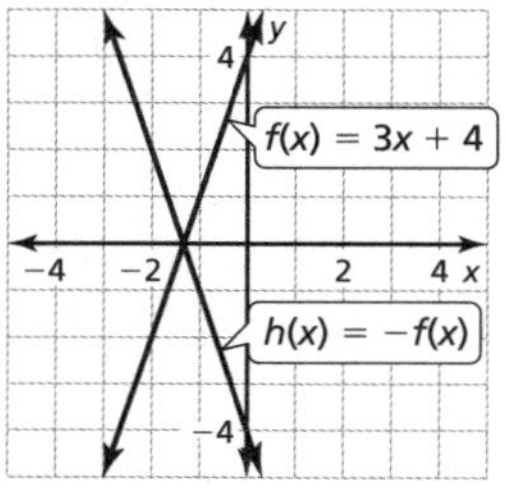

The graph of h is a reflection in the x-axis of the graph of f.

49.

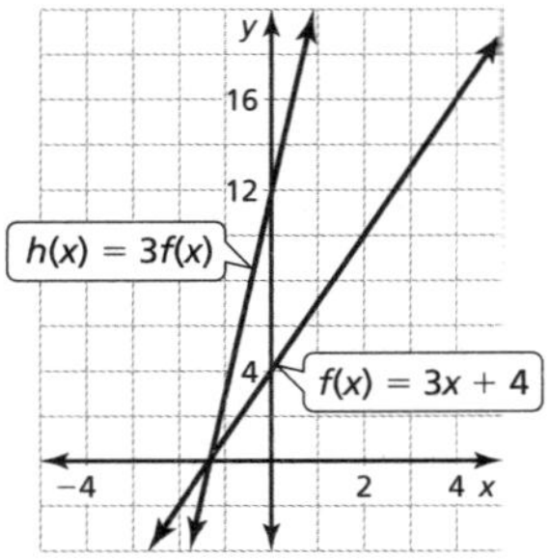

The graph of h is a vertical stretch of the graph of f by a factor of 3.

50.

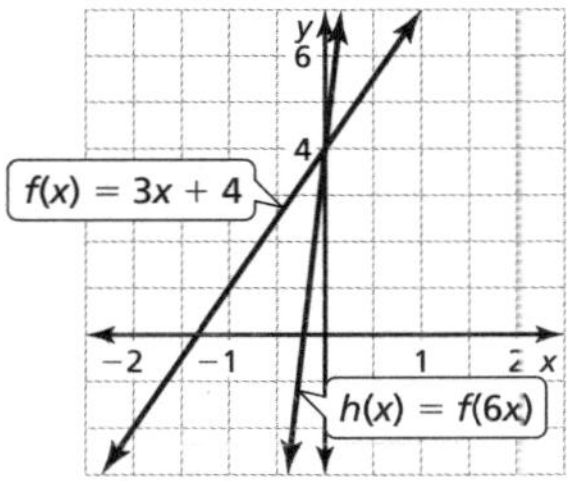

The graph of h is a horizontal shrink of the graph of f by a factor of $\frac{1}{6}$.

51.

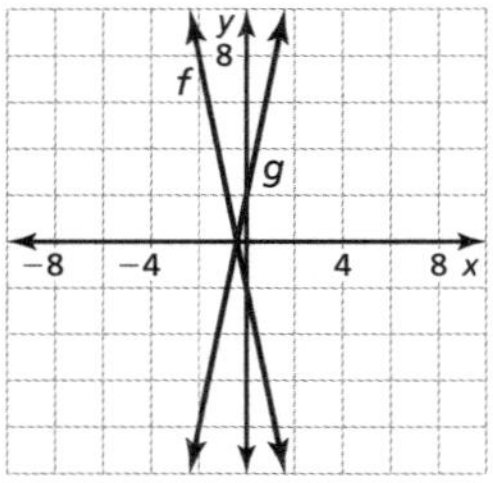

The graph of g is a reflection in the x-axis of the graph of f.

52. The graph of g is a horizontal stretch of the graph of f by a factor of 3.

53. $n = \frac{45}{28}$

54. positive: $x < 0$ and $x > 0$; negative: none; decreasing: $x < 0$; increasing $x > 0$; $y \to +\infty$ as $x \to -\infty$ and $y \to +\infty$ as $x \to +\infty$

55. positive: all real number; negative: none; decreasing: $x < 2$; increasing $x > 2$; $y \to +\infty$ as $x \to -\infty$ and $y \to +\infty$ as $x \to +\infty$

56.

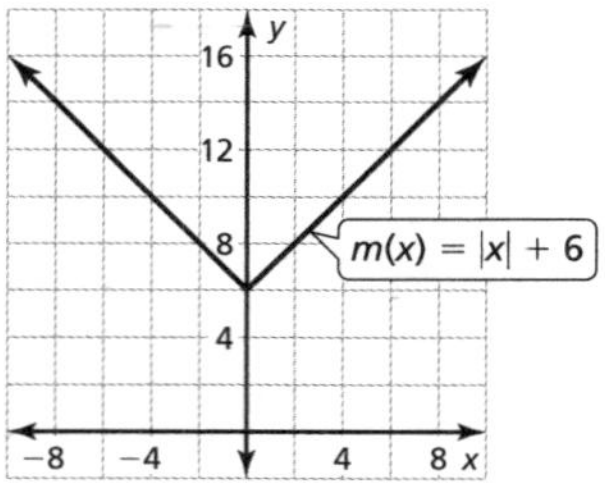

The graph of m is a vertical translation 6 units up of the graph of f; domain: all real numbers; range $y \geq 6$

57.

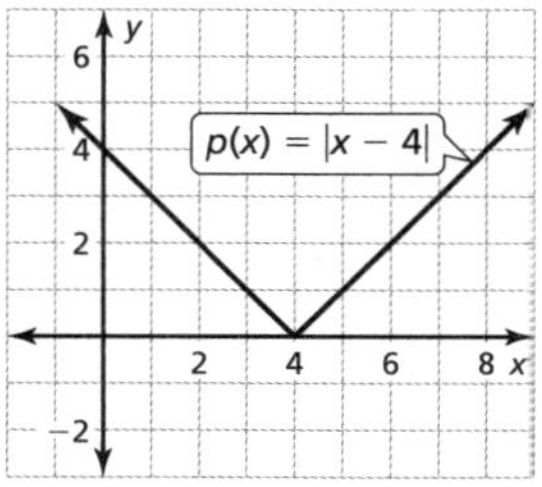

The graph of p is a horizontal translation 4 units right of the graph of f; domain: all real numbers; range $y \geq 0$

58. 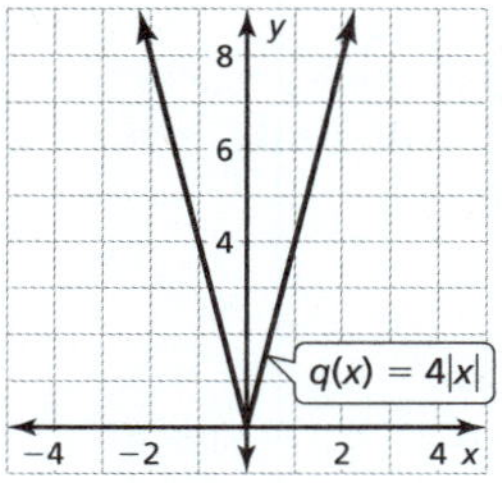

The graph of q is a vertical stretch of the graph of f by a factor of 4; domain: all real numbers; range $y \geq 0$

59. 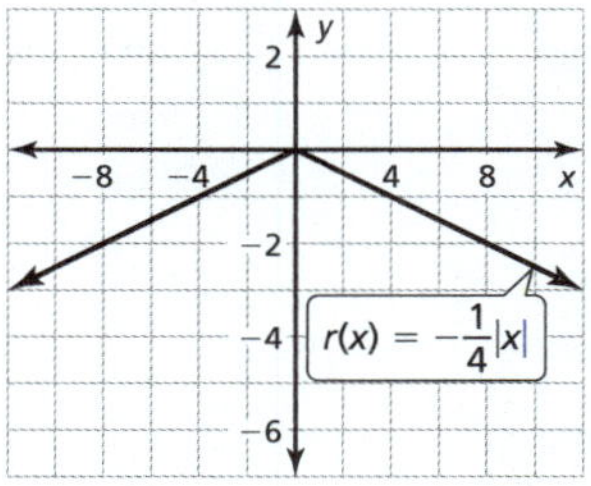

The graph of r is a vertical shrink of the graph of f by a factor of $\frac{1}{4}$ and a reflection in the x-axis; domain: all real numbers; range $y \leq 0$

60. $f(x) = |x - 9|$

61. $f(x) = \frac{1}{6}|x|$

62. The graph of g is a vertical stretch of the graph of f by a factor of 2.

63. The graph of g is a horizontal translation 2 units left of the graph of f.

64. $g(x) = 2|3x + 3| - 2$

65. a. 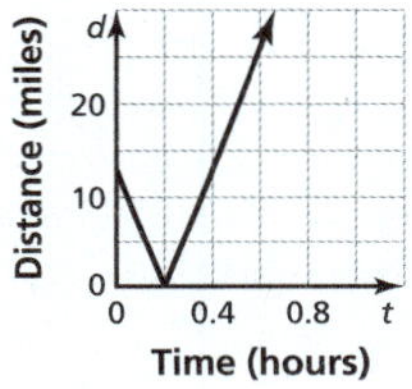

The t-intercept shows it takes 0.2 hour to reach the exit; The d-intercept shows you start 13 miles from the exit.

b. 1 h

Chapter 3 Practice Test

1. function; Every input has exactly one output; not linear; As x increases by 1, y changes by different amounts. The rate of change is not constant.
2. function; Every input has exactly one output; linear; It is in the form $y = mx + b$.
3. not a function; The input -2 has infinite output values.

4. 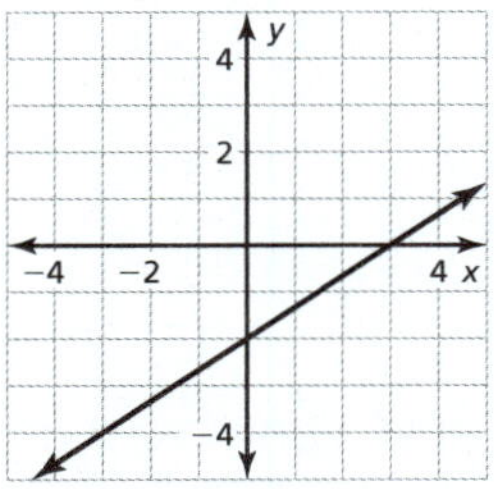

x-intercept: 3; y-intercept: -2; slope: $\frac{2}{3}$

5. 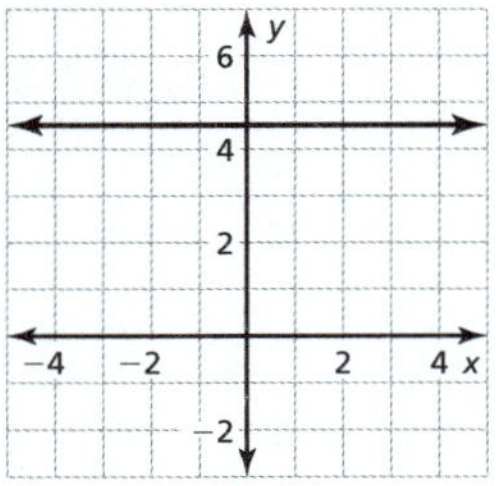

no x-intercept; y-intercept: 4.5; slope: 0

6. 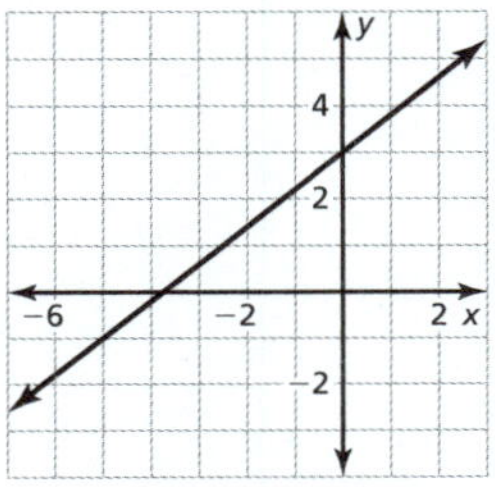

x-intercept: -3.75; y-intercept: 3; slope: $\frac{4}{5}$

7. 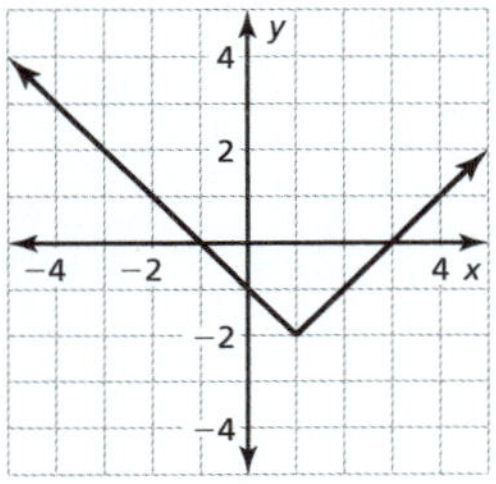

x-intercepts: -1, 3; y-intercept: -1

8. domain: all real numbers; range: $y \geq -2$; continuous; Because the domain is all real numbers, the domain is continuous.

9. positive: $x < -3$ and $x > 1$; negative: $-3 < x < 1$; decreasing: $x < -1$; increasing: $x > -1$; $y \to +\infty$ as $x \to +\infty$ and $y \to +\infty$ as $x \to -\infty$

10. 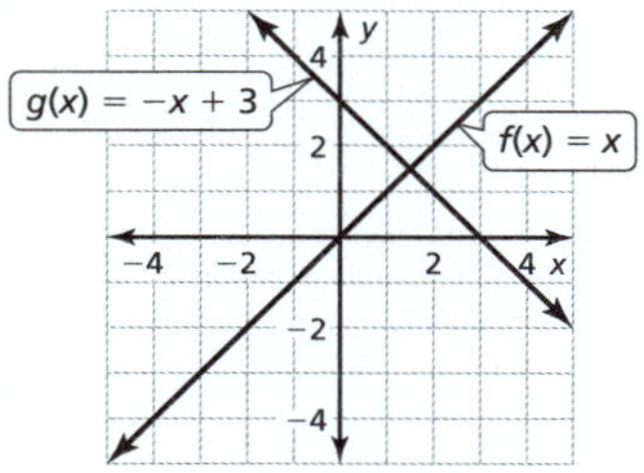

The graph of g is a reflection in the x-axis then a vertical translation 3 units up of the graph of f.

11. 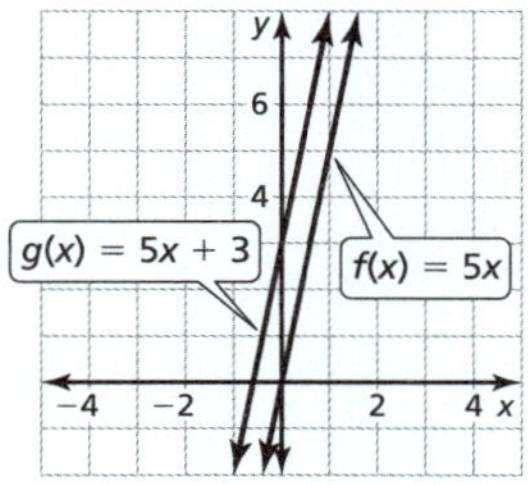

The graph of g is a vertical translation 3 units up of the graph of f.

12. The graph of g is a vertical shrink of the graph of f by a factor of $\frac{1}{3}$.

13. a. m is the dependent variable and r is the independent variable.

b. domain: 0, 1, 2, 3, 4, 5, 6, 7, 8, 9, 10; range: 0, 3, 6, 9, 12, 15, 18, 21, 24, 27, 30; discrete; The number of video games rented must be a whole number.

c. 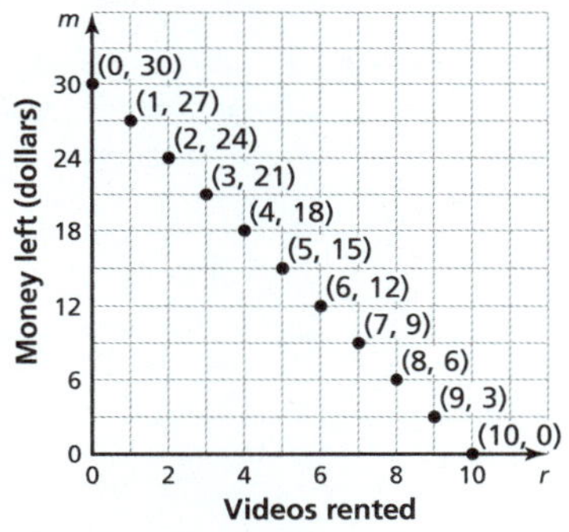

14. a. The slope is 125, so the climber ascends at a rate of 125 feet per hour; The y-intercept is 50, so the climber began the ascent at 50 feet above sea level.

b. 3.6 h; At the top, $f(x) = 500$. Setting 500 equal to $125x + 50$ and solving for x gives the time it takes to reach the top.

15. 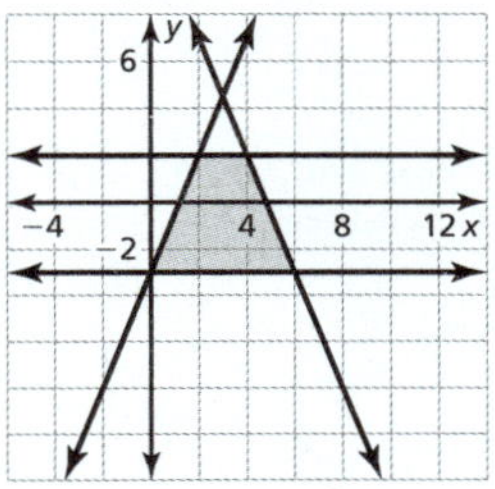

20 units^2

16. a. The number of downloads (in thousands) is the dependent variable and time is the independent variable.

b.

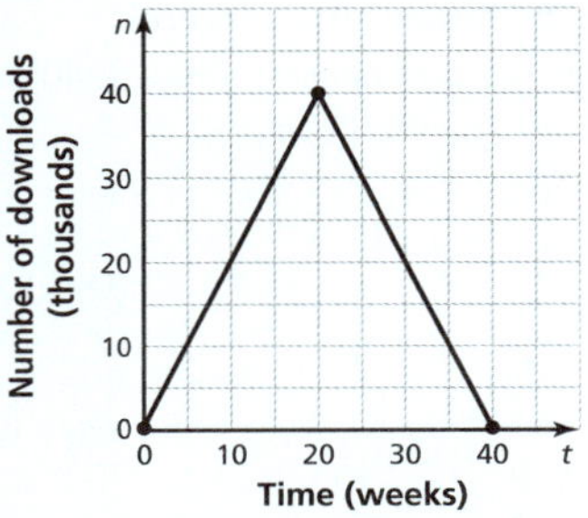

The graph of n is a vertical stretch of the graph of f by a factor of 4.

Chapter 3 B.E.S.T. Test Prep

1. 8 **2.** A **3.** 4.5 **4.** D
5. B, C, E, H **6.** 28 **7.** B **8.** B
9. A, B, D, E **10.** D **11.** 75 **12.** D

Chapter 4

Prepare with CalcChat

1. $(-5, -2)$
2. $(2, 0)$
3. C
4. E
5. $y = -5 + x$
6. $y = -\frac{1}{3} - 2x$
7. $y = 4x - 5$
8. $y = \frac{1}{4}x + 7$
9. $y = 4x - \frac{1}{2}$
10. $y = -\frac{3}{4}x - 1$
11. Points in Quadrant I move to Quadrant III, points in Quadrant II move to Quadrant IV, points in Quadrant III move to Quadrant I, points in Quadrant IV move to Quadrant II, points on the positive x- or y-axis move to the negative x- or y-axis respectively, points on the negative x- or y-axis move to the positive x- or y-axis respectively, and a point on the origin stays at the origin.

Section 4.1

4.1 Practice

1. $y = 2x + 9$ **3.** $y = -3x$ **5.** $y = \frac{2}{3}x - 8$
7. $y = \frac{1}{3}x + 2$ **9.** $y = -\frac{4}{3}x$ **11.** $y = -3x + 10$
13. $y = -4x - 24$ **15.** $f(x) = x + 2$ **17.** $f(x) = -\frac{1}{4}x - 2$
19. $f(x) = -10x - 4$ **21.** $f(x) = -2x + 1$
23. The slope and the y-intercept were substituted incorrectly: $y = 2x + 7$
25. a. $I = 24t$

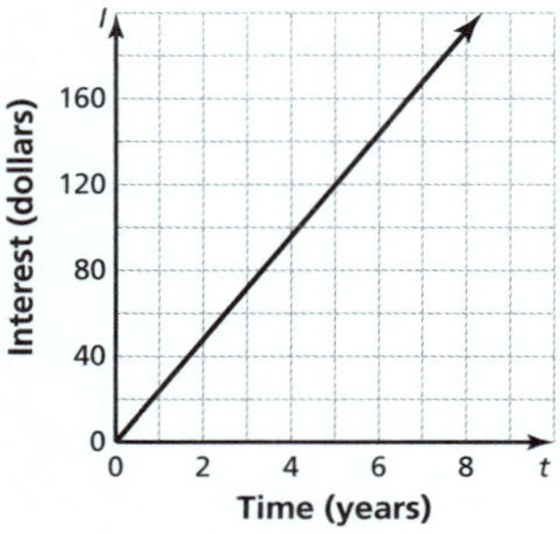

The interest earned each year is $24.

b. no

27. $11,300
29. a. about 5 years; You need to earn $480 in interest to cover the total cost of $1400; $480 = 920(0.10)t$, $t \approx 5.2$ years

b. about 2 years; $480 = 920(0.157)t$, $t \approx 3.3$ years, $5.2 - 3.3 = 1.9$

31. a. $P(x) = 55x - 800$;

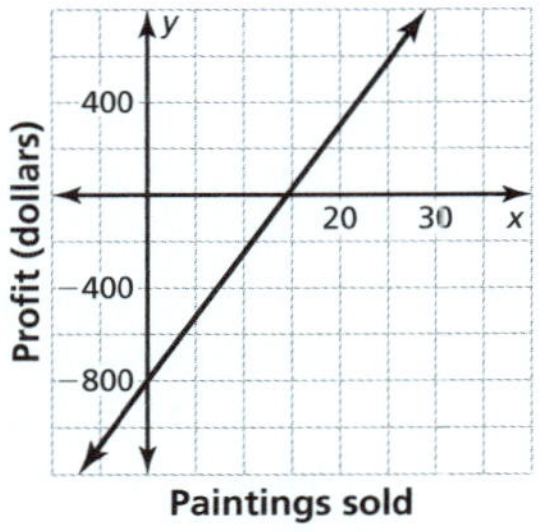

The slope of 55 means there is a $55 profit for each additional painting sold; the y-intercept of -800 means the painter starts with a debt of $800

b. 15 paintings; The x-intercept of about 14.5 represents the number of paintings the vendor will sell to reach a profit of $0. The profit is positive for each successive paining sold.

33. a. Service A: 12.5 miles or more; Service B: 12.5 miles or less; The services cost the same amount when $5 + 0.2x = 0.6x + 0$, or when $x = 12.5$; Service B has a y-intercept of 0 and Service A has a y-intercept of 5, making Service B initially less expensive.

b. Service A: 2.5 miles or more; Service B: 2.5 miles or less; The services cost the same amount when $1 + 0.2x = 0.6x + 0$, or when $x = 2.5$; Service B has a y-intercept of 0 and Service A has a y-intercept of 1, making Service B initially less expensive.

35. your friend; If f is a function, then the line is not vertical.
37. $y = \frac{5}{3}x - 1$
39. $f(x) = mx + b$; b is the y-intercept. m is the slope.

4.1 Review & Refresh

40. $y = \frac{1}{4}$
41. no solution
42. all real numbers
43. $y = -\frac{1}{3}x + 5$
44.

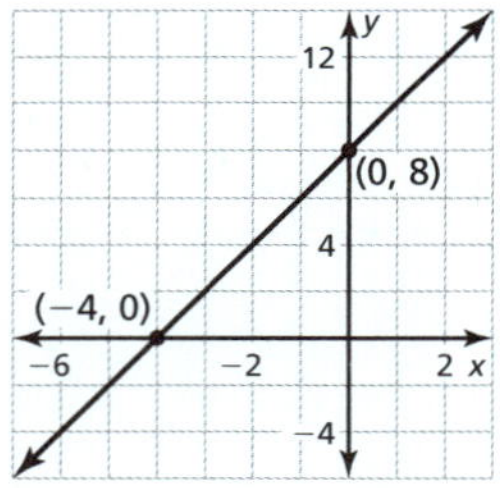

45. a. The graph of g is a vertical shrink of the graph of f by a factor of $\frac{1}{2}$.

b.

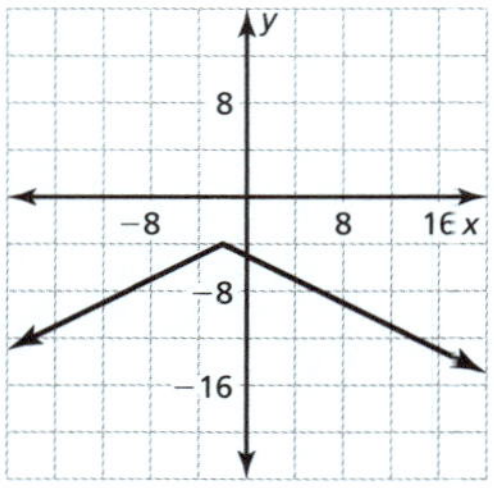

46. -3
47. slope: 0; y-intercept: 9.5

48. slope: -10; y-intercept: -7

49. not a solution

50. $a = 1.25$ represents the factor that your weekly earnings increase by

Section 4.2

4.2 Practice

1.

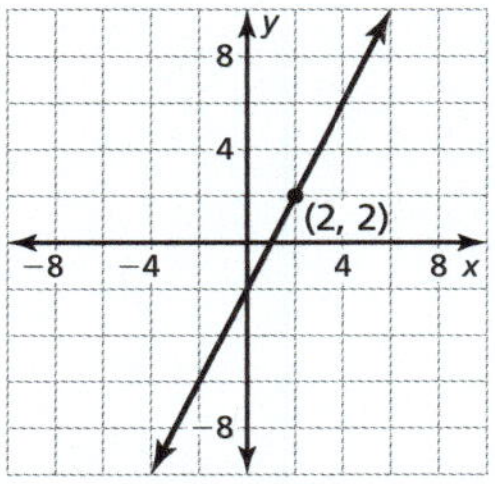

The x-intercept is 1 and the y-intercept is -2.

3.

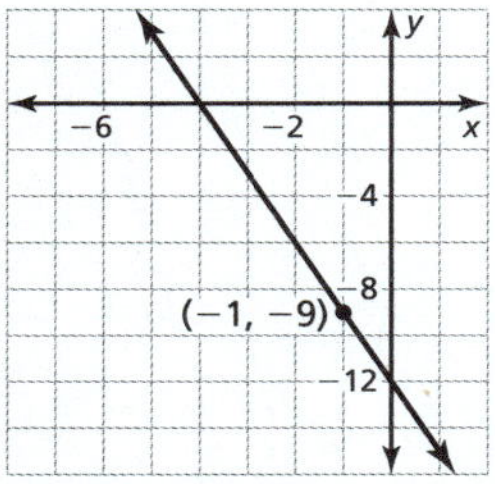

The x-intercept is -4 and the y-intercept is -12.

5. $y - 1 = 2(x - 2)$

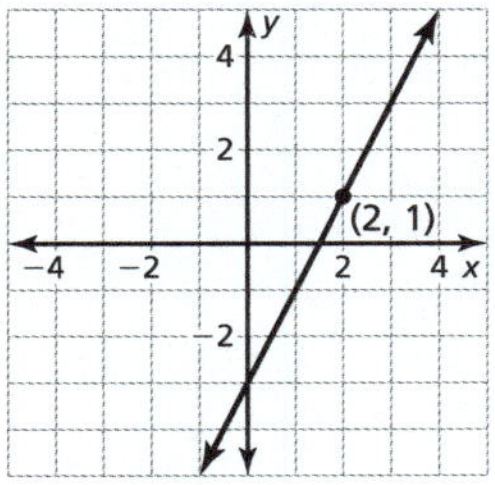

7. $y + 4 = -6(x - 7)$

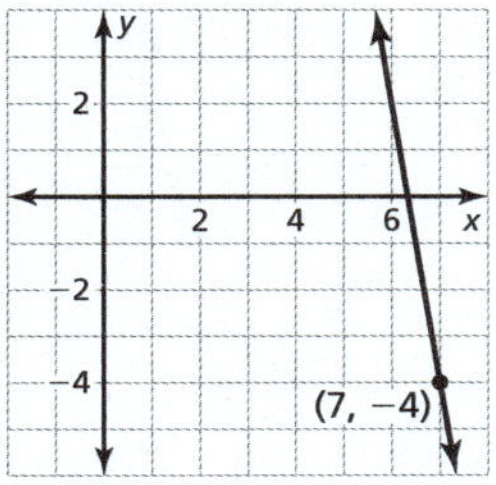

9. $y = -3\left(x - \frac{5}{6}\right)$

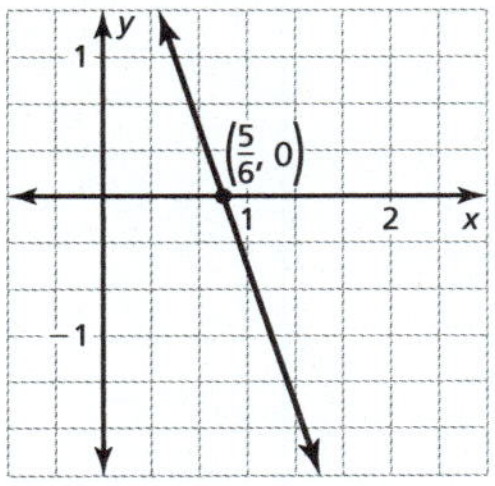

11. $y + 12 = -\frac{2}{5}(x - 5)$

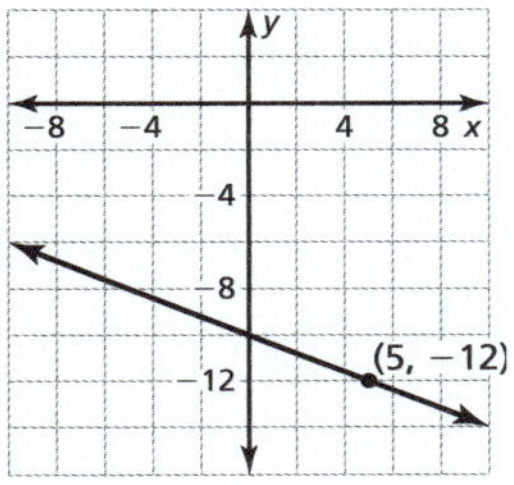

13. $y = 2x - 5$ **15.** $y = -\frac{1}{2}x + 1$ **17.** $y = -2x + 16$

19. $y = -9$ **21.** $y = \frac{2}{3}x + 7$ **23.** $f(x) = -3x + 4$

25. $f(x) = -\frac{1}{2}x$ **27.** $f(x) = \frac{1}{4}x + \frac{7}{4}$

29. no; y does not increase at a constant rate.

31. **a.** yes; The total cost increases at a constant rate.

b. \$49; \$104.50

c. 11 days

33. The value -5 should be subtracted from y, not added; $y - (-5) = -2(x - 4)$

35. **a.** $y = 0.2x$

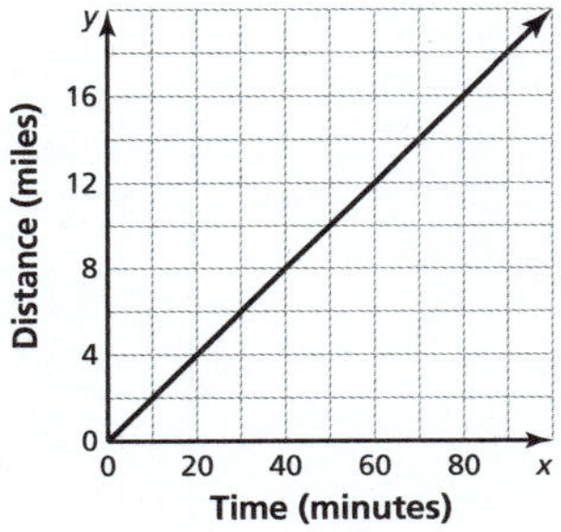

b. The slope of 0.2 means you bike 0.2 miles each additional minute and the y-intercept of 0 means you have biked 0 miles at the start of your ride

c. 48 miles; 4 hours = 240 minutes, and $0.2(240) = 48$

37. 21 kWh; 42 kWh; The slope of the equation is 3 because you save 3 kilowatt hours each day and the y-intercept is 0 because on day 0 you have not saved any kilowatt hours; $y = 3x$, so $3(7) = 21$ kWh saved in 7 days and $3(14) = 42$ kWh saved in 14 days.

39. $y = 2x - 30$; *Sample answer:* a person's distance from home if they start 30 miles from home and walk at a rate of 2 miles per hour; yes; The domain is $x \geq 0$ because x represent the time (in hours) spent walking.

41. **a.** *Sample answer:* when given a point on the line other than the y-intercept and the slope; when given the y-intercept and the slope of the line; I would not have to spend time simplifying the equations.

b. *Sample answer:* I prefer using point-slope form because I can quickly graph the point provided and then use the slope to find a second point on the line.

43. The graph of $y - 1 = 2(x + 3)$ is a horizontal translation 3 units left and a vertical translation 1 unit up of the graph of $y = 2x$; The graph of $y - k = m(x - h)$ is a translation h units horizontally and k units vertically of the graph of $y = mx$.

45. **a.** The domain of each account is the number of months until the account has no money left in it. Account A's domain: is $0 \leq x \leq 5\frac{1}{3}$; Account B's domain: $0 \leq x \leq 5$; Account C's domain is $0 \leq x \leq 4$; Account B; Account A

b. Account B; Account A

c. Account C; Account A

4.2 Review & Refresh

47. $\frac{1}{5}$ **48.** $-\frac{1}{8}$ **49.** $-\frac{7}{2}$ **50.** $\frac{2}{3}$

51. $y - 1 = \frac{2}{3}(x + 9)$

52. The graph of p is a horizontal translation 6 units right of the graph of $f(x) = |x|$. The graph of q is a vertical translation 6 units down of the graph of $f(x) = |x|$.

53. continuous; The number of years can be any value greater than or equal to 0.

54. $f(x) = -x + 2$

55. The graph of T is a vertical translation 25 units up of the graph of C.

56. $r < 2$ or $r \geq 7$

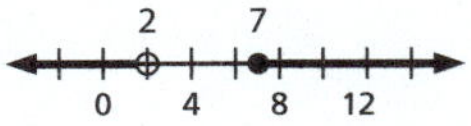

57.

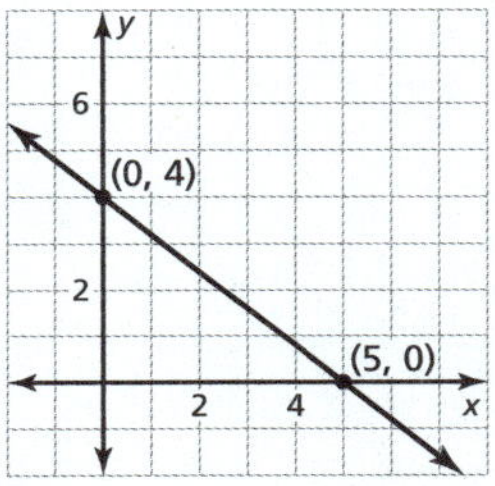

x-intercept: 5; y-intercept: 4

58.

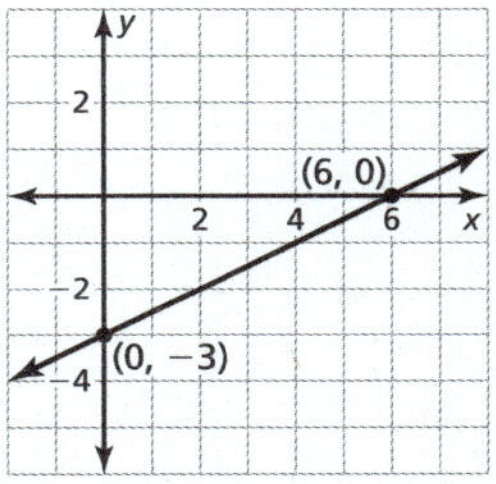

x-intercept: 6; y-intercept: -3

Section 4.3

4.3 Practice

1. $-5x + y = 4$ **3.** $-2x + y = -18$

5. $-\frac{4}{3}x + y = \frac{10}{3}$ **7.** $-x + y = 5$ **9.** $2x + y = 5$

11. $\frac{3}{2}x + y = -10$ **13.** $-x + y = 7$ **15.** $\frac{4}{3}x + y = -2$

17. slope: 1; y-intercept: -10; slope-intercept form: $y = x - 10$

19. slope: 3; y-intercept: 4; slope-intercept form: $y = 3x + 4$

21. $y = 3, x = 2$ **23.** $y = -1, x = 8$

25. 4; $4x + 3y = 5$ **27.** 4; $-x + 4y = 10$

29. a. $1.20x + 2.50y = 300$

b.

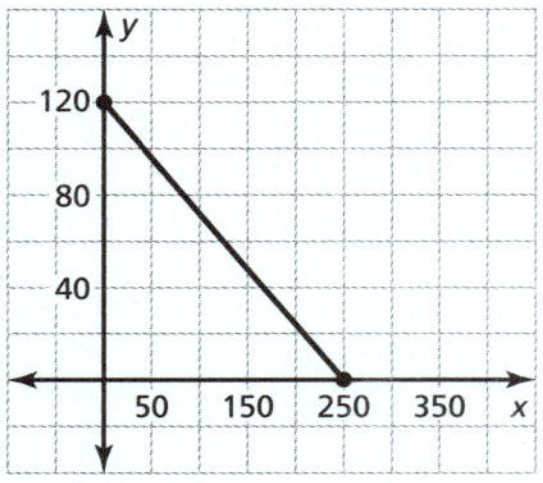

c. *Sample answer:* 0 Vinca plants and 120 Phlox plants, 50 Vinca plants and 96 Phlox plants, 150 Vinca plants and 48 Phlox plants, and 250 Vinca plants and 0 Phlox plants

31. no; The equation of a horizontal line is the same in all forms.

33. $\frac{b}{a}x + y = b$

35. $2\ell + 2w = 60$; *Sample answer:*

Length	Width
28	2
26	4
25	5
22	8
18	12

4.3 Review & Refresh

36. $y = -\frac{1}{3}x + 1$

37.

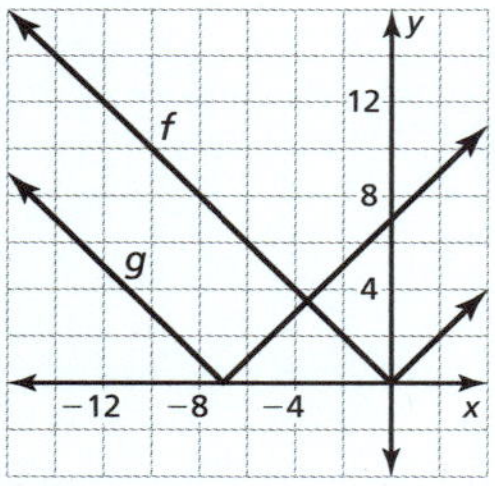

The graph of g is a horizontal translation left 7 units of the graph of f; domain: all reals; range: $y \geq 0$

38. $3x - 4y = -4$ **39.** $f(x) = \frac{2}{3}x + 7$

40.

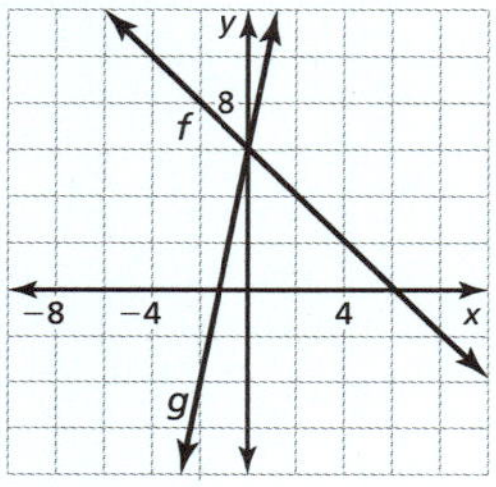

The graph of g is a reflection in the y-axis and a horizontal shrink of the graph of f by a factor of $\frac{1}{5}$.

41.

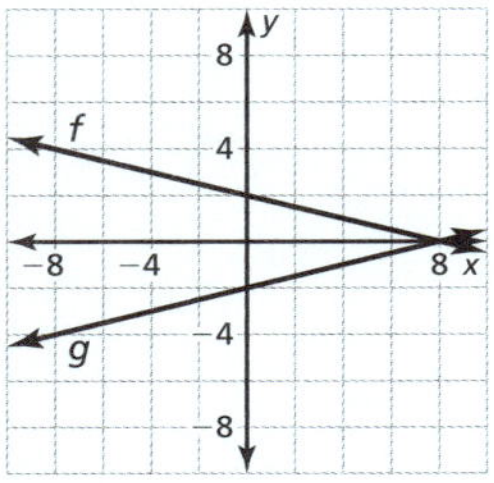

The graph of g is a reflection in the x-axis of the graph of f.

42.

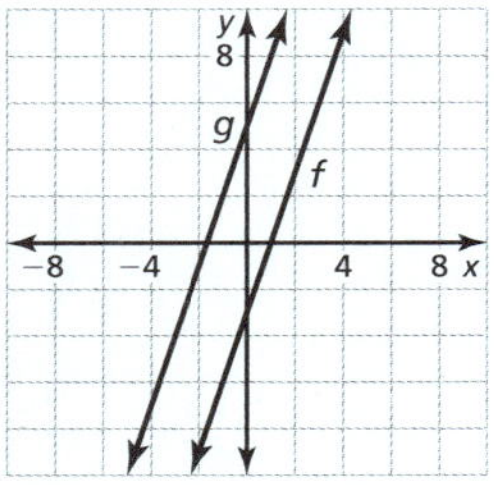

The graph of g is a horizontal translation left 2 units of the graph of f.

43.

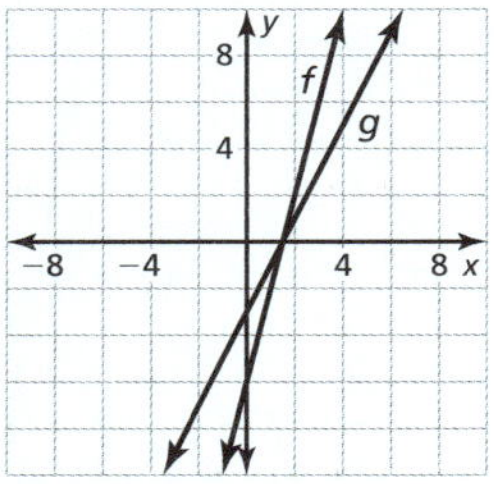

The graph of g is a vertical shrink of the graph of f by a factor of $\frac{1}{2}$.

44. $d(m) = 100 + 50m$

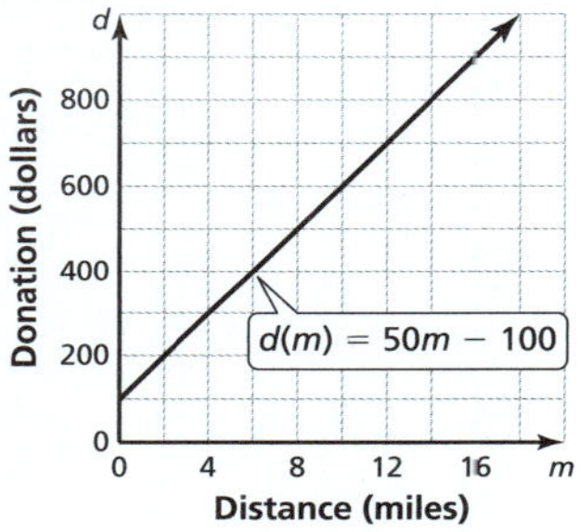

domain: $0 \leq m \leq 15$; range $100 \leq d(m) \leq 850$; The slope of 50 means another \$50 is donated for each additional mile and the y-intercept of 100 means the donation is \$100 for participating.

45. $x > -4$

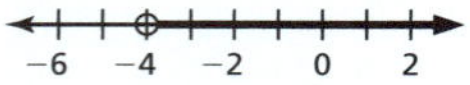

46. $y = \frac{5}{2}x - 7$

Section 4.4

4.4 Practice

1. lines a and b; They have the same slope.

3. lines a and c; They have the same slope.

5. none; None of the lines have the same slope.

7. $x = 0$ **9.** $y = -3x$ **11.** $y = \frac{1}{3}x + 2$

13. None are parallel or perpendicular; None of the lines have the same slope or slopes that are negative reciprocals of each other.

15. None are parallel; Lines b and c are perpendicular; None of the lines have the same slope and the slope of line b is the negative reciprocal of the slope of line c.

17. Lines a and b are parallel; Line c is perpendicular to lines a and b; Lines a and b have the same slope and the slope of line c is the negative reciprocal of the slopes of lines a and b.

19. $y = 5$

21. $y = 5x - 25$

23. $y = -\frac{1}{4}x + \frac{9}{4}$

25. $(-1, 1)$

27. Perpendicular lines have negative reciprocal slopes, not just reciprocal slopes; $y - (-5) = -3(x - 4)$; $y + 5 = -3x + 12$; $y = -3x + 7$

29. yes; no; Opposite sides are parallel but adjacent sides are not perpendicular, so it is a parallelogram but not a rectangle.

31. never; Perpendicular lines have opposite reciprocal slopes, so one must be positive and the other must be negative.

33. sometimes; They are perpendicular when the slopes are negative reciprocals, otherwise they will not be perpendicular.

35. no; The lines that form the angle are not perpendicular.

4.4 Review & Refresh

36. not a function; The input values of -1 and 1 are each paired with more than one output value.

37. 100 gal

38.

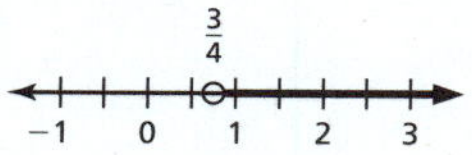

39.

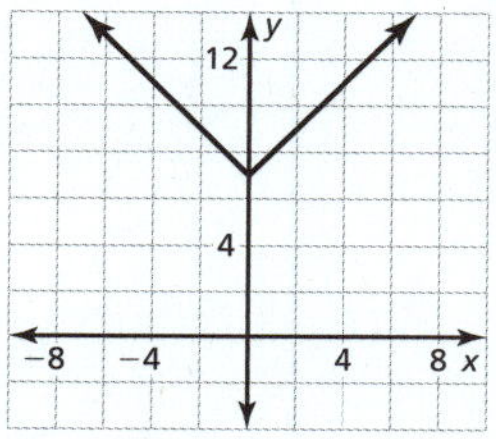

The graph of g is a vertical translation 7 units up of the graph of f; domain: all real numbers; range: $y \geq 7$

40.

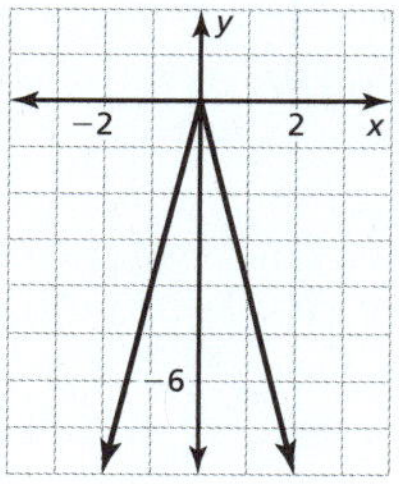

The graph of h is a reflection in the x-axis, and a vertical stretch by a factor of 4 of the graph of f; domain: all real numbers; range: $y \leq 0$

41.

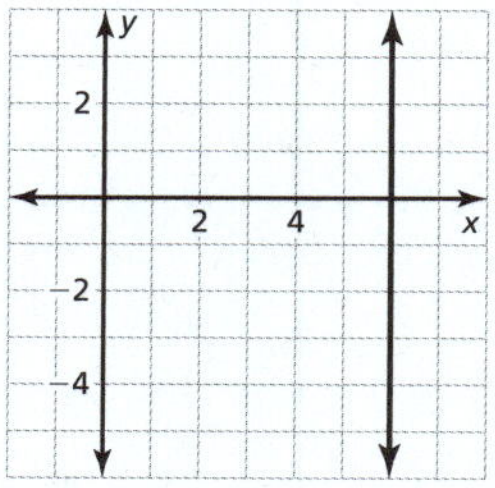

42.

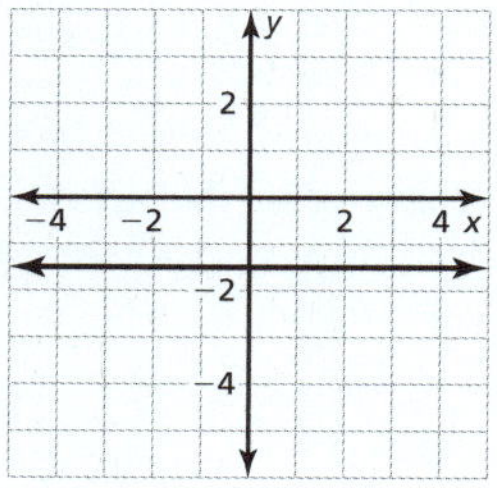

43. 1.41 kg, 1.42 kg, or 1.43 kg

44. a. $y = -4x + 19$

b. $y = \frac{1}{4}x + 2$

45. $5x + 2y = 8$

46. $a = -\frac{2}{3}$; $a = 6$

47. 279 in.^{2}

Section 4.5

4.5 Practice

1. a. \$800

b. 16 GB

c. increases

3. positive linear correlation

5. no correlation

7.

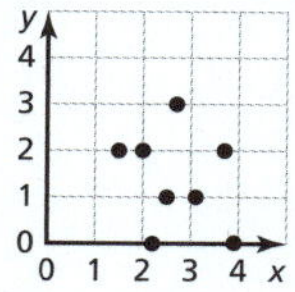

no correlation

9. a. $y = 1.55x - 12$

b. The slope of 1.55 means a homeowner saves about \$1550 on electric bills each year after installing solar panels. The y-intercept of -12 represents the total cost to install the solar panels was about \$12,000.

11. no; A line of fit should have about as many points above the line as below it, but does not have to pass through any data points.

13. a. *Sample answer:*

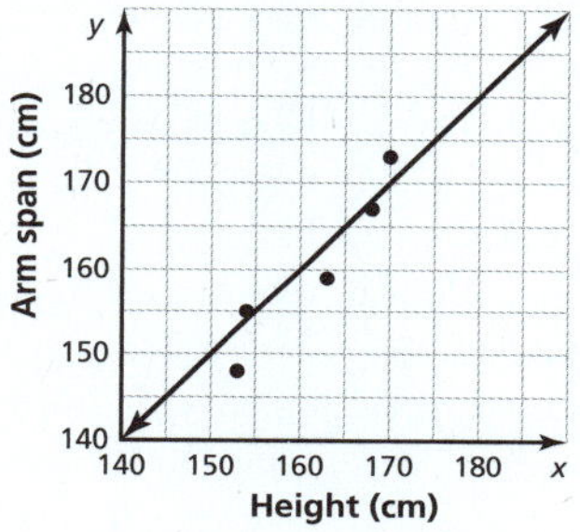

b. $y = x$ is the equation of the line of fit, where y is the length, in centimeters, of a person's arm span and x is the height, in centimeters, of the person. The coefficient of 1 means a person's arm span increases by about 1 centimeter for every 1 centimeter increase in height.

15. no; The data points do not have a linear trend.

4.5 Review & Refresh

17. no; The data points do not have a linear trend.

18. a. $y = -4x - 16$

b. $y = \frac{1}{4}x + 1$

19.

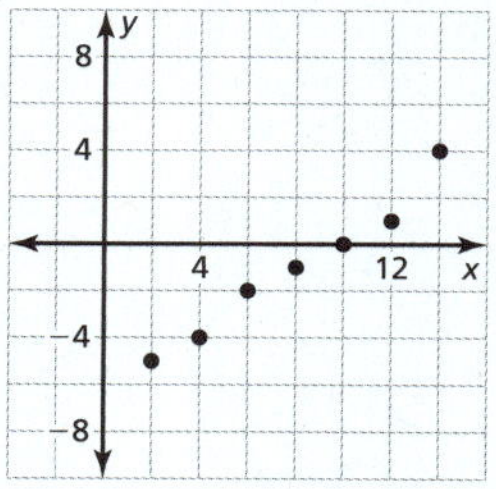

positive linear correlation

20.

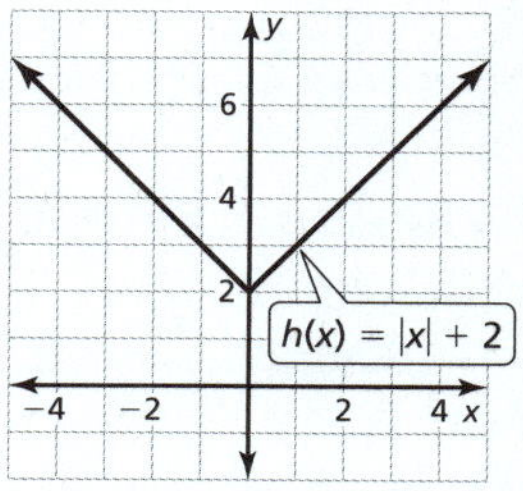

The graph of h is a vertical translation 2 units up of the graph of f.

21. 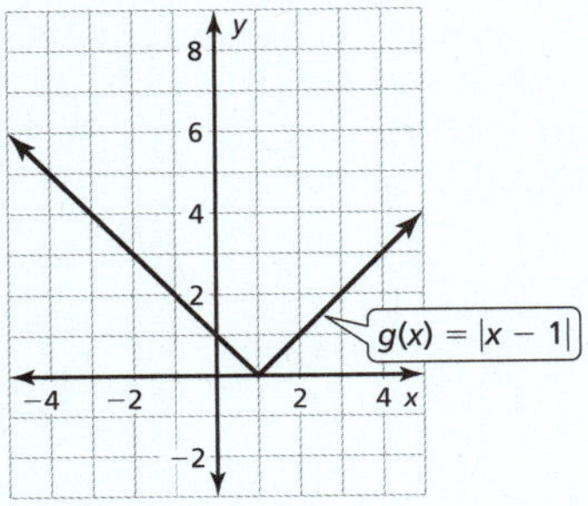

The graph of g is a horizontal translation 1 unit right of the graph of f.

22. Company A; You can keep the site running for 13 months at Company A. You can keep the site running for 10 months at Company B.
23. yes; y decreases at a constant rate; $y = -2.25x + 9.25$
24. $w = \frac{P - 2\ell}{2}$, or $w = \frac{1}{2}P - \ell$
25. $-9.5x + y = 1.2$

Section 4.6

4.6 Practice

1. weak positive correlation
3. 4; 2; 12; 1; yes
5. There is a negative correlation and a causal relationship because the more time you spend talking on the phone, the less charge there is left in the battery.
7. A correlation is unlikely. The number of hats you own is not related to the size of your head.
9. a. weak positive correlation
   b. The slope of 75 means the number of sent text messages increases by about 75 billion each year. The y-intercept of 1602 is an estimate of the number of billions of text messages sent in 2014, which is outside the range of the model.
   c. no; Increased the availability of texting devises over time may result in more text messages sent, but the passage of time does not cause more texts to be sent.
11. a. A; The data points plotted are relatively close to the line of fit with a positive slope.
    b. B; The data points plotted are relatively close to the line of fit with a negative slope.
    c. D; The data points plotted are loosely scattered about the line of fit with a negative slope.
    d. C; The data points plotted are loosely scattered about the line of fit with a positive slope.
13. your cousin; Not all absolute values of the residuals are relatively small. The data, excluding outlier (5, 8.5), do not appear to be linear.

4.6 Review & Refresh

15. $w \leq 25$

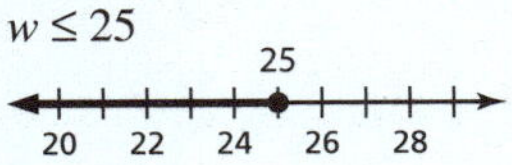

16. $y > -\frac{8}{3}$

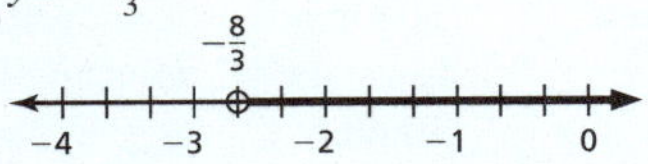

17. yes; no; There may be other factors that can cause an illness.
18. \$25
19. linear; The rate of change is constant.
20. $y = 12; x = -3$
21. weak positive linear correlation
22. $y = -2x - 6$
23. None are parallel; Lines a and b are perpendicular; None of the lines have the same slope and the slope of line a is the negative reciprocal of the slope of line b.
24. $d = -5, d = 5$
25. $b = \frac{31}{8}$
26. There is a strong positive linear correlation; As time increases, the diver ascends at a nearly constant rate.

Section 4.7

4.7 Practice

1. $y = 1.4x + 16$

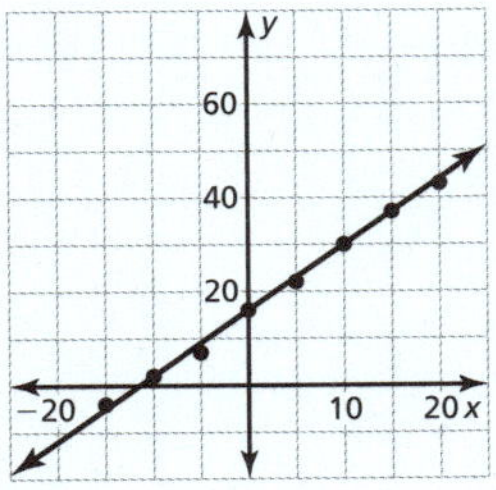

3. $y = 5x + 51$

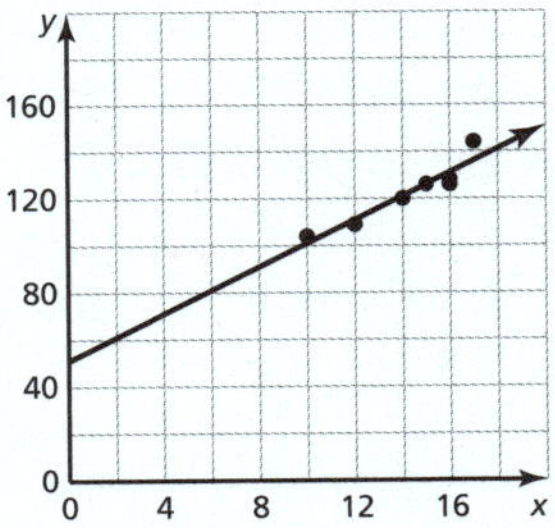

5. a. $y = x + 7$

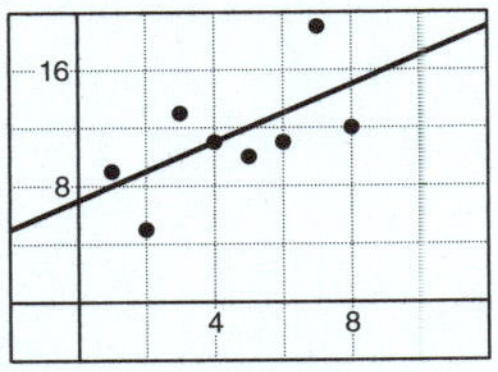

   b. The slope of 1 means the number of people who volunteer increases by about 1 each day. The y-intercept of 7 has no meaning in this context because there is no day 0.
7. a. $y = -0.2x + 20$; The slope of -0.2 means the selling price decreases by about \$200 for every increase in mileage of 1000 miles. The y-intercept of 20 has no meaning in this context because a used car cannot have 0 mileage.
   b. \$15,000
   c. \$18,800
9. *Sample answer:* The slope of the line of best fit represents the rate of change of the trend of the data; The y-intercept of the line of best fit represents the initial value of the trend of the data.
11. no; It is possible for none of the data to lie on the line of best fit.
13. Check students' work. Look for scatter plots with data and labels and a line of fit that represents the data. Conclusions should be based on the trend of the line of fit.

4.7 Review & Refresh

14. −5; 3
15. 0; 4.5
16. yes; Each input has a unique output.
17. 3; $3x + 5y = 15$

18. Interpolation is using a graph or its equation to approximate a value between two known values, and extrapolation is using a graph or its equation to predict a value outside the range of known values.

19. $y = -3x + 7$

20.

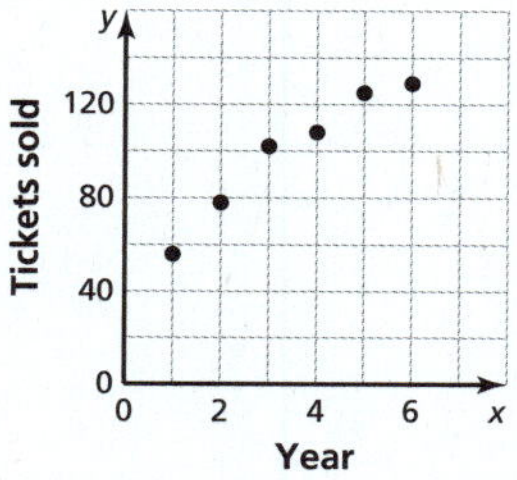

positive linear correlation

21. yes; no; There is a causal relationship between the time an athlete spends exercising and the calories they *burn*. But exercising does not cause them to *consume* more calories.

22. **a.** 357 shoppers

b. 297 shoppers

23. $x > 3$

Chapter 4 Review

1. $y = -\frac{1}{2}x + 1$ **2.** $y = \frac{2}{3}x + 3$ **3.** $1140

4. $y - 7 = -(x - 4)$; x-intercept 11; y-intercept 11

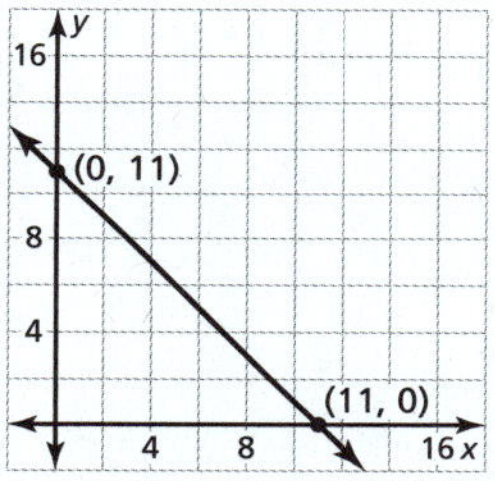

5. $f(x) = x - 5$

6. $f(x) = -4$

7. $f(x) = -\frac{5}{3}x + 18$

8. $y - \frac{C}{B} = -\frac{A}{B}(x - 0)$

9. $22.25

10. $2x + y = -6$

11. $x - 4y = -20$ **12.** $2x + y = -4$ **13.** $3x - 2y = -9$

14.

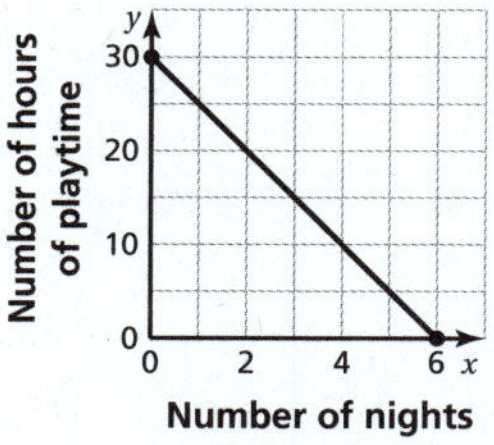

The x-intercept shows that you can board your dog for 6 nights when there are no hours of playtime. The y-intercept shows that you can have 30 hours of playtime for your dog when you do not leave your dog at the kennel for any nights.

15. Lines a and b are parallel; None of the lines are perpendicular; Lines a and b have the same slope and none of them have negative reciprocal slopes.

16. None of the lines are parallel; Lines b and c are perpendicular; None of the lines have the same slope and the slope of line b is the negative reciprocal of the slope of line c.

17. $y = -4x + 9$

18. $y = \frac{1}{2}x - 4$

19. 4 h

20. positive linear correlation

21. $y = 10.89x + 54.6$; The slope of 10.89 shows that the salary cap increases by about $10.89 million each year. The y-intercept of 54.6 represents the salary cap at the beginning of the season in 2013, in millions of dollars.

22. **a.**

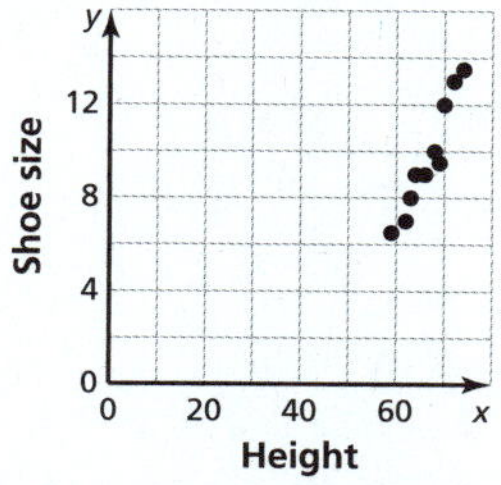

strong positive correlation

b. The slope of $\frac{1}{2}$ means that the shoe size increases by about half a size for each additional inch of height. The y-intercept of -21.5 has no meaning because height cannot be negative.

c. *Sample answer:* no; Height does not determine shoe size because other factors such as age, gender and genetics affect shoe size.

23. $y = -2.16x + 6.62$

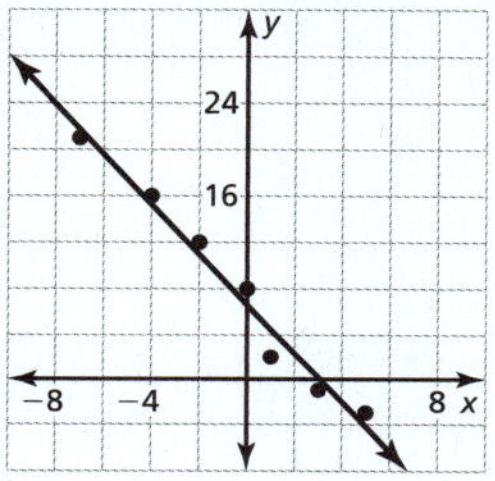

24. **a.** $y = 0.97x - 17.66$

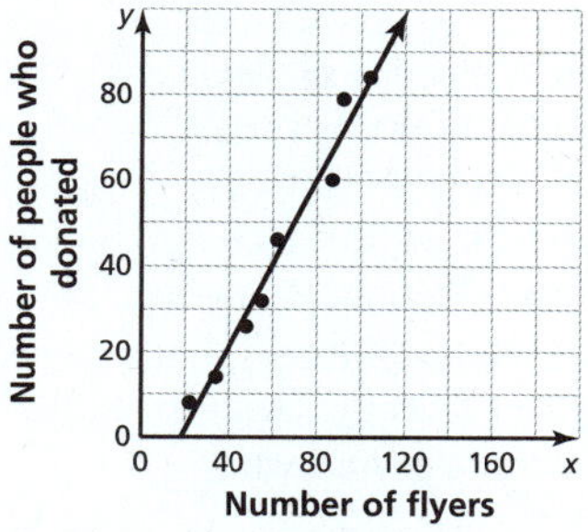

b. The slope of 0.97 means that the number of people who donate increases by about 1 person for each flyer. The y-intercept of -17.66 has no meaning since the number of people cannot be negative.

c. about 99 people

Chapter 4 Practice Test

1. $y = -3x + 6$

2. $y = 3x - 2$

3. $y - 1 = -4(x - 1)$

4. $f(x) = 3x + 6$

5. $3x - 2y = -10$

6. $x + y = -2$

7. a. $1.5x + 3y = 45$

b.

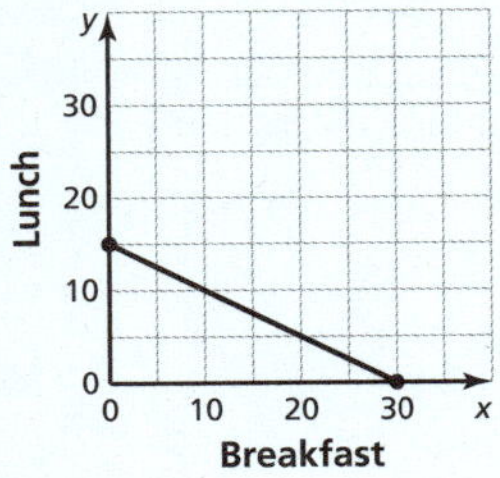

c. 13

8. None of the lines are parallel; Lines 1 and 2 are perpendicular; None of the lines have the same slope, but the slope of line 1 is the negative reciprocal of the slope of line 2.

9. $g(x) = -\frac{6}{5}x + \frac{34}{5}$

10. a.

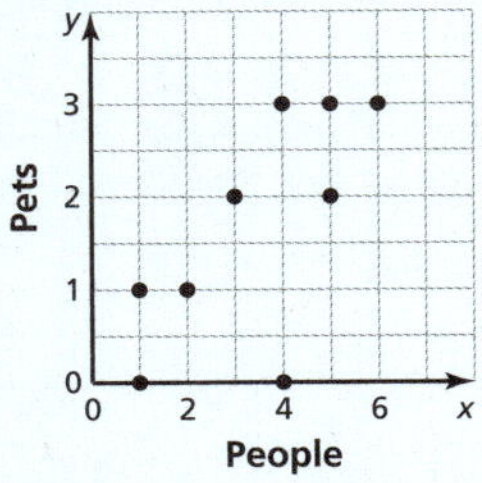

weak positive correlation

b. $y = 0.47x + 0.05$; The slope of about 0.47 means that the number of pets increases by 1 for every 2 people. The y-intercept of about 0.05 means that there are no pets if there are no people.

c. about 4 pets

11. a. *Sample answer:* $y = 0.2x + 309$; The slope of 0.2 means the attendance increases by about 1 person for every additional $5 spent on advertising. The y-intercept of 309 means that if no money is spent on advertising, about 309 people attend the festival.

b. more or less evenly dispersed about the horizontal axis; The line of best fit models the data well.

c. There may be a causal relationship in the data but the correlation may be caused by other factors, such as the quality of the attractions each year.

d. 2089 people

Chapter 4 B.E.S.T. Test Prep

1. A, B, C, F **2.** 12.4 **3.** D **4.** C
5. B, C, F **6.** $-\frac{7}{9}$ **7.** B **8.** A
9. A **10.** B, D, E

Chapter 5

Prepare with CalcChat

1.

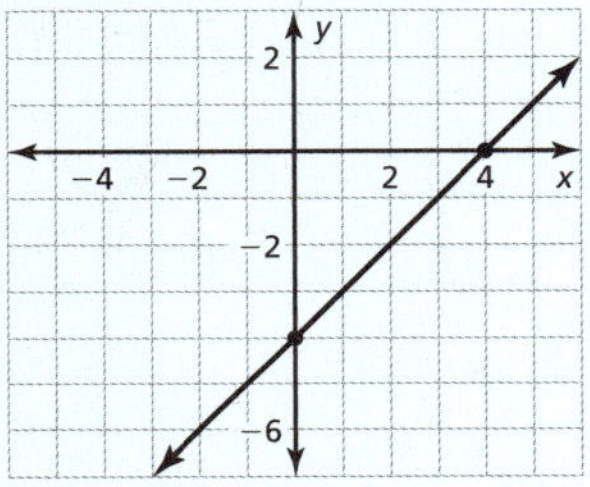

2.

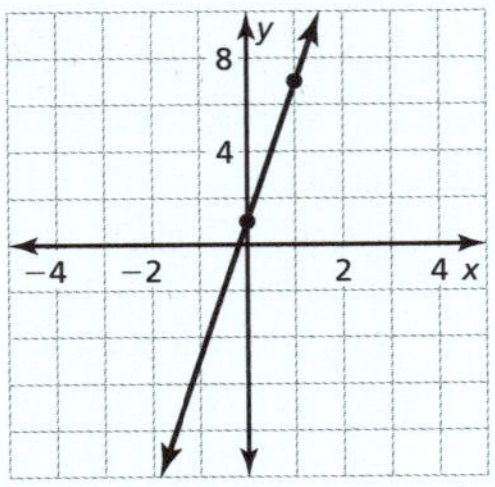

3.

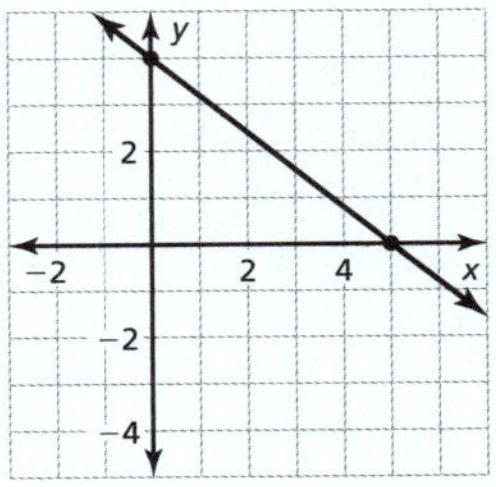

4.

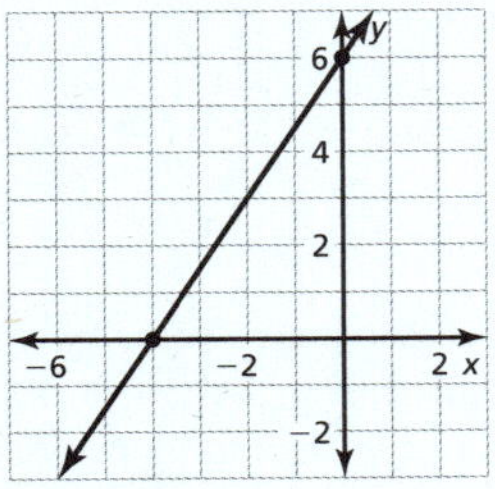

5. $m > 5$

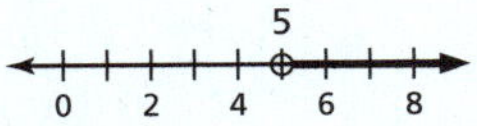

6. $t \le -4$

7. $a \le 9$

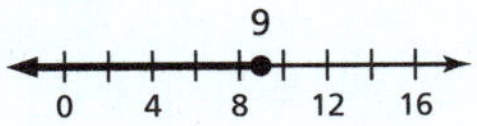

8. $z > 12$

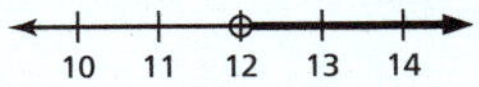

9. $k < 6$

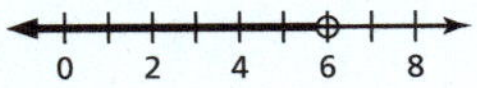

10. $w \ge -\frac{12}{5}$

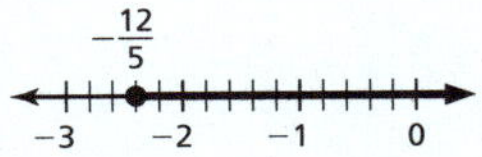

11. The two lines intersect.

Section 5.1

5.1 Practice

1. yes **3.** no **5.** no **7.** $(1, -3)$
9. $(3, 4)$ **11.** $(-9, -1)$ **13.** $(-1, 2)$
15. $(0, -5.5)$ **17.** $(10, 5)$ **19.** $(1.2, 1.4)$
21. The solution needs to be an ordered pair; (2, 3)
23. 30 min on the elliptical trainer, 10 min on the stationary bike
25. $m\angle X = 32°$, $m\angle Y = 58°$
27. a. yes; Because $y = 4.5x$ and $y = 3x + 1.5$ intersect at (1, 4.5), after one hour, you and your friend will be 4.5 miles from the trailhead.

b. you; 1.5 h; It will take you $18 \div 4.5 = 4$ hours, and your friend $(18 - 1.5) \div 3 = 5.5$ hours.

5.1 Review & Refresh

29. $y = 2x + 3$ **30.** $y = -3x + 20$
31. *Sample answer:* $y + 5 = \frac{2}{5}(x - 12)$; $y = \frac{2}{5}x - \frac{49}{5}$
32. $n = 5$ **33.** $r = -12$
34. $p = 8$ **35.** $k = 23$
36. positive linear correlation **37.** $(-4, 0)$
38. The model is a good fit. The absolute values of the residuals are relatively small.
39. x-intercept: $\frac{15}{2}$; y-intercept: 3
40. a. $y = 0.10x + 0.04$; The slope of 0.10 means the distance increases by about 0.10 mile for every minute spent running. The y-intercept of 0.04 has no meaning in this context because you cannot have run 0.04 miles at time 0.

b. about 1.24 mi

Section 5.2

5.2 Practice

1. *Sample answer:* Substitute $2y$ for x into $x + 4y = 30$.

3. *Sample answer:* Substitute $x - 15$ for $12y$ into $-3x + 12y = 3$.

5. *Sample answer:* Solve $x - y = -3$ for x then substitute that expression for x into $4x + 3y = -5$.

7. $(5, 3)$ **9.** $(-4, 5)$ **11.** $\left(4, \frac{3}{2}\right)$ **13.** $(6, 7)$

15. $(-9, 2)$

17. In Step 2, parenthesis should be used when substituting $3x + 4$ for $2y$. Because $4x - 4 = 12$, $x = 4$. The solution is $(4, 8)$.

19. 8 five-point problems, 30 two-point problems

21. *Sample answer:* $2x + y = 5$ and $2x - y = 55$

23. yes; Both equations have the term $-7x$, so you can substitute $42 - y$ for $-7x$ into the first equation and solve for y.

25. $x = 67, y = 23$ **27.** $a = 4, b = 5$ **29.** 47

5.2 Review & Refresh

31. $3x - 11$ **32.** $3d + 5$ **33.** $64v$ **34.** $\left(3, -\frac{1}{2}\right)$

35. **a.** 24 marbles

b. 32 times

36. $y = 3.21x - 16.38$

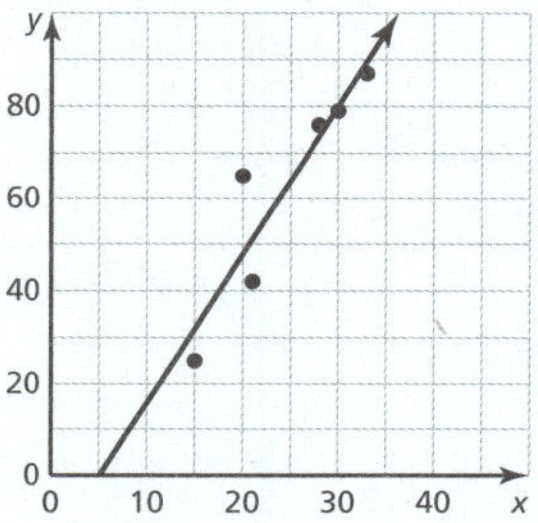

37. $a = -2$

38. *Sample answer:* There may be a correlation because it is likely that there are more car accidents when the weather results in wet or icy roads. There is no causal relationship because it is possible to have a large number of car accidents in good weather.

39.

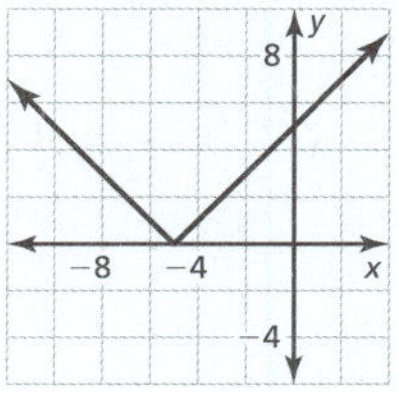

The graph of g is a horizontal translation 5 units left of the graph of f; domain: all real numbers; range: $y \geq 0$

40.

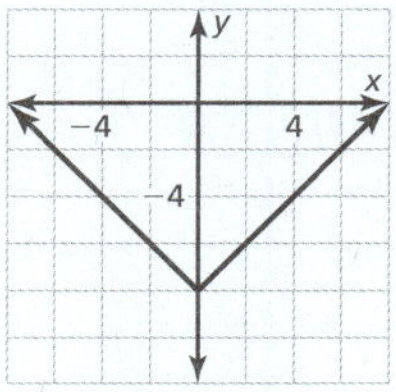

The graph of p is a vertical translation 8 units down of the graph of f; domain: all real numbers; range: $y \geq -8$

41. $(-3, 2)$

42. $x < \frac{1}{2}$ *or* $x > \frac{13}{2}$

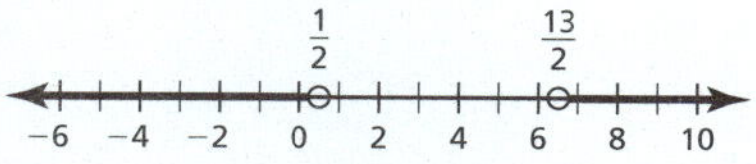

43. 80 shares of Stock A, 120 shares of Stock B

Section 5.3

5.3 Practice

1. $(1, 6)$ **3.** $(4, 5)$ **5.** $(-1, 2)$

7. $(0, -10)$ **9.** $(1, 1)$ **11.** $(8, 3)$

13. $(-7, -12)$ **15.** $(5, -3)$ **17.** \$14.95, \$4.50

19. $5x + x \neq 4x$; $6x = 24$, $x = 4$

21. $(2, -1)$; *Sample answer:* elimination because y has the same coefficient in both equations

23. $(4, 6)$; *Sample answer:* substitution because the second equation is already solved for y

25. $(-5, 3)$; *Sample answer:* elimination because multiplying the first equation by 2 creates two equations with the same coefficient for x

27. *Sample answer:* $3x + 4y = 12$ and $3x - 4y = 6$

29. C, D

31. 4.5 qt of 100% fruit juice, 1.5 qt of 20% fruit juice

33. Equation 1 can be rewritten as Equation 3 by adding $2(x + y)$ to the left and $2(6)$ to the right, and Equation 3 can be rewritten as Equation 1 by subtracting $2(x + y)$ from the left and $2(6)$ from the right. Because either system can be rewritten as the other. System 1 and System 2 have the same solution.

35. $(-5, 4, 2)$; *Sample answer:* Subtract Equation 2 from Equation 1. The resulting equation only has 1 variable, y, so use it to solve for y. Substitute this result in Equation 3 and solve for x. Substitute the values of x and y in Equation 2 and solve for z.

5.3 Review & Refresh

36. no solution **37.** $t = \frac{3}{8}$

38. *Sample answer:* Multiply each side of Equation 1 by 3. Add the equations to eliminate y. Solve the resulting equation for x. Substitute the value of x into one of the original equations and solve for y.

39. **a.** $y = \frac{2}{3}x + \frac{4}{3}$

b. $y = -\frac{3}{2}x - \frac{19}{2}$

40. $(-8, -30)$ **41.** $(0, -2)$

42. no; A vertical line can be drawn through more than one point on the graph.

43. not a solution

44.

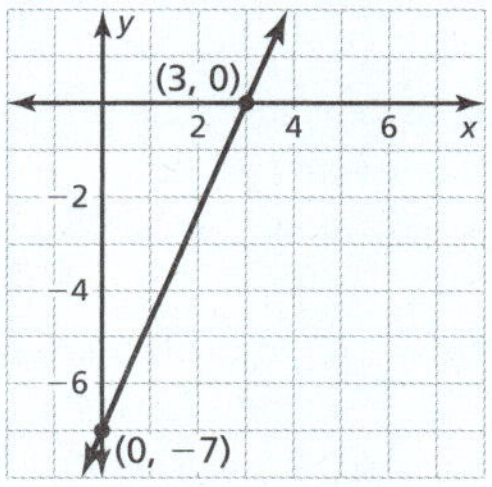

45. ★ $= 2$, ■ $= 7$ **46.** $d(5) = -1$

47. $c \le -22$

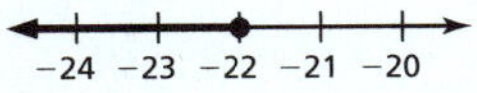

48. $y > -\frac{3}{2}$

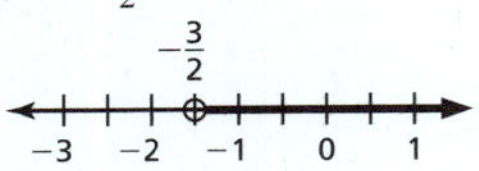

49. $z > 3$

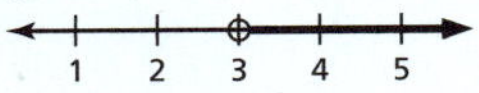

50. all real numbers

51. $6 < g < 26$

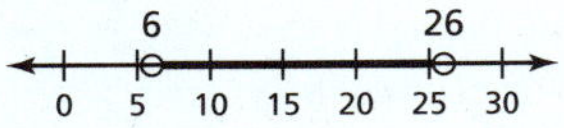

52. $r \le -1$ *or* $r \ge 6$

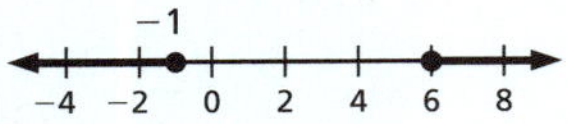

53.

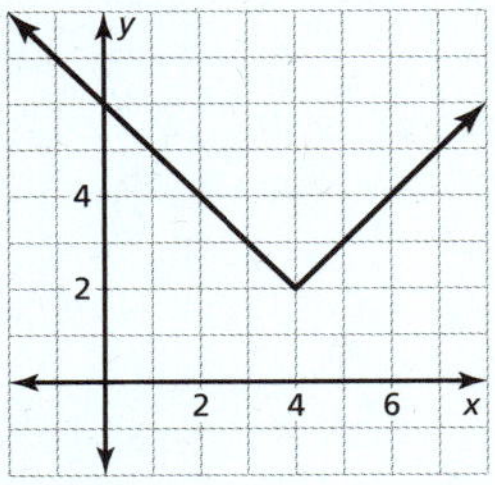

The graph of f is a vertical translation 1 unit down of the graph of g.

Section 5.4

5.4 Practice

1. $(0, -4)$; *Sample answer:* Substitute $-2x - 4$ in for y in the second equation.
3. infinitely many solutions; *Sample answer:* Add the equations.
5. infinitely many solutions; *Sample answer:* Multiple the second equation by 2 and then add the equations.
7. no solution; *Sample answer:* Multiply the first equation by 2 and the second equation by -3. Then add the equations.
9. $\left(\frac{2}{3}, -9\right)$; *Sample answer:* Substitute $3x - 14$ in for $\frac{4}{3}y$ in the second equation.
11. infinitely many solutions; The lines have the same slope and the same y-intercept, so they are the same line.
13. one solution; The lines have different slopes, so they will intersect.
15. no solution; The lines have the same slope but different y-intercepts, so they are parallel.
17. The lines are not parallel, so they must intersect.

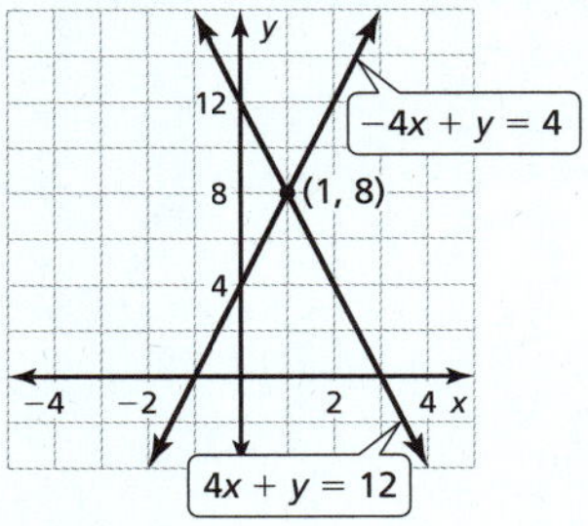

(1, 8)

19. There is not enough information to determine the price of 1 cup of dried fruit and 1 cup of almonds.
21. yes; The system $60c + 90b = 1950$ and $66c + 100b = 2160$ has a solution.
23. one; The lines have different slopes, so they will intersect at exactly one point.
25. **a.** *Sample answer:* $3x - 8y = 7$ and $5x - 4y = 9$
    b. *Sample answer:* $3x - 8y = 7$ and $3x - 8y = 10$
    c. *Sample answer:* $3x - 8y = 7$ and $6x - 16y = 14$
27. **a.** never; The intercepts are different, so they can never be equations for the same line.
    b. sometimes; When $a = b$, the lines are parallel and there is no solution.
    c. always; When $a > b$, the slopes are different and the lines intersect at one point.

5.4 Review & Refresh

29. $(-2, -2)$ **30.** $x = 3$ **31.** $x = 12, x = 2$

32. $(4, -1)$ **33.** $x = \dfrac{y + 8}{5z + 7}$

34. nonlinear; The rate of change is not constant.

35. linear; The rate of change is constant.

36. no solution; The slopes are the same, but y-intercepts are different, so the lines are parallel.

37. infinitely many solutions; The slopes and y-intercepts are the same, so they are the same line.

38. $-\frac{1}{4}$; *Sample answer:* $(8, -10)$

39. $g(12) = -7$ **40.** $(-22, -26)$

41. $d > 18.5$; Distances greater than 18.5 feet would break the women's long jump record.

Section 5.5

5.5 Practice

1. $x = -1$ **3.** $x = -2$

5. $x = 2$ **7.** $x = 3$

9. $x = 2$ **11.** $x = \frac{1}{4}$; one solution

13. all real numbers; infinitely many solutions

15. $x = 1$; one solution

17. all real numbers; infinitely many solutions

19. 4 seconds; Both underwater remote control vehicles will reach the same depth of 8 feet at 4 seconds because $-2(4) = -8$ and $-1.5(4) - 2 = -8$.

21. $x = -5$ **23.** $x = -2$ **25.** about 13 months

27. no; Only the x-coordinate is the solution, so the solution is $x = 4$.

29. *Sample answer:* $m = 1, b = 8$

31. **a.** 30 sec
b. you; 5 sec; When $d = 200$, $t = 40$ for you and $t = 45$ for your friend, and $45 - 40 = 5$ sec.

5.5 Review & Refresh

33. The graph of g is a vertical translation 2 units up of the graph of f.

34. The graph of g is a horizontal translation 1 unit right of the graph of f.

35. *Sample answer:*

Weight of car (pounds), x	2400	2500	2900	3000
Gas mileage (mi/gal), y	39	38	25	32

Weight of car (pounds), x	3400	3500	3700	5100
Gas mileage (mi/gal), y	30	24	21	16

36. $x = -6$ **37.** yes

38. 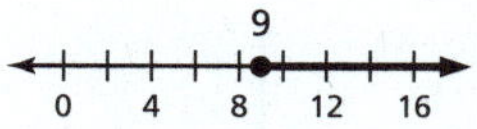

39. 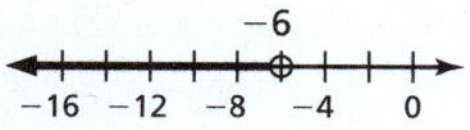

40. 12 small candles, 16 large candles

41. (4, 4); *Sample answer:* Substitute $-x + 8$ in for y in the second equation.

42. infinitely many solutions; *Sample answer:* Multiply the second equation by 2 and then add the equations.

43. $\left(-\frac{19}{2}, 2\right)$; *Sample answer:* Add the equations.

44. (4, 7); *Sample answer:* Substitute $\frac{3}{2}x + 1$ in for y in the second equation.

45. $x = 2$; one solution

46. $y + 2 = -\frac{2}{3}(x - 9)$

47. nonlinear; It cannot be written in the form $y = mx + b$.

Section 5.6

5.6 Practice

1. yes **3.** no **5.** yes **7.** no

9. no **11.** yes **13.** no

15. 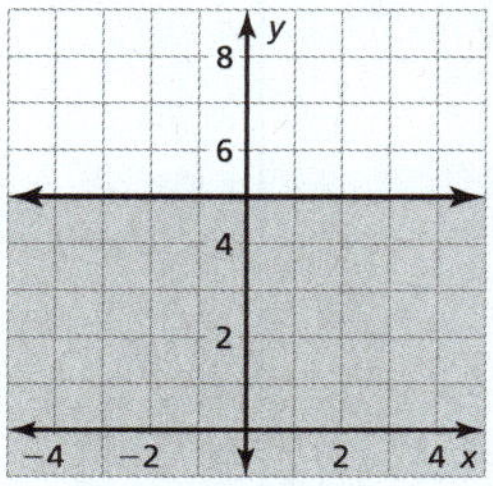

17. 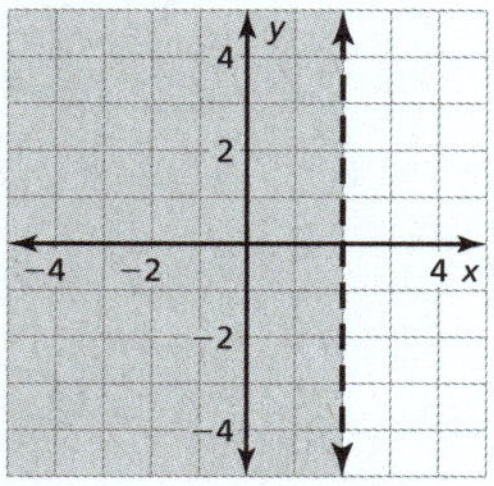

19. 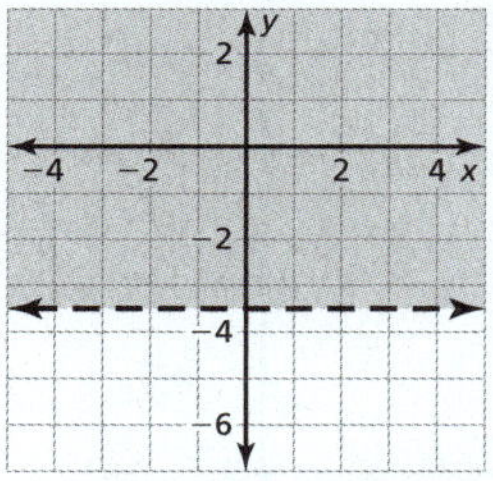

21. 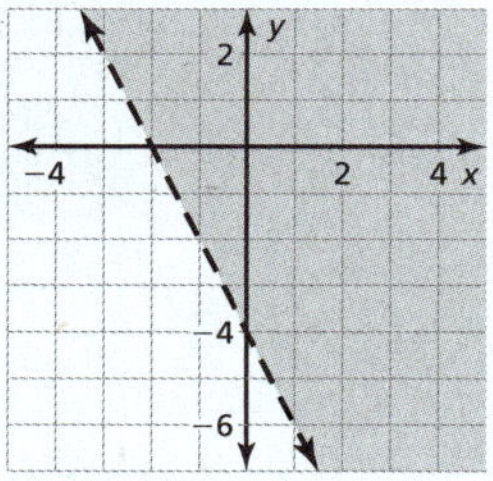

23. 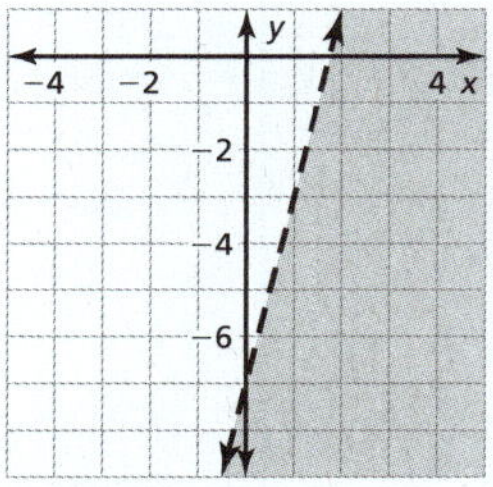

25. 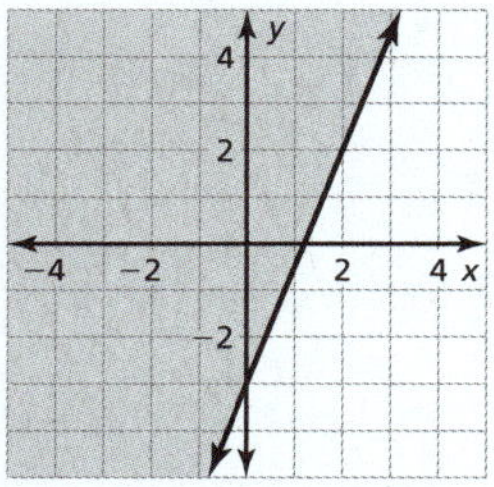

27. 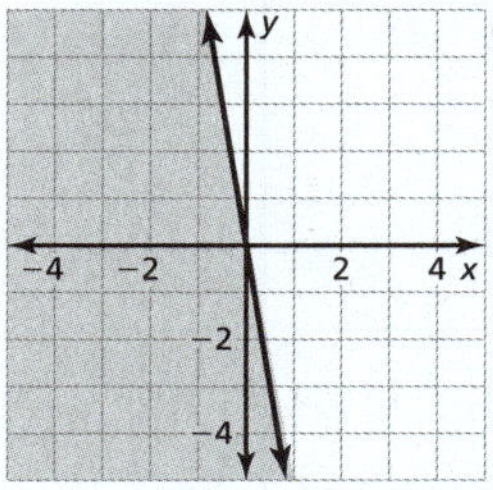

29. The line should be dashed.

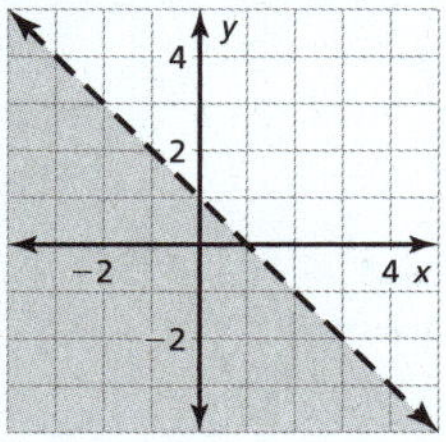

31. no; (12, 14) is not a solution of the inequality.

33. $y > 2x + 1$

35. $x + 5y \leq 25$

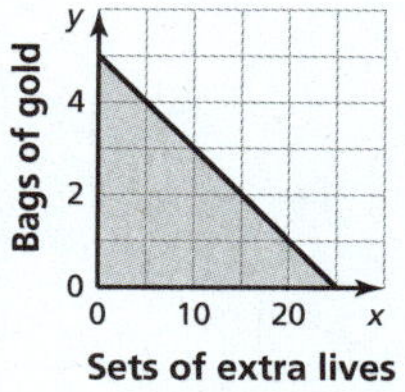

Sample answer: (15, 2), You can buy 15 sets of extra lives and 2 bags of gold; (8, 3), You can buy 8 sets of extra lives and 3 bags of gold.

37. $<$

39. yes; The graph of a proportional relationship passes through (0, 0) and a test point cannot be on the boundary line.

41. $y \leq 2x + 1$

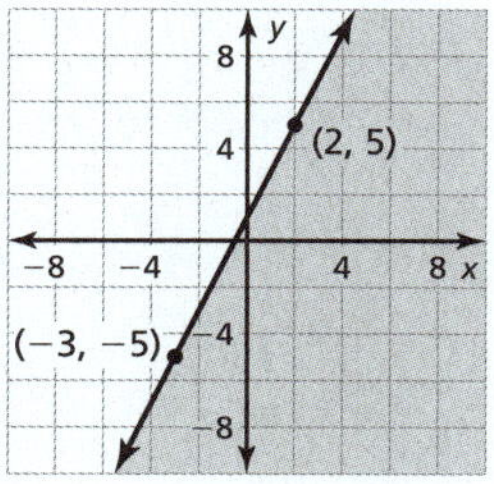

43. **a.** $75x + 40y \leq 1800$

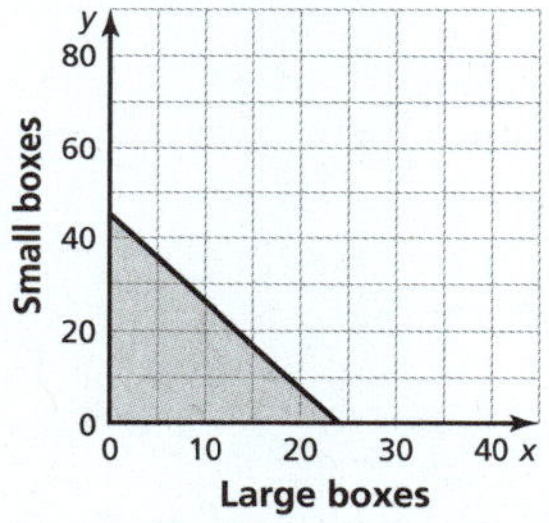

b. *Sample answer:* The number of boxes must be a positive whole number. It is also unlikely for 1 person to carry 45 boxes onto an elevator.

5.6 Review & Refresh

44. infinitely many solutions; *Sample answer:* Substitute $\frac{4}{5}x - 2$ in for y in the second equation.

45. positive: $x < -3$ and $x > 1$; negative: $-3 < x < 1$; increasing: $x > -1$; decreasing: $x < -1$; As $x \to -\infty$, $y \to +\infty$ and as $x \to +\infty$, $y \to +\infty$.

46. 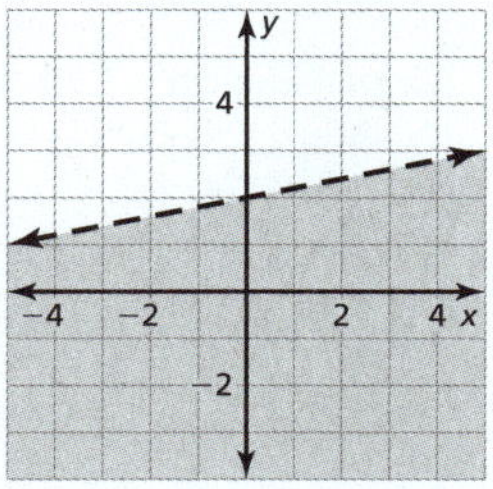

47. $6x + y = 13$

48. $-\frac{1}{4}x + y = 6$

49. $b = 3$ or $b = -3$; The coefficients of the y-terms should be the same or opposites to eliminate the variable y after addition or subtraction.

50. 32,600,000 **51.** $x = 3$ **52.** $x = 4$

53. $y > \frac{1}{2}x + 2$ **54.** $y \leq 3x - 3$

55. no; The input -5 has two outputs, 2 and 4.

Section 5.7

5.7 Practice

1. yes **3.** no **5.** no **7.** no

9. 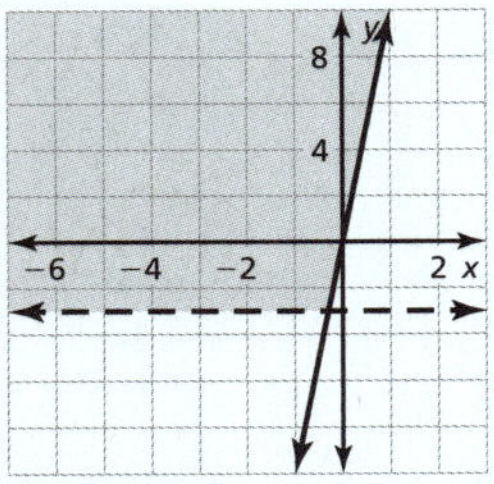

Sample answer: $(-2, 2)$

11. no solution

13. 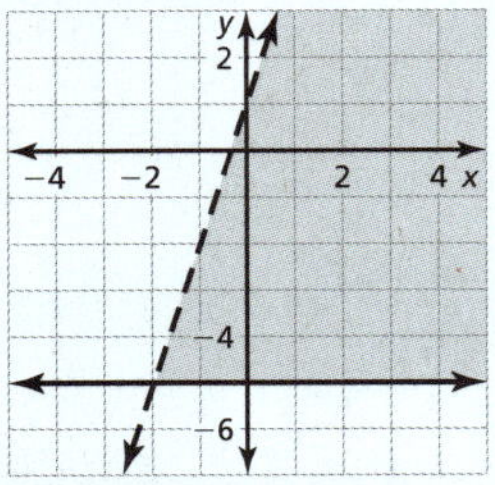

Sample answer: $(0, -3)$

15. 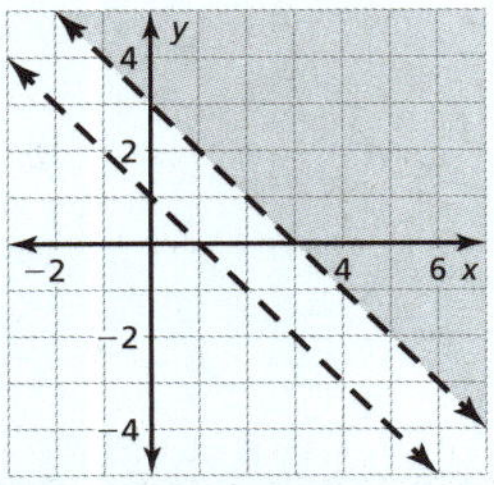

Sample answer: $(4, 3)$

17. 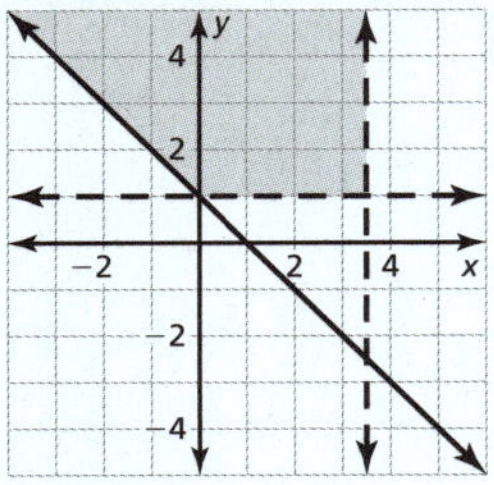

Sample answer: $(1, 3)$

19. $x \geq -1$ and $y < 3$

21. $y \geq \frac{2}{3}x - 2$ and $y \geq -3x + 2$

23. $y < -2x - 1$ and $y > -2x - 3$

25. The wrong region is shaded for $y > \frac{1}{2}x + 2$.

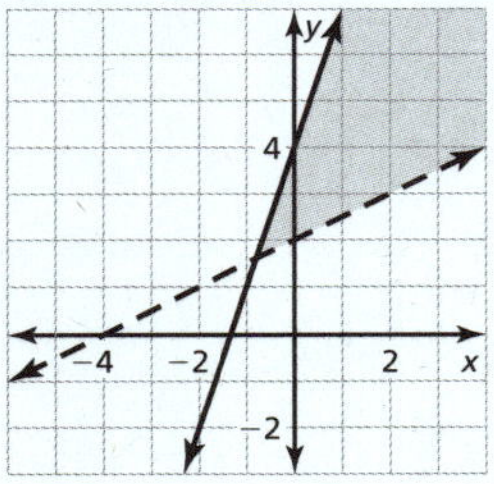

27. $x > 3$, $y \geq 2.5$, and $x + y \leq 7$

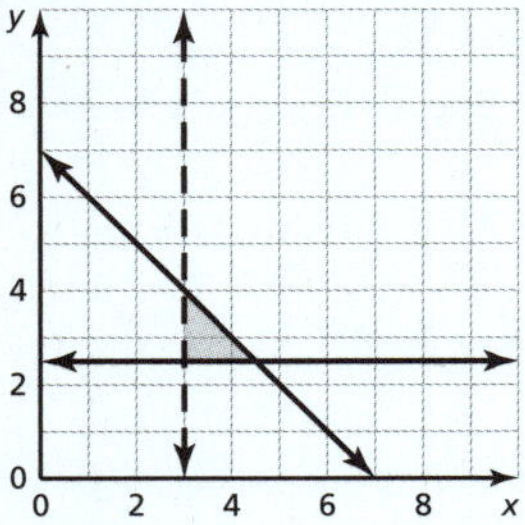

Sample answer: 3.5 hours traveling, 3 hours exploring

29. a. $x \leq 15$, $y \leq 10$, and $x + y \leq 20$; You can catch no more than 15 surfperch per day, no more than 10 rockfish per day, and no more than 20 total surfperch and rockfish per day.

b. yes; The point $(11, 9)$ is a solution of the system of linear inequalities.

31. *Sample answer:* \$300 on savings, \$500 on housing; $x + y < 1000$, $x \geq 200$, and $y \leq 600$

33. a. $x \geq -1$, $x \leq 6$, $y \geq -3$, and $y \leq 1$

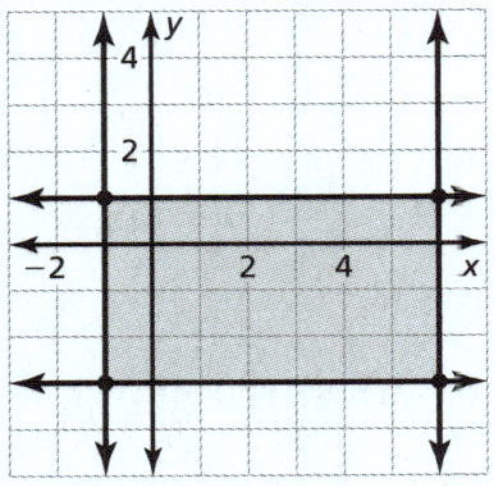

b. 28 square units

35. $y > -x$; $y < x$; and $x > 0$

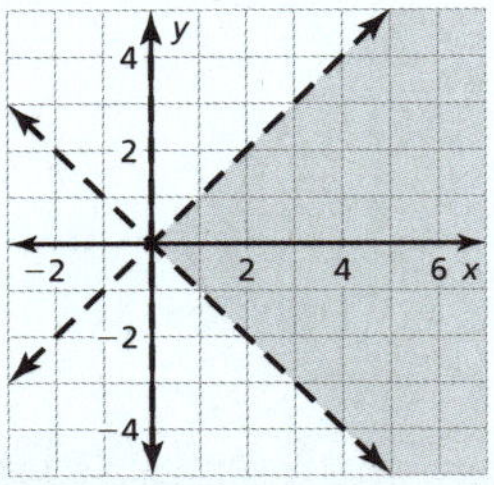

37. no; The half-planes could overlap depending on which side of the boundaries they are on.

39. *Sample answer:* $x > 2$ and $y > 3$

41. *Sample answer:* $y > 2$ and $y < -2$

43. a. 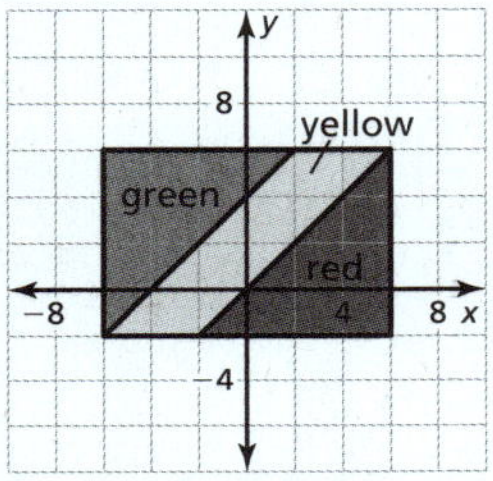

b. The Republic of Congo

c. Answers will vary. Check students' work.

45. a. *Sample answer:* 20 necklaces, 20 key chains; 10 necklaces, 30 key chains; 15 necklaces, 25 key chains; $0.5x + 0.25y \leq 20$, $2x + 3y \leq 120$

b. 30 necklaces, 20 key chains; \$460

5.7 Review & Refresh

46. 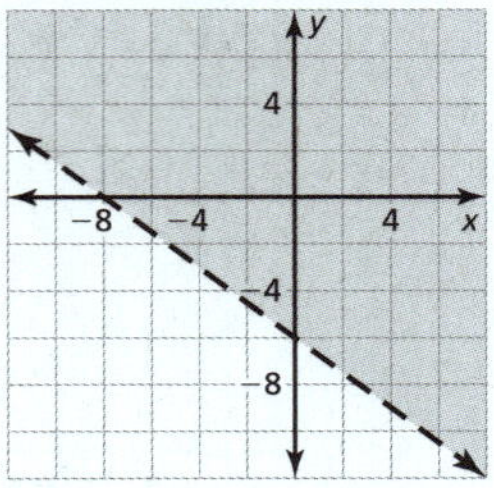

47. $(-13)^3$ **48.** x^6

49. $y \leq \frac{1}{3}x - 1$ and $y < -2x + 3$

50. $y = -\frac{1}{4}x - 1$ **51.** $x = 12$ **52.** $x = -\frac{1}{4}$

53. no solution; *Sample answer:* Multiply the first equation by 3 and the second equation by -5. Then add the equations.

54. $(-2, -5)$; *Sample answer:* Substitute $4x + 3$ in for y in the first equation.

55. $-2500 \le e \le -100$

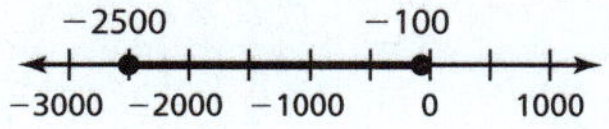

56. $x = -3$

57. *Sample answer:* $|x - 5| + 3 = 3$

58.

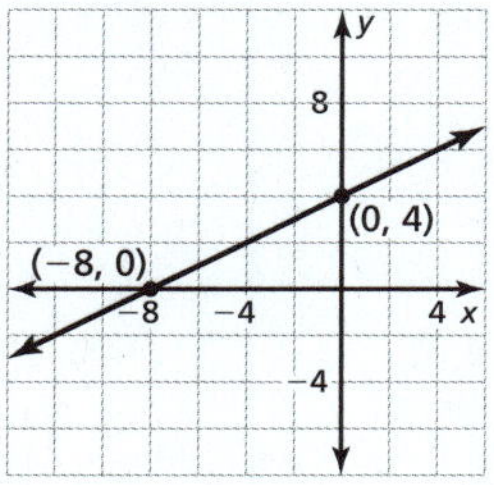

59.

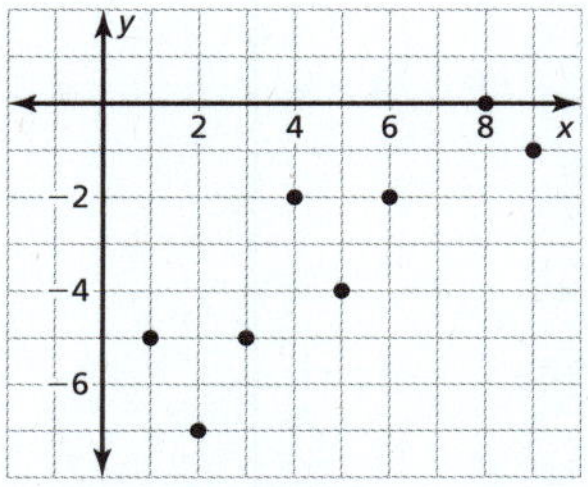

positive correlation

60.

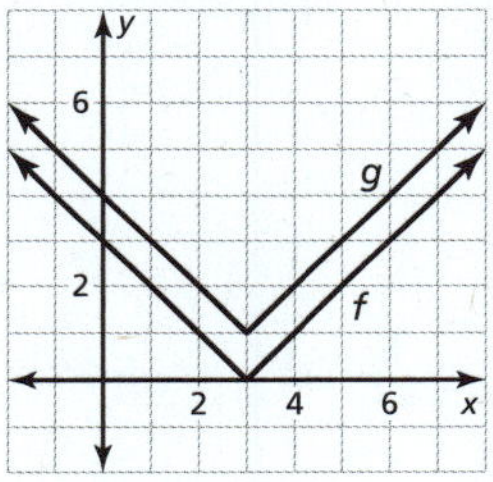

The graph of g is a vertical translation 1 unit up of the graph of f.

Chapter 5 Review

1. $(2, -5)$ **2.** $(1, -1)$ **3.** $(4, -1)$ **4.** $(3, 4)$

5. *Sample answer:* $y = 1.5x - 8.8$ and $y = -0.75x + 0.65$

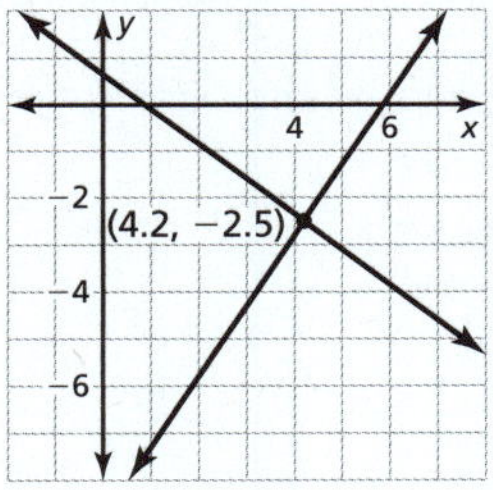

6. $(5a, 0)$ **7.** 3 years **8.** $(-2, -3)$ **9.** $(2, 1)$

10. $(2, 0)$ **11.** 8 brushes, 4 tubes of paint

12. $(2, -8)$ **13.** $(-2, 5)$

14. $\left(-\frac{9}{4}, -\frac{5}{2}\right)$ **15.** 2 touchdowns, 4 field goals

16. one solution; $x + (x + 2) = 2$, $x = 0$, and $y = 0 + 2 = 2$

17. no solution; $-x + (x + 2) = 1$, and $2 = 1$ is not true.

18. infinitely many solutions; $-2x + 2(x + 2) = 4$ and $4 = 4$ is true.

19. no solution; *Sample answer:* Substitute $y + 2$ in for x in the second equation.

20. $(0, 1)$; *Sample answer:* Multiply the first equation by 100 and the second equation by 5. Then add the equations.

21. infinitely many solutions; *Sample answer:* Solve the second equation for y and then substitute the result into the first equation.

22. $x = -3$ **23.** $x = -4$ **24.** $x = -9$ **25.** 2073

26.

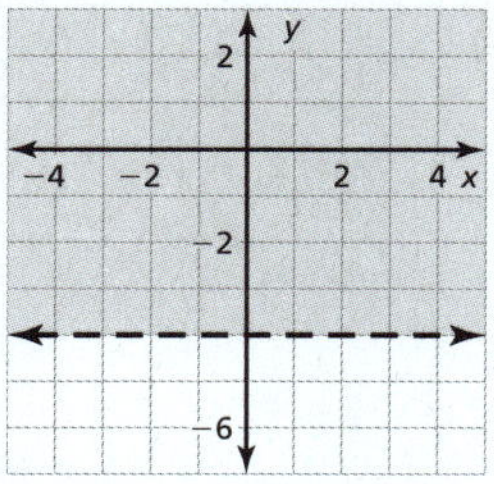

27.

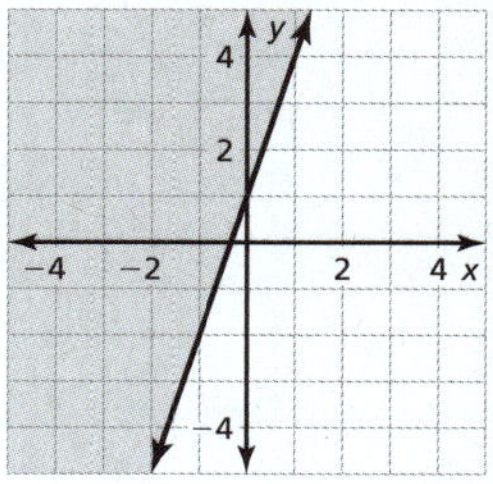

28.

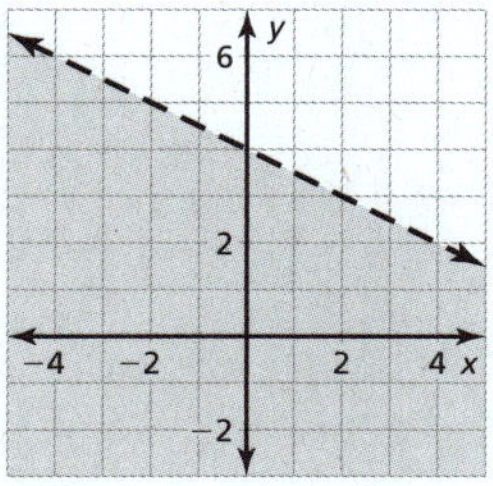

29. $y < -\frac{5}{4}x - 3$ **30.** $y \ge \frac{2}{3}x + \frac{4}{3}$ **31.** no solution

32.

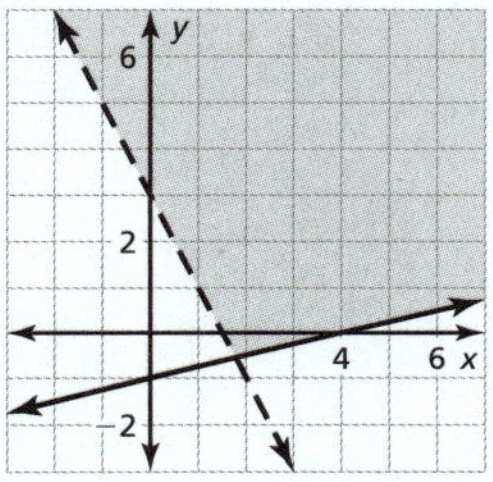

33.

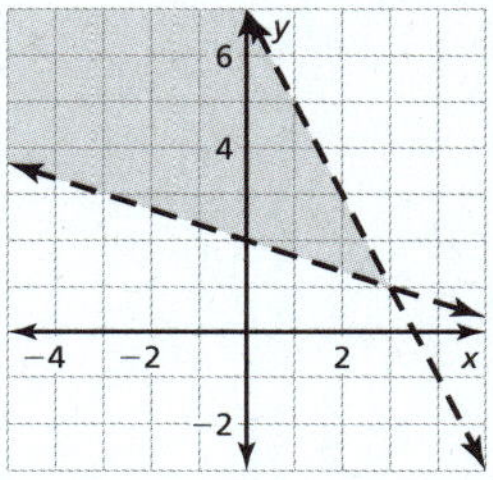

34. C; $y \le ax + b$ is shaded below the solid line and $y > ax - b$ is shaded above the dashed line, meaning the half-planes intersect between the lines.

35. B; $y \ge ax + b$ is shaded above the solid line and $y < ax - b$ is shaded below the dashed line, meaning the half-planes do not intersect.

36. A; $y < ax + b$ is shaded below the dashed line and $y \ge ax - b$ is shaded above the solid line, meaning the half-planes intersect between the lines.

Chapter 5 Practice Test

1. $(-3, 5)$; *Sample answer:* Add the equations.

2. $(-10, -1)$; *Sample answer:* Substitute $\frac{3}{5}x + 5$ in for y in the first equation.

3. infinitely many solutions; *Sample answer:* Substitute $4x + 4$ in for y in the second equation.

4. $(-17, -6)$; *Sample answer:* Substitute $y - 11$ in for x in the second equation.

5. no solution; *Sample answer:* Multiple the first equation by 3 and the second equation by -2. Then add the equations.

6. $(6, 23)$; *Sample answer:* Substitute $5x - 7$ in for y in the second equation.

7. $y < -\frac{1}{3}x + 3$ **8.** $y \ge 2x - 1$ **9.** no solution

10.

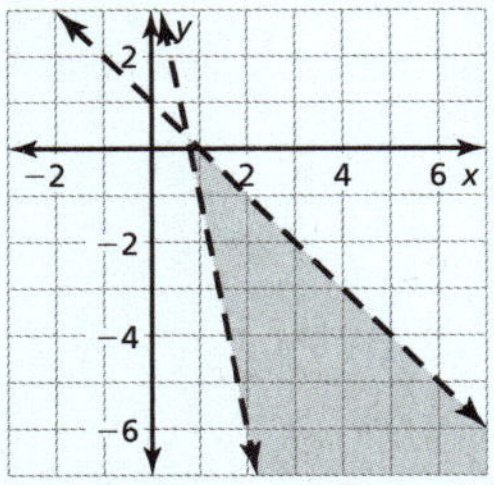

Sample answer: (3, −4)

11.

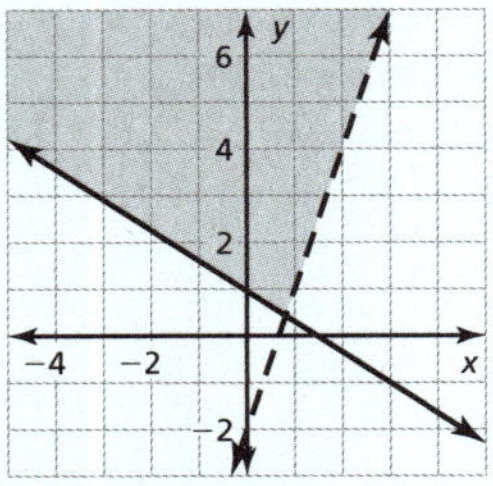

Sample answer: (−2, 5)

12. $x = 1.5$

13. **a.** no; The system $10g + 2q = 45.50$ and $5g + q = 22.75$ represents the situation and has infinitely many solutions.

b. yes; The solution of the system $10g + 2q = 45.50$ and $8g + 2q = 38.40$ is (3.55, 5). So, gasoline is \$3.55 per gallon and oil is \$5 per quart.

14.

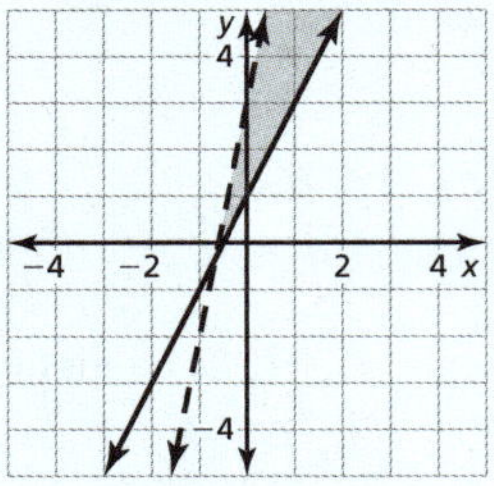

$2x + 1 \le y < 5x + 3$; *Sample answer:* $y \ge 2x + 1$ can be rewritten as $2x + 1 \le y$. Combining the inequalities results in $2x + 1 \le y < 5x + 3$.

15. **a.** $12x + 3y \le 60$

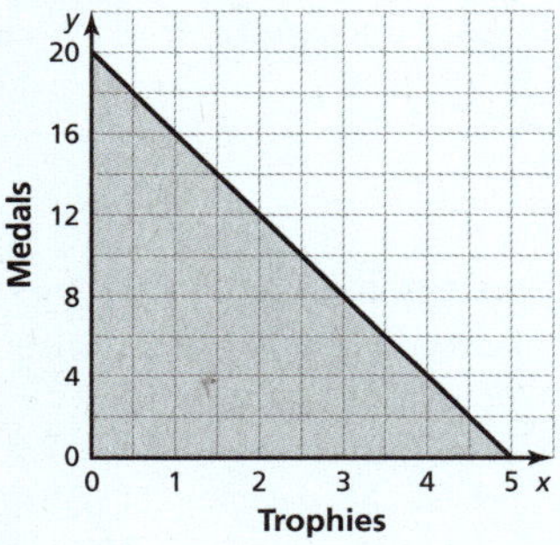

Sample answer: (2, 8); You can buy 2 trophies and 8 medals.

b. $12x + 3y \le 60$ and $x + y \ge 6$

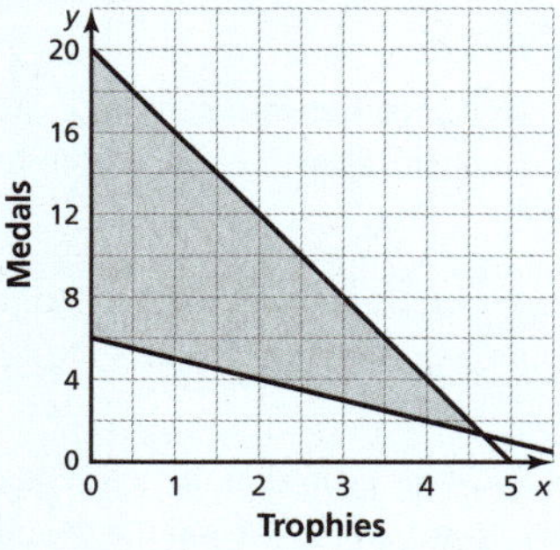

Sample answer: 2 trophies, 6 medals

Chapter 5 B.E.S.T. Test Prep

1. D **2.** A, B, D **3.** A, F **4.** \$541.20
5. C **6.** B **7.** B; A **8.** B
9. $x = -2$ **10.** B, D, E **11.** A, D

English-Spanish Glossary

English / Spanish

A

absolute deviation *(p. 149)* The absolute value of the difference of a number x and a given value.

desviación absoluta *(p. 149)* El valor absoluto de la diferencia entre un número x y un valor dado

absolute value equation *(p. 45)* An equation that contains an absolute value expression.

ecuación de valor absoluto *(p. 45)* Una ecuación que contiene una expresión de valor absoluto

absolute value function *(p. 268)* A function that contains an absolute value expression.

función de valor absoluto *(p. 268)* Una función que contiene una expresión de valor absoluto

absolute value inequality *(p. 147)* An inequality that contains an absolute value expression.

desigualdad de valor absoluto *(p. 147)* Una desigualdad que contiene una expresión de valor absoluto

asymptote *(p. 508)* A line that a graph approaches more and more closely

asíntota *(p. 508)* Una línea a la cual un gráfico se cerca cada vez más

average rate of change *(p. 753)* The slope of the line through $(a, f(a))$ and $(b, f(b))$ of a function $y = f(x)$ between $x = a$ and $x = b$.

tasa de variación media *(p. 753)* La pendiente de la línea a través de $(a, f(a))$ y $(b, f(b))$ de una función $y = f(x)$ entre $x = a$ y $x = b$

axis of symmetry *(p. 667)* The vertical line that divides a parabola into two symmetric parts.

eje de simetría *(p. 667)* La línea vertical que divide una parábola en dos partes simétricas

B

binomial *(p. 562)* A polynomial with two terms

binomio *(p. 562)* Un polinomio con dos términoso

bivariate data *(p. 883)* Data that measures two characteristics of a population

datos bivariados *(p. 883)* Datos que miden dos caracteristicas de una población

C

categorical data *(p. 883)* Data that consist of labels or nonnumerical entries that can be separated into different categories

datos categóricos *(p. 883)* Datos que consisten en etiquetas o valores no numéricos que pueden separarse en categorías distintas

causation *(p. 359)* When a change in one variable causes a change in another variable

causalidad *(p. 359)* Cuando un cambio en una variable causa un cambio en otra variable

closed *(p. 563)* When an operation performed on any two numbers in the set results in a number that is also in the set

operación interna *(p. 563)* Cuando una operación efectuada en dos números cualesquiera del conjunto da como resultado un número que también está en el conjunto

completing the square *(p. 831)* To add a constant c to an expression of the form $x^2 + bx$ so that $x^2 + bx + c$ is a perfect square trinomial

completando el cuadrado *(p. 831)* Agregar una constante c a una expresión de la forma $x^2 + bx$ para que $x^2 + bx + c$ sea un trinomio de cuadrado perfecto

compound inequality *(p. 133)* An inequality formed by joining two inequalities with the word "and" or the word "or"

desigualdad compuesta *(p. 133)* Una desigualdad formada por dos desigualdades con la palabra "y" o la palabra "o"

compound interest *(p. 534)* The interest earned on the principal and on previously earned interest

interés compuesto *(p. 534)* El interés obtenido en el principal y en intereses previamente obtenidos

GLOSSARY

conditional relative frequency *(p. 910)* The ratio of a joint relative frequency to the marginal relative frequency

frecuencia relativa condicional *(p. 910)* La razón de una frecuencia relativa conjunta a una frecuencia relativa marginal

constant function *(p. 237)* A linear equation written in the form $y = 0x + b$ or $y = b$

función constante *(p. 237)* Una ecuación lineal escrita bajo la forma $y = 0x + b$ o $y = b$

continuous domain *(p. 201)* A set of input values that consists of all numbers in an interval

dominio continuo *(p. 201)* Un conjunto de valores que consiste en todos los números en un intervalo

correlation *(p. 348)* A relationship between data sets

correlación *(p. 348)* Una relación entre conjuntos de datos

D

decreasing *(p. 190)* A function's graph moves down as x moves to the right

en disminución *(p. 190)* Una función cuyo gráfico desciende a medida que x avanza hacia la derecha

degree of a monomial *(p. 561)* The sum of the exponents of the variables in the monomial

grado de un monomio *(p. 561)* La suma de los exponentes de las variables en el monomio

degree of a polynomial *(p. 562)* The greatest degree of the terms in a polynomial

grado de un polinomio *(p. 562)* El grado mayor de los términos en un polinomio

dependent variable *(p. 179)* The variable that represents the output values of a function

variable dependiente *(p. 179)* La variable que representa los resultados de una función

descriptive statistics *(p. 920)* The branch of statistics that involves the organization, summarization, and display of data

estadistica descriptiva *(p. 920)* La rama de la estadística que implica la organización, resumen y presentación de datos

discrete domain *(p. 201)* A set of input values that consists of only certain numbers in an interval

dominio discreto *(p. 201)* Un conjunto de valores que consiste en solamente ciertos números en un intervalo

discriminant *(p. 851)* The expression $b^2 - 4ac$ in the Quadratic Formula

discriminante *(p. 851)* La expresión $b^2 - 4ac$ en la Fórmula Cuadrática

domain *(p. 177)* The set of all possible input values of a function

dominio *(p. 177)* El conjunto de todos los valores de entrada posibles de una función

E

end behavior *(p. 190)* The behavior of the graph of a function as x approaches positive infinity $(+\infty)$ or negative infinity $(-\infty)$

comportamiento de extremo *(p. 190)* El comportamiento del gráfico de una función según x se aproxima al infinito positivo $(+\infty)$ o al infinto negativo $(-\infty)$

equation *(p. 7)* A statement that two expressions are equal

ecuación *(p. 7)* Una afirmación de que dos expresiones son iguales

equivalent equations *(p. 7)* Equations that have the same solution(s)

ecuaciones equivalentes *(p. 7)* Ecuaciones que tienen las mismas soluciones

equivalent inequalities *(p. 103)* Inequalities that have the same solutions

desigualdades equivalentes *(p. 103)* Desigualdades que tienen las mismas soluciones

exponential decay *(p. 521)* When a quantity decreases by the same factor over equal intervals

decaimiento exponencial *(p. 521)* Cuando una cantidad disminuye por el mismo factor sobre intervalos iguales

exponential decay function *(p. 521)* A function of the form $y = a(1 - r)^x$, where $a > 0$ and $0 < r < 1$

función de decaimiento exponencial *(p. 521)* Una función de la forma $y = a(1 - r)^x$, donde $a > 0$ y $0 < r < 1$

exponential function *(p. 507)* A nonlinear function of the form $y = ab^x$, where $a \neq 0$, $b \neq 1$, and $b > 0$

función exponencial *(p. 507)* Una función no lineal de la forma $y = ab^x$, donde $a \neq 0$, $b \neq 1$, y $b > 0$

exponential growth *(p. 520)* When a quantity increases by the same factor over equal intervals

crecimiento exponencial *(p. 520)* Cuando una cantidad se incrementa por el mismo factor sobre intervalos iguales

exponential growth function *(p. 520)* A function of the form $y = a(1 + r)^x$, where $a > 0$ and $r > 0$

función de crecimiento exponencial *(p. 520)* Una función de la forma $y = a(1 + r)^x$, donde $a > 0$ y $r > 0$

extraneous solution *(p. 49)* An apparent solution that must be rejected because it does not satisfy the original equation

solución extraña *(p. 49)* Una solución aparente que debe ser rechazada porque no satisface la ecuación original

extrapolation *(p. 370)* To predict a value outside the range of known values using a graph or its equation

extrapolación *(p. 370)* Predecir un valor fuera del rango de valores conocidos usando un gráfico o su ecuación

F

factored completely *(p. 640)* A polynomial that is written as a product of unfactorable polynomials with integer coefficients

factorizado completamente *(p. 640)* Un polinomio que se escribe como un producto de polinomios no factorizables con coeficientes de números enteros

factored form *(p. 599)* A polynomial that is written as a product of factors

forma factorizada *(p. 599)* Un polinomio que se escribe como un producto de factores

factoring by grouping *(p. 639)* To use the Distributive Property to factor a polynomial with four terms

factorización por agrupamiento *(p. 639)* Uso de la propiedad distributiva para factorizar un polinomio con cuatro términos

family of functions *(p. 253)* A group of functions with similar characteristics

familia de funciones *(p. 253)* Un grupo de funciones con características similares

FOIL Method *(p. 578)* A shortcut for multiplying two binomials by finding the sum of the products of the first terms, outer terms, inner terms, and last terms

método FOIL o de multiplicación de binomios *(p. 578)* Un método rápido para multiplicar dos binomios encontrando la suma de los productos de los primeros términos, los segundos términos, los terceros términos y los últimos términos

formula *(p. 59)* A literal equation that shows how one variable is related to one or more other variables

fórmula *(p. 59)* Una ecuación literal que muestra cómo una variable está relacionada con una o más variables

function *(p. 175)* A relation that pairs each input with exactly one output

función *(p. 175)* Una relación que asocia cada valor exactamente con un resultado

function notation *(p. 214)* Another name for y denoted as $f(x)$ and read as "the value of f at x" or "f of x"

notación de función *(p. 214)* Otro nombre para y que se denota como $f(x)$ y que se lee como "el valor de f en x" o "f de x"

G

graph of an inequality *(p. 92)* A graph that shows the solution set of an inequality on a number line

gráfico de una desigualdad *(p. 92)* Un gráfico que muestra el conjunto de soluciones de una desigualdad en una línea numérica

graph of a linear inequality *(p. 445)* The graph in two variables that shows all the solutions of the inequality in a coordinate plane

gráfico de una desigualdad lineal *(p. 445)* El gráfico en dos variables que muestra todas las soluciones de la desigualdad en un plano coordenado

graph of a system of linear inequalities *(p. 456)* The graph of all the solutions of the system of linear inequalities

gráfico de un sistema de desigualdades lineales *(p. 456)* El gráfico de todas las soluciones del sistema de desigualdades lineales

H

half-planes *(p. 445)* Two regions of the coordinate plane divided by a boundary line

semiplanos *(p. 445)* Dos regiones del plano coordenado divididas por una línea limítrofe

horizontal shrink *(p. 255)* A transformation that causes the graph of a function to shrink toward the y-axis when all the x-coordinates are multiplied by a factor a, where $a > 1$

reducción horizontal *(p. 255)* Una transformación que hace que el gráfico de una función se reduzca hacia el eje y cuando todas las coordenadas x se multiplican por un factor a, donde $a > 1$

horizontal stretch *(p. 255)* A transformation that causes the graph of a function to stretch away from the y-axis when all the x-coordinates are multiplied by a factor a, where $0 < a < 1$

ampliación horizontal *(p. 255)* Una transformación que hace que el gráfico de una función se amplíe desde el eje y cuando todas las coordenadas x se multiplican por un factor a, donde $0 < a < 1$

I

identity *(p. 36)* An equation that is true for all values of the variable

identidad *(p. 36)* Una ecuación que es verdadera para todos los valores de la variable

increasing *(p. 190)* A function's graph moves up as x moves to the right

en aumento *(p. 190)* Una función cuyo gráfico asciende a medida que x avanza hacia la derecha

independent variable *(p. 179)* The variable that represents the input values of a function

variable independiente *(p. 179)* La variable que representa los valores de entrada de una función

index of a radical *(p. 498)* The value of n in the radical $\sqrt[n]{a}$

índice de un radical *(p. 498)* El valor de n en el radical $\sqrt[n]{a}$

inequality *(p. 89)* A mathematical sentence that compares expressions

desigualdad *(p. 89)* Una oración matemática que compara expresiones

inferential statistics *(p. 920)* The branch of statistics that involves using a sample to draw conclusions about a population

estadística inferencial *(p. 920)* La rama de la estadística que implica el uso de una muestra para sacar conclusiones acerca de una población

intercept form *(p. 723)* A quadratic function written in the form $f(x) = a(x - p)(x - q)$, where $a \neq 0$

forma factorizada *(p. 723)* Una ecuación cuadrática escrita en la forma $f(x) = a(x - p)(x - q)$, donde $a \neq 0$

interpolation *(p. 370)* To approximate a value between two known values using a graph or its equation

interpolación *(p. 370)* Aproximar un valor entre dos valores conocidos usando un gráfico o su ecuación

J

joint frequency *(p. 896)* Each entry in a two-way table

frecuencia conjunta *(p. 896)* Cada valor en una tabla de doble entrada

joint relative frequency *(p. 909)* The ratio of a joint frequency to the total number of values or observations

frecuencia relativa conjunta *(p. 909)* La razón de una frecuencia conjunta al número total de valores u observaciones

L

leading coefficient *(p. 562)* The coefficient of the first term of a polynomial written in standard form

coeficiente principal *(p. 562)* El coeficiente del primer término de un polinomio escrito en forma estándar

like radicals *(p. 796)* Radicals with the same index and radicand

radicales semejantes *(p. 796)* Radicales con el mismo índice y radicando

line of best fit *(p. 367)* A line that best models a set of data

línea de mejor ajuste *(p. 367)* Una línea que mejor modela un conjunto de datos

line of fit *(p. 349)* A line drawn on a scatter plot that is close to most of the data points

línea de ajuste *(p. 349)* Una línea dibujada en un diagrama de dispersión que está cerca a la mayoría de los puntos de datos

linear equation in one variable *(p. 7)* An equation that can be written in the form $ax + b = 0$, where a and b are constants and $a \neq 0$

ecuación lineal en una variable *(p. 7)* Una ecuación que puede escribirse en la forma $ax + b = 0$, donde a y b son constantes y $a \neq 0$

linear equation in two variables *(p. 198)* An equation that can be written in the form $y = mx + b$, where m and b are constants

ecuación lineal en dos variables *(p. 198)* Una ecuación que puede escribirse en la forma $y = mx + b$, donde m y b son constantes

linear function *(p. 198)* A function whose graph is a nonvertical line

función lineal *(p. 198)* Una función cuyo gráfico es una línea no vertical

linear inequality in two variables *(p. 444)* An inequality written in the form $ax + by < c$, $ax + by \leq c$, $ax + by > c$, or $ax + by \geq c$, where a, b, and c are real numbers

desigualdad lineal en dos variables *(p. 444)* Una desigualdad escrita en la forma $ax + by < c$, $ax + by \leq c$, $ax + by > c$, o $ax + by \geq c$, donde a, b y c son números reales

linear model *(p. 305)* A linear function that models a real-life situation

modelo lineal *(p. 305)* Una función lineal que modela una situación de la vida real

linear regression *(p. 367)* A method that uses technology to find a precise line of fit that models a set of data

regresión lineal *(p. 367)* Un método que emplea tecnología para hallar una línea precisa de ajuste que modela un conjunto de datos

literal equation *(p. 58)* An equation that has two or more variables

ecuación literal *(p. 58)* Una ecuación que tiene dos o más variables

M

margin of error *(p. 923)* The maximum expected difference between a sample result and the population parameter it is estimating

margen de error *(p. 923)* La máxima diferencia que se espera entre el resultado de una muestra y el parámetro de población que está estimando

marginal frequency *(p. 896)* The sums of the rows and columns in a two-way table

frecuencia marginales *(p. 896)* Las sumas de las hileras y columnas en una tabla de doble entrada

marginal relative frequency *(p. 909)* The sum of the joint relative frequencies in a row or a column

frecuencia relativa marginal *(p. 909)* La suma de las frecuencias relativas conjuntas en una hilera o columna

maximum value *(p. 693)* The y-coordinate of the vertex of the graph of $f(x) = ax^2 + bx + c$, where $a < 0$

valor máximo *(p. 693)* La coordenada y del vértice del gráfico de $f(x) = ax^2 + bx + c$, donde $a < 0$

minimum value *(p. 693)* The y-coordinate of the vertex of the graph of $f(x) = ax^2 + bx + c$, where $a > 0$

valor mínimo *(p. 693)* La coordenada y del vértice del gráfico de $f(x) = ax^2 + bx + c$, donde $a > 0$

misleading graph *(p. 887)* A statistical graph that is not drawn appropriately

gráfico engañoso *(p. 887)* Un gráfico estadístico que no está dibujado apropiadamente

monomial *(p. 561)* A number, a variable, or the product of a number and one or more variables with whole number exponents

monomio *(p. 561)* Un número, una variable o el producto de un número y una o más variables con exponentes en números enteros

N

nonlinear function *(p. 198)* A function that does not have a constant rate of change and whose graph is not a line

función no lineal *(p. 198)* Una función que no tiene una tasa constante de cambio y cuyo gráfico no es una línea

n*th root of *a *(p. 498)* For an integer n greater than 1, if $b^n = a$, then b is an nth root of a.

raíz de orden *n* de *a* *(p. 498)* Para un número entero n mayor que 1, si $b^n = a$, entonces b es una raíz de orden n de a.

numerical data *(p. 883)* Data that consist of numbers that represent counts or measurements

datos numéricos *(p. 883)* Datos compuestos por números que representan conteos o medidas

P

parabola *(p. 667)* The U-shaped graph of a quadratic function

parábola *(p. 667)* El gráfico en forma de U de una función cuadrática

parallel lines *(p. 337)* Two lines in the same plane that never intersect

líneas paralelas *(p. 337)* Dos líneas en el mismo plano que nunca se intersectan

parameter *(p. 919)* A numerical description of a population characteristic

parámetro *(p. 919)* Una descripción numérica de una característica de la población

GLOSSARY

parent function *(p. 253)* The most basic function in a family of functions

función principal *(p. 253)* La función más básica en una familia de funciones

perpendicular lines *(p. 338)* Two lines in the same plane that intersect to form right angles

líneas perpendiculares *(p. 338)* Dos líneas en el mismo plano que se intersectan para formar ángulos rectos

point-slope form *(p. 314)* A linear equation written in the form $y - y_1 = m(x - x_1)$

forma punto-pendiente *(p. 314)* Una ecuación lineal escrita en la forma $y - y_1 = m(x - x_1)$

polynomial *(p. 562)* A monomial or a sum of monomials

polinomio *(p. 562)* Un monomio o una suma de monomios

population *(p. 918)* The collection of all data, such as responses, measurements, or counts, that are of interest

población *(p. 918)* La recolección de datos, tales como respuestas, medidas o conteos que son de interés

Q

quadratic equation *(p. 807)* A nonlinear equation that can be written in the standard form $ax^2 + bx + c = 0$, where $a \neq 0$

ecuación cuadrática *(p. 807)* Una ecuación no lineal que puede escribirse en la forma estándar $ax^2 + bx + c = 0$, donde $a \neq 0$

Quadratic Formula *(p. 849)* The real solutions of the quadratic equation $ax^2 + bx + c = 0$ are

$x = \dfrac{-b \pm \sqrt{b^2 - 4ac}}{2a}$, where $a \neq 0$ and $b^2 - 4ac \geq 0$.

fórmula cuadrática *(p. 849)* Las soluciones reales de la ecuación cuadrática $ax^2 + bx + c = 0$ son

$x = \dfrac{-b \pm \sqrt{b^2 - 4ac}}{2a}$, donde $a \neq 0$ y $b^2 - 4ac \geq 0$.

quadratic function *(p. 667)* A nonlinear function that can be written in the standard form $y = ax^2 + bx + c$, where $a \neq 0$

función cuadrática *(p. 667)* Una ecuación no lineal que puede escribirse en la forma estándar $y = ax^2 + bx + c$, donde $a \neq 0$

qualitative data *(p. 883)* Data that consist of labels or nonnumerical entries that can be separated into different categories

datos cualitativos *(p. 883)* Datos que consisten en etiquetas o valores no numéricos que pueden separarse en categorías distintas

quantitative data *(p. 883)* Data that consist of numbers that represent counts or measurements

datos cuantitativos *(p. 883)* Datos que consisten en números que representan conteos o medidas

R

radical *(p. 498)* An expression of the form $\sqrt[n]{a}$

radical *(p. 498)* Una expresión de la forma $\sqrt[n]{a}$

radical expression *(p. 794)* An expression that contains a radical

expresión radical *(p. 794)* Una expresión que contiene un radical

range of a function *(p. 177)* The set of all possible output values of a function

rango de una función *(p. 177)* El conjunto de todos los resultados posibles de una función

rationalizing the denominator *(p. 795)* To eliminate a radical from the denominator of a fraction by multiplying by an appropriate form of 1

racionalización del denominador *(p. 795)* Eliminar un radical del denominador de una fracción multiplicando por una forma apropiada de 1

reflection *(p. 254)* A transformation that flips a graph over a line called the *line of reflection*

reflexión *(p. 254)* Una transformación que voltea un gráfico sobre una línea llamada la *línea de reflexión*

relation *(p. 175)* A pairing of inputs with outputs

relación *(p. 175)* Una pareja de valores con resultados

repeated roots *(p. 600)* Two or more roots of an equation that are the same number

raíces repetidas *(p. 600)* Dos o más raíces de una ecuación que son el mismo número

residual *(p. 357)* The difference of the y-value of a data point and the corresponding y-value found using the line of fit

residual *(p. 357)* La diferencia del valor y de un punto de datos y el valor y correspondiente usando la línea de ajuste

rise *(p. 235)* The change in y between any two points on a line

desplazamiento vertical *(p. 235)* El cambio en y entre cualesquiera dos puntos en una recta

roots *(p. 599)* The solutions of a polynomial equation

raíces *(p. 599)* Las soluciones deuna ecuación de polinomios

run *(p. 235)* The change in x between any two points on a line

desplazamiento horizontal *(p. 235)* El cambio en x entre cualesquiera dos puntos en una recta

S

sample *(p. 918)* A subset of a population

muestra *(p. 918)* Un subconjunto de una población

scatter plot *(p. 347)* A graph that shows the relationship between two data sets

diagrama de dispersión *(p. 347)* Un gráfico que muestra la relación entre dos conjuntos de datos

segmented bar graph *(p. 898)* A bar graph that displays bivariate categorical data by two or more bars divided into segments

gráfico de barras segmentadas *(p. 898)* Un gráfico de barras que muestra datos categóricos bivariados en dos o más barras divididas en segmentos

set-builder notation *(p. 136)* A way to use symbols to define a set in terms of the properties of the members of the set

notación constructiva de conjuntos *(p. 136)* Una manera de usar símbolos para definir un conjunto en términos de las propiedades de los elementos del conjunto

simplest form of a radical *(p. 794)* An expression involving a radical with index n that has no radicands with perfect nth powers as factors other than 1, no radicands that contain fractions, and no radicals that appear in the denominator of a fraction

mínima expresión de un radical *(p. 794)* Una expresión que conlleva un radical con índice n que no tiene radicandos con potencias perfectas de orden n como factores distintos a 1, que no tiene radicandos que contengan fracciones y que no tiene radicales que aparezcan en el denominador de una fracción

slope *(p. 235)* The rate of change between any two points on a line

pendiente *(p. 235)* La tasa de cambio entre dos puntos cualesquiera en una línea

slope-intercept form *(p. 237)* A linear equation written in the form $y = mx + b$

forma intersección-pendiente *(p. 237)* Una ecuación lineal escrita en la forma $y = mx + b$

solution of an equation *(p. 7)* A value that makes an equation true

solución de una ecuación *(p. 7)* Un valor que hace que una ecuación sea verdadera

solution of an inequality *(p. 90)* A value that makes an inequality true

solución de una desigualdad *(p. 90)* Un valor que hace que una desigualdad sea verdadera

solution of a linear equation in two variables *(p. 201)* An ordered pair (x, y) that makes an equation true

solución de una ecuación lineal en dos variables *(p. 201)* Un par ordenado (x, y) que hace que una ecuación sea verdadera

solution of a linear inequality in two variables *(p. 444)* An ordered pair (x, y) that makes the inequality true

solución de una desigualdad lineal en dos variables *(p. 444)* Un par ordenado (x, y) que hace que la desigualdad sea verdadera

solution set *(p. 90)* The set of all solutions of an inequality

conjunto de solucíones *(p. 90)* El conjunto de todas las soluciones de una desigualdad

solution of a system of linear equations *(p. 394)* An ordered pair that is a solution of each equation in the system

solución de un sistema de ecuaciones lineales *(p. 394)* Un par ordenado que es una solución de cada ecuación en el sistema

solution of a system of linear inequalities *(p. 454)* An ordered pair that is a solution of each inequality in the system

solución de un sistema de desigualdades lineales *(p. 454)* Un par ordenado que es una solución de cada desigualdad en el sistema

standard form of a linear equation *(p. 225)* A linear equation written in the form $Ax + By = C$, where A, B, and C are real numbers and A and B are not both zero

forma estándar de una ecuación lineal *(p. 225)* Una ecuación lineal escrita en la forma $Ax + By = C$, donde A, B y C son números reales y ni A ni B son cero

standard form of a polynomial *(p. 562)* A polynomial in one variable written with the exponents of the terms decreasing from left to right

forma estándar de un polinomio *(p. 562)* Un polinomio en una variable escrita con los exponentes de los términos decreciendo de izquierda a derecha

statistic *(p. 919)* A numerical description of a sample characteristic

estadística *(p. 919)* Una descripción numérica de una característica de la muestra

system of linear equations *(p. 394)* A set of two or more linear equations in the same variables

sistema de ecuaciones lineales *(p. 394)* Un conjunto de dos o más ecuaciones lineales en las mismas variables

system of linear inequalities *(p. 454)* A set of two or more linear inequalities in the same variables

sistema de desigualdades lineales *(p. 454)* Un conjunto de dos o más desigualdades lineales en las mismas variables

T

transformation *(p. 253)* A change in the size, shape, position, or orientation of a graph

transformación *(p. 253)* Un cambio en el tamaño, forma, posición u orientación de un gráfico

translation *(p. 253)* A transformation that shifts a graph horizontally and/or vertically but does not change the size, shape, or orientation of the graph

traslación *(p. 253)* Una transformación que desplaza un gráfico horizontal y/o verticalmente pero no cambia el tamaño, forma u orientación del gráfico

trinomial *(p. 562)* A polynomial with three terms

trinomio *(p. 562)* Un polinomio con tres términos

two-way table *(p. 896)* A frequency table that displays data collected from one source that belong to two different categories

tabla de doble entrada *(p. 896)* Una tabla de frecuencia que muestra los datos recogidos de una fuente que pertenece a dos categorías distintas

U

univariate data *(p. 883)* Data that measures one characteristic of a population

datos univariados *(p. 883)* Datos que miden una característica de una población

V

vertex *(p. 268)* The point where a graph changes direction

vértice *(p. 268)* El punto en donde un gráfico cambia de dirección

vertex form of an absolute value function *(p. 273)* An absolute value function written in the form $g(x) = a|x - h| + k$, where $a \neq 0$

forma de vértice de una función de valor absoluto *(p. 273)* Una función de valor absoluto escrita en la forma $g(x) = a|x - h| + k$, donde $a \neq 0$

vertex form of a quadratic function *(p. 708)* A quadratic function written in the form $f(x) = a(x - h)^2 + k$, where $a \neq 0$

forma de vértice de una función cuadrática *(p. 708)* Una función cuadrática escrita en la forma $f(x) = a(x - h)^2 + k$, donde $a \neq 0$

vertex of a parabola *(p. 667)* The lowest point on a parabola that opens up or the highest point on a parabola that opens down

vértice de una parábola *(p. 667)* El punto más bajo de una parábola que se abre hacia arriba o el punto más alto de una parábola que se abre hacia abajo

vertical shrink *(p. 255)* A transformation that causes the graph of a function to shrink toward the x-axis when all the y-coordinates are multiplied by a factor a, where $0 < a < 1$

reducción vertical *(p. 255)* Una transformación que hace que el gráfico de una función se reduzca hacia el eje x cuando todas las coordenadas y se multiplican por un factor a, donde $0 < a < 1$

vertical stretch *(p. 255)* A transformation that causes the graph of a function to stretch away from the x-axis when all the y-coordinates are multiplied by a factor a, where $a > 1$

ampliación vertical *(p. 255)* Una transformación que hace que el gráfico de una función se amplíe desde el eje x cuando todas las coordenadas y se multiplican por un factor a, donde $a > 1$

X

x-intercept *(p. 189)* The x-coordinate of a point where the graph intersects the x-axis

intersección x *(p. 189)* La coordenada x de un punto donde el gráfico interseca el eje x

Y

y-intercept *(p. 189)* The y-coordinate of a point where the graph intersects the y-axis

intersección y *(p. 189)* La coordenada y de un punto donde el gráfico interseca el eje y

Z

zero of a function *(p. 684)* An x-value of a function f for which $f(x) = 0$

Zero-Product Property *(p. 599)* If the product of two real numbers is 0, then at least one of the numbers is 0.

cero de una función *(p. 684)* Un valor x de una función f para el cual $f(x) = 0$

propiedad de producto cero *(p. 599)* Si el producto de dos números reales es 0, entonces al menos uno de los números es 0.

Index

A

B

C

INDEX

INDEX

P

INDEX

Q

R

S

INDEX

T

U

V

W

X

Y

Z

Reference

Properties

Properties of Equality

Addition Property of Equality
If $a = b$, then $a + c = b + c$.

Multiplication Property of Equality
If $a = b$, then $a \cdot c = b \cdot c, c \neq 0$.

Subtraction Property of Equality
If $a = b$, then $a - c = b - c$.

Division Property of Equality
If $a = b$, then $a \div c = b \div c, c \neq 0$.

Properties of Inequality

Addition Property of Inequality
If $a > b$, then $a + c > b + c$.
If $a < b$, then $a + c < b + c$.

Multiplication Property of Inequality ($c > 0$)
If $a > b$ and $c > 0$, then $ac > bc$.

If $a < b$ and $c > 0$, then $ac < bc$.

Multiplication Property of Inequality ($c < 0$)
If $a > b$ and $c < 0$, then $ac < bc$.
If $a < b$ and $c < 0$, then $ac > bc$.

Subtraction Property of Inequality
If $a > b$, then $a - c > b - c$.
If $a < b$, then $a - c < b - c$.

Division Property of Inequality ($c > 0$)
If $a > b$ and $c > 0$, then $\frac{a}{c} > \frac{b}{c}$.

If $a < b$ and $c > 0$, then $\frac{a}{c} < \frac{b}{c}$.

Division Property of Inequality ($c < 0$)
If $a > b$ and $c < 0$, then $\frac{a}{c} < \frac{b}{c}$.

If $a < b$ and $c < 0$, then $\frac{a}{c} > \frac{b}{c}$.

* The Properties of Inequality are also true for ≥ and ≤.

Properties of Exponents

Zero Exponent
$a^0 = 1$, where $a \neq 0$

Negative Exponent
$a^{-n} = \frac{1}{a^n}$, where $a \neq 0$

Product of Powers Property
$a^m \cdot a^n = a^{m+n}$

Quotient of Powers Property
$\frac{a^m}{a^n} = a^{m-n}$, where $a \neq 0$

Power of a Power Property
$(a^m)^n = a^{mn}$

Power of a Product Property
$(ab)^m = a^m b^m$

Power of a Quotient Property
$\left(\frac{a}{b}\right)^m = \frac{a^m}{b^m}$, where $b \neq 0$

Rational Exponents
$a^{m/n} = a^{(1/n) \cdot m} = (a^{1/n})^m = (\sqrt[n]{a})^m$ or $a^{m/n} = a^{m \cdot (1/n)} = (a^m)^{1/n} = \sqrt[n]{a^m}$

Properties of Absolute Value

$|a| \geq 0$

$|-a| = |a|$

$|ab| = |a||b|$

$\left|\frac{a}{b}\right| = \frac{|a|}{|b|}, b \neq 0$

Properties of Radicals

Product Property of Square Roots
$\sqrt{ab} = \sqrt{a} \cdot \sqrt{b}$, where $a \geq 0$ and $b \geq 0$

Quotient Property of Square Roots
$\sqrt{\frac{a}{b}} = \frac{\sqrt{a}}{\sqrt{b}}$, where $a \geq 0$ and $b > 0$

Other Properties

Property of Equality for Exponential Equations
If $b > 0$ and $b \neq 1$, then $b^x = b^y$ if and only if $x = y$.

Zero-Product Property
If a and b are real numbers and $ab = 0$, then $a = 0$ or $b = 0$.

Patterns

Square of a Binomial Pattern
$(a + b)^2 = a^2 + 2ab + b^2$
$(a - b)^2 = a^2 - 2ab + b^2$

Sum and Difference Pattern
$(a + b)(a - b) = a^2 - b^2$

Difference of Two Squares Pattern
$a^2 - b^2 = (a + b)(a - b)$

Perfect Square Trinomial Pattern
$a^2 + 2ab + b^2 = (a + b)^2$
$a^2 - 2ab + b^2 = (a - b)^2$

Formulas

Slope
$m = \dfrac{y_2 - y_1}{x_2 - x_1}$

Slope-intercept form
$y = mx + b$

Point-slope form
$y - y_1 = m(x - x_1)$

Standard form of a linear equation
$Ax + By = C$, where A and B are not both 0

Vertex form of an absolute value function
$f(x) = a|x - h| + k$, where $a \neq 0$

Standard form of a quadratic function
$f(x) = ax^2 + bx + c$, where $a \neq 0$

Vertex form of a quadratic function
$f(x) = a(x - h)^2 + k$, where $a \neq 0$

Intercept form of a quadratic function
$f(x) = a(x - p)(x - q)$, where $a \neq 0$

Quadratic Formula
$x = \dfrac{-b \pm \sqrt{b^2 - 4ac}}{2a}$, where $a \neq 0$ and $b^2 - 4ac \geq 0$

Exponential growth
$y = a(1 + r)^t$, where $a > 0$ and $r > 0$

Exponential decay
$y = a(1 - r)^t$, where $a > 0$ and $0 < r < 1$

Characteristics of Functions

Positive and Negative
A function is positive when its graph lies above the x-axis. A function is negative when its graph lies below the x-axis.

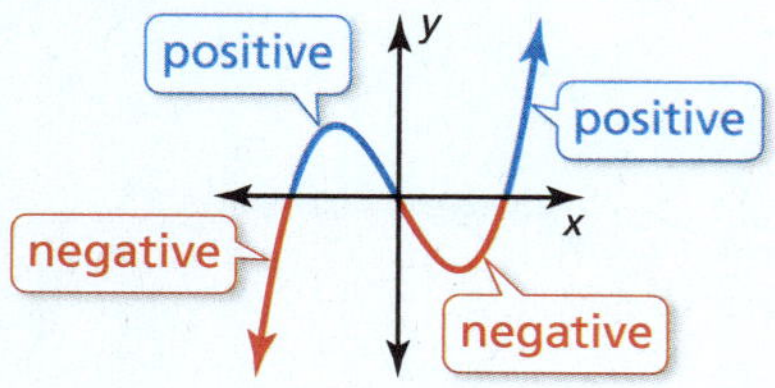

Increasing and Decreasing
A function is increasing when its graph moves up as x moves to the right. A function is decreasing when its graph moves down as x moves to the right.

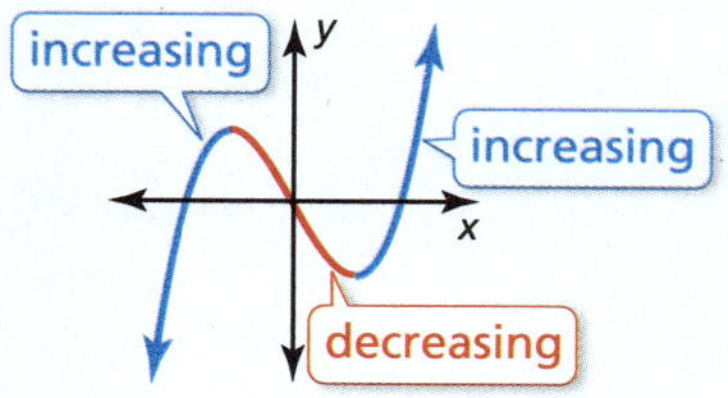

End Behavior
The end behavior of a function is the behavior of the graph as x approaches positive infinity $(+\infty)$ or negative infinity $(-\infty)$.

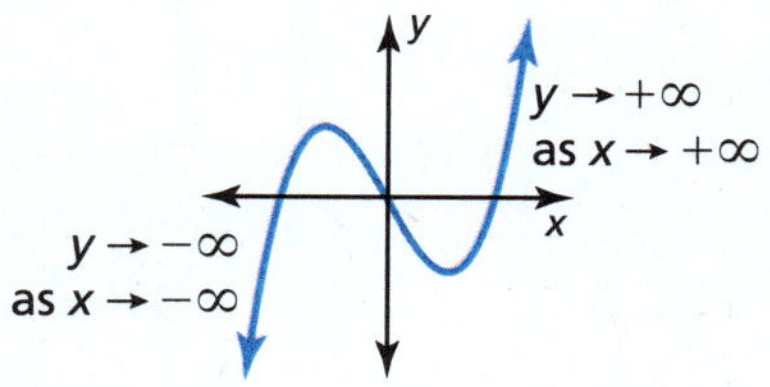

Perimeter, Area, and Volume Formulas

Square

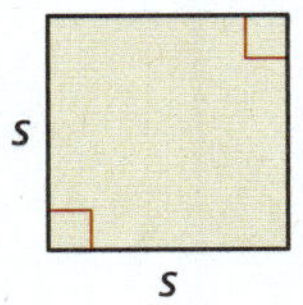

$P = 4s$
$A = s^2$

Rectangle

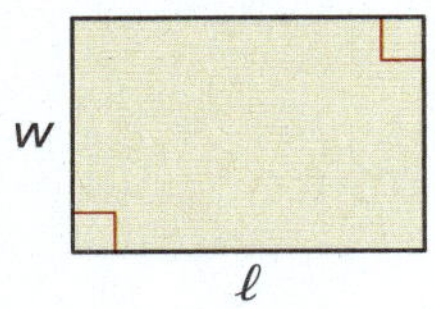

$P = 2\ell + 2w$
$A = \ell w$

Triangle

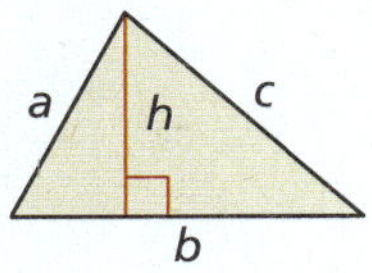

$P = a + b + c$
$A = \frac{1}{2}bh$

Circle

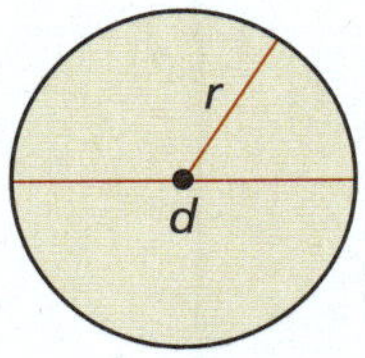

$C = \pi d$ or $C = 2\pi r$
$A = \pi r^2$

Parallelogram

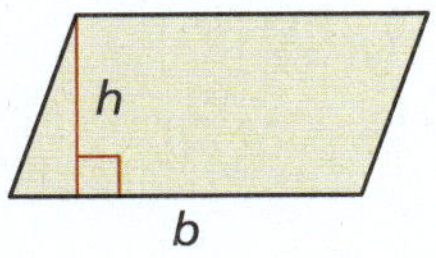

$A = bh$

Trapezoid

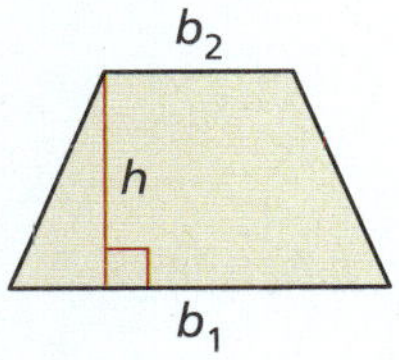

$A = \frac{1}{2}h(b_1 + b_2)$

Rhombus/Kite

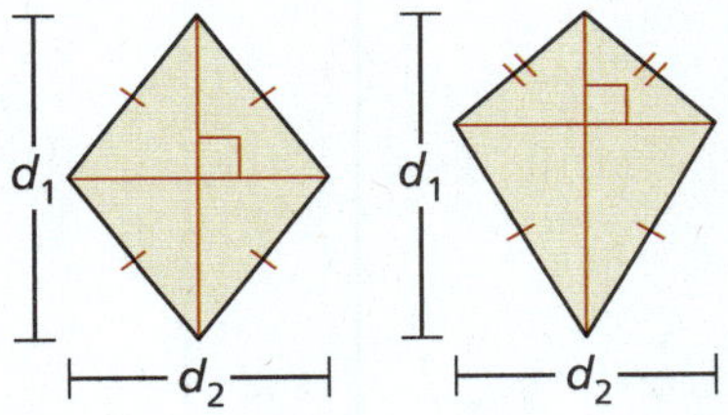

$A = \frac{1}{2}d_1 d_2$

Regular *n*-gon

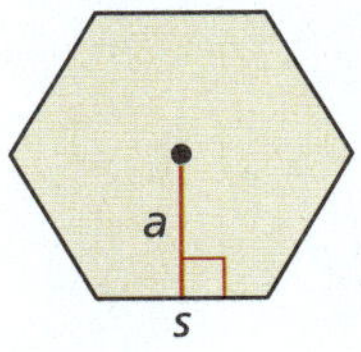

$A = \frac{1}{2}aP$ or $A = \frac{1}{2}a \bullet ns$

Prism

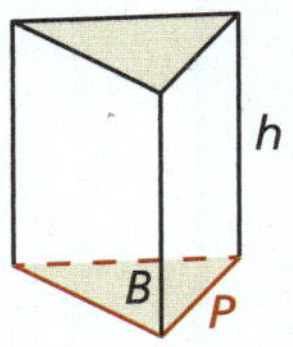

$L = Ph$
$S = 2B + L = aP + Ph$
$V = Bh$

Cylinder

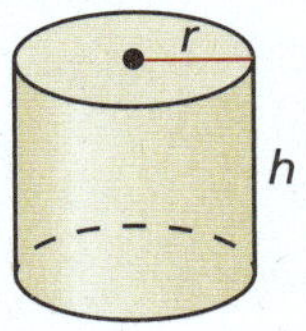

$L = 2\pi rh$
$S = 2B + L = 2\pi r^2 + 2\pi rh$
$V = \pi r^2 h$

Pyramid

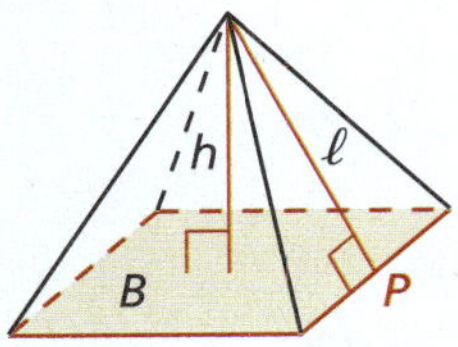

$L = \frac{1}{2}P\ell$
$S = B + L = B + \frac{1}{2}P\ell$
$V = \frac{1}{3}Bh$

Cone

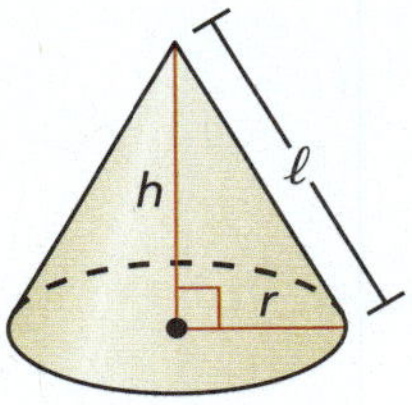

$L = \pi r\ell$

$S = B + L = \pi r^2 + \pi r\ell$

$V = \frac{1}{3}\pi r^2 h$

Sphere

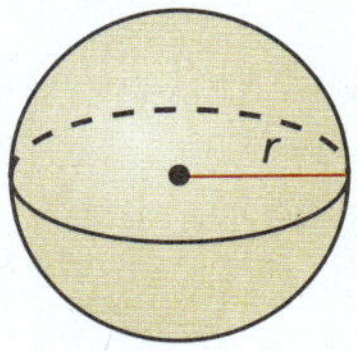

$S = 4\pi r^2$

$V = \frac{4}{3}\pi r^3$

Other Formulas

Pythagorean Theorem

$a^2 + b^2 = c^2$

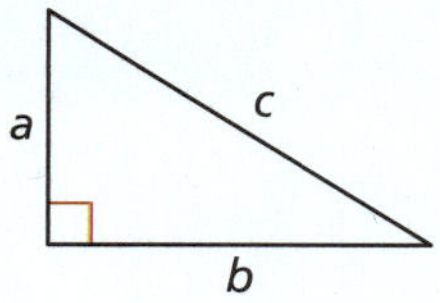

Simple Interest

$I = Prt$

Compound Interest

$y = P\left(1 + \frac{r}{n}\right)^{nt}$

Distance

$d = rt$

Conversions

U.S. Customary

1 foot = 12 inches
1 yard = 3 feet
1 mile = 5280 feet
1 mile = 1760 yards
1 acre = 43,560 square feet
1 cup = 8 fluid ounces
1 pint = 2 cups
1 quart = 2 pints
1 gallon = 4 quarts
1 gallon = 231 cubic inches
1 pound = 16 ounces
1 ton = 2000 pounds
1 cubic foot ≈ 7.5 gallons

U.S. Customary to Metric

1 inch = 2.54 centimeters
1 foot ≈ 0.3 meter
1 mile ≈ 1.61 kilometers
1 quart ≈ 0.95 liter
1 gallon ≈ 3.79 liters
1 cup ≈ 237 milliliters
1 pound ≈ 0.45 kilogram
1 ounce ≈ 28.3 grams
1 gallon ≈ 3785 cubic centimeters

Time

1 minute = 60 seconds
1 hour = 60 minutes
1 hour = 3600 seconds
1 year = 52 weeks

Temperature

$C = \frac{5}{9}(F - 32)$

$F = \frac{9}{5}C + 32$

Metric

1 centimeter = 10 millimeters
1 meter = 100 centimeters
1 kilometer = 1000 meters
1 liter = 1000 milliliters
1 kiloliter = 1000 liters
1 milliliter = 1 cubic centimeter
1 liter = 1000 cubic centimeters
1 cubic millimeter = 0.001 milliliter
1 gram = 1000 milligrams
1 kilogram = 1000 grams

Metric to U.S. Customary

1 centimeter ≈ 0.39 inch
1 meter ≈ 3.28 feet
1 meter ≈ 39.37 inches
1 kilometer ≈ 0.62 mile
1 liter ≈ 1.06 quarts
1 liter ≈ 0.26 gallon
1 kilogram ≈ 2.2 pounds
1 gram ≈ 0.035 ounce
1 cubic meter ≈ 264 gallons